Legal & Regulatory Environment of Business

Text & Cases for LSB 3213

Oklahoma State University

Author: Kenneth W. Clarkson, Roger LeRoy Miller, Frank B. Cross

CENGAGE
Learning·

Australia • Brazil • Japan • Korea • Mexico • Singapore • Spain • United Kingdom • United States

Legal & Regulatory Environment of Business: Text & Cases for LSB 3213, Oklahoma State University

Business Law: Text and Cases
Kenneth W. Clarkson, Roger LeRoy Miller, Frank B. Cross

©2018 Cengage Learning. All rights reserved.

For product information and technology assistance, contact us at
Cengage Learning Customer & Sales Support, 1-800-354-9706

For permission to use material from this text or product,
submit all requests online at **cengage.com/permissions**
Further permissions questions can be emailed to
permissionrequest@cengage.com

This book contains select works from existing Cengage Learning resources and was produced by Cengage Learning Custom Solutions for collegiate use. As such, those adopting and/or contributing to this work are responsible for editorial content accuracy, continuity and completeness.

Compilation © 2017 Cengage Learning
ISBN: 978-1-337-44666-2

Cengage Learning

Cengage Learning is a leading provider of customized learning solutions with office locations around the globe, including Singapore, the United Kingdom, Australia, Mexico, Brazil, and Japan. Locate your local office at:
www.international.cengage.com/region.

Cengage Learning products are represented in Canada by Nelson Education, Ltd.

For your lifelong learning solutions, visit **www.cengage.com/custom.**

Visit our corporate website at **www.cengage.com.**

Brief Contents

The Legal Environment of Business

CHAPTER

Law and Legal Reasoning

One of the most important functions of law in any society is to provide stability, predictability, and continuity so that people can know how to order their affairs. If any society is to survive, its citizens must be able to determine what is legally right and legally wrong. They must know what sanctions will be imposed on them if they commit wrongful acts. If they suffer harm as a result of others' wrongful acts, they must know how they can seek compensation. By setting forth the rights, obligations, and privileges of citizens, the law enables individuals to go about their business with confidence and a certain degree of predictability.

Although law has various definitions, they all are based on the general observation that **law** consists of *enforceable rules governing relationships among individuals and between individuals and their society*. These "enforceable rules" may consist of unwritten principles of behavior established by a nomadic tribe. They may be set forth in a law code, such as the Code of Hammurabi in ancient Babylon (c. 1780 B.C.E.) or the law code of one of today's European nations. They may consist of written laws and court decisions created by modern legislative and judicial bodies, as in the United States. Regardless of how such rules are created, they all have one thing in common: they establish rights, duties, and privileges that are consistent with the values and beliefs of their society or its ruling group.

In this introductory chapter, we first look at an important question for any student reading this text: How does the legal environment affect business decision making? We next describe the major sources of American law, the common law tradition, and some basic schools of legal thought. We conclude the chapter with sections offering practical guidance on several topics, including how to find the sources of law discussed in this chapter (and referred to throughout the text) and how to read and understand court opinions.

1–1 Business Activities and the Legal Environment

Laws and government regulations affect almost all business activities—from hiring and firing decisions to workplace safety, the manufacturing and marketing of products, business financing, and more. To make good business decisions, a basic knowledge of the laws and regulations governing these activities is beneficial—if not essential.

Realize also that in today's business world, a knowledge of "black-letter" law and what conduct can lead to legal **liability** is not enough. Businesspersons must develop critical thinking and legal reasoning skills so that they can evaluate how various laws might apply to a given situation and determine the best course of action. Businesspersons are also expected to make ethical decisions. Thus, the study of business law necessarily involves an ethical dimension.

1–1a Many Different Laws May Affect a Single Business Decision

As you will note, each chapter in this text covers specific areas of the law and shows how the legal rules in each area affect business activities. Although compartmentalizing the law in this fashion promotes conceptual clarity, it does not indicate the extent to which a number of different laws may apply to just one decision. Exhibit 1–1 illustrates the various areas of the law that may influence business decision making.

■ **EXAMPLE 1.1** When Mark Zuckerberg started Facebook as a Harvard student, he probably did not imagine all the legal challenges his company would face as a result of his business decisions.

- Shortly after Facebook was launched, others claimed that Zuckerberg had stolen their ideas for a social networking site. Their claims involved alleged theft of intellectual property, fraudulent misrepresentation, and

EXHIBIT 1-1 Areas of the Law That Can Affect Business Decision Making

Contracts

Environmental Law and Sustainability

Intellectual Property

Business Decision Making

Internet Law, Social Media, and Privacy

Torts

Sales

Product Liability

violations of partnership law and securities law. Facebook ultimately paid $65 million to settle those claims out of court.

• Facebook has been sued repeatedly for violating users' privacy (and federal laws) by tracking their Web site usage and by scanning private messages for purposes of data mining and user profiling. A class-action suit filed in Europe alleges that Facebook's data-use policies violate the law of the European Union. Facebook might have to pay millions in damages in this case.

• Facebook's business decisions have also come under scrutiny by federal regulators, such as the Federal Trade Commission (FTC). The company settled a complaint filed by the FTC alleging that Facebook had failed to keep "friends" lists and other user information private. ▪

1-1b Ethics and Business Decision Making

Merely knowing the areas of law that may affect a business decision is not sufficient in today's business world. Today, business decision makers need to consider not just whether a decision is legal, but also whether it is ethical.

Ethics generally is defined as the principles governing what constitutes right or wrong behavior. Often, as in several of the claims against Facebook discussed above, disputes arise in business because one party feels that he or she has been treated unfairly. Thus, the underlying reason for bringing some lawsuits is a breach of ethical duties (such as when a partner or employee attempts to secretly take advantage of a business opportunity).

Throughout this text, you will learn about the relationship between the law and ethics, as well as about some of the types of ethical questions that arise in business. For instance, all of the new unit-ending *Unit Application and Ethics* features include an *Ethical Connection* section that explores the ethical dimensions of a topic treated within the unit. We have also included *Ethical Questions* for each unit, as well as within the critical thinking sections of many of the cases presented in this text. *Ethics Today* features, which focus on ethical considerations in today's business climate, appear in selected chapters, including this chapter. *A Question of Ethics* case problem is included at the end of every chapter to introduce you to the ethical aspects of specific cases involving real-life situations.

1-2 Sources of American Law

American law has numerous sources. Often, these sources of law are classified as either primary or secondary.

Primary sources of law, or sources that establish the law, include the following:

1. The U.S. Constitution and the constitutions of the various states.
2. Statutory law—including laws passed by Congress, state legislatures, or local governing bodies.
3. Regulations created by administrative agencies, such as the Federal Trade Commission.
4. Case law and common law doctrines.

We describe each of these important sources of law in the following pages.

Secondary sources of law are books and articles that summarize and clarify the primary sources of law. Examples include legal encyclopedias, treatises, articles in law reviews, and compilations of law, such as the *Restatements of the Law* (which will be discussed later). Courts often refer to secondary sources of law for guidance in interpreting and applying the primary sources of law discussed here.

1–2a Constitutional Law

The federal government and the states have separate written constitutions that set forth the general organization, powers, and limits of their respective governments. **Constitutional law** is the law as expressed in these constitutions.

According to Article VI of the U.S. Constitution, the Constitution is the supreme law of the land. As such, it is the basis of all law in the United States. A law in violation of the Constitution, if challenged, will be declared unconstitutional and will not be enforced, no matter what its source. Because of its importance in the American legal system, we present the complete text of the U.S. Constitution in Appendix B.

The Tenth Amendment to the U.S. Constitution reserves to the states all powers not granted to the federal government. Each state in the union has its own constitution. Unless it conflicts with the U.S. Constitution or a federal law, a state constitution is supreme within the state's borders.

1–2b Statutory Law

Laws enacted by legislative bodies at any level of government, such as statutes passed by Congress or by state legislatures, make up the body of law known as **statutory law.** When a legislature passes a statute, that statute ultimately is included in the federal code of laws or the relevant state code of laws.

Statutory law also includes local **ordinances**—regulations passed by municipal or county governing units to deal with matters not covered by federal or state law. Ordinances commonly have to do with city or county land use (zoning ordinances), building and safety codes, and other matters affecting the local community.

A federal statute, of course, applies to all states. A state statute, in contrast, applies only within the state's borders. State laws thus may vary from state to state. No federal statute may violate the U.S. Constitution, and no state statute or local ordinance may violate the U.S. Constitution or the relevant state constitution.

Uniform Laws During the 1800s, the differences among state laws frequently created difficulties for businesspersons conducting trade and commerce among the states. To counter these problems, a group of legal scholars and lawyers formed the National Conference of Commissioners on Uniform State Laws, or NCCUSL (**www.uniformlaws.org**), in 1892. The NCCUSL still exists today. Its object is to draft **uniform laws** (model statutes) for the states to consider adopting.

Each state has the option of adopting or rejecting a uniform law. *Only if a state legislature adopts a uniform law does that law become part of the statutory law of that state.* Note that a state legislature may adopt all or part of a uniform law as it is written, or the legislature may rewrite the law however the legislature wishes. Hence, even though many states may have adopted a uniform law, those states' laws may not be entirely "uniform."

The earliest uniform law, the Uniform Negotiable Instruments Law, was completed by 1896 and adopted in every state by the 1920s (although not all states used exactly the same wording). Over the following decades, other acts were drawn up in a similar manner. In all, more than two hundred uniform acts have been issued by the NCCUSL since its inception. The most ambitious uniform act of all, however, was the Uniform Commercial Code.

The Uniform Commercial Code One of the most important uniform acts is the Uniform Commercial Code (UCC), which was created through the joint efforts of the NCCUSL and the American Law Institute.[1] The UCC was first issued in 1952 and has been adopted in all fifty states,[2] the District of Columbia, and the Virgin Islands.

The UCC facilitates commerce among the states by providing a uniform, yet flexible, set of rules governing commercial transactions. Because of its importance in the area of commercial law, we cite the UCC frequently in this text. We also present the full UCC in Appendix C. From time to time, the NCCUSL revises the articles contained in the UCC and submits the revised versions to the states for adoption.

1–2c Administrative Law

Another important source of American law is **administrative law,** which consists of the rules, orders, and decisions of administrative agencies. An **administrative agency** is a federal, state, or local government agency established to perform a specific function. Administrative law and procedures constitute a dominant element in the regulatory environment of business.

---

1. This institute was formed in the 1920s and consists of practicing attorneys, legal scholars, and judges.
2. Louisiana has not adopted Articles 2 and 2A (covering contracts for the sale and lease of goods), however.

Rules issued by various administrative agencies now affect almost every aspect of a business's operations. Regulations govern a business's capital structure and financing, its hiring and firing procedures, its relations with employees and unions, and the way it manufactures and markets its products. Regulations enacted to protect the environment also often play a significant role in business operations.

Federal Agencies At the national level, the cabinet departments of the executive branch include numerous **executive agencies.** The U.S. Food and Drug Administration, for instance, is an agency within the U.S. Department of Health and Human Services. Executive agencies are subject to the authority of the president, who has the power to appoint and remove their officers.

There are also major **independent regulatory agencies** at the federal level, such as the Federal Trade Commission, the Securities and Exchange Commission, and the Federal Communications Commission. The president's power is less pronounced in regard to independent agencies, whose officers serve for fixed terms and cannot be removed without just cause.

State and Local Agencies There are administrative agencies at the state and local levels as well. Commonly, a state agency (such as a state pollution-control agency) is created as a parallel to a federal agency (such as the Environmental Protection Agency). Just as federal statutes take precedence over conflicting state statutes, federal agency regulations take precedence over conflicting state regulations.

1–2d Case Law and Common Law Doctrines

The rules of law announced in court decisions constitute another basic source of American law. These rules include interpretations of constitutional provisions, of statutes enacted by legislatures, and of regulations created by administrative agencies.

Today, this body of judge-made law is referred to as **case law.** Case law—the doctrines and principles announced in cases—governs all areas not covered by statutory law or administrative law and is part of our common law tradition. We look at the origins and characteristics of the common law tradition in some detail in the pages that follow.

See Concept Summary 1.1 for a review of the sources of American law.

Concept Summary 1.1

Sources of American Law

Constitutional Law	• Law as expressed in the U.S. Constitution or state constitutions. • The U.S. Constitution is the supreme law of the land. • State constitutions are supreme within state borders to the extent that they do not conflict with the U.S. Constitution.
Statutory Law	• Statutes (including uniform laws) and ordinances enacted by federal, state, and local legislatures. • Federal statutes may not violate the U.S. Constitution. • State statutes and local ordinances may not violate the U.S. Constitution or the relevant state constitution.
Administrative Law	• The rules, orders, and decisions of federal, state, and local administrative agencies.
Case Law and Common Law Doctrines	• Judge-made law, including interpretations of constitutional provisions, of statutes enacted by legislatures, and of regulations created by administrative agencies.

1–3 The Common Law Tradition

Because of our colonial heritage, much of American law is based on the English legal system. Knowledge of this tradition is crucial to understanding our legal system today because judges in the United States still apply common law principles when deciding cases.

1–3a Early English Courts

After the Normans conquered England in 1066, William the Conqueror and his successors began the process of unifying the country under their rule. One of the means they used to do this was the establishment of the king's courts, or *curiae regis*.

Before the Norman Conquest, disputes had been settled according to the local legal customs and traditions in various regions of the country. The king's courts sought to establish a uniform set of customs for the country as a whole. What evolved in these courts was the beginning of the **common law**—a body of general rules that applied throughout the entire English realm. Eventually, the common law tradition became part of the heritage of all nations that were once British colonies, including the United States.

Courts of Law and Remedies at Law The early English king's courts could grant only very limited kinds of **remedies** (the legal means to enforce a right or redress a wrong). If one person wronged another in some way, the king's courts could award as compensation one or more of the following: (1) land, (2) items of value, or (3) money.

The courts that awarded this compensation became known as **courts of law,** and the three remedies were called **remedies at law.** (Today, the remedy at law normally takes the form of monetary **damages**—an amount given to a party whose legal interests have been injured.) This system made the procedure for settling disputes more uniform. When a complaining party wanted a remedy other than economic compensation, however, the courts of law could do nothing, so "no remedy, no right."

Courts of Equity When individuals could not obtain an adequate remedy in a court of law, they petitioned the king for relief. Most of these petitions were decided by an adviser to the king, called a *chancellor,* who had the power to grant new and unique remedies. Eventually, formal chancery courts, or **courts of equity,** were established. *Equity* is a branch of law—founded on notions of justice and fair dealing—that seeks to supply a remedy when no adequate remedy at law is available.

Remedies in Equity The remedies granted by the equity courts became known as **remedies in equity,** or equitable remedies. These remedies include specific performance, injunction, and rescission. *Specific performance* involves ordering a party to perform an agreement as promised. An *injunction* is an order to a party to cease engaging in a specific activity or to undo some wrong or injury. *Rescission* is the cancellation of a contractual obligation. We will discuss these and other equitable remedies in more detail in later chapters.

As a general rule, today's courts, like the early English courts, will not grant equitable remedies unless the remedy at law—monetary damages—is inadequate. ■ **EXAMPLE 1.2** Ted forms a contract (a legally binding agreement) to purchase a parcel of land that he thinks will be perfect for his future home. The seller **breaches** (fails to fulfill) this agreement. Ted could sue the seller for the return of any deposits or down payment he might have made on the land, but this is not the remedy he really wants. What Ted wants is to have a court order the seller to perform the contract. In other words, Ted will seek the equitable remedy of specific performance because monetary damages are inadequate in this situation. ■

Equitable Maxims In fashioning appropriate remedies, judges often were (and continue to be) guided by so-called **equitable maxims**—propositions or general statements of equitable rules. Exhibit 1–2 lists some important equitable maxims.

The last maxim listed in the exhibit—"Equity aids the vigilant, not those who rest on their rights"—merits special attention. It has become known as the equitable doctrine of **laches** (a term derived from the Latin *laxus,* meaning "lax" or "negligent"), and it can be used as a defense. A **defense** is an argument raised by the **defendant** (the party being sued) indicating why the **plaintiff** (the suing party) should not obtain the remedy sought. (Note that in equity proceedings, the party bringing a lawsuit is called the **petitioner,** and the party being sued is referred to as the **respondent.)**

The doctrine of laches arose to encourage people to bring lawsuits while the evidence was fresh. What constitutes a reasonable time, of course, varies according to the circumstances of the case. Time periods for different types of cases are now usually fixed by **statutes of limitations.** After the time allowed under a statute of limitations has expired, no action (lawsuit) can be brought, no matter how strong the case was originally.

EXHIBIT 1–2 Equitable Maxims

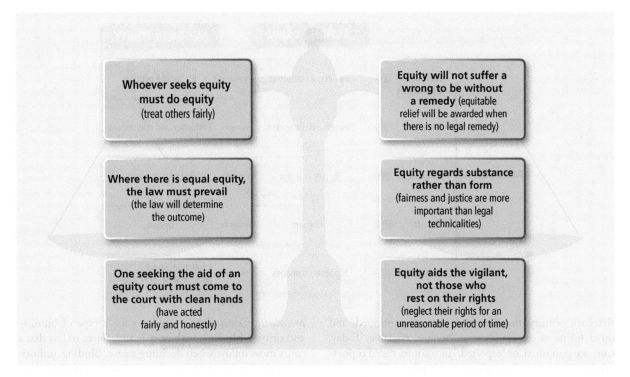

Whoever seeks equity must do equity (treat others fairly)

Equity will not suffer a wrong to be without a remedy (equitable relief will be awarded when there is no legal remedy)

Where there is equal equity, the law must prevail (the law will determine the outcome)

Equity regards substance rather than form (fairness and justice are more important than legal technicalities)

One seeking the aid of an equity court must come to the court with clean hands (have acted fairly and honestly)

Equity aids the vigilant, not those who rest on their rights (neglect their rights for an unreasonable period of time)

1–3b Legal and Equitable Remedies Today

The establishment of courts of equity in medieval England resulted in two distinct court systems: courts of law and courts of equity. The courts had different sets of judges and granted different types of remedies. During the nineteenth century, however, most states in the United States adopted rules of procedure that resulted in the combining of courts of law and equity. A party now may request both legal and equitable remedies in the same action, and the trial court judge may grant either or both forms of relief.

The distinction between legal and equitable remedies remains relevant to students of business law, however, because these remedies differ. To seek the proper remedy for a wrong, you must know what remedies are available. Additionally, certain vestiges of the procedures used when there were separate courts of law and equity still exist. For instance, a party has the right to demand a jury trial in an action at law, but not in an action in equity. Exhibit 1–3 summarizes the procedural differences (applicable in most states) between an action at law and an action in equity.

1–3c The Doctrine of *Stare Decisis*

One of the unique features of the common law is that it is *judge-made* law. The body of principles and doctrines that form the common law emerged over time as judges decided legal controversies.

Case Precedents and Case Reporters When possible, judges attempted to be consistent and to base their decisions on the principles suggested by earlier cases. They sought to decide similar cases in a similar way, and they considered new cases with care because they knew that their decisions would make new law. Each interpretation became part of the law on the subject and thus served as a legal **precedent.** A precedent is a decision that furnishes an example or authority for deciding subsequent cases involving identical or similar legal principles or facts.

In the early years of the common law, there was no single place or publication where court opinions, or written decisions, could be found. By the fourteenth century, portions of the most important decisions from each year were being gathered together and recorded in *Year Books*, which became useful references for lawyers and judges. In the

EXHIBIT 1–3 Procedural Differences between Actions at Law and Actions in Equity

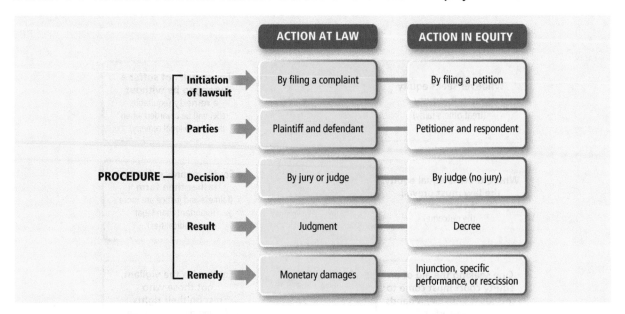

PROCEDURE		ACTION AT LAW	ACTION IN EQUITY
	Initiation of lawsuit	By filing a complaint	By filing a petition
	Parties	Plaintiff and defendant	Petitioner and respondent
	Decision	By jury or judge	By judge (no jury)
	Result	Judgment	Decree
	Remedy	Monetary damages	Injunction, specific performance, or rescission

sixteenth century, the *Year Books* were discontinued, and other forms of case publication became available. Today, cases are published, or "reported," in volumes called **reporters,** or *reports*—and are also posted online. We describe today's case reporting system in detail later in this chapter.

Stare Decisis and the Common Law Tradition

The practice of deciding new cases with reference to former decisions, or precedents, became a cornerstone of the English and American judicial systems. The practice formed a doctrine known as ***stare decisis***,[3] a Latin phrase meaning "to stand on decided cases."

Under the doctrine of *stare decisis*, judges are obligated to follow the precedents established within their jurisdictions. The term *jurisdiction* refers to a geographic area in which a court or courts have the power to apply the law. Once a court has set forth a principle of law as being applicable to a certain set of facts, that court must apply the principle in future cases involving similar facts. Courts of lower rank (within the same jurisdiction) must do likewise. Thus, *stare decisis* has two aspects:

1. A court should not overturn its own precedents unless there is a compelling reason to do so.
2. Decisions made by a higher court are binding on lower courts.

Controlling Precedents Precedents that must be followed within a jurisdiction are called *controlling*

precedents. Controlling precedents are a type of binding authority. A **binding authority** is any source of law that a court must follow when deciding a case. Binding authorities include constitutions, statutes, and regulations that govern the issue being decided, as well as court decisions that are controlling precedents within the jurisdiction. United States Supreme Court case decisions, no matter how old, remain controlling until they are overruled by a subsequent decision of the Supreme Court or changed by further legislation or a constitutional amendment.

Stare Decisis and Legal Stability The doctrine of *stare decisis* helps the courts to be more efficient because, if other courts have analyzed a similar case, their legal reasoning and opinions can serve as guides. *Stare decisis* also makes the law more stable and predictable. If the law on a subject is well settled, someone bringing a case can usually rely on the court to rule based on what the law has been in the past. See this chapter's *Ethics Today* feature for a discussion of how courts often defer to case precedent even when they disagree with the reasoning in the case.

Although courts are obligated to follow precedents, sometimes a court will depart from the rule of precedent if it decides that the precedent should no longer be followed. If a court decides that a ruling precedent is simply incorrect or that technological or social changes have rendered the precedent inapplicable, the court might rule contrary to the precedent. Cases that overturn precedent often receive a great deal of publicity.

■ **CASE IN POINT 1.3** The United States Supreme Court expressly overturned precedent in the case of

---

3. Pronounced *ster*-ay dih-*si*-ses.

ETHICS TODAY

Stare Decisis versus Spider-Man

Supreme Court Justice Elena Kagan, in a recent decision involving Marvel Comics' Spider-Man, ruled that, "What we can decide, we can undecide. But *stare decisis* teaches that we should exercise that authority sparingly." Citing a Spider-Man comic book, she went on to say that "in this world, with great power there must also come—great responsibility."[a] In its decision in the case—*Kimble v. Marvel Entertainment, LLC*—the Supreme Court applied *stare decisis* and ruled against Stephen Kimble, the creator of a toy related to the Spider-Man figure.[b]

Can a Patent Involving Spider-Man Last Super Long?

A patent is an exclusive right granted to the creator of an invention. Under U.S. law, patent owners generally possess that right for twenty years. Patent holders can license the use of their patents as they see fit during that period. In other words, they can allow others (called *licensees*) to use their invention in return for a fee (called *royalties*).

More than fifty years ago, the Supreme Court ruled in its *Brulotte* decision that a licensee cannot be forced to pay royalties to a patent holder after the patent has expired.[c] So if a licensee signs a contract to continue to pay royalties after the patent has expired, the contract is invalid and thus unenforceable.

At issue in the *Kimble* case was a contract signed between Marvel Entertainment and Kimble, who had invented a toy made up of a glove equipped with a valve and a canister of pressurized foam. The patented toy allowed people to shoot fake webs intended to look like Spider-Man's. In 1990, Kimble tried to cut a deal with Marvel Entertainment concerning his toy, but he was unsuccessful. Then Marvel started selling its own version of the toy.

When Kimble sued Marvel for patent infringement, he won. The result was a settlement that involved a licensing agreement between Kimble and Marvel with a lump-sum payment plus a royalty to Kimble of 3 percent of all sales of the toy. The agreement did not specify an end date for royalty payments to Kimble, and Marvel later sued to have the payments stop after the patent expired, consistent with the Court's earlier *Brulotte* decision.

A majority of the Supreme Court justices agreed with Marvel. As Justice Kagan said in the opinion, "Patents endow their holders with certain super powers, but only for a limited time." The court further noted that the fifty-year-old *Brulotte* decision was perhaps based on what today is an outmoded understanding of economics. That decision, according to some, may even hinder competition and innovation. But "respecting *stare decisis* means sticking to some wrong decisions."

The Ethical Side

In a dissenting opinion, Supreme Court Justice Samuel A. Alito, Jr., said, "The decision interferes with the ability of parties to negotiate licensing agreements that reflect the true value of a patent, and it disrupts contractual expectations. *Stare decisis* does not require us to retain this baseless and damaging precedent. . . . *Stare decisis* is important to the rule of law, but so are correct judicial decisions."

In other words, *stare decisis* holds that courts should adhere to precedent in order to promote predictability and consistency. But in the business world, shouldn't parties to contracts be able to, for example, allow a patent licensee to make smaller royalty payments that exceed the life of the patent? Isn't that a way to reduce the yearly costs to the licensee? After all, the licensee may be cash-strapped in its initial use of the patent. Shouldn't the parties to a contract be the ones to decide how long the contract should last?

Critical Thinking *When is the Supreme Court justified in not following the doctrine of stare decisis?*

---

a. "Spider-Man," *Amazing Fantasy* No. 15 (1962), p. 13.
b. 576 U.S. __, 135 S.Ct. 2401, 192 L.Ed.2d 463 (2015).
c. *Brulotte v. Thys Co.*, 379 U.S. 29, 85 S.Ct. 176 (1964).

Brown v. Board of Education of Topeka.[4] The Court concluded that separate educational facilities for whites and blacks, which it had previously upheld as constitutional,[5] were inherently unequal. The Supreme Court's departure from precedent in this case received a tremendous amount of publicity as people began to realize the ramifications of this change in the law. ■

Note that a lower court will sometimes avoid applying a precedent set by a higher court in its jurisdiction by

---

4. 347 U.S. 483, 74 S.Ct. 686, 98 L.Ed. 873 (1954).
5. See *Plessy v. Ferguson*, 163 U.S. 537, 16 S.Ct. 1138, 41 L.Ed. 256 (1896).

distinguishing the two cases based on their facts. When this happens, the lower court's ruling stands unless it is appealed to a higher court and that court overturns the decision.

When There Is No Precedent Occasionally, courts must decide cases for which no precedents exist, called *cases of first impression.* For instance, as you will read throughout this text, the Internet and certain other technologies have presented many new and challenging issues for the courts to decide.

■ **EXAMPLE 1.4** Google Glass is a Bluetooth-enabled, hands-free, wearable computer. A person using Google Glass can take photos and videos, surf the Internet, and do other things through voice commands. Many people expressed concerns about this new technology. Privacy advocates claimed that it is much easier to secretly film or photograph others with wearable video technology than with a camera or a smartphone. Indeed, numerous bars and restaurants, among others, banned the use of Google Glass to protect their patrons' privacy. Police officers were concerned about driver safety. A California woman was ticketed for wearing Google Glass while driving. But the court dismissed this case of first impression because it was not clear whether the device had been in operation at the time of the offense. ■

In deciding cases of first impression, courts often look at **persuasive authorities**—legal authorities that a court may consult for guidance but that are not binding on the court. A court may consider precedents from other jurisdictions, for instance, although those precedents are not binding. A court may also consider legal principles and policies underlying previous court decisions or existing statutes. Additionally, a court might look at issues of fairness, social values and customs, and public policy (governmental policy based on widely held societal values). Today, federal courts can also look at unpublished opinions (those not intended for publication in a printed legal reporter) as sources of persuasive authority.[6]

1–3d *Stare Decisis* and Legal Reasoning

In deciding what law applies to a given dispute and then applying that law to the facts or circumstances of the case, judges rely on the process of **legal reasoning.** Through the use of legal reasoning, judges harmonize their decisions with those that have been made before, as the doctrine of *stare decisis* requires.

Students of business law and the legal environment also engage in legal reasoning. For instance, you may be asked to provide answers for some of the case problems

that appear at the end of every chapter in this text. Each problem describes the facts of a particular dispute and the legal question at issue. If you are assigned a case problem, you will be asked to determine how a court would answer that question, and why. In other words, you will need to give legal reasons for whatever conclusion you reach.[7] We look next at the basic steps involved in legal reasoning and then describe some forms of reasoning commonly used by the courts in making their decisions.

Basic Steps in Legal Reasoning At times, the legal arguments set forth in court opinions are relatively simple and brief. At other times, the arguments are complex and lengthy. Regardless of the length of a legal argument, however, the basic steps of the legal reasoning process remain the same. These steps, which you can also follow when analyzing cases and case problems, form what is commonly referred to as the *IRAC method* of legal reasoning. IRAC is an acronym formed from the first letters of the words *Issue, Rule, Application,* and *Conclusion.* To apply the IRAC method, you ask the following questions:

1. **Issue**—*What are the key facts and issues?* Suppose that a plaintiff comes before the court claiming *assault* (words or acts that wrongfully and intentionally make another person fearful of immediate physical harm). The plaintiff claims that the defendant threatened her while she was sleeping. Although the plaintiff was unaware that she was being threatened, her roommate heard the defendant make the threat. The legal issue is whether the defendant's action constitutes the tort of assault, given that the plaintiff was unaware of that action at the time it occurred. (A tort is a wrongful act. As you will see later, torts fall under the governance of civil law rather than criminal law.)

2. **Rule**—*What rule of law applies to the case?* A rule of law may be a rule stated by the courts in previous decisions, a state or federal statute, or a state or federal administrative agency regulation. In our hypothetical case, the plaintiff **alleges** (claims) that the defendant committed a tort. Therefore, the applicable law is the common law of torts—specifically, tort law governing assault. Case precedents involving similar facts and issues thus would be relevant. Often, more than one rule of law will be applicable to a case.

3. **Application**—*How does the rule of law apply to the particular facts and circumstances of this case?* This step is often the most difficult because each case presents a unique set of facts, circumstances, and parties.

---

6. See Rule 32.1 of the Federal Rules of Appellate Procedure.

7. See Appendix A for further instructions on how to analyze case problems.

Although cases may be similar, no two cases are ever identical in all respects. Normally, judges (and lawyers and law students) try to find **cases on point**—previously decided cases that are as similar as possible to the one under consideration.

4. **Conclusion**—*What conclusion should be drawn?* This step normally presents few problems. Usually, the conclusion is evident if the previous three steps have been followed carefully.

There Is No One "Right" Answer Many people believe that there is one "right" answer to every legal question. In most legal controversies, however, there is no single correct result. Good arguments can usually be made to support either side of a legal controversy. Quite often, a case does not involve a "good" person suing a "bad" person. In many cases, both parties have acted in good faith in some measure or in bad faith to some degree. Additionally, each judge has her or his own personal beliefs and philosophy. At least to some extent, these personal factors shape the legal reasoning process. In short, the outcome of a particular lawsuit before a court cannot be predicted with certainty.

1–3e The Common Law Today

Today, the common law derived from judicial decisions continues to be applied throughout the United States. Common law doctrines and principles, however, govern only areas *not* covered by statutory or administrative law. In a dispute concerning a particular employment practice, for instance, if a statute regulates that practice, the statute will apply rather than the common law doctrine that applied before the statute was enacted. The common law tradition and its application are reviewed in Concept Summary 1.2.

Courts Interpret Statutes Even in areas governed by statutory law, judge-made law continues to be important because there is a significant interplay between statutory law and the common law. For instance, many statutes essentially codify existing common law rules, and regulations issued by various administrative agencies usually are based, at least in part, on common law principles. Additionally, the courts, in interpreting statutory law, often rely on the common law as a guide to what the legislators intended. Frequently, the applicability of a newly enacted statute does not become clear until a body of case law develops to clarify how, when, and to whom the statute applies.

Concept Summary 1.2

The Common Law Tradition

Origins of Common Law	The American legal system is based on the common law tradition, which originated in medieval England.
Legal and Equitable Remedies	Remedies at law (land, items of value, or money) and remedies in equity (including specific performance, injunction, and rescission of a contractual obligation) originated in the early English courts of law and courts of equity, respectively.
Case Precedents and the Doctrine of *Stare Decisis*	In the king's courts, judges attempted to make their decisions consistent with previous decisions, called precedents. This practice gave rise to the doctrine of *stare decisis*. This doctrine, which became a cornerstone of the common law tradition, obligates judges to abide by precedents established in their jurisdictions.
Common Law Today	The common law governs all areas not covered by statutory law or administrative laws. Courts interpret statutes and regulations.

Clearly, a judge's function is not to *make* the laws—that is the function of the legislative branch of government—but to interpret and apply them. From a practical point of view, however, the courts play a significant role in defining the laws enacted by legislative bodies, which tend to be expressed in general terms. Judges thus have some flexibility in interpreting and applying the law. It is because of this flexibility that different courts can, and often do, arrive at different conclusions in cases that involve nearly identical issues, facts, and applicable laws.

Restatements of the Law Clarify and Illustrate the Common Law The American Law Institute (ALI) has published compilations of the common law called *Restatements of the Law*, which generally summarize the common law rules followed by most states. There are *Restatements of the Law* in the areas of contracts, torts, agency, trusts, property, restitution, security, judgments, and conflict of laws. The *Restatements,* like other secondary sources of law, do not in themselves have the force of law, but they are an important source of legal analysis and opinion. Hence, judges often rely on them in making decisions.

Many of the *Restatements* are now in their second, third, or fourth editions. We refer to the *Restatements* frequently in subsequent chapters of this text, indicating in parentheses the edition to which we are referring. For instance, we refer to the third edition of the *Restatement of the Law of Contracts* as simply the *Restatement (Third) of Contracts.*

1–4 Schools of Legal Thought

How judges apply the law to specific cases, including disputes relating to the business world, depends in part on their philosophical approaches to law. Thus, the study of law, or **jurisprudence,** involves learning about different schools of legal thought and how the approaches to law characteristic of each school can affect judicial decision making.

1–4a The Natural Law School

An age-old question about the nature of law has to do with the finality of a nation's laws. What if a particular law is deemed to be a "bad" law by a substantial number of the nation's citizens? Must they obey that law? According to the **natural law** theory, a higher, or universal, law exists that applies to all human beings. Each written law should reflect the principles inherent in natural law. If it does not, then it loses its legitimacy and need not be obeyed.

The natural law tradition is one of the oldest and most significant schools of jurisprudence. It dates back to the days of the Greek philosopher Aristotle (384–322

B.C.E.), who distinguished between natural law and the laws governing a particular nation. According to Aristotle, natural law applies universally to all humankind.

The notion that people have "natural rights" stems from the natural law tradition. Those who claim that a specific foreign government is depriving certain citizens of their human rights, for instance, are implicitly appealing to a higher law that has universal applicability.

The question of the universality of basic human rights also comes into play in the context of international business operations. U.S. companies that have operations abroad often hire foreign workers as employees. Should the same laws that protect U.S. employees apply to these foreign employees? This question is rooted implicitly in a concept of universal rights that has its origins in the natural law tradition.

1–4b The Positivist School

Positive law, or national law, is the written law of a given society at a particular time. In contrast to natural law, it applies only to the citizens of that nation or society. Those who adhere to **legal positivism** believe that there can be no higher law than a nation's positive law.

According to the positivist school, there are no "natural rights." Rather, human rights exist solely because of laws. If the laws are not enforced, anarchy will result. Thus, whether a law is "bad" or "good" is irrelevant. The law is the law and must be obeyed until it is changed—in an orderly manner through a legitimate lawmaking process. A judge who takes this view will probably be more inclined to defer to an existing law than would a judge who adheres to the natural law tradition.

1–4c The Historical School

The **historical school** of legal thought emphasizes the evolutionary process of law by concentrating on the origin and history of the legal system. This school looks to the past to discover what the principles of contemporary law should be. The legal doctrines that have withstood the passage of time—those that have worked in the past—are deemed best suited for shaping present laws. Hence, law derives its legitimacy and authority from adhering to the standards that historical development has shown to be workable. Followers of the historical school are more likely than those of other schools to strictly follow decisions made in past cases.

1–4d Legal Realism

In the 1920s and 1930s, a number of jurists and scholars, known as *legal realists,* rebelled against the historical approach to law. **Legal realism** is based on the idea that law is just one of many institutions in society and that it is shaped by social forces and needs. Because the law is a human enterprise, this school reasons that judges should take social and economic realities into account when deciding cases.

Legal realists also believe that the law can never be applied with total uniformity. Given that judges are human beings with unique personalities, value systems, and intellects, different judges will obviously bring different reasoning processes to the same case. Female judges, for instance, might be more inclined than male judges to consider whether a decision might have a negative impact on the employment of women or minorities.

Legal realism strongly influenced the growth of what is sometimes called the **sociological school,** which views law as a tool for promoting justice in society. In the 1960s, for instance, the justices of the United States Supreme Court helped advance the civil rights movement by upholding long-neglected laws calling for equal treatment for all Americans, including African Americans and other minorities. Generally, jurists who adhere to this philosophy of law are more likely to depart from past decisions than are jurists who adhere to other schools of legal thought.

Concept Summary 1.3 reviews the schools of jurisprudential thought.

1–5 Classifications of Law

The law may be broken down according to several classification systems. One system, for instance, divides law into substantive law and procedural law. **Substantive law** consists of all laws that define, describe, regulate, and create legal rights and obligations. **Procedural law** consists of all laws that outline the methods of enforcing the rights established by substantive law.

Note that many statutes contain both substantive and procedural provisions. ■ **EXAMPLE 1.5** A state law that provides employees with the right to *workers' compensation benefits* for on-the-job injuries is a substantive law because it creates legal rights. Procedural laws establish the method by which an employee must notify the employer about an on-the-job injury, prove the injury, and periodically submit additional proof to continue receiving workers' compensation benefits. ■

Other classification systems divide law into federal law and state law, private law (dealing with relationships between private entities) and public law (addressing the relationship between persons and their governments), and national law and international law. Here we look at still another classification system, which divides law into

Concept Summary 1.3

Schools of Jurisprudential Thought

Natural Law School	One of the oldest and most significant schools of legal thought. Those who believe in natural law hold that there is a universal law applicable to all human beings.
Positivist School	A school of legal thought centered on the assumption that there is no law higher than the laws created by the government.
Historical School	A school of legal thought that stresses the evolutionary nature of law and looks to doctrines that have withstood the passage of time for guidance in shaping present laws.
Legal Realism	A school of legal thought that advocates a less abstract and more realistic and pragmatic approach to the law and takes into account customary practices and the circumstances surrounding the particular transaction.

civil law and criminal law. We also explain what is meant by the term *cyberlaw*.

1–5a Civil Law and Criminal Law

Civil law spells out the rights and duties that exist between persons and between persons and their governments, as well as the relief available when a person's rights are violated. Typically, in a civil case, a private party sues another private party who has failed to comply with a duty. (Note that the government can also sue a party for a civil law violation.) Much of the law that we discuss in this text is civil law, including contract law and tort law.

Criminal law, in contrast, is concerned with wrongs committed *against the public as a whole*. Criminal acts are defined and prohibited by local, state, or federal government statutes. Criminal defendants are thus prosecuted by public officials, such as a district attorney (D.A.), on behalf of the state, not by their victims or other private parties. Some statutes, such as those protecting the environment or investors, have both civil and criminal provisions.

1–5b Cyberlaw

The use of the Internet to conduct business has led to new types of legal issues. In response, courts have had to adapt traditional laws to situations that are unique to our age. Additionally, legislatures at both the federal and the state levels have created laws to deal specifically with such issues.

Frequently, people use the term **cyberlaw** to refer to the emerging body of law that governs transactions conducted via the Internet. Cyberlaw is not really a classification of law, though, nor is it a new *type* of law. Rather, it is an informal term used to refer to both new laws and modifications of traditional laws that relate to the online environment. Throughout this book, you will read how the law in a given area is evolving to govern specific legal issues that arise in the online context.

1–6 How to Find Primary Sources of Law

This text includes numerous references, or *citations,* to primary sources of law—federal and state statutes, the U.S. Constitution and state constitutions, regulations issued by administrative agencies, and court cases. A **citation** identifies the publication in which a legal authority—such as a statute or a court decision or other source—can be found. In this section, we explain how you can use citations to find primary sources of law. Note

that in addition to being published in sets of books, as described next, most federal and state laws and case decisions are available online.

1–6a Finding Statutory and Administrative Law

When Congress passes laws, they are collected in a publication titled *United States Statutes at Large.* When state legislatures pass laws, they are collected in similar state publications. Most frequently, however, laws are referred to in their codified form—that is, the form in which they appear in the federal and state codes. In these codes, laws are compiled by subject.

United States Code The *United States Code* (U.S.C.) arranges all existing federal laws by broad subject. Each of the fifty-two subjects is given a title and a title number. For instance, laws relating to commerce and trade are collected in Title 15, "Commerce and Trade." Each title is subdivided by sections. A citation to the U.S.C. includes both title and section numbers. Thus, a reference to "15 U.S.C. Section 1" means that the statute can be found in Section 1 of Title 15. ("Section" may be designated by the symbol §, and "Sections," by §§.)

In addition to the print publication, the federal government provides a searchable online database at **www.gpo.gov**. It includes the *United States Code,* the U.S. Constitution, and many other federal resources. (Click on "Libraries" and then "Core Documents of Our Democracy" to find these resources.)

Commercial publications of federal laws and regulations are also available. For instance, Thomson Reuters publishes the *United States Code Annotated* (U.S.C.A.). The U.S.C.A. contains the official text of the U.S.C., plus notes (annotations) on court decisions that interpret and apply specific sections of the statutes. The U.S.C.A. also includes additional research aids, such as cross-references to related statutes, historical notes, and library references. A citation to the U.S.C.A. is similar to a citation to the U.S.C.: "15 U.S.C.A. Section 1."

State Codes State codes follow the U.S.C. pattern of arranging law by subject. They may be called codes, revisions, compilations, consolidations, general statutes, or statutes, depending on the preferences of the states.

In some codes, subjects are designated by number. In others, they are designated by name. ■ **EXAMPLE 1.6** "13 Pennsylvania Consolidated Statutes Section 1101" means that the statute can be found in Title 13, Section 1101, of the Pennsylvania code. "California Commercial Code Section 1101" means that the statute can be found under the subject heading "Commercial Code" of the California code in Section 1101. Abbreviations are often used. For example, "13 Pennsylvania Consolidated Statutes Section 1101" is abbreviated "13 Pa. C.S. § 1101," and "California Commercial Code Section 1101" is abbreviated "Cal. Com. Code § 1101." ■

Administrative Rules Rules and regulations adopted by federal administrative agencies are initially published in the *Federal Register,* a daily publication of the U.S. government. Later, they are incorporated into the *Code of Federal Regulations* (C.F.R.). The C.F.R. is available online on the government database (**www.gpo.gov**).

Like the U.S.C., the C.F.R. is divided into titles. Rules within each title are assigned section numbers. A full citation to the C.F.R. includes title and section numbers. ■ **EXAMPLE 1.7** A reference to "17 C.F.R. Section 230.504" means that the rule can be found in Section 230.504 of Title 17. ■

1–6b Finding Case Law

Before discussing the case reporting system, we need to look briefly at the court system. There are two types of courts in the United States, federal courts and state courts. Both systems consist of several levels, or tiers, of courts. *Trial courts*, in which evidence is presented and testimony given, are on the bottom tier. Decisions from a trial court can be appealed to a higher court, which commonly is an intermediate *court of appeals*, or *appellate court*. Decisions from these intermediate courts of appeals may be appealed to an even higher court, such as a state supreme court or the United States Supreme Court.

State Court Decisions Most state trial court decisions are not published in books (except in New York and a few other states, which publish selected trial court opinions). Decisions from state trial courts are typically filed in the office of the clerk of the court, where the decisions are available for public inspection. (Increasingly, they can be found online as well.)

Written decisions of the appellate, or reviewing, courts, however, are published and distributed (in print and online). As you will note, most of the state court cases presented in this textbook are from state appellate courts. The reported appellate decisions are published in volumes called *reports* or *reporters,* which are numbered consecutively. State appellate court decisions are found in the state reporters of that particular state. Official reports are published by the state, whereas unofficial reports are published by nongovernment entities.

Regional Reporters. State court opinions appear in regional units of the West's National Reporter System, published by Thomson Reuters. Most lawyers and libraries have these reporters because they report cases more quickly and are distributed more widely than the state-published reporters. In fact, many states have eliminated their own reporters in favor of the National Reporter System.

The National Reporter System divides the states into the following geographic areas: *Atlantic* (A., A.2d, or A.3d), *North Eastern* (N.E. or N.E.2d), *North Western* (N.W. or N.W.2d), *Pacific* (P., P.2d, or P.3d), *South Eastern* (S.E. or S.E.2d), *South Western* (S.W., S.W.2d, or S.W.3d), and *Southern* (So., So.2d, or So.3d). (The *2d* and *3d* in the preceding abbreviations refer to *Second Series* and *Third Series*, respectively.) The states included in each of these regional divisions are indicated in Exhibit 1–4, which illustrates the National Reporter System.

Case Citations. After appellate decisions have been published, they are normally referred to (cited) by the name of the case and the volume, name, and page number of the reporter(s) in which the opinion can be found. The citation first lists the state's official reporter (if different from the National Reporter System), then the National Reporter, and then any other selected reporter. (Citing a reporter by volume number, name, and page number, in that order, is common to all citations. The year that the decision was issued is often included at the end in parentheses.) When more than one reporter is cited for the same case, each reference is called a *parallel citation.*

Note that some states have adopted a "public domain citation system" that uses a somewhat different format for the citation. For instance, in Wisconsin, a Wisconsin Supreme Court decision might be designated "2016 WI 40," meaning that the case was decided in the year 2016 by the Wisconsin Supreme Court and was the fortieth decision issued by that court during that year. Parallel citations to the *Wisconsin Reports* and the *North Western Reporter* are still included after the public domain citation.

■ **EXAMPLE 1.8** Consider the following case citation: *Summerhill, LLC v. City of Meridan,* 162 Conn.App. 469, 131 A.3d. 1225 (2016). We see that the opinion in this case can be found in Volume 162 of the official *Connecticut Appellate Court Reports*, on page 469. The parallel citation is to Volume 131 of the *Atlantic Reporter, Third Series*, page 1225. ■

When we present opinions in this text, in addition to the reporter, we give the name of the court hearing the case and the year of the court's decision. Sample citations to state court decisions are explained in Exhibit 1–5.

EXHIBIT 1–4 National Reporter System—Regional/Federal

Regional Reporters	Coverage Beginning	Coverage
Atlantic Reporter (A., A.2d, or A.3d)	1885	Connecticut, Delaware, District of Columbia, Maine, Maryland, New Hampshire, New Jersey, Pennsylvania, Rhode Island, and Vermont.
North Eastern Reporter (N.E. or N.E.2d)	1885	Illinois, Indiana, Massachusetts, New York, and Ohio.
North Western Reporter (N.W. or N.W.2d)	1879	Iowa, Michigan, Minnesota, Nebraska, North Dakota, South Dakota, and Wisconsin.
Pacific Reporter (P., P.2d, or P.3d)	1883	Alaska, Arizona, California, Colorado, Hawaii, Idaho, Kansas, Montana, Nevada, New Mexico, Oklahoma, Oregon, Utah, Washington, and Wyoming.
South Eastern Reporter (S.E. or S.E.2d)	1887	Georgia, North Carolina, South Carolina, Virginia, and West Virginia.
South Western Reporter (S.W., S.W.2d, or S.W.3d)	1886	Arkansas, Kentucky, Missouri, Tennessee, and Texas.
Southern Reporter (So., So.2d, or So.3d)	1887	Alabama, Florida, Louisiana, and Mississippi.

Federal Reporters		
Federal Reporter (F., F.2d, or F.3d)	1880	U.S. Circuit Courts from 1880 to 1912; U.S. Commerce Court from 1911 to 1913; U.S. District Courts from 1880 to 1932; U.S. Court of Claims (now called U.S. Court of Federal Claims) from 1929 to 1932 and since 1960; U.S. Courts of Appeals since 1891; U.S. Court of Customs and Patent Appeals since 1929; U.S. Emergency Court of Appeals since 1943.
Federal Supplement (F.Supp., F.Supp.2d, or F.Supp.3d)	1932	U.S. Court of Claims from 1932 to 1960; U.S. District Courts since 1932; U.S. Customs Court since 1956.
Federal Rules Decisions (F.R.D.)	1939	U.S. District Courts involving the Federal Rules of Civil Procedure since 1939 and Federal Rules of Criminal Procedure since 1946.
Supreme Court Reporter (S.Ct.)	1882	United States Supreme Court since the October term of 1882.
Bankruptcy Reporter (Bankr.)	1980	Bankruptcy decisions of U.S. Bankruptcy Courts, U.S. District Courts, U.S. Courts of Appeals, and the United States Supreme Court.
Military Justice Reporter (M.J.)	1978	U.S. Court of Military Appeals and Courts of Military Review for the Army, Navy, Air Force, and Coast Guard.

NATIONAL REPORTER SYSTEM MAP

EXHIBIT 1–5 How to Read Citations

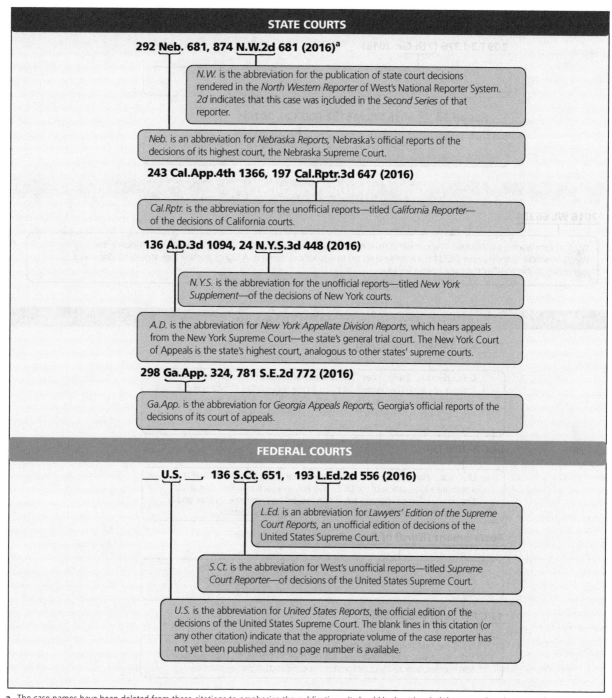

STATE COURTS

292 Neb. 681, 874 N.W.2d 681 (2016)[a]

N.W. is the abbreviation for the publication of state court decisions rendered in the *North Western Reporter* of West's National Reporter System. *2d* indicates that this case was included in the *Second Series* of that reporter.

Neb. is an abbreviation for *Nebraska Reports,* Nebraska's official reports of the decisions of its highest court, the Nebraska Supreme Court.

243 Cal.App.4th 1366, 197 Cal.Rptr.3d 647 (2016)

Cal.Rptr. is the abbreviation for the unofficial reports—titled *California Reporter*—of the decisions of California courts.

136 A.D.3d 1094, 24 N.Y.S.3d 448 (2016)

N.Y.S. is the abbreviation for the unofficial reports—titled *New York Supplement*—of the decisions of New York courts.

A.D. is the abbreviation for *New York Appellate Division Reports*, which hears appeals from the New York Supreme Court—the state's general trial court. The New York Court of Appeals is the state's highest court, analogous to other states' supreme courts.

298 Ga.App. 324, 781 S.E.2d 772 (2016)

Ga.App. is the abbreviation for *Georgia Appeals Reports,* Georgia's official reports of the decisions of its court of appeals.

FEDERAL COURTS

__ U.S. __ , 136 S.Ct. 651, 193 L.Ed.2d 556 (2016)

L.Ed. is an abbreviation for *Lawyers' Edition of the Supreme Court Reports*, an unofficial edition of decisions of the United States Supreme Court.

S.Ct. is the abbreviation for West's unofficial reports—titled *Supreme Court Reporter*—of decisions of the United States Supreme Court.

U.S. is the abbreviation for *United States Reports*, the official edition of the decisions of the United States Supreme Court. The blank lines in this citation (or any other citation) indicate that the appropriate volume of the case reporter has not yet been published and no page number is available.

a. The case names have been deleted from these citations to emphasize the publications. It should be kept in mind, however, that the name of a case is as important as the specific page numbers in the volumes in which it is found. If a citation is incorrect, the correct citation may be found in a publication's index of case names. In addition to providing a check on errors in citations, the date of a case is important because the value of a recent case as an authority is likely to be greater than that of older cases from the same court.

Continued

EXHIBIT 1–5 How to Read Citations—Continued

FEDERAL COURTS (Continued)

809 F.3d 376 (7th Cir. 2016)

7th Cir. is an abbreviation denoting that this case was decided in the U.S. Court of Appeals for the Seventh Circuit.

___ F.Supp.3d ___ 2016 WL 466132 (E.D.Cal. 2016)

E.D.Cal. is an abbreviation indicating that the U.S. District Court for the Eastern District of California decided this case.

WESTLAW® CITATIONS[b]

2016 WL 66334

WL is an abbreviation for Westlaw. The number 2016 is the year of the document that can be found with this citation in the Westlaw database. The number 66334 is a number assigned to a specific document. A higher number indicates that a document was added to the Westlaw database later in the year.

STATUTORY AND OTHER CITATIONS

18 U.S.C. Section 1961(1)(A)

U.S.C. denotes *United States Code*, the codification of *United States Statutes at Large*. The number 18 refers to the statute's U.S.C. title number and 1961 to its section number within that title. The number 1 in parentheses refers to a subsection within the section, and the letter A in parentheses to a subsection within the subsection.

UCC 2–206(1)(b)

UCC is an abbreviation for *Uniform Commercial Code*. The first number 2 is a reference to an article of the UCC, and 206 to a section within that article. The number 1 in parentheses refers to a subsection within the section, and the letter b in parentheses to a subsection within the subsection.

Restatement (Third) of Torts, Section 6

Restatement (Third) of Torts refers to the third edition of the American Law Institute's *Restatement of the Law of Torts*. The number 6 refers to a specific section.

17 C.F.R. Section 230.505

C.F.R. is an abbreviation for *Code of Federal Regulations*, a compilation of federal administrative regulations. The number 17 designates the regulation's title number, and 230.505 designates a specific section within that title.

b. Many court decisions that are not yet published or that are not intended for publication can be accessed through Westlaw, an online legal database.

Federal Court Decisions Federal district (trial) court decisions are published unofficially in the *Federal Supplement* (F.Supp. or F.Supp.2d), and opinions from the circuit courts of appeals (reviewing courts) are reported unofficially in the *Federal Reporter* (F., F.2d, or F.3d). Cases concerning federal bankruptcy law are published unofficially in the *Bankruptcy Reporter* (Bankr. or B.R.).

The official edition of the United States Supreme Court decisions is the *United States Reports* (U.S.), which is published by the federal government. Unofficial editions of Supreme Court cases include the *Supreme Court Reporter* (S.Ct.) and the *Lawyers' Edition of the Supreme Court Reports* (L.Ed. or L.Ed.2d). Sample citations for federal court decisions are also listed and explained in Exhibit 1–5.

Unpublished Opinions Many court opinions that are not yet published or that are not intended for publication can be accessed through Thomson Reuters Westlaw® (abbreviated in citations as "WL"), an online legal database. When no citation to a published reporter is available for cases cited in this text, we give the WL citation (such as 2016 WL 145734, which means it was case number 145734 decided in the year 2016). In addition, federal appellate court decisions that are designated as unpublished may appear in the *Federal Appendix* (Fed. Appx.) of the National Reporter System.

Old Case Law On a few occasions, this text cites opinions from old, classic cases dating to the nineteenth century or earlier. Some of these are from the English courts. The citations to these cases may not conform to the descriptions just presented because the reporters in which they were originally published were often known by the names of the persons who compiled the reporters.

1–7 How to Read and Understand Case Law

The decisions made by the courts establish the boundaries of the law as it applies to almost all business relationships. It thus is essential that businesspersons know how to read and understand case law.

The cases that we present in this text have been condensed from the full text of the courts' opinions and are presented in a special format. In approximately two-thirds of the cases (including the cases designated as *Classic* and *Spotlight*), we have summarized the background and facts, as well as the court's decision and remedy, in our own words. In those cases, we have included only selected excerpts from the court's opinion ("In the Language of the Court"). In the remaining one-third of the cases (labeled "Case Analysis"), we have provided a longer excerpt from the court's opinion without summarizing the background and facts or decision and remedy.

The following sections provide useful insights into how to read and understand case law.

1–7a Case Titles and Terminology

The title of a case, such as *Adams v. Jones*, indicates the names of the parties to the lawsuit. The *v.* in the case title stands for *versus*, which means "against." In the trial court, Adams was the plaintiff—the person who filed the suit. Jones was the defendant.

If the case is appealed, however, the appellate court will sometimes place the name of the party appealing the decision first, so the case may be called *Jones v. Adams* if Jones appealed. Because some appellate courts retain the trial court order of names, it is often impossible to distinguish the plaintiff from the defendant in the title of a reported appellate court decision. You must carefully read the facts of each case to identify the parties.

The following terms, phrases, and abbreviations are frequently encountered in court opinions and legal publications.

Parties to Lawsuits The party initiating a lawsuit is referred to as the *plaintiff* or *petitioner*, depending on the nature of the action. The party against whom a lawsuit is brought is the *defendant* or *respondent*. Lawsuits frequently involve more than one plaintiff and/or defendant.

When a case is appealed from the original court or jurisdiction to another court or jurisdiction, the party appealing the case is called the **appellant.** The **appellee** is the party against whom the appeal is taken. (In some appellate courts, the party appealing a case is referred to as the *petitioner*, and the party against whom the suit is brought or appealed is called the *respondent*.)

Judges and Justices The terms *judge* and *justice* are usually synonymous and represent two designations given to judges in various courts. All members of the United States Supreme Court, for instance, are referred to as justices. Justice is the formal title often given to judges of appellate courts, although this is not always true. In New York, a justice is a judge of the trial court (called the Supreme Court), and a member of the Court of Appeals (the state's highest court) is called a judge.

The term *justice* is commonly abbreviated to J., and *justices*, to JJ. A United States Supreme Court case might refer to Justice Sotomayor as Sotomayor, J., or to Chief Justice Roberts as Roberts, C.J.

Decisions and Opinions Most decisions reached by reviewing, or appellate, courts are explained in written **opinions.** The opinion contains the court's reasons for its decision, the rules of law that apply, and the judgment. You may encounter several types of opinions as you read appellate cases, including the following:

- When all the judges (or justices) agree, a *unanimous opinion* is written for the entire court.
- When there is not unanimous agreement, a **majority opinion** is generally written. It outlines the views of the majority of the judges deciding the case.
- A judge who agrees (concurs) with the majority opinion as to the result but not as to the legal reasoning often writes a **concurring opinion.** In it, the judge sets out the reasoning that he or she considers correct.
- A **dissenting opinion** presents the views of one or more judges who disagree with the majority view.
- Sometimes, no single position is fully supported by a majority of the judges deciding a case. In this situation, we may have a **plurality opinion.** This is the opinion that has the support of the largest number of judges, but the group in agreement is less than a majority.
- Finally, a court occasionally issues a ***per curiam* opinion** (*per curiam* is Latin for "of the court"), which does not indicate which judge wrote the opinion.

1–7b Sample Court Case

To illustrate the various elements contained in a court opinion, we present an annotated court opinion in Exhibit 1–6. The opinion is from an actual case that the United States Court of Appeals for the Eleventh Circuit decided in 2016.

Background of the Case In December 1955, on a bus in Montgomery, Alabama, Rosa Parks refused to give up her seat to a white man in violation of the city's segregation law. This "courageous act" sparked the modern civil rights movement. Parks's role in "the most significant social movement in the history of the United States" has been chronicled in books and movies, and featured on mementoes, some of which are offered for sale by Target Corp. The Rosa and Raymond Parks Institute for Self Development is a Michigan firm that owns the right to use Parks's name and likeness for commercial purposes. The Institute filed a suit in a federal district court against Target, alleging misappropriation in violation of the Institute's right of publicity. The court dismissed the complaint. The Institute appealed to the U.S. Court of Appeals for the Eleventh Circuit, arguing that Target's sales of books, movies, and other items that depict or discuss Rosa Parks and the modern civil rights movement violated Michigan law.

Editorial Practice You will note that triple asterisks (* * *) and quadruple asterisks (* * * *) frequently appear in the opinion. The triple asterisks indicate that we have deleted a few words or sentences from the opinion for the sake of readability or brevity. Quadruple asterisks mean that an entire paragraph (or more) has been omitted.

Additionally, when the opinion cites another case or legal source, the citation to the case or source has been omitted, again for the sake of readability and brevity. These editorial practices are continued in the other court opinions presented in this book. In addition, whenever we present a court opinion that includes a term or phrase that may not be readily understandable, a bracketed definition or paraphrase has been added.

Briefing Cases Knowing how to read and understand court opinions and the legal reasoning used by the courts is an essential step in undertaking accurate legal research. A further step is "briefing," or summarizing, the case.

Legal researchers routinely brief cases by reducing the texts of the opinions to their essential elements. Generally, when you brief a case, you first summarize the background and facts of the case, as the authors have done for most of the cases presented in this text. You then indicate the issue (or issues) before the court. An important element in the case brief is, of course, the court's decision on the issue and the legal reasoning used by the court in reaching that decision.

Detailed instructions on how to brief a case are given in Appendix A, which also includes a briefed version of the sample court case presented in Exhibit 1–6.

EXHIBIT 1–6 A Sample Court Case

This section contains the citation—the name of the case, the name of the court that heard the case, the year of the decision, and reporters in which the court's opinion can be found.	**Rosa and Raymond Parks Institute for Self Development v. Target Corporation** United States Court of Appeals, Eleventh Circuit, 812 F.3d 824 (2016).
This line provides the name of the judge (or justice) who authored the court's opinion.	*ROSENBAUM*, Circuit Judge: * * * *
In December 1955, on a bus in Montgomery, Alabama, Parks refused to give up her seat to a white man in violation of the city's segregation law.	[Rosa] **Parks's courageous act** inspired the Montgomery Bus Boycott and served as the **impetus** for the **modern Civil Rights Movement,** transforming the nation.
An *impetus* is a stimulus or a spark.	In response to Parks's arrest, for 381 days, 42,000 African–Americans boycotted Montgomery buses, until the United States Supreme Court held the Montgomery segregation law unconstitutional and ordered desegregation of the buses.
The *modern civil rights movement* (1954–1964) included mass demonstrations in which participants sought equality in public and private life at national, state, and local levels, as well as an end to state and local segregation and discrimination in schools, in the workplace and at the polls. The movement culminated in the enactment of two federal Civil Rights acts in 1957 and 1964.	Parks's refusal to **cede** ground in the face of continued injustice has made her among the most revered heroines of our national story; her role in American history cannot be over-emphasized. Indeed, the United States Congress * * * has credited Parks with "igniting the most significant social movement in the history of the United States."
To *cede* is to yield or surrender.	So it is not surprising that authors would write about Parks's story and artists would celebrate it with their works. The commemoration and dissemination of Parks's journey continues to entrench and embolden our pursuit of justice. And it is in the general public interest to relentlessly preserve, spotlight, and recount the story
A *right of publicity* is a person's right to the use of his or her name and likeness for a commercial purpose.	of Rosa Parks and the Civil Rights Movement—even when that interest allegedly conflicts with an individual **right of publicity.**
The court divides the opinion into three sections. The first section summarizes the factual background of the case.	**I.** The Rosa and Raymond Parks Institute for Self Development (the "Institute") is a Michigan * * * corporation that owns the name and likeness of the late Rosa Parks * * * .

Continued

EXHIBIT 1–6 A Sample Court Case—Continued

Target Corporation ("Target"), a national retail corporation headquartered in Minneapolis, Minnesota, operates more than 1,800 retail stores across the United States.

Target offered [for sale] seven books about Parks * * *, the * * * movie *The Rosa Parks Story*, and a * * * plaque that included * * * a picture of Parks.

* * * *

Misappropriation is the use of a person's name or likeness without his or her consent for a commercial purpose. This is commonly referred to as a violation of the individual's right of publicity.

* * * The Institute filed the underlying complaint in [a federal district court]. The Institute alleged claims for * * * **misappropriation** * * * for Target's sales of all items using the name and likeness of Rosa Parks.

Generally, the Institute complained that * * * Target had unfairly and "without the Institute's prior knowledge, or consent, used Parks's name, likeness, and image to sell products * * * for Target's own commercial advantage." * * * The district court dismissed the complaint, and this appeal followed.

The second major section of the opinion responds to the plaintiff's appeal.

II.

* * * In this case we apply * * * the **substantive law** of Michigan.

Substantive law is law that defines the rights and duties of persons with respect to each other. A federal court exercising jurisdiction based on diversity of citizenship—as in this case, where the two corporate parties are "citizens" of different states—applies the substantive law of the state in which the court sits (except in cases governed by federal law or the United States Constitution).

* * * *

Michigan's common-law right of publicity is founded upon the interest of the individual in the exclusive use of his own identity, in so far as it is represented by his name or likeness, and in so far as the use may be of benefit to him or to others. This * * * privacy right guards against the appropriation of the commercial value of a person's identity by using without consent the person's name, likeness, or other *indicia*

Indicia is a synonym for indications or signs.

of identity for the purpose of trade.

Privacy rights, however, are not absolute. * * * Individual rights must yield to the

Qualified privilege gives someone a limited right to act contrary to another person's right without the other person's having legal recourse for the act.

qualified privilege to communicate on matters of public interest.

* * * *

* * * The privilege attaches to matters of general public interest and extends

In this context, *bona fide* means sincerely and honestly.

to all communications made ***bona fide*** upon any subject matter where the party

EXHIBIT 1–6 A Sample Court Case—Continued

communicating has an interest or a [legal, moral, or social] duty to a person having a corresponding interest or duty.

* * * *

Of course, it is beyond dispute that Rosa Parks is a figure of great historical significance and the Civil Rights Movement a matter of legitimate and important public interest. And it is **uncontested** that * * * the * * * books * * * and the movie are all *bona fide* works * * * discussing Parks and her role in the Civil Rights Movement.

> Here, *uncontested* can mean unchallenged or accepted, as well as evident or obvious.

Similarly, the plaque depicts images and mentions dates and statements related to Parks and the Civil Rights Movement, in an effort to convey a message concerning Parks, her courage, and the results of her strength. Indeed, all of the works in question communicate information, express opinions, recite grievances, and protest claimed abuses on behalf of a movement whose existence and objectives continue to be of the highest public interest and concern.

* * * *

* * * The Institute has not articulated any argument as to why Michigan's qualified privilege for matters of public concern would not apply to these works, in light of the conspicuous historical importance of Rosa Parks. Nor can we conceive of any.

* * * Indeed, it is difficult to conceive of a discussion of the Civil Rights Movement without reference to Parks and her role in it. And Michigan law does not make discussion of these topics of public concern contingent on paying a fee. As a result, [the] books, the movie, and the plaque find protection in Michigan's qualified privilege protecting matters of public interest.

[III.]

> In the third major section of the opinion, the court states its decision.

In short, the district court did not err in dismissing the Institute's complaint. The district court's order is **AFFIRMED.**

> To *affirm* is to validate, to give legal force to.

Reviewing: Law and Legal Reasoning

Suppose that the California legislature passes a law that severely restricts carbon dioxide emissions from automobiles in that state. A group of automobile manufacturers files suit against the state of California to prevent the enforcement of the law. The automakers claim that a federal law already sets fuel economy standards nationwide and that fuel economy standards are essentially the same as carbon dioxide emission standards. According to the automobile manufacturers, it is unfair to allow California to impose more stringent regulations than those set by the federal law. Using the information presented in the chapter, answer the following questions.

1. Who are the parties (the plaintiffs and the defendant) in this lawsuit?
2. Are the plaintiffs seeking a legal remedy or an equitable remedy?
3. What is the primary source of the law that is at issue here?
4. Where would you look to find the relevant California and federal laws?

Debate This . . . *Under the doctrine of* stare decisis, *courts are obligated to follow the precedents established in their jurisdiction unless there is a compelling reason not to. Should U.S. courts continue to adhere to this common law principle, given that our government now regulates so many areas by statute?*

Terms and Concepts

administrative agency 4
administrative law 4
allege 10
appellant 19
appellee 19
binding authority 8
breach 6
case law 5
case on point 11
citation 14
civil law 14
common law 6
concurring opinion 20
constitutional law 4
court of equity 6
court of law 6
criminal law 14
cyberlaw 14
damages 6

defendant 6
defense 6
dissenting opinion 20
equitable maxims 6
executive agency 5
historical school 12
independent regulatory agency 5
jurisprudence 12
laches 6
law 2
legal positivism 12
legal realism 13
legal reasoning 10
liability 2
majority opinion 20
natural law 12
opinion 20
ordinance 4
persuasive authority 10

per curiam opinion 20
petitioner 6
plaintiff 6
plurality opinion 20
precedent 7
procedural law 13
remedy 6
remedy at law 6
remedy in equity 6
reporter 8
respondent 6
sociological school 13
stare decisis 8
statute of limitations 6
statutory law 4
substantive law 13
uniform law 4

Issue Spotters

1. Under what circumstances might a judge rely on case law to determine the intent and purpose of a statute? (See *Sources of American Law.*)

2. After World War II, several Nazis were convicted of "crimes against humanity" by an international court. Assuming that these convicted war criminals had not disobeyed any law of their country and had merely been following their government's orders, what law had they violated? Explain. (See *Schools of Legal Thought.*)

• **Check your answers to the Issue Spotters against the answers provided in Appendix D at the end of this text.**

Business Scenarios

1–1. Binding versus Persuasive Authority. A county court in Illinois is deciding a case involving an issue that has never been addressed before in that state's courts. The Iowa Supreme Court, however, recently decided a case involving a very similar fact pattern. Is the Illinois court obligated to follow the Iowa Supreme Court's decision on the issue? If the United States Supreme Court had decided a similar case, would that decision be binding on the Illinois court? Explain. (See *The Common Law Tradition*.)

1–2. Sources of Law. This chapter discussed a number of sources of American law. Which source of law takes priority in the following situations, and why? (See *Sources of American Law*.)

(a) A federal statute conflicts with the U.S. Constitution.

(b) A federal statute conflicts with a state constitutional provision.

(c) A state statute conflicts with the common law of that state.

(d) A state constitutional amendment conflicts with the U.S. Constitution.

1–3. *Stare Decisis*. In this chapter, we stated that the doctrine of *stare decisis* "became a cornerstone of the English and American judicial systems." What does *stare decisis* mean, and why has this doctrine been so fundamental to the development of our legal tradition? (See *The Common Law Tradition*.)

Business Case Problems

1–4. Spotlight on AOL—Common Law. AOL, LLC,

mistakenly made public the personal information of 650,000 of its members. The members filed a suit, alleging violations of California law. AOL asked the court to dismiss the suit on the basis of a "forum-selection clause" in its member agreement that designates Virginia courts as the place where member disputes will be tried. Under a decision of the United States Supreme Court, a forum-selection clause is unenforceable "if enforcement would contravene a strong public policy of the forum in which suit is brought." California courts have declared in other cases that the AOL clause contravenes a strong public policy. If the court applies the doctrine of *stare decisis*, will it dismiss the suit? Explain. [*Doe 1 v. AOL LLC*, 552 F.3d 1077 (9th Cir. 2009)] (See *The Common Law Tradition*.)

1–5. Business Case Problem with Sample Answer— Reading Citations. Assume that you want to read the entire

court opinion in the case of *Equal Employment Opportunity Commission v. Autozone, Inc.*, 809 F.3d 916 (7th Cir. 2016). Refer to the subsection entitled "Finding Case Law" in this chapter, and then explain specifically where you would find the court's opinion. (See *How to Find Primary Sources of Law*.)

• **For a sample answer to Problem 1–5, go to Appendix E at the end of this text.**

1–6. A Question of Ethics—The Common Law Tradition. On July 5, 1884, Dudley, Stephens, and Brooks—

"all able-bodied English seamen"—and a teenage English boy were cast adrift in a lifeboat following a storm at sea. They had no water with them in the boat, and all they had for sustenance were two one-pound tins of turnips. On July 24, Dudley proposed that one of the four in the lifeboat be sacrificed to save the others. Stephens agreed with Dudley, but Brooks refused to consent—and the boy was never asked for his opinion. On July 25, Dudley killed the boy, and the three men then fed on the boy's body and blood. Four days later, a passing vessel rescued the men. They were taken to England and tried for the murder of the boy. If the men had not fed on the boy's body, they would probably have died of starvation within the four-day period. The boy, who was in a much weaker condition, would likely have died before the rest. [*Regina v. Dudley and Stephens*, 14 Q.B.D. (Queen's Bench Division, England) 273 (1884)] (See *The Common Law Tradition*.)

(a) The basic question in this case is whether the survivors should be subject to penalties under English criminal law, given the men's unusual circumstances. Were the defendants' actions necessary but unethical? Explain your reasoning. What ethical issues might be involved here?

(b) Should judges ever have the power to look beyond the written "letter of the law" in making their decisions? Why or why not?

Legal Reasoning Group Activity

1–7. Court Opinions. Read through the subsection in this chapter entitled "Decisions and Opinions." (See *How to Read and Understand Case Law*.)

(a) One group will explain the difference between a concurring opinion and a majority opinion.

(b) Another group will outline the difference between a concurring opinion and a dissenting opinion.

(c) A third group will explain why judges and justices write concurring and dissenting opinions, given that these opinions will not affect the outcome of the case at hand, which has already been decided by majority vote.

Answers to the *Issue Spotters*

1. ***Under what circumstances might a judge rely on case law to determine the intent and purpose of a statute?*** Case law includes courts' interpretations of statutes, as well as constitutional provisions and administrative rules. Statutes often codify common law rules. For these reasons, a judge might rely on the common law as a guide to the intent and purpose of a statute.

2. ***Assuming that these convicted war criminals had not disobeyed any law of their country and had merely been following their government's orders, what law had they violated? Explain.*** At the time of the Nuremberg trials, "crimes against humanity" were new international crimes. The laws criminalized such acts as murder, extermination, enslavement, deportation, and other inhumane acts committed against any civilian population. These international laws derived their legitimacy from "natural law."

Natural law, which is the oldest and one of the most significant schools of jurisprudence, holds that governments and legal systems should reflect the moral and ethical ideals that are inherent in human nature. Because natural law is universal and discoverable by reason, its adherents believe that all other law is derived from natural law. Natural law therefore supersedes laws created by humans (national, or "positive," law), and in a conflict between the two, national or positive law loses its legitimacy.

The Nuremberg defendants asserted that they had been acting in accordance with German law. The judges dismissed these claims, reasoning that the defendants' acts were commonly regarded as crimes and that the accused must have known that the acts would be considered criminal. The judges clearly believed the tenets of natural law and expected that the defendants, too, should have been able to realize that their acts ran afoul of it. The fact that the "positivist law" of Germany at the time required them to commit these acts is irrelevant. Under natural law theory, the international court was justified in finding the defendants guilty of crimes against humanity.

Sample Answers for *Business Case Problems with Sample Answer*

Problem 1–5. *Reading Citations.* The court's opinion in this case—*Equal Employment Opportunity Commission v. Autozone, Inc.,* 809 F.3d 916 (7th Cir. 2016)—can be found in Volume 809 of *Federal Reporter, Third Series* on page 916. The U.S. Court of Appeals for the Seventh Circuit issued this opinion in 2016.

CHAPTER

Courts and Alternative Dispute Resolution

The United States has fifty-two court systems—one for each of the fifty states, one for the District of Columbia, and a federal system. Keep in mind that the federal courts are not superior to the state courts. They are simply an independent system of courts, which derives its authority from Article III, Section 2, of the U.S. Constitution. By the power given to it under the U.S. Constitution, Congress has extended the federal court system to U.S. territories such as Guam, Puerto Rico, and the Virgin Islands.[1]

As we shall see, the United States Supreme Court is the final controlling voice over all of these fifty-two systems, at least when questions of federal law are involved. The Supreme Court's decisions—whether on free speech and social media, health-care subsidies, environmental regulation, or same-sex marriage—represent the last word in the most controversial legal debates in our society. Nevertheless, many of the legal issues that arise in our daily lives, such as the use of social media by courts, employers, and law enforcement, have not yet come before the nation's highest court. The lower courts usually resolve such pressing matters, making these courts equally important in our legal system.

Although an understanding of our nation's court systems is beneficial for anyone, it is particularly crucial for businesspersons, who will likely face a lawsuit at some time during their careers. Anyone involved in business should be familiar with the basic requirements that must be met before a party can bring a lawsuit before a particular court.

---

1. In Guam and the Virgin Islands, territorial courts serve as both federal courts and state courts. In Puerto Rico, they serve only as federal courts.

2–1 The Judiciary's Role in American Government

The body of American law includes the federal and state constitutions, statutes passed by legislative bodies, administrative law, and the case decisions and legal principles that form the common law. These laws would be meaningless, however, without the courts to interpret and apply them. The essential role of the judiciary—the courts—in the American governmental system is to interpret the laws and apply them to specific situations.

2–1a Judicial Review

As the branch of government entrusted with interpreting the laws, the judiciary can decide, among other things, whether the laws or actions of the other two branches are constitutional. The process for making such a determination is known as **judicial review.** The power of judicial review enables the judicial branch to act as a check on the other two branches of government, in line with the system of checks and balances established by the U.S. Constitution.[2]

2–1b The Origins of Judicial Review in the United States

The power of judicial review is not mentioned in the U.S. Constitution (although many constitutional scholars believe that the founders intended the judiciary to have this power). The United States Supreme Court explicitly established this power in 1803 in the case *Marbury v. Madison*.[3] In that decision, the Court stated, "It is emphatically the province [authority] and duty of the Judicial Department to say what the law is. . . . If two laws conflict with each other, the courts must decide

---

2. In a broad sense, judicial review occurs whenever a court "reviews" a case or legal proceeding—as when an appellate court reviews a lower court's decision. When discussing the judiciary's role in American government, however, the term *judicial review* refers to the power of the judiciary to decide whether the actions of the other two branches of government violate the U.S. Constitution.

3. 5 U.S. (1 Cranch) 137, 2 L.Ed. 60 (1803).

on the operation of each. . . . [I]f both [a] law and the Constitution apply to a particular case, . . . the Court must determine which of these conflicting rules governs the case. This is of the very essence of judicial duty." Since the *Marbury v. Madison* decision, the power of judicial review has remained unchallenged. Today, this power is exercised by both federal and state courts.

2–2 Basic Judicial Requirements

Before a lawsuit can be brought before a court, certain requirements must be met. These requirements relate to jurisdiction, venue, and standing to sue. We examine each of these important concepts here.

2–2a Jurisdiction

In Latin, *juris* means "law," and *diction* means "to speak." Thus, "the power to speak the law" is the literal meaning of the term **jurisdiction.** Before any court can hear a case, it must have jurisdiction over the person (or company) against whom the suit is brought (the defendant) or over the property involved in the suit. The court must also have jurisdiction over the subject matter of the dispute.

Jurisdiction over Persons or Property Generally, a particular court can exercise *in personam* **jurisdiction** (personal jurisdiction) over any person or business that resides in a certain geographic area. A state trial court, for instance, normally has jurisdictional authority over residents (including businesses) of a particular area of the state, such as a county or district. A state's highest court (often called the state supreme court[4]) has jurisdictional authority over all residents within the state.

A court can also exercise jurisdiction over property that is located within its boundaries. This kind of jurisdiction is known as *in rem* **jurisdiction**, or "jurisdiction over the thing." ■ **EXAMPLE 2.1** A dispute arises over the ownership of a boat in dry dock in Fort Lauderdale, Florida. The boat is owned by an Ohio resident, over whom a Florida court normally cannot exercise personal jurisdiction. The other party to the dispute is a resident of Nebraska. In this situation, a lawsuit concerning the boat could be brought in a Florida state court on the basis of the court's *in rem* jurisdiction. ■

Long Arm Statutes and Minimum Contacts. Under the authority of a state **long arm statute,** a court can exercise personal jurisdiction over certain out-of-state defendants based on activities that took place within the state. Before a court can exercise jurisdiction, though, it must be demonstrated that the defendant had sufficient contacts, or *minimum contacts*, with the state to justify the jurisdiction.[5]

Generally, the minimum-contacts requirement means that the defendant must have sufficient connection to the state for the judge to conclude that it is fair for the state to exercise power over the defendant. For instance, if an out-of-state defendant caused an automobile accident within the state or breached a contract formed there, a court will usually find that minimum contacts exist to exercise jurisdiction over that defendant. Similarly, a state may exercise personal jurisdiction over a nonresident defendant that is sued for selling defective goods within the state.

■ **CASE IN POINT 2.2** An Xbox game system caught fire in Bonnie Broquet's home in Texas and caused substantial personal injuries. Broquet filed a lawsuit in a Texas court against Ji-Haw Industrial Company, a nonresident company that made the Xbox components. Broquet alleged that Ji-Haw's components were defective and had caused the fire. Ji-Haw argued that the Texas court lacked jurisdiction over it, but a state appellate court held that the Texas long arm statute authorized the exercise of jurisdiction over the out-of-state defendant.[6] ■

Corporate Contacts. Because corporations are considered legal persons, courts use the same principles to determine whether it is fair to exercise jurisdiction over a corporation. A corporation normally is subject to personal jurisdiction in the state in which it is incorporated, has its principal office, and/or is doing business.

Courts apply the minimum-contacts test to determine if they can exercise jurisdiction over out-of-state corporations. The minimum-contacts requirement is usually met if the corporation advertises or sells its products within the state, or places its goods into the "stream of commerce" with the intent that the goods be sold in the state. ■ **EXAMPLE 2.3** A business is incorporated under the laws of Maine but has a branch office and manufacturing plant in Georgia. The corporation also advertises and sells its products in Georgia. These activities would likely constitute sufficient contacts with the state of

---

4. As will be discussed shortly, a state's highest court is often referred to as the state supreme court, but there are exceptions. For instance, in New York the supreme court is a trial court.

5. The minimum-contacts standard was first established in *International Shoe Co. v. State of Washington*, 326 U.S. 310, 66 S.Ct. 154, 90 L.Ed. 95 (1945).

6. *Ji-Haw Industrial Co. v. Broquet*, 2008 WL 441822 (Tex.App.—San Antonio 2008).

Georgia to allow a Georgia court to exercise jurisdiction over the corporation. ∎

Some corporations do not sell or advertise their products in the general marketplace. Determining what constitutes minimum contacts in these situations can be more difficult. ∎ **CASE IN POINT 2.4** Independence Plating Corporation is a New Jersey corporation that provides metal-coating services. Its only office and all of its personnel are located in New Jersey, and it does not advertise out of state. Independence had a long-standing business relationship with Southern Prestige Industries, Inc., a North Carolina company. Eventually, Southern Prestige filed suit in North Carolina against Independence for defective workmanship. Independence argued that North Carolina did not have jurisdiction over it, but the court held that Independence had sufficient minimum contacts with the state to justify jurisdiction. The two parties had exchanged thirty-two separate purchase orders in a period of less than twelve months.[7] ∎

Jurisdiction over Subject Matter Subject-matter jurisdiction refers to the limitations on the types of cases a court can hear. Certain courts are empowered to hear certain kinds of disputes. In both the federal and the state court systems, there are courts of general (unlimited) jurisdiction and courts of limited jurisdiction.

A *court of general jurisdiction* can decide cases involving a broad array of issues. An example of a court of general jurisdiction is a state trial court or a federal district court.

In contrast, a *court of limited jurisdiction* can hear only specific types of cases. An example of a state court of limited jurisdiction is a probate court. **Probate courts** are state courts that handle only the disposition of a person's assets and obligations after that person's death, including issues relating to the custody and guardianship of children. An example of a federal court of limited subject-matter jurisdiction is a bankruptcy court. **Bankruptcy courts** handle only bankruptcy proceedings, which are governed by federal bankruptcy law.

A court's jurisdiction over subject matter is usually defined in the statute or constitution that created the court. In both the federal and the state court systems, a court's subject-matter jurisdiction can be limited by any of the following:

1. The subject of the lawsuit.
2. The sum in controversy.

3. Whether the case involves a felony (a serious type of crime) or a misdemeanor (a less serious type of crime).
4. Whether the proceeding is a trial or an appeal.

Original and Appellate Jurisdiction The distinction between courts of original jurisdiction and courts of appellate jurisdiction normally lies in whether the case is being heard for the first time. Courts having original jurisdiction are courts of the first instance, or trial courts. These are courts in which lawsuits begin, trials take place, and evidence is presented. In the federal court system, the *district courts* are trial courts. In the various state court systems, the trial courts are known by various names, as will be discussed shortly.

The key point here is that any court having original jurisdiction normally serves as a trial court. Courts having appellate jurisdiction act as reviewing, or appellate, courts. In general, cases can be brought before appellate courts only on appeal from an order or a judgment of a trial court or other lower courts.

Jurisdiction of the Federal Courts Because the federal government is a government of limited powers, the jurisdiction of the federal courts is limited. Federal courts have subject-matter jurisdiction in two situations: when a federal question is involved and when there is diversity of citizenship.

Federal Questions. Article III of the U.S. Constitution establishes the boundaries of federal judicial power. Section 2 of Article III states that "the judicial Power shall extend to all Cases, in Law and Equity, arising under this Constitution, the Laws of the United States, and Treaties made, or which shall be made, under their Authority."

In effect, this clause means that whenever a plaintiff's cause of action is based, at least in part, on the U.S. Constitution, a treaty, or a federal law, a **federal question** arises. Any lawsuit involving a federal question, such as a person's rights under the U.S. Constitution, can originate in a federal court. Note that in a case based on a federal question, a federal court will apply federal law.

Diversity of Citizenship. Federal district courts can also exercise original jurisdiction over cases involving **diversity of citizenship.** The most common type of diversity jurisdiction[8] requires *both* of the following:

---

7. *Southern Prestige Industries, Inc. v. Independence Plating Corp.*, 690 S.E.2d 768 (N.C. 2010).

8. Diversity jurisdiction also exists in cases between (1) a foreign country and citizens of a state or of different states and (2) citizens of a state and citizens or subjects of a foreign country. Cases based on these types of diversity jurisdiction occur infrequently.

1. The plaintiff and defendant must be residents of different states.
2. The dollar amount in controversy must exceed $75,000.

For purposes of diversity jurisdiction, a corporation is a citizen of both the state in which it is incorporated and the state in which its principal place of business is located.

A case involving diversity of citizenship can be filed in the appropriate federal district court. (If the case starts in a state court, it can sometimes be transferred, or "removed," to a federal court.) A large percentage of the cases filed in federal courts each year are based on diversity of citizenship. As noted before, a federal court will apply federal law in cases involving federal questions.

In a case based on diversity of citizenship, in contrast, a federal court will apply the relevant state law (which is often the law of the state in which the court sits).

The following case focused on whether diversity jurisdiction existed. A boat owner was severely burned when his boat exploded after being overfilled with fuel at a marina in the U.S. Virgin Islands. The owner filed a suit in a federal district court against the marina and sought a jury trial. The defendant argued that a plaintiff in an admiralty, or maritime, case (a case based on something that happened at sea) does not have a right to a jury trial unless the court has diversity jurisdiction. The defendant claimed that because both parties were citizens of the Virgin Islands, the court had no such jurisdiction.

Case Analysis 2.1

Mala v. Crown Bay Marina, Inc.
United States Court of Appeals, Third Circuit, 704 F.3d 239 (2013).

In the Language of the Court
SMITH, Circuit Judge.
* * * *

Kelley Mala is a citizen of the United States Virgin Islands. * * * He went for a cruise in his powerboat near St. Thomas, Virgin Islands. When his boat ran low on gas, he entered Crown Bay Marina to refuel. Mala tied the boat to one of Crown Bay's eight fueling stations and began filling his tank with an automatic gas pump. Before walking to the cash register to buy oil, Mala asked a Crown Bay attendant to watch his boat.

By the time Mala returned, the boat's tank was overflowing and fuel was spilling into the boat and into the water. The attendant manually shut off the pump and acknowledged that the pump had been malfunctioning in recent days. Mala began cleaning up the fuel, and at some point, the attendant provided soap and water. Mala eventually departed the marina, but as he did so, the engine caught fire and exploded. Mala was thrown into the water and was severely burned. His boat was unsalvageable.

* * * Mala sued Crown Bay in the District Court of the Virgin Islands.

Mala's * * * complaint asserted * * * that Crown Bay negligently maintained its gas pump. [Negligence is the failure to exercise the standard of care that a reasonable person would exercise in similar circumstances. Negligence can form the basis for a legal claim.] The complaint also alleged that the District Court had admiralty and diversity jurisdiction over the case, and it requested a jury trial.
* * * *

* * * Crown Bay filed a motion to strike Mala's jury demand. Crown Bay argued that plaintiffs generally do not have a jury-trial right in admiralty cases—only when the court also has diversity jurisdiction. And Crown Bay asserted that the parties were not diverse in this case * * *. In response to this motion, the District Court ruled that both Mala and Crown Bay were citizens of the Virgin Islands. The court therefore struck Mala's jury demand, but nevertheless opted to empanel an advisory jury. [The court could accept or reject the advisory jury's verdict.]

* * * At the end of the trial, the advisory jury returned a verdict of $460,000 for Mala—$400,000 for pain and suffering and $60,000 in compensatory

damages. It concluded that Mala was 25 percent at fault and that Crown Bay was 75 percent at fault. The District Court ultimately rejected the verdict and entered judgment for Crown Bay.
* * * *

This appeal followed.
* * * *

Mala * * * argues that the District Court improperly refused to conduct a jury trial. This claim ultimately depends on whether the District Court had diversity jurisdiction.

The Seventh Amendment [to the U.S. Constitution] creates a right to civil jury trials in federal court: "In Suits at common law * * * the right of trial by jury shall be preserved." Admiralty suits are not "Suits at common law," which means that when a district court has only admiralty jurisdiction the plaintiff does not have a jury-trial right. But [a federal statute] allows plaintiffs to pursue state claims in admiralty cases as long as the district court also has diversity jurisdiction. In such cases [the statute] preserves whatever jury-trial right exists with respect to the underlying state claims.

Case 2.1 Continues

Mala argues that the District Court had both admiralty and diversity jurisdiction. As a preliminary matter, the court certainly had admiralty jurisdiction. The alleged tort occurred on navigable water and bore a substantial connection to maritime activity.

The grounds for diversity jurisdiction are less certain. *District courts have jurisdiction only if the parties are completely diverse. This means that no plaintiff may have the same state or territorial citizenship as any defendant.* The parties agree that Mala was a citizen of the Virgin Islands. [Emphasis added.]

Unfortunately for Mala, the District Court concluded that Crown Bay also was a citizen of the Virgin Islands. Mala rejects this conclusion.

Mala bears the burden of proving that the District Court had diversity jurisdiction. Mala failed to meet that burden because he did not offer evidence that Crown Bay was anything other than a citizen of the Virgin Islands. Mala contends that Crown Bay admitted to being a citizen of Florida, but Crown Bay actually denied Mala's allegation.

Absent evidence that the parties were diverse, we are left with Mala's allegations. *Allegations are insufficient at trial. And they are especially insufficient on appeal,* where we review the District Court's underlying factual findings for clear error. Under this standard, we will not reverse unless we are left with the definite and firm conviction that Crown Bay was in fact a citizen of Florida. Mala has not presented any credible evidence that Crown Bay was a citizen of Florida—much less evidence that would leave us with the requisite firm conviction. [Emphasis added.]

* * * Accordingly, the parties were not diverse and Mala does not have a jury-trial right.

* * * *

* * * For these reasons we will affirm the District Court's judgment.

Legal Reasoning Questions

1. What is "diversity of citizenship"?

2. How does the presence—or lack—of diversity of citizenship affect a lawsuit?

3. What did the court conclude with respect to the parties' diversity of citizenship in this case?

Exclusive versus Concurrent Jurisdiction When both federal and state courts have the power to hear a case, as is true in lawsuits involving diversity of citizenship, **concurrent jurisdiction** exists. When cases can be tried only in federal courts or only in state courts, **exclusive jurisdiction** exists.

Federal courts have exclusive jurisdiction in cases involving federal crimes, bankruptcy, most patent and copyright claims, suits against the United States, and some areas of admiralty law. State courts also have exclusive jurisdiction over certain subjects—for instance, divorce and adoption.

When concurrent jurisdiction exists, a party may choose to bring a suit in either a federal court or a state court. Many factors can affect a party's decision to litigate in a federal versus a state court. Examples include the availability of different remedies, the distance to the respective courthouses, or the experience or reputation of a particular judge.

For instance, if the dispute involves a trade secret, a party might conclude that a federal court—which has exclusive jurisdiction over copyrights and patents—would have more expertise in the matter. In contrast, a plaintiff might choose to litigate in a state court if the court has a reputation for awarding substantial amounts of damages or if the judge is perceived as being pro-plaintiff. The concepts of exclusive and concurrent jurisdiction are illustrated in Exhibit 2–1.

Jurisdiction in Cyberspace The Internet's capacity to bypass political and geographic boundaries undercuts the traditional basis on which courts assert personal jurisdiction. As discussed, for a court to compel a defendant to come before it, the defendant must have a sufficient connection—that is, minimum contacts—with the state. When a defendant's only contacts with the state are through a Web site, however, it can be difficult to determine whether these contacts are sufficient for a court to exercise jurisdiction.

The "Sliding-Scale" Standard. The courts have developed a "sliding-scale" standard to determine when they can exercise personal jurisdiction over an out-of-state defendant based on the defendant's Web activities. The sliding-scale standard identifies three types of Internet business contacts and outlines the following rules for jurisdiction:

1. When the defendant conducts substantial business over the Internet (such as contracts and sales), jurisdiction is proper.

2. When there is some interactivity through a Web site, jurisdiction may be proper, depending on the

EXHIBIT 2–1 Exclusive and Concurrent Jurisdiction

Exclusive Federal Jurisdiction
(cases involving federal crimes, federal antitrust law, bankruptcy, patents, copyrights, trademarks, suits against the United States, some areas of admiralty law, and certain other matters specified in federal statutes)

Concurrent Jurisdiction
(most cases involving federal questions, diversity-of-citizenship cases)

Exclusive State Jurisdiction
(cases involving all matters not subject to federal jurisdiction—for example, divorce and adoption cases)

circumstances. Even a single contact can satisfy the minimum-contacts requirement in certain situations.

3. When a defendant merely engages in passive advertising on the Web, jurisdiction is never proper.[9] An Internet communication is typically considered passive if people have to voluntarily access it to read the message and active if it is sent to specific individuals.

■ **CASE IN POINT 2.5** Samantha Guffey lives in Oklahoma. She placed a winning bid on eBay for a used 2009 Volvo XC90 from Motorcars of Nashville, Inc. (MNI), a Tennessee corporation. Before she won the auction, she spoke with Otto Ostonakulov at the dealership. Later, Ostonakulov sent the necessary paperwork to Guffey in Oklahoma. She signed and returned it by mail, and he arranged for MNI to ship the Volvo to Oklahoma.

When the car was delivered to Guffey, she discovered it was not in the condition advertised. She filed a lawsuit in Oklahoma against MNI and Ostonakulov, alleging fraud and a violation of state consumer protection laws. Guffey's complaint alleged that the defendants were active "power sellers" on eBay, averaging twelve to twenty-five cars for sale every day. The sellers claimed that the Oklahoma court lacked jurisdiction over them, and a trial court dismissed the complaint. Guffey appealed. The reviewing court found that Oklahoma had jurisdiction because the sellers' "use of eBay to make multiple sales is systemic and appears to be a

core part of their business." They had negotiated with Guffey directly to sell her a vehicle in Oklahoma and had regularly used eBay to sell vehicles to remote parties in the past.[10] ■

International Jurisdictional Issues. Because the Internet is international in scope, it obviously raises international jurisdictional issues. The world's courts seem to be developing a standard that echoes the requirement of minimum contacts applied by the U.S. courts.

Most courts are indicating that minimum contacts—doing business within the jurisdiction, for instance—are enough to compel a defendant to appear and that a physical presence in the country is not necessary. The effect of this standard is that a business firm has to comply with the laws in any jurisdiction in which it targets customers for its products. This situation is complicated by the fact that many countries' laws on particular issues—free speech, for instance—are very different from U.S. laws.

The following case illustrates how federal courts apply a sliding-scale standard to determine if they can exercise jurisdiction over a foreign defendant whose only contact with the United States is through a Web site.

___
9. For a leading case on this issue, see *Zippo Manufacturing Co. v. Zippo Dot Com, Inc.*, 952 F.Supp. 1119 (W.D.Pa. 1997).

10. *Guffey v. Ostonakulov*, 2014 OK 6, 321 P.3d 971 (Ok.Sup. 2014). Note that a single sale on eBay does not necessarily form the basis for jurisdiction. Jurisdiction depends on whether the seller regularly uses eBay as a means for doing business with remote buyers. See *Hinners v. Robey*, 336 S.W.3d 891 (Ky.Sup. 2008).

Spotlight on Gucci

Case 2.2 Gucci America, Inc. v. Wang Huoqing

United States District Court, Northern District of California, 2011 WL 30972 (2011).

Company Profile *Gucci America, Inc., a New York corporation headquartered in New York City, is part of Gucci Group, a global fashion firm with offices in China, France, Great Britain, Italy, and Japan. Gucci makes and sells high-quality luxury goods, including footwear, belts, sunglasses, handbags, wallets, jewelry, fragrances, and children's clothing. In connection with its products, Gucci uses twenty-one federally registered trademarks. Gucci also operates a number of boutiques, some of which are located in California.*

Background and Facts Wang Huoqing, a resident of the People's Republic of China, operates numerous Web sites. When Gucci discovered that Wang Huoqing's Web sites offered for sale counterfeit goods—products bearing Gucci's trademarks but not genuine Gucci articles—it hired a private investigator in San Jose, California, to buy goods from the Web sites. The investigator purchased a wallet that was labeled Gucci but was counterfeit.

Gucci filed a trademark infringement lawsuit against Wang Huoqing in a federal district court in California seeking damages and an injunction to prevent further infringement. Wang Huoqing was notified of the lawsuit via e-mail but did not appear in court. Gucci asked the court to enter a default judgment—that is, a judgment entered when the defendant fails to appear. First, however, the court had to determine whether it had personal jurisdiction over Wang Huoqing based on the Internet sales.

In the Language of the Court

Joseph C. *SPERO*, United States Magistrate Judge.

* * * *

* * * Under California's long-arm statute, federal courts in California may exercise jurisdiction to the extent permitted by the Due Process Clause of the Constitution. The Due Process Clause allows federal courts to exercise jurisdiction where * * * the defendant has had sufficient minimum contacts with the forum to subject him or her to the specific jurisdiction of the court. The courts apply a three-part test to determine whether specific jurisdiction exists:

> (1) The nonresident defendant must do some act or consummate some transaction with the forum or perform some act by which he purposefully avails himself of the privilege of conducting activities in the forum, thereby invoking the benefits and protections of its laws; (2) the claim must be one which arises out of or results from the defendant's forum-related activities; and (3) exercise of jurisdiction must be reasonable.

* * * *

In order to satisfy the first prong of the test for specific jurisdiction, a defendant must have either purposefully availed itself of the privilege of conducting business activities within the forum or purposefully directed activities toward the forum. *Purposeful availment typically consists of action taking place in the forum that invokes the benefits and protections of the laws of the forum, such as executing or performing a contract within the forum.* To show purposeful availment, a plaintiff must show that the defendant "engage[d] in some form of affirmative conduct allowing or promoting the transaction of business within the forum state." [Emphasis added.]

"In the Internet context, the Ninth Circuit utilizes a sliding scale analysis under which 'passive' websites do not create sufficient contacts to establish purposeful availment, whereas interactive websites may create sufficient contacts, depending on how interactive the website is." * * * *Personal jurisdiction is appropriate where an entity is conducting business over the Internet and has offered for sale and sold its products to forum [California] residents.* [Emphasis added.]

Here, the allegations and evidence presented by Plaintiffs in support of the Motion are sufficient to show purposeful availment on the part of Defendant Wang Huoqing. Plaintiffs have alleged that Defendant operates "fully interactive Internet websites operating under the Subject Domain Names" and have presented evidence in the form of copies of web pages showing that the websites are, in fact, interactive.

Case 2.2 Continued

* * * Additionally, Plaintiffs allege Defendant is conducting counterfeiting and infringing activities within this Judicial District and has advertised and sold his counterfeit goods in the State of California. * * * Plaintiffs have also presented evidence of one actual sale within this district, made by investigator Robert Holmes from the website bag2do.cn.* * * Finally, Plaintiffs have presented evidence that Defendant Wang Huoqing owns or controls the twenty-eight websites listed in the Motion for Default Judgment. * * * Such commercial activity in the forum amounts to purposeful availment of the privilege of conducting activities within the forum, thus invoking the benefits and protections of its laws. Accordingly, the Court concludes that Defendant's contacts with California are sufficient to show purposeful availment.

Decision and Remedy *The U.S. District Court for the Northern District of California held that it had personal jurisdiction over the foreign defendant, Wang Huoqing. The court entered a default judgment against Wang Huoqing and granted Gucci an injunction.*

Critical Thinking

- **What If the Facts Were Different?** *Suppose that Gucci had not presented evidence that Wang Huoqing had made one actual sale through his Web site to a resident of the court's district (the private investigator). Would the court still have found that it had personal jurisdiction over Wang Huoqing? Why or why not?*
- **Legal Environment** *Is it relevant to the analysis of jurisdiction that Gucci America's principal place of business is in New York rather than California? Explain.*

Minimum Contacts and Smartphones. The widespread use of cellular phones, particularly smartphones, also complicates the determination of personal jurisdiction. People use their smartphones while traveling to make purchases, negotiate business deals, enter contracts, and download applications (apps). If a person traveling in another state (or nation) uses a smartphone to form a contract, does that forum have jurisdiction over the person? Is the party that creates an app subject to jurisdiction anywhere the app is downloaded or used? Because an app differs from a Web page, what degree of interactivity is required for apps to confer jurisdiction in the sliding-scale analysis? The courts will be addressing these questions in coming years and adapting traditional notions of jurisdiction to ever-changing technology.

Concept Summary 2.1 reviews the various types of jurisdiction, including jurisdiction in cyberspace.

2–2b Venue

Jurisdiction has to do with whether a court has authority to hear a case involving specific persons, property, or subject matter. **Venue**[11] is concerned with the most appropriate location for a trial. For instance, two state courts (or two federal courts) may have the authority to exercise jurisdiction over a case. Nonetheless, it may be

more appropriate or convenient to hear the case in one court than in the other.

The concept of venue reflects the policy that a court trying a case should be in the geographic neighborhood (usually the county) where the incident occurred or where the parties reside. Venue in a civil case typically is where the defendant resides or does business, whereas venue in a criminal case normally is where the crime occurred.

In some cases, pretrial publicity or other factors may require a change of venue to another community, especially in criminal cases in which the defendant's right to a fair and impartial jury has been impaired. Note, though, that venue has lost some significance in today's world because of the Internet and 24/7 news reporting. Courts now rarely grant requests for a change of venue. Because everyone has instant access to all information about a purported crime, courts reason that no community is more or less informed or prejudiced for or against a defendant.

2–2c Standing to Sue

Before a party can bring a lawsuit to court, that party must have **standing to sue,** or a sufficient stake in a matter to justify seeking relief through the court system. Standing means that the party that filed the action in court has a legally protected interest at stake in the litigation. At times, a person can have standing to sue on behalf of another person, such as a minor (child) or a mentally incompetent person.

---

11. Pronounced *ven*-yoo.

Concept Summary 2.1

Jurisdiction

Personal
Exists when a defendant:
- Is located in the court's territorial boundaries.
- Qualifies under state long arm statutes.
- Is a corporation doing business within the state.
- Advertises, sells, or places goods into commerce within the state.

Property
- Exists when the property that is subject to a lawsuit is located within the court's territorial boundaries.

Subject Matter
Limits the court's jurisdictional authority to particular types of cases.
- *General jurisdiction*—Exists when a court can hear cases involving a broad array of issues.
- *Limited jurisdiction*—Exists when a court is limited to a specific subject matter, such as probate or divorce.

Original
- Exists with courts that have the authority to hear a case for the first time (trial courts, district courts).

Appellate
- Exists with courts of appeal and review. Generally, appellate courts do not have original jurisdiction.

Federal
A federal court can exercise jurisdiction:
- When the plaintiff's cause of action involves a federal question (is based at least in part on the U.S. Constitution, a treaty, or a federal law).
- In cases between citizens of different states (or cases involving U.S. citizens and foreign countries or their citizens) when the amount in controversy exceeds $75,000 (diversity-of-citizenship jurisdiction).

Concurrent
- Exists when both federal and state courts have authority to hear the same case.

Exclusive
- Exists when only state courts or only federal courts have authority to hear a case.

Cyberspace
- The courts have developed a sliding-scale standard to use in determining when jurisdiction over a Web site owner or operator in another state is proper.

Standing can be broken down into three elements:

1. *Harm.* The party bringing the action must have suffered harm—an invasion of a legally protected interest—or must face imminent harm. The controversy must be real and substantial rather than hypothetical.
2. *Causation.* There must be a causal connection between the conduct complained of and the injury.
3. *Remedy.* It must be likely, as opposed to merely speculative, that a favorable court decision will remedy the injury suffered.

■ **CASE IN POINT 2.6** Harold Wagner obtained a loan through M.S.T. Mortgage Group to buy a house in Texas. After the sale, M.S.T. transferred its interest in the loan to another lender, which, in turn, assigned it to another lender (a common practice in the mortgage industry). Eventually, when Wagner failed to make the loan payments, CitiMortgage, Inc., notified him that it was going to foreclose on the property and sell the house.

Wagner filed a lawsuit, claiming that the lenders had improperly assigned the mortgage loan. In 2014, a federal district court ruled that Wagner lacked standing to contest the assignment. Under Texas law, only the parties directly involved in an assignment can challenge its validity. In this case, the assignment was between two lenders and did not directly involve Wagner.[12] ■

---

12. *Wagner v. CitiMortgage, Inc.*, 995 F.Supp.2d 621 (N.D.Tex. 2014).

2-3 The State and Federal Court Systems

Each state has its own court system. Additionally, there is a system of federal courts. The right-hand side of Exhibit 2–2 illustrates the basic organizational framework characteristic of the court systems in many states. The exhibit also shows how the federal court system is structured. We turn now to an examination of these court systems, beginning with the state courts.

2-3a The State Court Systems

No two state court systems are exactly the same. Typically, though, a state court system includes several levels, or tiers, of courts, as shown in Exhibit 2–2. State courts may include (1) trial courts of limited jurisdiction, (2) trial courts of general jurisdiction, (3) appellate courts (intermediate appellate courts), and (4) the state's highest court (often called the state supreme court).

Generally, any person who is a party to a lawsuit has the opportunity to plead the case before a trial court and then, if he or she loses, before at least one level of appellate court. If the case involves a federal statute or a federal constitutional issue, the decision of the state supreme court may be further appealed to the United States Supreme Court. Note that lawsuits can take years to resolve through the courts, especially since many states have experienced large cuts in court funding in recent years. In fact, the United States Supreme Court decided a

EXHIBIT 2–2 The State and Federal Court Systems

case in 2015 involving a trademark dispute that had been in the courts for more than sixteen years.[13]

The states use various methods to select judges for their courts. Usually, voters elect judges, but in some states judges are appointed. For instance, in Iowa, the governor appoints judges, and then the general population decides whether to confirm their appointment in the next general election. The states usually specify the number of years that judges will serve.

Trial Courts Trial courts are exactly what their name implies—courts in which trials are held and testimony is taken. State trial courts have either general or limited jurisdiction, as defined earlier.

General Jurisdiction. Trial courts that have general jurisdiction as to subject matter may be called county, district, superior, or circuit courts.[14] State trial courts of general jurisdiction have jurisdiction over a wide variety of subjects, including both civil disputes and criminal prosecutions. In some states, trial courts of general jurisdiction may hear appeals from courts of limited jurisdiction.

Limited Jurisdiction. Courts of limited jurisdiction as to subject matter are generally inferior trial courts or minor judiciary courts. Limited jurisdiction courts might include local municipal courts (which could include separate traffic courts and drug courts) and domestic relations courts (which handle divorce and child-custody disputes).

Small claims courts are inferior trial courts that hear only civil cases involving claims of less than a certain amount, such as $5,000 (the amount varies from state to state). Procedures in small claims courts are generally informal, and lawyers are not required (in a few states, lawyers are not even allowed). Decisions of small claims

courts and municipal courts may sometimes be appealed to a state trial court of general jurisdiction.

A few states have also established Islamic law courts, which are courts of limited jurisdiction that serve the American Muslim community. These courts decide cases with reference to the *sharia*, a system of law used in most Islamic countries that is derived from the Qur'an and the sayings and doings of Muhammad and his followers.

Appellate, or Reviewing, Courts Every state has at least one court of appeals (appellate court, or reviewing court), which may be an intermediate appellate court or the state's highest court. About three-fourths of the states have intermediate appellate courts.

Generally, courts of appeals do not conduct new trials, in which evidence is submitted to the court and witnesses are examined. Rather, an appellate court panel of three or more judges reviews the record of the case on appeal, which includes a transcript of the trial proceedings. The appellate court hears arguments from attorneys and determines whether the trial court committed an error.

Reviewing courts focus on questions of law, not questions of fact. A **question of fact** deals with what really happened in regard to the dispute being tried—such as whether a party actually burned a flag. A **question of law** concerns the application or interpretation of the law—such as whether flag-burning is a form of speech protected by the First Amendment to the U.S. Constitution. Only a judge, not a jury, can rule on questions of law.

Appellate courts normally defer (give significant weight) to the trial court's findings on questions of fact because the trial court judge and jury were in a better position to evaluate testimony. The trial court judge and jury can directly observe witnesses' gestures, demeanor, and other nonverbal behavior during the trial. An appellate court cannot.

In the following case, neither the administrative agency that initially ruled on the dispute nor the trial court to which the agency's decision was appealed made a finding on a crucial question of fact. Faced with that circumstance, what should a state appellate court do?

---

13. *B&B Hardware, Inc. v. Hargis Industries, Inc.,* ___ U.S. ___, 135 S.Ct. 1293, 191 L.Ed.2d 222 (2015).
14. The name in Ohio and Pennsylvania is Court of Common Pleas. The name in New York is Supreme Court, Trial Division.

Case 2.3

Johnson v. Oxy USA, Inc.

Court of Appeals of Texas, Houston—14th District, __ S.W.3d __ , 2016 WL 93559 (2016).

Background and Facts Jennifer Johnson was working as a finance analyst for Oxy USA, Inc., when Oxy changed the job's requirements. To meet the new standards, Johnson took courses to become a certified public accountant. Oxy's "Educational Assistance Policy" was to reimburse employees for the

Case 2.3 Continued

cost of such courses. Johnson further agreed that Oxy could withhold the reimbursed amount from her final paycheck if she quit Oxy within a year. When she resigned less than a year later, Oxy withheld that amount from her last check. Johnson filed a claim for the amount with the Texas Workforce Commission (TWC). The TWC ruled that she was not entitled to the unpaid wages. She filed a suit in a Texas state court against Oxy, alleging breach of contract. The court affirmed the TWC's ruling. Johnson appealed.

In the Language of the Court

Ken WISE, Justice

* * * *

* * * The trial court * * * held that Johnson's [claim for breach of contract was] barred by *res judicata* ["a matter judged"]. In a court of law, a claimant typically cannot pursue one remedy to an unfavorable outcome and then seek the same remedy in another proceeding before the same or a different tribunal. Res judicata *bars the relitigation of claims that have been finally adjudicated or that could have been litigated in the prior action.* [Emphasis added.]

Johnson argues that *res judicata* does not apply here because the TWC did not render a final judgment on the merits of her claim that Oxy misinterpreted its Educational Assistance Policy. Specifically, Johnson claims she was "denied the right of full adjudication of her claim because the TWC refused to consider her arguments at the administrative level as beyond its jurisdiction." To support this contention, Johnson points to the following excerpt from the * * * decision:

> * * * The TWC does not interpret contracts between employers and employee but only enforces the Texas Payday Law [the Texas state law that governs the timing of employees' paychecks]. * * * The question of whether the employer properly interpreted their policy on reimbursed educational expenses versus a business expense is a question for a different forum.

According to Johnson, this language shows that the TWC refused to consider the merits of the issue she raised as "beyond its reach." In contrast, the defendants contend that Johnson's claims are barred by *res judicata* because they are based on claims previously decided by the TWC.

* * * *

In Johnson's case, however, the TWC did not decide the key question of fact in dispute—whether Oxy violated its own Educational Assistance Policy when it withheld Johnson's final wages as reimbursement for the CPA courses. In fact, the TWC explicitly refused to do so, stating that the agency "does not interpret contracts between employers and employee." * * * Because this question goes to the heart of Johnson's breach of contract * * * claim, we hold that *res judicata* does not bar [that] claim. [Emphasis added.]

The defendants argue that because Johnson seeks to recover the same wages in this suit as she did in her claim with the TWC, *res judicata* must bar her common law cause of action. However, * * * *res judicata* would only bar a claim if TWC's order is considered final. * * * Here, the order in Johnson's case made no such findings with regard to the Educational Assistance Policy. The order expressly declined to address that issue. Therefore, * * * *res judicata* will not bar Johnson's breach of contract * * * claim.

Decision and Remedy *A state intermediate appellate court reversed the lower court's decision. "The TWC did not decide the key question of fact in dispute—whether Oxy violated its own Educational Assistance Policy when it withheld Johnson's final wages. In fact, the TWC explicitly refused to do so, stating that the agency 'does not interpret contracts between employers and employee.'" The appellate court remanded the case for a trial on the merits.*

Critical Thinking

- **Legal Environment** *Who can decide questions of fact? Who can rule on questions of law? Why?*
- **Global** *In some cases, a court may be asked to determine and interpret the law of a foreign country. Some states consider the issue of what the law of a foreign country requires to be a question of fact. Federal rules of procedure provide that this issue is a question of law. Which position seems more appropriate? Why?*

Highest State Courts The highest appellate court in a state is usually called the supreme court but may be designated by some other name. For instance, in both New York and Maryland, the highest state court is called the Court of Appeals. The highest state court in Maine and Massachusetts is the Supreme Judicial Court. In West Virginia, it is the Supreme Court of Appeals.

The decisions of each state's highest court on all questions of state law are final. Only when issues of federal law are involved can the United States Supreme Court overrule a decision made by a state's highest court. ■ **EXAMPLE 2.7** A city enacts an ordinance that prohibits citizens from engaging in door-to-door

advocacy without first registering with the mayor's office and receiving a permit. A religious group then sues the city, arguing that the law violates the freedoms of speech and religion guaranteed by the First Amendment. If the state supreme court upholds the law, the group could appeal the decision to the United States Supreme Court, because a constitutional (federal) issue is involved. ■

2–3b The Federal Court System

The federal court system is basically a three-tiered model consisting of (1) U.S. district courts (trial courts of general jurisdiction) and various courts of limited

---

MANAGERIAL STRATEGY

Should You Consent to Have Your Business Case Decided by a U.S. Magistrate Judge?

You have a strong case in a contract dispute with one of your business's suppliers. The supplier is located in another state. Your attorney did everything necessary to obtain your "day in court." The court in question is a federal district court. But you have just found out that your case may not be heard for several years—or even longer. Your attorney tells you that the case can be heard in just a few months if you consent to place it in the hands of a U.S. magistrate judge.[a] Should you consent?

A Short History of U.S. Magistrate Judges

Congress authorized the creation of a new federal judicial officer, the U.S. magistrate, in 1968 to help reduce delays in the U.S. district courts.[b] These junior federal officers were to conduct a wide range of judicial proceedings as set out by statute and as assigned by the district judges under whom they served. In 1979, Congress gave U.S. magistrates consent jurisdiction, which authorized them to conduct all civil trials as long as the parties consent.[c] Currently, magistrate judges dispose of over one million civil and criminal district court matters, which include motions and hearings.

The Selection and Quality of Magistrate Judges

As mentioned, federal district judges are nominated by the president, confirmed by the Senate, and appointed for life. In contrast, U.S. magistrate judges are selected by federal district court judges based on the recommenda-

tions of a merit screening committee. They serve an eight-year term (which can be renewed).

By statute, magistrate judges must be chosen through a merit selection process. Applicants are interviewed by a screening committee of lawyers and others from the district in which the position will be filled.[d] Political party affiliation plays no part in the process.

A variety of experienced attorneys, administrative law judges, state court judges, and others apply for magistrate judge positions. A typical opening receives about a hundred applicants. The merit selection panel selects the five most qualified, who are then voted on by federal district court judges.

Because the selection process for a magistrate judge is not the same as for a district judge, some critics have expressed concerns about the quality of magistrate judges. Some groups, such as People for the American Way, are not in favor of allowing magistrate judges the power to decide cases. These critics believe that because of their limited terms, they are not completely immune from outside pressure.

Business Questions

1. *If you were facing an especially complex legal dispute—one involving many facets and several different types of law—would you consent to allowing a U.S. magistrate judge to decide the case? Why or why not?*

2. *If you had to decide whether to allow a U.S. magistrate judge to hear your case, what information might you ask your attorney to provide concerning that individual?*

---

a. 28 U.S.C. Sec 636(c); *Roell v. Withrow*, 538 U.S. 580, 123 S.Ct. 1698, 155 L.Ed.2d 775 (2003).

b. Federal Magistrates Act, 82 Stat. 1107, October 17, 1968.

c. U.S.C. Section 636(c)(1).

d. 28 U.S.C. Section 631(b)(5).

jurisdiction, (2) U.S. courts of appeals (intermediate courts of appeals), and (3) the United States Supreme Court.

Unlike state court judges, who are usually elected, federal court judges—including the justices of the Supreme Court—are appointed by the president of the United States, subject to confirmation by the U.S. Senate. Federal judges receive lifetime appointments under Article III of the U.S. Constitution, which states that federal judges "hold their offices during good Behaviour." In the entire history of the United States, only seven federal judges have been removed from office through impeachment proceedings.

Certain federal court officers are not chosen in the way just described. This chapter's *Managerial Strategy* feature describes how U.S. magistrate judges are selected.

U.S. District Courts At the federal level, the equivalent of a state trial court of general jurisdiction is the district court. U.S. district courts have original jurisdiction in matters involving a federal question and concurrent jurisdiction with state courts when diversity jurisdiction exists. Federal cases typically originate in district courts. There are other federal courts with original, but special (or limited), jurisdiction, such as the federal bankruptcy courts and tax courts.

Every state has at least one federal district court. The number of judicial districts can vary over time, primarily owing to population changes and corresponding changes in caseloads. Today, there are ninety-four federal judicial districts. Exhibit 2–3 shows the boundaries of both the U.S. district courts and the U.S. courts of appeals.

U.S. Courts of Appeals In the federal court system, there are thirteen U.S. courts of appeals—referred to as U.S. circuit courts of appeals. Twelve of these courts (including the Court of Appeals for the D.C. Circuit) hear appeals from the federal district courts located within their respective judicial circuits (shown in Exhibit 2–3).[15]

---

15. Historically, judges were required to "ride the circuit" and hear appeals in different courts around the country, which is how the name "circuit court" came about.

EXHIBIT 2–3 Geographic Boundaries of the U.S. Courts of Appeals and U.S. District Courts

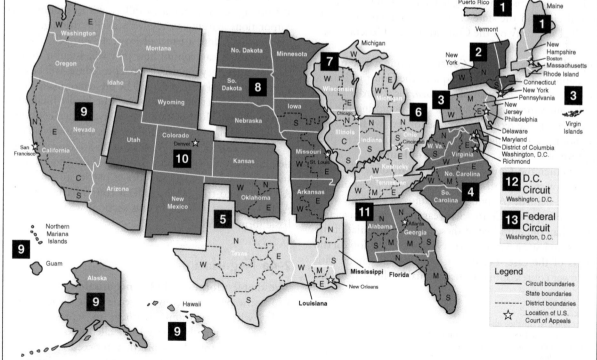

Source: Administrative Office of the United States Courts.

The Court of Appeals for the Thirteenth Circuit, called the Federal Circuit, has national appellate jurisdiction over certain types of cases, including those involving patent law and those in which the U.S. government is a defendant.

The decisions of a circuit court of appeals are binding on all courts within the circuit court's jurisdiction. These decisions are final in most cases, but appeal to the United States Supreme Court is possible.

The United States Supreme Court The highest level of the three-tiered federal court system is the United States Supreme Court. According to the U.S. Constitution, there is only one national Supreme Court. All other courts in the federal system are considered "inferior." Congress is empowered to create inferior courts as it deems necessary. The inferior courts that Congress has created include the second tier in our model—the U.S. circuit courts of appeals—as well as the district courts and the various federal courts of limited, or specialized, jurisdiction.

The United States Supreme Court consists of nine justices. Although the Supreme Court has original, or trial, jurisdiction in rare instances (set forth in Article III, Sections 1 and 2), most of its work is as an appeals court. The Supreme Court can review any case decided by any of the federal courts of appeals. It also has appellate authority over cases involving federal questions that have been decided in the state courts. The Supreme Court is the final authority on the Constitution and federal law.

Appeals to the Supreme Court. To bring a case before the Supreme Court, a party requests the Court to issue a writ of *certiorari*.[16] A **writ of *certiorari*** is an order issued by the Supreme Court to a lower court requiring the latter to send it the record of the case for review. The Court will not issue a writ unless at least four of the nine justices approve of it. This is called the **rule of four.**

Whether the Court will issue a writ of *certiorari* is entirely within its discretion, and most petitions for writs are denied. (Although thousands of cases are filed with the Supreme Court each year, it hears, on average, fewer than one hundred of these cases.)[17] A denial of the request to issue a writ of *certiorari* is not a decision on the merits of the case, nor does it indicate agreement with the lower court's opinion. Also, denial of the writ has no

value as a precedent. Denial simply means that the lower court's decision remains the law in that jurisdiction.

Petitions Granted by the Court. Typically, the Court grants petitions when cases raise important constitutional questions or when the lower courts have issued conflicting decisions on a significant issue. The justices, however, never explain their reasons for hearing certain cases and not others, so it is difficult to predict which type of case the Court might select.

Concept Summary 2.2 reviews the courts in the federal and state court systems.

2–4 Alternative Dispute Resolution

Litigation—the process of resolving a dispute through the court system—is expensive and time consuming. Litigating even the simplest complaint is costly, and because of the backlog of cases pending in many courts, several years may pass before a case is actually tried. For these and other reasons, more and more businesspersons are turning to **alternative dispute resolution (ADR)** as a means of settling their disputes.

The great advantage of ADR is its flexibility. Methods of ADR range from the parties sitting down together and attempting to work out their differences to multinational corporations agreeing to resolve a dispute through a formal hearing before a panel of experts. Normally, the parties themselves can control how they will attempt to settle their dispute. They can decide what procedures will be used, whether a neutral third party will be present or make a decision, and whether that decision will be legally binding or nonbinding. ADR also offers more privacy than court proceedings and allows disputes to be resolved relatively quickly.

Today, more than 90 percent of civil lawsuits are settled before trial using some form of ADR. Indeed, most states either require or encourage parties to undertake ADR prior to trial. Many federal courts have instituted ADR programs as well. In this section, we examine the basic forms of ADR.

2–4a Negotiation

The simplest form of ADR is **negotiation,** a process in which the parties attempt to settle their dispute informally, with or without attorneys to represent them. Attorneys frequently advise their clients to negotiate a settlement voluntarily before they proceed to trial. Parties may even try to negotiate a settlement during a trial or after the trial but before an appeal.

---

16. Pronounced sur-shee-uh-*rah*-ree.
17. From the mid-1950s through the early 1990s, the Supreme Court reviewed more cases per year than it has since then. In the Court's 1982–1983 term, for example, the Court issued written opinions in 151 cases. In contrast, during the Court's 2015–2016 term, the Court issued written opinions in only 81 cases.

Concept Summary 2.2

Types of Courts

Trial Courts	Trial courts are courts of original jurisdiction in which actions are initiated. • *State courts* —Courts of general jurisdiction can hear any case that has not been specifically designated for another court. Courts of limited jurisdiction include, among others, domestic relations courts, probate courts, municipal courts, and small claims courts. • *Federal courts* —The federal district court is the equivalent of the state trial court. Federal courts of limited jurisdiction include the bankruptcy courts and others shown in Exhibit 2–2.
Intermediate Appellate Courts	Courts of appeals are reviewing courts. Generally, appellate courts do not have original jurisdiction. • About three-fourths of the states have intermediate appellate courts. • In the federal court system, the U.S. circuit courts of appeals are the intermediate appellate courts.
Supreme Courts	The highest state court is that state's supreme court, although it may be called by some other name. • Appeal from state supreme courts to the United States Supreme Court is possible only if a federal question is involved. • The United States Supreme Court is the highest court in the federal court system and the final authority on the Constitution and federal law.

Negotiation traditionally involves just the parties themselves and (typically) their attorneys. The attorneys, though, are advocates—they are obligated to put their clients' interests first.

2–4b Mediation

In **mediation,** a neutral third party acts as a mediator and works with both sides in the dispute to facilitate a resolution. The mediator, who need not be a lawyer, usually charges a fee for his or her services (which can be split between the parties). States that require parties to undergo ADR before trial often offer mediation as one of the ADR options or (as in Florida) the only option.

During mediation, the mediator normally talks with the parties separately as well as jointly, emphasizes their points of agreement, and helps them to evaluate their options. Although the mediator may propose a solution (called a mediator's proposal), he or she does not make a decision resolving the matter.

One of the biggest advantages of mediation is that it is less adversarial than litigation. In mediation, the mediator takes an active role and attempts to bring the parties together so that they can come to a mutually satisfactory resolution. The mediation process tends to reduce the antagonism between the disputants, allowing them to resume their former relationship while minimizing hostility. For this reason, mediation is often the preferred form of ADR for disputes between business partners, employers and employees, or other parties involved in long-term relationships.

2–4c Arbitration

A more formal method of ADR is **arbitration,** in which an arbitrator (a neutral third party or a panel of experts) hears a dispute and imposes a resolution on the parties. Arbitration differs from other forms of ADR in that the third party hearing the dispute makes a decision for the parties. Exhibit 2–4 outlines the basic differences among the three traditional forms of ADR.

Usually, the parties in arbitration agree that the third party's decision will be *legally binding*, although the parties can also agree to *nonbinding* arbitration. In nonbinding arbitration, the parties can go forward with a lawsuit if they do not agree with the arbitrator's decision. Arbitration that is mandated by the courts often is not binding on the parties.

In some respects, formal arbitration resembles a trial, although usually the procedural rules are much less restrictive than those governing litigation. In a typical arbitration, the parties present opening arguments and ask for specific remedies. Both sides present evidence and may call and examine witnesses. The arbitrator then renders a decision.

The Arbitrator's Decision The arbitrator's decision is called an **award.** It is usually the final word on the matter. Although the parties may appeal an arbitrator's decision, a court's review of the decision will be much more restricted in scope than an appellate court's review of a trial court's decision. The general view is that because the parties were free to frame the issues and set the powers of the arbitrator at the outset, they cannot complain about the results. A court will set aside an award only in the event of one of the following:

1. The arbitrator's conduct or "bad faith" substantially prejudiced the rights of one of the parties.
2. The award violates an established public policy.
3. The arbitrator exceeded her or his powers—that is, arbitrated issues that the parties did not agree to submit to arbitration.

Arbitration Clauses Almost any commercial matter can be submitted to arbitration. Frequently, parties include an **arbitration clause** in a contract specifying that any dispute arising under the contract will be resolved through arbitration rather than through the court system. Parties can also agree to arbitrate a dispute *after* it arises.

Arbitration Statutes Most states have statutes (often based, in part, on the Uniform Arbitration Act) under which arbitration clauses will be enforced. Some state statutes compel arbitration of certain types of disputes, such as those involving public employees.

At the federal level, the Federal Arbitration Act (FAA), enacted in 1925, enforces arbitration clauses in contracts involving maritime activity and interstate commerce. As you will see in later chapters, the courts have defined *interstate commerce* broadly, and so arbitration

EXHIBIT 2–4 Basic Differences in the Traditional Forms of ADR

	Type of ADR		
	Negotiation	**Mediation**	**Arbitration**
Description	Parties meet informally with or without their attorneys and attempt to agree on a resolution. This is the simplest and least expensive method of ADR.	A neutral third party meets with the parties and emphasizes points of agreement to bring them toward resolution of their dispute, reducing hostility between the parties.	The parties present their arguments and evidence before an arbitrator at a formal hearing. The arbitrator renders a decision to resolve the parties' dispute.
Neutral Third Party Present?	No	Yes	Yes
Who Decides the Resolution?	The parties themselves reach a resolution.	The parties, but the mediator may suggest or propose a resolution.	The arbitrator imposes a resolution on the parties that may be either binding or nonbinding.

agreements involving transactions only slightly connected to the flow of interstate commerce may fall under the FAA. The FAA established a national policy favoring arbitration that the United States Supreme Court has continued to reinforce.[18]

■ **CASE IN POINT 2.8** Cleveland Construction, Inc. (CCI), was the general contractor on a project to build a grocery store in Houston, Texas. CCI hired Levco Construction, Inc., as a subcontractor. Their contract included an arbitration provision stating that any disputes would be resolved by arbitration in Ohio. When a dispute arose between the parties, Levco filed a suit against CCI in a Texas state court. CCI sought to compel arbitration in Ohio under the Federal Arbitration Act (FAA), but a Texas statute allows a party to void a contractual provision that requires arbitration outside Texas. Ultimately, a Texas appellate court held that the FAA preempted (took priority over) the state law. CCI could compel arbitration in Ohio.[19] ■

The Issue of Arbitrability The terms of an arbitration agreement can limit the types of disputes that the parties agree to arbitrate. Disputes can arise, however, when the parties do not specify limits or when the parties disagree on whether a particular matter is covered by their arbitration agreement.

When one party files a lawsuit to compel arbitration, it is up to the court to resolve the issue of *arbitrability*. That is, the court must decide whether the matter is one that must be resolved through arbitration. If the court finds that the subject matter in controversy is covered by the agreement to arbitrate, then it may compel arbitration.

Usually, a court will allow a claim to be arbitrated if the court finds that the relevant statute (the state arbitration statute or the FAA) does not exclude such claims. No party, however, will be ordered to submit a particular dispute to arbitration unless the court is convinced that the party has consented to do so. Additionally, the courts will not compel arbitration if it is clear that the arbitration rules and procedures are inherently unfair to one of the parties.

Mandatory Arbitration in the Employment Context A significant question for businesspersons has concerned mandatory arbitration clauses in employment contracts. Many employees claim they are at a disadvantage when they are forced, as a condition of being hired, to agree to arbitrate all disputes and thus waive their rights under statutes designed to protect employees.

The United States Supreme Court, however, has held that mandatory arbitration clauses in employment contracts are generally enforceable. ■ **CASE IN POINT 2.9** In a landmark decision, *Gilmer v. Interstate Johnson Lane Corp.*,[20] the Supreme Court held that a claim brought under a federal statute prohibiting age discrimination could be subject to arbitration. The Court concluded that the employee had waived his right to sue when he agreed, as part of a required application to be a securities representative, to arbitrate "any dispute, claim, or controversy" relating to his employment. ■

Since the *Gilmer* decision, some courts have refused to enforce one-sided arbitration clauses.[21] Nevertheless, the policy favoring enforcement of mandatory arbitration agreements in employment contracts remains strong.

■ **CASE IN POINT 2.10** Stephanie Cruise was hired by Kroger Co. to work in its deli. Her job application had included a clause requiring arbitration of "employment-related disputes." When Cruise was fired four years later, she filed a lawsuit claiming that Kroger had violated a number of laws prohibiting employment discrimination. Kroger filed a motion to compel arbitration. A state appellate court concluded that the arbitration clause in the employment application established that the parties had agreed to arbitrate their "employment-related disputes." Cruise's claims fell within the meaning of that agreement, and therefore she was required to arbitrate.[22] ■

2–4d Other Types of ADR

The three forms of ADR just discussed are the oldest and traditionally the most commonly used forms. In addition, a variety of newer types of ADR have emerged, including those described here.

1. In **early neutral case evaluation,** the parties select a neutral third party (generally an expert in the subject matter of the dispute) and explain their respective positions to that person. The case evaluator assesses the strengths and weaknesses of each party's claims.

2. In a **mini-trial,** each party's attorney briefly argues the party's case before the other party and a panel of representatives from each side who have the authority to settle the dispute. Typically, a neutral third party (usually an expert in the area being disputed) acts as

---

18. See, for example, *AT&T Mobility LLC v. Concepcion*, 563 U.S. 333, 131 S.Ct. 1740, 179 L.Ed.2d 742 (2010).

19. *Cleveland Construction, Inc. v. Levco Construction, Inc.*, 359 S.W.3d 843 (Tex.App. 2012).

20. 500 U.S. 20, 111 S.Ct. 1647, 114 L.Ed.2d 26 (1991).

21. See, for example, *Mohamed v. Uber Technologies, Inc.*, 2015 WL 3749716 (N.D.Cal. 2015); *Macias v. Excel Building Services, LLC*, 767 F.Supp.2d 1002 (N.D.Cal. 2011).

22. *Cruise v. Kroger Co.*, 233 Cal.App.4th 390, 183 Cal.Rptr.3d 17 (2015).

an adviser. If the parties fail to reach an agreement, the adviser renders an opinion as to how a court would likely decide the issue.

3. Numerous federal courts hold **summary jury trials,** in which the parties present their arguments and evidence and the jury renders a verdict. The jury's verdict is not binding, but it does act as a guide to both sides in reaching an agreement during the mandatory negotiations that immediately follow the trial.

4. Other alternatives being employed by the courts include summary proceedings, which dispense with some formal court procedures, and the appointment of special masters to assist judges in deciding complex issues.

2–4e Providers of ADR Services

ADR services are provided by both government agencies and private organizations. A major provider of ADR services is the American Arbitration Association (AAA), which handles more than 200,000 claims a year in its numerous offices worldwide. Most of the largest U.S. law firms are members of this nonprofit association.

Cases brought before the AAA are heard by an expert or a panel of experts in the area relating to the dispute and are usually settled quickly. Generally, about half of the panel members are lawyers. To cover its costs, the AAA charges a fee, paid by the party filing the claim. In addition, each party to the dispute pays a specified amount for each hearing day, as well as a special additional fee in cases involving personal injuries or property loss.

Hundreds of for-profit firms around the country also provide dispute-resolution services. Typically, these firms hire retired judges to conduct arbitration hearings or otherwise assist parties in settling their disputes. The judges follow procedures similar to those of the federal courts and use similar rules. Usually, each party to the dispute pays a filing fee and a designated fee for a hearing session or conference.

2–4f Online Dispute Resolution

An increasing number of companies and organizations are offering dispute-resolution services using the Internet. The settlement of disputes in these forums is known as **online dispute resolution (ODR).** The disputes resolved have most commonly involved rights to domain names (Web site addresses) or the quality of goods sold via the Internet, including goods sold through Internet auction sites.

Rules being developed in online forums may ultimately become a code of conduct for everyone who does business in cyberspace. Most online forums do not automatically apply the law of any specific jurisdiction. Instead, results are often based on general, universal legal principles. As with most offline methods of dispute resolution, any party may appeal to a court at any time.

ODR may be best for resolving small- to medium-sized business liability claims, which may not be worth the expense of litigation or traditional ADR methods. In addition, some cities use ODR as a means of resolving claims against them. ■ **EXAMPLE 2.11** New York City uses Cybersettle.com to resolve auto accident, sidewalk, and other personal-injury claims made against the city. Parties with complaints submit their demands, and the city submits its offers confidentially online. If an offer exceeds a demand, the claimant keeps half the difference as a bonus, plus the original claim. ■

2–5 International Dispute Resolution

Businesspersons who engage in international business transactions normally take special precautions to protect themselves in the event that a party with whom they are dealing in another country breaches an agreement. Often, parties to international contracts include special clauses in their contracts providing for how disputes arising under the contracts will be resolved. Sometimes, international treaties (formal agreements among several nations) even require parties to arbitrate any disputes.

2–5a Forum-Selection and Choice-of-Law Clauses

Parties to international transactions often include forum-selection and choice-of-law clauses in their contracts. These clauses designate the jurisdiction (court or country) where any dispute arising under the contract will be litigated and which nation's law will be applied.

When an international contract does not include such clauses, any legal proceedings arising under the contract will be more complex and attended by much more uncertainty. For instance, litigation may take place in two or more countries, with each country applying its own national law to the particular transactions.

Furthermore, even if a plaintiff wins a favorable judgment in a lawsuit litigated in the plaintiff's country, the defendant's country could refuse to enforce the court's judgment. The judgment may be enforced in the defendant's country for reasons of courtesy. The United States, for instance, will generally enforce a foreign court's decision if it is consistent with U.S. national law and policy. Other nations, however, may not be as accommodating as the United States, and the plaintiff may be left empty-handed.

2–5b Arbitration Clauses

International contracts also often include arbitration clauses that require a neutral third party to decide any contract disputes. Many of the institutions that offer arbitration, such as the International Chamber of Commerce or the Hong Kong International Arbitration Centre, have formulated model clauses for parties to use. In

international arbitration proceedings, the third party may be a neutral entity, a panel of individuals representing both parties' interests, or some other group or organization.

The United Nations Convention on the Recognition and Enforcement of Foreign Arbitral Awards[23] has been implemented in more than 145 countries, including the United States. This convention assists in the enforcement of arbitration clauses, as do provisions in specific treaties among nations. The American Arbitration Association provides arbitration services for international as well as domestic disputes.

---

23. June 10, 1958, 21 U.S.T. 2517, T.I.A.S. No. 6997 (the "New York Convention").

Reviewing: Courts and Alternative Dispute Resolution

Stan Garner resides in Illinois and promotes boxing matches for SuperSports, Inc., an Illinois corporation. Garner created the concept of "Ages" promotion—a three-fight series of boxing matches pitting an older fighter (George Foreman) against a younger fighter. The concept had titles for each of the three fights, including "Battle of the Ages." Garner contacted Foreman and his manager, who both reside in Texas, to sell the idea, and they arranged a meeting in Las Vegas, Nevada. During negotiations, Foreman's manager signed a nondisclosure agreement prohibiting him from disclosing Garner's promotional concepts unless the parties signed a contract. Nevertheless, after negotiations fell through, Foreman used Garner's "Battle of the Ages" concept to promote a subsequent fight. Garner filed a suit against Foreman and his manager in a federal district court located in Illinois, alleging breach of contract. Using the information presented in the chapter, answer the following questions.

1. On what basis might the federal district court in Illinois exercise jurisdiction in this case?
2. Does the federal district court have original or appellate jurisdiction?
3. Suppose that Garner had filed his action in an Illinois state court. Could an Illinois state court have exercised personal jurisdiction over Foreman or his manager? Why or why not?
4. Now suppose that Garner had filed his action in a Nevada state court. Would that court have had personal jurisdiction over Foreman or his manager? Explain.

Debate This . . .   *In this age of the Internet, when people communicate via e-mail, texts, tweets, Facebook, and Skype, is the concept of jurisdiction losing its meaning?*

Terms and Concepts

alternative dispute resolution (ADR) 40	federal question 28	online dispute resolution (ODR) 44
arbitration 41	*in personam* jurisdiction 27	probate court 28
arbitration clause 42	*in rem* jurisdiction 27	question of fact 36
award 42	judicial review 26	question of law 36
bankruptcy court 28	jurisdiction 27	rule of four 40
concurrent jurisdiction 30	litigation 40	small claims court 36
diversity of citizenship 28	long arm statute 27	standing to sue 33
early neutral case evaluation 43	mediation 41	summary jury trial 44
exclusive jurisdiction 30	mini-trial 43	venue 33
	negotiation 40	writ of *certiorari* 40

Issue Spotters

1. Sue uses her smartphone to purchase a video security system for her architectural firm from Tipton, Inc., a company located in a different state. The system arrives a month after the projected delivery date, is of poor quality, and does not function as advertised. Sue files a suit against Tipton in a state court. Does the court in Sue's state have jurisdiction over Tipton? What factors will the court consider in determining jurisdiction? (See *Basic Judicial Requirements.*)

2. The state in which Sue resides requires that her dispute with Tipton be submitted to mediation or nonbinding arbitration. If the dispute is not resolved, or if either party disagrees with the decision of the mediator or arbitrator, will a court hear the case? Explain. (See *Alternative Dispute Resolution.*)

- **Check your answers to the Issue Spotters against the answers provided in Appendix D at the end of this text.**

Business Scenarios

2–1. Standing. Jack and Maggie Turton bought a house in Jefferson County, Idaho, located directly across the street from a gravel pit. A few years later, the county converted the pit to a landfill. The landfill accepted many kinds of trash that cause harm to the environment, including major appliances, animal carcasses, containers with hazardous content warnings, leaking car batteries, and waste oil. The Turtons complained to the county, but the county did nothing. The Turtons then filed a lawsuit against the county alleging violations of federal environmental laws pertaining to groundwater contamination and other pollution. Do the Turtons have standing to sue? Why or why not? (See *Basic Judicial Requirements.*)

Business Case Problems

2–2. Venue. Brandy Austin used powdered infant formula manufactured by Nestlé USA, Inc., to feed her infant daughter. Austin claimed that a can of the formula was contaminated with *Enterobacter sakazakii* bacteria, causing severe injury to the infant. The bacteria can cause infections of the bloodstream and central nervous system—in particular, meningitis (inflammation of the tissue surrounding the brain or spinal cord). Austin filed an action against Nestlé in Hennepin County District Court in Minnesota. Nestlé argued for a change of venue because the alleged harm had occurred in South Carolina. Austin is a South Carolina resident and had given birth to her daughter in that state. Should the case be transferred to a South Carolina venue? Why or why not? [*Austin v. Nestlé USA, Inc.,* 677 F.Supp.2d 1134 (D.Minn. 2009)] (See *Basic Judicial Requirements.*)

2–3. Arbitration. PRM Energy Systems owned patents licensed to Primenergy to use in the United States. Their contract stated that "all disputes" would be settled by arbitration. Kobe Steel of Japan was interested in using the technology represented by PRM's patents. Primenergy agreed to let Kobe use the technology in Japan without telling PRM. When PRM learned about the secret deal, the firm filed a suit against Primenergy for fraud and theft. Does this dispute go to arbitration or to trial? Why? [*PRM Energy Systems v. Primenergy,* 592 F.3d 830 (8th Cir. 2010)] (See *Alternative Dispute Resolution.*)

2–4. Spotlight on the National Football League—Arbitration. Bruce Matthews played football for the Tennessee Titans. As part of his contract, he agreed to submit any dispute to arbitration. He also agreed that Tennessee law would determine all matters related to workers' compensation. After Matthews

retired, he filed a workers' compensation claim in California. The arbitrator ruled that Matthews could pursue his claim in California but only under Tennessee law. Should this award be set aside? Explain. [*National Football League Players Association v. National Football League Management Council,* 2011 WL 1137334 (S.D.Cal. 2011)] (See *Alternative Dispute Resolution.*)

2–5. Minimum Contacts. Seal Polymer Industries sold two freight containers of latex gloves to Med-Express, Inc., a company based in North Carolina. When Med-Express failed to pay the $104,000 owed for the gloves, Seal Polymer sued in an Illinois court and obtained a judgment against Med-Express. Med-Express argued that it did not have minimum contacts with Illinois because it was incorporated under North Carolina law and had its principal place of business in North Carolina. Therefore, the Illinois judgment based on personal jurisdiction was invalid. Was this argument alone sufficient to prevent the Illinois judgment from being collected against Med-Express in North Carolina? Why or why not? [*Seal Polymer Industries v. Med-Express, Inc.,* 725 S.E.2d 5 (N.C.App. 2012)] (See *Basic Judicial Requirements.*)

2–6. Arbitration. Horton Automatics and the Industrial Division of the Communications Workers of America, the union that represented Horton's workers, negotiated a collective bargaining agreement. If an employee's discharge for a workplace-rule violation was submitted to arbitration, the agreement limited the arbitrator to determining whether the rule was reasonable and whether the employee had violated it. When Horton discharged employee Ruben de la Garza, the union appealed to arbitration. The arbitrator found that de la Garza had violated a reasonable safety rule, but "was not totally convinced" that Horton should have treated the violation more seriously than other rule violations. The arbitrator ordered de la Garza reinstated. Can a court set aside this order? Explain. [*Horton Automatics v. The Industrial Division of the Communications Workers of America, AFL-CIO*, 2013 WL 59204 (5th Cir. 2013)] (See *Alternative Dispute Resolution*.)

2–7. Business Case Problem with Sample Answer—Corporate Contacts.

 LG Electronics, Inc., a South Korean company, and nineteen other foreign companies participated in the global market for cathode ray tube (CRT) products. CRTs were integrated as components in consumer goods, including television sets, and were sold for many years in high volume in the United States, including the state of Washington. The state filed a suit in a Washington state court against LG and the others, alleging a conspiracy to raise prices and set production levels in the market for CRTs in violation of a state consumer protection statute. The defendants filed a motion to dismiss the suit for lack of personal jurisdiction. Should this motion be granted? Explain. [*State of Washington v. LG Electronics, Inc.*, 341 P.3d 346 (Wash. App., Div. 1 2015)] (See *Basic Judicial Requirements*.)

• For a sample answer to Problem 2–7, go to Appendix E at the end of this text.

2–8. Appellate, or Reviewing, Courts.

Angelica Westbrook was employed as a collector for Franklin Collection Service, Inc. During a collection call, Westbrook told a debtor that a $15 processing fee was an "interest" charge. This violated company policy. Westbrook was fired. She filed a claim for unemployment benefits, which the Mississippi Department of Employment Security (MDES) approved. Franklin objected. At an MDES hearing, a Franklin supervisor testified that she had heard Westbrook make the false statement, although she admitted that there had been no similar incidents with Westbrook. Westbrook denied making the statement, but added that if she had said it, she did not remember it. The agency found that Franklin's reason for terminating Westbrook did not amount to the misconduct required to disqualify her for benefits and upheld the approval. Franklin appealed to a state intermediate appellate court. Is the court likely to uphold the agency's findings of fact? Explain. [*Franklin Collection Service, Inc. v. Mississippi Department of Employment Security*, 184 So.3d 330 (Miss.App. 2016)] (See *The State and Federal Court Systems*.)

2–9. A Question of Ethics—Agreement to Arbitrate.

 Nellie Lumpkin, who suffered from various illnesses, including dementia, was admitted to the Picayune Convalescent Center, a nursing home. Because of her mental condition, her daughter, Beverly McDaniel, filled out the admissions paperwork and signed the admissions agreement. It included a clause requiring parties to submit to arbitration any disputes that arose. After Lumpkin left the center two years later, she sued, through her husband, for negligent treatment and malpractice during her stay. The center moved to force the matter to arbitration. The trial court held that the arbitration agreement was not enforceable. The center appealed. [Covenant Health & Rehabilitation of Picayune, LP v. Lumpkin, 23 So.3d 1092 (Miss.App. 2009)] (See Alternative Dispute Resolution.)

(a) Should a dispute involving medical malpractice be forced into arbitration? This is a claim of negligent care, not a breach of a commercial contract. Is it ethical for medical facilities to impose such a requirement? Is there really any bargaining over such terms? Discuss fully.

(b) Should a person with limited mental capacity be held to an arbitration clause agreed to by the next of kin who signed on behalf of that person? Why or why not?

Legal Reasoning Group Activity

2–10. Access to Courts.

Assume that a statute in your state requires that all civil lawsuits involving damages of less than $50,000 be arbitrated. Such a case can be tried in court only if a party is dissatisfied with the arbitrator's decision. The statute also provides that if a trial does not result in an improvement of more than 10 percent in the position of the party who demanded the trial, that party must pay the entire cost of the arbitration proceeding. (See *Alternative Dispute Resolution*.)

(a) One group will argue that the state statute violates litigants' rights of access to the courts and trial by jury.

(b) Another group will argue that the statute does not violate litigants' right of access to the courts.

(c) A third group will evaluate how the determination on right of access would be changed if the statute was part of a pilot program that affected only a few judicial districts in the state.

Answers to the *Issue Spotters*

1. *Does the court in Sue's state have jurisdiction over Tipton? What factors will the court consider in determining jurisdiction?* Yes, the court in Sue's state has jurisdiction over Tipton on the basis of the company's minimum contacts with the state.

Courts look at the following factors in determining whether minimum contacts exist: the quantity of the contacts, the nature and quality of the contacts, the source and connection of the cause of action to the contacts, the interest of the forum state, and the convenience of the parties. Attempting to exercise jurisdiction without sufficient minimum contacts would violate the due process clause. Generally, courts have found that jurisdiction is proper when there is substantial business conducted online (with contracts, sales, and so on). Even when there is only some interactivity through a Web site, courts have sometimes held that jurisdiction is proper. Jurisdiction is not proper when there is merely passive advertising.

Here, all of these factors suggest that the defendant had sufficient minimum contacts with the state to justify the exercise of jurisdiction over the defendant. Two especially important factors were that the plaintiff sold the security system to a resident of the state and that litigating in the defendant's state would be relatively inconvenient for the plaintiff.

2. *If the dispute is not resolved, or if either party disagrees with the decision of the mediator or arbitrator, will a court hear the case? Explain.* Yes, if the dispute is not resolved, or if either party disagrees with the decision of the mediator or arbitrator, a court will hear the case. It is required that the dispute be submitted to mediation or arbitration, but this outcome is not binding.

Sample Answers for *Business Case Problems with Sample Answer*

Problem 2–7. *Corporate Contacts.* No, the defendants' motion to dismiss the suit for lack of personal jurisdiction should not be granted. A corporation normally is subject to jurisdiction in a state in which it is doing business. A court applies the minimum-contacts test to determine whether it can exercise jurisdiction over an out-of-state corporation. This requirement is met if the corporation sells its products within the state or places its goods in the "stream of commerce" with the intent that the goods be sold in the state.

In this problem, the state of Washington filed a suit in a Washington state court against LG Electronics, Inc., and nineteen other foreign companies that participated in the global market for cathode ray tube (CRT) products. The state alleged a conspiracy to raise prices and set production levels in the market for CRTs in violation of a state consumer protection statute. The defendants filed a motion to dismiss the suit for lack of personal jurisdiction. These goods were sold for many years in high volume in the United States, including the state of Washington. In other words, the corporations purposefully established minimum contacts in the state of Washington. This is a sufficient basis for a Washington state court to assert personal jurisdiction over the defendants.

In the actual case on which this problem is based, the court dismissed the suit for lack of personal jurisdiction. On appeal, a state intermediate appellate court reversed on the reasoning stated above.

CHAPTER

Court Procedures

American and English courts follow the *adversarial system of justice*. Although parties are allowed to represent themselves in court (called *pro se* representation),[1]

most parties to lawsuits hire attorneys to represent them. Each lawyer acts as his or her client's advocate. Each lawyer presents his or her client's version of the facts in such a way as to convince the judge (or the judge and jury, in a jury trial) that this version is correct. Most of the judicial procedures

that you will read about are rooted in the adversarial framework of the American legal system.

1. This right was definitively established in *Faretta v. California*, 422 U.S. 806, 95 S.Ct. 2525, 45 L.Ed.2d 562 (1975).

3–1 Procedural Rules

The parties to a lawsuit must comply with the procedural rules of the court in which the lawsuit is filed. Although people often think that substantive law determines the outcome of a case, procedural law can have a significant impact on a person's ability to pursue a legal claim. Procedural rules provide a framework for every dispute and specify what must be done at each stage of the litigation process.

Procedural rules are complex, and they vary from court to court and from state to state. There is a set of federal rules of procedure as well as various sets of rules for state courts. Additionally, the applicable procedures will depend on whether the case is a civil or criminal proceeding. All civil trials held in federal district courts are governed by the **Federal Rules of Civil Procedure (FRCP).**[2]

3–1a Stages of Litigation

Broadly speaking, the litigation process has three phases: pretrial, trial, and posttrial. Each phase involves specific procedures, as discussed throughout this chapter. Although civil lawsuits may vary greatly in terms of complexity, cost, and detail, they typically progress through the stages charted in Exhibit 3–1.

2. The United States Supreme Court has authority to establish these rules, as spelled out in 28 U.S.C. Sections 2071–2077. Generally, though, the federal judiciary appoints committees that make recommendations to the Supreme Court. The Court then publishes any proposed changes in the rules and allows for public comment before finalizing the rules.

To illustrate the procedures involved in a civil lawsuit, we will use a simple hypothetical case. The case arose from an automobile accident, which occurred when a car driven by Antonio Carvello, a resident of New Jersey, collided with a car driven by Jill Kirby, a resident of New York. The accident took place at an intersection in New York City. Kirby suffered personal injuries, which caused her to incur medical and hospital expenses as well as lost wages for four months. In all, she calculated that the cost to her of the accident was $500,000.[3] Carvello and Kirby have been unable to agree on a settlement, and Kirby now must decide whether to sue Carvello for the $500,000 compensation she feels she deserves.

3–1b Hire an Attorney

As mentioned, rules of procedure often affect the outcome of a dispute—a fact that highlights the importance of obtaining the advice of counsel. The first step taken by almost anyone contemplating a lawsuit is to seek the guidance of a licensed attorney.

In the hypothetical Kirby-Carvello case, assume that Kirby consults with a lawyer. The attorney will advise her regarding what she can expect in a lawsuit, her probability of success at trial, and the procedures that will be involved. If more than one court would have jurisdiction over the matter, the attorney will also discuss the advantages and disadvantages of filing in a particular court. In addition, the attorney will indicate how long it will take

3. For simplicity, we are ignoring damages for pain and suffering and for permanent disabilities, which plaintiffs in personal-injury cases often seek.

EXHIBIT 3–1 Stages in a Typical Lawsuit

- Accident, breach of contract, or other event
- The party hires a lawyer, who files a complaint and notifies (serves) the defendant
- Defendant's attorney files an answer or a motion to dismiss
- Pretrial discovery and more motions, pretrial conference
- Trial and perhaps posttrial motions and/or an appeal

to resolve the dispute through litigation in a particular court and provide an estimate of the costs involved.

The attorney will also inform Kirby of the legal fees that she will have to pay in an attempt to collect damages from the defendant, Carvello. Attorneys base their fees on such factors as the difficulty of the matter at issue, the attorney's experience and skill, and the amount of time involved. In the United States, legal fees range from $200 to $700 per hour or even higher (the average fee is between $200 and $450 per hour). The client normally must also pay various expenses related to the case (called "out-of-pocket" costs), such as court filing fees, travel expenses, and the costs of expert witnesses and investigators.

Types of Attorneys' Fees For a particular legal matter, an attorney may charge one type of fee or a combination of several types.

1. *Fixed fees* may be charged for the performance of such services as drafting a simple will.
2. *Hourly fees* may be charged for matters that will involve an indeterminate period of time. The amount of time required to bring a case to trial, for instance, probably cannot be precisely estimated in advance.
3. *Contingency fees* are fixed as a percentage (usually 33 percent) of a client's recovery in certain types of lawsuits, such as a personal-injury lawsuit.[4] If the

---

4. Contingency-fee arrangements are typically prohibited in criminal cases, divorce cases, and cases involving the distribution of assets after death.

lawsuit is unsuccessful, the attorney receives no fee, but the client will have to reimburse the attorney for all out-of-pocket costs incurred.

Because Kirby's claim involves a personal injury, her lawyer will likely take the case on a contingency-fee basis. In some cases, the winning party may be able to recover at least some portion of her or his attorneys' fees from the losing party.

Settlement Considerations Once an attorney has been retained, the attorney is required to pursue a resolution of the matter on the client's behalf. Nevertheless, the amount of resources an attorney will spend on a given case is affected by the time and funds the client wishes to devote to the process.

If the client is willing to pay for a lengthy trial and one or more appeals, the attorney may pursue those actions. Often, however, after learning of the substantial costs that litigation entails, a client may decide to pursue a settlement of the claim. Attempts to settle the case may be ongoing throughout the litigation process.

Another important consideration in deciding whether to pursue litigation is the defendant's ability to pay the damages sought. Even if Kirby is awarded damages, it may be difficult to enforce the court's judgment if the amount exceeds the limits of Carvello's automobile insurance policy. (We will discuss the problems involved in enforcing a judgment later in this chapter.)

3–2 Pretrial Procedures

The pretrial litigation process involves the filing of the *pleadings*, the gathering of evidence (called *discovery*), and possibly other procedures, such as a pretrial conference and jury selection.

3–2a The Pleadings

The *complaint* and *answer* (and other legal documents discussed below) are known as the **pleadings.** The pleadings inform each party of the other's claims, reveal the facts, and specify the issues (disputed questions) involved in the case. Because the rules of procedure vary depending on the jurisdiction of the court, the style and form of the pleadings may be different from those shown in this chapter.

The Plaintiff's Complaint Kirby's action against Carvello commences when her lawyer files a **complaint**[5] with the clerk of the appropriate court. Complaints can be lengthy or brief, depending on the complexity of the case and the rules of the jurisdiction. The complaint contains statements or allegations concerning the following:

1. *Jurisdiction.* Facts showing that the particular court has subject-matter and personal jurisdiction.
2. *Legal theory.* The facts establishing the plaintiff's claim and basis for relief.
3. *Remedy.* The remedy (such as an amount of damages) that the plaintiff is seeking.

Exhibit 3–2 illustrates how a complaint in the Kirby-Carvello case might appear. The complaint asserts facts indicating that the federal district court has subject-matter jurisdiction because of diversity of citizenship. It then gives a brief statement of the facts of the accident and alleges that Carvello negligently drove his vehicle through a red light, striking Kirby's car. The complaint alleges that Carvello's actions caused Kirby serious personal injury and property damage. The complaint goes on to state that Kirby is seeking $500,000 in damages. (In some state civil actions, the plaintiff need not specify the amount of damages sought.)

Service of Process. Before the court can exercise personal jurisdiction over the defendant (Carvello)—in effect, before the lawsuit can begin—the court must have proof that the defendant was notified of the lawsuit. Formally notifying the defendant of a lawsuit is called **service of process.**

The plaintiff must deliver, or serve, a copy of the complaint and a **summons** (a notice requiring the defendant to appear in court and answer the complaint) to the defendant. The summons notifies Carvello that he must file an answer to the complaint within a specified time period (twenty days in the federal courts) or suffer a default judgment against him. A **default judgment** in Kirby's favor would mean that she would be awarded the damages alleged in her complaint because Carvello failed to respond to the allegations. A typical summons is shown in Exhibit 3–3.

Method of Service. How service of process occurs depends on the rules of the court or jurisdiction in which the lawsuit is brought. Under the Federal Rules of Civil Procedure, anyone who is at least eighteen years of age and is not a party to the lawsuit can serve process in federal court cases. In state courts, the process server is often a county sheriff or an employee of an independent company that provides process service in the local area.

Usually, the server hands the summons and complaint to the defendant personally or leaves it at the defendant's residence or place of business. In some states, process can be served by mail if the defendant consents (accepts service). When the defendant cannot be reached, special rules provide for alternative means of service, such as publishing a notice in the local newspaper.

In some situations, courts allow service of process via e-mail, as long as it is reasonably calculated to provide notice and an opportunity to respond. Today, some judges have even allowed defendants to be served legal documents via social media, as discussed in this chapter's *Digital Update* feature.

In cases involving corporate defendants, the summons and complaint may be served on an officer or on a *registered agent* (representative) of the corporation. The name of a corporation's registered agent can usually be obtained from the secretary of state's office in the state where the company incorporated its business (and, frequently, from the secretary of state's office in any state where the corporation does business).

Waiver of Formal Service of Process. In many instances, the defendant is already aware that a lawsuit is being filed and is willing to waive (give up) her or his right to be served personally. The Federal Rules of Civil Procedure (FRCP) and many states' rules allow defendants to waive formal service of process, provided that certain procedures are followed.

In the Kirby case, for example, Kirby's attorney could mail to defendant Carvello a copy of the complaint, along with "Waiver of Service of Summons" forms for

---

5. Sometimes, the document filed with the court is called a *petition* or a *declaration* instead of a complaint.

EXHIBIT 3–2 A Typical Complaint

```
              IN THE UNITED STATES DISTRICT COURT
          FOR THE SOUTHERN DISTRICT OF NEW YORK


                                        CIVIL NO. 9-1047

   JILL KIRBY

                    Plaintiff,

   v.                                   COMPLAINT

   ANTONIO CARVELLO

                    Defendant.
```

The plaintiff brings this cause of action against the defendant, alleging as follows:

1. This action is between the plaintiff, who is a resident of the State of New York, and the defendant, who is a resident of the State of New Jersey. There is diversity of citizenship between the parties.
2. The amount in controversy, exclusive of interest and costs, exceeds the sum of $75,000.
3. On September 10th, 2017, the plaintiff, Jill Kirby, was exercising good driving habits and reasonable care in driving her car through the intersection of Boardwalk and Pennsylvania Avenue, New York City, New York, when the defendant, Antonio Carvello, negligently drove his vehicle through a red light at the intersection and collided with the plaintiff's vehicle.
4. As a result of the collision, the plaintiff suffered severe physical injury, which prevented her from working, and property damage to her car.

WHEREFORE, the plaintiff demands judgment against the defendant for the sum of $500,000 plus interest at the maximum legal rate and the costs of this action.

By _____*Joseph Roe*_____

Joseph Roe
Attorney for Plaintiff
100 Main Street
New York, New York

1/3/18

Carvello to sign. If Carvello signs and returns the forms within thirty days, formal service of process is waived.

Moreover, under the FRCP, defendants who agree to waive formal service of process receive additional time to respond to the complaint (sixty days, instead of twenty days). Some states provide similar incentives to encourage defendants to waive formal service of process and thereby reduce associated costs and foster cooperation between the parties.

The Defendant's Response Typically, the defendant's response to the complaint takes the form of an **answer.** In an answer, the defendant either admits or denies each of the allegations in the plaintiff's complaint and may also set forth defenses to those allegations.

Under the federal rules, any allegations that are not denied by the defendant will be deemed by the court to have been admitted. If Carvello admits to all of Kirby's allegations in his answer, a judgment will be entered for

EXHIBIT 3–3 A Typical Summons

```
                    UNITED STATES DISTRICT COURT
            FOR THE SOUTHERN DISTRICT OF NEW YORK

                                        CIVIL ACTION, FILE NO. 9-1047
    JILL KIRBY
                        Plaintiff,
    v.                                          SUMMONS
    ANTONIO CARVELLO

                        Defendant.


To the above-named Defendant:

You are hereby summoned and required to serve upon Joseph Roe,
plaintiff's attorney, whose address is 100 Main Street, New York, NY, an
answer to the complaint which is herewith served upon you, within 20 days
after service of this summons upon you, exclusive of the day of service.
If you fail to do so, judgment by default will be taken against you for
the relief demanded in the complaint.


C. H. Hynek                             January 3, 2018
_____                         _____
CLERK                                   DATE


John Dolan
_____
BY DEPUTY CLERK
```

Kirby. If Carvello denies Kirby's allegations, the matter will proceed further.

Affirmative Defenses. Carvello can also admit the truth of Kirby's complaint but raise new facts to show that he should not be held liable for Kirby's damages. This is called raising an **affirmative defense.**

Defendants in both civil and criminal cases can raise affirmative defenses. For example, Carvello could assert Kirby's own negligence as a defense by alleging that Kirby was driving negligently at the time of the accident. In some states, a plaintiff's contributory negligence operates as a complete defense. In most states, however, the plaintiff's own negligence constitutes only a partial defense.

Counterclaims. Carvello could also deny Kirby's allegations and set forth his own claim that the accident occurred as a result of Kirby's negligence and therefore she owes Carvello for damage to his car. This is appropriately called a **counterclaim.** If Carvello files a counterclaim, Kirby will have to submit an answer to the counterclaim.

3–2b Dismissals and Judgments before Trial

Many actions for which pleadings have been filed never come to trial. The parties may, for instance, negotiate a settlement of the dispute at any stage of the litigation process. There are also numerous procedural avenues for disposing of a case without a trial. Many of them involve one or the other party's attempts to get the case dismissed through the use of various motions.

A **motion** is a procedural request submitted to the court by an attorney on behalf of her or his client. When a motion is filed with the court, the filing party must also send to, or personally serve, the opposing party a *notice of*

DIGITAL UPDATE — Using Social Media for Service of Process

Historically, when process servers failed to reach a defendant at home, they attempted to serve process at the defendant's workplace, by mail, and by publication. In our digital age, does publication via social media qualify as legitimate service of process?

Can You Serve a Divorce Summons Through a Private Message on a Facebook Account?

Facebook has well over 1.6 billion active users per month. Assume that a man has a Facebook account and so does his spouse. He has moved out and is intentionally avoiding service of a divorce summons. Even a private investigator has not been able to deliver that summons. What to do? According to a New York state court ruling, the lawyer for the woman can serve the divorce summons through a private message from her Facebook account. "The past decade has . . . seen the advent and ascendancy of social media. . . . Thus, it would appear that the next frontier in the developing law of the service of process over the Internet is the use of social media sites as forums through which a summons can be delivered."[a]

An Increasing Use of Social Media for Service of Process

More and more courts are allowing service of process via Facebook and other social media. One New York City family court judge ruled that a divorced man could

serve his ex-wife through her active Facebook account. She had moved out of the house and provided no forwarding address. A Dallas district judge authorized service of process via social media, and other judges in that state have agreed with the ruling. A bill pending in the Texas state legislature would allow service via social media whenever a plaintiff can authenticate the social media account. Other states are considering similar legislation.

Not All Courts Agree, Though

In spite of these examples, the courts have not uniformly approved of using social media to serve process. In one federal district court case, the court pointed out the relative simplicity of creating a fake Facebook account and the court's resulting inability to verify the true owner of that account.[b] In another case, involving the Federal Trade Commission (FTC), the court did allow service of process via Facebook, but noted that "if the FTC were proposing to serve the defendants only by means of Facebook, as opposed to using Facebook as a supplemental means of service, a substantial question would arise whether that service comports with due process."[c]

Critical Thinking *In our connected world, is there any way a defendant could avoid service of process via social media?*

a. *Baido v. Blood-Dzraqu*, 48 Misc.3d 309, 5 N.Y.S.3d 709 (2015).
b. *Fortunato v. Chase Bank USA*, 2011 WL 5574884 (S.D.N.Y. 2011) and 2012 WL 2086950 (S.D.N.Y. 2012).
c. *FTC v. PCCare247, Inc.*, 2013 WL 841037 (S.D.N.Y. 2013).

---

motion. The notice of motion informs the opposing party that the motion has been filed. **Pretrial motions** include the motion to dismiss, the motion for judgment on the pleadings, and the motion for summary judgment, as well as the other motions listed in Exhibit 3–4.

Motion to Dismiss Either party can file a **motion to dismiss** asking the court to dismiss the case for the reasons stated in the motion. Normally, though, it is the defendant who requests dismissal.

A defendant can file a motion to dismiss if the plaintiff's complaint fails to state a claim for which relief (a remedy) can be granted. Such a motion asserts that even if the facts alleged in the complaint are true, they

do not give rise to any legal claim against the defendant. For example, if the allegations in Kirby's complaint do not constitute negligence on Carvello's part, Carvello can move to dismiss the case for failure to state a claim. Defendant Carvello could also file a motion to dismiss on the grounds that he was not properly served, that the court lacked jurisdiction, or that the venue was improper.

If the judge grants the motion to dismiss, the plaintiff generally is given time to file an amended complaint. If the judge denies the motion, the suit will go forward, and the defendant must then file an answer. Note that if Carvello wishes to discontinue the suit because, for example, an out-of-court settlement has been reached, he can likewise move for dismissal. The

EXHIBIT 3–4 Pretrial Motions

Motion to Dismiss	A motion (normally filed by the defendant) that asks the court to dismiss the case for a specified reason, such as lack of personal jurisdiction or failure to state a claim
Motion to Strike	A defendant's motion asking the court to strike (delete or remove) certain paragraphs from the complaint to better clarify the issues in dispute
Motion to Make More Definite or Certain	A motion by the defendant when the complaint is vague that asks the court to compel the plaintiff to clarify the cause of action
Motion for Judgment on the Pleadings	A motion by either party asking the court to enter judgment in his or her favor based on the pleadings because there are no facts in dispute
Motion to Compel Discovery	A motion asking the court to force the nonmoving party to comply with a discovery request
Motion for Summary Judgment	A motion asking the court to enter a judgment in his or her favor without a trial

court can also dismiss a case on its own motion. In the following case, one party filed a complaint against two others, alleging a breach of contract. The defendants filed a motion to dismiss on the ground that the venue was improper. The court denied the motion, and the defendants appealed.

Case Analysis 3.1

Espresso Disposition Corp. 1 v. Santana Sales & Marketing Group, Inc.

Florida Court of Appeal, Third District, 105 So.3d 592 (2013).

In the Language of the Court
CORTIÑAS, J. [Judge]
* * * *

Espresso Disposition Corporation 1 and Rowland Coffee Roasters, Inc. (collectively "Appellants") seek review of the trial court's order denying their motions to dismiss [Santana Sales & Marketing Group, Inc.'s ("Appellee's")] third amended complaint. Appellants claim that the trial court erred in denying their motions to dismiss because the plain and unambiguous language in the parties' * * * agreement contains a mandatory forum selection clause [a provision in a contract designating the court, jurisdiction, or tribunal that will decide any disputes arising under the contract] requiring that all lawsuits brought under the agreement shall be in Illinois.

Espresso Disposition Corporation 1 and Santana and Associates entered into the * * * agreement in 2002. The agreement provides for a mandatory forum selection clause in paragraph 8. The provision states:

Case 3.1 Continued

The venue with respect to any action pertaining to this Agreement shall be the State of Illinois. The laws of the State of Illinois shall govern the application and interpretation of this Agreement.

However, Appellee filed a lawsuit against Appellants alleging a breach of the agreement in Miami–Dade County, Florida. In fact, Appellee filed four subsequent complaints—an initial complaint, amended complaint, second amended complaint, and third amended complaint—after each and every previous pleading's dismissal was based upon venue as provided for in the agreement's mandatory forum selection clause. Appellee's third amended complaint alleges the forum selection clause was a mistake that was made at the time the agreement was drafted. Additionally, Appellee attached an affidavit [a sworn statement] which states that, in drafting the agreement, Appellee * * * copied a form version of an agreement between different parties, and by mistake, forgot to change the venue provision from Illinois to Florida. In response, Appellants filed their motions to dismiss the third amended complaint, which the trial court denied.

Florida appellate courts interpret a contractual forum selection clause under a *de novo* standard of review. [The courts review the issue anew, as if the lower courts had not ruled on the issue.] Likewise, as the trial court's order denying appellant's motion to dismiss is based on the interpretation of the contractual forum selection clause, this court's standard of review is *de novo*. Therefore, the narrow issue before this court is whether the * * *

agreement provides for a mandatory forum selection clause that is enforceable under Florida law.

Florida courts have long recognized that forum selection clauses such as the one at issue here are presumptively valid. *This is because forum selection clauses provide a degree of certainty to business contracts by obviating [preventing] jurisdictional struggles and by allowing parties to tailor the dispute resolution mechanism to their particular situation. Moreover, forum selection clauses reduce litigation over venue, thereby conserving judicial resources, reducing business expenses, and lowering consumer prices.* [Emphasis added.]

Because Florida law presumes that forum selection clauses are valid and enforceable, the party seeking to avoid enforcement of such a clause must establish that enforcement would be unjust or unreasonable. Under Florida law, the clause is only considered unjust or unreasonable if the party seeking avoidance establishes that enforcement would result in no forum at all. There is absolutely no set of facts that Appellee could plead and prove to demonstrate that Illinois state courts do not exist. Illinois became the twenty-first state in 1818, and has since established an extensive system of state trial and appellate courts. Clearly, Appellee failed to establish that enforcement would be unreasonable since the designated forum—Illinois— does not result in Appellee's having "no forum at all."

Further, as we have said on a number of occasions, if a forum selection clause unambiguously mandates that litigation be subject to an agreed upon forum, then it is error for the trial court to ignore the clause. Generally, the clause

is mandatory where the plain language used by the parties indicates exclusivity. Importantly, if the forum selection clause states or clearly indicates that any litigation must or shall be initiated in a specified forum, then it is mandatory. Here, the agreement's plain language provides that the venue for any action relating to a controversy under the agreement * * * "shall be the State of Illinois." The clear language unequivocally renders the forum selection clause mandatory.

Appellee would have us create an exception to our jurisprudence on mandatory forum selection clauses based on their error in cutting and pasting the clause from another agreement. Of course, the origin of "cutting and pasting" comes from the traditional practice of manuscript-editing whereby writers used to cut paragraphs from a page with editing scissors, that had blades long enough to cut an 8½ inch-wide page, and then physically pasted them onto another page. Today, the cut, copy, and paste functions contained in word processing software render unnecessary the use of scissors or glue. However, what has not been eliminated is the need to actually read and analyze the text being pasted, especially where it is to have legal significance. Thus, in reviewing the mandatory selection clause which Appellant seeks to enforce, we apply the legal maxim "be careful what you ask for" and enforce the pasted forum.

Accordingly, we reverse [the] trial court's denial of the motions to dismiss Appellee's third amended complaint on the basis of improper venue, and remand for entry of an order of dismissal.

Legal Reasoning Questions

1. Compare and contrast a motion to dismiss with other pretrial motions. Identify their chief differences.

2. Why did the appellants in this case file a motion to dismiss?

3. What is the effect of granting a motion to dismiss?

Motion for Judgment on the Pleadings At the close of the pleadings, either party may make a **motion for judgment on the pleadings.** This motion asks the court to decide the issue solely on the pleadings without proceeding to trial.

The judge will grant the motion only when there is no dispute over the facts of the case and the sole issue to be resolved is a question of law. For example, in the Kirby-Carvello case, if Carvello had admitted to all of Kirby's allegations in his answer and had raised no affirmative defenses, Kirby could file a motion for judgment on the pleadings.

In deciding a motion for judgment on the pleadings, the judge may consider only the evidence contained in the pleadings. In contrast, in a motion for summary judgment, discussed next, the court may consider evidence outside the pleadings, such as sworn statements and other materials that would be admissible as evidence at trial.

Motion for Summary Judgment Either party can file a **motion for summary judgment,** which asks the court to grant a judgment in that party's favor without a trial. The motion can be made before or during the trial. As with a motion for judgment on the pleadings, a court will grant a motion for summary judgment only if no facts are in dispute and the only question is how the law applies to the facts. In determining whether no facts are in contention, the court considers the evidence in the light most favorable to the other party.

To support a motion for summary judgment, a party can submit evidence obtained at any point before the trial that refutes the other party's factual claim. The evidence may consist of **affidavits** (sworn statements by parties or witnesses) or copies of documents, such as contracts, e-mails, and letters obtained through the course of discovery (discussed next).

Of course, the evidence must be *admissible* evidence—that is, evidence that the court would allow to be presented during the trial. As mentioned, the use of additional evidence is one feature that distinguishes the motion for summary judgment from the motion to dismiss and the motion for judgment on the pleadings.

On appeal of a court's grant or denial of a motion for summary judgment, the appellate court engages in *de novo* review—that is, it applies the same standard that the trial court applied. In the following case, an appellate court took a fresh look at the evidence that had been presented with a motion for summary judgment granted by the lower court.

Case 3.2

Lewis v. Twenty-First Century Bean Processing

United States Court of Appeals, Tenth Circuit, __ F.3d __, 2016 WL 66334 (2016).

Background and Facts Twenty-First Century Bean Processing hired Anthony Lewis, a forty-seven-year-old African American male, for a warehouse position, subject to a thirty-day probationary period. At the end of the period, Twenty-First Century evaluated Lewis's performance to determine whether he would remain an employee. The employer decided not to retain Lewis, who then filed a suit in a federal district court against Twenty-First Century. Lewis alleged discrimination on the basis of race and age in violation of Title VII of the Civil Rights Act and the Age Discrimination in Employment Act. Twenty-First Century filed a motion for summary judgment. As evidence, the employer presented proof concerning Lewis's job performance during the probationary period. The court granted the motion. Lewis appealed.

In the Language of the Court
Robert E. BACHARACH, Circuit Judge.
 * * * *

When a plaintiff alleges discrimination but offers no direct evidence of discrimination, the plaintiff bears the initial burden to establish a prima facie case of discrimination. [This requires a showing that (1) the plaintiff is a member of a protected class—a person defined by certain criteria, including race or age; (2) the plaintiff applied and was qualified for the job at issue; (3) the plaintiff was rejected by the employer; and (4) the employer filled the position with someone not in a protected class.] If a plaintiff

Case 3.2 Continued

establishes a prima facie *case, the burden shifts to the defendant to articulate a* * * * *nondiscriminatory reason for its actions.* If the defendant satisfies that burden, the employee would bear the burden to prove the defendant's actions were discriminatory, which the employee could do by showing defendant's proffered reason is a pretext for illegal discrimination. [Emphasis added.]

* * * *

Mr. Lewis alleges age discrimination under the Age Discrimination in Employment Act. * * * Mr. Lewis had not presented any direct evidence of discrimination [and] the court determined that Mr. Lewis had not established a *prima facie* case because he had failed to provide evidence that his work was satisfactory. In our view, that conclusion was proper. Therefore, we affirm the district court's grant of summary judgment to Twenty-First Century on the age discrimination claim.

* * * *

Mr. Lewis also alleges race discrimination under Title VII of the Civil Rights Act. Again finding no direct evidence of discrimination, * * * the court assumed without deciding that Mr. Lewis had established a *prima facie* case of race discrimination. Thus, the burden shifted to Twenty-First Century to show a nondiscriminatory reason for terminating Mr. Lewis.

As evidence of a non-discriminatory purpose, Twenty-First Century pointed out that Mr. Lewis had missed too many work days, slept at work, used his personal cellphone at work, and reacted argumentatively when warned about his cellphone usage. After finding that any one of these policy violations could serve as a nondiscriminatory reason for the firing, the court placed the burden on Mr. Lewis to show * * * that Twenty-First Century's explanation was pretextual [not legitimate]. The district court concluded that Mr. Lewis was unable to meet this burden, and we agree.

Decision and Remedy *The U.S. Court of Appeals for the Tenth Circuit affirmed the lower court's summary judgment. Of the twenty-five work days in the probationary period, Lewis was absent for four days, found sleeping twice, and seen several times texting and talking on his personal phone. When informed that this use of a phone was against company policy, Lewis argued with his superior.*

Critical Thinking

- **Legal Environment** *Should motions for summary judgment and other pretrial motions be abolished so that all lawsuits proceed to trial? Why or why not?*
- **What If the Facts Were Different?** *Suppose that at this stage of the litigation, Twenty-First Century had not been able to provide evidence in support of its asserted reason for Lewis's firing. What would have been the result? Why?*

3–2c Discovery

Before a trial begins, the parties can use a number of procedural devices to obtain information and gather evidence about the case. Kirby, for example, will want to know how fast Carvello was driving. She will also want to learn whether he had been drinking, was under the influence of medication, and was wearing corrective lenses if required by law to do so while driving.

The process of obtaining information from the opposing party or from witnesses prior to trial is known as **discovery.** Discovery includes gaining access to witnesses, documents, records, and other types of evidence.

In federal courts, the parties are required to make initial disclosures of relevant evidence to the opposing party. A court can impose sanctions on a party who fails to respond to discovery requests.

Discovery prevents surprises at trial by giving both parties access to evidence that might otherwise be hidden. This allows the litigants to learn as much as they can about what to expect at a trial before they reach the courtroom. Discovery also serves to narrow the issues so that trial time is spent on the main questions in the case. The following case shows how vital discovery can be to the outcome of litigation.

Case 3.3

Brothers v. Winstead

Supreme Court of Mississippi, 129 So.3d 906 (2014).

Background and Facts Phillips Brothers, LP (limited partnership), Harry Simmons, and Ray Winstead were the owners of Kilby Brake Fisheries, LLC (limited liability company), a catfish farm in Mississippi. For nearly eight years, Winstead operated a hatchery for the firm. During this time, the hatchery had only two profitable years. Consequently, Winstead was fired. He filed a suit in a Mississippi state court against Kilby Brake and its other owners, alleging a "freeze-out." (A freeze-out occurs when a majority of the owners of a firm exclude other owners from certain benefits of participating in the firm.)

The defendants filed a counterclaim of theft. To support this claim, the defendants asked the court to allow them to obtain documents from Winstead regarding his finances, particularly income from his Winstead Cattle Company. The court refused this request. A jury awarded Winstead more than $1.7 million, and the defendants appealed.

In the Language of the Court

WALLER, Chief Justice for the Court.
* * * *

During discovery, Winstead produced his tax returns from 2006 to 2009, which showed substantial income as coming from the Winstead Cattle Company. The only other income listed on Winstead's tax returns was from Kilby Brake * * *. Winstead had also produced [other documents showing income] from a fish farmer named Scott Kiker, which did not appear on his tax returns. [The documents supposedly involved income from sales of cattle.] Kilby Brake's theory was the entries for "cattle" represented income from sales of Kilby Brake fish Winstead was brokering and thus, it sought to compel [discovery] of all of the Winstead Cattle Company's financial records. Winstead [testified] in his deposition and again at trial that the Winstead Cattle Company did no actual business, and it was simply his hunting camp. The trial court denied Kilby Brake's motion to compel discovery into Winstead's finances.

* * * [Winstead was questioned about the forms he] had produced in discovery showing income from Kiker. Winstead testified that he would often act as a middle man if he knew of a farmer who was in need of fish and another who had fish for sale, taking a commission for brokering the deal.
* * * *

* * * Kiker testified that he had received a load of fish from Kilby Brake [but that] there was no paperwork on the transaction [and] that he sold this load of fish, gave Winstead a commission and did not pay Kilby Brake for the sales.

From the evidence noted above, we find the trial court's refusal to allow both discovery into the finances of Winstead and questions concerning Winstead Cattle Company on his tax return prevented Kilby Brake and the jury from finding out whether Winstead was selling fish from Kilby Brake and disguising it on his income tax returns * * *. Importantly, the decisions by the trial court denied Kilby Brake the ability to present its case as to what happened to the fish. The record shows there were years in which Winstead received substantial income from brokering fish sales, almost $20,000 in one year. He [testified] that Winstead Cattle Company did no business and was simply his hunting camp, yet it made significant amounts of money. [Emphasis added.]

Decision and Remedy *The Mississippi Supreme Court reversed the lower court's decision to deny discovery of information concerning Winstead's outside finances, especially regarding income from Winstead Cattle Company. The state supreme court remanded the case for a new trial.*

Critical Thinking

- **Ethical** *Does Winstead have an ethical duty to comply with the defendants' discovery request? Discuss.*
- **Legal Environment** *Did the defendants have a legitimate basis to make a discovery request for information regarding Winstead's outside income? Explain.*

Discovery Rules The FRCP and similar state rules set forth the guidelines for discovery activity. Generally, discovery is allowed regarding any matter that is relevant to the claim or defense of any party. Discovery rules also attempt to protect witnesses and parties from undue harassment, and to prevent privileged or confidential material from being disclosed. Only information that is relevant to the case at hand—or likely to lead to the discovery of relevant information—is discoverable.

If a discovery request involves privileged or confidential business information, a court can deny the request and can limit the scope of discovery in a number of ways. For instance, a court can require the party to submit the materials to the judge in a sealed envelope so that the judge can decide if they should be disclosed to the opposing party.

Depositions Discovery can involve the use of depositions. A **deposition** is sworn testimony by a party to the lawsuit or by any witness, recorded by an authorized court official. The person deposed gives testimony and answers questions asked by the attorneys from both sides. The questions and answers are recorded, sworn to, and signed. These answers, of course, will help the attorneys prepare their cases.

Depositions also give attorneys the opportunity to ask immediate follow-up questions and to evaluate how their witnesses will conduct themselves at trial. In addition, depositions can be employed in court to **impeach** (challenge the credibility of) a party or a witness who changes his or her testimony at the trial. Finally, a deposition can be used as testimony if the witness is not available at trial.

Interrogatories Discovery can also involve **interrogatories**—written questions for which written answers are prepared and then signed under oath. The main difference between interrogatories and written depositions is that interrogatories are directed to a party to the lawsuit (the plaintiff or the defendant), not to a witness. The party usually has thirty days to prepare answers.

The party's attorney often drafts the answers to interrogatories in a manner calculated to give away as little information as possible. Whereas depositions elicit candid answers not prepared in advance, interrogatories are designed to obtain accurate information about specific topics, such as how many contracts were signed and when. The scope of interrogatories is also broader because parties are obligated to answer questions, even if that means disclosing information from their records and files. As with discovery requests, a court can impose sanctions on a party who fails to answer interrogatories.

■ **CASE IN POINT 3.1** Ronald J. Hass (doing business as Valley Corp. and R. J. Hass Corp.) was a contractor who built a home for Ty and Karen Levine. Probuilders Specialty Insurance Co. provided commercial liability insurance for the contractor. Later, when the Levines sued Hass and his company for shoddy and incomplete work, Hass blamed the subcontractors. Probuilders provided Hass with legal representation, but the Levines won a judgment for more than $2 million. Then Probuilders sued Hass and his company, claiming that he had made misrepresentations to them regarding the facts of the case and seeking to avoid paying the judgment. Hass filed a counterclaim against Probuilders.

A dispute arose between Probuilders and Hass concerning discovery. Hass refused to respond fully to interrogatories and other discovery requests, and refused to give a deposition. Probuilders filed a motion to compel, and the court ordered Hass to respond to the discovery requests. Although Probuilders sent letters specifying what was needed, Hass continued to be evasive. The court imposed sanctions on Hass more than once. Ultimately, the court found that Hass had acted willfully and in bad faith, and recommended that his answers and counterclaim against Probuilders be dismissed.[6] ■

Requests for Admissions One party can serve the other party with a written request for an admission of the truth of matters relating to the trial. Any fact admitted under such a request is conclusively established as true for the trial. For example, Kirby can ask Carvello to admit that his driver's license was suspended at the time of the accident. A request for admission shortens the trial because the parties will not have to spend time proving facts on which they already agree.

Requests for Documents, Objects, and Entry upon Land A party can gain access to documents and other items not in her or his possession in order to inspect and examine them. Carvello, for example, can gain permission to inspect and copy Kirby's car repair bills. Likewise, a party can gain "entry upon land" to inspect the premises.

Requests for Examinations When the physical or mental condition of one party is in question, the opposing party can ask the court to order a physical or mental examination by an independent examiner. If the court agrees to make the order, the opposing party can obtain the results of the examination. Note that the court will

---

6. *Probuilders Specialty Insurance Co. v. Valley Corp.*, 2012 WL 6045753 (N.D.Cal. 2012).

make such an order only when the need for the information outweighs the right to privacy of the person to be examined.

Electronic Discovery Any relevant material, including information stored electronically, can be the object of a discovery request. The federal rules and most state rules (as well as court decisions) specifically allow individuals to obtain discovery of electronic "data compilations." Electronic evidence, or **e-evidence,** consists of all computer-generated or electronically recorded information, such as e-mail, voice mail, tweets, blogs, social media posts, spreadsheets, documents, and other data stored electronically.

E-evidence can reveal significant facts that are not discoverable by other means. Computers, smartphones, cameras, and other devices automatically record certain information about files—such as who created the file and when, and who accessed, modified, or transmitted it—on their hard drives. This information is called **metadata,** which can be thought of as "data about data." Metadata can be obtained only from the file in its electronic format—not from printed-out versions.

■ **EXAMPLE 3.2** In 2012, John McAfee, the programmer responsible for creating McAfee antivirus software, was wanted for questioning in the murder of his neighbor in Belize. McAfee left Belize and was on the run from police, but he allowed a journalist to come with him and photograph him. When the journalist posted photos of McAfee online, some metadata were attached to a photo. The police used the metadata to pinpoint the latitude and longitude of the image and subsequently arrested McAfee in Guatemala. ■

E-Discovery Procedures. The Federal Rules of Civil Procedure deal specifically with the preservation, retrieval, and production of electronic data. Although traditional interrogatories and depositions are still used to find out whether e-evidence exists, a party usually must hire an expert to retrieve the evidence in its electronic format. The expert uses software to reconstruct e-mail, text, and other exchanges to establish who knew what and when they knew it. The expert can even recover computer files that the user thought had been deleted.

Advantages and Disadvantages. Electronic discovery has significant advantages over paper discovery. Electronic versions of documents, e-mail, and text messages can provide useful—and often quite damaging—information about how a particular matter progressed over several weeks or months. E-discovery can uncover the proverbial smoking gun that will win the lawsuit. But it is also time consuming and expensive, especially when lawsuits involve large firms with multiple offices. Indeed, many firms are finding it difficult to fulfill their duty to preserve electronic evidence from a vast number of sources.

A party that fails to preserve e-evidence may find itself at such a disadvantage that it will settle a dispute rather than continue litigation. ■ **CASE IN POINT 3.3** Advanced Micro Devices, Inc. (AMD), sued Intel Corporation, one of the world's largest microprocessor suppliers, for violating antitrust laws. Immediately after the lawsuit was filed, Intel began collecting and preserving the electronic evidence on its servers and instructed its employees to retain documents and e-mails related to competition with AMD. Nevertheless, many employees saved only copies of the e-mails that they had received and not e-mails that they had sent. In addition, Intel did not stop its automatic e-mail deletion system, causing other information to be lost. In the end, although Intel produced data equivalent to "somewhere in the neighborhood of a pile 137 miles high" in paper, its failure to preserve e-discovery led it to settle the dispute.[7] ■

3–2d Pretrial Conference

After discovery has taken place and before the trial begins, the attorneys may meet with the trial judge in a **pretrial conference,** or hearing. Usually, the conference consists of an informal discussion between the judge and the opposing attorneys after discovery has taken place. The purpose is to explore the possibility of a settlement without trial and, if this is not possible, to identify the matters in dispute and to plan the course of the trial. In particular, the parties may attempt to establish ground rules to restrict the number of expert witnesses or discuss the admissibility or costs of certain types of evidence.

3–2e The Right to a Jury Trial

The Seventh Amendment to the U.S. Constitution guarantees the right to a jury trial for cases at law in *federal* courts when the amount in controversy exceeds $20. Most states have similar guarantees in their own constitutions (although the threshold dollar amount is higher than $20).

The right to a trial by jury need not be exercised, and many cases are tried without a jury. In most states and in federal courts, one of the parties must request a jury, or the judge presumes the parties waive this right. If there

---

7. *In re Intel Corp. Microprocessor Antitrust Litigation,* 2008 WL 2310288 (D.Del. 2008).

is no jury, the judge determines the truth of the facts alleged in the case.

3–2f Jury Selection

Before a jury trial commences, a panel of jurors must be selected. Although some types of trials require twelve-person juries, most civil matters can be heard by six-person juries. The jury selection process is known as *voir dire*.[8] In most jurisdictions, attorneys for the plaintiff and the defendant ask prospective jurors oral questions to determine whether they are biased or have any connection with a party to the action or with a prospective witness. In some jurisdictions, the judge may do all or part of the questioning based on written questions submitted by counsel for the parties.

During *voir dire*, a party may challenge a certain number of prospective jurors *peremptorily*—that is, ask that an individual not be sworn in as a juror without providing any reason. Alternatively, a party may challenge a prospective juror *for cause*—that is, provide a reason why an individual should not be sworn in as a juror. If the judge grants the challenge, the individual is asked to step down. A prospective juror, however, may not be excluded by the use of discriminatory challenges, such as those based on racial criteria or gender.

See Concept Summary 3.1 for a review of pretrial procedures.

3–3 The Trial

Various rules and procedures govern the trial phase of the litigation process. There are rules governing what kind of evidence will or will not be admitted during the trial, as well as specific procedures that the participants in the lawsuit must follow. For instance, a trial judge may instruct jurors not to communicate with anyone about the case or order reporters not to use social media to comment on the case while in the courtroom.

3–3a Opening Statements

At the beginning of the trial, both attorneys are allowed to make **opening statements** setting forth the facts that they expect to prove during the trial. The opening statement provides an opportunity for each lawyer to give a brief version of the facts and the supporting evidence that will be used during the trial. Then the plaintiff's case is presented. In our hypothetical case, Kirby's lawyer would introduce evidence (relevant documents, exhibits, and the testimony of witnesses) to support Kirby's position.

3–3b Rules of Evidence

Whether evidence will be admitted in court is determined by the **rules of evidence.** These are a series of rules that the courts have created to ensure that any evidence presented during a trial is fair and reliable. The Federal Rules of Evidence govern the admissibility of evidence in federal courts.

Evidence Must Be Relevant to the Issues Evidence will not be admitted in court unless it is relevant to the matter in question. **Relevant evidence** is evidence that tends to prove or disprove a fact in question or to establish the degree of probability of a fact or action. For instance, evidence that the defendant was in another person's home when the victim was shot would be relevant, because it would tend to prove that the defendant was not the shooter.

Hearsay Evidence Is Not Admissible Generally, hearsay is not admissible as evidence. **Hearsay** is testimony someone gives in court about a statement made by someone else who was not under oath at the time of the statement. Literally, it is what someone heard someone else say. If a witness in the Kirby-Carvello case testified in court concerning what he or she heard another observer say about the accident, for example, that testimony would be hearsay. Admitting hearsay into evidence carries many risks because, even though it may be relevant, there is no way to test its reliability.

3–3c Examination of Witnesses and Potential Motions

Because Kirby is the plaintiff, she has the burden of proving that her allegations are true. Her attorney begins the presentation of Kirby's case by calling the first witness for the plaintiff and examining, or questioning, the witness. (For both attorneys, the types of questions and the manner of asking them are governed by the rules of evidence.) This questioning is called **direct examination.**

After Kirby's attorney is finished, the witness is subject to **cross-examination** by Carvello's attorney. Then Kirby's attorney has another opportunity to question the witness in *redirect examination*, and Carvello's

---

8. Pronounced *vwahr deehr*. These verbs, based on Old French, mean "to speak the truth." In legal language, the phrase refers to the process of questioning jurors to learn about their backgrounds, attitudes, and similar attributes.

Concept Summary 3.1

Pretrial Procedures

The Pleadings	• *The plaintiff's complaint*—The plaintiff's statement of the cause of action and the parties involved, filed with the court by the plaintiff's attorney. After the filing, the defendant is notified of the suit through service of process. • *The defendant's response*—The defendant's response to the plaintiff's complaint may take the form of an answer, in which the defendant admits or denies the plaintiff's allegations. The defendant may also raise an affirmative defense and/or assert a counterclaim.
Pretrial Motions	• *Motion to dismiss*—See Exhibit 3–4. • *Motion for judgment* on the pleadings—May be made by either party and will be granted only if no facts are in dispute and only questions of law are at issue. • *Motion for summary judgment*—See Exhibit 3–4.
Discovery	The process of gathering evidence concerning the case, which may involve the following: • *Depositions* (sworn testimony by either party or any witness). • *Interrogatories* (in which parties to the action write answers to questions with the aid of their attorneys). • Requests for admissions, documents, examinations, or other information relating to the case. • Requests for electronically recorded information, such as e-mail, text messages, voice mail, and other data.
Pretrial Conference	• A pretrial hearing, at the request of either party or the court, to identify the matters in dispute after discovery has taken place and to explore the possibility of settling the dispute without a trial. If no settlement is possible, the parties plan the course of the trial.
Jury Selection	• In a jury trial, the selection of members of the jury from a pool of prospective jurors. During a process known as *voir dire*, the attorneys for both sides may challenge prospective jurors either for cause or peremptorily (for no cause).

attorney may follow the redirect examination with a *recross-examination*. When both attorneys have finished with the first witness, Kirby's attorney calls the succeeding witnesses in the plaintiff's case. Each witness is subject to examination by the attorneys in the manner just described.

Expert Witnesses As part of their cases, both the plaintiff and the defendant may present testimony from one or more expert witnesses, such as forensic scientists, physicians, and psychologists. An *expert witness* is a person who, by virtue of education, training, skill, or experience, has scientific, technical, or other specialized knowledge in a particular area beyond that of an average person. In Kirby's case, her attorney might hire an accident reconstruction specialist to establish Carvello's negligence or a physician to testify to the extent of Kirby's injuries.

Normally, witnesses can testify only about the facts of a case—that is, what they personally observed. When witnesses are qualified as experts in a particular field, however, they can offer their opinions and conclusions about the evidence in that field. Because numerous experts are available for hire and expert testimony is powerful and effective with juries, there is tremendous potential for abuse. Therefore, judges act as gatekeepers to ensure that the experts are qualified. If a party believes that the opponent's expert witness is not a qualified expert in the relevant field, that party can make a motion to prevent the witness from testifying.[9]

■ **CASE IN POINT 3.4** Yvette Downey bought a children's bedroom set from Bob's Discount Furniture Holdings, Inc. She later discovered that it was infested with bed bugs, which had spread throughout her home. Downey spoke with Edward Gordinier, a licensed and experienced exterminator, who identified the bedroom set as the source of the problem. Although Bob's retrieved the bedroom set and refunded the purchase price, it refused to pay for the costs of extermination or any other damages. Downey sued.

Before the trial, Downey's attorney named Gordinier as a witness but did not submit a written report describing his anticipated testimony or specifying his qualifications. The defendants filed a motion to prevent his testimony. The district court refused to allow Gordinier to testify, but that decision was reversed on appeal. The appellate court concluded that Gordinier was not the type of expert who regularly was hired by plaintiffs to testify in court, in which case a report would have been required. Gordinier was simply an expert on bugs, and he was allowed to give his opinion on the infestation.[10] ■

Possible Motion and Judgment At the conclusion of the plaintiff's case, the defendant's attorney may ask the judge to direct a verdict for the defendant on the ground that the plaintiff has presented no evidence to support her or his claim. This is called a **motion for a judgment as a matter of law** (or a **motion for a directed verdict** in state courts). In considering the motion, the judge looks at the evidence in the light most favorable to the plaintiff and grants the motion only if there is insufficient evidence to raise an issue of fact. (Motions for directed verdicts at this stage of a trial are seldom granted.)

Defendant's Evidence The defendant's attorney then presents the evidence and witnesses for the defendant's case. Witnesses are called and examined by the defendant's attorney. The plaintiff's attorney has the right to cross-examine them, and there may be a redirect examination and possibly a recross-examination.

At the end of the defendant's case, either attorney can move for a directed verdict. Again, the test is whether the jury can, through any reasonable interpretation of the evidence, find for the party against whom the motion has been made. After the defendant's attorney has finished introducing evidence, the plaintiff's attorney can present a **rebuttal** by offering additional evidence that refutes the defendant's case. The defendant's attorney can, in turn, refute that evidence in a **rejoinder.**

3–3d Closing Arguments, Jury Instructions, and Verdict

After both sides have rested their cases, each attorney presents a **closing argument.** In the closing argument, each attorney summarizes the facts and evidence presented during the trial and indicates why the facts and evidence support his or her client's claim. In addition to generally urging a verdict in favor of the client, the closing argument typically reveals the shortcomings of the points made by the opposing party during the trial.

Jury Instructions Attorneys usually present closing arguments whether or not the trial was heard by a jury. If it was a jury trial, the attorneys will have met with the judge before the closing arguments to determine how the jury will be instructed on the law. The attorneys can refer to these instructions in their closing arguments. After closing arguments are completed, the judge instructs the jury in the law that applies to the case (these instructions are often called *charges*). The jury then retires to the jury room to deliberate a verdict.

Juries are instructed on the standard of proof they must apply to the case. In most civil cases, the standard of proof is a *preponderance of the evidence.*[11] In other words, the plaintiff (Kirby in our hypothetical case) need only show that her factual claim is more likely to be true than the defendant's. (In a criminal trial, the prosecution has a higher standard of proof to meet—it must prove its case *beyond a reasonable doubt.*)

---

9. See Edward J. Imwinkelried, *The Methods of Attacking Scientific Evidence,* 5th ed. (2014).
10. *Downey v. Bob's Discount Furniture Holdings, Inc.,* 633 F.3d 1 (1st Cir. 2011).

11. Note that some civil claims must be proved by "clear and convincing evidence," meaning that the evidence must show that the truth of the party's claim is *highly* probable. This standard is often applied in situations that present a particular danger of deception, such as allegations of fraud.

Verdict Once the jury has reached a decision, it issues a **verdict** in favor of one party. The verdict specifies the jury's factual findings. In some cases, the jury also decides on the amount of the *award* (the compensation to be paid to the prevailing party). After the announcement of the verdict, which marks the end of the trial itself, the jurors are dismissed.

See Concept Summary 3.2 for a review of trial procedures.

3–4 Posttrial Motions

After the jury has rendered its verdict, either party may make a posttrial motion. The prevailing party usually requests that the court enter a judgment in accordance with the verdict. The nonprevailing party frequently files one of the motions discussed next.

3–4a Motion for a New Trial

At the end of the trial, the losing party may make a motion to set aside the adverse verdict and any judgment and to hold a new trial. After looking at all the evidence, the judge will grant the **motion for a new trial** only if she or he believes that the jury was in error and that it is not appropriate to grant judgment for the other side.

Usually, a new trial is granted only when the jury verdict is obviously the result of a misapplication of the law or a misunderstanding of the evidence presented at trial. A new trial can also be granted on the grounds of newly discovered evidence, misconduct by the participants during the trial (such as when a juror has made prejudicial and inflammatory remarks), or an error by the judge.

3–4b Motion for Judgment *N.O.V.*

If Kirby wins and if Carvello's attorney has previously moved for a judgment as a matter of law, then Carvello's

---

Concept Summary 3.2

Trial Procedure

Opening Statements	• Each party's attorney is allowed to present an opening statement indicating what the attorney will attempt to prove during the course of the trial.
Examination of Witnesses	• Plaintiff's introduction and direct examination of witnesses, cross-examination by defendant's attorney, possible redirect examination by plaintiff's attorney, and possible recross-examination by defendant's attorney. • Both the plaintiff and the defendant may present testimony from one or more expert witnesses. • At the close of the plaintiff's case, the defendant may make a motion for a directed verdict (or for judgment as a matter of law). If granted by the court, this motion will end the trial before the defendant presents witnesses. • Defendant's introduction and direct examination of witnesses, cross-examination by plaintiff's attorney, possible redirect examination by defendant's attorney, and possible recross-examination by plaintiff's attorney. • Possible rebuttal of defendant's argument by plaintiff's attorney, who presents more evidence. • Possible rejoinder by defendant's attorney to meet that evidence.
Closing Arguments, Jury Instructions, and Verdict	• Each party's attorney argues in favor of a verdict for his or her client. • The judge instructs (or charges) the jury as to how the law applies to the issue, and the jury retires to deliberate. • When the jury renders its verdict, the trial comes to an end.

attorney can make a second motion for a judgment as a matter of law (the terminology used in federal courts). State courts may use different terms for these motions.

In many state courts, if the defendant's attorney moved earlier for a directed verdict, he or she may now make a **motion for judgment *n.o.v.***—from the Latin *non obstante veredicto*, meaning "notwithstanding the verdict." Such a motion will be granted only if the jury's verdict was unreasonable and erroneous.

If the judge grants the motion, then the jury's verdict will be set aside, and a judgment will be entered in favor of the opposing party (Carvello). If the motion is denied, Carvello may then appeal the case. (Kirby may also appeal the case, even though she won at trial. She might appeal, for example, if she received a smaller monetary award than she had sought.)

3–5 The Appeal

Either party may appeal not only the jury's verdict but also the judge's ruling on any pretrial or posttrial motion. Many of the appellate court cases that appear in this text involve appeals of motions for summary judgment or other motions that were denied by trial court judges.

Note that a party must have legitimate grounds to file an appeal (some legal error) and that few trial court decisions are reversed on appeal. Moreover, the expenses associated with an appeal can be considerable.

3–5a Filing the Appeal

If Carvello decides to appeal the verdict in Kirby's favor, then his attorney must file a *notice of appeal* with the clerk of the trial court within a prescribed period of time. Carvello then becomes the *appellant* or *petitioner*. The clerk of the trial court sends to the reviewing court (usually an intermediate court of appeals) the *record on appeal*. The record contains all the pleadings, motions, and other documents filed with the court and a complete written transcript of the proceedings, including testimony, arguments, jury instructions, and judicial rulings.

Carvello's attorney will file an appellate **brief** with the reviewing court. The brief is a formal legal document outlining the facts and issues of the case, the judge's rulings or jury's findings that should be reversed or modified, the applicable law, and arguments on Carvello's behalf (citing applicable statutes and relevant cases as precedents). The attorney for the *appellee* (Kirby, in our hypothetical case) usually files an answering brief. Carvello's attorney can file a reply, although it is not required. The reviewing court then considers the case.

3–5b Appellate Review

A court of appeals does not hear any evidence. Rather, it reviews the record for errors of law. Its decision concerning a case is based on the record on appeal and the briefs and arguments. The attorneys present oral arguments, after which the case is taken under advisement. The court then issues a written opinion. In general, appellate courts do not reverse findings of fact unless the findings are unsupported or contradicted by the evidence.

An appellate court has the following options after reviewing a case:

1. The court can *affirm* the trial court's decision. (Most decisions are affirmed.)
2. The court can *reverse* the trial court's judgment if it concludes that the trial court erred or that the jury did not receive proper instructions.
3. The appellate court can *remand* (send back) the case to the trial court for further proceedings consistent with its opinion on the matter.
4. The court might also affirm or reverse a decision *in part*. For example, the court might affirm the jury's finding that Carvello was negligent but remand the case for further proceedings on another issue (such as the extent of Kirby's damages).
5. An appellate court can also *modify* a lower court's decision. If the appellate court decides that the jury awarded an excessive amount in damages, for example, the court might reduce the award to a more appropriate, or fairer, amount.

3–5c Higher Appellate Courts

If the reviewing court is an intermediate appellate court, the losing party may decide to appeal the decision to the state's highest court, usually called its supreme court. Although the losing party has a right to ask (petition) a higher court to review the case, the party does not have a right to have the case heard by the higher appellate court. Appellate courts normally have discretionary power and can accept or reject an appeal. Like the United States Supreme Court, state supreme courts generally deny most petitions for appeal.

If the petition for review is granted, new briefs must be filed before the state supreme court, and the attorneys may be allowed or requested to present oral arguments. Like the intermediate appellate courts, the state supreme court can reverse or affirm the lower appellate court's decision or remand the case. At this point, the case typically has reached its end (unless a federal question is at issue and one of the parties has legitimate grounds to seek review by a federal appellate court).

Concept Summary 3.3 reviews the options that the parties may pursue after the trial.

3–6 Enforcing the Judgment

The uncertainties of the litigation process are compounded by the lack of guarantees that any judgment will be enforceable. Even if the jury awards Kirby the full amount of damages requested ($500,000), for example, Carvello's auto insurance coverage might have lapsed. If so, the company would not pay any of the damages. Alternatively, Carvello's insurance policy might be limited to $250,000, meaning that Carvello personally would have to pay the remaining $250,000.

3–6a Requesting Court Assistance in Collecting the Judgment

If the defendant does not have the funds available to pay the judgment, the plaintiff can go back to the court and request that the court issue a writ of execution. A **writ of execution** is an order directing the sheriff to seize and sell the defendant's nonexempt assets, or property (certain assets are exempted by law from creditors' actions). The proceeds of the sale are then used to pay the damages owed, and any excess proceeds are returned to the defendant. Alternatively, the nonexempt property itself could be transferred to the plaintiff in lieu of an outright payment. (Creditors' remedies, discussed elsewhere in this text, may also be available.)

3–6b Availability of Assets

The problem of collecting a judgment is less pronounced when a party is seeking to satisfy a judgment against a defendant with substantial assets that can be easily located, such as a major corporation. Usually, one of the factors considered by the plaintiff and his or her attorney before a lawsuit is initiated is whether the defendant has sufficient assets to cover the amount of damages sought. In addition, during the discovery process, attorneys routinely seek information about the location of the defendant's assets that might potentially be used to satisfy a judgment.

Concept Summary 3.3

Posttrial Options

Posttrial Motions	• *Motion for a new trial*—If the judge believes that the jury was in error but is not convinced that the losing party should have won, the motion normally is granted. It can also be granted on the basis of newly discovered evidence, misconduct by the participants during the trial, or error by the judge. • *Motion for judgment n.o.v.* ("*notwithstanding the verdict*")—The party making the motion must have filed a motion for a directed verdict at the close of the presentation of evidence during the trial. The motion will be granted if the judge is convinced that the jury was in error.
The Appeal	Either party can appeal the trial court's judgment to an appropriate court of appeals. • *Filing the appeal*—The appealing party must file a notice of appeal with the clerk of the trial court, who forwards the record on appeal to the appellate court. Attorneys file appellate briefs. • *Appellate review*—The appellate court does not hear evidence but bases its opinion, which it issues in writing, on the record on appeal and the attorneys' briefs and oral arguments. The court may affirm or reverse all (or part) of the trial court's judgment and/or remand the case for further proceedings consistent with its opinion. Most decisions are affirmed on appeal. • *Further review*—In some cases, further review may be sought from a higher appellate court, such as a state supreme court. If a federal question is involved, the case may ultimately be appealed to the United States Supreme Court.

Reviewing: Court Procedures

Ronald Metzgar placed his fifteen-month-old son, Matthew, awake and healthy, in his playpen. Ronald left the room for five minutes and on his return found Matthew lifeless. A toy block had lodged in the boy's throat, causing him to choke to death. Ronald called 911, but efforts to revive Matthew were to no avail. There was no warning of a choking hazard on the box containing the block. Matthew's parents hired an attorney and sued Playskool, Inc., the manufacturer of the block, alleging that the manufacturer had been negligent in failing to warn of the block's hazard. Playskool filed a motion for summary judgment, arguing that the danger of a young child's choking on a small block was obvious. Using the information presented in the chapter, answer the following questions.

1. Suppose that the attorney the Metzgars hired agreed to represent them on a contingency-fee basis. What does that mean?
2. How would the Metzgars' attorney likely have served process (the summons and complaint) on Playskool, Inc.?
3. Should Playskool's request for summary judgment be granted? Why or why not?
4. Suppose that the judge denied Playskool's motion and the case proceeded to trial. After hearing all the evidence, the jury found in favor of the defendant. What options do the plaintiffs have at this point if they are not satisfied with the verdict?

Debate This ... *Some consumer advocates argue that attorneys' high contingency fees—sometimes reaching 40 percent—unfairly deprive winning plaintiffs of too much of their awards. Should the government cap contingency fees at, say, 20 percent of the award? Why or why not?*

Terms and Concepts

affidavit 56	hearsay 61	pleadings 50
affirmative defense 52	impeach 59	pretrial conference 60
answer 51	interrogatories 59	pretrial motion 53
brief 65	metadata 60	rebuttal 63
closing argument 63	motion 52	rejoinder 63
complaint 50	motion for a directed verdict 63	relevant evidence 61
counterclaim 52	motion for a judgment as a matter	rules of evidence 61
cross-examination 61	of law 63	service of process 50
default judgment 50	motion for a new trial 64	summons 50
deposition 59	motion for judgment *n.o.v.* 65	verdict 64
direct examination 61	motion for judgment on the	*voir dire* 61
discovery 57	pleadings 56	writ of execution 66
e-evidence 60	motion for summary judgment 56	
Federal Rules of Civil Procedure	motion to dismiss 53	
(FRCP) 48	opening statement 61	

Issue Spotters

1. At the trial, after Sue calls her witnesses, offers her evidence, and otherwise presents her side of the case, Tom has at least two choices between courses of actions. Tom can call his first witness. What else might he do? (See *The Trial*.)

2. After the trial, the judge issues a judgment that includes a grant of relief for Sue, but the relief is less than Sue wanted. Neither Sue nor Tom is satisfied with this result. Who can appeal to a higher court? (See *The Appeal*.)

• **Check your answers to the Issue Spotters against the answers provided in Appendix D at the end of this text.**

Business Scenarios

3–1. Discovery Rules. In the past, the rules of discovery were very restrictive, and trials often turned on elements of surprise. For example, a plaintiff would not necessarily know until the trial what the defendant's defense was going to be. In the last several decades, however, new rules of discovery have substantially changed this situation. Now each attorney can access practically all of the evidence that the other side intends to present at trial, with the exception of certain information—namely, the opposing attorney's work product. Work product is not a precise concept. Basically, it includes all of the attorney's thoughts on the case. Can you see any reason why such information should not be made available to the opposing attorney? Discuss fully. (See *Pretrial Procedures*.)

3–2. Motions. When and for what purpose is each of the following motions made? Which of them would be appropriate if a defendant claimed that the only issue between the parties was a question of law and that the law was favorable to the defendant's position? (See *Pretrial Procedures*.)

(a) A motion for judgment on the pleadings.

(b) A motion for a directed verdict.

(c) A motion for summary judgment.

(d) A motion for judgment *n.o.v.*

3–3. Motion for a New Trial. Washoe Medical Center, Inc., admitted Shirley Swisher for the treatment of a fractured pelvis. During her stay, Swisher suffered a fatal fall from her hospital bed. Gerald Parodi, the administrator of her estate, and others filed an action against Washoe seeking damages for the alleged lack of care in treating Swisher. During *voir dire*, when the plaintiffs' attorney returned a few minutes late from a break, the trial judge led the prospective jurors in a standing ovation. The judge joked with one of the prospective jurors, whom he had known in college, about his fitness to serve as a judge and personally endorsed another prospective juror's business. After the trial, the jury returned a verdict in favor of Washoe. The plaintiffs moved for a new trial, but the judge denied the motion. The plaintiffs then appealed, arguing that the tone set by the judge during *voir dire* prejudiced their right to a fair trial. Should the appellate court agree? Why or why not? (See *Posttrial Motions*.)

3–4. Discovery. Advance Technology Consultants, Inc. (ATC), contracted with RoadTrac, LLC, to provide software and client software systems for the products of global positioning satellite (GPS) technology being developed by RoadTrac. RoadTrac agreed to provide ATC with hardware with which ATC's software would interface. Problems soon arose, however. ATC claimed that RoadTrac's hardware was defective, making it difficult to develop the software. Road-Trac contended that its hardware was fully functional and that ATC had simply failed to provide supporting software.

ATC told RoadTrac that it considered their contract terminated. RoadTrac filed a suit in a Georgia state court against ATC alleging breach of contract. During discovery, RoadTrac requested ATC's customer lists and marketing procedures. ATC objected to providing this information because Road-Trac and ATC had become competitors in the GPS industry. Should a party to a lawsuit have to hand over its confidential business secrets as part of a discovery request? Why or why not? What limitations might a court consider imposing before requiring ATC to produce this material? (See *Pretrial Procedures*.)

Business Case Problems

3–5. Jury Misconduct. Michelle Fleshner worked for Pepose Vision Institute (PVI), a surgical practice. She was fired after she provided information to the U.S. Department of Labor about PVI's overtime pay policy. She sued for wrongful termination, and the jury awarded her $125,000. After the trial, a juror told PVI's attorneys that another juror had made anti-Semitic statements during jury deliberations. The comments concerned a witness who testified on PVI's behalf. According to the juror, the other juror said, about the witness: "She is a Jewish witch." "She is a penny-pinching Jew." "She was such a cheap Jew that she did not want to pay Plaintiff unemployment compensation." Another juror confirmed the remarks. PVI filed a motion for a new trial on the basis of juror misconduct. The trial judge held that the comments had not prevented a fair trial from occurring. PVI appealed. Do you think such comments are sufficient to require a new trial, or must a juror's bias be discovered during *voir dire* for it to matter? Explain. [*Fleshner v. Pepose Vision Institute*, 304 S.W.3d 81 (Mo. 2010)] (See *The Trial*.)

3–6. Service of Process. Dr. Kevin Bardwell owns Northfield Urgent Care, LLC, a Minnesota medical clinic. Northfield ordered flu vaccine from Clint Pharmaceuticals, a licensed distributer of flu vaccine located in Tennessee. The parties signed a credit agreement that specified that any disputes would be litigated in the Tennessee state courts. When Northfield failed to pay what it owed for the vaccine, Clint Pharmaceuticals filed a lawsuit in Tennessee and served process on the clinic via registered mail to Dr. Bardwell, the registered agent of Northfield.

Bardwell's wife, who worked as a receptionist at the clinic and handled inquiries on the clinic's Facebook site, signed for the letter. Bardwell did not appear on the trial date, however, and the Tennessee court entered a default judgment against Northfield. When Clint Pharmaceuticals attempted to collect on the judgment in Minnesota, Bardwell claimed that the judgment was unenforceable. He asserted that he had not been properly served because his wife was not a registered agent. Should the Minnesota court invalidate the Tennessee judgment? Was service of process proper when it was mailed to the defendant medical clinic and the wife of the physician who owned the clinic opened the letter? Explain. [*Clint Pharmaceuticals v. Northfield Urgent Care, LLC*, 2012 WL 3792546 (Minn.App. 2012).] (See *Pretrial Procedures*.)

3–7. Business Case Problem with Sample Answer—Discovery.

 Jessica Lester died from injuries suffered in an auto accident caused by the driver of a truck owned by Allied Concrete Co. Jessica's widower, Isaiah, filed a suit against Allied for damages. The defendant requested copies of all of Isaiah's Facebook photos and other postings. Before responding, Isaiah "cleaned up" his Facebook page. Allied suspected that some items had been deleted, including a photo of Isaiah holding a beer can while wearing a T-shirt that declared "I [heart] hotmoms." Can this material be recovered? If so, how? What effect might Isaiah's "postings" have on the result in this case? Discuss. [*Allied Concrete Co. v. Lester*, 736 S.E.2d 699 (2013)] (See *Pretrial Procedures*.)

- For a sample answer to Problem 3–7, go to Appendix E at the end of this text.

3–8. Motion for Summary Judgment.

Rebecca Nichols drove a truck for Tri-National Logistics, Inc. (TNI). On a delivery trip, Nichols's fellow driver, James Paris, made unwelcome sexual advances. Paris continued to make advances during a subsequent mandatory layover. Nichols reported this behavior to their employer. TNI nevertheless left her with Paris in Pharr, Texas, for another seven days with no alternative form of transportation before sending a driver to pick her up. She filed a suit in a federal district court against TNI, alleging discrimination on the basis of sex in violation of Title VII of the Civil Rights Act. Disputed facts included whether Nichols subjectively felt abused by Paris and whether their employer was aware of his conduct and failed to take appropriate action.

Could TNI successfully file a motion for summary judgment at this point? Explain. [*Nichols v. Tri-National Logistics, Inc,* 809 F.3d 981 (8th Cir. 2016)] (See *Pretrial Procedures*.)

3–9. A Question of Ethics—Service of Process.

 Narnia Investments, Ltd., filed a suit in a Texas state court against several defendants, including Harvestons Securities, Inc., a securities dealer. (Securities are investments that include stocks and bonds.) Harvestons is registered with the state of Texas. Thus, a party may serve a summons and a copy of a complaint on Harvestons by serving the Texas Securities Commissioner. In this case, the return of service indicated that process had been served on the commissioner "by delivering to JoAnn Kocerek defendant, in person, a true copy of this [summons] together with the accompanying copy(ies) of the [complaint]."

*Harvestons did not file an answer, and Narnia obtained a default judgment against the defendant for $365,000, plus attorneys' fees and interest. Five months after this judgment, Harvestons filed a motion for a new trial, which the court denied. Harvestons appealed to a state intermediate appellate court, claiming that it had not been served in strict compliance with the rules governing service of process. [*Harvestons Securities, Inc. v. Narnia Investments, Ltd., 218 S.W.3d 126 (Tex.App.—Houston 2007)]* (See *Pretrial Procedures*.)

(a) Harvestons asserted that Narnia's service was invalid, in part, because "the return of service states that process was delivered to 'JoAnn Kocerek'" and did not show that she "had the authority to accept process on behalf of Harvestons or the Texas Securities Commissioner." Should such a detail, if it is required, be strictly construed and applied? Should it apply in this case? Explain.

(b) Who is responsible for ensuring that service of process is accomplished properly? Was it accomplished properly in this case? Why or why not?

Legal Reasoning Group Activity

3–10. Court Procedures.

Bento Cuisine is a lunch-cart business. It occupies a street corner in Texarkana, a city that straddles the border of Arkansas and Texas. Across the street—and across the state line, which runs down the middle of the street—is Rico's Tacos. The two businesses compete for customers. Recently, Bento has begun to suspect that Rico's is engaging in competitive behavior that is illegal. Bento's manager overheard several of Rico's employees discussing these competitive tactics while on a break at a nearby Starbucks. Bento files a lawsuit against Rico's in a federal court based on diversity jurisdiction. (See *Pretrial Procedures*.)

(a) The first group will discuss whether Rico's could file a motion claiming that the federal court lacks jurisdiction over this dispute.

(b) The second group will assume that the case goes to trial. Bento's manager believes that Bento's has both the law and the facts on its side. Nevertheless, at the end of the trial, the jury decides against Bento, and the judge issues a ruling in favor of Rico's. If Bento is unwilling to accept this result, what are its options?

(c) As discussed in this chapter, hearsay is literally what a witness says he or she heard another person say. A third group will decide whether Bento's manager can testify about what he heard some of Rico's employees say to one another while at a coffee shop. This group will also discuss what makes the admissibility of hearsay evidence potentially unethical.

Answers to the *Issue Spotters*

1. *Tom can call his first witness. What else might he do?* Tom could file a motion for a directed verdict. This motion asks the judge to direct a verdict for Tom on the ground that Sue presented no evidence that would justify granting Sue relief. The judge grants the motion if there is insufficient evidence to raise an issue of fact.

2. *Who can appeal to a higher court?* Either a plaintiff or a defendant, or both, can appeal a judgment to a higher court. An appellate court can affirm, reverse, or remand a case, or take any of these actions in combination. To appeal successfully, it is best to appeal on the basis of an error of law, because appellate courts do not usually reverse on findings of fact.

Sample Answers for *Business Case Problems with Sample Answer*

Problem 3–7. *Discovery.* Yes. The items that were deleted from a Facebook page can be recovered. Normally, a party must hire an expert to recover material in an electronic format, and this can be time consuming and expensive.

Electronic evidence, or e-evidence, consists of all computer-generated or electronically recorded information, such as posts on Facebook and other social media sites. The effect that e-evidence can have in a case depends on its relevance and what it reveals. In the facts presented in this problem, Isaiah should be sanctioned—he should be required to cover Allied's cost to hire the recovery expert and attorney's fees to confront the misconduct. In a jury trial, the court might also instruct the jury to presume that any missing items are harmful to Isaiah's case. If all of the material is retrieved and presented at the trial, any prejudice to Allied's case might thereby be mitigated. If not, the court might go so far as to order a new trial.

In the actual case on which this problem is based, Allied hired an expert, who determined that Isaiah had in fact removed some photos and other items from his Facebook page. After the expert testified about the missing material, Isaiah provided Allied with all of it, including the photos that he had deleted. Allied sought a retrial, but the court instead reduced the amount of Isaiah's damages by the amount that it cost Allied to address his "misconduct."

CHAPTER

Business and the Constitution

Laws that govern business have their origin in the lawmaking authority granted by the U.S. Constitution, which is the supreme law in this country.[1] Neither Congress nor any state may pass a law that is in conflict with the Constitution.

Constitutional disputes frequently come before the courts. For instance, numerous states challenged the Obama administration's Affordable Care Act on constitutional grounds. The United States Supreme Court decided in 2012 that the provisions of this law, which required most Americans to have health insurance by 2014, did not exceed the constitutional authority of the federal government. The Court's decision in the matter continues to have a significant impact on the business environment.

1. See Appendix B for the full text of the U.S. Constitution.

4-1 The Constitutional Powers of Government

Following the Revolutionary War, the states adopted the Articles of Confederation. The Articles created a *confederal form of government* in which the states had the authority to govern themselves and the national government could exercise only limited powers. Problems soon arose because the nation was facing an economic crisis and state laws interfered with the free flow of commerce. A national convention was called, and the delegates drafted the U.S. Constitution. This document, after its ratification by the states in 1789, became the basis for an entirely new form of government.

4-1a A Federal Form of Government

The new government created by the U.S. Constitution reflected a series of compromises made by the convention delegates on various issues. Some delegates wanted sovereign power to remain with the states. Others wanted the national government alone to exercise sovereign power. The end result was a compromise—a **federal form of government** in which the national government and the states *share* sovereign power.

Federal Powers The Constitution sets forth specific powers that can be exercised by the national (federal) government. It further provides that the national government has the implied power to undertake actions necessary to carry out its expressly designated powers (or *enumerated powers*). All other powers are expressly "reserved" to the states under the Tenth Amendment to the U.S. Constitution.

Regulatory Powers of the States As part of their inherent **sovereignty** (power to govern themselves), state governments have the authority to regulate certain affairs within their borders. As mentioned, this authority stems, in part, from the Tenth Amendment, which reserves all powers not delegated to the national government to the states or to the people.

State regulatory powers are often referred to as **police powers.** The term encompasses more than just the enforcement of criminal laws. Police powers also give state governments broad rights to regulate private activities to protect or promote the public order, health, safety, morals, and general welfare. Fire and building codes, antidiscrimination laws, parking regulations, zoning restrictions, licensing requirements, and thousands of other state statutes have been enacted pursuant to states' police powers. Local governments, such as cities, also exercise police powers.[2] Generally, state laws enacted

2. Local governments derive their authority to regulate their communities from the state, because they are creatures of the state. In other words, they cannot come into existence unless authorized by the state to do so.

pursuant to a state's police powers carry a strong presumption of validity.

4–1b Relations among the States

The U.S. Constitution also includes provisions concerning relations among the states in our federal system. Particularly important are the *privileges and immunities clause* and the *full faith and credit clause.*

The Privileges and Immunities Clause Article IV, Section 2, of the Constitution provides that the "Citizens of each State shall be entitled to all Privileges and Immunities of Citizens in the several States." This clause is often referred to as the interstate **privileges and immunities clause.**[3] It prevents a state from imposing unreasonable burdens on citizens of another state—particularly with regard to means of livelihood or doing business.

When a citizen of one state engages in basic and essential activities in another state (the "foreign state"), the foreign state must have a *substantial reason* for treating the nonresident differently than its own residents. Basic activities include transferring property, seeking employment, and accessing the court system. The foreign state must also establish that its reason for the discrimination is *substantially related* to the state's ultimate purpose in adopting the legislation or regulating the activity.[4]

The Full Faith and Credit Clause Article IV, Section 1, of the U.S. Constitution provides that "Full Faith and Credit shall be given in each State to the public Acts, Records, and judicial Proceedings of every other State." This clause, which is referred to as the **full faith and credit clause,** applies only to civil matters. It ensures that rights established under deeds, wills, contracts, and similar instruments in one state will be honored by other states. It also ensures that any judicial decision with respect to such property rights will be honored and enforced in all states.

The legal issues raised by same-sex marriage involve, among other things, the full faith and credit clause, because that clause requires each state to honor marriage decrees issued by another state. See this chapter's *Managerial Strategy* feature for a discussion of marriage equality laws.

The full faith and credit clause has contributed to the unity of American citizens because it protects their legal rights as they move about from state to state. It also protects the rights of those to whom they owe obligations, such as persons who have been awarded monetary damages by courts. The ability to enforce such rights is extremely important for the conduct of business in a country with a very mobile citizenry.

4–1c The Separation of Powers

To make it more difficult for the national government to use its power arbitrarily, the Constitution provided for three branches of government. The legislative branch makes the laws, the executive branch enforces the laws, and the judicial branch interprets the laws. Each branch performs a separate function, and no branch may exercise the authority of another branch.

Additionally, a system of **checks and balances** allows each branch to limit the actions of the other two branches, thus preventing any one branch from exercising too much power. Some examples of these checks and balances include the following:

1. The legislative branch (Congress) can enact a law, but the executive branch (the president) has the constitutional authority to veto that law.
2. The executive branch is responsible for foreign affairs, but treaties with foreign governments require the advice and consent of the Senate.
3. Congress determines the jurisdiction of the federal courts, and the president appoints federal judges, with the advice and consent of the Senate. The judicial branch has the power to hold actions of the other two branches unconstitutional.[5]

4–1d The Commerce Clause

To prevent states from establishing laws and regulations that would interfere with trade and commerce among the states, the Constitution expressly delegated to the national government the power to regulate interstate commerce. Article I, Section 8, of the U.S. Constitution explicitly permits Congress "[t]o regulate Commerce with foreign Nations, and among the several States, and with the Indian Tribes." This clause, referred to as the **commerce clause,** has had a greater impact on business than any other provision in the Constitution. The commerce clause provides the basis for the national government's extensive regulation of state and even local affairs.

---

3. Interpretations of this clause commonly use the terms *privilege* and *immunity* synonymously. Generally, the terms refer to certain rights, benefits, or advantages enjoyed by individuals.
4. This test was first announced in *Supreme Court of New Hampshire v. Piper,* 470 U.S. 274, 105 S.Ct. 1272, 84 L.Ed.2d 205 (1985). For another example, see *Lee v. Miner,* 369 F.Supp.2d 527 (D.Del. 2005).

5. The power of judicial review was established by the United States Supreme Court in *Marbury v. Madison,* 5 U.S. (1 Cranch) 137, 2 L.Ed. 60 (1803).

MANAGERIAL STRATEGY — Marriage Equality and the Constitution

The debate over same-sex marriage has been raging across the country for years. The legal issues raised by marriage equality involve privacy rights and equal protection. Although marriage equality may not appear at first glance to be business related, it is an important legal issue for managers. Companies like Barilla Pasta, Chick-fil-A, Exxon Mobil, and Target Corporation have lost significant business for purportedly supporting anti-gay organizations and legislation.

The Definition of Marriage

Before 1996, federal law did not define marriage, and the U.S. government recognized any marriage that was recognized by a state. Then Congress passed the Defense of Marriage Act (DOMA), which explicitly defined marriage as a union of one man and one woman. DOMA was later challenged, and a number of federal courts found it to be unconstitutional in the context of bankruptcy, public employee benefits, and estate taxes. In 2013, the United States Supreme Court struck down part of DOMA as unconstitutional.[a] Today, once again, no federal law defines marriage.

Bans on Same-Sex Marriage Eliminated by the Supreme Court

During this period, federal courts became increasingly likely to invalidate state bans on same-sex marriage. In 2013, a federal district court held that Utah's same-sex marriage ban was unconstitutional.[b] In 2014, federal district courts in Arkansas, Mississippi, and Oklahoma struck down state same-sex marriage bans.[c] Moreover, public sentiment on the issue had shifted, and more states recognized the rights of same-sex couples. By 2015, thirty-seven states, as well as the District of Columbia, had legalized same-sex marriage.

In 2015, the United States Supreme Court determined that the remaining state-level prohibitions on same-sex marriage were unconstitutional. In a landmark decision, the Court ruled that the Fourteenth Amendment requires individual states to (1) issue marriage licenses to same-sex couples and (2) recognize same-sex marriages performed in other states.[d]

The landmark Supreme Court decision requiring all states to recognize same-sex marriage means that businesses must make adjustments. Company policies need to be revised to specify how same-sex partners will be treated in terms of family and medical leave, health-insurance coverage, pensions, and other benefits.

Business Questions

1. *Can a business manager's religious beliefs legally factor into the business's hiring and treatment of same-sex partners? Why or why not?*

2. *Must business owners in all states provide the same benefits to employees in a same-sex union as they do to heterosexual couples?*

---

a. *Windsor v. United States,* ___ U.S. ___, 133 S.Ct. 2675, 186 L.Ed.2d 808 (2013).
b. *Kitchen v. Herbert,* 961 F.Supp.2d 1181 (D.Utah 2013).
c. *Campaign for Southern Equality v. Bryant,* 64 F.Supp.3d 906 (S.D. Miss. 2014); *Jernigan v. Crane,* 64 F.Supp.3d 1260 (E.D.Ark. 2014); and *Bishop v. U.S. ex rel. Holder,* 962 F.Supp.2d 1252 (N.D. Okla. 2014).
d. *Obergefell v. Hodges,* ___ U.S. ___, 135 S.Ct. 2584, 192 L.Ed.2d 609 (2015).

Initially, the courts interpreted the commerce clause to apply only to commerce between the states (*interstate* commerce) and not commerce within the states (*intrastate* commerce). That changed in 1824, however, when the United States Supreme Court decided the landmark case of *Gibbons v. Ogden.*[6] The Court held that commerce within the states could also be regulated by the national government as long as the commerce *substantially affected* commerce involving more than one state.

The Expansion of National Powers under the Commerce Clause As the nation grew and faced new kinds of problems, the commerce clause became a vehicle for the additional expansion of the national government's regulatory powers. Even activities that seemed purely local in nature came under the regulatory reach of the national government if those activities were deemed to substantially affect interstate commerce. In 1942, the Supreme Court held that wheat production by an individual farmer intended wholly for consumption on his own farm was subject to federal regulation.[7]

The following *Classic Case* involved a challenge to the scope of the national government's constitutional authority to regulate local activities.

---

6. 22 U.S. (9 Wheat.) 1, 6 L.Ed. 23 (1824).

7. *Wickard v. Filburn,* 317 U.S. 111, 63 S.Ct. 82, 87 L.Ed. 122 (1942).

Heart of Atlanta Motel v. United States

Supreme Court of the United States, 379 U.S. 241, 85 S.Ct. 348, 13 L.Ed.2d 258 (1964).

Background and Facts In the 1950s, the United States Supreme Court ruled that racial segregation imposed by the states in school systems and other public facilities violated the Constitution. Privately owned facilities were not affected until Congress passed the Civil Rights Act of 1964, which prohibited racial discrimination in "establishments affecting interstate commerce."

The owner of the Heart of Atlanta Motel, in violation of the Civil Rights Act of 1964, refused to rent rooms to African Americans. The motel owner brought an action in a federal district court to have the Civil Rights Act declared unconstitutional on the ground that Congress had exceeded its constitutional authority to regulate commerce by enacting the statute.

The owner argued that his motel was not engaged in interstate commerce but was "of a purely local character." The motel, however, was accessible to state and interstate highways. The owner advertised nationally, maintained billboards throughout the state, and accepted convention trade from outside the state (75 percent of the guests were residents of other states).

The district court ruled that the act did not violate the Constitution and enjoined (prohibited) the owner from discriminating on the basis of race. The motel owner appealed. The case ultimately went to the United States Supreme Court.

In the Language of the Court

Mr. Justice *CLARKE* delivered the opinion of the Court.
* * * *

While the Act as adopted carried no congressional findings, the record of its passage through each house is replete with evidence of the burdens that discrimination by race or color places upon interstate commerce * * *. This testimony included the fact that our people have become increasingly mobile with millions of all races traveling from State to State; that Negroes in particular have been the subject of discrimination in transient accommodations, having to travel great distances to secure the same; that often they have been unable to obtain accommodations and have had to call upon friends to put them up overnight. * * * These exclusionary practices were found to be nationwide, the Under Secretary of Commerce testifying that there is "no question that this discrimination in the North still exists to a large degree" and in the West and Midwest as well * * *. This testimony indicated a qualitative as well as quantitative effect on interstate travel by Negroes. The former was the obvious impairment of the Negro traveler's pleasure and convenience that resulted when he continually was uncertain of finding lodging. As for the latter, there was evidence that this uncertainty stemming from racial discrimination had the effect of discouraging travel on the part of a substantial portion of the Negro community * * *. We shall not burden this opinion with further details since the voluminous testimony presents overwhelming evidence that discrimination by hotels and motels impedes interstate travel.
* * * *

It is said that the operation of the motel here is of a purely local character. But, assuming this to be true, "if it is interstate commerce that feels the pinch, it does not matter how local the operation that applies the squeeze." * * * *Thus the power of Congress to promote interstate commerce also includes the power to regulate the local incidents thereof, including local activities in both the States of origin and destination, which might have a substantial and harmful effect upon that commerce.* [Emphasis added.]

Decision and Remedy *The United States Supreme Court upheld the constitutionality of the Civil Rights Act of 1964. The power of Congress to regulate interstate commerce permitted the enactment of legislation that could halt local discriminatory practices.*

Impact of This Case on Today's Law *If the United States Supreme Court had invalidated the Civil Rights Act of 1964, the legal landscape of the United States would be much different today. The act prohibits discrimination based on race, color, national origin, religion, or gender in all "public accommodations," including hotels and restaurants.*

Case 4.1 Continues

Case 4.1 Continued

The act also prohibits discrimination in employment based on these criteria. Although state laws now prohibit many of these forms of discrimination as well, the protections available vary from state to state—and it is not certain whether such laws would have been passed had the outcome in this case been different.

Critical Thinking

- **What If the Facts Were Different?** *If this case had involved a small, private retail business that did not advertise nationally, would the result have been the same? Why or why not?*

The Commerce Clause Today Today, at least theoretically, the power over commerce authorizes the national government to regulate almost every commercial enterprise in the United States. The breadth of the commerce clause permits the national government to legislate in areas in which Congress has not explicitly been granted power. Only occasionally has the Supreme Court curbed the national government's regulatory authority under the commerce clause.[8]

The Supreme Court has, for instance, allowed the federal government to regulate noncommercial activities relating to medical marijuana that take place wholly within a state's borders. ■ **CASE IN POINT 4.1** More than half the states, including California, have adopted laws that legalize marijuana for medical purposes (and a handful of states now permit the recreational use of marijuana). Marijuana possession, however, is illegal under the federal Controlled Substances Act (CSA).[9] After the federal government seized the marijuana that two seriously ill California women were using on the advice of their physicians, the women filed a lawsuit. They argued that it was unconstitutional for the federal statute to prohibit them from using marijuana for medical purposes that were legal within the state.

The Supreme Court, though, held that Congress has the authority to prohibit the *intrastate* possession and noncommercial cultivation of marijuana as part of a larger regulatory scheme (the CSA).[10] In other words, the federal government may still prosecute individuals for possession of marijuana regardless of whether they reside in a state that allows the medical or recreational use of marijuana. ■

The "Dormant" Commerce Clause The Supreme Court has interpreted the commerce clause to mean that the national government has the *exclusive* authority to regulate commerce that substantially affects trade and commerce among the states. This express grant of authority to the national government is often referred to as the "positive" aspect of the commerce clause. But this positive aspect also implies a negative aspect—that the states do *not* have the authority to regulate interstate commerce. This negative aspect of the commerce clause is often referred to as the "dormant" (implied) commerce clause.

The dormant commerce clause comes into play when state regulations affect interstate commerce. In this situation, the courts weigh the state's interest in regulating a certain matter against the burden that the state's regulation places on interstate commerce. Because courts balance the interests involved, it is difficult to predict the outcome in a particular case. State laws that alter conditions of competition to favor in-state interests over out-of-state competitors in a market (such as wineries or construction workers) are usually invalidated, however.[11]

■ **CASE IN POINT 4.2** Maryland imposed personal income taxes on its residents at the state level and the county level. Maryland residents who paid income tax in another state were allowed a credit against the *state* portion of their Maryland taxes, but not the *county* portion. Several Maryland residents who had earned profits in and paid taxes to other states but had not received a credit against their county tax liability sued. They claimed that Maryland's system discriminated against intrastate commerce because those who earned income in other states paid more taxes than residents whose only income came from within Maryland. When the case reached the United States Supreme Court in 2015, the

---

8. See, for example, *United States v. Morrison*, 529 U.S. 598, 120 S.Ct. 1740, 146 L.Ed.2d 658 (2000), holding that the federal Violence Against Women Act violated Congress's commerce clause authority.

9. 21 U.S.C. Sections 801 *et seq.*

10. *Gonzales v. Raich*, 545 U.S. 1, 125 S.Ct. 2195, 162 L.Ed.2d 1 (2005).

11. See *Family Winemakers of California v. Jenkins*, 592 F.3d 1 (1st Cir. 2010); and *Tri-M Group, LLC v. Sharp*, 638 F.3d 406 (3d Cir. 2011).

Court held that Maryland's personal income tax scheme violated the dormant commerce clause.[12] ■

4-1e The Supremacy Clause and Federal Preemption

Article VI of the U.S. Constitution, commonly referred to as the **supremacy clause,** provides that the Constitution, laws, and treaties of the United States are "the supreme Law of the Land." When there is a direct conflict between a federal law and a state law, the state law is rendered invalid. Because some powers are *concurrent* (shared by the federal government and the states), however, it is necessary to determine which law governs in a particular circumstance.

Preemption When Congress chooses to act exclusively in a concurrent area, **preemption** occurs. In this circumstance, a valid federal statute or regulation will take precedence over a conflicting state or local law or regulation on the same general subject.

Congressional Intent Often, it is not clear whether Congress, in passing a law, intended to preempt an entire subject area. In these situations, the courts determine whether Congress intended to exercise exclusive power.

No single factor is decisive as to whether a court will find preemption. Generally, though, congressional intent to preempt will be found if a federal law regulating an activity is so pervasive, comprehensive, or detailed that the states have little or no room to regulate in that area. Also, when a federal statute creates an agency to enforce the law, matters that may come within the agency's jurisdiction will likely preempt state laws.

■ **CASE IN POINT 4.3** A man who alleged that he had been injured by a faulty medical device (a balloon catheter that was inserted into his artery following a heart attack) sued the manufacturer. The case ultimately came before the United States Supreme Court. The Court noted that the relevant federal law (the Medical Device Amendments of 1976) had included a preemption provision. Furthermore, the device had passed the U.S. Food and Drug Administration's rigorous premarket approval process. Therefore, the Court ruled that the federal regulation of medical devices preempted the man's state law claims.[13] ■

4-1f The Taxing and Spending Powers

Article I, Section 8, of the U.S. Constitution provides that Congress has the "Power to lay and collect Taxes, Duties, Imposts, and Excises." Section 8 further requires uniformity in taxation among the states, and thus Congress may not tax some states while exempting others.

In the distant past, if Congress attempted to regulate indirectly, by taxation, an area over which it had no authority, the courts would invalidate the tax. Today, however, if a tax measure is reasonable, it generally is held to be within the national taxing power. Moreover, the expansive interpretation of the commerce clause almost always provides a basis for sustaining a federal tax.

Article I, Section 8, also gives Congress its spending power—the power "to pay the Debts and provide for the common Defence and general Welfare of the United States." Congress can spend revenues not only to carry out its expressed powers but also to promote any objective it deems worthwhile, so long as it does not violate the Bill of Rights. The spending power necessarily involves policy choices, with which taxpayers (and politicians) may disagree.

4–2 Business and the Bill of Rights

The importance of a written declaration of the rights of individuals caused the first Congress of the United States to submit twelve amendments to the U.S. Constitution to the states for approval. Ten of these amendments, known as the **Bill of Rights,** were adopted in 1791 and embody a series of protections for the individual against various types of interference by the federal government.[14]

The protections guaranteed by these ten amendments are summarized in Exhibit 4–1.[15] Some of these constitutional protections apply to business entities as well as individuals. For example, corporations exist as separate legal entities, or *legal persons,* and enjoy many of the same rights and privileges as *natural persons* do.

---

12. *Comptroller of Treasury of Maryland v. Wynne,* ___ U.S. ___, 135 S.Ct. 1787, 191 L.Ed.2d 813 (2015).
13. *Riegel v. Medtronic, Inc.,* 552 U.S. 312, 128 S.Ct. 999, 169 L.Ed.2d 892 (2008).

14. Another of these proposed amendments was ratified more than two hundred years later (in 1992) and became the Twenty-seventh Amendment to the Constitution. See Appendix B.
15. See the Constitution in Appendix B for the complete text of each amendment.

EXHIBIT 4–1 Protections Guaranteed by the Bill of Rights

First Amendment:	Guarantees the freedoms of religion, speech, and the press and the rights to assemble peaceably and to petition the government.
Second Amendment:	States that the right of the people to keep and bear arms shall not be infringed.
Third Amendment:	Prohibits, in peacetime, the lodging of soldiers in any house without the owner's consent.
Fourth Amendment:	Prohibits unreasonable searches and seizures of persons or property.
Fifth Amendment:	Guarantees the rights to *indictment* (formal accusation) by a grand jury, to due process of law, and to fair payment when private property is taken for public use. The Fifth Amendment also prohibits compulsory self-incrimination and double jeopardy (trial for the same crime twice).
Sixth Amendment:	Guarantees the accused in a criminal case the right to a speedy and public trial by an impartial jury and with counsel. The accused has the right to cross-examine witnesses against him or her and to solicit testimony from witnesses in his or her favor.
Seventh Amendment:	Guarantees the right to a trial by jury in a civil case involving at least twenty dollars.
Eighth Amendment:	Prohibits excessive bail and fines, as well as cruel and unusual punishment.
Ninth Amendment:	Establishes that the people have rights in addition to those specified in the Constitution.
Tenth Amendment:	Establishes that those powers neither delegated to the federal government nor denied to the states are reserved to the states and to the people.

4–2a Limits on Federal and State Governmental Actions

As originally intended, the Bill of Rights limited only the powers of the national government. Over time, however, the United States Supreme Court "incorporated" most of these rights into the protections against state actions afforded by the Fourteenth Amendment to the Constitution.

The Fourteenth Amendment The Fourteenth Amendment, passed in 1868 after the Civil War, provides, in part, that "[n]o State shall . . . deprive any person of life, liberty, or property, without due process of law." Starting in 1925, the Supreme Court began to define various rights and liberties guaranteed in the U.S. Constitution as constituting "due process of law," which was required of state governments under that amendment.

Today, most of the rights and liberties set forth in the Bill of Rights apply to state governments as well as the national government. In other words, neither the federal government nor state governments can deprive persons of those rights and liberties.

Judicial Interpretation The rights secured by the Bill of Rights are not absolute. Many of the rights

guaranteed by the first ten amendments are set forth in very general terms. The Second Amendment states that people have a right to keep and bear arms, but it does not describe the extent of this right. As the Supreme Court has noted, this right does not mean that people can "keep and carry any weapon whatsoever in any manner whatsoever and for whatever purpose."[16] Legislatures can prohibit the carrying of concealed weapons or certain types of weapons, such as machine guns.

Ultimately, the United States Supreme Court, as the final interpreter of the Constitution, gives meaning to these rights and determines their boundaries. Changing public views on controversial topics, such as privacy in an era of terrorist threats or the rights of gay men and lesbians, can affect the way the Supreme Court decides a case.

4–2b Freedom of Speech

A democratic form of government cannot survive unless people can freely voice their political opinions and criticize government actions or policies. Freedom of speech,

---

16. *District of Columbia v. Heller,* 554 U.S. 570, 128 S.Ct. 2783, 171 L.Ed.2d 637 (2008).

particularly political speech, is thus a prized right, and traditionally the courts have protected this right to the fullest extent possible.

Symbolic speech—gestures, movements, articles of clothing, and other forms of expressive conduct—is also given substantial protection by the courts. The Supreme Court has held that the burning of the American flag as part of a peaceful protest is a constitutionally protected form of expression.[17] Similarly, wearing a T-shirt with a photo of a presidential candidate is a constitutionally protected form of expression. ■ **EXAMPLE 4.4** As a form of expression, Nate has gang signs tattooed on his torso, arms, neck, and legs. If a reasonable person would interpret this conduct as conveying a message, then it might be a protected form of symbolic speech. ■

Reasonable Restrictions A balance must be struck between a government's obligation to protect its citizens and those citizens' exercise of their rights. Expression—oral, written, or symbolized by conduct—is therefore subject to reasonable restrictions. Reasonableness is analyzed on a case-by-case basis.

Content-Neutral Laws. Laws that regulate the time, manner, and place, but not the content, of speech receive less scrutiny by the courts than do laws that restrict the content of expression. If a restriction imposed by the government is content neutral, then a court may allow it. To be content neutral, the restriction must be aimed at combatting some societal problem, such as crime or drug abuse, and not be aimed at suppressing the expressive conduct or its message.

Courts have often protected nude dancing as a form of symbolic expression but typically allow content-neutral laws that ban all public nudity. ■ **CASE IN POINT 4.5** Ria Ora was charged with dancing nude at an annual "anti-Christmas" protest in Harvard Square in Cambridge, Massachusetts, under a statute banning public displays of open and gross lewdness. Ora argued that the statute was overbroad and unconstitutional, and a trial court agreed. On appeal, however, a state appellate court upheld the statute as constitutional in situations in which there was an unsuspecting or unwilling audience.[18] ■

Laws That Restrict the Content of Speech. Any law that regulates the content of expression must serve a compelling state interest and must be narrowly written to achieve that interest. Under the **compelling government**

interest test, the government's interest is balanced against the individual's constitutional right to free expression. For the statute to be valid, there must be a compelling government interest that can be furthered only by the law in question.

The United States Supreme Court has held that schools may restrict students' speech at school events. ■ **CASE IN POINT 4.6** Some high school students held up a banner saying "Bong Hits 4 Jesus" at an off-campus but school-sanctioned event. The Supreme Court ruled that the school did not violate the students' free speech rights when school officials confiscated the banner and suspended the students for ten days. Because the banner could reasonably be interpreted as promoting drugs, the Court concluded that the school's actions were justified. Several justices disagreed, however, noting that the majority's holding creates an exception that will allow schools to censor any student speech that mentions drugs.[19] ■

Corporate Political Speech Political speech by corporations also falls within the protection of the First Amendment. Many years ago, the United States Supreme Court struck down as unconstitutional a Massachusetts statute that prohibited corporations from making political contributions or expenditures that individuals were permitted to make.[20] The Court has also held that a law forbidding a corporation from including inserts with its bills to express its views on controversial issues violates the First Amendment.[21]

Corporate political speech continues to be given significant protection under the First Amendment. ■ **CASE IN POINT 4.7** In *Citizens United v. Federal Election Commission,*[22] the Supreme Court issued a landmark decision that overturned a twenty-year-old precedent on campaign financing. The case involved Citizens United, a nonprofit corporation that runs a *political action committee* (an organization that registers with the government and campaigns for or against political candidates).

Citizens United had produced a film called *Hillary: The Movie* that was critical of Hillary Clinton, who was seeking the Democratic nomination for presidential candidate. Campaign-finance law restricted Citizens United from broadcasting the movie. The Court ruled that these

---

17. *Texas v. Johnson,* 491 U.S. 397, 109 S.Ct. 2533, 105 L.Ed.2d 342 (1989).
18. *Commonwealth v. Ora,* 451 Mass. 125, 883 N.E.2d 1217 (2008).
19. *Morse v. Frederick,* 551 U.S. 393, 127 S.Ct. 2618, 168 L.Ed.2d 290 (2007).
20. *First National Bank of Boston v. Bellotti,* 435 U.S. 765, 98 S.Ct. 1407, 55 L.Ed.2d 707 (1978).
21. *Consolidated Edison Co. v. Public Service Commission,* 447 U.S. 530, 100 S.Ct. 2326, 65 L.Ed.2d 319 (1980).
22. 558 U.S. 310, 130 S.Ct. 876, 175 L.Ed.2d 753 (2010).

restrictions were unconstitutional and that the First Amendment prevents limits from being placed on independent political expenditures by corporations. ■

Commercial Speech The courts also give substantial protection to *commercial speech,* which consists of communications—primarily advertising and marketing—made by business firms that involve only their commercial interests. The protection given to commercial speech under the First Amendment is less extensive than that afforded to noncommercial speech, however.

A state may restrict certain kinds of advertising, for instance, in the interest of preventing consumers from being misled. States also have a legitimate interest in roadside beautification and therefore may impose restraints on billboard advertising. ■ **EXAMPLE 4.8** Café Erotica, a nude dancing establishment, sues the state after being denied a permit to erect a billboard along an interstate highway in Florida. Because the law directly advances a substantial government interest in highway beautification and safety, a court will likely find that it is not an unconstitutional restraint on commercial speech. ■

Generally, a restriction on commercial speech will be considered valid as long as it meets three criteria:

1. It must seek to implement a substantial government interest.
2. It must directly advance that interest.
3. It must go no further than necessary to accomplish its objective.

At issue in the following case was whether a government agency had unconstitutionally restricted commercial speech when it prohibited the inclusion of a certain illustration on beer labels.

Spotlight on Beer Labels

Case 4.2 Bad Frog Brewery, Inc. v. New York State Liquor Authority

United States Court of Appeals, Second Circuit, 134 F.3d 87 (1998).

Background and Facts Bad Frog Brewery, Inc., makes and sells alcoholic beverages. Some of the beverages feature labels that display a drawing of a frog making the gesture generally known as "giving the finger." Bad Frog's authorized New York distributor, Renaissance Beer Company, applied to the New York State Liquor Authority (NYSLA) for brand label approval, as required by state law before the beer could be sold in New York.

The NYSLA denied the application, in part, because "the label could appear in grocery and convenience stores, with obvious exposure on the shelf to children of tender age." Bad Frog filed a suit in a federal district court against the NYSLA, asking for, among other things, an injunction against the denial of the application. The court granted summary judgment in favor of the NYSLA. Bad Frog appealed to the U.S. Court of Appeals for the Second Circuit.

In the Language of the Court

Jon O. *NEWMAN,* Circuit Judge:

＊＊＊＊

＊＊＊ To support its asserted power to ban Bad Frog's labels [NYSLA advances] ＊＊＊ the State's interest in "protecting children from vulgar and profane advertising" ＊＊＊.

[This interest is] substantial ＊＊＊. *States have a compelling interest in protecting the physical and psychological wellbeing of minors* ＊＊＊. [Emphasis added.]

＊＊＊＊

＊＊＊ NYSLA endeavors to advance the state interest in preventing exposure of children to vulgar displays by taking only the limited step of barring such displays from the labels of alcoholic beverages. *In view of the wide currency of vulgar displays throughout contemporary society, including comic books targeted directly at children, barring such displays from labels for alcoholic beverages cannot realistically be expected to reduce children's exposure to such displays to any significant degree.* [Emphasis added.]

＊＊＊ If New York decides to make a substantial effort to insulate children from vulgar displays in some significant sphere of activity, at least with respect to materials likely to be seen by children, NYSLA's label prohibition might well be found to make a justifiable contribution to the material

Case 4.2 Continued

advancement of such an effort, but its currently isolated response to the perceived problem, applicable only to labels on a product that children cannot purchase, does not suffice. * * * A state must demonstrate that its commercial speech limitation is part of a substantial effort to advance a valid state interest, not merely the removal of a few grains of offensive sand from a beach of vulgarity.

* * * *

* * * Even if we were to assume that the state materially advances its asserted interest by shielding children from viewing the Bad Frog labels, it is plainly excessive to prohibit the labels from all use, including placement on bottles displayed in bars and taverns where parental supervision of children is to be expected. Moreover, to whatever extent NYSLA is concerned that children will be harmfully exposed to the Bad Frog labels when wandering without parental supervision around grocery and convenience stores where beer is sold, that concern could be less intrusively dealt with by placing restrictions on the permissible locations where the appellant's products may be displayed within such stores.

Decision and Remedy *The U.S. Court of Appeals for the Second Circuit reversed the judgment of the district court and remanded the case for the entry of a judgment in favor of Bad Frog. The NYSLA's ban on the use of the labels lacked a "reasonable fit" with the state's interest in shielding minors from vulgarity. In addition, the NYSLA had not adequately considered alternatives to the ban.*

Critical Thinking
- **What If the Facts Were Different?** *If Bad Frog had sought to use the offensive label to market toys instead of beer, would the court's ruling likely have been the same? Why or why not?*
- **Legal Environment** *Whose interests are advanced by the banning of certain types of advertising?*

Unprotected Speech The United States Supreme Court has made it clear that certain types of speech will not be protected under the First Amendment. Unprotected speech includes fighting words, or words that are likely to incite others to respond violently. It also includes speech that harms the good reputation of another, or defamatory speech. In addition, speech that violates criminal laws (threatening speech or possession of child pornography, for instance) is not constitutionally protected.

Threatening Speech. Note that in the case of threatening speech, the speaker must have posed a "true threat"— that is, must have meant to communicate a serious intent to commit an unlawful, violent act against a particular person or group. ■ **CASE IN POINT 4.9** After Anthony Elonis's wife, Tara, left him and took their two children, Elonis was upset and experienced problems at work. A coworker filed five sexual harassment reports against him. When Elonis posted a photograph of himself in a Halloween costume holding a toy knife to the coworker's neck, he was fired from his job. Elonis then began posting violent statements on his Facebook page, mostly focusing on his former wife and talking about killing her.

Elonis continued to post statements about killing his wife and eventually was arrested and prosecuted for his online posts. Elonis was convicted by a jury of violating a statute and ordered to serve time in prison. He appealed

to the United States Supreme Court, which held that it is not enough that a reasonable person might view the defendant's Facebook posts as threats. Elonis must have intended to issue threats or known that his statements would be viewed as threats to be convicted of a crime. The Court reversed Elonis's conviction and remanded the case back to the lower court to determine if there was sufficient evidence of intent.[23] ■

Obscene Speech. The First Amendment, as interpreted by the Supreme Court, also does not protect obscene speech. Numerous state and federal statutes make it a crime to disseminate and possess obscene materials, including child pornography. Objectively defining obscene speech has proved difficult, however. It is even more difficult to prohibit the dissemination of obscenity and pornography online.

Most of Congress's attempts to pass legislation protecting minors from pornographic materials on the Internet have been struck down on First Amendment grounds when challenged in court. One exception is a law that requires public schools and libraries to install **filtering software** on computers to keep children from accessing adult content.[24] Such software is designed to

---

23. *Elonis v. United States*, ___ U.S. ___, 135 S.Ct. 2001, 192 L.Ed.2d 1 (2015).
24. Children's Internet Protection Act (CIPA), 17 U.S.C. Sections 1701–1741.

prevent persons from viewing certain Web sites based on a site's Internet address or its **meta tags,** or key words. The Supreme Court held that the act does not unconstitutionally burden free speech because it is flexible and libraries can disable the filters for any patrons who ask.[25]

Another exception is a law that makes it a crime to intentionally distribute *virtual child pornography*—which uses computer-generated images, not actual people—without indicating that it is computer-generated.[26] In a case challenging the law's constitutionality, the Supreme Court held that the statute is valid because it does not prohibit a substantial amount of protected speech.[27] Nevertheless, because of the difficulties of policing the Internet, as well as the constitutional complexities of prohibiting obscenity through legislation, online obscenity remains a legal issue.

4–2c Freedom of Religion

The First Amendment states that the government may neither establish any religion nor prohibit the free exercise of religious practices. The first part of this constitutional provision is referred to as the **establishment clause,** and the second part is known as the **free exercise clause**. Government action, both federal and state, must be consistent with this constitutional mandate.

The Establishment Clause The establishment clause prohibits the government from establishing a state-sponsored religion, as well as from passing laws that promote (aid or endorse) religion or show a preference for one religion over another. Although the establishment clause involves the separation of church and state, it does not require a complete separation.

Applicable Standard. Establishment clause cases often involve such issues as the legality of allowing or requiring school prayers, using state-issued vouchers to pay tuition at religious schools, and teaching creation theories versus evolution. Federal or state laws that do not promote or place a significant burden on religion are constitutional even if they have some impact on religion. For a government law or policy to be constitutional, it must not have the primary effect of promoting or inhibiting religion.

Religious Displays. Religious displays on public property have often been challenged as violating the establishment clause, and the United States Supreme Court has ruled on a number of such cases. Generally, the Court has focused on the proximity of the religious display (such as a Christian Christmas symbol) to nonreligious symbols (such as reindeer and candy canes) or symbols from different religions (such as a menorah, a nine-branched candelabrum used in celebrating Hanukkah).

The Supreme Court took a slightly different approach when it held that public displays having historical, as well as religious, significance do not necessarily violate the establishment clause.[28] Still, historical significance must be carefully weighed against religious elements in establishment clause cases.

■ **CASE IN POINT 4.10** Mount Soledad is a prominent hill near San Diego. There has been a forty-foot cross on top of Mount Soledad since 1913. In the 1990s, a war memorial with six walls listing the names of veterans was constructed next to the cross. The site was privately owned until 2006, when Congress authorized the property's transfer to the federal government "to preserve a historically significant war memorial."

Steve Trunk and the Jewish War Veterans filed lawsuits claiming that the cross violated the establishment clause because it endorsed the Christian religion. A federal appellate court agreed, finding that the primary effect of the memorial as a whole sent a strong message of endorsement of Christianity and exclusion of non-Christian veterans. The court noted that although not all cross displays at war memorials violate the establishment clause, the cross in this case physically dominated the site. Additionally, it was originally dedicated to religious purposes, had a long history of religious use, and was the only portion visible to drivers on the freeway below.[29] ■

The Free Exercise Clause The free exercise clause guarantees that people can hold any religious beliefs they want or can hold no religious beliefs. The constitutional guarantee of personal freedom restricts only the actions of the government, however, and not those of individuals or private businesses.

Restrictions Must Be Necessary. The government must have a compelling state interest for restricting the free exercise of religion, and the restriction must be the only way to further that interest. ■ **CASE IN POINT 4.11** Gregory Holt, an inmate in an Arkansas state prison, was a devout Muslim who wished to grow a beard in accord with his religious beliefs. The Arkansas Department of

---

25. *United States v. American Library Association,* 539 U.S. 194, 123 S.Ct. 2297, 156 L.Ed.2d 221 (2003).

26. The Prosecutorial Remedies and Other Tools to End the Exploitation of Children Today Act (Protect Act), 18 U.S.C. Section 2252A(a)(5)(B).

27. *United States v. Williams,* 553 U.S. 285, 128 S.Ct. 1830, 170 L.Ed.2d 650 (2008).

28. *Van Orden v. Perry,* 545 U.S. 677, 125 S.Ct. 2854, 162 L.Ed.2d 607 (2005). The Court held that a six-foot-tall monument of the Ten Commandments on the Texas state capitol grounds did not violate the establishment clause because the Ten Commandments have historical significance.

29. *Trunk v. City of San Diego,* 629 F.3d 1099 (9th Cir. 2011).

Correction prohibited inmates from growing beards (except for medical reasons). Holt asked for an exemption to grow a half-inch beard on religious grounds, and prison officials denied his request. Holt filed a suit in a federal district court against Ray Hobbs, the director of the department, and others.

A federal statute prohibits the government from taking any action that substantially burdens the religious exercise of an institutionalized person unless the action constitutes the least restrictive means of furthering a compelling governmental interest. The defendants argued that beards compromise prison safety—a compelling government interest—because contraband can be hidden in them and because an inmate can quickly shave his beard to disguise his identity.

The district court dismissed Holt's suit, and the dismissal was affirmed on appeal. Holt then appealed to the United States Supreme Court. The Court noted that "an item of contraband would have to be very small indeed to

be concealed by a 1/2–inch beard." Moreover, the Court reasoned that the department could satisfy its security concerns by simply searching the beard, the way it already searches prisoners' hair and clothing. The Court concluded that the department's grooming policy, which prevented Holt from growing a half-inch beard, violated his right to exercise his religious beliefs.[30] ∎

Restrictions Must Not Be a Substantial Burden. To comply with the free exercise clause, a government action must not place a substantial burden on religious practices. A burden is substantial if it pressures an individual to modify his or her behavior and to violate his or her beliefs.

At issue in the following case was whether forcing a state prison inmate to choose between daily nutrition and a religious practice is a substantial burden.

---

30. *Holt v. Hobbs*, ___ U.S. ___, 135 S.Ct. 853, 190 L.Ed.2d 747 (2015).

Case Analysis 4.3

Thompson v. Holm
United States Court of Appeals, Seventh Circuit, 809 F.3d 376 (2016).

In the Language of the Court
ROVNER, Circuit Judge.
Michael Thompson, a Muslim inmate incarcerated at Waupun Correctional Institution in Wisconsin, sued members of the prison staff for violating his right under the First Amendment to exercise his religion freely. The violation occurred, Thompson says, when for two days prison staff prevented him from fasting properly during Ramadan.

* * * A central religious practice of the Islamic faith is a sunrise-to-sunset fast during the month of Ramadan. The prison normally accommodates this practice by providing Ramadan "meal bags" at sunset to each Muslim prisoner listed as eligible. The prison's chaplain determines eligibility. Each Ramadan meal bag contains two meals: the post-sunset dinner and the next morning's pre-sunrise breakfast. A prisoner who eats at the prison cafeteria during Ramadan forfeits his right to the meal bags for the rest of the month-long fast. Thompson, a practicing Muslim, began fasting for Ramadan after sunrise on August 11—the first day of Ramadan. He

received his daily meal bags until August 21, about one-third into the month.

* * * Thompson says that shortly before August 21, as he was on his way back to his cell, Randall Lashock, a prison guard, handed him a meal bag. When Thompson arrived at his cell, he found that a guard had already left a meal bag for him there. Thompson could not leave his cell to return the extra bag without risking a conduct violation, so he left one of the two bags unopened for Lashock to retrieve. Lashock asserts that when he later retrieved that extra meal bag from Thompson's cell, he found Thompson eating from both bags.

Thompson received no meal bags on August 21 and 22. Lashock was supposed to deliver the Ramadan meal bags to every prisoner on the eligibility list. But on those two days, Lashock brought Thompson nothing, even though * * * he remained on the list. Receiving no meals, and learning from [prison guards] Bruce Bleich and Matthew Larson when he complained to them that he would have to go to the cafeteria if he wanted

to eat, Thompson felt pressure to break his fast by going to the cafeteria. But he knew that under the prison's policy he could not do that without forfeiting meal bags for the rest of the month-long fast. He also had hunger pangs and felt tired and unwell. Because of his hunger, exhaustion, and anxiety, he missed one of his morning prayers and did not properly experience Ramadan, which is meant to be a time of peace and focus.

* * * *

While he was receiving no meal bags, Thompson asked other prison officials to explain why Lashock was not bringing him food * * * . Bleich and Larson told him that Captain William Holm had ordered his name removed from the list because he had stolen a meal bag; they too refused to bring him any meals. But Holm * * * did not remove Thompson from the list and had no authority to do so; only the chaplain could do that.

* * * On August 23, Thompson received a Ramadan meal bag at sunset

Case 4.3 Continues

Case 4.3 Continued

and continued to receive a bag each day until the end of Ramadan.

Thompson [filed a suit in a federal district court against] Lashock, Holm, Bleich, and Larson * * * for violating his First Amendment rights, and the defendants moved for summary judgment. * * * They argued the lack of meal bags for two days did not substantially burden Thompson's free-exercise rights.

Thompson responded that the defendants unlawfully withheld his meal bags. * * * By forcing him to choose between adequate nutrition and a central tenet of his religion, the defendants substantially burdened his free-exercise rights.

[The court] granted the defendants' motion for summary judgment. The judge ruled that receiving no meal bags for just two days was not a substantial burden on Thompson's free-exercise rights because he kept fasting, praying, and reading the Koran.

On appeal Thompson challenges the entry of summary judgment.

We begin our analysis by asking whether the denial of meal bags substantially burdened Thompson's free exercise rights. The answer is yes. *Without the meal bags, Thompson was forced to choose between foregoing adequate nutrition or violating a central tenet of his religion. Facing that choice for "only" two days was not, as defendants argue, a "de minimis" [minimal] burden.* Not only did Thompson receive no proper meal for 55 hours, leaving him weak and tired, he did not know if he would ever be put back on the Ramadan list and get regular food. This uncertainty put pressure on him to resign himself to the cafeteria; the anxiety left him unable to practice Ramadan properly. [Emphasis added.]

* * * *

We next consider whether Thompson produced sufficient evidence that all the defendants were personally involved in imposing this burden. Once again, the answer is yes. We consider the defendants individually, beginning with Lashock. He was responsible for delivering the meal bags to all inmates on the eligibility list. Yet he personally denied them to Thompson for two days even though * * * Thompson remained on the list. As to Holm, * * * Holm lied about whether he had removed Thompson from the meal list. Finally, as to Bleich and Larson, they also bear responsibility for depriving Thompson of his food. By (falsely) telling Thompson that Holm had removed him from the religious meal list, refusing to bring him any meals, and warning him to go to the cafeteria if he wanted to eat, * * * they were involved in a joint effort to pressure Thompson to break his fast.

* * * *

Accordingly, we VACATE the judgment. This case is REMANDED for further proceedings consistent with this order.

Legal Reasoning Questions

1. What is the standard for determining whether a restriction on a religious practice is constitutional under the First Amendment?

2. How did that standard apply to the prison guards' conduct in this case?

3. Were all of the guards personally involved in the alleged violation of the First Amendment? Explain.

Public Welfare Exception. When religious *practices* work against public policy and the public welfare, the government can act. For instance, the government can require that a child receive certain types of vaccinations or medical treatment if his or her life is in danger—regardless of the child's or parent's religious beliefs. When public safety is an issue, an individual's religious beliefs often have to give way to the government's interest in protecting the public.

■ **EXAMPLE 4.12** A woman of the Muslim faith may choose not to appear in public without a scarf, known as a *hijab*, over her head. Nevertheless, due to public safety concerns, many courts today do not allow the wearing of any headgear (hats or scarves) in courtrooms. ■

4–2d Searches and Seizures

The Fourth Amendment protects the "right of the people to be secure in their persons, houses, papers, and effects."

Before searching or seizing private property, law enforcement officers must usually obtain a **search warrant**—an order from a judge or other public official authorizing the search or seizure. Because of the strong government interest in protecting the public, however, a warrant normally is not required for seizures of spoiled or contaminated food. Nor are warrants required for searches of businesses in such highly regulated industries as liquor, guns, and strip mining.

To obtain a search warrant, law enforcement officers must convince a judge that they have reasonable grounds, or **probable cause,** to believe a search will reveal evidence of a specific illegality. To establish probable cause, the officers must have trustworthy evidence that would convince a reasonable person that the proposed search or seizure is more likely justified than not.

■ **CASE IN POINT 4.13** Citlalli Flores was driving across the border into the United States from Tijuana, Mexico, when a border protection officer became suspicious because she was acting nervous and looking around inside her car.

On further inspection, the officer found thirty-six pounds of marijuana hidden in the car's quarter panels. Flores claimed that she had not known about the marijuana.

Flores was arrested for importing marijuana into the United States. She then made two jail-recorded phone calls in which she asked her cousin to delete whatever he felt needed to be removed from Flores's Facebook page. The government got a warrant to search Flores's Facebook messages, where they found references to her "carrying" or "bringing" marijuana into the United States that day. Flores's Facebook posts were later used as evidence against her at trial, and she was convicted.

On appeal, the court held that the phone calls had given the officers probable cause to support a warrant to search Flores's social networking site for incriminating statements. Her conviction was affirmed.[31] ■

4–2e Self-Incrimination

The Fifth Amendment guarantees that no person "shall be compelled in any criminal case to be a witness against himself." Thus, in any court proceeding, an accused person cannot be forced to give testimony that might subject him or her to any criminal prosecution. The guarantee applies to both federal and state proceedings because the due process clause of the Fourteenth Amendment (discussed shortly) extends the protection to state courts.

The Fifth Amendment's guarantee against self-incrimination extends only to natural persons. Neither corporations nor partnerships receive Fifth Amendment protection. When a partnership is required to produce business records, it must therefore do so even if the information provided incriminates the individual partners of the firm. In contrast, sole proprietors and sole practitioners (those who individually own their businesses) cannot be compelled to produce their business records. These individuals have full protection against self-incrimination because they function in only one capacity, and there is no separate business entity.

4–3 Due Process and Equal Protection

Other constitutional guarantees of great significance to Americans are mandated by the *due process clauses* of the Fifth and Fourteenth Amendments and the *equal protection clause* of the Fourteenth Amendment.

4–3a Due Process

Both the Fifth and Fourteenth Amendments provide that no person shall be deprived "of life, liberty, or property, without due process of law." The **due process clause** of these constitutional amendments has two aspects—procedural and substantive. Note that the due process clause applies to "legal persons" (that is, corporations), as well as to individuals.

Procedural Due Process *Procedural* due process requires that any government decision to take life, liberty, or property must be made equitably. In other words, the government must give a person proper notice and an opportunity to be heard. Fair procedures must be used in determining whether a person will be subjected to punishment or have some burden imposed on her or him.

Fair procedure has been interpreted as requiring that the person have at least an opportunity to object to a proposed action before an impartial, neutral decision maker (who need not be a judge). ■ **EXAMPLE 4.14** Doyle Burns, a nursing student in Kansas, poses for a photograph standing next to a placenta used as a lab specimen. Although she quickly deletes the photo from her library, it ends up on Facebook. When the director of nursing sees the photo, Burns is expelled. She sues for reinstatement and wins. The school violated Burns's due process rights by expelling her from the nursing program for taking a photo without giving her an opportunity to present her side to school authorities. ■

Substantive Due Process *Substantive* due process focuses on the content of legislation rather than the fairness of procedures. Substantive due process limits what the government may do in its legislative and executive capacities. Legislation must be fair and reasonable in content and must further a legitimate governmental objective.

If a law or other governmental action limits a fundamental right, the state must have a legitimate and compelling interest to justify its action. Fundamental rights include interstate travel, privacy, voting, marriage and family, and all First Amendment rights. Thus, for instance, a state must have a substantial reason for taking any action that infringes on a person's free speech rights.

In situations not involving fundamental rights, a law or action does not violate substantive due process if it rationally relates to any legitimate government purpose. It is almost impossible for a law or action to fail the "rationality" test. Under this test, almost any business regulation will be upheld as reasonable.

---

31. *United States v. Flores*, 830 F.3d 1028 (9th Cir. 2015).

4–3b Equal Protection

Under the Fourteenth Amendment, a state may not "deny to any person within its jurisdiction the equal protection of the laws." The United States Supreme Court has interpreted the due process clause of the Fifth Amendment to make the **equal protection clause** applicable to the federal government as well. Equal protection means that the government cannot enact laws that treat similarly situated individuals differently.

Equal protection, like substantive due process, relates to the substance of a law or other governmental action. When a law or action limits the liberty of *all* persons, it may violate substantive due process. When a law or action limits the liberty of *some* persons but not others, it may violate the equal protection clause. ■ **EXAMPLE 4.15** If a law prohibits all advertising on the sides of trucks, it raises a substantive due process question. If the law makes an exception to allow truck owners to advertise their own businesses, it raises an equal protection issue. ■

In an equal protection inquiry, when a law or action distinguishes between or among individuals, the basis for the distinction—that is, the classification—is examined. Depending on the classification, the courts apply different levels of scrutiny, or "tests," to determine whether the law or action violates the equal protection clause. The courts use one of three standards: strict scrutiny, intermediate scrutiny, or the "rational basis" test.

Strict Scrutiny If a law or action prohibits or inhibits some persons from exercising a fundamental right, the law or action will be subject to "strict scrutiny" by the courts. Under this standard, the classification must be necessary to promote a *compelling state interest.*

Compelling state interests include remedying past unconstitutional or illegal discrimination but do not include correcting the general effects of "society's discrimination." ■ **EXAMPLE 4.16** For a city to give preference to minority applicants in awarding construction contracts, it normally must identify past unconstitutional or illegal discrimination against minority construction firms. Because the policy is based on suspect traits (race and national origin), it will violate the equal protection clause *unless* it is necessary to promote a compelling state interest. ■ Generally, few laws or actions survive strict-scrutiny analysis by the courts.

Intermediate Scrutiny Another standard, that of *intermediate scrutiny,* is applied in cases involving discrimination based on gender or legitimacy (children born out of wedlock). Laws using these classifications must be *substantially related to important government*

objectives. ■ **EXAMPLE 4.17** An important government objective is preventing illegitimate teenage pregnancies. Males and females are not similarly situated in this regard because only females can become pregnant. Therefore, a law that punishes men but not women for statutory rape will be upheld even though it treats men and women unequally. ■

The state also has an important objective in establishing time limits (called *statutes of limitation*) for how long after an event a particular type of action can be brought. Nevertheless, the limitation period must be substantially related to the important objective of preventing fraudulent or outdated claims. ■ **EXAMPLE 4.18** A state law requires illegitimate children to bring paternity suits within six years of their births in order to seek support from their fathers. A court will strike down this law if legitimate children are allowed to seek support from their parents at any time. Distinguishing between support claims on the basis of legitimacy is not related to the important government objective of preventing fraudulent or outdated claims. ■

The "Rational Basis" Test In matters of economic or social welfare, a classification will be considered valid if there is any conceivable *rational basis* on which the classification might relate to a legitimate government interest. It is almost impossible for a law or action to fail the rational basis test.

■ **CASE IN POINT 4.19** A Kentucky statute prohibits businesses that sell substantial amounts of staple groceries or gasoline from applying for a license to sell wine and liquor. A local grocer (Maxwell's Pic-Pac) filed a lawsuit against the state, alleging that the statute and the regulation were unconstitutional under the equal protection clause. The court applied the rational basis test and ruled that the statute and regulation were rationally related to a legitimate government interest in reducing access to products with high alcohol content.

The court cited the problems caused by alcohol, including drunk driving, and noted that the state's interest in limiting access to such products extends to the general public. Grocery stores and gas stations pose a greater risk of exposing members of the public to alcohol. For these and other reasons, the state can restrict these places from selling wine and liquor.[32] ■

4–4 Privacy Rights

The U.S. Constitution does not explicitly mention a general right to privacy. In a 1928 Supreme Court case,

32. *Maxwell's Pic-Pac, Inc. v. Dehner,* 739 F.3d 936 (6th Cir. 2014).

Olmstead v. United States,[33] Justice Louis Brandeis stated in his dissent that the right to privacy is "the most comprehensive of rights and the right most valued by civilized men." The majority of the justices at that time, however, did not agree with Brandeis.

It was not until the 1960s that the Supreme Court endorsed the view that the Constitution protects individual privacy rights. In a landmark 1965 case, *Griswold v. Connecticut,*[34] the Supreme Court held that a constitutional right to privacy was implied by the First, Third, Fourth, Fifth, and Ninth Amendments.

Today, privacy rights receive protection under various federal statutes as well the U.S. Constitution. State constitutions and statutes also secure individuals' privacy rights, often to a significant degree. Privacy rights are also protected to an extent under tort law, consumer law, and employment law.

4–4a Federal Privacy Legislation

In the last several decades, Congress has enacted a number of statutes that protect the privacy of individuals in various areas of concern. Most of these statutes deal with personal information collected by governments or private businesses.

In the 1960s, Americans were sufficiently alarmed by the accumulation of personal information in government files that they pressured Congress to pass laws permitting individuals to access their files. Congress responded by passing the Freedom of Information Act, which allows any person to request copies of any information on her or him contained in federal government files. Congress later enacted the Privacy Act, which also gives persons the right to access such information.

In the 1990s, responding to the growing need to protect the privacy of individuals' health records—particularly computerized records—Congress passed the Health Insurance Portability and Accountability Act (HIPAA).[35] This act defines and limits the circumstances in which an individual's "protected health information" may be used or disclosed by health-care providers, health-care plans, and others. These and other major federal laws protecting privacy rights are listed and briefly described in Exhibit 4–2.

---

33. 277 U.S. 438, 48 S.Ct. 564, 72 L.Ed. 944 (1928).
34. 381 U.S. 479, 85 S.Ct. 1678, 14 L.Ed.2d 510 (1965).

35. HIPAA was enacted as Pub. L. No. 104-191 (1996) and is codified in 29 U.S.C.A. Sections 1181 *et seq.*

EXHIBIT 4–2 Federal Legislation Relating to Privacy

Freedom of Information Act (1966)	Provides that individuals have a right to obtain access to information about them collected in government files.
Privacy Act (1974)	Protects the privacy of individuals about whom the federal government has information. Regulates agencies' use and disclosure of data, and gives individuals access to and a means to correct inaccuracies.
Electronic Communications Privacy Act (1986)	Prohibits the interception of information communicated by electronic means.
Health Insurance Portability and Accountability Act (1996)	Requires health-care providers and health-care plans to inform patients of their privacy rights and of how their personal medical information may be used. States that medical records may not be used for purposes unrelated to health care or disclosed without permission.
Financial Services Modernization Act (Gramm-Leach-Bliley Act) (1999)	Prohibits the disclosure of nonpublic personal information about a consumer to an unaffiliated third party unless strict disclosure and opt-out requirements are met.

4–4b The USA Patriot Act and the USA Freedom Act

The USA Patriot Act was passed by Congress in the wake of the terrorist attacks of September 11, 2001.[36] The Patriot Act has given government officials increased authority to monitor Internet activities (such as e-mail and Web site visits) and to gain access to personal financial information and student information. Law enforcement officials can track the telephone and e-mail communications of one party to find out the identity of the other party or parties. Privacy advocates argue that this law adversely affects the constitutional rights of all Americans, and it has been widely criticized in the media.

While the bulk of the Patriot Act is permanent law, its most controversial surveillance provisions had to be reauthorized every four years and expired in June 2015. Most of the expired provisions were restored by the USA Freedom Act, which extends surveillance authority through 2019.[37] The Freedom Act did amend a portion of the Patriot Act in an attempt to stop the National Security Agency (NSA) from collecting mass phone data. (Note, however, that the act still allows the data to be collected by private phone companies, and the NSA can obtain data about targeted individuals through these companies.)

36. The Uniting and Strengthening America by Providing Appropriate Tools Required to Intercept and Obstruct Terrorism Act of 2001, also known as the USA Patriot Act, was enacted as Pub. L. No. 107-56 (2001) and last reauthorized by Pub. L. No. 112-114 (2011).

37. The full title of this statute is Uniting and Strengthening America by Fulfilling Rights and Ending Eavesdropping, Dragnet-collection and Online Monitoring, H.R. 3361.

Reviewing: Business and the Constitution

A state legislature enacted a statute that required any motorcycle operator or passenger on the state's highways to wear a protective helmet. Jim Alderman, a licensed motorcycle operator, sued the state to block enforcement of the law. Alderman asserted that the statute violated the equal protection clause because it placed requirements on motorcyclists that were not imposed on other motorists. Using the information presented in the chapter, answer the following questions.

1. Why does this statute raise equal protection issues instead of substantive due process concerns?
2. What are the three levels of scrutiny that the courts use in determining whether a law violates the equal protection clause?
3. Which standard of scrutiny, or test, would apply to this situation? Why?
4. Applying this standard, is the helmet statute constitutional? Why or why not?

Debate This . . . *Legislation aimed at "protecting people from themselves" concerns the individual as well as the public in general. Protective helmet laws are just one example of such legislation. Should individuals be allowed to engage in unsafe activities if they choose to do so?*

Terms and Concepts

Bill of Rights 75
checks and balances 71
commerce clause 71
compelling government interest 77
due process clause 83
equal protection clause 84
establishment clause 80

federal form of government 70
filtering software 79
free exercise clause 80
full faith and credit clause 71
meta tag 80
police powers 70
preemption 75

privileges and immunities clause 71
probable cause 82
search warrant 82
sovereignty 70
supremacy clause 75
symbolic speech 77

Issue Spotters

1. Can a state, in the interest of energy conservation, ban all advertising by power utilities if conservation could be accomplished by less restrictive means? Why or why not? (See *Business and the Bill of Rights*.)

2. Suppose that a state imposes a higher tax on out-of-state companies doing business in the state than it imposes on in-state companies. Is this a violation of equal protection if the only reason for the tax is to protect the local firms from out-of-state competition? Explain. (See *The Constitutional Powers of Government*.)

- **Check your answers to the Issue Spotters against the answers provided in Appendix D at the end of this text.**

Business Scenarios

4–1. Commerce Clause. A Georgia state law requires the use of contoured rear-fender mudguards on trucks and trailers operating within Georgia state lines. The statute further makes it illegal for trucks and trailers to use straight mudguards. In approximately thirty-five other states, straight mudguards are legal. Moreover, in Florida, straight mudguards are explicitly required by law. There is some evidence suggesting that contoured mudguards might be a little safer than straight mudguards. Discuss whether this Georgia statute violates any constitutional provisions. (See *The Constitutional Powers of Government*.)

4–2. Equal Protection. With the objectives of preventing crime, maintaining property values, and preserving the quality of urban life, New York City enacted an ordinance to regulate the locations of adult entertainment establishments. The ordinance expressly applied to female, but not male, topless entertainment. Adele Buzzetti owned the Cozy Cabin, a New York City cabaret that featured female topless dancers. Buzzetti and an anonymous dancer filed a suit in a federal district court against the city, asking the court to block the enforcement of the ordinance. The plaintiffs argued, in part, that the ordinance violated the equal protection clause. Under the equal protection clause, what standard applies to the court's consideration of this ordinance? Under this test, how should the court rule? Why? (See *Due Process and Equal Protection*.)

Business Case Problems

4–3. Spotlight on Plagiarism—Due Process. The Russ

College of Engineering and Technology of Ohio University announced in a press conference that it had found "rampant and flagrant plagiarism" in the theses of mechanical engineering graduate students. Faculty singled out for "ignoring their ethical responsibilities" included Jay Gunasekera, chair of the department. Gunasekera was prohibited from advising students. He filed a suit against Dennis Irwin, the dean of Russ College, for violating his due process rights. What does due process require in these circumstances? Why? [*Gunasekera v. Irwin*, 551 F.3d 461 (6th Cir. 2009)] (See *Due Process and Equal Protection*.)

4–4. Business Case Problem with Sample Answer— The Dormant Commerce Clause. In 2001, Puerto Rico

enacted a law that requires specific labels on cement sold in Puerto Rico and imposes fines for any violations of these requirements. The law prohibits the sale or distribution of cement manufactured outside Puerto Rico that does not carry a required label warning that the cement may not be used in government-financed construction projects. Antilles Cement Corp., a Puerto Rican firm that imports foreign cement, filed a complaint in federal court, claiming that this law violated the dormant commerce clause. (The dormant commerce clause doctrine applies not only to commerce among the states and U.S. territories, but also to international commerce.) Did the 2001 Puerto Rican law violate the dormant commerce clause? Why or why not? [*Antilles Cement Corp. v. Fortuno*, 670 F.3d 310 (1st Cir. 2012)] (See *The Constitutional Powers of Government*.)

- **For a sample answer to Problem 4–4, go to Appendix E at the end of this text.**

4–5. Freedom of Speech. Mark Wooden sent an e-mail to an alderwoman for the city of St. Louis. Attached was a nineteen-minute audio file that compared her to the biblical character Jezebel. The audio said she was a "bitch in the Sixth Ward," spending too much time with the rich and powerful and too little time with the poor. In a menacing, maniacal tone, Wooden said that he was "dusting off a sawed-off shotgun," called himself a "domestic terrorist," and referred to the assassination of President John Kennedy, the murder of federal judge John Roll, and the shooting of Representative Gabrielle Giffords. Feeling threatened, the alderwoman called the police. Wooden was convicted of harassment under a state criminal statute. Was this conviction unconstitutional under the First Amendment? Discuss. [*State of Missouri v. Wooden*, 388 S.W.3d 522 (Mo. 2013)] (See *Business and the Bill of Rights*.)

4–6. Equal Protection. Abbott Laboratories licensed SmithKline Beecham Corp. to market an Abbott human immunodeficiency virus (HIV) drug in conjunction with one of SmithKline's drugs. Abbott then increased the price of its drug fourfold, forcing SmithKline to increase its prices and thereby driving business to Abbott's own combination drug. SmithKline filed a suit in a federal district court against Abbott. During jury selection, Abbott struck the only self-identified gay person among the potential jurors. (The pricing of HIV drugs is of considerable concern in the gay community.) Could the equal protection clause be applied to prohibit discrimination based on sexual orientation in jury selection? Discuss. [*SmithKline Beecham Corp. v. Abbott Laboratories,* 740 F.3d 471 (9th Cir. 2014)] (See *Due Process and Equal Protection.*)

4–7. Procedural Due Process. Robert Brown applied for admission to the University of Kansas School of Law. Brown answered "no" to questions on the application asking if he had a criminal history and acknowledged that a false answer constituted "cause for . . . dismissal." In fact, Brown had criminal convictions for domestic battery and driving under the influence. He was accepted for admission to the school. When school officials discovered his history, however, he was notified of their intent to dismiss him and given an opportunity to respond in writing. He demanded a hearing. The officials refused to grant Brown a hearing and then expelled him. Did the school's actions deny Brown due process? Discuss. [*Brown v. University of Kansas,* 599 Fed.Appx. 833 (10th Cir. 2015)] (See *Due Process and Equal Protection.*)

4–8. The Commerce Clause. Regency Transportation, Inc., operates a freight business throughout the eastern United States. Regency maintains its corporate headquarters, four warehouses, and a maintenance facility and terminal location for repairing and storing vehicles in Massachusetts. All of the vehicles in Regency's fleet were bought in other states. Massachusetts imposes a use tax on all taxpayers subject to its jurisdiction, including those that do business in interstate commerce, as Regency does. When Massachusetts imposed the tax on the purchase price of each tractor and trailer in Regency's fleet, the trucking firm challenged the assessment as discriminatory under the commerce clause. What is the chief consideration under the commerce clause when a state law affects interstate commerce?

Is Massachusetts's use tax valid? Explain. [*Regency Transportation, Inc. v. Commissioner of Revenue,* 473 Mass. 459, 42 N.E.3d 1133 (2016)] (See *The Constitutional Powers of Government.*)

4–9. A Question of Ethics—Defamation. *Aric Toll owns and manages the Balboa Island Village Inn, a restaurant and bar in Newport Beach, California. Anne Lemen lives across from the inn. Lemen complained to the authorities about the inn's customers, whom she called "drunks" and "whores." She referred to Aric's wife as "Madam Whore" and told neighbors that the owners were involved in illegal drugs and prostitution. Lemen told Ewa Cook, a bartender at the Inn, that Cook "worked for Satan." She repeated her statements to potential customers, and the inn's sales dropped more than 20 percent. The inn filed a suit against Lemen. [Balboa Island Village Inn, Inc. v. Lemen, 40 Cal.4th 1141, 156 P.3d 339 (2007)]* (See *Business and the Bill of Rights.*)

(a) Are Lemen's statements about the inn's owners, customers, and activities protected by the U.S. Constitution? Should such statements be protected? In whose favor should the court rule? Why?

(b) Did Lemen behave unethically in the circumstances of this case? Explain.

4–10. Special Case Analysis—Freedom of Religion. Go to Case Analysis 4.3, *Thompson v. Holm.* Read the excerpt, and answer the following questions.

(a) Issue: The focus in this case was on an allegation of the violation of which clause of the U.S. Constitution, and by what means?

(b) Rule of Law: What is required to establish that this clause has been violated?

(c) Applying the Rule of Law: How did the court determine whether the claim of a violation was supported in this case?

(d) Conclusion: What did the federal appellate court conclude with respect to the plaintiff's claim, and what did the court order as the next step in the case?

Legal Reasoning Group Activity

4–11. Free Speech and Equal Protection. For many years, New York City has had to deal with the vandalism and defacement of public property caused by unauthorized graffiti. In an effort to stop the damage, the city banned the sale of aerosol spray-paint cans and broad-tipped indelible markers to persons under twenty-one years of age. The new rules also prohibited people from possessing these items on property other than their own. Within a year, five people under age twenty-one were cited for violations of these regulations, and 871 individuals were arrested for actually making graffiti.

Lindsey Vincenty and other artists wished to create graffiti on legal surfaces, such as canvas, wood, and clothing. Unable to buy supplies in the city or to carry them into the city from elsewhere, Vincenty and others filed a lawsuit on behalf of themselves and other young artists against Michael

Bloomberg, the city's mayor, and others. The plaintiffs claimed that, among other things, the new rules violated their right to freedom of speech.

(a) One group will argue in favor of the plaintiffs and provide several reasons why the court should hold that the city's new rules violate the plaintiffs' freedom of speech. (See *Business and the Bill of Rights.*)

(b) Another group will develop a counterargument that outlines the reasons why the new rules do not violate free speech rights. (See *Business and the Bill of Rights.*)

(c) A third group will argue that the city's ban violates the equal protection clause because it applies only to persons under age twenty-one. (See *Due Process and Equal Protection.*)

Answers to the *Issue Spotters*

1. *Can a state, in the interest of energy conservation, ban all advertising by power utilities if conservation could be accomplished by less restrictive means? Why or why not?* No. Even if commercial speech is neither related to illegal activities nor misleading, it may be restricted if a state has a substantial interest that cannot be achieved by less restrictive means. In this case, the interest in energy conservation is substantial, but it could be achieved by less restrictive means. That would be the utilities' defense against the enforcement of this state law.

2. *Is this a violation of equal protection if the only reason for the tax is to protect the local firms from out-of-state competition? Explain.* Yes. The tax would limit the liberty of some persons (out-of-state businesses), so it is subject to a review under the equal protection clause. Protecting local businesses from out-of-state competition is not a legitimate government objective. Thus, such a tax would violate the equal protection clause.

Sample Answers for *Business Case Problems with Sample Answer*

Problem 4–4. *The Dormant Commerce Clause.* The court ruled that, like a state, Puerto Rico generally may not enact policies that discriminate against out-of-state commerce. The law requiring companies that sell cement in Puerto Rico to place certain labels on their products is clearly an attempt to regulate the cement market. The law imposed labeling regulations that affect transactions between the citizens of Puerto Rico and private companies. State laws that on their face discriminate against foreign commerce are almost always invalid, and this Puerto Rican law is such a law. The discriminatory labeling requirement placed sellers of cement manufactured outside Puerto Rico at a competitive disadvantage. This law therefore contravenes the dormant commerce clause.

CHAPTER

Business Ethics

One of the most complex issues businesspersons and corporations face is ethics. It is not as well defined as the law, and yet it can have substantial impacts on a firm's finances and reputation, especially when the firm is involved in a well-publicized scandal. Some scandals arise from activities that are legal, but are ethically questionable. Other scandals arise from conduct that is both illegal and unethical.

Consider, for example, Volkswagen's corporate executives, who were accused of cheating on the pollution emissions tests of millions of vehicles that were sold in the United States. Volkswagen admitted in 2015 that it had installed "defeat device" software in its diesel models. The software detected when the car was being tested and changed its performance to improve the test outcome. As a result, the diesel cars showed low emissions—a feature that made the cars more attractive to today's consumers. Ultimately, millions of Volkswagen vehicles were recalled, and the company suffered its first quarterly loss in fifteen years.

5–1 Business Ethics

At the most basic level, the study of **ethics** is the study of what constitutes right or wrong behavior. It is a branch of philosophy focusing on morality and the way moral principles are derived and implemented. Ethics has to do with the fairness, justness, rightness, or wrongness of an action.

The study of **business ethics** typically looks at the decisions businesses make or have to make and whether those decisions are right or wrong. It has to do with how businesspersons apply moral and ethical principles in making their decisions. Those who study business ethics also evaluate what duties and responsibilities exist or should exist for businesses.

In this book, we include an *Application and Ethics* feature at the end of each unit to expand on the concepts of business ethics discussed in that unit. We also cover ethical issues in *Ethics Today* features that appear in a number of chapters.

5–1a Why Is Studying Business Ethics Important?

Over the last hundred years, the public perception of the corporation has changed from an entity that primarily generates revenues for its owners to an entity that participates in society as a corporate citizen. Originally, the only goal or duty of a corporation was to maximize profits. Although many people today may view this idea as greedy or inhumane, the rationale for the profit-maximization theory is still valid.

Profit Maximization In theory, if all firms strictly adhere to the goal of profit maximization, resources flow to where they are most highly valued by society. Corporations can focus on their strengths, and other entities that are better suited to deal with social problems and perform charitable acts can specialize in those activities. The government, through taxes and other financial allocations, can shift resources to those other entities to perform public services. Thus, in an ideal world, profit maximization leads to the most efficient allocation of scarce resources.

The Rise of Corporate Citizenship Over the years, as resources purportedly were not sufficiently reallocated to cover the costs of social needs, many people became dissatisfied with the profit-maximization theory. Investors and others began to look beyond profits and dividends and to consider the **triple bottom line**—a corporation's profits, its impact on people, and its impact on the planet. Magazines and Web sites began to rank companies based on their environmental impacts and their ethical decisions. The corporation came to be viewed as a "citizen" that was expected to participate in bettering communities and society.

Even so, many still believe that corporations are fundamentally profit-making entities that should have no responsibility other than profit maximization.

5–1b The Importance of Ethics in Making Business Decisions

Whether one believes in profit maximization or corporate citizenship, ethics is important in making business decisions. When making decisions, a business should evaluate:

1. The legal implications of each decision.
2. The public relations impact.
3. The safety risks for consumers and employees.
4. The financial implications.

This four-part analysis will assist the firm in making decisions that not only maximize profits but also reflect good corporate citizenship.

Long-Run Profit Maximization In attempting to maximize profits, corporate executives and employees have to distinguish between *short-run* and *long-run* profit maximization. In the short run, a company may increase its profits by continuing to sell a product even though it knows that the product is defective. In the long run, though, because of lawsuits, large settlements, and bad publicity, such unethical conduct will cause profits to suffer. Thus, business ethics is consistent only with long-run profit maximization. An overemphasis on short-term profit maximization is the most common reason that ethical problems occur in business.

■ **CASE IN POINT 5.1** When the powerful narcotic painkiller OxyContin was first marketed, its manufacturer, Purdue Pharma, claimed that it was unlikely to lead to drug addiction or abuse. Internal company documents later showed that the company's executives knew that OxyContin could be addictive, but kept this risk a secret to boost sales and maximize short-term profits.

Subsequently, Purdue Pharma and three former executives pleaded guilty to criminal charges that they had misled regulators, patients, and physicians about OxyContin's risks of addiction. Purdue Pharma agreed to pay $600 million in fines and other payments. The three former executives agreed to pay $34.5 million in fines and were barred from federal health programs for a period of fifteen years. Thus, the company's focus on maximizing profits in the short run led to unethical conduct that hurt profits in the long run.[1] ■

1. *United States v. Purdue Frederick Co.*, 495 F.Supp.2d 569 (W.D.Va. 2007).

The Internet Can Ruin Reputations In the past, negative information or opinions about a company might remain hidden. Now, however, cyberspace provides a forum where disgruntled employees, unhappy consumers, or special interest groups can post derogatory remarks. Thus, the Internet has increased the potential for a major corporation (or other business) to suffer damage to its reputation or loss of profits through negative publicity.

Wal-Mart and Nike in particular have been frequent targets for advocacy groups that believe those corporations exploit their workers. Although some of these assertions may be unfounded or exaggerated, the courts generally have refused to consider them *defamatory* (a tort giving rise to a civil lawsuit). Most courts regard online attacks as expressions of opinion protected by the First Amendment. Even so, corporations often incur considerable expense in running marketing campaigns to thwart bad publicity and may even face legal costs if the allegations lead to litigation.

Image Is Everything The study of business ethics is concerned with the purposes of a business and how that business achieves those purposes. Thus, business ethics is concerned not only with the image of the business, but also with the impact that the business has on the environment, customers, suppliers, employees, and the global economy.

Unethical corporate decision making can negatively affect suppliers, consumers, the community, and society as a whole. It can also have a negative impact on the reputation of the company and the individuals who run that company. Hence, an in-depth understanding of business ethics is important to the long-run viability of any corporation today.

5–1c The Relationship of Law and Ethics

Because the law does not codify all ethical requirements, compliance with the law is not always sufficient to determine "right" behavior. Laws have to be general enough to apply in a variety of circumstances. Laws are broad in their purpose and their scope. They prohibit or require certain actions to avoid significant harm to society.

When two competing companies secretly agree to set prices on products, for instance, society suffers harm—typically, the companies will charge higher prices than they could if they continued to compete. This harm inflicted on consumers has negative consequences for the economy, and so colluding to set prices is an illegal activity. Similarly, when a company is preparing to issue stock, the law requires certain disclosures to potential investors. This requirement is meant to prevent harms that come with uninformed investing. Such harms occurred in the 1920s and may have contributed to the stock market crash and the Great Depression.

Moral Minimum Compliance with the law is sometimes called the **moral minimum.** If people and entities merely comply with the law, they are acting at the lowest ethical level society will tolerate. The study of ethics goes beyond those legal requirements to evaluate what is right for society. The following case illustrates some consequences of a businessperson's failure to meet the moral minimum.

Case 5.1

Scott v. Carpanzano

United States Court of Appeals, Fifth Circuit, 556 Fed.Appx. 288 (2014).

Background and Facts Rick Scott deposited $2 million into an escrow account maintained by a company owned by Salvatore Carpanzano. Immediately after the deposit was made, in violation of the escrow agreement, the funds were withdrawn. When Scott was unable to recover his money, he filed a suit against Salvatore Carpanzano and others, including Salvatore's daughter Carmela Carpanzano. In the complaint, Scott made no allegations of acts or knowledge on Carmela's part.

Salvatore failed to cooperate with discovery and did not respond to attempts to contact him by certified mail, regular mail, or e-mail. Salvatore also refused to make an appearance in the court and did not finalize a settlement negotiated between the parties' attorneys. Carmela denied that she was involved in her father's business or the Scott transaction. The court found that the defendants had intentionally failed to respond to the litigation and issued a judgment for more than $6 million in Scott's favor. The defendants appealed to the U.S. Court of Appeals for the Fifth Circuit.

In the Language of the Court
PER CURIAM [By the Whole Court].
  * * * *

A willful default is an *intentional failure to respond to litigation.* The district court found that [the] Defendants willfully defaulted based on evidence that the Defendants were aware of the proceedings against them and that [their] attorneys were specifically instructed not to enter an appearance [participate] in this case. [Emphasis added.]

The evidence substantially supports the district court's finding as to Mr. Carpanzano. First, Mr. Carpanzano's first attorney withdrew [from the case] because Mr. Carpanzano failed to cooperate with the discovery process and refused to appear as requested and ordered. Second, * * * Mr. Carpanzano instructed his second set of attorneys to negotiate settlement of this matter but not to enter an appearance in the district court. Significantly, Mr. Carpanzano never denies this allegation. Third, * * * Mr. Carpanzano and his attorneys were well aware that the case was proceeding toward default and * * * were in communication with each other during this time. Fourth, * * * once final execution of settlement papers was at hand, Mr. Carpanzano also ceased communication with his second set of attorneys and did not finalize the settlement. Finally, other than ambiguously suggesting that a health condition (unsupported by any evidence of what the condition was) and absence from the country (unsupported by any evidence that electronic communication was not possible from that country) prevented him from defending this action, Mr. Carpanzano offers no real reason why he did not answer the * * * complaint.
  * * * *

By contrast, the record does not support the district court's finding that * * * Ms. [Carmela] Carpanzano also willfully defaulted.

* * * Ms. Carpanzano repeatedly indicated that [she was] relying on Mr. Carpanzano * * * to make sure [her] interests were protected. Nothing in the record contradicts this assertion. While [her] reliance on Mr. Carpanzano acting with the attorneys he retained may have been negligent, it does not amount to an intentional failure to respond to litigation.

Case 5.1 Continues

Case 5.1 Continued

* * * *

* * * [Furthermore] the * * * complaint * * * contains no factual allegations of acts or omissions on the part of Ms. Carpanzano. It does not allege that she ever was in contact with Scott, that she was in control of the * * * escrow account, or that she wrongfully transferred any funds out of the account. Nor does it allege any intent or knowledge on the part of Ms. Carpanzano * * *. Indeed, an examination of the complaint reveals that there is not a sufficient basis in the pleadings for the judgment * * * entered against Ms. Carpanzano.

The defenses presented by Ms. Carpanzano to the district court assert that she had no knowledge of the details of her father's business transactions, she did not personally enter into any contracts with Scott or seek to defraud him, and * * * she had limited involvement in the facts of this case.

* * * *

* * * Even if Scott were able to prove the entirety of the * * * complaint, we fail to see how it would justify a judgment * * * against Ms. Carpanzano.

Decision and Remedy *The U.S. Court of Appeals for the Fifth Circuit affirmed the judgment against Salvatore, but reversed the decision against Carmela. Scott had made no allegations of acts on Carmela's part.*

Critical Thinking

- **Ethical** *Are Salvatore's actions likely to affect his business's ability to profit in the long run? Discuss.*
- **Legal Environment** *Did Carmela Carpanzano meet the minimum acceptable standard for ethical business behavior? Explain.*

Ethical Requirements The study of ethics goes beyond legal requirements to evaluate what is right for society. Businesspersons thus must remember that an action that is legal is not necessarily ethical. For instance, a company's refusal to negotiate liability claims for alleged injuries because of a faulty product is legal. But it may not be ethical if the reason the business refuses to negotiate is to increase the injured party's legal costs and force the person to drop a legitimate claim.

Private Company Codes of Ethics Most companies attempt to link ethics and law through the creation of internal codes of ethics. Company codes are not law. Instead, they are rules that the company sets forth that it can also enforce (by terminating an employee who does not follow them, for instance). Codes of conduct typically outline the company's policies on particular issues and indicate how employees are expected to act.

■ **EXAMPLE 5.2** Google's code of conduct starts with the motto "Don't be evil." The code then makes general statements about how Google promotes integrity, mutual respect, and the highest standard of ethical business conduct. Google's code also provides specific rules on a number of issues, such as privacy, drugs and alcohol, conflicts of interest, co-worker relationships, and confidentiality.

It even has a dog policy. The company takes a stand against employment discrimination that goes further than the law requires—it prohibits discrimination based on sexual orientation, gender identity or expression, and veteran status. ■

Industry Ethical Codes Numerous industries have also developed their own codes of ethics. The American Institute of Certified Public Accountants (AICPA) has a comprehensive Code of Professional Conduct for the ethical practice of accounting. The American Bar Association has model rules of professional conduct for attorneys, and the American Nurses Association has a code of ethics that applies to nurses. These codes can give guidance to decision makers facing ethical questions.

Violation of an industry code may result in discipline of an employee or sanctions against a company from the industry organization. Remember, though, that these internal codes are not laws, so their effectiveness is determined by the commitment of the industry or company leadership to enforcing the codes.

■ **CASE IN POINT 5.3** National Football League (NFL) rules require footballs to be inflated to a minimum air pressure (pounds per square inch, or psi) as measured by the referees. This rule gained attention when the New

England Patriots played the Indianapolis Colts for the American Football Conference championship in early 2015. After Tom Brady, the Patriots quarterback, threw a pass that was intercepted, officials became suspicious that the football was underinflated. The game continued after NFL officials verified the psi in all the footballs, and the Patriots won.

Nevertheless, allegations continued that Brady and the Patriots had deflated balls during the game—a controversy popularly known as "deflategate." The NFL performed an investigation, and after arbitration, the league announced that Brady would be suspended for four games. Brady appealed, and a federal district court vacated the arbitrator's decision to suspend, but a federal appellate court reinstated Brady's suspension in 2016. The reviewing court held that the arbitrator had grounds to suspend Brady for being generally aware that the team had intentionally released air from the game balls.[2] ■

"Gray Areas" in the Law Because it is often highly subjective and subject to change over time without any sort of formal process, ethics is less certain than law. But the law can also be uncertain. Numerous "gray areas" in the law make it difficult to predict with certainty how a court will apply a given law to a particular action. In addition, laws frequently change.

5–2 Business Ethics and Social Media

Most young people may think of social media— Facebook, Flickr, Instagram, Tumblr, Twitter, Pinterest, Google+, LinkedIn, VR, and the like—as simply ways to communicate rapidly. Businesses, though, often face ethical issues with respect to these same social media platforms.

5–2a Hiring Procedures

In the past, to learn about a prospective employee, an employer would ask the candidate's former employers for references. Today, employers are likely to also conduct Internet searches to discover what job candidates have posted on their Facebook pages, blogs, and tweets.

On the one hand, job candidates may be judged by what they post on social media. On the other hand,

though, they may be judged because they *do not* participate in social media. Given that the vast majority of younger people do use social media, some employers have decided that the failure to do so raises a red flag. In either case, many people believe that judging a job candidate based on what she or he does outside the work environment is unethical.

5–2b The Use of Social Media to Discuss Work-Related Issues

Because so many Americans use social media daily, they often discuss work-related issues there. Numerous companies have strict guidelines about what is appropriate and inappropriate for employees to say when making posts on their own or others' social media accounts. A number of companies have fired employees for such activities as criticizing other employees or managers through social media outlets. Until recently, such disciplinary measures were considered ethical and legal.

Responsibility of Employers Today, in contrast, a ruling by the National Labor Relations Board (NLRB—the federal agency that investigates unfair labor practices) has changed the legality of such actions. ■ **EXAMPLE 5.4** At one time, Costco's social media policy specified that its employees should not make statements that would damage the company, harm another person's reputation, or violate the company's policies. Employees who violated these rules were subject to discipline and could be fired.

The NLRB ruled that Costco's social media policy violated federal labor law, which protects employees' right to engage in "concerted activities." Employees can freely associate with each other and have conversations about common workplace issues without employer interference. This right extends to social media posts. Therefore, an employer cannot broadly prohibit its employees from criticizing the company or co-workers, supervisors, or managers via social media. ■

Responsibility of Employees While most of the discussion in this chapter concerns the ethics of business management, employee ethics is also an important issue. For instance, is it ethical for employees to make negative posts in social media about other employees or, more commonly, about managers? After all, negative comments about managers reflect badly on those managers, who often are reluctant to respond via social media to such criticism. Disgruntled employees may exaggerate the negative qualities of managers whom they do not like.

---

2. *National Football League Management Council v. National Football League Players Association*, 820 F.3d 527 (2d Cir. 2016).

Some may consider the decision by the National Labor Relations Board outlined in *Example 5.4* to be too lenient toward employees and too stringent toward management. There is likely to be an ongoing debate about how to balance employees' right to free expression against employers' right to prevent the spreading of inaccurate negative statements across the Internet.

5–3 Ethical Principles and Philosophies

As Dean Krehmeyer, executive director of the Business Roundtable's Institute for Corporate Ethics, once said, "Evidence strongly suggests being ethical—doing the right thing—pays." Even if ethics "pays," though, instilling ethical business decision making into the fabric of a business organization is no small task.

How do business decision makers decide whether a given action is the "right" one for their firms? What ethical standards should be applied? Broadly speaking, **ethical reasoning**—the application of morals and ethics to a situation—applies to businesses just as it does to individuals. As businesses make decisions, they must analyze their alternatives in a variety of ways, one of which is the ethical implications of each alternative.

Generally, the study of ethics is divided into two major categories—duty-based ethics and outcome-based ethics. **Duty-based ethics** is rooted in the idea that every person has certain duties to others, including both humans and the planet. **Outcome-based ethics** focuses on the impacts of a decision on society or on key *stakeholders*.

5–3a Duty-Based Ethics

Duty-based ethics focuses on the obligations of the corporation. It deals with standards for behavior that traditionally were derived from revealed truths, religious authorities, or philosophical reasoning. These standards involve concepts of right and wrong, duties owed, and rights to be protected. Corporations today often describe these values or duties in their mission statements or strategic plans. Some companies base their statements on a nonreligious rationale, while others derive their values from religious doctrine.

Religious Ethical Principles Nearly every religion has principles or beliefs about how one should treat others. In the Judeo-Christian tradition, which is the dominant religious tradition in the United States, the Ten Commandments of the Old Testament establish these fundamental rules for moral action. The principles of the Muslim faith are set out in the Qur'an, and Hindus find their principles in the four Vedas.

Religious rules generally are absolute with respect to the behavior of their adherents. ■ **EXAMPLE 5.5** The commandment "Thou shalt not steal" is an absolute mandate for a person who believes that the Ten Commandments reflect revealed truth. Even a benevolent motive for stealing (such as Robin Hood's) cannot justify the act because the act itself is inherently immoral and thus wrong. ■

For businesses, religious principles can be a unifying force for employees or a rallying point to increase employee motivation. They can also present problems, however, because different owners, suppliers, employees, and customers may have different religious backgrounds. Taking an action based on religious principles, especially when those principles address socially or politically controversial topics, can lead to negative publicity and even to protests or boycotts.

Principles of Rights Another view of duty-based ethics focuses on basic rights. The principle that human beings have certain fundamental rights (to life, freedom, and the pursuit of happiness, for example) is deeply embedded in Western culture.

Those who adhere to this **principle of rights,** or "rights theory," believe that a key factor in determining whether a business decision is ethical is how that decision affects the rights of others. These others include the firm's owners, its employees, the consumers of its products or services, its suppliers, the community in which it does business, and society as a whole.

Conflicting Rights. A potential dilemma for those who support rights theory is that they may disagree on which rights are most important. When considering all those affected by a business decision to downsize a firm, for example, how much weight should be given to employees relative to shareholders? Which employees should be laid off first—those with the highest salaries or those who have worked there for less time (and have less seniority)? How should the firm weigh the rights of customers relative to the community, or employees relative to society as a whole?

Resolving Conflicts. In general, rights theorists believe that whichever right is stronger in a particular circumstance takes precedence. ■ **EXAMPLE 5.6** Murray

Chemical Corporation has to decide whether to keep a chemical plant in Utah open, thereby saving the jobs of a hundred and fifty workers, or shut it down. Closing the plant will avoid contaminating a river with pollutants that might endanger the health of tens of thousands of people. In this situation, a rights theorist can easily choose which group to favor because the value of the right to health and well-being is obviously stronger than the basic right to work. Not all choices are so clear-cut, however. ■

Kantian Ethical Principles Duty-based ethical standards may also be derived solely from philosophical reasoning. The German philosopher Immanuel Kant (1724–1804) identified some general guiding principles for moral behavior based on what he thought to be the fundamental nature of human beings. Kant believed that human beings are qualitatively different from other physical objects and are endowed with moral integrity and the capacity to reason and conduct their affairs rationally.

People Are Not a Means to an End. Based on this view of human beings, Kant said that when people are treated merely as a means to an end, they are being treated as the equivalent of objects and are being denied their basic humanity. For instance, a manager who treats subordinates as mere profit-making tools is less likely to retain motivated and loyal employees than a manager who respects employees. Management research has shown that, in fact, employees who feel empowered to share their thoughts, opinions, and solutions to problems are happier and more productive.

Categorical Imperative. When a business makes unethical decisions, it often rationalizes its action by saying that the company is "just one small part" of the problem or that its decision has had "only a small impact." A central theme in Kantian ethics is that individuals should evaluate their actions in light of the consequences that would follow if everyone in society acted in the same way. This **categorical imperative** can be applied to any action.

■ **EXAMPLE 5.7** CHS Fertilizer is deciding whether to invest in expensive equipment that will decrease profits but will also reduce pollution from its factories. If CHS has adopted Kant's categorical imperative, the decision makers will consider the consequences if every company invested in the equipment (or if no company did so). If the result would make the world a better place (less polluted), CHS's decision would be clear. ■

5–3b Outcome-Based Ethics: Utilitarianism

In contrast to duty-based ethics, outcome-based ethics focuses on the consequences of an action, not on the nature of the action itself or on any set of preestablished moral values or religious beliefs. Outcome-based ethics looks at the impacts of a decision in an attempt to maximize benefits and minimize harms.

The premier philosophical theory for outcome-based decision making is **utilitarianism,** a philosophical theory developed by Jeremy Bentham (1748–1832) and modified by John Stuart Mill (1806–1873)—both British philosophers. "The greatest good for the greatest number" is a paraphrase of the major premise of the utilitarian approach to ethics.

Cost-Benefit Analysis Under a utilitarian model of ethics, an action is morally correct, or "right," when, among the people it affects, it produces the greatest amount of good for the greatest number or creates the least amount of harm for the fewest people. When an action affects the majority adversely, it is morally wrong. Applying the utilitarian theory thus requires the following steps:

1. A determination of which individuals will be affected by the action in question.
2. A **cost-benefit analysis,** which involves an assessment of the negative and positive effects of alternative actions on these individuals.
3. A choice among alternative actions that will produce maximum societal utility (the greatest positive net benefits for the greatest number of individuals).

Thus, if expanding a factory would provide hundreds of jobs but generate pollution that could endanger the lives of thousands of people, a utilitarian analysis would find that saving the lives of thousands creates greater good than providing jobs for hundreds.

Problems with the Utilitarian Approach There are problems with a strict utilitarian analysis. In some situations, an action that produces the greatest good for the most people may not seem to be the most ethical. ■ **EXAMPLE 5.8** Phazim Company is producing a drug that will cure a disease in 85 percent of patients, but the other 15 percent will experience agonizing side effects and a horrible, painful death. A quick utilitarian analysis would suggest that the drug should be produced and marketed because the majority of patients will benefit. Many people, however, have significant concerns about manufacturing a drug that will cause such harm to anyone. ■

5–3c Corporate Social Responsibility

In pairing duty-based concepts with outcome-based concepts, strategists and theorists developed the idea of the corporate citizen. **Corporate social responsibility (CSR)** combines a commitment to good citizenship with a commitment to making ethical decisions, improving society, and minimizing environmental impact.

CSR is a relatively new concept in the history of business, but a concept that becomes more important every year. Although CSR is not imposed on corporations by law, it does involve a commitment to self-regulation in a way that attends to the text and intent of the law as well as to ethical norms and global standards. A survey of U.S. executives undertaken by the Boston College Center for Corporate Citizenship found that more than 70 percent of those polled agreed that corporate citizenship must be treated as a priority. More than 60 percent said that good corporate citizenship added to their companies' profits.

CSR can be a successful strategy for companies, but corporate decision makers must not lose track of the two descriptors in the title: *corporate* and *social.* The company must link the responsibility of citizenship with the strategy and key principles of the business. Incorporating both the social and the corporate components of CSR and making ethical decisions can help companies grow and prosper. CSR is most successful when a company undertakes activities that are significant and related to its business operations.

The Social Aspects of CSR Because business controls so much of the wealth and power in this country, business has a responsibility to use that wealth and power in socially beneficial ways. Thus, the social aspect requires that corporations demonstrate that they are promoting goals that society deems worthwhile and are moving toward solutions to social problems. Companies may be judged on how much they donate to social causes, as well as how they conduct their operations with respect to employment discrimination, human rights, environmental concerns, and similar issues.

Some corporations publish annual social responsibility reports, which may also be called corporate sustainability (referring to the capacity to endure) or citizenship reports. ■ **EXAMPLE 5.9** The software company Symantec Corporation issues corporate responsibility reports to demonstrate its focus on critical environmental, social, and governance issues. In its 2014 report, Symantec pointed out that 88 percent of facilities it owns or leases on a long-term basis are certified as environmentally friendly by the LEED program. LEED stands for Leadership in Energy and Environmental Design. Certification requires the achievement of high standards for energy efficiency, material usage in construction, and other environmental qualities. ■

The Corporate Aspects of CSR Arguably, any socially responsible activity will benefit a corporation. A corporation may see an increase in goodwill from the local community for creating a park, for instance. A corporation that is viewed as a good citizen may see an increase in sales.

At times, the benefit may not be immediate. Constructing a new plant that meets the high LEED standards may cost more initially. Nevertheless, over the life of the building, the savings in maintenance and utilities may more than make up for the extra cost of construction.

Surveys of college students about to enter the job market confirm that young people are looking for socially responsible employers. Socially responsible activities may thus cost a corporation now, but may lead to more impressive and more committed employees. Corporations that engage in meaningful social activities retain workers longer, particularly younger ones.

■ **EXAMPLE 5.10** Pacific Gas and Electric (PG&E) in California sends its employees out on Earth Day to help clean and restore state parks. PG&E also provides free solar panels for new Habitat for Humanity homes and donates food to the needy. LinkedIn employees participate in an "InDay" every month to donate time and resources to the community. Zappos donates large amounts of its goods to charities and pays its employees for time off if they are volunteering. ■

Stakeholders One view of CSR stresses that corporations have a duty not just to shareholders, but also to other groups affected by corporate decisions—called **stakeholders.** The rationale for this "stakeholder view" is that, in some circumstances, one or more of these other groups may have a greater stake in company decisions than the shareholders do.

Under this approach, a corporation considers the impact of its decisions on its employees, customers, creditors, suppliers, and the community in which it operates. Stakeholders could also include advocacy groups such as environmental groups and animal rights groups. To avoid making a decision that may be perceived as unethical and result in negative publicity or protests, a corporation should consider the impact of its decision on the stakeholders.

The most difficult aspect of the stakeholder analysis is determining which group's interests should receive greater weight if the interests conflict. For instance, companies that are struggling financially sometimes lay off workers to reduce labor costs. But in recent years, some corporations have given greater weight to employees' interests and have found ways to avoid slashing their workforces. Companies finding alternatives to layoffs included Dell (extended unpaid holidays), Cisco Systems (four-day end-of-year shutdowns), Motorola (salary cuts), and Honda (voluntary unpaid vacation time).

5–4 Making Ethical Business Decisions

Even if officers, directors, and others in a company want to make ethical decisions, it is not always clear what is ethical in a given situation. Thinking beyond things that are easily measured, such as profits, can be challenging. Although profit projections are not always accurate, they are more objective than considering the personal impacts of decisions on employees, shareholders, customers, and the community. But this subjective component of decision making potentially has a great potential influence on a company's profits.

Companies once considered leaders in their industry, such as Enron and the worldwide accounting firm Arthur Andersen, were brought down by the unethical behavior of a few. A two-hundred-year-old British investment banking firm, Barings Bank, was destroyed by the actions of one employee and a few of his friends. Clearly, ensuring that all employees get on the ethical business decision-making "bandwagon" is crucial in today's fast-paced world.

Individuals entering the global corporate community, even in entry-level positions, must be prepared to make hard decisions. Sometimes, there is no "good" answer to the questions that arise. Therefore, it is important to have tools to help in the decision-making process and to create a framework for organizing those tools. Business decisions can be complex and may involve legal concerns, financial questions, possibly health and safety concerns, and ethical components.

5–4a A Systematic Approach

Organizing the ethical concerns and issues and approaching them systematically can help a businessperson eliminate various alternatives and identify the strengths and weaknesses of the remaining alternatives. Ethics consultant Leonard H. Bucklin of Corporate-Ethics.US™ has devised a procedure that he calls Business Process Pragmatism™. It involves five steps:

Step 1: Inquiry. First, the decision maker must understand the problem. This step involves identifying the parties involved (the stakeholders) and collecting the relevant facts. Once the ethical problem or problems are clarified, the decision maker lists any relevant legal and ethical principles that will guide the decision.

Step 2: Discussion. In this step, the decision maker lists possible actions. The ultimate goals for the decision are determined, and each option is evaluated using the laws and ethical principles listed in Step 1.

Step 3: Decision. In this step, those participating in the decision making work together to craft a consensus decision or consensus plan of action for the corporation.

Step 4: Justification. In this step, the decision maker articulates the reasons for the proposed action or series of actions. Generally, these reasons should come from the analysis done in Step 3. This step essentially results in documentation to be shared with stakeholders explaining why the proposal is an ethical solution to the problem.

Step 5: Evaluation. This final step occurs once the decision has been made and implemented. The solution should be analyzed to determine if it was effective. The results of this evaluation may be used in making future decisions.

5–4b The Importance of Ethical Leadership

Talking about ethical business decision making is meaningless if management does not set standards. Furthermore, managers must apply the same standards to themselves as they do to the company's employees. See this chapter's *Digital Update* feature for a discussion of an ethical dilemma that has arisen from the increased use of digital technology by employees after work hours.

Attitude of Top Management One of the most important ways to create and maintain an ethical

DIGITAL UPDATE — Should Employees Have a "Right of Disconnecting"?

Almost all jobs today involve digital technology, whether it be e-mail, Internet access, or smartphone use. Most employees, when interviewed, say that digital technology increases their productivity and flexibility.

The downside is what some call an "electronic leash"—meaning that employees are constantly connected and end up working when they are not "at work." Over one-third of full-time workers, for example, say that they frequently check e-mails outside normal working hours.

Do Workers Have the Right to Disconnect?

Because the boundaries between being "at work" and being "at leisure" can be so hazy, some labor unions in other countries have attempted to pass rules that allow employees to disconnect from e-mail and other work-related digital communication during nonworking hours. For instance, a French labor union representing high-tech workers signed an agreement with a large business association recognizing a "right of disconnecting." In Germany, Volkswagen and BMW no longer forward e-mail to staff from company servers after the end of the workday. Other German firms have declared that workers are not expected to check e-mail on weekends and holidays. The government is considering legislating such restrictions nationwide.

The Thorny Issue of Overtime and the Fair Labor Standards Act

Payment for overtime work is strictly regulated under the Fair Labor Standards Act (FLSA). According to the United States Supreme Court, in this context, *work* is "physical or mental exertion (whether burdensome or not) controlled or required by the employer and pursued necessarily for the benefit of the employer and his business."[a]

This definition was extended to off-duty work if such work is an "integral and indispensable part of [employees'] activities."[b]

Today's modern digital connectivity raises issues about the definition of *work*. Employees at several major companies, including Black & Decker, T-Mobile, and Verizon, have sued for unpaid overtime related to smartphone use. In another case, a police sergeant has sued the city of Chicago, claiming that he should have been paid overtime for hours spent using his personal digital assistant (PDA).[c] The police department issues PDAs to officers and requires them to respond to work-related text messages, e-mails, and voice mails not only while on duty, but also while off duty. Off-duty responses are not compensated by the city.

Not All Employees Demand the "Right to Disconnect"

According to a recent Gallup poll, 79 percent of full-time employees had either strongly positive or somewhat positive views of using computers, e-mail, tablets, and smartphones to work remotely outside of normal business hours. According to the same poll, 17 percent of them report "better overall lives" because of constant online connectivity with their work. Finally, working remotely after business hours apparently does not necessarily result in additional work-related stress.

Critical Thinking *From an ethical point of view, is there any difference between calling subordinates during off hours for work-related questions and sending them e-mails or text messages?*

a. *Tennessee Coal, Iron & R. Co. v. Muscoda Local No. 123*, 321 U.S. 590, 64 S.Ct. 698, 8 L.Ed. 949 (1944). Although Congress later passed a statute that superseded the holding in this case, the statute gave the courts broad authority to interpret the FLSA's definition of *work*. 29 U.S.C. Section 251(a). See *Integrity Staffing Solutions, Inc. v. Busk*, ___ U.S. ___, 135 S.Ct. 513, 190 L.Ed.2d 410 (2014).

b. *Steiner v. Mitchell*, 350 U.S. 247, 76 S.Ct. 330, 100 L.Ed. 267 (1956).

c. *Allen v. City of Chicago*, 2014 WL 5461856 (N.D.Ill. 2014).

workplace is for top management to demonstrate its commitment to ethical decision making. A manager who is not totally committed to an ethical workplace rarely succeeds in creating one. Management's behavior, more than anything else, sets the ethical tone of a firm. Employees take their cues from management.

Managers have found that discharging even one employee for ethical reasons has a tremendous impact as a deterrent to unethical behavior in the workplace. This is true even if the company has a written code of ethics. If management does not enforce the company code, the code is essentially nonexistent.

The administration of a university may have had a similar concept in mind in the following case when it applied the school's professionalism standard to a student who had engaged in serious misconduct.

Al-Dabagh v. Case Western Reserve University

United States Court of Appeals, Sixth Circuit, 777 F.3d 355 (2015).

Background and Facts The curriculum at Case Western Reserve University School of Medicine identifies nine "core competencies." At the top of the list is professionalism, which includes "ethical, honest, responsible and reliable behavior." The university's Committee on Students determines whether a student has met the professionalism requirements.

Amir Al-Dabagh enrolled at the school and did well academically. But he sexually harassed fellow students, often asked an instructor not to mark him late for class, received complaints from hospital staff about his demeanor, and was convicted of driving while intoxicated. The Committee on Students unanimously refused to certify him for graduation and dismissed him from the university.

He filed a suit in a federal district court against Case Western, alleging a breach of good faith and fair dealing. The court ordered the school to issue a diploma. Case Western appealed.

In the Language of the Court

SUTTON, Circuit Judge.
    * * * *

    * * * Case Western's student handbook * * * makes clear that the only thing standing between Al-Dabagh and a diploma is the Committee on Students' finding that he lacks professionalism. Unhappily for Al-Dabagh, that is an academic judgment. And *we can no more substitute our personal views for the Committee's when it comes to an academic judgment than the Committee can substitute its views for ours when it comes to a judicial decision.* [Emphasis added.]
    * * * *

    * * * *The Committee's professionalism determination is an academic judgment. That conclusion all but resolves this case. We may overturn the Committee only if it substantially departed from accepted academic norms when it refused to approve Al-Dabagh for graduation.* And given Al-Dabagh's track record—one member of the Committee does not recall encountering another student with Al-Dabagh's "repeated professionalism issues" in his quarter century of experience—we cannot see how it did. [Emphasis added.]

    To the contrary, Al-Dabagh insists: The Committee's decision was a "punitive disciplinary measure" that had nothing to do with academics. * * * His argument fails to wrestle with the prominent place of professionalism in the university's academic curriculum—which itself is an academic decision courts may not lightly disturb.

    Even if professionalism is an academic criterion, Al-Dabagh persists that the university defined it too broadly. As he sees it, the only professional lapses that matter are the ones linked to academic performance. That is not how we see it or for that matter how the medical school sees it. That many professionalism-related cases involve classroom incidents does not establish that only classroom incidents are relevant to the professionalism inquiry * * * . Our own standards indicate that professionalism does not end at the courtroom door. Why should hospitals operate any differently? As for the danger that an expansive view of professionalism might forgive, or provide a cloak for, arbitrary or discriminatory behavior, we see no such problem here. Nothing in the record suggests that the university had impermissible motives or acted in bad faith in this instance. And nothing in our deferential standard prevents us from invalidating genuinely objectionable actions when they occur.

Decision and Remedy *The U.S. Court of Appeals for the Sixth Circuit reversed the lower court's order to issue a diploma to Al-Dabagh. The federal appellate court found nothing to indicate that Case Western had "impermissible motives," acted in bad faith, or dealt unfairly with Al-Dabagh.*

Critical Thinking

- **What If the Facts Were Different?** *Suppose that Case Western had tolerated Al-Dabagh's conduct and awarded him a diploma. What impact might that had on other students at the school? Why?*

Behavior of Owners and Managers Certain types of behavior on the part of managers and owners contribute to unethical behavior among employees. Managers who set unrealistic production or sales goals increase the probability that employees will act unethically. If a sales quota can be met only through high-pressure, unethical sales tactics, employees will try to act "in the best interest of the company" and will continue to behave unethically. A manager who looks the other way when she or he knows about an employee's unethical behavior also sets an example—one indicating that ethical transgressions will be accepted.

Business owners and managers sometimes take more active roles in fostering unethical and illegal conduct. This sort of misbehavior can have negative consequences for the owners and managers and their business. Not only can a court sanction them, but it can also issue an injunction that prevents them from engaging in similar patterns of conduct in the future.

■ **CASE IN POINT 5.11** John Robert Johnson, Jr., took a truck that needed repair along with its fifteen-ton trailer to Bubba Shaffer, doing business as Shaffer's Auto and Diesel Repair, LLC. The truck was supposedly fixed, and Johnson paid the bill, but the truck continued to leak oil and water. Johnson returned the truck to Shaffer, who again claimed to have fixed the problem. Johnson paid the second bill. The problems with the truck continued, however, so Johnson returned the truck and trailer to Shaffer a third time.

Johnson was given a verbal estimate of $1,000 for the repairs, but Shaffer ultimately sent an invoice for $5,863. Johnson offered to settle for $2,480, the amount of the initial estimate ($1,000), plus the costs of parts and shipping. Shaffer refused the offer and would not return Johnson's truck or trailer until full payment was made. Shaffer retained possession for almost four years and also charged Johnson a storage fee of $50 a day and 18 percent interest on the $5,863. Johnson sued for unfair trade practices and won. The court awarded him $3,500 in damages plus attorneys' fees and awarded Shaffer $1,000 (the amount of his estimate).[3] ■

The following case further demonstrates the types of situations that can occur when management demonstrates a lack of concern about ethics.

3. *Johnson Construction Co. v. Shaffer*, 87 So.3d 203 (La.App. 2012).

Case Analysis 5.3

Moseley v. Pepco Energy Services, Inc.
United States District Court, District of New Jersey, 2011 WL 1584166 (2011).

In the Language of the Court
Joseph H. *RODRIGUEZ*, District Judge.

* * * Plaintiff Moseley is an employee of Defendant Pepco Energy Services, Inc. ("PES"). He has been employed by PES or its corporate predecessors for over twenty-five years. PES, a subsidiary of Defendant Pepco Holdings, Inc. ("PHI"), provides deregulated energy and energy-related services for residential, small business, and large commercial customers.
* * * *

In 1998, Thomas Herzog held the position of Vice President of CTS. * * * In or around 2002, CTS merged with Potomic Electric Power Company, Inc., and each company became a subsidiary of PHI. Following the merger, according to Plaintiff, he continued to work for PHI, still as Maintenance Manager at Midtown Thermal, until December 31, 2009.
* * * *

Following the 2002 merger with PHI, employees were required to complete an annual ethics survey. By March of 2007, Plaintiff and two co-workers had discussed their respective observations of Herzog's conduct, which they deemed questionable and possibly unethical. Specifically, they felt that Herzog improperly used company assets and improperly hired immediate family members and friends who did not appear on the payroll. The three decided to disclose this information on PHI's annual "Ethics Survey."

The three planned to reveal that Herzog employed his daughter, Laurie, as his secretary in the summer of 2005 and the beginning of 2006 without posting the position first and in violation of PHI's anti-nepotism policy.
* * * *

Next, Herzog hired his girlfriend's daughter as his secretary after his daughter had gone back to school. Plaintiff believed this was in violation of Company policy because the position again was not posted. Herzog also hired his son as a project manager, again through a third party independent contractor, Walter Ratai. Plaintiff thought this was wrong because (1) Herzog circumvented the Company's hiring process, (2) it violated Company policy, and (3) Herzog's son was being paid $75.00/hr, which was more than Plaintiff was making. * * *

Case 5.3 Continued

In addition, Plaintiff had learned that Herzog was improperly using the Company's Eagles' tickets for personal use. Finally, Herzog had leased a new SUV with Company funds, but which was not approved by the Company.
* * * *

[After the surveys were completed, an] investigation ensued. Following the investigation, effective on or about May 10, 2007, Herzog was escorted out of the building. * * * On March 8, 2008, Plaintiff received his annual performance evaluation * * *; for the first time in twenty-three years, Plaintiff's performance review was negative. Plaintiff feels that this negative performance review was a further act of retaliation for his disclosure of Herzog's conduct.
* * * *

On or about June 11, 2008 the Plant/Operations Manager position was posted * * *. Plaintiff applied for the position, but it was offered to [another person]. Plaintiff alleges that he "was not promoted to the position of Plant/ Operations Manager despite his experience performing the job for the previous two and a half years, qualifications for same and seniority, as a direct and proximate result of his prior complaints and/or disclosures regarding the Herzog illegal conduct and activities."
* * * *

The New Jersey Legislature enacted the Conscientious Employee Protection Act (CEPA) to "protect and encourage employees to report illegal or unethical workplace activities." * * * CEPA prohibits a New Jersey employer from taking "retaliatory action" against an employee who objects to "any activity, policy or practice which the employee reasonably believes" is in violation of applicable law. * * * "To prevail on a claim under

this provision, a plaintiff must establish that: (1) he reasonably believed that [the complained-of] conduct was violating a law or rule or regulation promulgated pursuant to law; (2) he objected to the conduct; (3) an adverse employment action was taken against him; and (4) a causal connection exists between the whistleblowing activity and the adverse employment action.
* * * *

The first element of the prima facie case [a case sufficient to be sent to the jury] under CEPA is that the Plaintiff reasonably believed that the complained-of conduct (1) was violating a "law, rule, or regulation promulgated pursuant to law, including any violation involving deception of, or misrepresentation to, any shareholder, investor, client, patient, customer, employee, former employee, retiree or pensioner of the employer or any governmental entity"; or "(2) is fraudulent or criminal, including any activity, policy or practice of deception or misrepresentation which the employee reasonably believes may defraud any shareholder, investor, client, patient, customer, employee, former employee, retiree or pensioner of the employer or any governmental entity."

Although Defendants have argued that Plaintiff merely disclosed a violation of Company policy, Moseley has testified that in March 2007, he reported what he believed to be "unethical conduct, misappropriation of company funds, and theft" by his direct supervisor. * * * *Moreover, a plaintiff need not demonstrate that there was a violation of the law or fraud, but instead that he "reasonably believed" that to be the case.* The facts in this case support an objectively reasonable belief that a violation of law or

fraudulent conduct was being committed by Plaintiff's supervisor. [Emphasis added.]

Regarding the causal connection between Plaintiff's whistleblowing activity and the negative adverse employment actions taken against him, Plaintiff stresses that he was employed by the Defendants for twenty-five years without a negative employment evaluation or any form of discipline until immediately after he disclosed the wrongful conduct of his supervisor. Not only did Plaintiff then receive a negative performance evaluation, but the posted position of Plant Manager was given to [another], despite [the other's] alleged past negative history and despite that Plaintiff asserts he had been acting in that job for over two years. Plaintiff contends that this is sufficient evidence of pretext.

The Court is unable to find as a matter of law that Defendants' inferences prevail or that a jury could not reasonably adopt a contrary inference of retaliation. There are questions of fact as to how much the individuals responsible for Plaintiff's negative performance evaluations knew about Plaintiff's complaints. "[A] finding of the required causal connection may be based solely on circumstantial evidence that the person ultimately responsible for an adverse employment action was aware of an employee's whistle-blowing activity." Because jurors may infer a causal connection from the surrounding circumstances, as well as temporal proximity, the Court will not grant summary judgment. [Emphasis added.]
* * * *

IT IS ORDERED on this 26th day of April, 2011 that Defendants' motion for summary judgment is hereby DENIED.

Legal Reasoning Questions

1. Using duty-based ethical principles, what facts or circumstances in this case would lead Moseley to disclose Herzog's behavior?

2. Using outcome-based ethical principles, what issues would Moseley have to analyze in making the decision to report Herzog's behavior? What would be the risks to Moseley? The benefits?

3. Under the Business Process Pragmatism™ steps, what alternatives might Moseley have had in this situation?

The Sarbanes-Oxley Act Congress enacted the Sarbanes-Oxley Act[4] to help reduce corporate fraud and unethical management decisions. The act requires companies to set up confidential systems so that employees and others can "raise red flags" about suspected illegal or unethical auditing and accounting practices.

Some companies have implemented online reporting systems to accomplish this goal. In one such system, employees can click on an on-screen icon that anonymously links them with NAVEX Global, an organization based in Oregon. Through NAVEX Global, employees can report suspicious accounting practices, sexual harassment, and other possibly unethical behavior. NAVEX, in turn, alerts management personnel or the audit committee at the designated company to the possible problem.

5–5 Global Business Ethics

Just as different religions have different moral codes, different countries, regions, and even states have different ethical expectations and priorities. Some of these differences are based in religious values, whereas others are cultural in nature. Such differences make it even more difficult to determine what is ethical in a particular situation. For instance, in certain countries the consumption of alcohol is forbidden for religious reasons. It would be considered unethical for a U.S. business to produce alcohol in those countries and employ local workers to assist in alcohol production.

International transactions often involve issues related to employment and financing. Congress has addressed some of these issues, not eliminating the ethical components but clarifying some of the conflicts between the ethics of the United States and the ethics of other nations. For instance, the Civil Rights Act and the Foreign Corrupt Practices Act have clarified the U.S. ethical position on employment issues and bribery in foreign nations. (Other nations, including Mexico, have also enacted laws that prohibit bribery.)

5–5a Monitoring the Employment Practices of Foreign Suppliers

Many businesses contract with companies in developing nations to produce goods, such as shoes and clothing, because the wage rates in those nations are significantly lower than those in the United States. But what if one of those contractors hires women and children at

below-minimum-wage rates or requires its employees to work long hours in a workplace full of health hazards? What if the company's supervisors routinely engage in workplace conduct that is offensive to women? What if plants located abroad routinely violate labor and environmental standards?

■ **EXAMPLE 5.12** Pegatron Corporation, a company based in China, manufactures and supplies parts to Apple, Inc., for iPads and other Apple products. After an explosion at a Pegatron factory in Shanghai, allegations surfaced that the conditions at the factory violated labor and environmental standards. Similar allegations were made about other Apple suppliers.

Apple started to evaluate practices at companies in its supply chain and to communicate its ethics policies to them. Its audits revealed numerous violations. Apple released a list of its suppliers for the first time and issued a lengthy "Supplier Responsibility Report" detailing supplier practices. Numerous facilities had withheld worker pay as a disciplinary measure. Some had falsified pay records and forced workers to use machines without safeguards. Others had engaged in unsafe environmental practices, such as dumping wastewater on neighboring farms. Apple terminated its relationship with one supplier and turned over its findings to the Fair Labor Association for further inquiry. ■

Given today's global communications network, few companies can assume that their actions in other nations will go unnoticed by "corporate watch" groups that discover and publicize unethical corporate behavior. As a result, U.S. businesses today usually take steps to avoid such adverse publicity—either by refusing to deal with certain suppliers or by arranging to monitor their suppliers' workplaces to make sure that the employees are not being mistreated.

5–5b The Foreign Corrupt Practices Act

Another ethical problem in international business dealings has to do with the legitimacy of certain side payments to government officials. In the United States, the majority of contracts are formed within the private sector. In many foreign countries, however, government officials make the decisions on most major construction and manufacturing contracts because of extensive government regulation and control over trade and industry.

Side payments to government officials in exchange for favorable business contracts are not unusual in such countries, nor have they been considered unethical. In the past, U.S. corporations doing business in these nations largely followed the dictum "When in Rome, do as the Romans do."

In the 1970s, however, the U.S. media uncovered a number of business scandals involving large side

---

4. 15 U.S.C. Sections 7201 *et seq.*

payments by U.S. corporations to foreign representatives for the purpose of securing advantageous international trade contracts. In response to this unethical behavior, Congress passed the Foreign Corrupt Practices Act[5] (FCPA), which prohibits U.S. businesspersons from bribing foreign officials to secure beneficial contracts.

Prohibition against the Bribery of Foreign Officials The first part of the FCPA applies to all U.S. companies and their directors, officers, shareholders, employees, and agents. This part prohibits the bribery of most officials of foreign governments if the purpose of the payment is to motivate the official to act in his or her official capacity to provide business opportunities.

The FCPA does not prohibit payments made to minor officials whose duties are ministerial. A ministerial action is a routine activity, such as the processing of paperwork, with little or no discretion involved in the action. These payments are often referred to as "grease," or facilitating payments. They are meant to accelerate the performance of administrative services that might otherwise be carried out at a slow pace. Thus, for instance, if a firm makes a payment to a minor official to speed up an import licensing process, the firm has not violated the FCPA.

Generally, the act, as amended, permits payments to foreign officials if such payments are lawful within the foreign country. Payments to private foreign companies or other third parties are permissible—unless the U.S. firm knows that the payments will be passed on to a foreign government in violation of the FCPA. The U.S. Department of Justice also uses the FCPA to prosecute foreign companies suspected of bribing officials outside the United States.

Accounting Requirements In the past, bribes were often concealed in corporate financial records. Thus, the second part of the FCPA is directed toward accountants.

All companies must keep detailed records that "accurately and fairly" reflect their financial activities. Their accounting systems must provide "reasonable assurance" that all transactions entered into by the companies are accounted for and legal. These requirements assist in detecting illegal bribes. The FCPA prohibits any person from making false statements to accountants or false entries in any record or account.

■ **CASE IN POINT 5.13** Noble Corporation, an international provider of offshore drilling services and equipment, was operating some drilling rigs offshore in Nigeria. Mark Jackson and James Ruehlen were officers at Noble. The U.S. government accused Noble of bribing Nigerian government officials and charged Jackson and Ruehlen individually with violating the FCPA's accounting provisions. Jackson and Ruehlen allegedly assisted in the bribery because they repeatedly allowed allegedly illegal payments to be posted on Noble's books as legitimate operating expenses.[6] ■

Penalties for Violations The FCPA provides that business firms that violate the act may be fined up to $2 million. Individual officers or directors who violate the FCPA may be fined up to $100,000 (the fine cannot be paid by the company) and may be imprisoned for up to five years. These statutory amounts can be significantly increased under the Alternative Fines Act[7] (up to twice the amount of any gain that the defendant obtained by making the corrupt payment).

Today, the U.S. government is actively seeking out violators and has around 150 FCPA investigations going on at any given time. In recent years, a high percentage of the total fines imposed by the Department of Justice have come from FCPA cases.

---

5. 15 U.S.C. Sections 78dd-1 *et seq.*

6. *S.E.C. v. Jackson*, 908 F.Supp.2d 834 (S.D.Tex—Houston Div. 2012).
7. 18 U.S.C. Section 3571.

Reviewing: Business Ethics

James Stilton is the chief executive officer (CEO) of RightLiving, Inc., a company that buys life insurance policies at a discount from terminally ill persons and sells the policies to investors. RightLiving pays the terminally ill patients a percentage of the future death benefit (usually 65 percent) and then sells the policies to investors for 85 percent of the value of the future benefit. The patients receive the cash to use for medical and other expenses. The investors are "guaranteed" a positive return on their investment, and RightLiving profits on the difference between the purchase and sale prices. Stilton is aware that some sick patients might obtain insurance policies through fraud (by not revealing the illness on the insurance application). Insurance companies that discover this will cancel the policy and refuse to pay.

Continues

Stilton believes that most of the policies he has purchased are legitimate, but he knows that some probably are not. Using the information presented in this chapter, answer the following questions.

1. Would a person who adheres to the principle of rights consider it ethical for Stilton not to disclose the potential risk of cancellation to investors? Why or why not?
2. Using Immanuel Kant's categorical imperative, are the actions of RightLiving, Inc., ethical? Why or why not?
3. Under utilitarianism, are Stilton's actions ethical? Why or why not? What difference does it make if most of the policies are legitimate?
4. Using the Business Process Pragmatism™ steps discussed in this chapter, discuss the decision process Stilton should use in deciding whether to disclose the risk of fraudulent policies to potential investors.

Debate This . . . *Executives in large corporations are ultimately rewarded if their companies do well, particularly as evidenced by rising stock prices. Consequently, should we let those who run corporations decide what level of negative side effects of their goods or services is "acceptable"?*

Terms and Concepts

business ethics 89
categorical imperative 95
corporate social responsibility
  (CSR) 96
cost-benefit analysis 95

duty-based ethics 94
ethical reasoning 94
ethics 89
moral minimum 91
outcome-based ethics 94

principle of rights 94
stakeholders 96
triple bottom line 89
utilitarianism 95

Issue Spotters

1. Acme Corporation decides to respond to what it sees as a moral obligation to correct for past discrimination by adjusting pay differences among its employees. Does this raise an ethical conflict between Acme and its employees? Between Acme and its shareholders? Explain your answers. (See *Making Ethical Business Decisions.*)

2. Delta Tools, Inc., markets a product that under some circumstances is capable of seriously injuring consumers. Does Delta have an ethical duty to remove this product from the market, even if the injuries result only from misuse? Why or why not? (See *Making Ethical Business Decisions.*)

• **Check your answers to the Issue Spotters against the answers provided in Appendix D at the end of this text.**

Business Scenarios

5–1. Business Ethics. Jason Trevor owns a commercial bakery in Blakely, Georgia, that produces a variety of goods sold in grocery stores. Trevor is required by law to perform internal tests on food produced at his plant to check for contamination. On three occasions, the tests of food products containing peanut butter were positive for salmonella contamination. Trevor was not required to report the results to U.S. Food and Drug Administration officials, however, so he did not. Instead, Trevor instructed his employees to simply repeat the

tests until the results were negative. Meanwhile, the products that had originally tested positive for salmonella were eventually shipped out to retailers.

Five people who ate Trevor's baked goods that year became seriously ill, and one person died from a salmonella infection. Even though Trevor's conduct was legal, was it unethical for him to sell goods that had once tested positive for salmonella? Why or why not? (See *Business Ethics.*)

Business Case Problems

5–2. Spotlight on Pfizer, Inc.—Corporate Social Responsibility.

 Methamphetamine (meth) is an addictive drug made chiefly in small toxic labs (STLs) in homes, tents, barns, or hotel rooms. The manufacturing process is dangerous and often results in explosions, burns, and toxic fumes. Government entities spend time and resources to find and destroy STLs, imprison meth dealers and users, treat addicts, and provide services for affected families. Meth cannot be made without ingredients that are also used in cold and allergy medications. Arkansas has one of the highest numbers of STLs in the United States. To recoup the costs of fighting the meth epidemic, twenty counties in Arkansas filed a suit against Pfizer, Inc., which makes cold and allergy medications. What is Pfizer's ethical responsibility here, and to whom is it owed? Why? [*Ashley County, Arkansas v. Pfizer, Inc.,* 552 F.3d. 659 (8th Cir. 2009)] (See *Ethical Principles and Philosophies.*)

5–3. Business Case Problem with Sample Answer—Online Privacy.

 Facebook, Inc., launched a program called "Beacon" that automatically updated the profiles of users on Facebook's social networking site when those users had any activity on Beacon "partner" sites. For example, one partner site was Blockbuster.com. When a user rented or purchased a movie through Blockbuster.com, the user's Facebook profile would be updated to share the purchase. The Beacon program was set up as a default setting, so users never consented to the program, but they could opt out. What are the ethical implications of an opt-in program versus an opt-out program in social media? [*Lane v. Facebook, Inc.,* 696 F.3d 811 (9th Cir. 2011)] (See *Business Ethics and Social Media.*)

- **For a sample answer to Problem 5-3, go to Appendix E at the end of this text.**

5–4. Business Ethics on a Global Scale.

After the fall of the Soviet Union, the new government of Azerbaijan began converting certain state-controlled industries to private ownership. Ownership in these companies could be purchased through a voucher program. Frederic Bourke, Jr., and Viktor Kozeny wanted to purchase the Azerbaijani oil company, SOCAR, but it was unclear whether the Azerbaijani president would allow SOCAR to be put up for sale. Kozeny met with one of the vice presidents of SOCAR (who was also the son of the president of Azerbaijan) and other Azerbaijani leaders to discuss the sale of SOCAR. To obtain their cooperation, Kozeny set up a series of parent and subsidiary companies through which the Azerbaijani leaders would eventually receive two-thirds of the SOCAR profits without ever investing any of their own funds. In return, the Azerbaijani leaders would attempt to use their influence to convince the president to put SOCAR up for sale. Assume that Bourke and Kozeny are operating out of a U.S. company. Discuss the ethics of this scheme, both in terms of the Foreign Corrupt Practices Act (FCPA) and as a general ethical issue. What duties did Kozeny have under the FCPA? [*United States v. Kozeny,* 667 F.3d 122 (2d Cir. 2011)] (See *Making Ethical Business Decisions.*)

5–5. Business Ethics.

Mark Ramun worked as a manager for Allied Erecting and Dismantling Co., where he had a tense relationship with his father, who was Allied's president. After more than ten years, Mark left Allied, taking 15,000 pages of Allied's documents on DVDs and CDs, which constituted trade secrets. Later, he joined Genesis Equipment & Manufacturing, Inc., a competitor. Genesis soon developed a piece of equipment that incorporated elements of Allied equipment. How might business ethics have been violated in these circumstances? Discuss. [*Allied Erecting and Dismantling Co. v. Genesis Equipment & Manufacturing, Inc.,* 511 Fed.Appx. 398 (6th Cir. 2013)] (See *Business Ethics.*)

5–6. Business Ethics.

Stephen Glass made himself infamous as a dishonest journalist by fabricating material for more than forty articles for *The New Republic* magazine and other publications. He also fabricated supporting materials to delude *The New Republic*'s fact checkers. At the time, he was a law student at Georgetown University. Once suspicions were aroused, Glass tried to avoid detection. Later, Glass applied for admission to the California bar. The California Supreme Court denied his application, citing "numerous instances of dishonesty and disingenuousness" during his "rehabilitation" following the exposure of his misdeeds. How do these circumstances underscore the importance of ethics? Discuss. [*In re Glass,* 58 Cal.4th 500, 316 P.3d 1199 (2014)] (See *Business Ethics.*)

5–7. Business Ethics.

Operating out of an apartment in Secane, Pennsylvania, Hratch Ilanjian convinced Vicken Setrakian, the president of Kenset Corp., that he was an international businessman who could help Kenset turn around its business in the Middle East. At Ilanjian's insistence, Setrakian provided confidential business documents. Claiming that they had an agreement, Ilanjian demanded full, immediate payment and threatened to disclose the confidential information to a Kenset supplier if payment was not forthcoming. Kenset denied that they had a contract and filed a suit in a federal district court against Ilanjian, seeking return of the documents. During discovery, Ilanjian was uncooperative. Who behaved unethically in these circumstances? Explain. [*Kenset Corp. v. Ilanjian,* 600 Fed.Appx. 827 (3rd Cir. 2015)] (See *Business Ethics.*)

5–8. Business Ethics.

Priscilla Dickman worked as a medical technologist at the University of Connecticut Health Center. Dickman's supervisor received complaints that she was getting nonbusiness-related phone calls and was absent from her work area when she should have been working. Based on e-mails and other documents found on Dickman's work computer, the state investigated her for violations of state law. She was convicted of conducting "personal business for financial gain on state time utilizing state resources." Separate criminal investigations resulted in convictions for forgery and filing an unrelated fraudulent insurance claim. She "retired" from her job and filed a claim with the state of Connecticut against the health center, alleging that her former employer had initiated the investigations to harass her and force her to quit. For lack of "credible evidence or legal support," the claim was dismissed. Which of these acts, if any, were unethical? Why? [*Dickman v. University of Connecticut Health Center*, 162 Conn.App. 441, ___ A.3d ___ (2016)] (See *Business Ethics*.)

5–9. A Question of Ethics—Consumer Rights.

 Best Buy, a national electronics retailer, offered a credit card that allowed users to earn "reward points" that could be redeemed for discounts on Best Buy goods. After reading a newspaper advertisement for the card, Gary Davis applied for, and was given, a credit card. As part of the application process, he visited a Web page containing Frequently Asked Questions as well as terms and conditions for the card. He clicked on a button affirming that he understood the terms and conditions. When Davis received his card, it came with seven brochures about the card and the reward point program. As he read the brochures, he discovered that a $59 annual fee would be charged for the card. Davis went back to the Web pages he had visited and found a statement that the card "may" have an annual fee. Davis sued, claiming that the company did not adequately disclose the fee. [Davis v. HSBC Bank Nevada, N.A., 691 F.3d 1152 (9th Cir. 2012)] (See Business Ethics.)

(a) Online applications frequently have click-on buttons or check boxes for consumers to acknowledge that they have read and understand the terms and conditions of applications or purchases. Often, the terms and conditions are so long that they cannot all be seen on one screen and users must scroll to view the entire document. Is it unethical for companies to put terms and conditions, especially terms that may cost the consumer, in an electronic document that is too long to read on one screen? Why or why not? Does this differ from having a consumer sign a hard-copy document with terms and conditions printed on it? Why or why not?

(b) The Truth-in-Lending Act requires that credit terms be clearly and conspicuously disclosed in application materials. Assuming that the Best Buy credit-card materials had sufficient legal disclosures, discuss the ethical aspects of businesses strictly following the language of the law as opposed to following the intent of the law.

Legal Reasoning Group Activity

5–10. Global Business Ethics. Pfizer, Inc., developed a new antibiotic called Trovan (trovafloxacinmesylate). Tests showed that in animals Trovan had life-threatening side effects, including joint disease, abnormal cartilage growth, liver damage, and a degenerative bone condition. Several years later, an epidemic of bacterial meningitis swept across Nigeria. Pfizer sent three U.S. physicians to test Trovan on children who were patients in Nigeria's Infectious Disease Hospital. Pfizer did not obtain the patients' consent, alert them to the risks, or tell them that Médecins Sans Frontières (Doctors without Borders) was providing an effective conventional treatment at the same site. Eleven children died in the experiment, and others were left blind, deaf, paralyzed, or brain damaged. Rabi Abdullahi and other Nigerian children filed a suit in a U.S. federal court against Pfizer, alleging a violation of a customary international law norm prohibiting involuntary medical experimentation on humans. (See *Global Business Ethics*.)

(a) One group should use the principles of ethical reasoning discussed in this chapter to develop three arguments that Pfizer's conduct was a violation of ethical standards.

(b) A second group should take a pro-Pfizer position and argue that the company did not violate any ethical standards (and counter the first group).

(c) A third group should come up with proposals for what Pfizer might have done differently to avert the consequences.

UNIT   Application and Ethics

"Arbitration, No Class Actions"

It is nearly impossible to apply for credit, obtain phone or Internet service, or buy goods online without agreeing to submit any claim arising from the deal to arbitration. This is also true with respect to employment—job applicants are generally informed by a potential employer that "any controversy or claim arising out of or relating to this employment application shall be settled by arbitration."[1]

By including arbitration clauses in consumer and employment contracts, businesses can prevent customers and employees from getting their day in court. Claims removed from consideration by the courts in favor of arbitration have involved theft, fraud, sexual harassment, employment discrimination, and other serious issues.

Class Action

A *class action* is a suit in which a large number of plaintiffs file a complaint as a group. A class action can increase the efficiency of the legal process and lower the costs to the parties. It can be an important method by which plaintiffs with similar claims seek relief. More importantly, a class action may be the best means by which the costs of wrongdoing can be imposed on a wrongdoer.

Best Means to Stop a Bad Practice In some circumstances, a class-action suit may be the only practical method for a group of individuals to stop an allegedly harmful business practice. For example, suppose a business pads all of its customers' bills with an unexpected fee—adding up to millions in profit for the business. An individual customer may find it too costly to bring suit against the business or even to engage in arbitration to contest the charge. But a number of customers together could afford to fight the charge.

Groundless Claims and High Fees "Arbitration, No Class Actions," states the terms of use for Budget Rent a Car System, Inc.[2] Everyone who rents a car from Budget must agree to these terms. Businesses, such as Budget, assert that class-action suits are fomented by lawyers, who make millions of dollars in fees. Businesses claim that they have no choice but to settle such claims, even those that are groundless. Arbitration, they argue, can prevent these consequences.

Arbitration

Arbitration is a method of alternative dispute resolution in which a dispute is submitted to a third party (an arbitrator), who listens to the parties, reviews the evidence, and renders a decision. Arbitration clauses can be mandatory or voluntary. A dispute that is subject to mandatory

Continues

---

1. American Arbitration Association, *Drafting Dispute Resolution Clauses: A Practical Guide*, https://www.adr.org/aaa/ShowPDF?doc=ADRSTG_002540 (Nov. 6, 2015).
2. Budget Rent a Car System, Inc., *Terms of Use*, http://www.budget.com /budgetWeb/html/en/customer/termsofuse.html (Nov. 6, 2015).

Application and Ethics

arbitration must be resolved through arbitration. The parties give up their right to sue in court, participate in a class action, or appeal the arbitration decision.

Professional and Unbiased Businesses argue that class-action suits are unnecessary because individuals can more easily resolve their complaints through arbitration. With arbitration, disputes can be resolved quickly without complicated procedures, the limits of judicial rules, or the time constraints of a crowded court's schedule.

Proponents of arbitration also contend that arbitrators can act professionally and without bias. The American Arbitration Association and JAMS, the two largest arbitration firms, claim to ensure a professional and unbiased process. These organizations require an arbitrator to disclose any conflict of interest before taking a case, for instance.

Biased and Unprofessional Opponents of arbitration emphasize that a party's right to appeal an arbitrator's handling of a case and its outcome is limited. Questions about a witness's testimony, a party's handling of the evidence, an arbitrator's potential conflict of interest, and many other issues are not grounds for appeal to a court.

Arbitrators often depend for their business on a company against whom a customer or employee may have a grievance. An arbitrator may handle many cases involving the same company and may therefore consider the company his or her client. For this reason, critics argue that an arbitrator is more likely to rule in favor of the business, regardless of the merits of a claim against it.

What Do the Courts Say?

Most plaintiffs who are blocked from pursuing their claim as a group drop their case. Furthermore, in four out of five class actions filed between 2014 and 2016, judges remanded the disputes to arbitration. During the same period, only about five hundred consumers went to arbitration over a dispute of $2,500 or less. Among those contesting a credit card or loan fee, two-thirds received no award of money in arbitration.

In other words, individual consumers whose only recourse against a company is arbitration do not normally prevail in their claims. Despite this history, recent decisions by the United States Supreme Court upheld the use of arbitration clauses in consumer and merchant contracts to prohibit class-action suits.

Class Actions Interfere with Arbitration Vincent and Liza Concepcion, along with other consumers, filed a class action in a California state court against AT&T Mobility LLC, alleging that the company had promised them a free phone if they agreed to service but actually charged them $30.22 for the phone. AT&T responded that a class-action ban in an arbitration clause in the customers' contracts barred the suit. The court ruled that the ban was unconscionable.

AT&T appealed to the United States Supreme Court, which reasoned that "requiring the availability of class-wide arbitration interferes with fundamental attributes of arbitration." The main purpose of the federal law that applied in this case—the Federal Arbitration Act—"is to ensure the enforcement of arbitration agreements according to their terms." This conclusion relegated *state* law on this issue, including California's ruling, to the sidelines.[3]

---

3. *AT&T Mobility LLC v. Concepcion*, 563 U.S. 333, 131 S.Ct. 1740, 179 L.Ed.2d 742 (2011).

UNIT   Application and Ethics

Arbitration Clauses Trump Class Actions Meanwhile, Alan Carlson, the owner of the restaurant Italian Colors, pursued a suit against American Express Company over the fee that the company assessed merchants to process American Express credit-card charges. Carlson argued that a class-action ban in an arbitration clause in the company's merchant contract prevented merchants from exercising their *federal* right to fight a monopoly. None of the merchants could afford to fight the charge individually.

On appeal, the Supreme Court ruled in favor of American Express. The Court stated that federal antitrust "laws do not guarantee an affordable procedural path to the vindication of every claim."[4] Under this decision, an arbitration clause can outlaw a class action even if it is the only realistic, practical way to bring a case.

More recently, the U.S. Court of Appeals for the Fifth Circuit concluded that employers who require prospective employees to sign mandatory arbitration agreements do not violate the National Labor Relations Act.[5]

Ethical Connection

Some persons would contend that a business's principal ethical obligation is to make a profit for its owners. Others might propose that a business take a number of stakeholders' perspectives into account when deciding on a course of action. Still others might insist that a business has a responsibility to act chiefly in the best interests of society. And there may be some who would impose a different ethical standard—religious, philosophical, or political.

Whichever standard is applied, a business has an interest in staying in business. Sometimes, a class action may be based on a groundless claim and brought for the sole purpose of generating a fee for the lawyer who brings it. There is no ethical requirement for a business to exhaust its assets to litigate or settle such a case.

Other times, though, a class action may be the best means of curbing a bad business practice. In that circumstance, engaging in harmful conduct and then cutting off an important means of redress for those harmed by the conduct cannot be seen as ethical.

Ethics Question *Is it unethical for a business to include an arbitration clause with a class-action ban in its contracts with customers, employees, and other businesses? Discuss.*

Critical Thinking *Many businesses include opt-out provisions in their arbitration clauses, but few consumers and employees take advantage of them. Why?*

---

4. *American Express Co. v. Italian Colors Restaurant*, 570 U.S. 333, 133 S.Ct. 2304, 186 L.Ed.2d 417 (2013).
5. *Murphy Oil USA, Inc. v. National Labor Relations Board*, 808 F.3d 1013 (5th Cir. 2015).

Answers to the *Issue Spotters*

1. *Does this raise an ethical conflict between Acme's employees? Between Acme and its employees? Between Acme and its shareholders? Explain your answers.* When a corporation decides to respond to what it sees as a moral obligation to correct for past discrimination by adjusting pay differences among its employees, an ethical conflict is raised between the firm and its employees and between the firm and its shareholders. This dilemma arises directly out of the effect such a decision has on the firm's profits. If satisfying this obligation increases profitability, then the dilemma is easily resolved in favor of "doing the right thing."

2. *Does Delta have an ethical duty to remove this product from the market, even if the injuries result only from misuse? Why or why not?* Maybe. On the one hand, it is not the company's "fault" when a product is misused. Also, keeping the product on the market is not a violation of the law, and stopping sales would hurt profits. On the other hand, suspending sales could reduce suffering and could stop potential negative publicity.

Sample Answers for *Business Case Problems with Sample Answer*

Problem 5–3. *Online Privacy.* Facebook created a program that makes decisions for users. Using duty-based ethics, many believe that privacy is an extremely important right that should be fiercely protected. Accordingly, any program that has a default of giving out information is unethical. Facebook should create the program as an opt-in program. In addition, under the Kantian categorical imperative, if every company created opt-out programs that disclosed potentially personal information, the concept of privacy may be reduced to a theoretical concept only.

One could argue that this reduction or elimination of privacy would not make the world a better place. From a utilitarian or outcome-based approach, the benefits of an opt-out program might be in ease of creation and start up, as well as ease of recruiting partner programs. The detriment is the elimination of choice on the part of users to disclose information about themselves. An opt-in program maintains that user control but may be harder to start, as it requires more marketing up front in order to convince users to opt in.

Torts and Crimes

BUSINESS LAW

CLARKSON · MILLER · CROSS

CHAPTER

Tort Law

Part of doing business today—and, indeed, part of everyday life—is the risk of being involved in a lawsuit. The list of circumstances in which businesspersons can be sued is long and varied. A customer who is injured by a security guard at a business establishment, for instance, may sue the business owner, claiming that the security guard's conduct was intentionally wrongful. A person who slips and falls at a retail store may sue the company for negligence.

Any time that one party's allegedly wrongful conduct causes injury to another, an action may arise under the law of *torts* (the word *tort* is French for "wrong"). Through tort law, society compensates those who have suffered injuries as a result of the wrongful conduct of others. Many of the lawsuits brought by or against business firms are based on various tort theories.

6–1 The Basis of Tort Law

Two notions serve as the basis of all **torts:** wrongs and compensation. Tort law is designed to compensate those who have suffered a loss or injury due to another person's wrongful act. In a tort action, one person or group brings a lawsuit against another person or group to obtain compensation (monetary damages) or other relief for the harm suffered.

6–1a The Purpose of Tort Law

Generally, the purpose of tort law is to provide remedies for the violation of various *protected interests.* Society recognizes an interest in personal physical safety. Thus, tort law provides remedies for acts that cause physical injury or that interfere with physical security and freedom of movement. Society also recognizes an interest in protecting property, and tort law provides remedies for acts that cause destruction of or damage to property.

6–1b Damages Available in Tort Actions

Because the purpose of tort law is to compensate the injured party for the damage suffered, you need to have an understanding of the types of damages that plaintiffs seek in tort actions. Note that legal usage distinguishes between the terms *damage* and *damages. Damage* refers to harm or injury to persons or property, while **damages** refers to monetary compensation for such harm or injury.

Compensatory Damages A plaintiff is awarded **compensatory damages** to compensate or reimburse the plaintiff for actual losses. Thus, the goal is to make the plaintiff whole and put her or him in the same position that she or he would have been in had the tort not occurred. Compensatory damages awards are often broken down into *special damages* and *general damages.*

Special damages compensate the plaintiff for quantifiable monetary losses, such as medical expenses and lost wages and benefits (now and in the future). Special damages might also be awarded to compensate for extra costs, the loss of irreplaceable items, and the costs of repairing or replacing damaged property.

■ **CASE IN POINT 6.1** Seaway Marine Transport operates the *Enterprise,* a large cargo ship, which has twenty-two hatches for storing coal. When the *Enterprise* positioned itself to receive a load of coal on the shores of Lake Erie, in Ohio, it struck a land-based coal-loading machine operated by Bessemer & Lake Erie Railroad Company. A federal court found Seaway liable and awarded $522,000 in special damages to compensate Bessemer for the cost of repairing the damage to the loading boom.[1] ■

General damages compensate individuals (not companies) for the nonmonetary aspects of the harm suffered, such as pain and suffering. A court might award general damages for physical or emotional pain and suffering, loss of companionship, loss of consortium (losing

---

1. *Bessemer & Lake Erie Railroad Co. v. Seaway Marine Transport,* 357 F.3d 596 (6th Cir. 2010).

the emotional and physical benefits of a spousal relationship), disfigurement, loss of reputation, or loss or impairment of mental or physical capacity.

Punitive Damages Occasionally, the courts also award **punitive damages** in tort cases to punish the wrongdoer and deter others from similar wrongdoing. Punitive damages are appropriate only when the defendant's conduct was particularly egregious (flagrant) or reprehensible (blameworthy).

Usually, this means that punitive damages are available in *intentional* tort actions and only rarely in negligence lawsuits (negligence actions will be discussed later in this chapter). They may be awarded, however, in suits involving *gross negligence*. Gross negligence can be defined as an intentional failure to perform a manifest duty in reckless disregard of the consequences of such a failure for the life or property of another.

Courts exercise great restraint in granting punitive damages to plaintiffs in tort actions because punitive damages are subject to limitations under the due process clause of the U.S. Constitution. The United States Supreme Court has held that to the extent that an award of punitive damages is grossly excessive, it furthers no legitimate purpose and violates due process requirements.[2] Consequently, an appellate court will sometimes reduce the amount of punitive damages awarded to a plaintiff on the ground that it is excessive and thereby violates the due process clause.

Legislative Caps on Damages State laws may limit the amount of damages—both punitive and general—that can be awarded to the plaintiff. More than half of the states have placed caps ranging from $250,000 to $750,000 on noneconomic general damages (such as for pain and suffering), especially in medical malpractice suits. More than thirty states have limited punitive damages, with some imposing outright bans.

6-1c Classification of Torts

There are two broad classifications of torts: *intentional torts* and *unintentional torts* (torts involving negligence). The classification of a particular tort depends largely on how the tort occurs (intentionally or negligently) and the surrounding circumstances. Intentional torts result from the intentional violation of person or property (fault plus intent). Negligence results from the breach of a duty to act reasonably (fault without intent).

---

2. *State Farm Mutual Automobile Insurance Co. v. Campbell*, 538 U.S. 408, 123 S.Ct. 1513, 155 L.Ed.2d 585 (2003).

6-1d Defenses

Even if a plaintiff proves all the elements of a tort, the defendant can raise a number of legally recognized *defenses* (reasons why the plaintiff should not obtain damages). A successful defense releases the defendant from partial or full liability for the tortious act.

The defenses available may vary depending on the specific tort involved. A common defense to intentional torts against persons, for instance, is *consent*. When a person consents to the act that damages her or him, there is generally no liability. The most widely used defense in negligence actions is *comparative negligence*.

In addition, most states have a *statute of limitations* that establishes the time limit (often two years from the date of discovering the harm) within which a particular type of lawsuit can be filed. After that time period has run, the plaintiff can no longer file a claim.

6-2 Intentional Torts against Persons

An **intentional tort,** as the term implies, requires intent. The **tortfeasor** (the one committing the tort) must intend to commit an act, the consequences of which interfere with another's personal or business interests in a way not permitted by law. An evil or harmful motive is not required—in fact, the person committing the action may even have a beneficial motive for doing what turns out to be a tortious act.

In tort law, *intent* means only that the person intended the consequences of his or her act or knew with substantial certainty that specific consequences would result from the act. The law generally assumes that individuals intend the *normal* consequences of their actions. Thus, forcefully pushing another—even if done in jest—is an intentional tort (if injury results), because the object of a strong push can ordinarily be expected to fall down.

In addition, intent can be transferred when a defendant intends to harm one individual, but unintentionally harms a second person. This is called **transferred intent.** ■ **EXAMPLE 6.2** Alex swings a bat intending to hit Blake but misses and hits Carson instead. Carson can sue Alex for the tort of battery (discussed shortly) because Alex's intent to harm Blake can be transferred to Carson. ■

6-2a Assault

An **assault** is any intentional and unexcused threat of immediate harmful or offensive contact—words or acts that create a reasonably believable threat. An assault can occur even if there is no actual contact with the plaintiff, provided that the defendant's conduct creates a reasonable apprehension of imminent harm in the plaintiff. Tort law aims to protect individuals from having to expect harmful or offensive contact.

6–2b Battery

If the act that created the apprehension is *completed* and results in harm to the plaintiff, it is a **battery**—an unexcused and harmful or offensive physical contact *intentionally* performed. ■ **EXAMPLE 6.3** Ivan threatens Jean with a gun and then shoots her. The pointing of the gun at Jean is an assault. The firing of the gun (if the bullet hits Jean) is a battery. ■

The contact can be harmful, or it can be merely offensive (such as an unwelcome kiss). Physical injury need not occur. The contact can involve any part of the body or anything attached to it—for instance, a hat, a purse, or a jacket. The contact can be made by the defendant or by some force set in motion by the defendant, such as a rock thrown by the defendant. Whether the contact is offensive is determined by the *reasonable person standard*.[3]

If the plaintiff shows that there was contact, and the jury (or judge, if there is no jury) agrees that the contact was offensive, then the plaintiff has a right to compensation. A plaintiff may be compensated for the emotional harm or loss of reputation resulting from a battery, as well as for physical harm. A defendant may assert self-defense or defense of others in an attempt to justify his or her conduct.

6–2c False Imprisonment

False imprisonment is the intentional confinement or restraint of another person's activities without justification. False imprisonment interferes with the freedom to move without restraint. The confinement can be accomplished through the use of physical barriers, physical restraint, or threats of physical force. Moral pressure does not constitute false imprisonment. It is essential that the person being restrained does not wish to be restrained. (The plaintiff's consent to the restraint bars any liability.)

Businesspersons often face suits for false imprisonment after they have attempted to confine a suspected shoplifter for questioning. Under the "privilege to detain" granted to merchants in most states, a merchant can use *reasonable force* to detain or delay persons suspected of shoplifting and hold them for the police. Although laws pertaining to this privilege vary from state to state, generally any detention must be conducted in a *reasonable* manner and for only a *reasonable* length of time. Undue force or unreasonable detention can lead to liability for the business.

Cities and counties may also face lawsuits for false imprisonment if they detain individuals without reason. ■ **CASE IN POINT 6.4** Police arrested Adetokunbo Shoyoye for riding the subway without a ticket and for a theft that had been committed by someone who had stolen his identity. A court ordered him to be released, but a county employee mistakenly confused Shoyoye's paperwork with that of another person who was scheduled to be sent to state prison. As a result, instead of being released, Shoyoye was held in county jail for more than two weeks. Shoyoye later sued the county for false imprisonment and won.[4] ■

6–2d Intentional Infliction of Emotional Distress

The tort of *intentional infliction of emotional distress* involves an intentional act that amounts to extreme and outrageous conduct resulting in severe emotional distress to another. To be **actionable** (capable of serving as the ground for a lawsuit), the act must be extreme and outrageous to the point that it exceeds the bounds of decency accepted by society.

Outrageous Conduct Courts in most jurisdictions are wary of emotional distress claims and confine them to situations involving truly outrageous behavior. Generally, repeated annoyances (such as those experienced by a person who is being stalked), coupled with threats, are enough. Acts that cause indignity or annoyance alone usually are not sufficient.

■ **EXAMPLE 6.5** A father attacks a man who has had consensual sexual relations with the father's nineteen-year-old daughter. The father handcuffs the man to a steel pole and threatens to kill him unless he leaves town immediately. The father's conduct may be sufficiently extreme and outrageous to be actionable as an intentional infliction of emotional distress. ■

Limited by the First Amendment When the outrageous conduct consists of speech about a public figure,

---

3. The *reasonable person standard* is an "objective" test of how a reasonable person would have acted under the same circumstances. See "The Duty of Care and Its Breach" later in this chapter.

4. *Shoyoye v. County of Los Angeles*, 203 Cal.App.4th 947, 137 Cal.Rptr.3d 839 (2012).

the First Amendment's guarantee of freedom of speech also limits emotional distress claims.

■ **CASE IN POINT 6.6** *Hustler* magazine once printed a false advertisement that showed a picture of the late Reverend Jerry Falwell and described him as having lost his virginity to his mother in an outhouse while he was drunk. Falwell sued the magazine for intentional infliction of emotional distress and won, but the United States Supreme Court overturned the decision. The Court held that parodies of public figures are protected under the First Amendment from intentional infliction of emotional distress claims. (The Court uses the same standards that apply to public figures in defamation lawsuits, discussed next.)[5] ■

6–2e Defamation

The freedom of speech guaranteed by the First Amendment is not absolute. The courts are required to balance the vital guarantee of free speech against other pervasive and strong social interests, including society's interest in preventing and redressing attacks on reputation.

Defamation of character involves wrongfully hurting a person's good reputation. The law imposes a general duty on all persons to refrain from making false, defamatory *statements of fact* about others. Breaching this duty in writing or other permanent form (such as a digital recording) involves the tort of **libel.** Breaching this duty orally involves the tort of **slander.** The tort of defamation also arises when a false statement of fact is made about a person's product, business, or legal ownership rights to property.

Establishing defamation involves proving the following elements:

1. The defendant made a false statement of fact.
2. The statement was understood as being about the plaintiff and tended to harm the plaintiff's reputation.
3. The statement was published to at least one person other than the plaintiff.
4. If the plaintiff is a public figure, she or he must also prove *actual malice,* discussed later in the chapter.

The following case involved the application of free speech guarantees to online reviews of professional services.

---

5. *Hustler Magazine, Inc. v. Falwell*, 485 U.S. 46, 108 S.Ct. 876, 99 L.Ed.2d 41 (1988). For another example of how the courts protect parody, see *Busch v. Viacom International, Inc.*, 477 F.Supp.2d 764 (N.D.Tex. 2007), involving a false endorsement of televangelist Pat Robertson's diet shake.

Case Analysis 6.1

Blake v. Giustibelli

District Court of Appeal of Florida, Fourth District, 182 So.3d 881, 41 Fla.L.Weekly D122 (2016).

In the Language of the Court
CIKLIN, C.J. [Chief Judge]

* * * *

[Ann-Marie] Giustibelli represented Copia Blake in a dissolution of marriage proceeding brought against Peter Birzon. After a breakdown in the attorney-client relationship between Giustibelli and her client[,] Blake, and oddly, Birzon as well, took to the Internet to post defamatory reviews of Giustibelli. In response, Giustibelli brought suit [in a Florida state court against Blake and Birzon], pleading a count for libel.

Blake's and Birzon's posted Internet reviews contained the following statements:

This lawyer represented me in my divorce. She was combative and explosive and took my divorce to a level of anger which caused major suffering of my minor children. She insisted I was an emotionally abused wife who couldn't make rational decisions which caused my case to drag on in the system for a year and a half so her FEES would continue to multiply!! She misrepresented her fees with regards to the contract I initially signed. The contract she submitted to the courts for her fees were 4 times her original quote and pages of the original had been exchanged to support her claims, only the signature page was the same. Shame on me that I did not have an original copy, but like an idiot * * * I trusted my lawyer. Don't mistake sincerity for honesty because I assure you, that in this attorney's case, they are NOT the same thing. She absolutely perpetuates

the horrible image of attorneys who are only out for the money and themselves. Although I know this isn't the case and there are some very good honest lawyers out there, Mrs. Giustibelli is simply not one of the "good ones." Horrible horrible experience. Use anyone else, it would have to be a better result.

* * * *

No integrity. Will say one thing and do another. Her fees outweigh the truth. Altered her charges to 4 times the original quote with no explanation. Do not use her. Don't mistake sincerity for honesty. In her case, they're not at all the same. Will literally lie to your face if it means more money for her. Get someone else.

Case 6.1 Continues

* * * Anyone else would do a superior effort for you.

* * * *

I accepted an initial VERY fair offer from my ex. Mrs. Giustibelli convinced me to "crush" him and that I could have permanent etc. Spent over a year (and 4 times her original estimate) to arrive at the same place we started at. Caused unnecessary chaos and fear with my kids, convinced me that my ex cheated (which he didn't), that he was hiding money (which he wasn't), and was mad at ME when I realized her fee circus had gone on long enough and finally said "stop." Altered her fee structures, actually replaced original documents with others to support her charges and generally gave the kind of poor service you only hear about. I'm not a disgruntled ex-wife. I'm just the foolish person who believes that a person's word should be backed by integrity. Not even remotely true in this case. I've had 2 prior attorneys and never ever have I seen ego and monies be so blatantly out of control.

Both Blake and Birzon admitted to posting the reviews on various Internet sites. The evidence showed that Blake had agreed to pay her attorney the amount reflected on the written retainer agreement—$300 an hour. Blake and Birzon both admitted at trial that Giustibelli had not charged Blake four times more than what was quoted in the agreement. The court entered judgment in favor of Giustibelli and awarded punitive damages of $350,000.

On appeal, Blake and Birzon argue that their Internet reviews constituted statements of opinion and thus were protected by the First Amendment and not actionable as defamation. We disagree. *An action for libel will lie for a false and unprivileged publication by letter, or otherwise, which exposes a person to distrust, hatred, contempt, ridicule or obloquy [censure or disgrace] or which causes such person to be avoided, or which has a tendency to injure such person in their office, occupation, business or employment.* [Emphasis added.]

Here, all the reviews contained allegations that Giustibelli lied to Blake regarding the attorney's fee. Two of the reviews contained the allegation that Giustibelli falsified a contract. These are factual allegations, and the evidence showed they were false.

* * * *

Affirmed.

Legal Reasoning Questions

1. What is the standard for the protection of free speech guaranteed by the First Amendment?

2. How did this standard apply to the statements posted online by Blake and Birzon?

3. The First Amendment normally protects statements of opinion, and this can be an effective defense against a charge of defamation. Does it seem reasonable to disregard this defense, however, if *any* assertion of fact within a statement of opinion is false? Explain.

Statement-of-Fact Requirement Often at issue in defamation lawsuits (including online defamation) is whether the defendant made a statement of fact or a *statement of opinion*. Statements of opinion normally are not actionable, because they are protected under the First Amendment.

In other words, making a negative statement about another person is not defamation unless the statement is false and represents something as a fact rather than a personal opinion. ■ **EXAMPLE 6.7** The statement "Lane cheats on his taxes," if false, can lead to liability for defamation. The statement "Lane is a jerk" cannot constitute defamation because it is clearly an opinion. ■

The Publication Requirement The basis of the tort of defamation is the publication of a statement or statements that hold an individual up to contempt, ridicule, or hatred. *Publication* here means that the defamatory statements are communicated (either intentionally or accidentally) to persons other than the defamed party.

The courts have generally held that even dictating a letter to a secretary constitutes publication, although the publication may be privileged (a concept that will be explained shortly). Moreover, if a third party merely overhears defamatory statements by chance, the courts usually hold that this also constitutes publication. Defamatory statements made via the Internet are actionable as well. Note also that any individual who repeats or republishes defamatory statements normally is liable even if that person reveals the source of the statements.

■ **CASE IN POINT 6.8** Eddy Ramirez, a meat cutter at Costco Wholesale Corporation, was involved in a workplace incident with a coworker, and Costco gave him a notice of suspension. After an investigation in which coworkers were interviewed, Costco fired Ramirez. Ramirez sued, claiming that the suspension notice was defamatory. The court ruled in Costco's favor. Ramirez could not establish defamation, because he had not shown that the suspension notice was published to any third parties. Costco did nothing beyond what was necessary to investigate the events that led to Ramirez's termination.[6] ■

Damages for Libel Once a defendant's liability for libel is established, general damages are presumed as a matter of law. General damages are designed to compensate the plaintiff for nonspecific harms such as disgrace or dishonor in the eyes of the community, humiliation, injured reputation, and emotional distress—harms that are difficult to measure. In other words, to recover damages, the plaintiff need not prove that he or she was actually harmed in any specific way as a result of the libelous statement.

Damages for Slander In contrast to cases alleging libel, in a case alleging slander, the plaintiff must prove *special damages* to establish the defendant's liability. The plaintiff must show that the slanderous statement caused her or him to suffer actual economic or monetary losses.

Unless this initial hurdle of proving special damages is overcome, a plaintiff alleging slander normally cannot go forward with the suit and recover any damages. This requirement is imposed in slander cases because oral statements have a temporary quality. In contrast, a libelous (written) statement has the quality of permanence and can be circulated widely, especially through tweets and blogs. Also, libel usually results from some degree of deliberation by the author.

Slander *Per Se* Exceptions to the burden of proving special damages in cases alleging slander are made for certain types of slanderous statements. If a false statement constitutes "slander *per se*," it is actionable with no proof of special damages required. In most states, the following four types of declarations are considered to be slander *per se:*

1. A statement that another has a "loathsome" disease (such as a sexually transmitted disease).
2. A statement that another has committed improprieties while engaging in a profession or trade.
3. A statement that another has committed or has been imprisoned for a serious crime.

4. A statement that a person is unchaste or has engaged in serious sexual misconduct. (This usually applies only to unmarried persons and sometimes only to women.)

Defenses to Defamation Truth is normally an absolute defense against a defamation charge. In other words, if a defendant in a defamation case can prove that the allegedly defamatory statements of fact were true, normally no tort has been committed.

■ **CASE IN POINT 6.9** David McKee, a neurologist, went to examine a patient who had been transferred from the intensive care unit (ICU) to a private room. In the room were family members of the patient, including his son. The patient's son later made the following post on a "rate your doctor" Web site: "[Dr. McKee] seemed upset that my father had been moved [into a private room]. Never having met my father or his family, Dr. McKee said 'When you weren't in ICU, I had to spend time finding out if you transferred or died.' When we gaped at him, he said 'Well, 44 percent of hemorrhagic strokes die within 30 days. I guess this is the better option.'"

McKee filed suit for defamation but lost. The court found that all the statements made by the son were essentially true, and truth is a complete defense to a defamation action.[7] ■ In other words, true statements are not actionable no matter how disparaging. Even the presence of minor inaccuracies of expression or detail does not render basically true statements false.

Other defenses to defamation may exist if the speech is privileged or if it concerns a public figure. We discuss these defenses next. Note that the majority of defamation actions are filed in state courts, and state laws differ somewhat in the defenses they allow.

Privileged Communications. In some circumstances, a person will not be liable for defamatory statements because she or he enjoys a **privilege,** or immunity. Privileged communications are of two types: absolute and qualified.[8] Only in judicial proceedings and certain government proceedings is an *absolute privilege* granted. Thus, statements made by attorneys and judges in the courtroom during a trial are absolutely privileged, as are statements made by government officials during legislative debate.

---

6. *Ramirez v. Costco Wholesale Corp.*, 2014 WL 2696737 (Ct.Sup.Ct. 2014).

7. *McKee v. Laurion*, 825 N.W.2d 725 (Minn.Sup. 2013).
8. Note that the term *privileged communication* in this context is not the same as privileged communication between a professional, such as an attorney, and his or her client.

In other situations, a person will not be liable for defamatory statements because he or she has a *qualified,* or *conditional, privilege.* An employer's statements in written evaluations of employees, for instance, are protected by a qualified privilege. Generally, if the statements are made in good faith and the publication is limited to those who have a legitimate interest in the communication, the statements fall within the area of qualified privilege.

■ **EXAMPLE 6.10** Jorge has worked at Google for five years and is being considered for a management position. His supervisor, Lydia, writes a memo about Jorge's performance to those evaluating him for the position. The memo contains certain negative statements, which Lydia honestly believes are true. If Lydia limits the disclosure of the memo to company representatives, her statements will likely be protected by a qualified privilege. ■

Public Figures. Politicians, entertainers, professional athletes, and others in the public eye are considered **public figures.** Public figures are regarded as "fair game." False and defamatory statements about public figures that are published in the media will not constitute defamation unless the statements are made with **actual malice.**[9] To be made with actual malice, a statement must be made *with either knowledge of its falsity or a reckless disregard of the truth.*

Statements made about public figures, especially when they are communicated via a public medium, usually relate to matters of general interest. They are made about people who substantially affect all of us. Furthermore, public figures generally have some access to a public medium for answering belittling falsehoods about themselves. For these reasons, public figures have a greater burden of proof in defamation cases—to show actual malice—than do private individuals.

■ **CASE IN POINT 6.11** *In Touch* magazine published a story about a former call girl who claimed to have slept with legendary soccer player David Beckham more than once. Beckham sued *In Touch* magazine for libel, seeking $25 million in damages. He said that he had never met the woman, had not cheated on his wife with her, and had not paid her for sex. After months of litigation, a federal district court dismissed the case because Beckham could not show that the magazine had acted with actual malice. Whether or not the statements in the article were accurate, there was no evidence that the defendants had made the statements with knowledge of their falsity or reckless disregard for the truth.[10] ■

---

9. *New York Times Co. v. Sullivan,* 376 U.S. 254, 84 S.Ct. 710, 11 L.Ed.2d 686 (1964).
10. *Beckham v. Bauer Pub. Co., L.P.,* 2011 WL 977570 (2011).

6–2f Invasion of Privacy

A person has a right to solitude and freedom from prying public eyes—in other words, to privacy. The courts have held that certain amendments to the U.S. Constitution imply a right to privacy. Some state constitutions explicitly provide for privacy rights, as do a number of federal and state statutes.

Tort law also safeguards these rights through the tort of *invasion of privacy.* Generally, to sue successfully for an invasion of privacy, a person must have a reasonable expectation of privacy, and the invasion must be highly offensive. (See this chapter's *Digital Update* feature for a discussion of how invasion of privacy claims can arise when someone posts pictures or videos taken with digital devices.)

Invasion of Privacy under the Common Law
The following four acts qualify as an invasion of privacy under the common law:

1. *Intrusion into an individual's affairs or seclusion.* Invading someone's home or searching someone's briefcase or laptop without authorization is an invasion of privacy. This tort has been held to extend to eavesdropping by wiretap, unauthorized scanning of a bank account, compulsory blood testing, and window peeping. ■ **EXAMPLE 6.12** A female sports reporter for ESPN is digitally videoed while naked through the peephole in the door of her hotel room. She will probably win a lawsuit against the man who took the video and posted it on the Internet. ■

2. *False light.* Publication of information that places a person in a false light is also an invasion of privacy. For instance, writing a story that attributes to a person ideas and opinions not held by that person is an invasion of privacy. (Publishing such a story could involve the tort of defamation as well.) ■ **EXAMPLE 6.13** An Iowa newspaper prints an article saying that nineteen-year-old Yassine Alam is part of the terrorist organization Islamic State of Iraq (ISIL). Next to the article is a photo of Yassine's brother, Salaheddin. Salaheddin can sue the paper for putting him in a false light by using his photo. If the report is not true, and Yassine is not involved with ISIL, Yassine can sue the paper for defamation. ■

3. *Public disclosure of private facts.* This type of invasion of privacy occurs when a person publicly discloses private facts about an individual that an ordinary person would find objectionable or embarrassing. A newspaper account of a private citizen's sex life or financial affairs could be an actionable invasion of

DIGITAL UPDATE — Revenge Porn and Invasion of Privacy

Nearly every digital device today takes photos and videos at virtually no cost. Software allows the recording of conversations via Skype. Many couples immortalize their "private moments" using such digital devices. One partner may take a racy selfie and send it as an attachment to a text message to the other partner, for example.

Occasionally, after a couple breaks off their relationship, one of them seeks a type of digital revenge. The result, called revenge porn, has been defined in the Cyber Civil Rights Initiative as "the online distribution of sexually explicit images of a non-consenting individual with the intent to humiliate that person."

Until relatively recently, few states had criminal statutes that covered revenge porn. Therefore, victims have sued on the basis of (1) invasion of privacy, (2) public disclosure of private facts, and (3) intentional infliction of emotional distress.

It Is More Than Just Pictures and Videos

Perhaps the worst form of revenge porn occurs when the perpetrator provides detailed information about the victim. Such information may include the victim's name, Facebook page, address, and phone number, as well as the victim's workplace and children's names. This information, along with the sexually explicit photos and videos, are posted on hosting Web sites. Many such Web sites have been shut down, as was the case with IsAnybodyDown? and Texxxan.com. But others are still active, usually with offshore servers and foreign domain name owners.

The Injurious Results of Revenge Porn

Of course, victims of revenge porn suffer extreme embarrassment. They may also have their reputations ruined. Some have lost their jobs. Others have been unable to obtain jobs because employers have seen their pictures online. A number of victims have been stalked in the physical world and harassed online and offline. When attempts to have offending photos removed from Web sites have failed, victims have changed their phone numbers and sometimes their names.

A Class-Action Lawsuit

Hollie Toups, along with twenty-two other female plaintiffs, sued the domain name registrar and Web hosting company GoDaddy in a Texas court. Although GoDaddy did not create the defamatory and offensive material at issue, GoDaddy knew of the content and did not remove it. The plaintiffs asserted causes of action "for intentional infliction of emotional distress," among other claims.

Additionally, the plaintiffs argued that "by its knowing participation in these unlawful activities, GoDaddy has also committed the intentional Texas tort of invasion of privacy . . . as well as intrusion on Plaintiffs' right to seclusion, the public disclosure of their private facts, [and] the wrongful appropriation of their names and likenesses. . . ." GoDaddy sought to dismiss the case, and an appeals court eventually granted the motion to dismiss.[a]

Another Texas woman had better luck. The woman's ex-boyfriend had uploaded videos of her to YouTube and other sites. At the time she made the complaint, revenge porn was not a crime in Texas. Nevertheless, in a jury trial in 2014, she won a $500,000 award. Since then, a handful of states have made revenge porn a crime. In 2015, a California man, Kevin Bollaert, was convicted for creating a revenge porn Web site and sentenced to serve eighteen years in prison.

Critical Thinking *Should domain name hosting companies be liable for revenge porn?*

a. *GoDaddy.com, LLC. v. Toups,* 429 S.W.3d 752 (Tex.App.—Beaumont 2014).

---

privacy. This is so even if the information revealed is true, because it should not be a matter of public concern.

4. *Appropriation of identity.* Using a person's name, picture, likeness, or other identifiable characteristic for commercial purposes without permission is also an invasion of privacy. An individual's right to privacy normally includes the right to the exclusive use of her or his identity. ■ **EXAMPLE 6.14** An advertising agency asks a singer with a distinctive voice and stage presence to take part in a marketing campaign for a new automobile. The singer rejects the offer. If the

agency then uses someone who imitates the singer's voice and dance moves in the ad, it will be actionable as an appropriation of identity. ∎

Appropriation Statutes Most states today have codified the common law tort of appropriation of identity in statutes that establish the distinct tort of **appropriation,** or **right of publicity.** States differ as to the degree of likeness that is required to impose liability for appropriation, however.

Some courts have held that even when an animated character in a video or a video game is made to look like an actual person, there are not enough similarities to constitute appropriation. ∎ **CASE IN POINT 6.15** Robert Burck is a street entertainer in New York City who has become famous as "The Naked Cowboy." Burck performs wearing only a white cowboy hat, white cowboy boots, and white underwear. He carries a guitar strategically placed to give the illusion of nudity. Burck sued Mars, Inc., the maker of M&Ms candy, over a video it showed on billboards in Times Square that depicted a blue M&M dressed exactly like The Naked Cowboy. The court, however, held that the use of Burck's signature costume did not amount to appropriation.[11] ∎

---

11. *Burck v. Mars, Inc.,* 571 F.Supp.2d 446 (S.D.N.Y. 2008).

6–2g Fraudulent Misrepresentation

A misrepresentation leads another to believe in a condition that is different from the condition that actually exists. Although persons sometimes make misrepresentations accidentally because they are unaware of the existing facts, the tort of **fraudulent misrepresentation (fraud),** involves *intentional* deceit for personal gain. The tort includes several elements:

1. A misrepresentation of material facts or conditions with knowledge that they are false or with reckless disregard for the truth.
2. An intent to induce another party to rely on the misrepresentation.
3. A justifiable reliance on the misrepresentation by the deceived party.
4. Damages suffered as a result of that reliance.
5. A causal connection between the misrepresentation and the injury suffered.

For fraud to occur, more than mere **puffery,** or *seller's talk,* must be involved. Fraud exists only when a person represents as a fact something he or she knows is untrue. For instance, it is fraud to claim that the roof of a building does not leak when one knows that it does. Facts are objectively ascertainable, whereas seller's talk (such as "I am the best accountant in town") is not, because the use of the word *best* is subjective.

In the following case, the court considered each of the elements of fraud.

Case 6.2

Revell v. Guido

New York Supreme Court, Appellate Division, Third Department, 124 A.D.3d 1006, 2 N.Y.S.3d 252 (2015).

Background and Facts Joseph Guido bought a parcel of land in Stillwater, New York, that contained nine rental houses. The houses shared a waste disposal system that was defective. Guido had a new septic system installed. When town officials discovered sewage on the property, Guido had the system partially replaced. Prospective buyers, including Danny Revell, were given a property information sheet that stated, "Septic system totally new—each field totally replaced." In response to a questionnaire from the buyers' bank, Guido denied any knowledge of environmental problems.

A month after the buyers bought the houses, the septic system failed and required substantial repairs. The lender foreclosed on the property. The buyers filed a suit in a New York state court against Guido and his firm, Real Property Solutions, LLC, alleging fraud. A jury found fraud and awarded damages. The court issued a judgment in the plaintiffs' favor. The defendants appealed.

In the Language of the Court

EGAN, Jr., J.: [Judge:]
* * * *

To prevail upon their cause of action for fraud, plaintiffs were required to establish that defendants, with the intent to deceive, misrepresented or omitted a material fact that they knew to be false and that plaintiffs,

Case 6.2 Continued

in turn, justifiably relied upon such misrepresentation or omission, thereby incurring damages. As to the misrepresentation element, plaintiffs point to the statement made on the property information sheet * * * , as well as Guido's responses to certain of the inquiries contained on the environmental questionnaire. In this regard, the record reflects that the [replacement] septic system * * * was not "totally new," as it retained the original pump house structure and, more to the point, utilized the holding tanks that originally were part of the system * * * . There also is no question that Guido provided false answers to various inquiries posed on the environmental questionnaire. For example, Guido disavowed any knowledge of "governmental notification relating to past or recurrent violations of environmental laws with respect to the property * * * "—despite having been advised by the Town of Stillwater * * * that partially treated sewage was discovered on the property. [Emphasis added.]

As to the intent element, * * * given the arguably cavalier [offhand] manner in which Guido completed the environmental questionnaire, as well as his extensive knowledge regarding the * * * problems with the original septic system * * * , the jury could properly find that Guido made the cited misrepresentations with the intent to deceive plaintiffs.

With respect to the issue of justifiable reliance, Revell * * * conducted a visual inspection of the property prior to making an offer and did not observe any conditions indicative of a problem with the septic system. * * * If a septic system was represented to be "totally new" and a visual inspection of the property did not reveal any red flags, [that is,] boggy areas, odors or liquids bubbling up to the surface, one would assume that the system was working properly. * * * The jury [could] find that plaintiffs' reliance upon the representation contained in the property information sheet was reasonable.

* * * *

Nor are we persuaded that plaintiffs failed to tender sufficient admissible proof to substantiate the damages awarded by the jury. During the trial, the parties stipulated to the admission into evidence of a binder containing, among other things, an abundance of receipts, invoices, billing statements and canceled checks detailing plaintiffs' expenditures related to the subject property—and plaintiffs' forensic accountant, in turn, utilized such documents to arrive at a damages figure. * * * We are satisfied that plaintiffs tendered sufficient admissible proof to sustain the damages awarded by the jury.

Decision and Remedy *The state intermediate appellate court affirmed the lower court's judgment in the plaintiffs' favor. The facts of the case and the plaintiffs' proof met all of the requirements for establishing fraud.*

Critical Thinking

- **Legal Environment** *Financing for the purchase of the property was conditioned on the bank's review of Guido's answers to the environmental questionnaire. How could the court conclude that the plaintiffs justifiably relied on misrepresentations made to the bank? Explain.*
- **What If the Facts Were Different?** *If a visual inspection of the property had revealed "boggy areas, odors or liquids bubbling up to the surface" indicating that the septic system was not working properly, would the outcome of this case have been different?*

Statement of Fact versus Opinion Normally, the tort of fraudulent misrepresentation occurs only when there is reliance on a *statement of fact*. Sometimes, however, reliance on a *statement of opinion* may involve the tort of fraudulent misrepresentation if the individual making the statement of opinion has superior knowledge of the subject matter. For instance, when a lawyer makes a statement of opinion about the law in a state in which the lawyer is licensed to practice, a court might treat it as a statement of fact.

Negligent Misrepresentation Sometimes, a tort action can arise from misrepresentations that are made negligently rather than intentionally. The key difference between intentional and negligent misrepresentation is whether the person making the misrepresentation had actual knowledge of its falsity. Negligent misrepresentation requires only that the person making the statement or omission did not have a reasonable basis for believing its truthfulness.

Liability for negligent misrepresentation usually arises when the defendant who made the misrepresentation owed a duty of care to the plaintiff to supply correct information. (We discuss the duty of care in more detail later in the chapter.) Statements or omissions made by attorneys and accountants to their clients, for instance, can lead to liability for negligent misrepresentation.

6–2h Abusive or Frivolous Litigation

Tort law recognizes that people have a right not to be sued without a legally just and proper reason, and therefore it protects individuals from the misuse of litigation. Torts related to abusive litigation include malicious prosecution and abuse of process. If a party initiates a lawsuit out of malice and without a legitimate legal reason, and ends up losing the suit, that party can be sued for *malicious prosecution*. *Abuse of process* can apply to any person using a legal process against another in an improper manner or to accomplish a purpose for which the process was not designed.

The key difference between the torts of abuse of process and malicious prosecution is the level of proof. Unlike malicious prosecution, abuse of process is not limited to prior litigation and does not require the plaintiff to prove malice. It can be based on the wrongful use of subpoenas, court orders to attach or seize real property, or other types of formal legal process.

Concept Summary 6.1 reviews intentional torts against persons.

Concept Summary 6.1

Intentional Torts against Persons

Assault and Battery	Any unexcused and intentional act that causes another person to be apprehensive of immediate harm is an assault. An assault resulting in physical contact is a battery.
False Imprisonment	An intentional confinement or restraint of another person's movement without justification.
Intentional Infliction of Emotional Distress	An intentional act that amounts to extreme and outrageous conduct resulting in severe emotional distress to another.
Defamation (Libel or Slander)	A false statement of fact, not made under privilege, that is communicated to a third person and that causes damage to a person's reputation. For public figures, the plaintiff must also prove that the statement was made with actual malice.
Invasion of Privacy	Publishing or otherwise making known or using information relating to a person's private life and affairs, with which the public has no legitimate concern, without that person's permission or approval.
Fraudulent Misrepresentation (Fraud)	A false representation made by one party, through misstatement of facts or through conduct, with the intention of deceiving another and on which the other reasonably relies to his or her detriment.
Abusive or Frivolous Litigation	The filing of a lawsuit without legitimate grounds and with malice. Alternatively, the use of a legal process in an improper manner.

6-2i Wrongful Interference

The torts known as *business torts* generally involve wrongful interference with another's business rights. Public policy favors free competition, and these torts protect against tortious interference with legitimate business. Business torts involving wrongful interference generally fall into two categories: interference with a contractual relationship and interference with a business relationship.

Wrongful Interference with a Contractual Relationship Three elements are necessary for wrongful interference with a contractual relationship to occur:

1. A valid, enforceable contract must exist between two parties.
2. A third party must know that this contract exists.
3. This third party must *intentionally induce* a party to the contract to breach the contract.

■ **CASE IN POINT 6.16** A landmark case in this area involved an opera singer, Joanna Wagner, who was under contract to sing for a man named Lumley for a specified period of years. A man named Gye, who knew of this contract, nonetheless "enticed" Wagner to refuse to carry out the agreement, and Wagner began to sing for Gye. Gye's action constituted a tort because it interfered with the contractual relationship between Wagner and Lumley. (Wagner's refusal to carry out the agreement also entitled Lumley to sue Wagner for breach of contract.)[12] ■

The body of tort law relating to wrongful interference with a contractual relationship has increased greatly in recent years. In principle, any lawful contract can be the basis for an action of this type. The contract could be between a firm and its employees or a firm and its customers. Sometimes, a competitor of a firm lures away one of the firm's key employees. In this situation, the original employer can recover damages from the competitor only if it can be shown that the competitor knew of the contract's existence and intentionally induced the breach.

Wrongful Interference with a Business Relationship Businesspersons devise countless schemes to attract customers. They are prohibited, however, from unreasonably interfering with another's business in their attempts to gain a greater share of the market.

There is a difference between *competitive practices* and *predatory behavior*—actions undertaken with the intention of unlawfully driving competitors completely out of the market. Attempting to attract customers in general is a legitimate business practice, whereas specifically

---

12. *Lumley v. Gye*, 118 Eng.Rep. 749 (1853).

---

targeting the customers of a competitor is more likely to be predatory. A plaintiff claiming predatory behavior must show that the defendant used predatory methods to intentionally harm an established business relationship or gain a prospective economic advantage.

■ **EXAMPLE 6.17** A shopping mall contains two athletic shoe stores: Joe's and Ultimate Sport. Joe's cannot station an employee at the entrance of Ultimate Sport's to divert customers to Joe's by telling them that Joe's will beat Ultimate Sport's prices. This type of activity constitutes the tort of wrongful interference with a business relationship, which is commonly considered to be an unfair trade practice. If this activity were permitted, Joe's would reap the benefits of Ultimate Sport's advertising. ■

Defenses to Wrongful Interference A person will not be liable for the tort of wrongful interference with a contractual or business relationship if it can be shown that the interference was justified or permissible. Bona fide competitive behavior—such as marketing and advertising strategies—is a permissible interference even if it results in the breaking of a contract.

■ **EXAMPLE 6.18** Taylor Meats advertises so effectively that it induces Sam's Restaurant to break its contract with Burke's Meat Company. In that situation, Burke's Meat Company will be unable to recover against Taylor Meats on a wrongful interference theory. The public policy that favors free competition through advertising outweighs any possible instability that such competitive activity might cause in contractual relations. ■

6–3 Intentional Torts against Property

Intentional torts against property include trespass to land, trespass to personal property, conversion, and disparagement of property. These torts are wrongful actions that interfere with individuals' legally recognized rights with regard to their land or personal property.

The law distinguishes real property from personal property. *Real property* is land and things permanently attached to the land, such as a house. *Personal property* consists of all other items, including cash and securities (such as stocks and bonds).

6–3a Trespass to Land

A **trespass to land** occurs when a person, without permission, does any of the following:

1. Enters onto, above, or below the surface of land that is owned by another.
2. Causes anything to enter onto land owned by another.
3. Remains on land owned by another or permits anything to remain on it.

Actual harm to the land is not an essential element of this tort, because the tort is designed to protect the right of an owner to exclusive possession.

Common types of trespass to land include walking or driving on another's land, shooting a gun over another's land, and throwing rocks at a building that belongs to someone else. Another common form of trespass involves constructing a building so that part of it extends onto an adjoining landowner's property.

Establishing Trespass Before a person can be a trespasser, the real property owner (or another person in actual and exclusive possession of the property, such as a renter) must establish that person as a trespasser. For instance, "posted" trespass signs expressly establish as a trespasser a person who ignores these signs and enters onto the property. A guest in your home is not a trespasser, unless he or she has been asked to leave and refuses. Any person who enters onto another's property to commit an illegal act (such as a thief entering a lumberyard at night to steal lumber) is impliedly a trespasser, with or without posted signs.

Liability for Harm At common law, a trespasser is liable for any damage caused to the property and generally cannot hold the owner liable for injuries that the trespasser sustains on the premises. This common law rule is being modified in many jurisdictions, however, in favor of a *reasonable duty of care* rule that varies depending on the status of the parties.

For instance, a landowner may have a duty to post a notice that guard dogs patrol the property. Also, if young children are attracted to the property by some object, such a swimming pool or a sand pile, and are injured, the landowner may be held liable (under the *attractive nuisance doctrine*). Still, an owner can normally use reasonable force to remove a trespasser from the premises or detain the trespasser for a reasonable time without liability for damages.

Defenses against Trespass to Land One defense to a claim of trespass is to show that the trespass was warranted, such as when a trespasser enters a building to assist someone in danger. Another defense exists when the trespasser can show that she or he had a *license* to come onto the land.

A **licensee** is one who is invited (or allowed to enter) onto the property of another for the licensee's benefit. A person who enters another's property to read an electric meter, for example, is a licensee. When you purchase a ticket to attend a movie or sporting event, you are licensed to go onto the property of another to view that movie or event.

Note that licenses to enter onto another's property are *revocable* by the property owner. If a property owner asks an electric meter reader to leave and she or he refuses to do so, the meter reader at that point becomes a trespasser.

6–3b Trespass to Personal Property

Whenever any individual wrongfully takes or harms the personal property of another or otherwise interferes with the lawful owner's possession and enjoyment of personal property, **trespass to personal property** occurs. This tort may also be called *trespass to chattels* or *trespass to personalty*.[13] In this context, harm means not only destruction of the property, but also anything that diminishes its value, condition, or quality.

Trespass to personal property involves intentional meddling with a possessory interest (one arising from possession), including barring an owner's access to personal property. ■ **EXAMPLE 6.19** Kelly takes Ryan's business law book as a practical joke and hides it so that Ryan is unable to find it for several days before the final examination. Here, Kelly has engaged in a trespass to personal property (and also *conversion,* the tort discussed next). ■

If it can be shown that trespass to personal property was warranted, then a complete defense exists. Most states, for instance, allow automobile repair shops to hold a customer's car (under what is called an *artisan's lien*) when the customer refuses to pay for repairs already completed.

6–3c Conversion

Any act that deprives an owner of personal property or of the use of that property without the owner's permission and without just cause can constitute **conversion.** Even the taking of electronic records and data may form the basis of a conversion claim. Often, when conversion occurs, a trespass to personal property also occurs. The original taking of the personal property from the owner was a trespass. Wrongfully retaining the property is conversion.

---

13. Pronounced *per-sun-ul-tee.*

Failure to Return Goods Conversion is the civil side of crimes related to theft, but it is not limited to theft. Even when the rightful owner consented to the initial taking of the property, so no theft or trespass occurred, a failure to return the property may still be conversion. ■ **EXAMPLE 6.20** Chen borrows Mark's iPad mini to use while traveling home from school for the holidays. When Chen returns to school, Mark asks for his iPad back, but Chen says that he gave it to his little brother for Christmas. In this situation, Mark can sue Chen for conversion, and Chen will have to either return the iPad or pay damages equal to its replacement value. ■

Intention Conversion can occur even when a person mistakenly believed that she or he was entitled to the goods. In other words, good intentions are not a defense against conversion. Someone who buys stolen goods, for instance, may be sued for conversion even if he or she did not know the goods were stolen. If the true owner of the goods sues the buyer, the buyer must either return the property to the owner or pay the owner the full value of the property.

Conversion can also occur from an employee's unauthorized use of a credit card. ■ **CASE IN POINT 6.21** Nicholas Mora worked for Welco Electronics, Inc., but had also established his own company, AQM Supplies. Mora used Welco's credit card without permission and deposited more than $375,000 into AQM's account, which he then transferred to his personal account. Welco sued. A California court held that Mora was liable for conversion. The court reasoned that when Mora misappropriated Welco's credit card and used it, he took part of Welco's credit balance with the credit-card company.[14] ■

6-3d Disparagement of Property

Disparagement of property occurs when economically injurious falsehoods are made about another's product or property rather than about another's reputation (as in the tort of defamation). *Disparagement of property* is a general term for torts that can be more specifically referred to as *slander of quality* or *slander of title*.

Slander of Quality The publication of false information about another's product, alleging that it is not what its seller claims, constitutes the tort of **slander of quality,** or **trade libel.** To establish trade libel, the plaintiff must prove that the improper publication caused a third person to refrain from dealing with the plaintiff and that the plaintiff sustained economic damages (such as lost profits) as a result.

An improper publication may be both a slander of quality and a defamation of character. For instance, a statement that disparages the quality of a product may also, by implication, disparage the character of a person who would sell such a product.

Slander of Title When a publication falsely denies or casts doubt on another's legal ownership of property, resulting in financial loss to the property's owner, the tort of **slander of title** occurs. Usually, this is an intentional tort in which someone knowingly publishes an untrue statement about another's ownership of certain property with the intent of discouraging a third person from dealing with the person slandered. For instance, it would be difficult for a car dealer to attract customers after competitors published a notice that the dealer's stock consisted of stolen automobiles.

See Concept Summary 6.2 for a review of intentional torts against property.

6-4 Unintentional Torts—Negligence

The tort of **negligence** occurs when someone suffers injury because of another's failure to live up to a required *duty of care*. In contrast to intentional torts, in torts involving negligence, the tortfeasor neither wishes to bring about the consequences of the act nor believes that they will occur. The person's conduct merely creates a risk of such consequences. If no risk is created, there is no negligence.

Moreover, the risk must be foreseeable. In other words, it must be such that a reasonable person engaging in the same activity would anticipate the risk and guard against it. In determining what is reasonable conduct, courts consider the nature of the possible harm.

Many of the actions giving rise to the intentional torts discussed earlier in the chapter constitute negligence if the element of intent is missing (or cannot be proved). ■ **EXAMPLE 6.22** Juan walks up to Maya and intentionally shoves her. Maya falls and breaks her arm as a result. In this situation, Juan is liable for the intentional tort of battery. If Juan carelessly bumps into Maya, however, and she falls and breaks her arm as a result, Juan's action constitutes negligence. In either situation, Juan has committed a tort. ■

---

14. *Welco Electronics, Inc. v. Mora,* 223 Cal.App.4th 202, 166 Cal.Rptr.3d 877 (2014).

Concept Summary 6.2

Intentional Torts against Property

Trespass to Land	The invasion of another's real property without consent or privilege. Once a person is expressly or impliedly established as a trespasser, the property owner has specific rights, which may include the right to detain or remove the trespasser.
Trespass to Personal Property	The intentional interference with an owner's right to use, possess, or enjoy his or her personal property without the owner's consent.
Conversion	The wrongful possession or use of another person's personal property without just cause.
Disparagement of Property	Any economically injurious falsehood that is made about another's product or property; an inclusive term for the torts of *slander of quality* and *slander of title*.

To succeed in a negligence action, the plaintiff must prove each of the following:

1. *Duty.* The defendant owed a duty of care to the plaintiff.
2. *Breach.* The defendant breached that duty.
3. *Causation.* The defendant's breach caused the plaintiff's injury.
4. *Damages.* The plaintiff suffered a legally recognizable injury.

6–4a The Duty of Care and Its Breach

Central to the tort of negligence is the concept of a **duty of care.** The basic principle underlying the duty of care is that people are free to act as they please so long as their actions do not infringe on the interests of others. When someone fails to comply with the duty to exercise reasonable care, a potentially tortious act may have been committed.

Failure to live up to a standard of care may be an act (accidentally setting fire to a building) or an omission (neglecting to put out a campfire). It may be a careless act or a carefully performed but nevertheless dangerous act that results in injury. In determining whether the duty of care has been breached, courts consider several factors:

1. The nature of the act (whether it is outrageous or commonplace).
2. The manner in which the act was performed (cautiously versus heedlessly).
3. The nature of the injury (whether it is serious or slight).

Creating even a very slight risk of a dangerous explosion might be unreasonable, whereas creating a distinct possibility of someone's burning his or her fingers on a stove might be reasonable.

The Reasonable Person Standard Tort law measures duty by the **reasonable person standard.** In determining whether a duty of care has been breached, the courts ask how a reasonable person would have acted in the same circumstances. The reasonable person standard is said to be objective. It is not necessarily how a particular person *would* act. It is society's judgment of how an ordinarily prudent person *should* act. If the so-called reasonable person existed, he or she would be careful, conscientious, even tempered, and honest.

The degree of care to be exercised varies, depending on the defendant's occupation or profession, her or his relationship with the plaintiff, and other factors. Generally, whether an action constitutes a breach of the duty of care is determined on a case-by-case basis. The outcome depends on how the judge (or jury) decides that a reasonable person in the position of the defendant would have acted in the particular circumstances of the case.

Note that the courts frequently use the reasonable person standard in other areas of law as well as in negligence cases. Indeed, the principle that individuals are required to exercise a reasonable standard of care in their activities is a pervasive concept in business law.

The Duty of Landowners Landowners are expected to exercise reasonable care to protect individuals coming onto their property from harm. In some jurisdictions, landowners may even have a duty to protect trespassers against certain risks. Landowners who rent or lease premises to tenants are expected to exercise reasonable care to ensure that the tenants and their guests are not harmed in common areas, such as stairways, entryways, and laundry rooms.

The Duty to Warn Business Invitees of Risks. Retailers and other business operators who explicitly or implicitly invite persons to come onto their premises have a duty to exercise reasonable care to protect these **business invitees.** The duty normally requires storeowners to warn business invitees of foreseeable risks, such as construction zones or wet floors, about which the owners knew or *should have known.*

■ **EXAMPLE 6.23** Liz enters Kwan's neighborhood market, slips on a wet floor, and sustains injuries as a result. If there was no sign or other warning that the floor was wet at the time Liz slipped, the owner, Kwan, would be liable for damages. A court would hold that Kwan was negligent because he failed to exercise a reasonable degree of care to protect customers against foreseeable risks about which he knew or should have known. That a patron might slip on the wet floor and be injured was a foreseeable risk, and Kwan should have taken care to avoid this risk or warn the customer of it. ■

A business owner also has a duty to discover and remove any hidden dangers that might injure a customer or other invitee. Hidden dangers might include uneven surfaces or defects in the pavement of a parking lot or a walkway, or merchandise that has fallen off shelves in a store.

Obvious Risks Provide an Exception. Some risks are so obvious that an owner need not warn of them. For instance, a business owner does not need to warn customers to open a door before attempting to walk through it. Other risks, however, even though they may seem obvious

to a business owner, may not be so in the eyes of another, such as a child. In addition, even if a risk is obvious, a business owner is not necessarily excused from the duty to protect customers from foreseeable harm from that risk.

■ **CASE IN POINT 6.24** Giorgio's Grill is a restaurant in Florida that becomes a nightclub after hours. At those times, traditionally, as the manager of Giorgio's knew, the staff and customers throw paper napkins into the air as the music plays. The napkins land on the floor, but no one picks them up. One night, Jane Izquierdo went to Giorgio's. Although she had been to the club on prior occasions and knew about the napkin-throwing tradition, she slipped and fell, breaking her leg. She sued Giorgio's for negligence, but lost at trial because a jury found that the risk of slipping on the napkins was obvious. A state appellate court reversed, however, holding that the obviousness of a risk does not discharge a business owner's duty to its invitees to maintain the premises in a safe condition.[15] ■

The Duty of Professionals Persons who possess superior knowledge, skill, or training are held to a higher standard of care than others. Professionals—including physicians, dentists, architects, engineers, accountants, and lawyers, among others—are required to have a standard minimum level of special knowledge and ability. In determining what constitutes reasonable care in the case of professionals, the law takes their training and expertise into account. Thus, an accountant's conduct is judged not by the reasonable person standard, but by the reasonable accountant standard.

If a professional violates his or her duty of care toward a client, the client may bring a suit against the professional, alleging **malpractice,** which is essentially professional negligence. For instance, a patient might sue a physician for *medical malpractice.* A client might sue an attorney for *legal malpractice.*

6–4b Causation

Another element necessary to a negligence action is *causation.* If a person breaches a duty of care and someone suffers injury, the person's act must have caused the harm for it to constitute the tort of negligence.

Courts Ask Two Questions In deciding whether the requirement of causation is met, the court must address two questions:

---

15. *Izquierdo v. Gyroscope, Inc.,* 946 So.2d 115 (Fla.App. 2007).

1. *Is there causation in fact?* Did the injury occur because of the defendant's act, or would it have occurred anyway? If the injury would not have occurred without the defendant's act, then there is causation in fact.

   Causation in fact usually can be determined by use of the *but for* test: "but for" the wrongful act, the injury would not have occurred. This test seeks to determine whether there was a cause-and-effect relationship between the act and the injury suffered. In theory, causation in fact is limitless. One could claim, for example, that "but for" the creation of the world, a particular injury would not have occurred. Thus, as a practical matter, the law has to establish limits, and it does so through the concept of proximate cause.

2. *Was the act the proximate, or legal, cause of the injury?* **Proximate cause,** or *legal cause,* exists when the connection between an act and an injury is strong enough to justify imposing liability. Proximate cause asks whether the injuries sustained were foreseeable or were too remotely connected to the incident to trigger liability. Judges use proximate cause to limit the scope of the defendant's liability to a subset of the total number of potential plaintiffs that might have been harmed by the defendant's actions.

   ■ **EXAMPLE 6.25** Ackerman carelessly leaves a campfire burning. The fire not only burns down the forest but also sets off an explosion in a nearby chemical plant that spills chemicals into a river, killing all the fish for twenty miles downstream and ruining the economy of a tourist resort. Should Ackerman be liable to the resort owners? To the tourists whose vacations were ruined? These are questions of proximate cause that a court must decide. ■

Both of these causation questions must be answered in the affirmative for liability in tort to arise. If there is causation in fact but a court decides that the defendant's action is not the proximate cause of the plaintiff's injury, the causation requirement has not been met. Therefore, the defendant normally will not be liable to the plaintiff.

Foreseeability Questions of proximate cause are linked to the concept of foreseeability because it would be unfair to impose liability on a defendant unless the defendant's actions created a foreseeable risk of injury. Generally, if the victim or the consequences of a harm done were unforeseeable, there is no proximate cause.

Probably the most cited case on the concept of foreseeability and proximate cause is the *Palsgraf* case, which established foreseeability as the test for proximate cause. ■ **CASE IN POINT 6.26** Helen Palsgraf was waiting for a train on a station platform. A man carrying a package was rushing to catch a train that was moving away from a platform across the tracks from Palsgraf. As the man attempted to jump aboard the moving train, he seemed unsteady and about to fall. A railroad guard on the car reached forward to grab him, and another guard on the platform pushed him from behind to help him board the train.

In the process, the man's package, which (unknown to the railroad guards) contained fireworks, fell on the railroad tracks and exploded. There was nothing about the package to indicate its contents. The repercussions of the explosion caused weighing scales at the other end of the train platform to fall on Palsgraf, causing injuries for which she sued the railroad company. At the trial, the jury found that the railroad guards had been negligent in their conduct. The railroad company appealed. New York's highest state court held that the railroad company was not liable to Palsgraf. The railroad had not been negligent toward her, because injury to her was not foreseeable.[16] ■

6–4c The Injury Requirement and Damages

For tort liability to arise, the plaintiff must have suffered a *legally recognizable* injury. To recover damages, the plaintiff must have suffered some loss, harm, wrong, or invasion of a protected interest. Essentially, the purpose of tort law is to compensate for legally recognized harms and injuries resulting from wrongful acts. If no harm or injury results from a given negligent action, there is nothing to compensate, and no tort exists.

For instance, if you carelessly bump into a passerby, who stumbles and falls as a result, you may be liable in tort if the passerby is injured in the fall. If the person is unharmed, however, there normally can be no lawsuit for damages, because no injury was suffered.

Compensatory damages are the norm in negligence cases. A court will award punitive damages only if the defendant's conduct was grossly negligent, reflecting an intentional failure to perform a duty with reckless disregard of the consequences to others.

6–4d Good Samaritan Statutes

Most states now have what are called **Good Samaritan statutes.**[17] Under these statutes, someone who is aided voluntarily by another cannot turn around and sue the "Good Samaritan" for negligence. These laws were passed largely to protect physicians and medical personnel who

---

16. *Palsgraf v. Long Island Railroad Co.,* 248 N.Y. 339, 162 N.E. 99 (1928).
17. These laws derive their name from the Good Samaritan story in the Bible. In the story, a traveler who had been robbed and beaten lay along the roadside, ignored by those passing by. Eventually, a man from the region of Samaria (the "Good Samaritan") stopped to render assistance to the injured person.

volunteer their services in emergency situations to those in need, such as individuals hurt in car accidents.

6–4e Dram Shop Acts

Many states have also passed **dram shop acts,**[18] under which a bar's owner or bartender may be held liable for injuries caused by a person who became intoxicated while drinking at the bar. The owner or bartender may also be held responsible for continuing to serve a person who was already intoxicated.

Some states' statutes also impose liability on *social hosts* (persons hosting parties) for injuries caused by guests who became intoxicated at the hosts' homes. Under these statutes, it is unnecessary to prove that the bar owner, bartender, or social host was negligent. ■ **EXAMPLE 6.27** Jane hosts a Super Bowl party at which Brett, a minor, sneaks alcoholic drinks. Jane is potentially liable for damages resulting from Brett's drunk driving after the party. ■

6–5 Defenses to Negligence

Defendants often defend against negligence claims by asserting that the plaintiffs have failed to prove

---

18. Historically, a dram was a small unit of liquid, and distilled spirits (strong alcoholic liquor) were sold in drams. Thus, a dram shop was a place where liquor was sold in drams.

the existence of one or more of the required elements for negligence. Additionally, there are three basic *affirmative* defenses in negligence cases (defenses that a defendant can use to avoid liability even if the facts are as the plaintiff states): *assumption of risk, superseding cause,* and *contributory and comparative negligence.*

6–5a Assumption of Risk

A plaintiff who voluntarily enters into a risky situation, knowing the risk involved, will not be allowed to recover. This is the defense of **assumption of risk,** which requires two elements:

1. Knowledge of the risk.
2. Voluntary assumption of the risk.

The defense of assumption of risk is frequently asserted when the plaintiff was injured during a recreational activity that involves known risk, such as skiing or skydiving. (Courts do not apply the assumption of risk doctrine in emergency situations.)

Assumption of risk can apply not only to participants in sporting events, but also to spectators and bystanders who are injured while attending those events. In the following *Spotlight Case,* the issue was whether a spectator at a baseball game voluntarily assumed the risk of being hit by an errant ball thrown while the players were warming up before the game.

Spotlight on the Seattle Mariners

Case 6.3 Taylor v. Baseball Club of Seattle, LP
Court of Appeals of Washington, 132 Wash.App. 32, 130 P.3d 835 (2006).

Background and Facts Delinda Taylor went to a Seattle Mariners baseball game at Safeco Field with her boyfriend and her two minor sons. Their seats were four rows up from the field along the right field foul line. They arrived more than an hour before the game so that they could see the players warm up and get their autographs. When she walked in, Taylor saw that a Mariners pitcher, Freddy Garcia, was throwing a ball back and forth with José Mesa right in front of their seats.

As Taylor stood in front of her seat, she looked away from the field, and a ball thrown by Mesa got past Garcia and struck her in the face, causing serious injuries. Taylor sued the Mariners for the allegedly negligent warm-up throw. The Mariners filed a motion for summary judgment in which they argued that Taylor, a longtime Mariners fan, was familiar with baseball and the inherent risk of balls entering the stands. Thus, the motion asserted, Taylor had assumed the risk of her injury. The trial court granted the motion and dismissed Taylor's case. Taylor appealed.

In the Language of the Court
DWYER, J. [Judge]
* * * *

* * * For many decades, courts have required baseball stadiums to screen some seats—generally those behind home plate—to provide protection to spectators who choose it.

Case 6.3 Continues

Case 6.3 Continued

A sport spectator's assumption of risk and a defendant sports team's duty of care are accordingly discerned under the doctrine of primary assumption of risk. * * * "Implied *primary* assumption of risk arises where a plaintiff has impliedly consented (often in advance of any negligence by defendant) to relieve defendant of a duty to plaintiff regarding specific *known* and appreciated risks."

* * * *

Under this implied primary assumption of risk, defendant must show that plaintiff had full subjective understanding of the specific risk, both its nature and presence, and that he or she voluntarily chose to encounter the risk.

* * * It is undisputed that the warm-up is part of the sport, that spectators such as Taylor purposely attend that portion of the event, and that the Mariners permit ticket-holders to view the warm-up.

* * * We find the fact that Taylor was injured during warm-up is not legally significant because that portion of the event is necessarily incident to the game.

* * * *

Here, there is no evidence that the circumstances leading to Taylor's injury constituted an unusual danger. It is undisputed that it is the normal, every-day practice at all levels of baseball for pitchers to warm up in the manner that led to this incident. *The risk of injuries such as Taylor's are within the normal comprehension of a spectator who is familiar with the game.* Indeed, the possibility of an errant ball entering the stands is part of the game's attraction for many spectators. [Emphasis added.]

* * * The record contains substantial evidence regarding Taylor's familiarity with the game. She attended many of her sons' baseball games, she witnessed balls entering the stands, she had watched Mariners' games both at the Kingdome and on television, and she knew that there was no screen protecting her seats, which were close to the field. In fact, as she walked to her seat she saw the players warming up and was excited about being in an unscreened area where her party might get autographs from the players and catch balls.

Decision and Remedy *The state intermediate appellate court affirmed the lower court's judgment. As a spectator who chose to sit in an unprotected area of seats, Taylor voluntarily undertook the risk associated with being hit by an errant baseball thrown during the warm-up before the game.*

Critical Thinking

- **What If the Facts Were Different?** *Would the result in this case have been different if it had been Taylor's minor son, rather than Taylor herself, who had been struck by the ball? Should courts apply the doctrine of assumption of risk to children? Discuss.*
- **Legal Environment** *What is the basis underlying the defense of assumption of risk? How does that basis support the court's decision in this case?*

6–5b Superseding Cause

An unforeseeable intervening event may break the causal connection between a wrongful act and an injury to another. If so, the intervening event acts as a **superseding cause**—that is, it relieves the defendant of liability for injuries caused by the intervening event.

■ EXAMPLE 6.28 While riding his bicycle, Derrick negligently runs into Julie, who is walking on the sidewalk. As a result of the impact, Julie falls and fractures her hip. While she is waiting for help to arrive, a small aircraft crashes nearby and explodes, and some of the fiery debris hits her, causing her to sustain severe burns. Derrick will be liable for the damages related to Julie's fractured hip, because the risk of injuring her with his bicycle was foreseeable. Normally, though, Derrick will not be liable for the burns caused by the plane crash, because he could not have foreseen the risk that a plane would crash nearby and injure Julie. ■

6–5c Contributory Negligence

All individuals are expected to exercise a reasonable degree of care in looking out for themselves. In the past, under the common law doctrine of **contributory negligence,** a plaintiff who was also negligent (who failed to exercise a reasonable degree of care) could not recover anything from the defendant. Under this rule, no matter how insignificant the plaintiff's negligence was relative to the defendant's negligence, the plaintiff would be precluded from recovering any damages. Today, only a few jurisdictions still follow this doctrine.

6–5d Comparative Negligence

In most states, the doctrine of contributory negligence has been replaced by a **comparative negligence** standard. Under this standard, both the plaintiff's and the defendant's negligence are computed, and the liability for damages is distributed accordingly.

Some jurisdictions have adopted a "pure" form of comparative negligence that allows the plaintiff to recover, even if the extent of his or her fault is greater than that of the defendant. Under pure comparative negligence, if the plaintiff was 80 percent at fault and the defendant 20 percent at fault, the plaintiff can recover 20 percent of his or her damages.

Many states' comparative negligence statutes, however, contain a "50 percent" rule that prevents the plaintiff from recovering any damages if she or he was more than 50 percent at fault. Under this rule, a plaintiff who was 35 percent at fault can recover 65 percent of his or her damages, but a plaintiff who was 65 percent (more than 50 percent) at fault can recover nothing.

Reviewing: Tort Law

Elaine Sweeney went to Ragged Mountain Ski Resort in New Hampshire with a friend. Elaine went snow tubing down a run designed exclusively for snow tubers. There were no Ragged Mountain employees present in the snow-tube area to instruct Elaine on the proper use of a snow tube. On her fourth run down the trail, Elaine crossed over the center line between snow-tube lanes, collided with another snow tuber, and was injured. Elaine filed a negligence action against Ragged Mountain seeking compensation for the injuries that she sustained. Two years earlier, the New Hampshire state legislature had enacted a statute that prohibited a person who participates in the sport of skiing from suing a ski-area operator for injuries caused by the risks inherent in skiing. Using the information presented in the chapter, answer the following questions.

1. What defense will Ragged Mountain probably assert?
2. The central question in this case is whether the state statute establishing that skiers assume the risks inherent in the sport bars Elaine's suit. What would your decision be on this issue? Why?
3. Suppose that the court concludes that the statute applies only to skiing and not to snow tubing. Will Elaine's lawsuit be successful? Explain.
4. Now suppose that the jury concludes that Elaine was partly at fault for the accident. Under what theory might her damages be reduced in proportion to the degree to which her actions contributed to the accident and her resulting injuries?

Debate This . . . *Each time a state legislature enacts a law that applies the assumption of risk doctrine to a particular sport, participants in that sport suffer.*

Terms and Concepts

Issue Spotters

1. Jana leaves her truck's motor running while she enters a Kwik-Pik Store. The truck's transmission engages, and the vehicle crashes into a gas pump, starting a fire that spreads to a warehouse on the next block. The warehouse collapses, causing its billboard to fall and injure Lou, a bystander. Can Lou recover from Jana? Why or why not? (See *Unintentional Torts—Negligence*.)

2. A water pipe bursts, flooding a Metal Fabrication Company utility room and tripping the circuit breakers on a panel in the room. Metal Fabrication contacts Nouri, a licensed electrician with five years' experience, to check the damage and turn the breakers back on. Without testing for short circuits, which Nouri knows that he should do, he tries to switch on a breaker. He is electrocuted, and his wife sues Metal Fabrication for damages, alleging negligence. What might the firm successfully claim in defense? (See *Defenses to Negligence*.)

- **Check your answers to the Issue Spotters against the answers provided in Appendix D at the end of this text.**

Business Scenarios

6–1. Defamation. Richard is an employee of the Dun Construction Corp. While delivering materials to a construction site, he carelessly backs Dun's truck into a passenger vehicle driven by Green. This is Richard's second accident in six months. When the company owner, Dun, learns of this latest accident, a heated discussion ensues, and Dun fires Richard. Dun is so angry that he immediately writes a letter to the union of which Richard is a member and to all other construction companies in the community, stating that Richard is the "worst driver in the city" and that "anyone who hires him is asking for legal liability." Richard files a suit against Dun, alleging libel on the basis of the statements made in the letters. Discuss the results. (See *Intentional Torts against Persons*.)

6–2. Liability to Business Invitees. Kim went to Ling's Market to pick up a few items for dinner. It was a stormy day, and the wind had blown water through the market's door each time it opened. As Kim entered through the door, she slipped and fell in the rainwater that had accumulated on the floor. The manager knew of the weather conditions but had not posted any sign to warn customers of the water hazard. Kim injured her back as a result of the fall and sued Ling's for damages. Can Ling's be held liable for negligence? Discuss. (See *Unintentional Torts—Negligence*.)

Business Case Problems

6–3. Spotlight on Intentional Torts—Defamation.

 Sharon Yeagle was an assistant to the vice president of student affairs at Virginia Polytechnic Institute and State University (Virginia Tech). As part of her duties, Yeagle helped students participate in the Governor's Fellows Program. The *Collegiate Times*, Virginia Tech's student newspaper, published an article about the university's success in placing students in the program. The article's text surrounded a block quotation attributed to Yeagle with the phrase "Director of Butt Licking" under her name. Yeagle sued the *Collegiate Times* for defamation. She argued that the phrase implied the commission of sodomy and was therefore actionable. What is *Collegiate Times* defense to this claim? [*Yeagle v. Collegiate Times*, 497 S.E.2d 136 (Va. 1998)] (See *Intentional Torts against Persons*.)

6–4. Intentional Infliction of Emotional Distress.

While living in her home country of Tanzania, Sophia Kiwanuka signed an employment contract with Anne Margareth Bakilana, a Tanzanian living in Washington, D.C. Kiwanuka traveled to the United States to work as a babysitter and maid in Bakilana's house. When Kiwanuka arrived, Bakilana confiscated her passport, held her in isolation, and forced her to work long hours under threat of having her deported. Kiwanuka worked seven days a week without breaks and was subjected to regular verbal and psychological abuse by Bakilana. Kiwanuka filed a complaint against Bakilana for intentional infliction of emotional distress, among other claims. Bakilana argued that Kiwanuka's complaint should be dismissed because the allegations were insufficient to show outrageous intentional conduct that resulted in severe emotional distress.

If you were the judge, in whose favor would you rule? Why? [*Kiwanuka v. Bakilana,* 844 F.Supp.2d 107 (D.D.C. 2012)] (See *Intentional Torts against Persons.*)

6–5. Business Case Problem with Sample Answer—Negligence. At the Weatherford Hotel in Flagstaff, Arizona, in Room 59, a balcony extends across thirty inches of the room's only window, leaving a twelve-inch gap with a three-story drop to the concrete below. A sign prohibits smoking in the room but invites guests to "step out onto the balcony" to smoke. Toni Lucario was a guest in Room 59 when she climbed out of the window and fell to her death. Patrick McMurtry, her estate's personal representative, filed a suit against the Weatherford. Did the hotel breach a duty of care to Locario? What might the Weatherford assert in its defense? Explain. [*McMurtry v. Weatherford Hotel, Inc.,* 231 Ariz. 244, 293 P.3d 520 (2013)] (See *Unintentional Torts—Negligence.*)

• **For a sample answer to Problem 6–5, go to Appendix E at the end of this text.**

6–6. Negligence. Ronald Rawls and Zabian Bailey were in an auto accident in Bridgeport, Connecticut. Bailey rear-ended Rawls at a stoplight. Evidence showed it was more likely than not that Bailey failed to apply his brakes in time to avoid the collision, failed to turn his vehicle to avoid the collision, failed to keep his vehicle under control, and was inattentive to his surroundings. Rawls filed a suit in a Connecticut state court against his insurance company, Progressive Northern Insurance Co., to obtain benefits under an underinsured motorist clause, alleging that Bailey had been negligent. Could Rawls collect? Discuss. [*Rawls v. Progressive Northern Insurance Co.,* 310 Conn. 768, 83 A.3d 576 (2014)] (See *Unintentional Torts—Negligence.*)

6–7. Negligence. Charles Robison, an employee of West Star Transportation, Inc., was ordered to cover an unevenly loaded flatbed trailer with a 150-pound tarpaulin (a waterproof cloth). The load included uncrated equipment and pallet crates of different heights, about thirteen feet off the ground at its highest point. While standing on the load, manipulating the tarpaulin without safety equipment or assistance, Robison fell and sustained a traumatic head injury. He filed a suit against West Star to recover for his injury. Was West Star "negligent in failing to provide a reasonably safe place to work," as Robison claimed? Explain. [*West Star Transportation, Inc. v. Robison,* 457 S.W.3d 178 (Tex.App.—Amarillo 2015)] (See *Unintentional Torts—Negligence.*)

6–8. Negligence. DSC Industrial Supply and Road Rider Supply are located in North Kitsap Business Park in Seattle, Washington. Both firms are owned by Paul and Suzanne Marshall. The Marshalls had outstanding commercial loans from Frontier Bank. The bank dispatched one of its employees, Suzette Gould, to North Kitsap to "spread Christmas cheer" to the Marshalls as an expression of appreciation for their business. Approaching the entry to Road Rider, Gould tripped over a concrete "wheel stop" and fell, suffering a broken arm and a dislocated elbow. The stop was not clearly visible, it had not been painted a contrasting color, and it was not marked with a sign. Gould had not been aware of the stop before she tripped over it. Is North Kitsap liable to Gould for negligence? Explain. [*Gould v. North Kitsap Business Park Management, LLC,* 2016 WL 236455 (2016)] (See *Unintentional Torts—Negligence.*)

6–9. A Question of Ethics—Wrongful Interference. *White Plains Coat & Apron Co. is a New York–based linen rental business. Cintas Corp. is a competitor. White Plains had five-year exclusive contracts with some of its customers. As a result of Cintas's soliciting of business, dozens of White Plains' customers breached their contracts and entered into rental agreements with Cintas. White Plains filed a suit against Cintas, alleging wrongful interference.* [White Plains Coat & Apron Co. v. Cintas Corp., *8 N.Y.3d 422, 867 N.E.2d 381 (2007)*] (See *Intentional Torts against Persons.*)

(a) What are the two important policy interests at odds in wrongful interference cases? Which of these interests should be accorded priority?

(b) The U.S. Court of Appeals for the Second Circuit asked the New York Court of Appeals to answer a question: Is a general interest in soliciting business for profit a sufficient defense to a claim of wrongful interference with a contractual relationship? What do you think? Why?

Legal Reasoning Group Activity

6–10. Negligence. Donald and Gloria Bowden hosted a cookout at their home in South Carolina, inviting mostly business acquaintances. Justin Parks, who was nineteen years old, attended the party. Alcoholic beverages were available to all of the guests, even those who, like Parks, were between the ages of eighteen and twenty-one. Parks consumed alcohol at the party and left with other guests. One of these guests detained Parks at the guest's home to give Parks time to "sober up." Parks then drove himself from this guest's home and was killed in a one-car accident. At the time of death, he had a blood alcohol content of 0.291 percent, which exceeded the state's limit for driving a motor vehicle. Linda Marcum, Parks's mother, filed a suit in a South Carolina state court against the Bowdens and others, alleging that they were negligent. (See *Unintentional Torts—Negligence.*)

(a) The first group will present arguments in favor of holding the social hosts liable in this situation.

(b) The second group will formulate arguments against holding the social hosts liable based on principles in this chapter.

(c) The third group will determine the reasons why some courts do not treat social hosts the same as parents who serve alcoholic beverages to their underage children.

Answers to the *Issue Spotters*

1. ***Can Lou recover from Jana? Why or why not?*** Probably. To recover on the basis of negligence, the injured party as a plaintiff must show that the truck's owner owed the plaintiff a duty of care, that the owner breached that duty, that the plaintiff was injured, and that the breach caused the injury.

In this situation, the owner's actions breached the duty of reasonable care. The billboard falling on the plaintiff was the direct cause of the injury, not the plaintiff's own negligence. Thus, liability turns on whether the plaintiff can connect the breach of duty to the injury. This involves the test of proximate cause—the question of foreseeability. The consequences to the injured party must have been a foreseeable result of the owner's carelessness.

2. ***What might the firm successfully claim in defense?*** The company might defend against this electrician's claim by asserting that the electrician should have known of the risk and, therefore, the company had no duty to warn. According to the problem, the danger is common knowledge in the electrician's field and should have been apparent to this electrician, given his years of training and experience. In other words, the company most likely had no need to warn the electrician of the risk.

The firm could also raise comparative negligence. Both parties' negligence, if any, could be weighed and the liability distributed proportionately. The defendant could also assert assumption of risk, claiming that the electrician voluntarily entered into a dangerous situation, knowing the risk involved.

Sample Answers for *Business Case Problems with Sample Answer*

Problem 6–5. *Negligence.* Negligence requires proof that (1) the defendant owed a duty of care to the plaintiff, (2) the defendant breached that duty, (3) the defendant's breach caused the plaintiff's injury, and (4) the plaintiff suffered a legally recognizable injury. With respect to the duty of care, a business owner has a duty to use reasonable care to protect business invitees. This duty includes an obligation to discover and correct or warn of unreasonably dangerous conditions that the owner of the premises should reasonably foresee might endanger an invitee. Some risks are so obvious that an owner need not warn of them. But even if a risk is obvious, a business owner may not be excused from the duty to protect its customers from foreseeable harm.

Because Lucario was the Weatherford's business invitee, the hotel owed her a duty of reasonable care to make its premises safe for her use. The balcony ran nearly the entire width of the window in Lucario's room. She could have reasonably believed that the window was a means of access to the balcony. The window/balcony configuration was dangerous, however, because the window opened wide enough for an adult to climb out, but the twelve-inch gap between one side of the window and the balcony was unprotected. This unprotected gap opened to a drop of more than three stories to a concrete surface below.

Should the hotel have anticipated the potential harm to a guest who opened the window in Room 59 and attempted to access the balcony? The hotel encouraged guests to "step out onto the balcony" to smoke. The dangerous condition of the window/balcony configuration could have been remedied at a minimal cost. These circumstances could be perceived as creating an "unreasonably dangerous" condition. And it could be concluded that the hotel created or knew of the condition and failed to take reasonable steps to warn of it or correct it. Of course, the Weatherford might argue that the window/ balcony configuration was so obvious that the hotel was not liable for Lucario's fall.

In the actual case on which this problem is based, the court concluded that the Weatherford did not breach its duty of care to Lucario. On McMurtry's appeal, a state intermediate appellate court held that this conclusion was in error, vacated the lower court's judgment in favor of the hotel on this issue, and remanded the case.

CHAPTER

Strict Liability and Product Liability

In this chapter, we look at a category of tort called **strict liability,** or *liability without fault.* Under the doctrine of strict liability, a person who engages in certain activities can be held responsible for any harm that results to others, even if the person used the utmost care.

We then look at an area of tort law of particular importance to businesspersons—product liability. The manufacturers and sellers of products may incur **product liability** when product defects cause injury or property damage to consumers, users, or bystanders.

Although multimillion-dollar product liability claims often involve big automakers, pharmaceutical companies, or tobacco companies, many businesses face potential liability. For instance, a number of product liability lawsuits have been filed claiming that energy drinks like Monster, Red Bull, and Rockstar have serious adverse effects—especially on young people. A man who swallowed a bone fragment while eating sued McDonald's in 2015 for allegedly defective chicken McNuggets.

Product liability lawsuits also reach across international borders. Takata Corporation, a global company that supplies seat belts, airbags, and other automobile safety systems, is being sued by hundreds of plaintiffs in the United States. Takata manufactured allegedly defective airbags, which violently exploded and ejected metal debris, resulting in injuries and deaths.[1] Takata has already paid a $70 million penalty to the National Highway Safety Administration for failing to promptly disclose defects in its airbags, millions of which have now been recalled.

---

1. *In re Takata Airbag Products Liability Litigation,* 84 F.Supp.3d 1371 (2015).

7–1 Strict Liability

The modern concept of strict liability traces its origins, in part, to an English case decided in 1868. ■ **CASE IN POINT 7.1** In the coal-mining area of Lancashire, England, the Rylands, who were mill owners, had constructed a reservoir on their land. Water from the reservoir broke through a filled-in shaft of an abandoned coal mine nearby and flooded the connecting passageways in an active coal mine owned by Fletcher.

Fletcher sued the Rylands, and the court held that the defendants (the Rylands) were liable, even though the circumstances did not fit within existing tort liability theories. The court held that a "person who for his own purposes brings on his land and collects and keeps there anything likely to do mischief if it escapes . . . is *prima facie*[2] answerable for all the damage which is the natural consequence of its escape."[3] ■

---

2. *Prima facie* is Latin for "at first sight." Legally, it refers to a fact that is presumed to be true unless contradicted by evidence.
3. *Rylands v. Fletcher,* 3 L.R.–E & I App. [Law Reports, English & Irish Appeal Cases] (H.L. [House of Lords] 1868).

British courts liberally applied the doctrine that emerged from the case. Initially, though, few U.S. courts accepted the doctrine, presumably because the courts were worried about its effect on the expansion of American business. Today, however, the doctrine of strict liability is the norm rather than the exception.

7–1a Abnormally Dangerous Activities

Strict liability for damages proximately caused by an abnormally dangerous, or ultrahazardous, activity is one application of strict liability. Courts apply the doctrine of strict liability in these situations because of the extreme risk of the activity. Abnormally dangerous activities are those that involve a high risk of serious harm to persons or property that cannot be completely guarded against by the exercise of reasonable care.

Activities such as blasting or storing explosives qualify as abnormally dangerous, for instance. Even if blasting with dynamite is performed with all reasonable care, there is still a risk of injury. Considering the potential for harm, it seems reasonable to ask the person engaged in the activity to pay for injuries caused by that activity. Although there is no fault, there is still responsibility because of the dangerous nature of the undertaking.

Similarly, persons who keep wild animals are strictly liable for any harm inflicted by the animals. The basis for applying strict liability is that wild animals, should they escape from confinement, pose a serious risk of harm to people in the vicinity. Even an owner of domestic animals (such as dogs or horses) may be strictly liable for harm caused by those animals if the owner knew, or should have known, that the animals were dangerous or had a propensity to harm others.

7–1b Application of Strict Liability to Product Liability

A significant application of strict liability is in the area of product liability—liability of manufacturers and sellers for harmful or defective products. Liability here is a matter of social policy and is based on two factors:

1. The manufacturer can better bear the cost of injury because it can spread the cost throughout society by increasing the prices of its goods.
2. The manufacturer is making a profit from its activities and therefore should bear the cost of injury as an operating expense.

We discuss product liability in detail next. Strict liability is also applied in certain types of *bailments* (a bailment exists when goods are transferred temporarily into the care of another).

7–2 Product Liability

Those who make, sell, or lease goods can be held liable for physical harm or property damage caused by those goods to a consumer, user, or bystander. This is called *product liability.* Product liability may be based on the theories of negligence, misrepresentation, strict liability, and warranties. Multiple theories of liability can be, and often are, asserted in the same case. We look here at product liability based on negligence and on misrepresentation.

7–2a Based on Negligence

Negligence is the failure to exercise the degree of care that a reasonable, prudent person would have exercised under the circumstances. If a manufacturer fails to exercise "due care" to make a product safe, a person who is injured by the product may sue the manufacturer for negligence.

Due Care Must Be Exercised Manufacturers must use due care in all of the following areas:

1. Designing the product.
2. Selecting the materials.
3. Using the appropriate production process.
4. Assembling and testing the product.
5. Placing adequate warnings on the label to inform the user of dangers of which an ordinary person might not be aware.
6. Inspecting and testing any purchased components used in the product.

Privity of Contract Not Required A product liability action based on negligence does not require *privity of contract* between the injured plaintiff and the defendant-manufacturer. **Privity of contract** refers to the relationship that exists between the parties to a contract. Privity is the reason that normally only the parties to a contract can enforce that contract.

In the context of product liability law, though, privity is not required. A person who is injured by a defective product may bring a negligence suit even though he or she was not the one who actually purchased the product—and thus is not in privity. A manufacturer, seller, or lessor is liable for failure to exercise due care to *any person* who sustains an injury proximately caused by a negligently made (defective) product.

A 1916 landmark decision established this exception to the privity requirement. ■ **CASE IN POINT 7.2** Donald MacPherson suffered injuries while riding in a Buick automobile that suddenly collapsed because one of the wheels was made of defective wood. The spokes crumbled into fragments, throwing MacPherson out of the vehicle and injuring him.

MacPherson had purchased the car from a Buick dealer, but he brought a lawsuit against the manufacturer, Buick Motor Company, alleging negligence. Buick itself had not made the wheel but had bought it from another manufacturer. There was evidence, though, that the defects could have been discovered by a reasonable inspection by Buick and that no such inspection had taken place. The primary issue was whether Buick owed a duty of care to anyone except the immediate purchaser of the car—that is, the Buick dealer. Although Buick itself had not manufactured the wheel, New York's highest state court held that Buick had a duty to inspect the wheels and that Buick "was responsible for the finished product." Therefore, Buick was liable to MacPherson for the injuries he sustained. [4] ■

---

4. *MacPherson v. Buick Motor Co.,* 217 N.Y. 382, 111 N.E. 1050 (1916).

"Cause in Fact" and Proximate Cause In a product liability suit based on negligence, as in any action alleging that the defendant was negligent, the plaintiff must show that the defendant's conduct was the "cause in fact" of an injury. "Cause in fact" requires showing that "but for" the defendant's action, the injury would not have occurred.

It must also be determined that the defendant's act was the *proximate cause* of the injury. This determination focuses on the foreseeability of the consequences of the act and whether the defendant should be held legally responsible. For proximate cause to become a relevant issue, however, a plaintiff first must establish cause in fact. The cause of a serious accident was at issue in the following case.

Case Analysis 7.1

Schwarck v. Arctic Cat, Inc.

Court of Appeals of Michigan, __ Mich.App. __, 2016 WL 191992 (2016).

In the Language of the Court

PER CURIAM. [By the Whole Court]
* * * *

* * * Karen Schwarck * * * was operating an Arctic Cat [660 snowmobile] near Mackinac Island's Grand Hotel [in Michigan] with her sister, Edith Bonno, as passenger. The sisters met their demise when the Arctic Cat went, in reverse, backward through a wooden fence and over the West Bluff of the Island.

[Donald Schwarck and Joshua Bonno] the spouses of decedents, as their personal representatives, filed this action [in a Michigan state court] against defendant Arctic Cat [the manufacturer of the 660]. Plaintiffs alleged that the Arctic Cat 660 was negligently designed * * * without a backup alarm that operated throughout all the reverse travel positions and as a result proximately caused decedents' injuries.

Defendant filed a motion for summary [judgment]. Defendant denied the existence of a "silent reverse zone," but argued that even if such a zone existed, it was not a cause of the accident because the alarm was intended as a warning to bystanders and not as an indicator of shift position for operators.
* * * *

* * * The court issued its decision and order in favor of defendant. [The plaintiffs appealed.]
* * * *

There is no dispute that on the day of the accident decedent Schwarck was driving the Arctic Cat 660 * * * and that she attempted to execute a three-point

or K-turn * * * . To make the turn decedent Schwarck had to turn left to face north, stop, reverse south, stop, and then complete the turn to drive east. * * * Plaintiffs argue that after decedent Schwarck reversed, she stopped a second time and shifted forward, and not hearing the reverse alarm, believed she was in forward, and accelerated. As a result, the craft went in reverse through the fence and off the bluff.

The trial court determined that there were no material questions of fact on * * * the operability of the reverse alarm. * * * It was undisputed that an inspection of the Arctic Cat post-accident showed the reverse alarm to be operable.
* * * *

* * * [But] the court's conclusion that the reverse alarm was working at the time of the accident does not determine whether its operational process constituted a product defect. Plaintiffs' claim was that the reverse alarm was defective because it did not sound during the entire time the vehicle was in reverse. Plaintiffs' causation theory was that the Arctic Cat's reverse alarm caused decedent Schwarck to be confused about whether she was in forward or reverse gear and that the confusion led to the accident that caused decedents' deaths.

[Plaintiffs' expert John Frackelton, an accident reconstructionist and snowmobile mechanic,] observed that the shift lever traveled from full reverse to full forward in a distance of four inches. Frackelton's testing revealed that when the lever was shifted all the way down

and pressed against the reverse buffer switch, the switch sounded a chime and the snowmobile was in full reverse mode. Frackelton experimented with the lever, shifting it up toward forward gear, an inch at a time. For the next two inches of shift travel forward, the reverse alarm did not sound, but the snowmobile was still in reverse. Frackelton observed that it was only in the last or fourth inch of shift travel that the snowmobile was in full forward.

* * * Frackelton observed that the transition from full reverse to full forward was smooth and accomplished with little pressure. He opined that an operator could "become accustomed to the highly repeatable return performance." On two occasions, however, Frackelton pushed the gearshift forward and the Arctic Cat did not return to forward gear as expected.

* * * Frackelton's opinion * * * creates a material question of fact as to whether the alarm failed to sound at all times when the gear was in reverse. Defendant argues that the alarm served its intended purpose which is to notify bystanders and not operators that the snowmobile is in reverse and that it was unreasonable for decedent Schwarck to rely on the alarm to determine the gear of the snowmobile. *The fact that the manufacturer's intended purpose for the alarm was to warn third-parties is not dispositive of the issue of whether decedent Schwarck relied on the alarm to*

determine her gear or whether that reliance was reasonable or a foreseeable misuse of the alarm and snowmobile. Decedent Schwarck is assumed to have acted with due care for her own safety. Her widower averred that, based upon his observations, decedent Schwarck had a practice and routine of relying upon the sounding of the alarm as a signal that she was in reverse. Evidence from Frackelton's test runs also demonstrate that despite manual control of the shift lever, the lever could stop just short of the forward position and prevent the snowmobile from going into drive. [Emphasis added.]

Reasonable minds could differ as to whether a reverse alarm that does not sound throughout the reverse trajectory or only operates in a partial manner is defective.

* * * *

Legal cause becomes a relevant issue after cause in fact has been established. * * * *To establish legal cause, the plaintiff*

*must show that it was foreseeable that the defendant's conduct may create a risk of harm to the victim, and * * * that the result of that conduct and intervening causes were foreseeable. * * ** It is foreseeable that an operator of the Arctic Cat may rely on the sound of the reverse alarm to indicate when the snowmobile is no longer in reverse and experience unexpected travel backward because the alarm does not sound during the entire reverse gear. It is further foreseeable that unanticipated reverse travel may cause a risk of harm to the operator. * * * Frackelton's tests regarding speed velocity without aggressive throttle demonstrate how the Arctic Cat can travel almost thirty feet in just 5.4 seconds. Not only can an operator of the Arctic Cat find him or herself unexpectedly travelling in reverse, but also doing so quickly. Plaintiffs' other expert [Lila Laux, a psychologist and engineer] testified * * * that time is * * * required for the operator to determine how to respond to the

unexpected stimuli, to engage the brake, and for the brake to activate. [Emphasis added.]

A jury could infer that traveling backward when one thought he or she would go forward is an unexpected stimulus. It is also a reasonable inference, from the opinions of both plaintiffs' experts, that it was foreseeable that the operator would be surprised by the rearward motion. Given the evidence, reasonable minds may differ as to whether decedent Schwarck did not or could not correct the snowmobile's rearward direction in the time allotted.

Based on the whole record, there is evidence that warrants submission of this case to a jury to determine whether the reverse alarm was defective and whether that defect caused decedent Schwarck and Bonno's deaths.

* * * *

[The trial court's judgment is] vacated and remanded for proceedings consistent with this opinion.

Legal Reasoning Questions

1. According to the plaintiffs, what was the product defect at the center of this case? According to the defendant, why was this not a defect?

2. How did the plaintiffs use evidence to support their claim?

3. Why did the court conclude that this case should be submitted to a jury? Explain.

7–2b Misrepresentation

When a user or consumer is injured as a result of a manufacturer's or seller's fraudulent misrepresentation, the basis of liability may be the tort of fraud. In this situation, the misrepresentation must have been made knowingly or with reckless disregard for the facts. The intentional mislabeling of packaged cosmetics, for instance, or the intentional concealment of a product's defects would constitute fraudulent misrepresentation.

In addition, the misrepresentation must be of a material fact, and the seller must have intended to induce the buyer's reliance on the misrepresentation. Misrepresentation on a label or advertisement is enough to show an intent to induce the reliance of anyone who may use the

product. In addition, the buyer must have relied on the misrepresentation.

7–3 Strict Product Liability

As mentioned earlier, under the doctrine of strict liability, people may be liable for the results of their acts regardless of their intentions or their exercise of reasonable care. In addition, liability does not depend on privity of contract. Thus, the injured party does not have to be the buyer, as required under contract warranty theories. In the 1960s, courts applied the doctrine of strict liability in several landmark cases involving manufactured goods, and it has since become a common method of holding manufacturers liable.

7–3a Strict Product Liability and Public Policy

The law imposes strict product liability as a matter of public policy. This public policy rests on a threefold assumption:

1. Consumers should be protected against unsafe products.
2. Manufacturers and distributors should not escape liability for faulty products simply because they are not in privity of contract with the ultimate user of those products.
3. Manufacturers and distributors can better bear the costs associated with injuries caused by their products, because they can ultimately pass the costs on to all consumers in the form of higher prices.

Development of the Doctrine California was the first state to impose strict product liability in tort on manufacturers. ■ **CASE IN POINT 7.3** William Greenman was injured when his Shopsmith combination power tool threw off a piece of wood that struck him in the head. He sued the manufacturer, claiming that he had followed the product's instructions and the product must be defective. In a landmark decision, *Greenman v. Yuba Power Products, Inc.,*[5] the California Supreme Court set out the reason for applying tort law rather than contract law (including laws governing warranties) in cases involving consumers who were injured by defective products.

According to the *Greenman* court, the "purpose of such liability is to [e]nsure that the costs of injuries resulting from defective products are borne by the manufacturers . . . rather than by the injured persons who are powerless to protect themselves." ■ Today, the majority of states recognize strict product liability, although some state courts limit its application to situations involving personal injuries (rather than property damage).

Stated Public Policy Public policy may be expressed in a statute or in the common law. Sometimes, public policy may be revealed in a court's interpretation of a statute, as in the following case.

---

5. 59 Cal.2d 57, 377 P.2d 897, 27 Cal.Rptr. 697 (1962).

Spotlight on Injuries from Vaccines

Case 7.2 Bruesewitz v. Wyeth, LLC

Supreme Court of the United States, 562 U.S. 223, 131 S.Ct. 1068, 179 L.Ed.2d 1 (2011).

Company Profile *Wyeth, LLC—a subsidiary of Pfizer, Inc.—is an international pharmaceutical and health-care company with its corporate headquarters in Madison, New Jersey. Wyeth develops, makes, and markets medical therapies, clinical programs, nutritional supplements, prescription drugs, and other health-care products, including over-the-counter medications. Wyeth was incorporated in 1926. In 1994, the company bought Lederle Laboratories. Since 1948, Lederle had been making the diphtheria, tetanus, and pertussis (DTP) vaccine for children.*

Background and Facts When Hannah Bruesewitz was six months old, her pediatrician administered a dose of the DTP vaccine according to the Centers for Disease Control's recommended childhood immunization schedule. Within twenty-four hours, Hannah began to experience seizures. She suffered more than one hundred seizures during the next month. Her doctors diagnosed her with "residual seizure disorder" and "developmental delay."

Hannah's parents, Russell and Robalee Bruesewitz, filed a claim for relief in the U.S. Court of Federal Claims under the National Childhood Vaccine Injury Act (NCVIA). The NCVIA had set up a no-fault compensation program for persons injured by vaccines. The claim was denied. The Bruesewitzes then filed a suit in a state court against Wyeth, LLC, the maker of the vaccine, alleging strict product liability. The suit was moved to a federal district court. The court held that the claim was preempted by the NCVIA, which includes provisions protecting manufacturers from liability for "a vaccine's unavoidable, adverse side effects." The U.S. Court of Appeals for the Third Circuit affirmed the district court's judgment. The Bruesewitzes appealed to the United States Supreme Court.

Case 7.2 Continued

In the Language of the Court

Justice *SCALIA* delivered the opinion of the Court.

* * * *

In the 1970's and 1980's vaccines became, one might say, victims of their own success. They had been so effective in preventing infectious diseases that the public became much less alarmed at the threat of those diseases, and much more concerned with the risk of injury from the vaccines themselves.

Much of the concern centered around vaccines against * * * DTP, which were blamed for children's disabilities * * * . This led to a massive increase in vaccine-related tort litigation. * * * This destabilized the DTP vaccine market, causing two of the three domestic manufacturers to withdraw.

* * * *

To stabilize the vaccine market and facilitate compensation, Congress enacted the NCVIA in 1986. The Act establishes a no-fault compensation program designed to work faster and with greater ease than the civil tort system. A person injured by a vaccine, or his legal guardian, may file a petition for compensation in the United States Court of Federal Claims.

* * * *

Successful claimants receive compensation for medical, rehabilitation, counseling, special education, and vocational training expenses; diminished earning capacity; pain and suffering; and $250,000 for vaccine-related deaths. Attorney's fees are provided * * * . These awards are paid out of a fund created by a * * * tax on each vaccine dose.

The *quid pro quo* [something done in exchange] for this, designed to stabilize the vaccine market, was the provision of significant tort-liability protections for vaccine manufacturers. * * * *Manufacturers are generally immunized from liability * * * if they have complied with all regulatory requirements * * * . * * * And most relevant to the present case, the Act expressly eliminates liability for a vaccine's unavoidable, adverse side effects.* [Emphasis added.]

* * * *

The Act's structural *quid pro quo* leads to the * * * conclusion: The vaccine manufacturers fund from their sales an informal, efficient compensation program for vaccine injuries; in exchange they avoid costly tort litigation.

Decision and Remedy *The United States Supreme Court affirmed the lower court's judgment. The NCVIA preempted the Bruesewitzes' claim against Wyeth for compensation for the injury to their daughter caused by the DTP vaccine's side effects. The Court found that the NCVIA's compensation program strikes a balance between paying victims harmed by vaccines and protecting the vaccine industry from collapsing under the costs of tort liability.*

Critical Thinking

- **Economic** *What is the public policy expressed by the provisions of the NCVIA?*
- **Political** *If the public wants to change the policy outlined in this case, which branch of the government—and at what level—should be lobbied to make the change? Explain.*

7–3b The Requirements for Strict Product Liability

After the *Restatement (Second) of Torts* was issued in 1964, Section 402A became a widely accepted statement of how the doctrine of strict liability should be applied to sellers of goods (including manufacturers, processors, assemblers, packagers, bottlers, wholesalers, distributors, retailers, and lessors). The bases for an action in strict liability that are set forth in Section 402A can be summarized as a set of six requirements.

1. The product must be in a *defective condition* when the defendant sells it.

2. The defendant must normally be engaged in the *business of selling* (or otherwise distributing) that product.

3. The product must be *unreasonably dangerous* to the user or consumer because of its defective condition (in most states).

4. The plaintiff must incur *physical harm* to self or property by use or consumption of the product.

5. The defective condition must be the *proximate cause* of the injury or damage.
6. The *goods must not have been substantially changed* from the time the product was sold to the time the injury was sustained.

Depending on the jurisdiction, if these requirements are met, a manufacturer's liability to an injured party can be almost unlimited.

Proving a Defective Condition Under these requirements, in any action against a manufacturer, seller, or lessor, the plaintiff need not show why or in what manner the product became defective. The plaintiff does, however, have to prove that the product was defective at the time it left the hands of the seller or lessor. The plaintiff must also show that this defective condition made the product "unreasonably dangerous" to the user or consumer.

Unless evidence can be presented to support the conclusion that the product was defective when it was sold or leased, the plaintiff will not succeed. If the product was delivered in a safe condition and subsequent mishandling made it harmful to the user, the seller or lessor normally is not strictly liable.

Unreasonably Dangerous Products The *Restatement* recognizes that many products cannot be made entirely safe for all uses. Thus, sellers or lessors are liable only for products that are *unreasonably* dangerous. A court could consider a product so defective as to be an **unreasonably dangerous product** in either of the following situations:

1. The product was dangerous beyond the expectation of the ordinary consumer.
2. A less dangerous alternative was *economically* feasible for the manufacturer, but the manufacturer failed to produce it.

As will be discussed next, a product may be unreasonably dangerous due to the manufacturing process, the design, or the warning.

7–3c Product Defects

The *Restatement (Third) of Torts: Products Liability* defines the three types of product defects that have traditionally been recognized in product liability law—manufacturing defects, design defects, and inadequate warnings.

Manufacturing Defects According to Section 2(a) of the *Restatement (Third) of Torts,* a product "contains a manufacturing defect when the product departs from

its intended design even though all possible care was exercised in the preparation and marketing of the product." Basically, a manufacturing defect is a departure from a product unit's design specifications that results in products that are physically flawed, damaged, or incorrectly assembled. A glass bottle that is made too thin and explodes in a consumer's face is an example of a product with a manufacturing defect.

Quality Control. Usually, manufacturing defects occur when a manufacturer fails to assemble, test, or check the quality of a product adequately. Liability is imposed on the manufacturer (and on the wholesaler and retailer) regardless of whether the manufacturer's quality control efforts were "reasonable." The idea behind holding defendants strictly liable for manufacturing defects is to encourage greater investment in product safety and stringent quality control standards.

Expert Testimony. Cases involving allegations of a manufacturing defect are often decided based on the opinions and testimony of experts. ■ **CASE IN POINT 7.4** Kevin Schmude purchased an eight-foot stepladder and used it to install radio-frequency shielding in a hospital room. While Schmude was standing on the ladder, it collapsed, and he was seriously injured. He filed a lawsuit against the ladder's maker, Tricam Industries, Inc., based on a manufacturing defect.

Experts testified that the preexisting holes in the ladder's top cap did not properly line up with the holes in the rear right rail and backing plate. As a result of the misalignment, the rear legs of the ladder were not securely fastened in place, causing the ladder to fail. A jury concluded that this manufacturing defect made the ladder unreasonably dangerous and awarded Schmude more than $677,000 in damages.[6] ■

Design Defects Unlike a product with a manufacturing defect, a product with a design defect is made in conformity with the manufacturer's design specifications. Nevertheless, the product results in injury to the user because the design itself was faulty. A product "is defective in design when the foreseeable risks of harm posed by the product could have been reduced or avoided by the adoption of a reasonable alternative design by the seller or other distributor, or a predecessor in the commercial chain of distribution, and the omission of the alternative design renders the product not reasonably safe."[7]

---

6. *Schmude v. Tricam Industries, Inc.,* 550 F.Supp.2d 846 (E.D.Wis. 2008).
7. *Restatement (Third) of Torts: Products Liability,* Section 2(b).

Test for Design Defects. To successfully assert a design defect, a plaintiff has to show that:

1. A reasonable alternative design was available.
2. As a result of the defendant's failure to adopt the alternative design, the product was not reasonably safe.

In other words, a manufacturer or other defendant is liable only when the harm was reasonably preventable.

Factors to Be Considered. According to the *Restatement,* a court can consider a broad range of factors in deciding claims of design defects. These include the magnitude and probability of the foreseeable risks, as well as the relative advantages and disadvantages of the product as it was designed and as it could have been designed.

Risk-Utility Analysis. Most courts engage in a risk-utility analysis to determine whether the risk of harm from the product as designed outweighs its utility to the user and to the public. ■ **CASE IN POINT 7.5** Benjamin Riley, the county sheriff, was driving his Ford F-150 pickup truck near Ehrhardt, South Carolina, when it collided with another vehicle. The impact caused Riley's truck to leave the road and roll over. The driver's door of the truck opened in the collision, and Riley was ejected and killed.

Riley's widow, Laura, as the representative of his estate, filed a product liability suit against Ford Motor Company. She alleged that the design of the door-latch system of the truck allowed the door to open in the collision. A state court awarded the estate $900,000 in damages "because of the stature of Riley and what he's done in life, what he's contributed to his family."

Ford appealed, but the court found that a reasonable alternative design was available for the door-latch system. Evidence showed that Ford was aware of the safety problems presented by the current system (a rod-linkage system). After conducting a risk-utility analysis of a different system (a cable-linkage system), Ford had concluded that the alternative system was feasible and perhaps superior. The state's highest court affirmed the damages award.[8] ■

Consumer-Expectation Test. Other courts apply the consumer-expectation test to determine whether a product's design was defective. Under this test, a product is unreasonably dangerous when it fails to perform in the manner that would reasonably be expected by an ordinary consumer.

■ **CASE IN POINT 7.6** A representative from Wilson Sporting Goods Company gave Edwin Hickox an umpire's mask that was designed to be safer than other such masks. The mask had a newly designed throat guard that angled forward instead of extending straight down. Hickox was wearing the mask while working as an umpire at a game when he was struck by a ball and injured. He suffered a concussion and damage to his inner ear, which caused permanent hearing loss.

Hickox and his wife sued Wilson for product liability based on a defective design and won. Wilson appealed. The reviewing court affirmed the jury's verdict. The design was defective because "an ordinary consumer would have expected the mask to perform more safely than it did." The evidence presented to the jury had shown that Wilson's mask was more dangerous than comparable masks sold at the time.[9] ■

Inadequate Warnings A product may also be deemed defective because of inadequate instructions or warnings. A product will be considered defective "when the foreseeable risks of harm posed by the product could have been reduced or avoided by the provision of reasonable instructions or warnings by the seller or other distributor . . . and the omission of the instructions or warnings renders the product not reasonably safe."[10] Generally, a seller must also warn consumers of the harm that can result from the *foreseeable misuse* of its product.

Content of Warnings. Important factors for a court to consider include the risks of a product, the "content and comprehensibility" and "intensity of expression" of warnings and instructions, and the "characteristics of expected user groups."[11] Courts apply a "reasonableness" test to determine if the warnings adequately alert consumers to the product's risks. For instance, children will likely respond readily to bright, bold, simple warning labels, whereas educated adults might need more detailed information. For more on tips on making sure a product's warnings are adequate, see this chapter's *Managerial Strategy* feature.

■ **CASE IN POINT 7.7** Jeffrey Johnson went to an emergency room for an episode of atrial fibrillation, a heart rhythm disorder. Dr. David Hahn used a defibrillator manufactured by Medtronic, Inc., to deliver electric shocks to Johnson's heart. The defibrillator had synchronous and asynchronous modes, and it reverted to the

---

8. *Riley v. Ford Motor Co.,* 414 S.C. 185, 777 S.E.2d 824 (2015).

9. *Wilson Sporting Goods Co. v. Hickox,* 59 A.3d 1267 (D.C.App. 2013).
10. *Restatement (Third) of Torts: Products Liability,* Section 2(c).
11. *Restatement (Third) of Torts: Products Liability,* Section 2, Comment h.

MANAGERIAL
STRATEGY

When Is a Warning Legally Bulletproof?

A company can sell a perfectly manufactured and designed product, yet still face product liability lawsuits for failure to provide appropriate warnings. According to the *Restatement (Third) of Torts*, a product may be deemed defective because of inadequate instructions or warnings when the foreseeable risks of harm posed by the product could have been reduced by reasonable warnings offered by the seller or other distributor.

Manufacturers and distributors have a duty to warn users of any hidden dangers of their products. Additionally, they have a duty to instruct users in how to use the product to avoid any dangers. Warnings generally must be clear and specific. They must also be conspicuous.

When No Warning Is Required

Not all products have to provide warnings. People are expected to know that knives can cut fingers, for example, so a seller need not place a bright orange label on each knife sold reminding consumers of this danger. Most household products are generally safe when used as intended.

In a New Jersey case, an appeals court reviewed a product liability case against the manufacturer of a Razor A–type kick scooter. A ten-year-old boy was injured when he fell and struck his face on the scooter's handlebars. The padded end caps on the handlebars had deteriorated, and the boy's mother had thrown them away, exposing the metal ends.

The boy and his mother sued, claiming that the manufacturer was required to provide a warning to prevent injuries of this type. The appellate court noted, however, that the plaintiffs were not able to claim that the Razor A was defective. "Lacking evidence that Razor A's end-cap design was defective, plaintiffs cannot show that Razor A had a duty to warn of such a defect, and

therefore cannot make out their failure to warn claim."[a]

Warnings on Medications

In a case involving a prescription medication, a woman suffered neurological disorders after taking a generic drug to treat her gastroesophageal reflux disease. Part of her complaint asserted strict liability for failure to warn. The plaintiff claimed that the manufacturer had not updated its label to indicate that usage should not exceed twelve weeks. The reviewing court reasoned that "The adequacy of the instructions . . . made no difference to the outcome . . . because [the plaintiff alleges that her prescribing physician] did not read those materials."[b]

In contrast, in a 2014 Pennsylvania case, a family was awarded over $10 million in a lawsuit against Johnson & Johnson for defective warnings on bottles of children's Motrin. A three-year-old girl suffered burns over 84 percent of her skin, experienced brain damage, and went blind after suffering a reaction to the drug. The drug did have a specific warning label that instructed consumers to stop taking the medication and contact a physician in the event of an allergic reaction. Nonetheless, Johnson & Johnson was found liable for failing to warn about the known risk of severe side effects.[c]

Business Questions

1. *To protect themselves, manufacturers have been forced to include lengthy safety warnings for their products. What might be the downside of such warnings?*

2. *Does a manufacturer have to create safety warnings for every product? Why or why not?*

a. *Vann v. Toys R Us*, 2014 WL3537937 (N.J.Sup. A.D. 2014).
b. *Brinkley v. Pfizer, Inc.*, 772 F.3d 1133 (8th Cir. 2014).
c. *Maya v. Johnson and Johnson*, 97 A.3d 1203, 2014 PA Super. 152 (2014).

asynchronous mode after each use. Hahn intended to deliver synchronized shocks, which would have required him to select the synchronous mode for each shock. But Hahn did not read the device's instructions, which Medtronic had provided both in a manual and on the device itself. As a result, the physician delivered one synchronized shock, followed by twelve asynchronous shocks that endangered Johnson's life.

Johnson and his wife filed a product liability suit against Medtronic, asserting that Medtronic had provided

inadequate warnings about the defibrillator and that the device had a design defect. A Missouri appellate court held that the Johnsons could not pursue a claim based on the inadequacy of Medtronic's warnings, but they could pursue a claim alleging a design defect. The court reasoned that, in some cases, "a manufacturer may be held liable where it chooses to warn of the danger . . . rather than preclude the danger by design."[12] ■

12. *Johnson v. Medtronic, Inc.*, 365 S.W.3d 226 (Mo.App. 2012).

Obvious Risks. There is no duty to warn about risks that are obvious or commonly known. Warnings about such risks do not add to the safety of a product and could even detract from it by making other warnings seem less significant. As will be discussed later in the chapter, the obviousness of a risk and a user's decision to proceed in the face of that risk may be a defense in a product liability suit based on an inadequate warning.

■ **EXAMPLE 7.8** Sixteen-year-old Lana White attempts to do a back flip on a trampoline and fails. She is paralyzed as a result. There are nine warning labels affixed to the trampoline, an instruction manual with safety warnings, and a placard at the entrance advising users not to do flips. If White sues the manufacturer for inadequate warnings in this situation, she is likely to lose. The warning labels are probably sufficient to make the risks obvious and insulate the manufacturer from liability for her injuries. ■

Risks that may seem obvious to some users, though, will not be obvious to all users, especially when the users are likely to be children. A young child may not be able to read or understand warning labels or comprehend the risk of certain activities. To avoid liability, the manufacturer would have to prove that the warnings it provided were adequate to make the risk of injury obvious to a young child.[13]

State Laws and Constitutionality. An action alleging that a product is defective due to an inadequate label can be based on state law, but that law must not violate the U.S. Constitution. ■ **CASE IN POINT 7.9** California once enacted a law imposing restrictions and a labeling requirement on the sale or rental of "violent video games" to minors. Although the video game industry had adopted a voluntary rating system for games, the legislators deemed those labels inadequate.

The Video Software Dealers Association and the Entertainment Software Association immediately filed a suit in federal court to invalidate the law, and the law was struck down. The state appealed to the United States Supreme Court. The Court found that the definition of a violent video game in California's law was unconstitutionally vague and violated the First Amendment's guarantee of freedom of speech.[14] ■

7–3d Market-Share Liability

Ordinarily, in all product liability claims, a plaintiff must prove that the defective product that caused his or her injury was the product of a specific defendant. In a few situations, however, courts have dropped this requirement when plaintiffs could not prove which of many distributors of a harmful product supplied the particular product that caused the injuries. Under a theory of **market-share liability,** a court can hold each manufacturer responsible for a percentage of the plaintiff's damages that is equal to the percentage of its market share.

■ **CASE IN POINT 7.10** Suffolk County Water Authority (SCWA) is a municipal water supplier in New York. SCWA discovered the presence of a toxic chemical—perchlorethylene (PCE), which is used by dry cleaners and others—in its local water. SCWA filed a product liability lawsuit against Dow Chemical Corporation and other companies that manufactured and distributed PCE. Dow filed a motion to dismiss the case for failure to state a claim, since SCWA could not identify each defendant whose allegedly defective product caused the water contamination.

A state trial court refused to dismiss the action, holding that SCWA's allegations were sufficient to invoke market-share liability. Under market-share liability, the burden of identification shifts to defendants if the plaintiff establishes a *prima facie* case on every element of the claim except identification of the specific defendant. (A *prima facie* case is one in which the plaintiff has presented sufficient evidence for the claim to go forward.)[15] ■

Many jurisdictions do not recognize the market-share theory of liability because they believe that it deviates too significantly from traditional legal principles. Jurisdictions that do recognize market-share liability apply it only when it is difficult to determine which company made a particular product.

7–3e Other Applications of Strict Product Liability

Almost all courts extend the strict liability of manufacturers and other sellers to injured bystanders. Thus, if a defective forklift that will not go into reverse injures a passerby, that individual can sue the manufacturer for product liability (and possibly also sue the forklift operator for negligence).

Strict product liability also applies to suppliers of component parts. ■ **EXAMPLE 7.11** Toyota buys brake pads from a subcontractor and puts them in Corollas without changing their composition. If those pads are defective, both the supplier of the brake pads and Toyota will be held strictly liable for the injuries caused by the defects. ■

---

13. See, for example, *Bunch v. Hoffinger Industries, Inc.*, 123 Cal.App.4th 1278, 20 Cal.Rptr.3d 780 (2004).

14. *Video Software Dealers Association v. Schwarzenegger*, 556 F.3d 950 (9th Cir. 2009); *Brown v. Entertainment Merchants Association*, ___ U.S. ___, 131 S.Ct. 2729, 180 L.Ed.2d 708 (2011).

15. *Suffolk County Water Authority v. Dow Chemical Co.*, 44 Misc.3d 569, 987 N.Y.S.2d 819 (N.Y.Sup. 2014).

7–4 Defenses to Product Liability

Defendants in product liability suits can raise a number of defenses. One defense, of course, is to show that there is no basis for the plaintiff's claim. Thus, for instance, in an action based on negligence, If a defendant can show that the plaintiff has *not* met the requirements for such an action (such as causation), then generally the defendant will not be liable.

Similarly, in a case involving strict product liability, a defendant can claim that the plaintiff failed to meet one of the requirements. For instance, if the defendant shows that the goods were altered after they were sold, normally the defendant will not be held liable.

In the following case, a product's safety switch had been disabled before the plaintiff used the product.

Case 7.3

VeRost v. Mitsubishi Caterpillar Forklift America, Inc.

New York Supreme Court, Appellate Division, Fourth Department, 124 A.D.3d 1219, 1 N.Y.S.3d 589 (2015).

Background and Facts Drew VeRost was employed at a manufacturing facility in Buffalo, New York, owned by Nuttall Gear, LLC. While operating a forklift at Nuttall's facility, VeRost climbed out of the seat and attempted to engage a lever on the vehicle. As he stood on the front of the forklift and reached for the lever with his hand, he inadvertently stepped on the vehicle's gearshift. The activated gears caused part of the forklift to move backward, injuring him. He filed a suit in a New York state court against the forklift's maker, Mitsubishi Caterpillar Forklift America, Inc., and others, asserting claims in product liability.

The defendants established that the vehicle had been manufactured with a safety switch that would have prevented the accident had it not been disabled after delivery to Nuttall. The court issued a summary judgment in the defendants' favor. VeRost appealed.

In the Language of the Court
MEMORANDUM:
* * * *

The forklift in question was manufactured by defendant Mitsubishi Caterpillar Forklift America, Inc. (MCFA), and sold new to Nuttall Gear by defendants Buffalo Lift Trucks, Inc. (Buffalo Lift) and Mullen Industrial Handling Corp. (Mullen). The forklift as manufactured was equipped with a seat safety switch that would render the forklift inoperable if the operator was not in the driver's seat. At the time of the accident, however, someone had intentionally disabled the safety switch by installing a "jumper wire" under the seat of the forklift. As a result, the forklift still had power when the operator was not in the driver's seat. Of the 10 forklifts owned by Nuttall Gear, seven had "jumper wires" installed that disabled the safety switches.

The complaint asserts causes of action against MCFA, Buffalo Lift and Mullen sounding in strict products liability, alleging, *inter alia* ["among other things"], that the forklift was defectively designed and that those defendants failed to provide adequate "warnings for the safe operation, maintenance repair and servicing of the forklift." * * * Following discovery, the * * * defendants * * * each moved for summary judgment dismissing the complaint against them, contending that the forklift was safe when it was manufactured and delivered to Nuttall Gear, and that it was thereafter rendered unsafe by a third party who deactivated the safety switch. * * * [The] Supreme Court [of New York] granted the motions and dismissed the complaint in its entirety, and this appeal ensued.

We conclude that the court properly granted the motions of the * * * defendants. * * * *A manufacturer, who has designed and produced a safe product, will not be liable for injuries resulting from substantial alterations or modifications of the product by a third party which render the product defective or otherwise unsafe.* Here, the * * * defendants established as a matter of law that the forklift was not defectively designed by establishing that, when it was manufactured and delivered to Nuttall Gear, it had a safety switch that would have prevented plaintiff's accident, and a third party thereafter made a substantial modification to the forklift by disabling the safety switch. [Emphasis added.]

Decision and Remedy *The state intermediate appellate court affirmed the lower court's judgment in Mitsubishi's favor. To succeed in an action based on product liability, the goods at issue must not have been substantially changed from the time the product was sold to the time the injury was sustained. VeRost could not meet this requirement.*

Critical Thinking

- **Legal Environment** *Could VeRost succeed in an action against Nuttall, alleging that the company's failure to maintain the forklift in a safe condition constituted negligence? Discuss.*

7–4a Preemption

A defense that has been successfully raised by defendants in recent years is preemption—that government regulations preempt claims for product liability (see *Spotlight Case* 7.2). An injured party may not be able to sue the manufacturer of defective products that are subject to comprehensive federal regulatory schemes.

■ **CASE IN POINT 7.12** Medical devices are subject to extensive government regulation and undergo a rigorous premarket approval process. The United States Supreme Court decided in *Riegel v. Medtronic, Inc.,* that a man who was injured by an approved medical device (a balloon catheter) could not sue its maker for product liability. The Court reasoned that Congress had created a comprehensive scheme of federal safety oversight for medical devices. The U.S. Food and Drug Administration is required to review the design, labeling, and manufacturing of medical devices before they are marketed to make sure that they are safe and effective. Because premarket approval is a "rigorous process," it preempts all common law claims challenging the safety or effectiveness of a medical device that has been approved.[16] ■

Since the *Medtronic* decision, some courts have extended the preemption defense to other product liability actions. Other courts have been unwilling to deny an injured party relief simply because the federal government was supposed to ensure a product's safety.[17] Even the United States Supreme Court refused to extend the preemption defense to preclude a drug maker's liability in one subsequent case.[18]

7–4b Assumption of Risk

Assumption of risk can sometimes be used as a defense in a product liability action. To establish assumption of risk, the defendant must show the following:

1. The plaintiff knew and appreciated the risk created by the product defect.
2. The plaintiff voluntarily assumed the risk—by express agreement or by words or conduct—even though it was unreasonable to do so.

Some states do not allow the defense of assumption of risk in strict product liability claims, however. ■ **CASE IN POINT 7.13** When Savannah Boles became a customer of Executive Tans, she signed a contract. One part of the contract stated that signers used the company's tanning booths at their own risk. It also released the manufacturer and others from liability for any injuries.

Later, Boles's fingers were partially amputated when they came into contact with a tanning booth's fan. Boles sued the manufacturer for strict product liability. The Colorado Supreme Court held that assumption of risk was not applicable because strict product liability is driven by public-policy considerations. The theory focuses on the nature of the product rather than the conduct of either the manufacturer or the person injured.[19] ■

7–4c Product Misuse

Similar to the defense of voluntary assumption of risk is that of **product misuse,** which occurs when a product is used for a purpose for which it was not intended. The courts have severely limited this defense, however, and it is now recognized as a defense *only when the particular use was not foreseeable.* If the misuse is reasonably foreseeable, the seller must take measures to guard against it.

---

16. *Riegel v. Medtronic, Inc.,* 552 U.S. 312, 128 S.Ct. 999, 169 L.Ed.2d 892 (2008).

17. See, for example, *McGuan v. Endovascular Technologies, Inc.,* 182 Cal. App.4th 974, 106 Cal.Rptr.3d 277 (2010), and *Paduano v. American Honda Motor Co.,* 169 Cal.App.4th 1453, 88 Cal.Rptr.3d 90 (2009).

18. *Wyeth v. Levine,* 555 U.S. 555, 129 S.Ct. 1187, 173 L.Ed.2d 51 (2009).

19. *Boles v. Sun Ergoline, Inc.,* 223 P.3d 724 (Col.Sup.Ct. 2010).

CASE IN POINT 7.14 David Stults developed bronchiolitis obliterans ("popcorn lung") from consuming multiple bags of microwave popcorn daily for several years. When Stults filed a lawsuit against the popcorn manufacturers, they asked the court for a summary judgment in their favor. The court denied the defendants' motion and found that a manufacturer has a duty to warn of dangers associated with reasonably foreseeable misuses of a product. If it is foreseeable that a person might consume several bags of microwave popcorn a day, then the manufacturer might have to warn users about the potential health risks associated with doing so.[20] ■

7–4d Comparative Negligence (Fault)

Comparative negligence, or fault, can also affect strict liability claims. Today, courts in many jurisdictions consider the negligent or intentional actions of both the plaintiff and the defendant when apportioning liability and damages. A defendant may be able to limit some of its liability if it can show that the plaintiff's misuse of the product contributed to his or her injuries.

When proved, comparative negligence differs from other defenses in that it does not completely absolve the defendant of liability. It can, however, reduce the total amount of damages that will be awarded to the plaintiff. Note that some jurisdictions allow only intentional conduct to affect a plaintiff's recovery, whereas other states allow ordinary negligence to be used as a defense to product liability.

7–4e Commonly Known Dangers

The dangers associated with certain products (such as matches and sharp knives) are so commonly known that, as mentioned, manufacturers need not warn users of those dangers. If a defendant succeeds in convincing the court that a plaintiff's injury resulted from a *commonly known danger*, the defendant will not be liable.

CASE IN POINT 7.15 In a classic example from 1957, Marguerite Jamieson was injured when an elastic exercise rope slipped off her foot and struck her in the eye, causing a detachment of the retina. Jamieson claimed that the manufacturer should be liable because it had failed to warn users that the exerciser might slip off a foot in such a manner.

The court stated that to hold the manufacturer liable in these circumstances "would go beyond the reasonable dictates of justice in fixing the liabilities of manufacturers." After all, stated the court, "almost every physical object can be inherently dangerous or potentially dangerous in a sense. . . . A manufacturer cannot manufacture a knife that will not cut or a hammer that will not mash a thumb or a stove that will not burn a finger. The law does not require [manufacturers] to warn of such common dangers."[21] ■

7–4f Knowledgeable User

A related defense is the *knowledgeable user* defense. If a particular danger (such as electrical shock) is or should be commonly known by particular users of a product (such as electricians), the manufacturer need not warn these users of the danger.

CASE IN POINT 7.16 The parents of teenagers who had become overweight and developed health problems filed a product liability suit against McDonald's. The plaintiffs claimed that the fast-food chain had failed to warn customers of the adverse health effects of eating its food. The court rejected this claim, however, based on the knowledgeable user defense.

The court found that it is well known that the food at McDonald's contains high levels of cholesterol, fat, salt, and sugar and is therefore unhealthful. The court stated: "If consumers know (or reasonably should know) the potential ill health effects of eating at McDonald's, they cannot blame McDonald's if they, nonetheless, choose to satiate their appetite with a surfeit [excess] of supersized McDonald's products."[22] ■

7–4g Statutes of Limitations and Repose

Statutes of limitations restrict the time within which an action may be brought. The statute of limitations for product liability cases varies according to state law. Usually, the injured party must bring a product liability claim within two to four years. Often, the running of the prescribed period is **tolled** (that is, suspended) until the party suffering an injury has discovered it or should have discovered it.

To ensure that sellers and manufacturers will not be left vulnerable to lawsuits indefinitely, many states have passed **statutes of repose,** which place *outer* time limits on product liability actions. For instance, a statute of repose may require that claims be brought within twelve years from the date of sale or manufacture of the defective product. If the plaintiff does not bring an action before the prescribed period expires, the seller cannot be held liable.

Concept Summary 7.1 reviews the possible defenses in product liability actions.

---

20. *Stults v. International Flavors and Fragrances, Inc.,* 31 F.Supp.3d 1015 (N.D. Iowa 2014).

21. *Jamieson v. Woodward & Lothrop,* 247 F.2d 23 (D.C.Cir. 1957).
22. *Pelman v. McDonald's Corp.,* 237 F.Supp.2d 512 (S.D.N.Y. 2003).

Concept Summary 7.1

Defenses to Product Liability

Preemption	If the product is subject to comprehensive federal safety regulations
Assumption of Risk	When the user or consumer knew the risk and voluntarily assumed it
Product Misuse	If the consumer misused the product in an unforeseeable way
Comparative Negligence	Apportions liability if the defendant was also negligent
Commonly Known Dangers	If the product was commonly known to be dangerous
Knowledgeable User	If the particular danger is commonly known by particular users of the product
Statutory Time Periods	If the statute of limitations or statute of repose period has expired

Reviewing: Strict Liability and Product Liability

Shalene Kolchek bought a Great Lakes Spa from Val Porter, a dealer who was selling spas at the state fair. Kolchek signed an installment contract. Porter then handed her the manufacturer's paperwork and arranged for the spa to be delivered and installed for her. Three months later, Kolchek left her six-year-old daughter, Litisha, alone in the spa. While exploring the spa's hydromassage jets, Litisha stuck her index finger into one of the jet holes and was unable to remove her finger from the jet.

Litisha yanked hard, injuring her finger, then panicked and screamed for help. Kolchek was unable to remove Litisha's finger, and the local police and rescue team were called to assist. After a three-hour operation that included draining the spa, sawing out a section of the spa's plastic molding, and slicing the jet casing, Litisha's finger was freed. Following this procedure, the spa was no longer functional. Litisha was taken to the local emergency room, where she was told that a bone in her finger was broken in two places. Using the information presented in the chapter, answer the following questions.

1. Under which theories of product liability can Kolchek sue Porter to recover for Litisha's injuries?
2. Would privity of contract be required for Kolchek to succeed in a product liability action against Great Lakes? Explain.
3. For an action in strict product liability against Great Lakes, what six requirements must Kolchek meet?
4. What defenses to product liability might Porter or Great Lakes be able to assert?

Debate This . . . *All liability suits against tobacco companies for lung cancer should be thrown out of court now and forever.*

Terms and Concepts

market-share liability 143	product misuse 145	tolling 146
privity of contract 135	statute of repose 146	unreasonably dangerous
product liability 134	strict liability 134	product 140

Issue Spotters

1. Rim Corporation makes tire rims that it sells to Superior Vehicles, Inc., which installs them on cars. One set of rims is defective, which an inspection would reveal. Superior does not inspect the rims. The car with the defective rims is sold to Town Auto Sales, which sells the car to Uri. Soon, the car is in an accident caused by the defective rims, and Uri is injured. Is Superior Vehicles liable? Explain your answer. (See *Strict Product Liability*.)

2. Bensing Company manufactures generic drugs for the treatment of heart disease. A federal law requires generic drug makers to use labels that are identical to the labels on brand-name versions of the drugs. Hunter Rothfus purchased Bensing's generic drugs in Ohio and wants to sue Bensing for defective labeling based on its failure to comply with Ohio state common law (rather than the federal labeling requirements). What defense might Bensing assert to avoid liability under state law? (See *Defenses to Product Liability*.)

• **Check your answers to the Issue Spotters against the answers provided in Appendix D at the end of this text.**

Business Scenarios

7–1. Strict Liability. Danny and Marion Klein were injured when part of a fireworks display went astray and exploded near them. They sued Pyrodyne Corp., the pyrotechnic company that was hired to set up and discharge the fireworks. The Kleins alleged, among other things, that the company should be strictly liable for damages caused by the fireworks display. Will the court agree with the Kleins? What factors will the court consider in making its decision? Discuss fully. (See *Strict Liability*.)

7–2. Product Liability. Jason Clark, an experienced hunter, bought a paintball gun. Clark practiced with the gun and knew how to screw in the carbon dioxide cartridge, pump the gun, and use its safety and trigger. Although Clark was aware that he could purchase protective eyewear, he chose not to buy it.

Clark had taken gun safety courses and understood that it was "common sense" not to shoot anyone in the face. Clark's friend, Chris Wright, also owned a paintball gun and was similarly familiar with the gun's use and its risks.

Clark, Wright, and their friends played a game that involved shooting paintballs at cars whose occupants also had the guns. One night, while Clark and Wright were cruising with their guns, Wright shot at Clark's car, but hit Clark in the eye. Clark filed a product liability lawsuit against the manufacturer of Wright's paintball gun to recover for the injury. Clark claimed that the gun was defectively designed. During the trial, Wright testified that his gun "never malfunctioned." In whose favor should the court rule? Why? (See *Product Liability*.)

Business Case Problems

7–3. Design Defects. Yun Tung Chow tried to unclog a floor drain in the kitchen of the restaurant where he worked. He used a drain cleaner called Lewis Red Devil Lye that contained crystalline sodium hydroxide. The product label said to wear eye protection, to put one tablespoon of lye directly into the drain, and to keep one's face away from the drain because there could be dangerous backsplash.

Without eye protection, Chow mixed three tablespoons of lye in a can and poured that mixture down the drain while bending over it. Liquid splashed back into his face, causing injury. He brought a product liability suit based on inadequate warnings and design defect. The trial court granted summary judgment to the manufacturer, and Chow appealed. An expert for Chow stated that the product was defective because it had a tendency to backsplash. Is that a convincing argument? Why or why not? [*Yun Tung Chow v. Reckitt & Coleman, Inc.,* 69 A.D.3d 413, 891 N.Y.S.2d 402 (N.Y.A.D. 1 Dept. 2010)] (See *Strict Product Liability*.)

7–4. Strict Product Liability. David Dobrovolny bought a new Ford F-350 pickup truck. A year later, the truck spontaneously caught fire in Dobrovolny's driveway. The truck was destroyed, but no other property was damaged, and no one was injured. Dobrovolny filed a suit in a Nebraska state court against Ford Motor Co. on a theory of strict product liability to recover the cost of the truck. Nebraska limits the application of strict product liability to situations involving personal injuries. Is Dobrovolny's claim likely to succeed? Why or why not? Is there another basis for liability on which he might recover? Explain. [*Dobrovolny v. Ford Motor Co.,* 281 Neb. 86, 793 N.W.2d 445 (2011)] (See *Strict Product Liability*.)

7–5. Product Misuse. Five-year-old Cheyenne Stark was riding in the backseat of her parents' Ford Taurus. Cheyenne was not sitting in a booster seat. Instead, she was using a seatbelt designed by Ford, but was wearing the shoulder belt behind her back. The car was involved in a collision. As a result, Cheyenne suffered a spinal cord injury and was paralyzed from the waist down. The family filed a suit against Ford Motor Co., alleging that the seatbelt was defectively designed. Could Ford successfully claim that Cheyenne had misused the seatbelt? Why or why not? [*Stark v. Ford Motor Co.*, 365 N.C. 468, 723 S.E.2d 753 (2012)] (See *Defenses to Product Liability.*)

7–6. Business Case Problem with Sample Answer—Product Liability. While driving on Interstate 40 in North Carolina, Carroll Jett became distracted by a texting system in the cab of his tractor-trailer truck. He smashed into several vehicles that were slowed or stopped in front of him, injuring Barbara and Michael Durkee and others. The injured motorists filed a suit in a federal district court against Geologic Solutions, Inc., the maker of the texting system, alleging product liability. Was the accident caused by Jett's inattention or the texting device? Should a manufacturer be required to design a product that is incapable of distracting a driver? Discuss. [*Durkee v. Geologic Solutions, Inc.*, 2013 WL 14717 (4th Cir. 2013)] (See *Product Liability.*)

- For a sample answer to Problem 7–6, go to Appendix E at the end of this text.

7–7. Strict Product Liability. Medicis Pharmaceutical Corp. makes Solodyn, a prescription oral antibiotic. Medicis warns physicians that "autoimmune syndromes, including drug-induced lupus-like syndrome," may be associated with use of the drug. Amanda Watts had chronic acne. Her physician prescribed Solodyn. Information included with the drug did not mention the risk of autoimmune disorders, and Watts was not otherwise advised of it. She was prescribed the drug twice, each time for twenty weeks. Later, she experienced debilitating joint pain and, after being hospitalized, was diagnosed with lupus. On what basis could Watts recover from Medicis in an action grounded in product liability? Explain. [*Watts v. Medicis Pharmaceutical Corp.*, 236 Ariz. 511, 342 P.3d 847 (2015)] (See *Strict Product Liability.*)

7–8. Strict Product Liability. Duval Ford, LLC, sold a new Ford F-250 pick-up truck to David Sweat. Before taking delivery, Sweat ordered a lift kit to be installed on the truck by a Duval subcontractor. Sweat also replaced the tires and modified the suspension system to increase the towing capacity. Later, through Burkins Chevrolet, Sweat sold the truck to Shaun Lesnick. Sweat had had no problems with the truck's steering or suspension, but Lesnick did. He had the steering repaired and made additional changes, including installing a steering stabilizer and replacing the tires. Two months later, Lesnick was driving the truck when the steering and suspension suddenly failed, and the truck flipped over, causing Lesnick severe injuries. Could Lesnick successfully claim that Duval and Burkins had failed to warn him of the risk of a lifted truck? Explain. [*Lesnick v. Duval Ford, LLC*, 41 Fla.L.Weekly D281, __ So.3d __ (Fla.Dist.Ct.App., 1 Dist. 2016)] (See *Strict Product Liability.*)

7–9. A Question of Ethics—Dangerous Products. Susan Calles lived with her four daughters—Amanda, age eleven; Victoria, age five; and Jenna and Jillian, age three. In March 1998, Calles bought an Aim N Flame utility lighter, which she stored on the top shelf of her kitchen cabinet. A trigger can ignite the Aim N Flame after an "ON/OFF" switch is slid to the "on" position. On the night of March 31, Calles and Victoria left to get videos. Jenna and Jillian were in bed, and Amanda was watching television. Calles returned to find fire trucks and emergency vehicles around her home. Robert Finn, a fire investigator, determined that Jenna had started a fire using the lighter. Jillian suffered smoke inhalation, was hospitalized, and died on April 21. Calles filed a suit in an Illinois state court against Scripto-Tokai Corp., which distributed the Aim N Flame, and others. In her suit, which was grounded, in part, in strict liability claims, Calles alleged that the lighter was an "unreasonably dangerous product." Scripto filed a motion for summary judgment. [*Calles v. Scripto-Tokai Corp.*, 224 Ill.2d 247, 864 N.E.2d 249, 309 Ill. Dec. 383 (2007)] (See *Strict Product Liability.*)

(a) A product is "unreasonably dangerous" when it is dangerous beyond the expectation of the ordinary consumer. Whose expectation—Calles's or Jenna's—applies? Does the lighter pass this test? Explain.

(b) Calles presented evidence as to the likelihood and seriousness of injury from lighters that do not have child-safety devices. Scripto argued that the Aim N Flame is an alternative source of fire and is safer than a match. Calles admitted that she knew the dangers presented by lighters in the hands of children. Scripto admitted that it had been a defendant in several suits for injuries under similar circumstances. How should the court rule? Why?

Legal Reasoning Group Activity

7–10. Product Liability. Bret D'Auguste was an experienced skier when he rented equipment to ski at Hunter Mountain Ski Bowl in New York. When D'Auguste entered an extremely difficult trail, he noticed immediately that the surface consisted of ice with almost no snow. He tried to exit the steeply declining trail by making a sharp right turn, but in the attempt, his left ski snapped off. D'Auguste lost his balance, fell, and slid down the mountain, striking his face and head against a fence along the trail. According to a report by a rental shop employee, one of the bindings on D'Auguste's skis had a "cracked heel housing." D'Auguste filed a lawsuit against the bindings' manufacturer on a theory of strict product liability. The manufacturer filed a motion for summary judgment. (See *Product Liability.*)

(a) The first group will take the position of the manufacturer and develop an argument for why the court should *grant* the summary judgment motion and dismiss the strict product liability claim.

(b) The second group will take the position of D'Auguste and formulate a basis for why the court should *deny* the motion and allow the strict product liability claim.

Answers to the *Issue Spotters*

1. *Is Superior Vehicles liable? Explain your answer.* Yes. The manufacturer is liable for the injuries to the user of the product. A manufacturer is liable for its failure to exercise due care to any person who sustains an injury proximately caused by a negligently made (defective) product.

2. *What defense might Bensing assert to avoid liability under state law?* Bensing can assert the defense of preemption. An injured party may not be able to sue the manufacturer of defective products that are subject to comprehensive federal regulatory schemes. If the federal government has a comprehensive regulatory scheme (such as it does with medical devices and vaccines), then it is assumed that the rules were designed to ensure a product's safety, and the federal rules will preempt any state regulations. Therefore, Bensing could not be held liable under state law if it complied with the federal drug-labeling requirements.

Sample Answers for *Business Case Problems with Sample Answer*

Problem 7–6. *Product Liability.* Here, the accident was caused by Jett's inattention, not by the texting device in the cab of his truck. In a product liability case based on a design defect, the plaintiff has to prove that the product was defective at the time it left the hands of the seller or lessor. The plaintiff must also show that this defective condition made it "unreasonably dangerous" to the user or consumer. If the product was delivered in a safe condition and subsequent mishandling made it harmful to the user, the seller or lessor normally is not liable. To successfully assert a design defect, a plaintiff has to show that a reasonable alternative design was available and that the defendant failed to use it.

The plaintiffs could contend that the defendant manufacturer of the texting device owed them a duty of care because injuries to vehicle drivers and passengers, and others on the roads, were reasonably foreseeable due to the product's design, which (1) required the driver to divert his eyes from the road to view an incoming text from the dispatcher, and (2) permitted the receipt of texts while the vehicle was moving. But manufacturers are not required to design a product incapable of distracting a driver. The duty owed by a manufacturer to the user or consumer of a product does not require guarding against hazards that are commonly known or obvious or protecting against injuries that result from a user's careless conduct. That is what happened here.

In the actual case on which this problem is based, the court reached the same conclusion, based on the reasoning stated above, and an intermediate appellate court affirmed the judgment.

CHAPTER

Intellectual Property Rights

Intellectual property is any property that results from intellectual, creative processes—the products of an individual's mind. Although it is an abstract term for an abstract concept, intellectual property is nonetheless familiar to almost everyone. The apps for your iPhone, iPad, or Samsung Galaxy, the movies you see, and the music you listen to are all forms of intellectual property.

More than two hundred years ago, the framers of the U.S. Constitution recognized the importance of protecting creative works in Article I, Section 8. Statutory protection of these rights began in the 1940s and continues to evolve to meet the needs of modern society. In today's global economy, however, protecting intellectual property in one country is no longer sufficient. The United States is participating in various international agreements to secure ownership rights in intellectual property in other countries.

Whether locally or globally, businesspersons have a vital need to protect their rights in intellectual property, which may be more valuable than their physical property, such as machines and buildings. Consider, for instance, the importance of intellectual property rights to technology companies, such as Apple, Inc., and Samsung. These two companies have been involved in patent litigation over the designs of their smartphones for several years.

8–1 Trademarks and Related Property

A **trademark** is a distinctive mark, motto, device, or implement that a manufacturer stamps, prints, or otherwise affixes to the goods it produces so that they can be identified on the market and their origins made known. In other words, a trademark is a source indicator. At common law, the person who used a symbol or mark to identify a business or product was protected in the use of that trademark. Clearly, by using another's trademark, a business could lead consumers to believe that its goods were made by the other business. The law seeks to avoid this kind of confusion.

In the following classic case, the defendants argued that the Coca-Cola trademark was entitled to no protection under the law because the term did not accurately represent the product.

The Coca-Cola Co. v. The Koke Co. of America
Supreme Court of the United States, 254 U.S. 143, 41 S.Ct. 113, 65 L.Ed.189 (1920).

Company Profile *John Pemberton, an Atlanta pharmacist, invented a caramel-colored, carbonated soft drink in 1886. His bookkeeper, Frank Robinson, named the beverage Coca-Cola after two of the ingredients, coca leaves and kola nuts. Asa Candler bought the Coca-Cola Company in 1891, and within seven years, he had made the soft drink available throughout the United States, as well as in parts of Canada and Mexico. Candler continued to sell Coke aggressively and to open up new markets, reaching Europe before 1910. In doing so, however, he attracted numerous competitors, some of which tried to capitalize directly on the Coke name.*

Case 8.1 Continued

Background and Facts The Coca-Cola Company sought to enjoin (prevent) the Koke Company of America and other beverage companies from, among other things, using the word *Koke* for their products. The Koke Company of America and other beverage companies contended that the Coca-Cola trademark was a fraudulent representation and that Coca-Cola was therefore not entitled to any help from the courts. The Koke Company and the other defendants alleged that the Coca-Cola Company, by its use of the Coca-Cola name, represented that the beverage contained cocaine (from coca leaves), which it no longer did. The trial court granted the injunction against the Koke Company, but the appellate court reversed the lower court's ruling. Coca-Cola then appealed to the United States Supreme Court.

In the Language of the Court

Mr. Justice *HOLMES* delivered the opinion of the Court.

* * * *

* * * Before 1900 the beginning of [Coca-Cola's] good will was more or less helped by the presence of cocaine, a drug that, like alcohol or caffeine or opium, may be described as a deadly poison or as a valuable [pharmaceutical item, depending on the speaker's purposes]. The amount seems to have been very small,[a] but it may have been enough to begin a bad habit and after the Food and Drug Act of June 30, 1906, if not earlier, long before this suit was brought, it was eliminated from the plaintiff's compound.

* * * Since 1900 the sales have increased at a very great rate corresponding to a like increase in advertising. The name now characterizes a beverage to be had at almost any soda fountain. It means a single thing coming from a single source, and well known to the community. It hardly would be too much to say that the drink characterizes the name as much as the name the drink. In other words *Coca-Cola probably means to most persons the plaintiff's familiar product to be had everywhere rather than a compound of particular substances.* * * * Before this suit was brought the plaintiff had advertised to the public that it must not expect and would not find cocaine, and had eliminated everything tending to suggest cocaine effects except the name and the picture of [coca] leaves and nuts, which probably conveyed little or nothing to most who saw it. It appears to us that it would be going too far to deny the plaintiff relief against a palpable [readily evident] fraud because possibly here and there an ignorant person might call for the drink with the hope for incipient cocaine intoxication. The plaintiff's position must be judged by the facts as they were when the suit was begun, not by the facts of a different condition and an earlier time. [Emphasis added.]

Decision and Remedy *The district court's injunction was allowed to stand. The competing beverage companies were enjoined from calling their products Koke.*

Impact of This Case on Today's Law *In this early case, the United States Supreme Court made it clear that trademarks and trade names (and nicknames for those marks and names, such as the nickname "Coke" for "Coca-Cola") that are in common use receive protection under the common law. This holding is significant historically because it is the predecessor to the federal statute later passed to protect trademark rights—the Lanham Act of 1946. In many ways, this act represented a codification of common law principles governing trademarks.*

Critical Thinking

- **What If the Facts Were Different?** *Suppose that Coca-Cola had been trying to make the public believe that its product contained cocaine. Would the result in this case likely have been different? Why or why not?*

---

a. In reality, until 1903 the amount of active cocaine in each bottle of Coke was equivalent to one "line" of cocaine.

8-1a Statutory Protection of Trademarks

Statutory protection of trademarks and related property is provided at the federal level by the Lanham Act of 1946.[1] The Lanham Act was enacted, in part, to protect manufacturers from losing business to rival companies that used confusingly similar trademarks. The act incorporates the common law of trademarks and provides remedies for owners of trademarks who wish to enforce their claims in federal court. Many states also have trademark statutes.

Trademark Dilution In 1995, Congress amended the Lanham Act by passing the Federal Trademark Dilution Act,[2] which allowed trademark owners to bring suits in federal court for trademark **dilution.** In 2006, Congress further amended the law on trademark dilution by passing the Trademark Dilution Revision Act (TDRA).[3]

Under the TDRA, to state a claim for trademark dilution, a plaintiff must prove the following:

1. The plaintiff owns a famous mark that is distinctive.
2. The defendant has begun using a mark in commerce that allegedly is diluting the famous mark.
3. The similarity between the defendant's mark and the famous mark gives rise to an *association* between the marks.
4. The association is likely to impair the distinctiveness of the famous mark or harm its reputation.

Trademark dilution laws protect "distinctive" or "famous" trademarks (such as Rolls Royce, McDonald's, Starbucks, and Apple) from certain unauthorized uses. Such a mark is protected even when the use is on noncompeting goods or is unlikely to cause confusion. More than half of the states have also enacted trademark dilution laws.

Marks Need Not Be Identical Note that a famous mark may be diluted by the use of an *identical* mark or by the use of a *similar* mark.[4] A similar mark is more likely to lessen the value of a famous mark when the companies using the marks provide related goods or compete against each other in the same market.

■ **CASE IN POINT 8.1** Samantha Lundberg opened a business called "Sambuck's Coffeehouse," in Astoria, Oregon, even though she knew that "Starbucks" was one of the largest coffee chains in the nation. Starbucks Corporation filed a dilution lawsuit, and a federal court ruled that use of the "Sambuck's" mark constituted trademark dilution because it created confusion for consumers. Not only was there a "high degree" of similarity between the marks, but also both companies provided coffee-related services and marketed their services through "stand-alone" retail stores. Therefore, the use of the similar mark (Sambuck's) reduced the value of the famous mark (Starbucks).[5] ■

8-1b Trademark Registration

Trademarks may be registered with the state or with the federal government. To register for protection under federal trademark law, a person must file an application with the U.S. Patent and Trademark Office in Washington, D.C. Under current law, a mark can be registered (1) if it is currently in commerce or (2) if the applicant intends to put it into commerce within six months.

In special circumstances, the six-month period can be extended by thirty months. Thus, the applicant would have a total of three years from the date of notice of trademark approval to make use of the mark and file the required use statement. Registration is postponed until the mark is actually used. During this waiting period, any applicant can legally protect his or her trademark against a third party who previously has neither used the mark nor filed an application for it.

Registration is renewable between the fifth and sixth years after the initial registration and every ten years thereafter (every twenty years for those trademarks registered before 1990).

8-1c Trademark Infringement

Registration of a trademark with the U.S. Patent and Trademark Office gives notice on a nationwide basis that the trademark belongs exclusively to the registrant. The registrant is also allowed to use the symbol ® to indicate that the mark has been registered. Whenever that trademark is copied to a substantial degree or used in its entirety by another, intentionally or unintentionally, the trademark has been *infringed* (used without authorization).

When a trademark has been infringed, the owner of the mark has a cause of action against the infringer. To succeed in a trademark infringement action, the owner must show that the defendant's use of the mark created a likelihood of confusion about the origin of the defendant's goods or services. The owner need not prove that

---

1. 15 U.S.C. Sections 1051–1128.
2. 15 U.S.C. Section 1125.
3. Pub. L. No. 103-312, 120 Stat. 1730 (2006).
4. See *Louis Vuitton Malletier S.A. v. Haute Diggity Dog, LLC*, 507 F.3d 252 (4th Cir. 2007); and *Moseley v. V Secret Catalogue, Inc.*, 537 U.S. 418, 123 S.Ct. 1115, 155 L.Ed.2d 1 (2003).

5. *Starbucks Corp. v. Lundberg*, 2005 WL 3183858 (D.Or. 2005).

the infringer acted intentionally or that the trademark was registered (although registration does provide proof of the date of inception of the trademark's use).

The most commonly granted remedy for trademark infringement is an *injunction* to prevent further infringement. Under the Lanham Act, a trademark owner that successfully proves infringement can recover actual damages, plus the profits that the infringer wrongfully received from the unauthorized use of the mark. A court can also order the destruction of any goods bearing the unauthorized trademark. In some situations, the trademark owner may also be able to recover attorneys' fees.

At the center of the following case was an injunction granted in an earlier dispute between two brothers prohibiting one of them from using trademarks owned by the other, including a mark featuring their shared last name.

Case 8.2

LFP IP, LLC v. Hustler Cincinnati, Inc.

United States Court of Appeals, Sixth Circuit, 810 F.3d 424 (2016).

Background and Facts Brothers Jimmy and Larry Flynt owned "The Hustler Club," a bar and nightclub in Cincinnati, Ohio. Larry opened Hustler clubs in other Ohio cities. Within a few years, he also began publishing *Hustler,* a sexually explicit magazine. Larry formed LFP IP, Inc., and other corporations to conduct his enterprises. Many of them used the trademarks "HUSTLER" and "LARRY FLYNT," which LFP owned. Jimmy opened his own store, Hustler Cincinnati, and paid LFP licensing fees to use the "HUSTLER" mark.

When the store stopped paying the fees, LFP filed a suit in a federal district court against the store's corporate owner, alleging trademark infringement. The court issued an injunction prohibiting Jimmy from using the "HUSTLER" mark. Later, he opened a store called "FLYNT Sexy Gifts." LFP claimed that this name was likely to cause confusion with the "LARRY FLYNT" mark. The court modified the injunction to limit Jimmy's use of the "Flynt" name without "Jimmy." Jimmy appealed.

In the Language of the Court

SUTTON, Circuit Judge.

* * * *

Courts * * * may exercise their sound judicial discretion to modify an injunction if the circumstances, whether of law or fact, obtaining at the time of its issuance have changed, or new ones have since arisen.

* * * The [district] court * * * applied the traditional test for trademark infringement under federal law, asking whether (1) Larry and his companies owned the LARRY FLYNT trademark, (2) Jimmy used the mark in commerce, and (3) the use was likely to cause confusion. The court found all three elements satisfied * * * . Because the original injunction was tailored to prevent trademark infringement by [Jimmy] and because Jimmy had committed new violations, the district court acted appropriately when it modified its initial grant of relief to cover Jimmy's conduct at the [new] outlet.

The district court's modified injunction was also suitably tailored to the changed circumstances. Balancing the competing interests of Larry and Jimmy, the court permitted Jimmy to use his full name while protecting Larry's interest in the LARRY FLYNT trademark.

* * * *

Jimmy * * * takes issue with some of the factual findings that the district court used to justify the modified injunction.

But none of the district court's factual findings is clearly erroneous. * * * Larry * * * presented evidence that he used the mark in connection with a wide range of adult entertainment products, including the kinds of products sold at Jimmy's store. Because *product use * * * marks the salient [most noticeable] indicator of ownership in trademark-infringement actions,* the district court reasonably found that Larry * * * owned the LARRY FLYNT trademark with respect to retail goods. The court also reasonably found that Larry began using the mark on adult entertainment products before Jimmy did. * * * And * * * Larry's company * * * continued to use that mark in commerce. [Emphasis added.]

In claiming an absence of evidence of consumer confusion, Jimmy missteps. Some of the evidence comes from Jimmy himself. When asked about instances where a consumer has been confused, in terms of whether or not Jimmy was the owner of the store, Jimmy responded, "I have experienced the

Case 8.2 Continues

Case 8.2 Continued confusion in the names, you know. Jimmy and Larry Flynt, in this market area, is somewhat synonymous with Hustler or with Flynt. You're not going to get around that."

Decision and Remedy *The U.S. Court of Appeals for the Sixth Circuit affirmed the lower court's modification of the injunction. The injunction was initially tailored to prevent Jimmy's infringement of his brother's marks. When Jimmy committed a new violation by opening "FLYNT Sexy Gifts," the district court acted appropriately in modifying the injunction to cover this conduct.*

Critical Thinking
- **E-Commerce** *Could Jimmy use his last name—the name that he shares with his brother—as a domain name? Why or why not?*
- **What If the Facts Were Different?** *Suppose that Jimmy had used the marks at the center of this case on an entirely different line of goods, not adult entertainment products. Would the result have been the same? Explain.*

8–1d Distinctiveness of the Mark

A trademark must be sufficiently distinctive to enable consumers to identify the manufacturer of the goods easily and to distinguish between those goods and competing products.

Strong Marks Fanciful, arbitrary, or suggestive trademarks are generally considered to be the most distinctive (strongest) trademarks. These marks receive automatic protection because they serve to identify a particular product's source, as opposed to describing the product itself.

Fanciful and Arbitrary Trademarks. Fanciful trademarks use invented words, such as "Xerox" for one manufacturer's copiers and "Google" for a search engine. Arbitrary trademarks use common words in an uncommon way that is not descriptive of the product, such as "Dutch Boy" as a name for paint.

Even a single letter used in a particular style can be an arbitrary trademark. ■ **CASE IN POINT 8.2** Sports entertainment company ESPN sued Quiksilver, Inc., a maker of youth-oriented clothing, alleging trademark infringement. ESPN claimed that Quiksilver's clothing used the stylized "X" mark that ESPN uses in connection with the "X Games" ("extreme" sports competitions).

Quiksilver filed counterclaims for trademark infringement and dilution, arguing that it had a long history of using the stylized X on its products. ESPN had created the X Games in the mid-1990s, and Quiksilver had been using the X mark since 1994. ESPN asked the court to dismiss Quiksilver's counterclaims, but the court refused, holding that the X on Quiksilver's clothing is clearly an arbitrary mark. The court found that the two Xs are

"similar enough that a consumer might well confuse them." Therefore, Quicksilver could continue its claim for trademark infringement.[6] ■

Suggestive Trademarks. Suggestive trademarks indicate something about a product's nature, quality, or characteristics, without describing the product directly. These marks require imagination on the part of the consumer to identify the characteristic.

"Dairy Queen," for instance, suggests an association between its products and milk, but it does not directly describe ice cream. "Blu-ray" is a suggestive mark that is associated with the high-quality, high-definition video contained on a particular type of optical data storage disc. Although blue-violet lasers are used to read blu-ray discs, the term *blu-ray* does not directly describe the disc.

Secondary Meaning Descriptive terms, geographic terms, and personal names are not inherently distinctive and do not receive protection under the law until they acquire a secondary meaning. A secondary meaning may arise when customers begin to associate a specific term or phrase (such as *London Fog*) with specific trademarked items (coats with "London Fog" labels) made by a particular company.

Whether a secondary meaning becomes attached to a name usually depends on how extensively the product is advertised, the market for the product, the number of sales, and other factors. ■ **CASE IN POINT 8.3** Unity Health Plans Insurance Corporation has been a health maintenance organization (HMO) insurer in Wisconsin since 1955. In 2013, another health-care provider, Iowa

---
6. *ESPN, Inc. v. Quiksilver, Inc.*, 586 F.Supp.2d 219 (S.D.N.Y. 2008).

Health System, began rebranding itself (changing its name and marketing) as UnityPoint Health. When the company expanded into Wisconsin, where Unity Health already had an established presence, Unity Health filed a trademark infringement suit in federal court.

The court found that Unity Health was a descriptive mark, and thus not inherently distinctive. But the court also held that the Unity Health mark had acquired a secondary meaning, largely because it had been used for so long and so exclusively by one health insurer in Wisconsin. It made no difference to the court that only one part of the mark (Unity) was common to both trademarks. To allow Iowa Health Systems to use the mark UnityPoint Health in Wisconsin would likely create confusion for consumers. Therefore, the court issued an injunction and blocked Iowa Health from using the trademark Unity-Point Health.[7] ■

Once a secondary meaning is attached to a term or name, a trademark is considered distinctive and is protected. Even a color can qualify for trademark protection, as did the color schemes used by some state university sports teams, including Ohio State University and Louisiana State University.[8]

■ **CASE IN POINT 8.4** Federal Express Corporation (FedEx) provides transportation and delivery services worldwide using the logo FedEx in a specific color combination. FedEx sued a competitor, JetEx Management Services, Inc., for using the same color combination and a similar name and logo. JetEx also mimicked FedEx's trademarked slogan ("The World on Time" for FedEx, and "Keeping the World on Time" for JetEx). FedEx alleged trademark infringement and dilution, among other claims. A federal district court in New York granted a permanent injunction to block JetEx from using the infringing mark in FedEx colors.[9] ■

Generic Terms Generic terms that refer to an entire class of products, such as *bicycle* and *computer,* receive no protection, even if they acquire secondary meanings. A particularly thorny problem arises when a trademark acquires generic use. For instance, *aspirin* and *thermos* were originally the names of trademarked products, but today the words are used generically. Other trademarks that have acquired generic use are *escalator, trampoline, raisin bran, dry ice, lanolin, linoleum, nylon,* and *cornflakes.*

A trademark does not become generic simply because it is commonly used, however. ■ **CASE IN POINT 8.5** In 2014, David Elliot and Chris Gillespie sought to register numerous domain names, including "googledisney.com" and "googlenewstvs.com." (A *domain name* is part of an Internet address, such as "cengage.com.") They were unable to register the names because all of them used the word *google,* a trademark of Google, Inc.

Elliot and Gillespie brought an action in federal court to have the Google trademark cancelled because it had become a generic term. They argued that because most people now use *google* as a verb ("to google") when referring to searching the Internet with any search engine (not just Google), the term should no longer be protected. The court held that even if people do use the word *google* as a verb, it is still a protected trademark if consumers associate the noun with one company. The court concluded that "the primary significance of the word *google* to a majority of the public who utilize Internet search engines is a designation of the Google search engine."[10] ■

8–1e Service, Certification, and Collective Marks

A **service mark** is essentially a trademark that is used to distinguish the *services* (rather than the products) of one person or company from those of another. For instance, each airline has a particular mark or symbol associated with its name. Titles and character names used in radio and television are frequently registered as service marks.

Other marks protected by law include certification marks and collective marks. A **certification mark** is used by one or more persons, other than the owner, to certify the region, materials, mode of manufacture, quality, or other characteristic of specific goods or services. Certification marks include "Good Housekeeping Seal of Approval" and "UL Tested."

When used by members of a cooperative, association, or other organization, a certification mark is referred to as a **collective mark.** ■ **EXAMPLE 8.6** Collective marks appear at the ends of motion picture credits to indicate the various associations and organizations that participated in the making of the films. The union marks found on the tags of certain products are also collective marks. ■

8–1f Trade Dress

The term **trade dress** refers to the image and overall appearance of a product. Trade dress is a broad concept

---

7. *Unity Health Plans Insurance Co. v. Iowa Health System,* 995 F.Supp.2d 874 (W.D.Wis. 2014).

8. *Board of Supervisors of Louisiana State University v. Smack Apparel Co.,* 438 F.Supp.2d 653 (E.D.La. 2006). See also *Abraham v. Alpha Chi Omega,* 781 F.Supp.2d 396 (N.D.Tex. 2011).

9. *Federal Express Corp. v. JetEx Management Services, Inc.,* 2014 WL 4628983 (E.D.N.Y. 2014).

10. *Elliot v. Google,* 45 F.Supp.3d 1156 (D.Ariz. 2014).

and can include either all or part of the total image or overall impression created by a product or its packaging.

■ **EXAMPLE 8.7** The distinctive decor, menu, layout, and style of service of a particular restaurant may be regarded as trade dress. Trade dress can also include the layout and appearance of a catalogue, the use of a lighthouse as part of the design of a golf hole, the fish shape of a cracker, or the G-shaped design of a Gucci watch. ■

Basically, trade dress is subject to the same protection as trademarks. In cases involving trade dress infringement, as in trademark infringement cases, a major consideration is whether consumers are likely to be confused by the allegedly infringing use.

8-1g Counterfeit Goods

Counterfeit goods copy or otherwise imitate trademarked goods, but they are not the genuine trademarked goods. The importation of goods that bear counterfeit (fake) trademarks poses a growing problem for U.S. businesses, consumers, and law enforcement. In addition to the negative financial effects on legitimate businesses, certain counterfeit goods, such as pharmaceuticals and nutritional supplements, can present serious public health risks.

The Stop Counterfeiting in Manufactured Goods Act The Stop Counterfeiting in Manufactured Goods Act[11] (SCMGA) was enacted to combat counterfeit goods. The act makes it a crime to traffic intentionally in or attempt to traffic in counterfeit goods or services, or to knowingly use a counterfeit mark on or in connection with goods or services.

Before this act, the law did not prohibit the creation or shipment of counterfeit labels that were not attached to any product. Therefore, counterfeiters would make labels and packaging bearing another's trademark, ship the labels to another location, and then affix them to an inferior product to deceive buyers. The SCMGA closed this loophole by making it a crime to knowingly traffic in counterfeit labels, stickers, packaging, and the like, regardless of whether the items are attached to any goods.

Penalties for Counterfeiting Persons found guilty of violating the SCMGA may be fined up to $2 million or imprisoned for up to ten years (or more if they are repeat offenders). If a court finds that the statute was violated, it must order the defendant to forfeit the counterfeit products (which are then destroyed), as well as any property

used in the commission of the crime. The defendant must also pay restitution to the trademark holder or victim in an amount equal to the victim's actual loss.

■ **CASE IN POINT 8.8** Charles Anthony Jones pleaded guilty to trafficking of counterfeit prescription erectile dysfunction drugs. The court sentenced Jones to thirty-seven months in prison and ordered him to pay $633,019 in restitution. Jones appealed, arguing that the amount awarded was more than the pharmaceutical companies' actual losses. The court agreed. The pharmaceutical companies were entitled only to their lost net profits rather than the retail price of the genuine drugs.[12] ■

Combating Foreign Counterfeiters Although Congress has enacted statutes against counterfeit goods, the United States cannot prosecute foreign counterfeiters because our national laws do not apply to them. One effective tool that U.S. officials have used to combat online sales of counterfeit goods is to obtain a court order to close down the domain names of Web sites that sell such goods. For instance, U.S. agents have shut down hundreds of domain names on the Monday after Thanksgiving ("Cyber Monday"). Shutting down the Web sites, particularly on key shopping days, prevents some counterfeit goods from entering the United States. Europol, an international organization, has also used this tactic.

8-1h Trade Names

Trademarks apply to *products*. A **trade name** indicates part or all of a business's name, whether the business is a sole proprietorship, a partnership, or a corporation. Generally, a trade name is directly related to a business and its goodwill.

A trade name may be protected as a trademark if the trade name is also the name of the company's trademarked product—for example, Coca-Cola. Unless it is also used as a trademark or service mark, a trade name cannot be registered with the federal government. Trade names are protected under the common law, but only if they are unusual or fancifully used. The word *Safeway*, for example, was sufficiently fanciful to obtain protection as a trade name for a grocery chain.

8-1i Licensing

One way to avoid litigation and still make use of another's trademark or other form of intellectual property is to obtain a license to do so. A **license** in this context is an agreement, or contract, permitting the use of a

---

11. Pub. L. No. 109-181 (2006), which amended 18 U.S.C. Sections 2318–2320.

12. *United States v. Jones*, 616 Fed.Appx. 726 (5th Cir. 2015).

trademark, copyright, patent, or trade secret for certain purposes. The party that owns the intellectual property rights and issues the license is the *licensor,* and the party obtaining the license is the *licensee.* The licensee generally pays fees, or *royalties,* for the privilege of using the intellectual property.

A license grants only the rights expressly described in the license agreement. A licensor might, for example, allow the licensee to use the trademark as part of its company or domain name, but not otherwise use the mark on any products or services. Disputes frequently arise over licensing agreements, particularly when the license involves Internet uses.

■ **CASE IN POINT 8.9** George V Restauration S.A. and others owned and operated the Buddha Bar Paris, a restaurant with an Asian theme in Paris, France. One of the owners allowed Little Rest Twelve, Inc., to use the Buddha Bar trademark and its associated concept in New York City under the name *Buddha Bar NYC.* Little Rest paid royalties for its use of the Buddha Bar mark and advertised Buddha Bar NYC's affiliation with Buddha Bar Paris. This connection was also noted on its Web site and in the media.

When a dispute arose, the owners of Buddha Bar Paris withdrew their permission for Buddha Bar NYC's use of their mark, but Little Rest continued to use it. The owners of the mark filed a suit in a New York state court against Little Rest. The court granted an injunction to prevent Little Rest from using the mark.[13] ■

8–2 Patents

A **patent** is a grant from the government that gives an inventor the exclusive right to make, use, or sell his or her invention for a period of twenty years. Patents for designs, as opposed to those for inventions, are given for a fourteen-year period. The applicant must demonstrate to the satisfaction of the U.S. Patent and Trademark Office that the invention, discovery, process, or design is novel, useful, and not obvious in light of current technology.

Until recently, U.S. patent law differed from the laws of many other countries because the first person to invent a product obtained the patent rights rather than the first person to file for a patent. It was often difficult to prove who invented an item first, however, which prompted Congress to change the system in 2011 by passing the

America Invents Act.[14] Now the first person to file an application for a patent on a product or process will receive patent protection. In addition, the new law established a nine-month limit for challenging a patent on any ground.

The period of patent protection begins on the date the patent application is filed, rather than when the patent is issued, which may sometimes be years later. After the patent period ends (either fourteen or twenty years later), the product or process enters the public domain, and anyone can make, sell, or use the invention without paying the patent holder.

8–2a Searchable Patent Databases

A significant development relating to patents is the availability online of the world's patent databases. The Web site of the U.S. Patent and Trademark Office (www.uspto.gov) provides searchable databases covering U.S. patents granted since 1976. The Web site of the European Patent Office (www.epo.org) provides online access to 50 million patent documents in more than seventy nations through a searchable network of databases.

Businesses use these searchable databases in many ways. Companies may conduct patent searches to list or inventory their patents, which are valuable assets. Patent searches may also be conducted to study trends and patterns in a specific technology or to gather information about competitors in the industry.

8–2b What Is Patentable?

Under federal law, "[w]hoever invents or discovers any new and useful process, machine, manufacture, or composition of matter, or any new and useful improvement thereof, may obtain a patent therefor, subject to the conditions and requirements of this title."[15] Thus, to be patentable, the applicant must prove that the invention, discovery, process, or design is *novel, useful,* and *not obvious* in light of current technology.

In sum, almost anything is patentable, except the laws of nature, natural phenomena, and abstract ideas (including algorithms[16]). Even artistic methods and works of art, certain business processes, and the structures of storylines

---

13. *George V Restauration S.A. v. Little Rest Twelve, Inc.,* 58 A.D.3d 428, 871 N.Y.S.2d 65 (2009).

14. The full title of this law is the Leahy-Smith America Invents Act, Pub. L. No. 112-29 (2011), which amended 35 U.S.C. Sections 1, 41, and 321.

15. 35 U.S.C. Section 101.

16. An *algorithm* is a step-by-step procedure, formula, or set of instructions for accomplishing a specific task. An example is the set of rules used by a search engine to rank the listings contained within its index in response to a query.

are patentable, provided that they are novel and not obvious.[17]

Plants that are reproduced asexually (by means other than from seed), such as hybrid or genetically engineered plants, are patentable in the United States, as are genetically engineered (or cloned) microorganisms and animals. ■ **CASE IN POINT 8.10** Monsanto, Inc., sells its patented genetically modified (GM) seeds to farmers to help them achieve higher yields from crops using fewer pesticides. It requires farmers who buy GM seeds to sign licensing agreements promising to plant the seeds for only one crop and to pay a technology fee for each acre planted. To ensure compliance, Monsanto has many full-time employees whose job is to investigate and prosecute farmers who use the GM seeds illegally. Monsanto has filed nearly 150 lawsuits against farmers in the United States and has been awarded more than $15 million in damages (not including out-of-court settlement amounts).[18] ■

8–2c Patent Infringement

If a firm makes, uses, or sells another's patented design, product, or process without the patent owner's permission, that firm commits the tort of patent infringement. Patent infringement may occur even though the patent owner has not put the patented product into commerce. Patent infringement may also occur even though not all features or parts of a product are copied. (To infringe the patent on a process, however, all steps or their equivalent must be copied.) To read about an important issue in patent infringement today, see this chapter's *Digital Update* feature.

Patent Infringement Lawsuits and High-Tech Companies Obviously, companies that specialize in developing new technology stand to lose significant profits if someone "makes, uses, or sells" devices that incorporate their patented inventions. Because these firms are the holders of numerous patents, they are frequently involved in patent infringement lawsuits (as well as other types of intellectual property disputes).

■ **CASE IN POINT 8.11** Apple sued Samsung in federal court alleging that Samsung's Galaxy smartphones and tablets that use Google's HTC Android operating system infringe on Apple's patents. Apple has design patents that cover its devices' graphical user interface (the display of icons on the home screen), shell, and screen and button design. Apple has also patented the way information is displayed on iPhones and other devices, the way windows pop open, and the way information is scaled and rotated.

A jury found that Samsung had willfully infringed five of Apple's patents and awarded damages. The parties appealed. A judge later reduced the amount of damages awarded on the patent claims, but litigation between the two companies has continued. In 2015, a federal appellate court held that elements of the physical design of these two manufacturers' mobile devices and their on-screen icons were functional and thus not protected under the Lanham Act. A product feature is functional and not protected as trade dress if it is essential to the article's use or purpose or affects the cost or quality of the article. [19] ■

Patent Infringement and Foreign Sales Many companies that make and sell electronics and computer software and hardware are based in foreign nations (for instance, Samsung Electronics Company is a Korean firm). Foreign firms can apply for and obtain U.S. patent protection on items that they sell within the United States. Similarly, U.S. firms can obtain protection in foreign nations where they sell goods.

In the United States, the Supreme Court has narrowly construed patent infringement as it applies to exported software, however. As a general rule, under U.S. law, no patent infringement occurs when a patented product is made and sold in another country. ■ **CASE IN POINT 8.12** AT&T Corporation holds a patent on a device used to digitally encode, compress, and process recorded speech. AT&T brought an infringement case against Microsoft Corporation, which admitted that its Windows operating system incorporated software code that infringed on AT&T's patent.

The United States Supreme Court held that Microsoft was liable only for infringement in the United States and not for the Windows-based computers produced in foreign locations. The Court reasoned that Microsoft had not "supplied" the software for the computers but had only electronically transmitted a master copy, which the foreign manufacturers copied and loaded onto the computers.[20] ■

---

17. For a United States Supreme Court case discussing the obviousness requirement, see *KSR International Co. v. Teleflex, Inc.*, 550 U.S. 398, 127 S.Ct. 1727, 167 L.Ed.2d 705 (2007).
18. See, for example, *Monsanto Co. v. Bowman*, 657 F.3d 1341 (Fed.Cir. 2011); and *Monsanto Co. v. Scruggs*, 2009 WL 1228318 (Fed.Cir. 2009).
19. *Apple, Inc. v. Samsung Electronics Co.*, 926 F.Supp.2d 1110 (N.D.Cal. 2013); 786 F.3d 983 (Fed. Cir. 2015).
20. *Microsoft Corp. v. AT&T Corp.*, 550 U.S. 437, 127 S.Ct. 1746, 167 L.Ed.2d 737 (2007).

DIGITAL UPDATE — The Problem of Patent Trolls

In recent years, a huge number of patent infringement lawsuits have been filed against software and technology firms. Many patent cases involve companies defending real innovations, but some lawsuits are "shakedowns" by patent trolls.

Patent trolls—more formally called nonpracticing entities (NPEs) or patent assertion entities (PAEs)—are firms that do not make or sell products or services but are in the business of patent litigation. These firms buy patents and then try to enforce them against companies that *do* sell products or services, demanding licensing fees and threatening infringement lawsuits. Patent trolls usually target online businesses.

"I'm Going to Sue You Unless You Pay Me to Go Away"

Patent trolls literally bank on the fact that when threatened with infringement suits, most companies would rather pay to settle than engage in costly litigation, even if they believe they could win.

Consider an example. Soverain Software, LLC, sued dozens of online retailers, including Amazon, Avon, Home Depot, Macy's, Nordstrom, Kohl's, RadioShack, The Gap, and Victoria's Secret. Soverain claimed that it owned patents that covered nearly any use of online shopping-cart technology and that all these retailers had infringed on its patents. Amazon paid millions to settle with Soverain, as did most of the other defendants.

Interestingly, one online retailer, Newegg, Inc., refused to pay Soverain and ultimately won in court. In 2013, a federal appellate court held that the shopping-cart patent claim was invalid on the ground of obviousness because the technology for it had already existed before Soverain obtained its patent.[a]

The Role of Software Patents

The patent troll problem is concentrated in software patents, which often include descriptions of what the software does rather than the computer code involved. Many software patents are vaguely worded and overly broad. In the United States, both the patent system and the courts have had difficulty evaluating and protecting such patents.

As a result, nearly any business that uses basic technology can be a target of patent trolls. In fact, *more than 60 percent of all new patent cases* are filed by patent trolls. The firms most commonly targeted by patent trolls are large technology companies, including AT&T, Google, Apple, Samsung, Amazon, and Verizon. In one recent year, "AT&T was sued for patent infringement by patent trolls 54 times—more than once a week."[b]

Critical Thinking *Some argue that the best way to stop patent trolls from taking advantage of the system would be to eliminate software patents completely and pass a law that makes software unpatentable. Would this be fair to software and technology companies? Why or why not?*

a. *Soverain Software, LLC v. Newegg, Inc.*, 728 F.3d 1332 (Fed. Cir. 2013), *cert.* denied, 134 S.Ct. 910 (2014).
b. Roger Parloff, "Taking on the Patent Trolls," *Fortune*, February 27, 2014.

8–2d Remedies for Patent Infringement

If a patent is infringed, the patent holder may sue for relief in federal court. The patent holder can seek an injunction against the infringer and can also request damages for royalties and lost profits. In some cases, the court may grant the winning party reimbursement for attorneys' fees and costs. If the court determines that the infringement was willful, the court can triple the amount of damages awarded (treble damages).

In the past, permanent injunctions were routinely granted to prevent future infringement. Today, however, according to the United States Supreme Court, a patent holder must prove that it has suffered irreparable injury and that the public interest would not be *disserved* by a permanent injunction.[21] Thus, courts have discretion to decide what is equitable in the circumstances and to consider what is in the public interest rather than just the interests of the parties.

■ **CASE IN POINT 8.13** Cordance Corporation developed some of the technology and software that automates Internet communications. Cordance sued Amazon.com, Inc., for patent infringement, claiming that Amazon's one-click purchasing interface infringed on one of Cordance's patents. After a jury found Amazon guilty of infringement, Cordance requested the court to issue a permanent injunction against Amazon's infringement or,

21. *eBay, Inc. v. MercExchange, LLC*, 547 U.S. 388, 126 S.Ct. 1837, 164 L.Ed.2d 641 (2006).

alternatively, to order Amazon to pay Cordance an ongoing royalty.

The court refused to issue a permanent injunction because Cordance had not proved that it would otherwise suffer irreparable harm. Cordance and Amazon were not direct competitors in the relevant market. Cordance had never sold or licensed the technology infringed by Amazon's one-click purchasing interface and had presented no market data or evidence to show how the infringement negatively affected Cordance. The court also refused to impose an ongoing royalty on Amazon.[22] ■

8–3 Copyrights

A **copyright** is an intangible property right granted by federal statute to the author or originator of a literary or artistic production of a specified type. The Copyright Act of 1976,[23] as amended, governs copyrights. Works created after January 1, 1978, are automatically given statutory copyright protection for the life of the author plus 70 years. For copyrights owned by publishing houses, the copyright expires 95 years from the date of publication or 120 years from the date of creation, whichever comes first. For works by more than one author, the copyright expires 70 years after the death of the last surviving author.[24]

When copyright protection ends, works enter into the *public domain*. Intellectual property, such as songs and other published works, that have entered into the public domain belong to everyone and are not protected by copyright or patent laws.

■ **CASE IN POINT 8.14** The popular character Sherlock Holmes originated in stories written by Arthur Conan Doyle and published from 1887 through 1927. Over the years, elements of the characters and stories created by Doyle have appeared in books, movies, and television series, including *Elementary* on CBS and *Sherlock* on BBC.

Before 2013, those who wished to use the copyrighted Sherlock material had to pay a licensing fee to Doyle's estate. Then, in 2013, the editors of a book of Holmes-related stories filed a lawsuit in federal court claiming that the basic Sherlock Holmes story elements introduced before 1923 should no longer be protected. The

court agreed and ruled that these elements have entered the public domain—that is, the copyright has expired, and they can be used without permission.[25] ■

8–3a Registration

Copyrights can be registered with the U.S. Copyright Office (www.copyright.gov) in Washington, D.C. Registration is not required, however. A copyright owner no longer needs to place the symbol © or the term *Copr.* or *Copyright* on the work to have the work protected against infringement. Chances are that if somebody created it, somebody owns it.

Generally, copyright owners are protected against the following:

1. Reproduction of the work.
2. Development of derivative works.
3. Distribution of the work.
4. Public display of the work.

8–3b What Is Protected Expression?

Works that are copyrightable include books, records, films, artworks, architectural plans, menus, music videos, product packaging, and computer software. To be protected, a work must be "fixed in a durable medium" from which it can be perceived, reproduced, or communicated. As noted, protection is automatic, and registration is not required.

Section 102 of the Copyright Act explicitly states that it protects original works that fall into one of the following categories:

1. Literary works (including newspaper and magazine articles, computer and training manuals, catalogues, brochures, and print advertisements).
2. Musical works and accompanying words (including advertising jingles).
3. Dramatic works and accompanying music.
4. Pantomimes and choreographic works (including ballets and other forms of dance).
5. Pictorial, graphic, and sculptural works (including cartoons, maps, posters, statues, and even stuffed animals).
6. Motion pictures and other audiovisual works (including multimedia works).
7. Sound recordings.
8. Architectural works.

22. *Cordance Corp. v. Amazon.com, Inc.*, 730 F.Supp.2d 333 (D.Del. 2010).
23. 17 U.S.C. Sections 101 *et seq.*
24. These time periods reflect the extensions of the length of copyright protection enacted by Congress in the Copyright Term Extension Act of 1998, 17 U.S.C. Section 302. The United States Supreme Court upheld the constitutionality of the act in 2003. See *Eldred v. Ashcroft*, 537 U.S. 186, 123 S.Ct. 769, 154 L.Ed.2d 683 (2003).
25. *Klinger v. Conan Doyle Estate, Ltd.*, 988 F.Supp.2d 879 (N.D.Ill. 2013).

Section 102 Exclusions Generally, anything that is not an original expression will not qualify for copyright protection. Facts widely known to the public are not copyrightable. Page numbers are not copyrightable because they follow a sequence known to everyone. Mathematical calculations are not copyrightable.

Furthermore, it is not possible to copyright an *idea.* Section 102 of the Copyright Act specifically excludes copyright protection for any "idea, procedure, process, system, method of operation, concept, principle, or discovery, regardless of the form in which it is described, explained, illustrated, or embodied." Thus, anyone can freely use the underlying ideas or principles embodied in a work.

What is copyrightable is the particular way in which an idea is *expressed.* Whenever an idea and an expression are inseparable, the expression cannot be copyrighted. An idea and its expression, then, must be separable to be copyrightable. Thus, for the design of a useful item to be copyrightable, the way it looks must be separate from its utilitarian (functional) purpose.

■ **CASE IN POINT 8.15** Inhale, Inc., registered a copyright on a hookah—a device for smoking tobacco by filtering the smoke through water held in a container at the base. Starbuzz Tobacco, Inc., sold hookahs with water containers shaped exactly like the Inhale containers.

Inhale filed a suit in a federal district court against Starbuzz for copyright infringement. The court determined that the shape of the water container on Inhale's hookahs was not copyrightable. The U.S. Court of Appeals for the Ninth Circuit affirmed the judgment. "The shape of a container is not independent of the container's utilitarian function—to hold the contents within its shape—because the shape accomplishes the function."[26] ■

---

26. *Inhale, Inc. v. Starbuzz Tobacco, Inc.,* 755 F.3d 1038 (2014).

Compilations of Facts Unlike ideas, *compilations* of facts are copyrightable. Under Section 103 of the Copyright Act, a compilation is "a work formed by the collection and assembling of preexisting materials or data that are selected, coordinated, or arranged in such a way that the resulting work as a whole constitutes an original work of authorship."

The key requirement in the copyrightability of a compilation is originality. If the facts are selected, coordinated, or arranged in an original way, they can qualify for copyright protection. Therefore, the White Pages of a telephone directory do not qualify for copyright protection, because they simply list alphabetically names and telephone numbers. The Yellow Pages of a directory can be copyrightable, provided the information is selected, coordinated, or arranged in an original way. Similarly, a compilation of information about yachts listed for sale has qualified for copyright protection.[27]

8–3c Copyright Infringement

Whenever the form or expression of an idea is copied, an infringement of copyright has occurred. The reproduction does not have to be exactly the same as the original, nor does it have to reproduce the original in its entirety. If a substantial part of the original is reproduced, the copyright has been infringed.

In the following case, rapper Curtis Jackson—better known as "50 Cent"—was the defendant in a suit that claimed his album *Before I Self-Destruct,* and the film of the same name, infringed the copyright of Shadrach Winstead's book *The Preacher's Son—But the Streets Turned Me into a Gangster.*

---

27. *BUC International Corp. v. International Yacht Council, Ltd.,* 489 F.3d 1129 (11th Cir. 2007).

Case Analysis 8.3

Winstead v. Jackson
United States Court of Appeals, Third Circuit, 509 Fed.Appx. 139 (2013).

In the Language of the Court
PER CURIAM. [By the Whole Court]
 * * * *

 * * * Winstead filed his * * * complaint in the United States District Court for the District of New Jersey, claiming that Jackson's album/CD and film derived their contents from, and infringed the copyright of, his book.
 * * * *

 * * * The District Court dismissed Winstead's * * * complaint * * * , concluding that Jackson * * * did not improperly copy protected aspects of Winstead's book.
 * * * *

Winstead appeals.
 * * * *

Here, it is not disputed that Winstead is the owner of the copyrighted property * * * . However, *not all copying is copyright infringement, so even if actual copying is proven, the court must decide, by comparing the allegedly infringing work with the original work, whether the copying was unlawful. Copying may be proved inferentially by showing that the allegedly infringing work is substantially similar to the copyrighted*

Case 8.3 Continues

work. A court compares the allegedly infringing work with the original work, and considers whether a "lay-observer" would believe that the copying was of protectable aspects of the copyrighted work. The inquiry involves distinguishing between the author's expression and the idea or theme that he or she seeks to convey or explore, because the former is protected and the latter is not. The court must determine whether the allegedly infringing work is similar because it appropriates the unique expressions of the original work, or merely because it contains elements that would be expected when two works express the same idea or explore the same theme. [Emphasis added.]

* * * A lay observer would not believe that Jackson's album/CD and film copied protectable aspects of Winstead's book. Jackson's album/CD is comprised of 16 individual songs, which explore drug-dealing, guns and money, vengeance, and other similar clichés of hip hop gangsterism. Jackson's fictional film is the story of a young man who turns to violence when his mother is killed in a drive-by shooting. The young man takes revenge by killing the man who killed his mother, and then gets rich by becoming an "enforcer" for a powerful criminal. He takes up with a woman who eventually betrays him, and is shot to death by her boyfriend, who has just been released from prison. The movie ends with his younger brother vowing to seek vengeance. Winstead's book purports to be autobiographical and tells the story of a young man whose beloved father was a Bishop in the church. The protagonist was angry as a child because his stepmother abused him, but he found acceptance and self-esteem on the streets of Newark because he was physically powerful. He earned money robbing and beating people, went to jail, returned to crime upon his release, and then made even more money. The protagonist discusses his time at Rahway State Prison in great and compelling detail. The story ends when the protagonist learns that his father has passed away; he conveys his belief that this tragedy has led to his redemption, and he hopes that others might learn from his mistakes.

* * * Although Winstead's book and Jackson's works share similar themes and setting, the story of an angry and wronged protagonist who turns to a life of violence and crime has long been a part of the public domain [and is therefore not protected by copyright law]. Winstead argues * * * that a protagonist asking for God's help when his father dies, cutting drugs with mixing agents to maximize profits, and complaining about relatives who are addicts and steal the product, are protectable, but these things are not unique. To the extent that Jackson's works contain these elements, they are to be expected when two works express the same idea about "the streets" or explore the same theme. Winstead argues that not every protagonist whose story concerns guns, drugs, and violence in an urban setting winds up in prison or loses a parent, but this argument only serves to illustrate an important difference between his book and Jackson's film. Jackson's protagonist never spends any time in prison, whereas Winstead's protagonist devotes a considerable part of his story to his incarcerations.

In addition, Winstead's book and Jackson's works are different with respect to character, plot, mood, and sequence of events. Winstead's protagonist embarks on a life of crime at a very young age, but is redeemed by the death of his beloved father. Jackson's protagonist turns to crime when he is much older and only after his mother is murdered. He winds up dead at a young age, unredeemed. Winstead's book is hopeful; Jackson's film is characterized * * * by moral apathy. It is true that both works involve the loss of a parent and the protagonist's recognition of the parent's importance in his life, but nowhere does Jackson appropriate anything unique about Winstead's expression of this generic topic.

Winstead contends that direct phrases from his book appear in Jackson's film. * * * He emphasizes these phrases: "Yo, where is my money at," "I would never have done no shit like that to you," "my father, my strength was gone," "he was everything to me," and "I did not know what to do," but, like the phrases "putting the work in," "get the dope, cut the dope," "let's keep it popping," and "the strong take from the weak but the smart take from everybody," they are either common in general or common with respect to hip hop culture, and do not enjoy copyright protection. The average person reading or listening to these phrases in the context of an overall story or song would not regard them as unique and protectable. Moreover, words and short phrases do not enjoy copyright protection. The similarity between Winstead's book and the lyrics to Jackson's songs on the album/CD is even more tenuous. "Stretching the dope" and "bloodshot red eyes" are common phrases that do not enjoy copyright protection. A side-by-side comparison of Winstead's book and the lyrics from Jackson's album/CD do not support a claim of copyright infringement.

For the foregoing reasons, we will affirm the order of the District Court dismissing [Winstead's] complaint.

Legal Reasoning Questions

1. Which expressions of an original work are protected by copyright law?

2. Is all copying copyright infringement? If not, what is the test for determining whether a creative work has been unlawfully copied?

3. How did the court in this case determine whether the defendant's work infringed on the plaintiff's copyright?

Remedies for Copyright Infringement Those who infringe copyrights may be liable for damages or criminal penalties. These range from actual damages or statutory damages, imposed at the court's discretion, to criminal proceedings for willful violations.

Actual damages are based on the harm caused to the copyright holder by the infringement, while statutory damages, not to exceed $150,000, are provided for under the Copyright Act. Criminal proceedings may result in fines and/or imprisonment. A court can also issue a permanent injunction against a defendant when the court deems it necessary to prevent future copyright infringement.

■ **CASE IN POINT 8.16** Rusty Carroll operated an online term paper business, R2C2, Inc., that offered up to 300,000 research papers for sale at nine Web sites. Individuals whose work was posted on these Web sites without their permission filed a lawsuit against Carroll for copyright infringement. Because Carroll had repeatedly failed to comply with court orders regarding discovery, the court found that the copyright infringement was likely to continue unless an injunction was issued. The court therefore issued a permanent injunction prohibiting Carroll and R2C2 from selling any term paper without sworn documentary evidence that the paper's author had given permission.[28] ■

The "Fair Use" Exception An exception to liability for copyright infringement is made under the "fair use" doctrine. In certain circumstances, a person or organization can reproduce copyrighted material without paying royalties. Section 107 of the Copyright Act provides as follows:

[T]he fair use of a copyrighted work, including such use by reproduction in copies or phonorecords or by any other means specified by [Section 106 of the Copyright Act], for purposes such as criticism, comment, news reporting, teaching (including multiple copies for classroom use), scholarship, or research, is not an infringement of copyright. In determining whether the use made of a work in any particular case is a fair use the factors to be considered shall include—

(1) the purpose and character of the use, including whether such use is of a commercial nature or is for nonprofit educational purposes;
(2) the nature of the copyrighted work;
(3) the amount and substantiality of the portion used in relation to the copyrighted work as a whole; and
(4) the effect of the use upon the potential market for or value of the copyrighted work.

What Is Fair Use? Because these guidelines are very broad, the courts determine whether a particular use is fair on a case-by-case basis. Thus, anyone who reproduces copyrighted material may be committing a violation. In determining whether a use is fair, courts have often considered the fourth factor to be the most important.

■ **CASE IN POINT 8.17** A number of research universities, in partnership with Google, Inc., agreed to digitize books from their libraries and create a repository for them. Eighty member institutions (including many colleges and universities) contributed more than ten million works into the HathiTrust Digital Library. Some authors complained that this book scanning violated their rights and sued the HathiTrust and several associated entities for copyright infringement.

The court, however, sided with the defendants and held that making digital copies for the purposes of online search was a fair use. The library's searchable database enabled researchers to find terms of interest in the digital volumes—but not to read the volumes online. Therefore, the court concluded that the digitization did not provide a substitute that damaged the market for the original works.[29] ■

The First Sale Doctrine Section 109(a) of the Copyright Act provides that the owner of a particular item that is copyrighted can, without the authority of the copyright owner, sell or otherwise dispose of it. This rule is known as the first sale doctrine.

Under this doctrine, once a copyright owner sells or gives away a particular copy of a work, the copyright owner no longer has the right to control the distribution of that copy. Thus, for instance, a person who buys a copyrighted book can sell it to someone else. The first sale doctrine also applies to a person who receives promotional CDs, such as a music critic or radio programmer.[30]

■ **CASE IN POINT 8.18** Supap Kirtsaeng, a citizen of Thailand, was a graduate student at the University of Southern California. He enlisted friends and family in Thailand to buy copies of textbooks there and ship them to him in the United States. Kirtsaeng resold the textbooks on eBay, where he eventually made about $100,000.

John Wiley & Sons, Inc., had printed eight of those textbooks in Asia. Wiley sued Kirtsaeng in federal district court for copyright infringement. Kirtsaeng argued that Section 109(a) of the Copyright Act allows the first purchaser-owner of a book to sell it without the copyright owner's permission. The trial court held in favor of Wiley, and that decision was affirmed on appeal. Kirtsaeng then appealed to the United States Supreme Court, which ruled

28. *Weidner v. Carroll*, 2010 WL 310310 (S.D.Ill. 2010).
29. *Authors Guild, Inc., v. HathiTrust*, 755 F.3d 87 (2d Cir. 2014).
30. See, for example, *UMG Recordings, Inc. v. Augusto*, 628 F.3d 1175 (9th Cir. 2011).

in Kirtsaeng's favor. The first sale doctrine applies even to goods purchased abroad and resold in the United States.[31] ■

8–3d Copyright Protection for Software

The Computer Software Copyright Act amended the Copyright Act to include computer programs in the list of creative works protected by federal copyright law.[32] Generally, copyright protection extends to those parts of a computer program that can be read by humans, such as the "high-level" language of a source code. Protection also extends to the binary-language object code, which is readable only by the computer, and to such elements as the overall structure, sequence, and organization of a program.

Not all aspects of software are protected, however. Courts typically have not extended copyright protection to the "look and feel"—the general appearance, command structure, video images, menus, windows, and other screen displays—of computer programs. (Note that copying the "look and feel" of another's product may be a violation of trade dress or trademark laws, however.) Sometimes it can be difficult for courts to decide which particular aspects of software are protected.

■ **CASE IN POINT 8.19** Oracle America, Inc., is a software company that owns numerous application programming interfaces, or API packages. Oracle grants licenses to others to use these API packages to write applications in the Java programming language. Java is open and free for anyone to use, but using it requires an interface. When Google began using some of Oracle's API packages to run Java on its Android mobile devices, Oracle sued for copyright infringement. Google argued that the software packages were command structure and, as such, not protected under copyright law. Ultimately, a federal appellate court concluded that the API packages were source code and were entitled to copyright protection.[33] ■

8–4 Trade Secrets

The law of trade secrets protects some business processes and information that are not, or cannot be, patented, copyrighted, or trademarked. A **trade secret** is basically information of commercial value, such as customer lists, plans, and research and development. Trade secrets may also include pricing information, marketing methods, production techniques, and generally anything that makes an individual company unique and that would have value to a competitor.

Unlike copyright and trademark protection, protection of trade secrets extends to both ideas and their expression. For this reason, and because there are no registration or filing requirements for trade secrets, trade secret protection may be well suited for software.

Of course, a company's trade secrets must be disclosed to some persons, particularly to key employees. Businesses generally attempt to protect their trade secrets by having all employees who use a protected process or information agree in their contracts, or in confidentiality agreements, never to divulge it.

8–4a State and Federal Law on Trade Secrets

Under Section 757 of the *Restatement of Torts,* those who disclose or use another's trade secret, without authorization, are liable to that other party if either of the following is true:

1. They discovered the secret by improper means.
2. Their disclosure or use constitutes a breach of a duty owed to the other party.

Stealing confidential business data by industrial espionage, such as by tapping into a competitor's computer, is a theft of trade secrets without any contractual violation and is actionable in itself.

Trade secrets have long been protected under the common law. Today, nearly every state has enacted trade secret laws based on the Uniform Trade Secrets Act.[34] Additionally, the Economic Espionage Act[35] makes the theft of trade secrets a federal crime.

8–4b Trade Secrets in Cyberspace

Computer technology is undercutting many business firms' ability to protect their confidential information, including trade secrets. For example, a dishonest employee could e-mail trade secrets in a company's computer to a competitor or a future employer. If e-mail is not an option, the employee might walk out with the information on a flash drive.

Misusing a company's social media account is yet another way in which employees may appropriate trade secrets. ■ **CASE IN POINT 8.20** Noah Kravitz worked for a company called PhoneDog for four years as a product reviewer and video blogger. PhoneDog provided him with the Twitter account "@PhoneDog_Noah." Kravitz's popularity grew, and he had approximately 17,000

31. *Kirtsaeng v. John Wiley & Sons, Inc.,* ___ U.S. ___, 133 S.Ct. 1351, 185 L.Ed.2d 392 (2013).
32. Pub. L. No. 96-517 (1980), amending 17 U.S.C. Sections 101, 117.
33. *Oracle America, Inc. v. Google Inc.,* 750 F.3d 1339 (Fed.Cir. 2014).
34. The Uniform Trade Secrets Act, as drafted by the National Conference of Commissioners on Uniform State Laws (NCCUSL), can be found at uniformlaws.org.
35. 18 U.S.C. Sections 1831–1839.

followers by the time he quit. PhoneDog requested that Kravitz stop using the Twitter account. Although Kravitz changed his handle to "@noahkravitz," he continued to use the account. PhoneDog subsequently sued Kravitz for misappropriation of trade secrets, among other things. Kravitz moved for a dismissal, but the court found that the complaint adequately stated a cause of action for

misappropriation of trade secrets and allowed the suit to continue.[36] ∎

Exhibit 8–1 outlines trade secrets and other forms of intellectual property discussed in this chapter.

36. *PhoneDog v. Kravitz,* 2011 WL 5415612 (N.D.Cal. 2011). See also *Mintel Learning Technology, Inc. v. Ambrow Education Holding Ltd.,* 2012 WL 762126 (N.D.Cal. 2012).

EXHIBIT 8–1 Forms of Intellectual Property

	PATENTS	COPYRIGHTS	TRADEMARKS	TRADE SECRETS
Definition	A grant from the government that gives an inventor exclusive rights to an invention.	The right of an author or originator of a literary or artistic work, or other production that falls within a specified category, to have the exclusive use of that work for a given period of time.	Any distinctive word, name, symbol, or device (image or appearance), or combination thereof, that an entity uses to distinguish its goods or services from those of others. The owner has the exclusive right to use that mark or trade dress.	Any information that a business possesses and that gives the business an advantage over competitors (including formulas, lists, patterns, plans, processes, and programs).
How Acquired	By filing a patent application with the U.S. Patent and Trademark Office and receiving its approval.	Automatic (once the work or creation is put in tangible form). Only the *expression* of an idea (and not the idea itself) can be protected by copyright.	1. At common law, ownership created by use of the mark. 2. Registration with the appropriate federal or state office gives notice and is permitted if the mark is currently in use or will be within the next six months.	Through the originality and development of the information and processes that constitute the business secret and are unknown to others.
Duration	Twenty years from the date of the application; for design patents, fourteen years.	For authors: the life of the author, plus 70 years. For publishers: 95 years after the date of publication or 120 years after creation.	Unlimited, as long as it is in use. To continue notice by registration, the owner must renew by filing between the fifth and sixth years, and thereafter, every ten years.	Unlimited, so long as not revealed to others. Once revealed to others, it is no longer a trade secret.
Remedy for Infringement	Monetary damages, Including royalties and lost profits, *plus* attorneys' fees. Damages may be tripled for intentional infringements.	Actual damages plus profits received by the party who infringed *or* statutory damages under the Copyright Act, *plus* costs and attorneys' fees in either situation.	1. Injunction prohibiting the future use of the mark. 2. Actual damages plus profits received by the party who infringed (can be increased under the Lanham Act). 3. Destruction of articles that infringed. 4. *Plus* costs and attorneys' fees.	Monetary damages for misappropriation (the Uniform Trade Secrets Act also permits punitive damages if willful), *plus* costs and attorneys' fees.

8–5 International Protection for Intellectual Property

For many years, the United States has been a party to various international agreements relating to intellectual property rights. For instance, the Paris Convention of 1883, to which almost 180 countries are signatory, allows parties in one country to file for patent and trademark protection in any of the other member countries. Other international agreements in this area include the Berne Convention, the Trade-Related Aspects of Intellectual Property Rights (known as the TRIPS agreement), the Madrid Protocol, and the Anti-Counterfeiting Trade Agreement.

8–5a The Berne Convention

Under the Berne Convention, if a U.S. citizen writes a book, every country that has signed the convention must recognize the U.S. author's copyright in the book. Also, if a citizen of a country that has not signed the convention first publishes a book in one of the 169 countries that have signed, all other countries that have signed the convention must recognize that author's copyright. Copyright notice is not needed to gain protection under the Berne Convention for works published after March 1, 1989.

In 2011, the European Union altered its copyright rules under the Berne Convention to extend the period of royalty protection for musicians from fifty years to seventy years. This decision aids major record labels as well as performers and musicians who previously faced losing royalties from sales of their older recordings. The profits of musicians and record companies have been shrinking for years because of the sharp decline in sales of compact discs and the rise in illegal downloads.

8–5b The TRIPS Agreement

The Berne Convention and other international agreements have given some protection to intellectual property on a worldwide level. None of them, however, has been as significant and far reaching in scope as the TRIPS agreement. Representatives from more than one hundred nations signed the TRIPS agreement in 1994.

Establishes Standards and Procedures The TRIPS agreement established, for the first time, standards for the international protection of intellectual property rights, including patents, trademarks, and copyrights for movies, computer programs, books, and music. Each member country of the World Trade Organization must include in its domestic laws broad intellectual property rights and effective remedies (including civil and criminal penalties) for violations of those rights.

Each member nation must also ensure that legal procedures are available for parties who wish to bring actions for infringement of intellectual property rights. Additionally, a related document established a mechanism for settling disputes among member nations.

Prohibits Discrimination Generally, the TRIPS agreement forbids member nations from discriminating against foreign owners of intellectual property rights in the administration, regulation, or adjudication of those rights. In other words, a member nation cannot give its own nationals (citizens) favorable treatment without offering the same treatment to nationals of all other member countries. ■ **EXAMPLE 8.21** A U.S. software manufacturer brings a suit for the infringement of intellectual property rights under Germany's national laws. Because Germany is a member of the TRIPS agreement, the U.S. manufacturer is entitled to receive the same treatment as a German manufacturer. ■

8–5c The Madrid Protocol

In the past, one of the difficulties in protecting U.S. trademarks internationally was the time and expense required to apply for trademark registration in foreign nations. The filing fees and procedures for trademark registration vary significantly among individual countries. The Madrid Protocol, which was signed into law in 2003, may help to resolve these problems.

The Madrid Protocol is an international treaty that has been signed by about a hundred countries. Under its provisions, a U.S. company wishing to register its trademark abroad can submit a single application and designate other member countries in which the company would like to register its mark. The treaty was designed to reduce the costs of international trademark protection by more than 60 percent.

Although the Madrid Protocol may simplify and reduce the cost of trademark registration in foreign countries, it remains to be seen whether it will provide significant benefits to trademark owners. Even with an easier registration process, there are still questions as to whether all member countries will enforce the law and protect the mark.

8–5d The Anti-Counterfeiting Trade Agreement

In 2011, Australia, Canada, Japan, Korea, Morocco, New Zealand, Singapore, and the United States signed the Anti-Counterfeiting Trade Agreement (ACTA), an international treaty to combat global counterfeiting and piracy. Other nations have since signed the agreement.

Goals and Provisions The goals of the treaty are to increase international cooperation, facilitate the best law enforcement practices, and provide a legal framework to combat counterfeiting. ACTA applies not only to counterfeit physical goods, such as medications, but also to pirated copyrighted works being distributed via the Internet. The idea is to create a new standard of enforcement for intellectual property rights that goes beyond the TRIPS agreement and encourages international cooperation and information sharing among signatory countries.

Border Searches Under ACTA, member nations are required to establish border measures that allow officials, on their own initiative, to search commercial shipments of imports and exports for counterfeit goods. The treaty neither requires nor prohibits random border searches of electronic devices, such as laptops, tablet devices, and smartphones, for infringing content.

If border authorities reasonably believe that any goods in transit are counterfeit, the treaty allows them to keep the suspect goods unless the owner proves that the items are authentic and noninfringing. The treaty allows member nations, in accordance with their own laws, to order online service providers to furnish information about suspected trademark and copyright infringers, including their identities.

Reviewing: Intellectual Property Rights

Two computer science majors, Trent and Xavier, have an idea for a new video game, which they propose to call Hallowed. They form a business and begin developing their idea. Several months later, Trent and Xavier run into a problem with their design and consult a friend, Brad, who is an expert in designing computer source codes. After the software is completed but before Hallowed is marketed, a video game called Halo 2 is released for both the Xbox and the Playstation systems. Halo 2 uses source codes similar to those of Hallowed and imitates Hallowed's overall look and feel, although not all the features are alike. Using the information presented in the chapter, answer the following questions.

1. Would the name *Hallowed* receive protection as a trademark or as trade dress? Explain.
2. If Trent and Xavier had obtained a patent on Hallowed, would the release of Halo 2 have infringed on their patent? Why or why not?
3. Based only on the facts described above, could Trent and Xavier sue the makers of Halo 2 for copyright infringement? Why or why not?
4. Suppose that Trent and Xavier discover that Brad took the idea of Hallowed and sold it to the company that produced Halo 2. Which type of intellectual property issue does this raise?

Debate This . . . *Congress has amended copyright law several times so that copyright holders now have protection for many decades. Was Congress right in extending these copyright time periods?*

Terms and Concepts

certification mark 155	intellectual property 150	trade dress 155
collective mark 155	license 156	trade name 156
copyright 160	patent 157	trade secret 164
dilution 152	service mark 155	trademark 150

Issue Spotters

1. Roslyn, a food buyer for Organic Cornucopia Food Company, decides to go into business for herself as Roslyn's Kitchen. She contacts Organic's suppliers, offering to buy their entire harvest for the next year. She also contacts Organic's customers, offering to sell her products at prices lower than Organic's prices. Has Roslyn violated any of the intellectual property rights discussed in this chapter? Explain. (See *Trade Secrets*.)

2. Global Products develops, patents, and markets software. World Copies, Inc., sells Global's software without the maker's permission. Is this patent infringement? If so, how might Global save the cost of suing World for infringement and at the same time profit from World's sales? (See *Patents*.)

- **Check your answers to the Issue Spotters against the answers provided in Appendix D at the end of this text.**

Business Scenarios

8–1. Fair Use. Professor Wise is teaching a summer seminar in business torts at State University. Several times during the course, he makes copies of relevant sections from business law texts and distributes them to his students. Wise does not realize that the daughter of one of the textbook authors is a member of his seminar. She tells her father about Wise's copying activities, which have taken place without her father's or his publisher's permission. Her father sues Wise for copyright infringement. Wise claims protection under the fair use doctrine. Who will prevail? Explain. (See *Copyrights*.)

8–2. Patent Infringement. John and Andrew Doney invented a hard-bearing device for balancing rotors. Although they obtained a patent for their invention from the U.S. Patent and Trademark Office, it was never used as an automobile wheel balancer. Some time later, Exetron Corp. produced an automobile wheel balancer that used a hard-bearing device with a support plate similar to that of the Doneys' device. Given that the Doneys had not used their device for automobile wheel balancing, does Exetron's use of a similar device infringe on the Doneys' patent? Why or why not? (See *Patents*.)

Business Case Problems

8–3. Spotlight on Macy's—Copyright Infringement.
 United Fabrics International, Inc., bought a fabric design from an Italian designer and registered a copyright to it with the U.S. Copyright Office. When Macy's, Inc., began selling garments with a similar design, United filed a copyright infringement suit against Macy's. Macy's argued that United did not own a valid copyright to the design and so could not claim infringement. Does United have to prove that the copyright is valid to establish infringement? Explain. [*United Fabrics International, Inc. v. C&J Wear, Inc.*, 630 F.3d 1255 (9th Cir. 2011)] (See *Copyrights*.)

8–4. Theft of Trade Secrets. Hanjuan Jin, a citizen of China, worked as a software engineer for Motorola for many years in a division that created proprietary standards for cellular communications. Contrary to Motorola's policies, Jin also secretly began working as a consultant for Lemko Corp., as well as with Sun Kaisens, a Chinese software company, and with the Chinese military. She started corresponding with Sun Kaisens's management about a possible full-time job in China. Jin took several medical leaves of absence from Motorola to return to Beijing and work with Sun Kaisens and the military.

After one of these medical leaves, Jin returned to Motorola. Over a period of several days, Jin accessed and downloaded thousands of documents on her personal laptop and on pen drives. When, later, she attempted to board a flight to China from Chicago, she was randomly searched by U.S. Customs

and Border Protection officials at the airport. U.S. officials discovered the downloaded Motorola documents. Are there any circumstances under which Jin could avoid being prosecuted for theft of trade secrets? If so, what are these circumstances? Discuss fully. [*United States v. Hanjuan Jin*, 833 F.Supp.2d 977 (N.D.Ill. 2012)] (See *Trade Secrets*.)

8–5. Copyright Infringement. SilverEdge Systems Software hired Catherine Conrad to perform a singing telegram. SilverEdge arranged for James Bendewald to record Conrad's performance of her copyrighted song to post on its Web site. Conrad agreed to wear a microphone to assist in the recording, told Bendewald what to film, and asked for an additional fee only if SilverEdge used the video for a commercial purpose. Later, the company chose to post a video of a different performer's singing telegram instead. Conrad filed a suit in a federal district court against SilverEdge and Bendewald for copyright infringement. Are the defendants liable? Explain. [*Conrad v. Bendewald*, 500 Fed.Appx. 526 (7th Cir. 2013)] (See *Copyrights*.)

8–6. Business Case Problem with Sample Answer—Patents. The U.S. Patent and Trademark Office (PTO)
 denied Raymond Gianelli's application for a patent for a "Rowing Machine"—an exercise machine on which a user *pulls* on handles to perform a rowing motion against a selected resistance. The PTO considered the device obvious in light of a previously patented "Chest Press Apparatus for Exercising

Regions of the Upper Body"—an exercise machine on which a user *pushes* on handles to overcome a selected resistance. On what ground might this result be reversed on appeal? Discuss. [*In re Gianelli*, 739 F.3d 1375 (Fed. Cir. 2014)] (See *Patents.*)

- **For a sample answer to Problem 8–6, go to Appendix E at the end of this text.**

8–7. Patents. Rodney Klassen was employed by the U.S. Department of Agriculture (USDA). Without the USDA's authorization, Klassen gave Jim Ludy, a grape grower, plant material for two unreleased varieties of grapes. For almost two years, most of Ludy's plantings bore no usable fruit, none of the grapes were sold, and no plant material was given to any other person. The plantings were visible from publicly accessible roads, but none of the vines were labeled, and the variety could not be identified by simply viewing the vines. Under patent law, an applicant may not obtain a patent for an invention that is in public use for more than one year before the date of the application. Could the USDA successfully apply for patents on the two varieties given to Ludy? Explain. [*Delano Farms Co. v. California Table Grape Commission*, 778 F.3d 1243 (Fed. Cir. 2015)] (See *Patents.*)

8–8. Copyright. Savant Homes, Inc., is a custom home designer and builder. Using what it called the "Anders Plan," Savant built a model house in Windsor, Colorado. This was a ranch house with two bedrooms on one side and a master suite on the other, separated by a combined family room, dining room, and kitchen. Ron and Tammie Wagner toured the Savant house. The same month, the Wagners hired builder Douglas Collins and his firm, Douglas Consulting, LLC, to build a house for them in Windsor. After it was built, Savant filed a suit in a federal district court against Collins for copyright infringement, alleging that the builder had copied the Anders Plan in the design and construction of the Wagner house. Collins showed that the Anders Plan consisted of standard elements and standard arrangements of elements. In these circumstances, has infringement occurred? Explain.

[*Savant Homes, Inc. v. Collins*, 809 F.3d 1133 (10th Cir. 2016)] (See *Copyrights.*)

8–9. A Question of Ethics—Copyright Infringement.
 Custom Copies, Inc., prepares and sells coursepacks, which contain compilations of readings for college courses. A teacher selects the readings and delivers a syllabus to the copy shop, which obtains the materials from a library, copies them, and binds the copies. Blackwell Publishing, Inc., which owns the copyright to some of the materials, filed a suit, alleging copyright infringement. Custom Copies filed a motion to dismiss for failure to state a claim. [Blackwell Publishing, Inc. v. Custom Copies, Inc., 2006 WL 1529503 (N.D.Fla. 2006)] (See *Copyrights.*)

(a) Custom Copies argued, in part, that creating and selling did not "distribute" the coursepacks. Does a copy shop violate copyright law if it only copies materials for coursepacks? Does the copying fall under the "fair use" exception? Should the court grant the defendant's motion? Why or why not?

(b) What is the potential impact of copying and selling a book or journal without the permission of, and the payment of royalties or a fee to, the copyright owner? Explain.

8–10. Special Case Analysis—Copyright Infringement. Go to Case Analysis 8.3, *Winstead v. Jackson*. Read the excerpt, and answer the following questions. (See *Copyrights.*)

(a) Issue: This case focused on an allegation of copyright infringement involving what parties and which creative works?

(b) Rule of Law: What is the test for determining whether a creative work infringes the copyright of another work?

(c) Applying the Rule of Law: How did the court determine whether the claim of copyright infringement was supported in this case?

(d) Conclusion: Was the defendant liable for copyright infringement? Why or why not?

Legal Reasoning Group Activity

8–11. Patents. After years of research, your company develops a product that might revolutionize the green (environmentally conscious) building industry. The product is made from relatively inexpensive and widely available materials combined in a unique way that can substantially lower the heating and cooling costs of residential and commercial buildings. The company has registered the trademark it intends to use on the product and has filed a patent application with the U.S. Patent and Trademark Office. (See *Patents.*)

(a) One group should provide three reasons why this product does or does not qualify for patent protection.

(b) Another group should develop a four-step procedure for how your company can best protect its intellectual property rights (trademark, trade secret, and patent) and prevent domestic and foreign competitors from producing counterfeit goods or cheap knockoffs.

(c) Another group should list and explain three ways your company can utilize licensing.

Answers to the *Issue Spotters*

1. Has Roslyn violated any of the intellectual property rights discussed in this chapter? Explain. Yes, Roslyn has committed theft of trade secrets. Lists of suppliers and customers cannot be patented, copyrighted, or trademarked, but the information they contain is protected against appropriation by others as trade secrets. And most likely, Roslyn signed a contract agreeing not to use this information outside her employment by Organic. But even without this contract, Organic could make a convincing case against its ex-employee for a theft of trade secrets.

2. Is this patent infringement? If so, how might Global save the cost of suing World for infringement and at the same time profit from World's sales? This is patent infringement. A software maker in this situation might best protect its product, save litigation costs, and profit from its patent by the use of a license. In the context of this problem, a license would grant permission to sell a patented item. (A license can be limited to certain purposes and to the licensee only.)

Sample Answers for *Business Case Problems with Sample Answer*

Problem 8–6. Patents. One ground on which the denial of the patent application in this problem could be reversed on appeal is that the design of Raymond Gianelli's "Rowing Machine" is *not obvious* in light of the design of the "Chest Press Apparatus for Exercising Regions of the Upper Body."

To obtain a patent, an applicant must demonstrate to the satisfaction of the U.S. Patent and Trademark Office (PTO) that the invention, discovery, process, or design is novel, useful, and not obvious in light of current technology. In this problem, the PTO denied Gianelli's application for a patent for his "Rowing Machine"—an exercise machine on which a user *pulls* on handles to perform a rowing motion against a selected resistance to strengthen the back muscles. The PTO considered the device obvious in light of a patented "Chest Press Apparatus for Exercising Regions of the Upper Body"—a chest press exercise machine on which a user *pushes* on handles to overcome a selected resistance. But it can be easily argued that it is *not* obvious to modify a machine with handles designed to be *pushed* into one with handles designed to be *pulled*. In fact, anyone who has used exercise machines knows that a way to cause injury is to use a machine in a manner not intended by the manufacturer.

In the actual case on which this problem is based, the U.S. Court of Appeals for the Federal Circuit reversed the PTO's denial of Gianelli's application for a patent, based on the reasoning stated above.

Contracts and E-Contracts

CHAPTER

Nature and Terminology

Contract law deals with, among other things, the formation and keeping of promises. A **promise** is a declaration by a person (the *promisor*) to do or not to do a certain act. As a result, the person to whom the promise is made (the *promisee*) has a right to expect or demand that something either will or will not happen in the future.

Like other types of law, contract law reflects our social values, interests, and expectations at a given point in time. It shows, for instance, to what extent our society allows people to make promises or commitments that are legally binding. It distinguishes between promises that create only *moral* obligations (such as a promise to take a friend to lunch) and promises that are legally binding (such as a promise to pay for items ordered online).

Contract law also demonstrates which excuses our society accepts for breaking certain types of promises.

In addition, it indicates which promises are considered to be contrary to public policy—against the interests of society as a whole—and therefore legally invalid. When the person making a promise is a child or is mentally incompetent, for instance, a question will arise as to whether the promise should be enforced. Resolving such questions is the essence of contract law.

11–1 An Overview of Contract Law

Before we look at the numerous rules that courts use to determine whether a particular promise will be enforced, it is necessary to understand some fundamental concepts of contract law. In this section, we describe the sources and general function of contract law and introduce the objective theory of contracts.

11–1a Sources of Contract Law

The common law governs all contracts except when it has been modified or replaced by statutory law, such as the Uniform Commercial Code (UCC), or by administrative agency regulations. Contracts relating to services, real estate, employment, and insurance, for instance, generally are governed by the common law of contracts.

Contracts for the sale and lease of goods, however, are governed by the UCC—to the extent that the UCC has modified general contract law. In the discussion of general contract law that follows, we indicate in footnotes the areas in which the UCC has significantly altered common law contract principles.

11–1b The Function of Contract Law

No aspect of modern life is entirely free of contractual relationships. You acquire rights and obligations, for example, when you borrow funds, buy or lease a house, obtain insurance, and purchase goods or services. Contract law is designed to provide stability and predictability, as well as certainty, for both buyers and sellers in the marketplace.

Contract law assures the parties to private agreements that the promises they make will be enforceable. Clearly, many promises are kept because the parties involved feel a moral obligation to keep them or because keeping a promise is in their mutual self-interest. The **promisor** (the person making the promise) and the **promisee** (the person to whom the promise is made) may also decide to honor their agreement for other reasons. In business agreements, the rules of contract law are often followed to avoid potential disputes.

By supplying procedures for enforcing private contractual agreements, contract law provides an essential condition for the existence of a market economy. Without a legal framework of reasonably assured expectations within which to make long-run plans, businesspersons would be able to rely only on the good faith of others.

Duty and good faith are usually sufficient to obtain compliance with a promise. When price changes or adverse economic factors make contract compliance costly, however, these elements may not be enough. Contract law is necessary to ensure compliance with a promise or to entitle the innocent party to some form of relief.

11–1c The Definition of a Contract

A **contract** is "a promise or a set of promises for the breach of which the law gives a remedy, or the performance of which the law in some way recognizes as a duty."[1] Put simply, a contract is an agreement that can be enforced in court. It is formed by two or more parties who agree to perform or to refrain from performing some act now or in the future.

Generally, contract disputes arise when there is a promise of future performance. If the contractual promise is not fulfilled, the party who made it is subject to the sanctions of a court. That party may be required to pay damages for failing to perform the contractual promise. In a few instances, the party may be required to perform the promised act.

11–1d The Objective Theory of Contracts

In determining whether a contract has been formed, the element of intent is of prime importance. In contract law, intent is determined by what is called the **objective theory of contracts,** not by the personal or subjective intent, or belief, of a party.

The theory is that a party's intention to enter into a legally binding agreement, or contract, is judged by outward, objective facts. The facts are as interpreted by a *reasonable* person, rather than by the party's own secret, subjective intentions. Objective facts may include:

1. What the party said when entering into the contract.
2. How the party acted or appeared (intent may be manifested by conduct as well as by oral or written words).
3. The circumstances surrounding the transaction.

■ **CASE IN POINT 11.1** Pan Handle Realty, LLC, built a luxury home in Westport, Connecticut. Robert Olins signed a lease for the property and gave Pan Handle a check for the amount of the annual rent—$138,000. Olins planned to move into the home on January 28, but

on January 27, Olins's bank informed Pan Handle that payment had been stopped on the rental check. Olins then told Pan Handle that he was "unable to pursue any further interest in the property."

When Pan Handle was not able to find a new tenant, it filed a lawsuit in a Connecticut state court against Olins, alleging that he had breached the lease. Olins argued that when he signed the lease, he did not intend to be bound by it. The court ruled in Pan Handle's favor and awarded $138,000 in damages, plus $8,000 for utilities, interest, and attorneys' fees. The decision was affirmed on appeal. The objective fact, as supported by the evidence, was that the parties intended to be bound by the lease when they signed it. The fact that Olins had a change of heart after signing the contract was irrelevant.[2] ■

11–2 Elements of a Contract

The many topics that will be discussed in the following chapters on contract law require an understanding of the basic elements of a valid contract and the way in which a contract is created. It is also necessary to understand the types of circumstances in which even legally valid contracts will not be enforced.

11–2a Requirements of a Valid Contract

The following list briefly describes the four requirements that must be met before a valid contract exists. If any of these elements is lacking, no contract will have been formed. (Each requirement will be explained more fully in subsequent chapters.)

1. *Agreement.* An agreement to form a contract includes an *offer* and an *acceptance.* One party must offer to enter into a legal agreement, and another party must accept the terms of the offer.
2. *Consideration.* Any promises made by the parties to the contract must be supported by legally sufficient and bargained-for *consideration* (something of value received or promised, such as money, to convince a person to make a deal).
3. *Contractual capacity.* Both parties entering into the contract must have the contractual *capacity* to do so. The law must recognize them as possessing characteristics that qualify them as competent parties.
4. *Legality.* The contract's purpose must be to accomplish some goal that is legal and not against public policy.

---

1. *Restatement (Second) of Contracts,* Section 1. *Restatements of the Law* are scholarly books that restate the existing common law principles distilled from court opinions as sets of rules on particular topics. Courts often refer to the *Restatements* for guidance. The *Restatement* dealing with contracts will be referred to throughout the material on contract law. *Second* in the title indicates that this *Restatement* is in its second edition. A third edition is being drafted.

2. *Pan Handle Realty, LLC v. Olins,* 140 Conn.App. 556, 59 A.3d 842 (2013).

An agreement to form a contract can modify the terms of a previous contract. When a dispute concerns whether this occurred, the offer and acceptance of both agreements can be reviewed to determine their effect. As in every case involving a contract, the parties' *subjective* beliefs with respect to the terms are irrelevant, particularly in the absence of any evidence to support those beliefs. At issue in the following case was the effect of an offer and acceptance on a previous agreement between a university and an associate professor.

Case Analysis 11.1

Weston v. Cornell University

New York Supreme Court, Appellate Division, Third Department, 136 A.D.3d 1094, 24 N.Y.S.3d 448 (2016).

In the Language of the Court

ROSE, J. [Judge]

* * * *

Defendant [Cornell University in Ithaca, New York] appointed plaintiff [Leslie Weston] to an associate professorship in 1998 for an initial term of five years. The 1998 offer letter described the position as being "with tenure," but it stated that, although no problems were anticipated, the offer of tenure would have to be confirmed by defendant's review process shortly after plaintiff's arrival on campus. For a variety of reasons, plaintiff delayed her tenure submission for five years and, when she finally submitted it, she was not awarded tenure. In 2003, defendant gave plaintiff a two-year extension of her appointment, this time as an "associate professor without tenure," to allow her an opportunity to improve and resubmit her tenure package. Plaintiff resubmitted her request for tenure in 2005, but it was again denied, resulting in her eventual termination. Plaintiff then commenced this action [in a New York state court] seeking * * * to recover for breach of contract. * * * Following the completion of discovery, defendant moved for summary judgment dismissing the complaint * * * . The Supreme Court [a New York state trial court] denied that portion of the motion seeking dismissal of the breach of contract claim. Defendant now appeals.

Contrary to defendant's argument, Supreme Court properly found that issues of fact exist as to whether defendant's 1998 offer letter reflects an intent to assure plaintiff that she would be granted tenure. * * * The terms of the letter are ambiguous. Accordingly, Supreme Court properly relied upon extrinsic evidence to determine the parties' intent.[a] Based upon the affidavit of the then-chair of defendant's department who hired plaintiff and wrote the 1998 offer letter, as well as correspondence from the dean and associate dean of the college in which plaintiff's department was located, Supreme Court appropriately declined to award summary judgment to defendant with respect to the 1998 offer of tenure.

However, we must agree with defendant's alternative argument that the terms of its original offer were materially modified by plaintiff's acceptance of its 2003 offer to extend her appointment. *Defendant's 2003 letter offering to extend her appointment unambiguously replaced the "with tenure" language contained in the 1998 offer letter by restating her job title as "associate professor without tenure."* Defendant also points to plaintiff's deposition testimony, in which she explicitly acknowledged that she understood the 2003 letter to be a modification of the original terms of her employment agreement and agreed—albeit reluctantly—to the new terms. Significantly, plaintiff further admitted that defendant was "not guaranteeing her tenure in any case after this letter." [Emphasis added.]

In response to this *prima facie* showing by defendant, plaintiff contends that, regardless of what she agreed to in 2003, her oft-repeated assertions of her belief that defendant still owed her tenure based upon the original letter suffice to preclude summary judgment. Aside from plaintiff's own opinions on the matter, however, there is nothing in the record to indicate that any alleged guarantee of tenure remained beyond the date of the 2003 letter. Accordingly, we find that plaintiff's subjective beliefs and unsupported arguments regarding the 2003 modification of her employment agreement are insufficient to raise triable issues of fact to defeat defendant's motion for summary judgment dismissing the breach of contract cause of action.

ORDERED that the order is modified * * * by reversing so much thereof as partially denied defendant's motion for summary judgment; said motion granted in its entirety and breach of contract cause of action dismissed.

---

a. *Extrinsic evidence*, which is evidence outside the contract itself, will be discussed later in this chapter.

Legal Reasoning Questions

1. What did the plaintiff seek in this action? What was the legal ground for her claim? What was her principal contention regarding the offers and acceptances at the center of this case?

2. Why did the trial court deny the defendant's motion for summary judgment to dismiss the plaintiff's claim?

3. Why did the appellate court modify the trial court's denial of the defendant's motion?

11–2b Defenses to the Enforceability of a Contract

Even if all of the requirements listed above are satisfied, a contract may be unenforceable if the following requirements are not met. These requirements typically are raised as *defenses* to the enforceability of an otherwise valid contract.

1. *Voluntary consent.* The consent of both parties must be voluntary. For instance, if a contract was formed as a result of fraud, undue influence, mistake, or duress, the contract may not be enforceable.
2. *Form.* The contract must be in whatever form the law requires. Some contracts must be in writing to be enforceable.

11–3 Types of Contracts

There are many types of contracts. They are categorized based on legal distinctions as to their formation, performance, and enforceability.

11–3a Contract Formation

Contracts can be classified according to how and when they are formed. Exhibit 11–1 shows three such classifications, and the following subsections explain them in greater detail.

Bilateral versus Unilateral Contracts Every contract involves at least two parties. The **offeror** is the party making the offer. The **offeree** is the party to whom the offer is made. Whether the contract is classified as *bilateral* or *unilateral* depends on what the offeree must do to accept the offer and bind the offeror to a contract.

Bilateral Contracts. If the offeree can accept simply by promising to perform, the contract is a **bilateral contract.** Hence, a bilateral contract is a "promise for a promise." No performance, such as payment of funds or delivery of goods, need take place for a bilateral contract to be formed. The contract comes into existence at the moment the promises are exchanged.

■ **EXAMPLE 11.2** Jacob offers to buy Ann's smartphone for $200. Jacob tells Ann that he will give her the $200 for the smartphone next Friday, when he gets paid. Ann accepts Jacob's offer and promises to give him the smartphone when he pays her on Friday. Jacob and Ann have formed a bilateral contract. ■

Unilateral Contracts. If the offer is phrased so that the offeree can accept the offer only by completing the contract performance, the contract is a **unilateral contract.** Hence, a unilateral contract is a "promise for an act." In other words, a unilateral contract is formed not at the moment when promises are exchanged but at the moment when the contract is *performed.*

■ **EXAMPLE 11.3** Reese says to Celia, "If you drive my car from New York to Los Angeles, I'll give you $1,000." Only on Celia's completion of the act—bringing the car to Los Angeles—does she fully accept Reese's offer to pay $1,000. If she chooses not to accept the offer to drive the car to Los Angeles, there are no legal consequences. ■

Contests, Lotteries, and Prizes. Contests, lotteries, and other competitions involving prizes are examples of offers

EXHIBIT 11–1 Classifications Based on Contract Formation

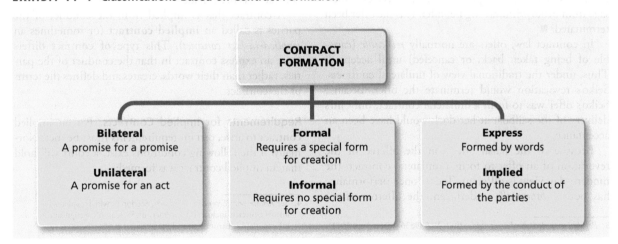

CONTRACT FORMATION		
Bilateral A promise for a promise **Unilateral** A promise for an act	**Formal** Requires a special form for creation **Informal** Requires no special form for creation	**Express** Formed by words **Implied** Formed by the conduct of the parties

to form unilateral contracts. If a person complies with the rules of the contest—such as by submitting the right lottery number at the right place and time—a unilateral contract is formed. The organization offering the prize is then bound to a contract to perform as promised in the offer. If the person fails to comply with the contest rules, however, no binding contract is formed.

■ **CASE IN POINT 11.4** John Rogalski entered a poker tournament sponsored by Little Poker League (LPL) that lasted several months. During the final event, all contestants signed an agreement that said LPL would pay the tournament winner's entry fee and travel expenses to the World Series of Poker (WSOP). The agreement also stated that if the winner did not attend the WSOP, he or she would relinquish the WSOP seat and return the expense money to LPL.

Rogalski won and accepted $2,500 for travel-related expenses from the sponsor, but he did not attend the WSOP. He then filed a suit for $10,000 against LPL, arguing that it had advertised that the winner could choose to receive the cash value of the prizes ($12,500) instead of going to the WSOP. Rogalski claimed that he had accepted LPL's offer by participating in the tournament. The court rejected this argument and found in favor of LPL. The contract was formed when Rogalski signed the WSOP agreement. Under the contest rules as stated in that agreement, Rogalski had to return the $2,500 to LPL.[3] ■

Revocation of Offers for Unilateral Contracts. A problem arises in unilateral contracts when the promisor attempts to *revoke* (cancel) the offer after the promisee has begun performance but before the act has been completed. ■ **EXAMPLE 11.5** Seiko offers to buy Jin's sailboat, moored in San Francisco, on delivery of the boat to Seiko's dock in Newport Beach, three hundred miles south of San Francisco. Jin rigs the boat and sets sail. Shortly before his arrival at Newport Beach, Jin receives a message from Seiko withdrawing her offer. Has the offer been terminated? ■

In contract law, offers are normally *revocable* (capable of being taken back, or canceled) until accepted. Thus, under the traditional view of unilateral contracts, Seiko's revocation would terminate the offer. Because Seiko's offer was to form a unilateral contract, only Jin's delivery of the sailboat at her dock would have been an acceptance.

Because of the harsh effect on the offeree of the revocation of an offer to form a unilateral contract, the modern-day view is different. Today, once performance has been *substantially* undertaken, the offeror cannot

revoke the offer. Thus, in *Example 11.5*, even though Jin has not yet accepted the offer by complete performance, Seiko is normally prohibited from revoking it. Jin can deliver the boat and bind Seiko to the contract.

Formal versus Informal Contracts Another classification system divides contracts into formal contracts and informal contracts. **Formal contracts** are contracts that require a special form or method of creation (formation) to be enforceable.[4] One example is *negotiable instruments,* which include checks, drafts, promissory notes, bills of exchange, and certificates of deposit. Negotiable instruments are formal contracts because, under the Uniform Commercial Code (UCC), a special form and language are required to create them.

Letters of credit, which are frequently used in international sales contracts, are another type of formal contract. Letters of credit are agreements to pay contingent on the purchaser's receipt of invoices and *bills of lading* (documents evidencing receipt of, and title to, goods shipped).

Informal contracts (also called *simple contracts*) include all other contracts. No special form is required (except for certain types of contracts that must be in writing), as the contracts are usually based on their substance rather than their form. Typically, businesspersons put their contracts in writing (including electronic records) to ensure that there is some proof of a contract's existence should disputes arise.

Express versus Implied Contracts Contracts may also be categorized as *express* or *implied*. In an **express contract,** the terms of the agreement are fully and explicitly stated in words, oral or written. A signed lease for an apartment or a house is an express written contract. If one classmate calls another on the phone and agrees to buy her textbooks from last semester for $200, an express oral contract has been made.

A contract that is implied from the conduct of the parties is called an **implied contract** (or sometimes an *implied-in-fact contract*). This type of contract differs from an express contract in that the conduct of the parties, rather than their words, creates and defines the terms of the contract.

Requirements for Implied Contracts. For an implied contract to arise, certain requirements must be met. Normally, if the following conditions exist, a court will hold that an implied contract was formed:

---

3. *Rogalski v. Little Poker League, LLC,* 2011 Wl 589636 (Minn.App. 2011).

4. See *Restatement (Second) of Contracts,* Section 6, which explains that formal contracts include (1) contracts under seal, (2) recognizances, (3) negotiable instruments, and (4) letters of credit.

1. The plaintiff furnished some service or property.
2. The plaintiff expected to be paid for that service or property, and the defendant knew or should have known that payment was expected.
3. The defendant had a chance to reject the services or property and did not.

■ **EXAMPLE 11.6** Alex, a small-business owner, needs an accountant to complete his tax return. He drops by a local accountant's office, explains his situation to the accountant, and learns what fees she charges. The next day, he returns and gives the receptionist all of the necessary documents to complete his return. Then he walks out without saying anything further to the accountant. In this situation, Alex has entered into an implied contract to pay the accountant the usual fees for her services. The contract is implied because of Alex's conduct and hers. She expects to be paid for completing the tax return, and by bringing in the records she will need to do the job, Alex has implied an intent to pay her. ■

Mixed Contracts with Express and Implied Terms.
Note that a contract may be a mixture of an express contract and an implied contract. In other words, a contract may contain some express terms and some implied terms. During the construction of a home, for instance, the homeowner often asks the builder to make changes in the original specifications.

■ **CASE IN POINT 11.7** Lamar Hopkins hired Uhrhahn Construction & Design, Inc., for several projects in building his home. For each project, the parties signed a written contract that was based on a cost estimate and specifications and that required changes to the agreement to be in writing. While the work was in progress, however, Hopkins repeatedly asked Uhrhahn to deviate from the contract specifications, which Uhrhahn did. None of these requests was made in writing.

One day, Hopkins asked Uhrhahn to use Durisol blocks instead of the cinder blocks specified in the original contract, indicating that the cost would be the same. Uhrhahn used the Durisol blocks but demanded extra payment when it became clear that the Durisol blocks were more complicated to install. Although Hopkins had paid for the other deviations from the contract that he had orally requested, he refused to pay Uhrhahn for the substitution of the Durisol blocks. Uhrhahn sued for breach of contract. The court found that Hopkins, through his conduct, had waived the provision requiring written contract modification and created an implied contract to pay the extra cost of installing the Durisol blocks.[5] ■

Among other implied terms, all contracts include an implied covenant of good faith and fair dealing. This implied term requires the parties to perform in accord with the contract and the parties' reasonable expectations under it. In the following case, the plaintiff claimed that the defendant had breached both the express terms of the parties' contract and the implied covenant of good faith and fair dealing.

---

5. *Uhrhahn Construction & Design, Inc. v. Hopkins*, 179 P.3d 808 (Utah App. 2008).

Case 11.2

Vukanovich v. Kine

Court of Appeals of Oregon, 268 Or.App. 623, 342 P.3d 1075 (2015).

Background and Facts Mark Vukanovich and Larry Kine agreed under a "Letter of Understanding" to work together to buy a certain parcel of real property in Eugene, Oregon, from Umpqua Bank. They expressly agreed to develop the property and to split the cost and profits equally. Vukanovich shared confidential financial information with Kine that he would not otherwise have shared. The bank agreed to accept $1.6 million for the property, and a closing date was set. Kine then said that he no longer wanted to pursue the deal with Vukanovich or to buy the property. The closing did not occur.

A month later, without Vukanovich's knowledge, Kine made a new offer to buy the property. At about the same time, Vukanovich made his own new offer. The bank accepted Kine's offer. Vukanovich filed a suit in an Oregon state court against Kine, alleging breach of contract. The jury returned a verdict in favor of Vukanovich, awarding him $686,000 on the breach of contract claim and other damages, but the court entered a judgment in favor of Kine. Vukanovich appealed.

In the Language of the Court
LAGESEN, J. [Judge]
* * * *

Case 11.2 Continues

Case 11.2 Continued

*** *Plaintiff's claim for breach of contract was predicated [based] on the theory that defendant breached both the express terms of the parties' "Letter of Understanding" and the implied covenant of good faith and fair dealing, damaging plaintiff by cutting plaintiff* * * * out of an ownership interest in the property and the profits generated by the property.* [Emphasis added.]

* * * Based on the evidence presented at trial, the jury could permissibly find that plaintiff and defendant entered into a contract to buy the property together and that defendant breached the express terms of that contract when, after the bank accepted the parties' joint offer to purchase the property * * *, defendant refused to close on the purchase and subsequently repudiated [renounced] the contract, even though defendant had the capacity to close the agreed upon * * * purchase of the property. The jury also could permissibly find that defendant lied to plaintiff about the reasons for not closing the * * * purchase of the property from the bank and used confidential information provided by plaintiff to develop a more lucrative plan for the property that cut out plaintiff, thereby breaching the implied covenant of good faith and fair dealing. Finally, the jury could find that defendant's breaches damaged plaintiff—that, but for those breaches, the * * * purchase would have been completed, and plaintiff would have been a part owner of the property and would have been entitled to a share of the profits that the property was expected to earn.

* * * Defendant argues that * * * after the agreement was undisputedly terminated * * *, both plaintiff and defendant made separate attempts to purchase the property. Defendant contends that his efforts to purchase the property after the contract was terminated could not constitute a breach of the parties' contract because, at that point in time, both parties understood that the agreement was over and were engaging in similar conduct.

The problem with defendant's argument is that plaintiff ultimately did not predicate his breach of contract claim on defendant's conduct of purchasing the property separately from plaintiff. Although the complaint identified defendant's separate purchase of the property as "among" the breaches committed by defendant, plaintiff's focus at trial * * * was on * * * defendant's refusal to complete the purchase of the property with plaintiff, his surreptitious [secret] use of the information that plaintiff had provided him to devise a more favorable transaction for himself * * *, and his lies to plaintiff about his reasons for not closing the deal. It is the evidence of that conduct, not the evidence of defendant's conduct following the termination of the contract, that permits the finding that defendant breached the parties' contract, damaging plaintiff by causing the planned * * * purchase of the property to fail.

Decision and Remedy *A state intermediate appellate court reinstated the jury verdict. The court ruled that there was sufficient evidence to permit the jury to find that Kine had "breached both the express terms of the parties' Letter of Understanding and the implied covenant of good faith and fair dealing."*

Critical Thinking
- **Economic** *What did the amount of the jury's award of $686,000 in damages represent? Explain.*

11–3b Contract Performance

Contracts are also classified according to the degree to which they have been performed. A contract that has been fully performed on both sides is called an **executed contract.** A contract that has not been fully performed by the parties is called an **executory contract.** If one party has fully performed but the other has not, the contract is said to be executed on the one side and executory on the other, but the contract is still classified as executory.

■ **EXAMPLE 11.8** Jackson, Inc., agreed to buy ten tons of coal from the Northern Coal Company. Northern delivered the coal to Jackson's steel mill, where it is being burned. At this point, the contract is executed on the part of Northern and executory on Jackson's part. After Jackson pays Northern, the contract will be executed on both sides. ■

11–3c Contract Enforceability

A **valid contract** has the elements necessary to entitle at least one of the parties to enforce it in court. Those elements, as mentioned earlier, consist of (1) an agreement (offer and acceptance), (2) supported by legally sufficient consideration, (3) made by parties who have the legal capacity to enter into the contract, and (4) a legal purpose.

As you can see in Exhibit 11–2, valid contracts may be enforceable, voidable, or unenforceable. Additionally, a contract may be referred to as a *void contract*. We look next at the meaning of the terms *voidable, unenforceable,* and *void* in relation to contract enforceability.

Voidable Contracts A **voidable contract** is a valid contract but one that can be avoided at the option of one or both of the parties. The party having the option can elect either to avoid any duty to perform or to *ratify* (make valid) the contract. If the contract is avoided, both parties are released from it. If it is ratified, both parties must fully perform their respective legal obligations.

For instance, contracts made by minors generally are voidable at the option of the minor (with certain exceptions). Contracts made by mentally incompetent persons and intoxicated persons may also be voidable. Additionally, contracts entered into under fraudulent conditions are voidable at the option of the defrauded party. Contracts entered into under legally defined duress or undue influence are also voidable.

Unenforceable Contracts An **unenforceable contract** is one that cannot be enforced because of certain legal defenses against it. It is not unenforceable because a party failed to satisfy a legal requirement of the contract. Rather, it is a valid contract rendered unenforceable by some statute or law. For instance, certain contracts must be in writing, and if they are not, they will not be enforceable except in certain exceptional circumstances.

Void Contracts A **void contract** is no contract at all. The terms *void* and *contract* are contradictory. None of the parties have any legal obligations if a contract is void. A contract can be void because one of the parties was determined by a court to be mentally incompetent, for instance, or because the purpose of the contract was illegal.

To review the various types of contracts, see Concept Summary 11.1.

11–4 Quasi Contracts

Express contracts and implied contracts are actual or true contracts formed by the words or actions of the parties. **Quasi contracts,** or contracts *implied in law,* are not actual contracts. Rather, they are fictional contracts that courts can impose on the parties "as if" the parties had entered into an actual contract. (The word *quasi* is Latin for "as if.")

Quasi contracts are equitable rather than legal contracts. Usually, they are imposed to avoid the *unjust enrichment* of one party at the expense of another. The doctrine of unjust enrichment is based on the theory that individuals should not be allowed to profit or enrich themselves inequitably at the expense of others.

EXHIBIT 11–2 Enforceable, Voidable, Unenforceable, and Void Contracts

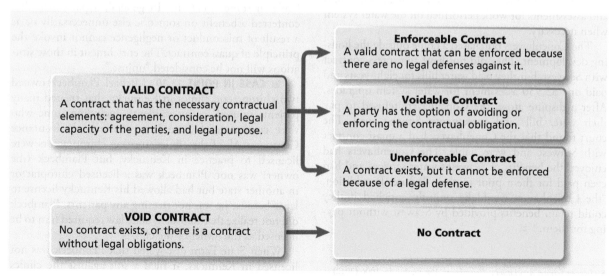

Concept Summary 11.1

Types of Contracts

Formation	• *Bilateral*—A promise for a promise. • *Unilateral*—A promise for an act—that is, acceptance is the completed performance of the act. • *Formal*—Requires a special form for creation. • *Informal*—Requires no special form for creation. • *Express*—Formed by words, such as oral, written, or a combination. • *Implied*—Formed by the conduct of the parties.
Performance	• *Executed*—A fully performed contract. • *Executory*—A contract not fully performed.
Enforceability	• *Valid*—The contract has the necessary contractual elements: agreement (offer and acceptance), consideration, legal capacity of the parties, and legal purpose. • *Voidable*—One party has the option of avoiding or enforcing the contractual obligation. • *Unenforceable*—A contract exists, but it cannot be enforced because of a legal defense. • *Void*—No contract exists, or there is a contract without legal obligations.

■ **CASE IN POINT 11.9** Seawest Services Association operated a water distribution system that served homes inside a housing development (full members) and some homes located outside the subdivision (limited members). Both full and limited members paid water bills and assessments for work performed on the water system when necessary.

The Copenhavers purchased a home outside the housing development. They did not have an express contract with Seawest, but they paid water bills for eight years and paid one $3,950 assessment for water system upgrades. After a dispute arose, the Copenhavers refused to pay their water bills and assessments. Seawest sued. The court found that the Copenhavers had a quasi contract with Seawest and were liable. The Copenhavers had enjoyed the benefits of Seawest's water services and had even paid for them prior to their dispute. In addition, "the Copenhavers would be unjustly enriched if they could retain benefits provided by Seawest without paying for them."[6] ■

---

6. *Seawest Services Association v. Copenhaver*, 166 Wash.App. 1006 (2012).

11–4a Limitations on Quasi-Contractual Recovery

Although quasi contracts exist to prevent unjust enrichment, the party obtaining the enrichment is not held liable in some situations. In general, a party who has conferred a benefit on someone else unnecessarily or as a result of misconduct or negligence cannot invoke the principle of quasi contract. The enrichment in those situations will not be considered "unjust."

■ **CASE IN POINT 11.10** Michael Plambeck owned two chiropractic clinics in Kentucky that treated many patients injured in car accidents, including some who were customers of State Farm Automobile Insurance Company. All of the clinics' treating chiropractors were licensed to practice in Kentucky, but Plambeck (the owner) was not. Plambeck was a licensed chiropractor in another state but had allowed his Kentucky license to lapse because he was not treating any patients. Plambeck did not realize that Kentucky state law required him to be licensed as the owner of the clinics.

When State Farm discovered that Plambeck was not licensed in Kentucky, it filed a suit against the clinics seeking to recover payments it had made on behalf of its customers. The trial court awarded State Farm $577,124 in damages for unjust enrichment, but the appellate court reversed. The court reasoned that State Farm had a legal duty to pay for the chiropractic treatment of its customers and could not avoid paying for the services because the clinics' owner was not licensed. The payments did not constitute unjust enrichment, because the patients had, in fact, received treatment by licensed chiropractors.[7] ■

11–4b When an Actual Contract Exists

The doctrine of quasi contract generally cannot be used when there is an *actual contract* that covers the matter in controversy. A remedy already exists if a party is unjustly enriched as a result of a breach of contract: the non-breaching party can sue the breaching party for breach of contract.

■ **EXAMPLE 11.11** Fung contracts with Cameron to deliver a furnace to a building owned by Grant. Fung delivers the furnace, but Cameron never pays Fung. Grant has been unjustly enriched in this situation, to be sure. Fung, however, cannot recover from Grant in quasi contract, because Fung had an actual contract with Cameron. Fung already has a remedy—he can sue for breach of contract to recover the price of the furnace from Cameron. The court does not need to impose a quasi contract in this situation to achieve justice. ■

---

7. *State Farm Automobile Insurance Co. v. Newburg Chiropractic, P.S.C.,* 741 F.3d 661 (6th Cir. 2013).

11–5 Interpretation of Contracts

Sometimes, parties agree that a contract has been formed but disagree on its meaning or legal effect. One reason this may happen is that one of the parties is not familiar with the legal terminology used in the contract. To an extent, *plain language* laws (enacted by the federal government and a majority of the states) have helped to avoid this difficulty. Sometimes, though, a dispute may arise over the meaning of a contract simply because the rights or obligations under the contract are not expressed clearly—no matter how "plain" the language used.

In this section, we look at some common law rules of contract interpretation. These rules, which have evolved over time, provide the courts with guidelines for deciding disputes over how contract terms or provisions should be interpreted. Exhibit 11–3 provides a brief graphic summary of how these rules are applied.

11–5a The Plain Meaning Rule

When a contract's writing is clear and unequivocal, a court will enforce it according to its obvious terms. The meaning of the terms must be determined from the *face of the instrument*—from the written document alone. This is sometimes referred to as the *plain meaning rule*. The words—and their plain, ordinary meaning—determine the intent of the parties at the time that they entered into the contract. A court is bound to give effect to the contract according to this intent.

EXHIBIT 11–3 Rules of Contract Interpretation

WRITTEN CONTRACT

The Plain Meaning Rule
If a court determines that the terms of the contract are clear from the written document alone, the plain meaning rule will apply, and the contract will be enforced according to what it clearly states.

Other Rules of Interpretation
If a court finds that there is a need to determine the parties' intentions from the terms of the contract, the court will apply a number of well-established rules of interpretation. For example, one rule of interpretation states that specific wording will be given greater weight than general wording.

Ambiguity A court will consider a contract to be unclear, or ambiguous, in the following situations:

1. When the intent of the parties cannot be determined from the contract's language.
2. When the contract lacks a provision on a disputed term.
3. When a term is susceptible to more than one interpretation.
4. When there is uncertainty about a provision.

Extrinsic Evidence If a contract term is ambiguous, a court may interpret the ambiguity against the party who drafted the term. The court may also consider *extrinsic evidence* when a term is ambiguous. **Extrinsic evidence** is any evidence not contained in the document itself—such as the testimony of parties and witnesses, additional agreements or communications, or other relevant information.

The admissibility of extrinsic evidence can significantly affect the court's interpretation of ambiguous contractual provisions and thus the outcome of litigation. When a contract is clear and unambiguous, a court cannot consider extrinsic evidence. The following case illustrates these points.

Spotlight on Columbia Pictures

Case 11.3 Wagner v. Columbia Pictures Industries, Inc.
California Court of Appeal, Second District, 146 Cal.App.4th 586, 52 Cal.Rptr.3d 898 (2007).

Background and Facts Actor Robert Wagner entered into an agreement with Spelling-Goldberg Productions (SGP) "relating to *Charlie's Angels* (herein called the 'series')." The contract entitled Wagner to 50 percent of the net profits that SGP received from broadcasting the series and from all ancillary, music, and subsidiary rights in connection with the series. SGP hired Ivan Goff and Ben Roberts to write the series, under a contract subject to the Writers Guild of America Minimum Basic Agreement (MBA).[a] The MBA stipulates that the writer of a television show retains the right to make and market films based on the material, subject to the producer's right to buy this right if the writer decides to sell it within five years.

The first *Charlie's Angels* episode aired in 1976. In 1982, SGP sold its rights to the series to Columbia Pictures Industries, Inc. Thirteen years later, Columbia bought the movie rights to the material from Goff's and Roberts's heirs. In 2000 and 2003, Columbia produced and distributed two *Charlie's Angels* films. Wagner filed a suit in a California state court against Columbia, claiming a share of the profits from the films. The court granted Columbia's motion for summary judgment. Wagner appealed to a state intermediate appellate court.

In the Language of the Court
JOHNSON, Acting P.J. [Presiding Judge]
* * * *

Wagner contends the "subsidiary rights" provision in the agreement with SGP entitles him * * * to 50 percent of the net profits from the two "Charlie's Angels" films.
* * * *

Wagner introduced evidence of the history of the negotiations underlying the "Charlie's Angels" contract in support of his [contention].

This history begins with a contract the Wagners [Wagner and his wife, Natalie Wood] entered into with SGP to star in a television movie-of-the-week, "Love Song." As compensation for Wagner and Wood acting in "Love Song," SGP agreed to pay them a fixed amount plus one-half the net profits * * * .
* * * *

In the * * * "Love Song" contract net profits were not limited to monies received "for the right to exhibit the Photoplay." Instead they were defined as the net of "all monies received by Producer as consideration for the right to exhibit the Photoplay, and exploitation of all ancillary, music and subsidiary rights in connection therewith."
* * * *

---

a. The Writers Guild of America is an association of screen and television writers that negotiates industry-wide agreements with motion picture and television producers.

Case 11.3 Continued

Wagner's argument is simple and straightforward. The net profits provision in the "Love Song" agreement was intended to give the Wagners a one-half share in the net profits received by SGP "from all sources" without limitation as to source or time. The "Charlie's Angels" agreement was based on the "Love Song" agreement and defines net profits in identical language. Therefore, the "Charlie's Angels" agreement should also be interpreted as providing the Wagners with a 50 percent share in SGP's income "from all sources" without limitation as to source or time. Since Columbia admits it stands in SGP's shoes with respect to SGP's obligations under the "Charlie's Angels" agreement, Columbia is obligated to pay Wagner * * * 50 percent of the net profits derived from the "Charlie's Angels" movies.

* * * *

The problem with Wagner's extrinsic evidence is that it does not explain the ["Charlie's Angels"] contract language, it contradicts it. *Under the parol evidence rule,*[b] *extrinsic evidence is not admissible to contradict express terms in a written contract or to explain what the agreement was. The agreement is the writing itself. Parol evidence cannot be admitted to show intention independent of an unambiguous written instrument.* [Emphasis added.]

Even if the Wagners and SGP intended the Wagners would share in the net profits "from any and all sources" they did not say so in their contract. What they said in their contract was the Wagners would share in "all monies actually received by Producer, as consideration for the right to exhibit photoplays of the series, and from the exploitation of all ancillary, music and subsidiary rights in connection therewith." For a right to be "subsidiary" or "ancillary," meaning supplementary or subordinate, there must be a primary right to which it relates. The only primary right mentioned in the contract is "the right to exhibit photoplays of the series." Thus the Wagners were entitled to share in the profits from the exploitation of the movie rights to "Charlie's Angels" if those rights were exploited by Columbia as ancillary or subsidiary rights of its primary "right to exhibit photoplays of the series" but not if those rights were acquired by Columbia independently from its right to exhibit photoplays.

Decision and Remedy *The state intermediate appellate court affirmed the lower court's summary judgment in favor of Columbia. The contract "unambiguously" stated the conditions under which the parties were to share the films' profits, and those conditions had not occurred.*

Critical Thinking

- **What If the Facts Were Different?** *How might the result in this case have been different if the court had admitted Wagner's evidence of the* Love Song *contract?*
- **Legal Environment** *Under what circumstances would Wagner have been entitled to a share of the profits from the* Charlie's Angels *movies even though the evidence of the* Love Song *contract was irrelevant?*

---

b. The *parol evidence rule* prohibits the parties from introducing in court evidence of an oral agreement that contradicts the written terms of a contract.

11–5b Other Rules of Interpretation

Generally, a court will interpret the language to give effect to the parties' intent as *expressed in their contract.* This is the primary purpose of the rules of interpretation—to determine the parties' intent from the language used in their agreement and to give effect to that intent. A court normally will not make or remake a contract, nor will it interpret the language according to what the parties *claim* their intent was when they made it.

Rules the Courts Use The courts use the following rules in interpreting contractual terms:

1. As far as possible, a reasonable, lawful, and effective meaning will be given to all of a contract's terms.
2. A contract will be interpreted as a whole. Individual, specific clauses will be considered subordinate to the contract's general intent. All writings that are a part of the same transaction will be interpreted together.
3. Terms that were the subject of separate negotiation will be given greater consideration than standardized terms and terms that were not negotiated separately.
4. A word will be given its ordinary, commonly accepted meaning, and a technical word or term will be given its technical meaning, unless the parties clearly intended something else.

5. Specific and exact wording will be given greater consideration than general language.
6. Written or typewritten terms will prevail over pre-printed ones.
7. Because a contract should be drafted in clear and unambiguous language, a party who uses ambiguous expressions is held to be responsible for the ambiguities. Thus, when the language has more than one meaning, it will be interpreted against the party who drafted the contract.
8. Evidence of *usage of trade, course of dealing,* and *course of performance* may be admitted to clarify the meaning of an ambiguously worded contract. (We will define and discuss these terms in a later chapter.)

Express Terms Usually Given the Most Weight

Express terms (terms expressly stated in the contract) are given the greatest weight, followed by course of performance, course of dealing, and custom and usage of trade—in that order. When considering custom and usage, a court will look at the trade customs and usage common to the particular business or industry and to the locale in which the contract was made or is to be performed.

■ **CASE IN POINT 11.12** Jessica Robbins bought a house in Tennessee. U.S. Bank financed the purchase, and Tennessee Farmers Mutual Insurance Company issued the homeowner's insurance policy. The policy included a clause that promised payment to the bank for losses unless the loss was due to an "increase in hazard" about which the bank knew but did not tell the insurer. When Robbins fell behind on her mortgage payments, the bank started foreclosure proceedings. No one told the insurer. Robbins filed for bankruptcy, which postponed foreclosure.

Meanwhile, the house was destroyed in a fire. The bank filed a claim under the policy, but the insurer refused to pay because it had not been told by the bank of an "increase in hazard"—the foreclosure. The bank then filed a lawsuit. The court found that the plain meaning of the words "increase in hazard" in the policy referred to physical conditions on the property that posed a risk, not to events such as foreclosure. Thus, the bank was not required to notify the insurer under the terms of the policy, and the lack of notice did not invalidate the coverage.[8] ■

---

8. *U.S. Bank, N.A. v. Tennessee Farmers Mutual Insurance Co.*, 277 S.W.3d 381 (Tenn.Sup.Ct. 2009).

Reviewing: Nature and Terminology

Mitsui Bank hired Ross Duncan as a branch manager in one of its Southern California locations. At that time, Duncan received an employee handbook informing him that Mitsui would review his performance and salary level annually. In 2016, Mitsui decided to create a new lending program to help financially troubled businesses stay afloat. It hired Duncan to be the credit development officer (CDO) and gave him a written compensation plan. Duncan's compensation was to be based on the program's success and involved a bonus and commissions based on the volume of new loans and sales. The written plan also stated, "This compensation plan will be reviewed and potentially amended after one year and will be subject to such review and amendment annually thereafter."

Duncan's efforts as CDO were successful, and the program he developed grew to represent 25 percent of Mitsui's business in 2016 and 40 percent in 2017. Nevertheless, Mitsui refused to give Duncan a raise in 2016. Mitsui also amended his compensation plan to significantly reduce his compensation and to change his performance evaluation schedule to every six months. When he had still not received a raise by 2018, Duncan resigned as CDO and filed a lawsuit alleging breach of contract. Using the information presented in the chapter, answer the following questions.

1. What are the four requirements of a valid contract?
2. Did Duncan have a valid contract with Mitsui for employment as CDO? If so, was it a bilateral or a unilateral contract?
3. What are the requirements of an implied contract?
4. Can Duncan establish an implied contract based on the employment manual or the written compensation plan? Why or why not?

Debate This . . . *Companies should be able to make or break employment contracts whenever and however they wish.*

Terms and Concepts

bilateral contract 219	implied contract 220	promisor 216
contract 217	informal contract 220	quasi contract 223
executed contract 222	objective theory of contracts 217	unenforceable contract 223
executory contract 222	offeree 219	unilateral contract 219
express contract 220	offeror 219	valid contract 222
extrinsic evidence 226	promise 216	void contract 223
formal contract 220	promisee 216	voidable contract 223

Issue Spotters

1. Dyna tells Ed that she will pay him $1,000 to set fire to her store so that she can collect under a fire insurance policy. Ed sets fire to the store, but Dyna refuses to pay. Can Ed recover? Why or why not? (See *Elements of a Contract*.)

2. Alison receives a notice of property taxes due from a local tax collector. The notice is for tax on Jerry's property, but Alison believes that the tax is on her property and pays it. Can Alison recover from Jerry the amount that she paid? Why or why not? (See *Quasi Contracts*.)

• **Check your answers to the Issue Spotters against the answers provided in Appendix D at the end of this text.**

Business Scenarios

11–1. Unilateral Contract. Rocky Mountain Races, Inc., sponsors the "Pioneer Trail Ultramarathon," with an advertised first prize of $10,000. The rules require the competitors to run 100 miles from the floor of Blackwater Canyon to the top of Pinnacle Mountain. The rules also provide that Rocky reserves the right to change the terms of the race at any time. Monica enters the race and is declared the winner. Rocky offers her a prize of $1,000 instead of $10,000. Did Rocky and Monica have a contract? Explain. (See *Types of Contracts*.)

11–2. Implied Contract. Janine was hospitalized with severe abdominal pain and placed in an intensive care unit. Her doctor told the hospital personnel to order around-the-clock nursing care for Janine. At the hospital's request, a nursing services firm, Nursing Services Unlimited, provided two weeks of in-hospital care and, after Janine was sent home, an additional two weeks of at-home care. During the at-home period of care, Janine was fully aware that she was receiving the benefit of the nursing services. Nursing Services later billed Janine $4,000 for the nursing care, but Janine refused to pay on the ground that she had never contracted for the services, either orally or in writing. In view of the fact that no express contract was ever formed, can Nursing Services recover the $4,000 from Janine? If so, under what legal theory? Discuss. (See *Types of Contracts*.)

Business Case Problems

11–3. Spotlight on Taco Bell—Implied Contract.
 Thomas Rinks and Joseph Shields developed Psycho Chihuahua, a caricature of a Chihuahua dog with a "do-not-back-down" attitude. They promoted and marketed the character through their company, Wrench, L.L.C. Ed Alfaro and Rudy Pollak, representatives of Taco Bell Corp., learned of Psycho Chihuahua and met with Rinks and Shields to talk about using the character as a Taco Bell "icon." Wrench sent artwork, merchandise, and marketing ideas to Alfaro, who promoted the character within Taco Bell. Alfaro asked Wrench to propose terms for Taco Bell's use of Psycho Chihuahua. Taco Bell did not accept Wrench's terms, but Alfaro continued to promote the character within the company.

Meanwhile, Taco Bell hired a new advertising agency, which proposed an advertising campaign involving a Chihuahua. When Alfaro learned of this proposal, he sent the Psycho Chihuahua materials to the agency. Taco Bell made a Chihuahua the focus of its marketing but paid nothing to Wrench. Wrench filed a suit against Taco Bell in a federal court claiming that it had an implied contract with Taco Bell and that Taco Bell breached that contract. Do these facts satisfy the requirements for an implied contract? Why or why not? [*Wrench, L.L.C. v. Taco Bell Corp.*, 256 F.3d 446 (6th Cir. 2001), *cert.* denied, 534 U.S. 1114, 122 S.Ct. 921, 151 L.Ed.2d 805 (2002)] (See *Types of Contracts*.)

11–4. Business Case Problem with Sample Answer—Quasi Contract. Robert Gutkowski, a sports marketing
 expert, met numerous times with George Steinbrenner, the owner of the New York Yankees, to discuss the Yankees Entertainment and Sports Network (YES). Gutkowski was paid as a

consultant. Later, he filed a suit, seeking an ownership share in YES. There was no written contract for the share, but he claimed that there were discussions about his being a part owner. Does Gutkowski have a valid claim for payment? Discuss. [*Gutkowski v. Steinbrenner*, 680 F.Supp.2d 602 (S.D.N.Y. 2010)] (See *Quasi Contracts*.)

- For a sample answer to Problem 11–4, go to Appendix E at the end of this text.

11–5. Quasi Contract. Kim Panenka asked to borrow $4,750 from her sister, Kris, to make a mortgage payment. Kris deposited a check for that amount into Kim's bank account. Hours later, Kim asked to borrow another $1,100. Kris took a cash advance on her credit card and deposited this amount into Kim's account. When Kim did not repay the amounts, Kris filed a suit, arguing that she had "loaned" Kim the money. Can the court impose a contract between the sisters? Explain. [*Panenka v. Panenka*, 331 Wis.2d 731, 795 N.W.2d 493 (2011)] (See *Quasi Contracts*.)

11–6. Implied Contracts. Ralph Ramsey insured his car with Allstate Insurance Co. He also owned a house on which he maintained a homeowner's insurance policy with Allstate. Bank of America had a mortgage on the house and paid the insurance premiums on the homeowner's policy from Ralph's account. After Ralph died, Allstate canceled the car insurance. Ralph's son Douglas inherited the house. The bank continued to pay the premiums on the homeowner's policy, but from Douglas's account, and Allstate continued to renew the insurance. When a fire destroyed the house, Allstate denied coverage, however, claiming that the policy was still in Ralph's name. Douglas filed a suit in a federal district court against the insurer. Was Allstate liable under the homeowner's policy? Explain. [*Ramsey v. Allstate Insurance Co.*, 514 Fed.Appx. 554 (6th Cir. 2013)] (See *Types of Contracts*.)

11–7. Quasi Contracts. Lawrence M. Clarke, Inc., was the general contractor for construction of a portion of a sanitary sewer system in Billings, Michigan. Clarke accepted Kim Draeger's proposal to do the work for a certain price. Draeger arranged with two subcontractors to work on the project. The work provided by Draeger and the subcontractors proved unsatisfactory. All of the work fell under Draeger's contract with Clarke. Clarke filed a suit in a Michigan state court against Draeger, seeking to recover damages on a theory of quasi contract. The court awarded Clarke $900,000 in damages on that theory. A state intermediate appellate court reversed this award. Why? [*Lawrence M. Clarke, Inc. v. Draeger*, 2015 WL 205182 (Mich.App. 2015)] (See *Quasi Contracts*.)

11–8. Interpretation of Contracts. Lehman Brothers, Inc. (LBI), wrote a letter to Mary Ortegón offering her employment as LBI's "Business Chief Administrative Officer in Its Fixed Income Division." The offer included a salary of $150,000 per year and an annual "minimum bonus" of $350,000. The letter stated that the bonus would be paid unless Ortegón resigned or was terminated for certain causes. In other words, the bonus was not a "signing" bonus—it was clearly tied to her performance on the job. Ortegón accepted the offer. Before she started work, however, LBI rescinded it. Later, LBI filed for bankruptcy in a federal court. Ortegón filed a claim with the court for the amount of the bonus on the ground that LBI had breached its contract with her by not paying it. Can extrinsic evidence be admitted to interpret the meaning of the bonus term? Explain. [*Ortegón v. Giddens*, ___ F.3d ___, 2016 WL 125268 (2d Cir. 2016)] (See *Interpretation of Contracts*.)

11–9. A Question of Ethics—Unilateral Contracts. *International Business Machines Corp. (IBM) hired Niels Jensen in 2000 as a software sales representative. According to the brochure on IBM's "Sales Incentive Plan" (SIP), "the more you sell, the more earnings for you." But "the SIP program does not constitute a promise by IBM. IBM reserves the right to modify the program at any time." Jensen was given a "quota letter" that said he would be paid $75,000 as a base salary and, if he attained his quota, an additional $75,000 as incentive pay. Jensen closed a deal worth more than $24 million to IBM. When IBM paid him less than $500,000 as a commission, Jensen filed a suit. He argued that the SIP was a unilateral offer that became a binding contract when he closed the sale. [Jensen v. International Business Machines Corp., 454 F.3d 382 (4th Cir. 2006)] (See Types of Contracts.)*

(a) Would it be fair to the employer for the court to hold that the SIP brochure and the quota letter created a unilateral contract if IBM did not *intend* to create such a contract? Would it be fair to the employee to hold that *no* contract was created? Explain.

(b) The "Sales Incentives" section of IBM's brochure included a clause providing that "management will decide if an adjustment to the payment is appropriate" when an employee closes a large transaction. Does this affect your answers to the questions above? From an ethical perspective, would it be fair to hold that a contract exists despite these statements? Why or why not?

Legal Reasoning Group Activity

11–10. Contracts. Review the basic requirements for a valid contract listed at the beginning of this chapter. Now consider the relationship created when a student enrolls in a college or university. (See *Elements of a Contract*.)

(a) One group should analyze and discuss whether a contract has been formed between the student and the college or university.

(b) A second group should assume that there is a contract and explain whether it is bilateral or unilateral.

Answers to the *Issue Spotters*

1. *Can Ed recover? Why or why not?* No. This contract, although not fully executed, is for an illegal purpose and therefore is void. A void contract gives rise to no legal obligation on the part of any party. A contract that is void is no contract. There is nothing to enforce.

2. *Can Alison recover from Jerry the amount that she paid? Why or why not?* Yes, because a person who is unjustly enriched at the expense of another can be required to account for the benefit under the theory of quasi contract. The parties here did not have a contract, but the law will impose one to avoid the unjust enrichment.

Sample Answers for *Business Case Problems with Sample Answer*

Problem 11–4. *Quasi Contract.* Gutkowski does not have a valid claim for payment, nor should he recover on the basis of a quasi contract. Quasi contracts are imposed by courts on parties in the interest of fairness and justice. Usually, a quasi contract is imposed to avoid the unjust enrichment of one party at the expense of another. Gutkowski was compensated as a consultant. For him to establish a claim that he is due more compensation based on unjust enrichment, he must have proof. As it is, he has only his claim that there were discussions about his being a part owner of YES. Discussions and negotiations are not a basis for recovery on a quasi contract. In the actual case on which this problem is based, the court dismissed Gutkowski's claim for payment.

CHAPTER

Agreement in Traditional and E-Contracts

Contract law developed over time to meet society's need to know with certainty what kinds of promises, or contracts, will be enforced and the point at which a valid and binding contract is formed. For a contract to be considered valid and enforceable, four basic requirements—agreement, consideration, contractual capacity, and legality—must be met. In this chapter, we look closely at the first of these requirements, *agreement*.

Agreement is required to form a contract, whether it is formed in the traditional way (on paper) or online.

In today's world, many contracts are formed via the Internet. We discuss online offers and acceptances and examine some laws that have been created to apply to electronic contracts, or *e-contracts*, in the latter part of this chapter.

12–1 Agreement

An essential element for contract formation is **agreement**—the parties must agree on the terms of the contract and manifest to each other their *mutual assent* (agreement) to the same bargain. Ordinarily, agreement is evidenced by two events: an *offer* and an *acceptance*. One party offers a certain bargain to another party, who then accepts that bargain.

An agreement does not necessarily have to be in writing. Both parties, however, must manifest their assent, or voluntary consent, to the same bargain. Once an agreement is reached, if the other elements of a contract (consideration, capacity, and legality—discussed in subsequent chapters) are present, a valid contract is formed. Generally, the contract creates enforceable rights and duties between the parties.

Because words often fail to convey the precise meaning intended, the law of contracts generally adheres to the *objective theory of contracts*. Under this theory, a party's words and conduct are held to mean whatever a reasonable person in the offeree's position would think they meant.

12–1a Requirements of the Offer

An **offer** is a promise or commitment to do or refrain from doing some specified action in the future. The party making an offer is called the *offeror*, and the party to whom the offer is made is called the *offeree*. Under the common law, three elements are necessary for an offer to be effective:

1. The offeror must have a serious intention to become bound by the offer.
2. The terms of the offer must be reasonably certain, or definite, so that the parties and the court can ascertain the terms of the contract.
3. The offer must be communicated to the offeree.

Once an effective offer has been made, the offeree's acceptance of that offer creates a legally binding contract (providing the other essential elements for a valid and enforceable contract are present).

Intention The first requirement for an effective offer is a serious intent on the part of the offeror. Serious intent is not determined by the subjective intentions, beliefs, and assumptions of the offeror. Rather, it is determined by what a reasonable person in the offeree's position would conclude that the offeror's words and actions meant. Offers made in obvious anger, jest, or undue excitement do not meet the serious-and-objective-intent test. A reasonable person would realize that such offers were not made seriously. Because these offers are not effective, an offeree's acceptance does not create an agreement.

■ **EXAMPLE 12.1** Linda and Dena ride to school each day in Dena's new automobile, which has a market value of $20,000. One cold morning, they get into the car, but the car will not start. Dena yells in anger, "I'll sell this car to anyone for $500!" Linda drops $500 on Dena's lap. A reasonable person—taking into consideration Dena's frustration and the obvious difference in value between the market price of the car and the proposed purchase price—would realize that Dena's offer was not made with serious and objective intent. No agreement is formed. ■

In the classic case presented next, the court considered whether an offer made "after a few drinks" met the serious-and-objective-intent requirement.

Lucy v. Zehmer

Supreme Court of Appeals of Virginia, 196 Va. 493, 84 S.E.2d 516 (1954).

Background and Facts W. O. Lucy, the plaintiff, filed a suit against A. H. and Ida Zehmer, the defendants, to compel the Zehmers to transfer title of their property, known as the Ferguson Farm, to the Lucys (W. O. and his wife) for $50,000, as the Zehmers had allegedly agreed to do. Lucy had known A. H. Zehmer for fifteen or twenty years and for the last eight years or so had been anxious to buy the Ferguson Farm from him. One night, Lucy stopped to visit the Zehmers in the combination restaurant, filling station, and motor court they operated. While there, Lucy tried to buy the Ferguson Farm once again. This time he tried a new approach. According to the trial court transcript, Lucy said to Zehmer, "I bet you wouldn't take $50,000 for that place." Zehmer replied, "Yes, I would too; you wouldn't give fifty." Throughout the evening, the conversation returned to the sale of the Ferguson Farm for $50,000. All the while, the men continued to drink whiskey and engage in light conversation.

Eventually, Lucy enticed Zehmer to write up an agreement to the effect that the Zehmers would sell the Ferguson Farm to Lucy for $50,000 complete. Later, Lucy sued Zehmer to compel him to go through with the sale. Zehmer argued that he had been drunk and that the offer had been made in jest and hence was unenforceable. The trial court agreed with Zehmer, and Lucy appealed.

In the Language of the Court
BUCHANAN, J. [Justice] delivered the opinion of the court.
* * * *

In his testimony, Zehmer claimed that he "was high as a Georgia pine," and that the transaction "was just a bunch of two doggoned drunks bluffing to see who could talk the biggest and say the most." That claim is inconsistent with his attempt to testify in great detail as to what was said and what was done.
* * * *

The appearance of the contract, the fact that it was under discussion for forty minutes or more before it was signed; Lucy's objection to the first draft because it was written in the singular, and he wanted Mrs. Zehmer to sign it also; the rewriting to meet that objection and the signing by Mrs. Zehmer; the discussion of what was to be included in the sale, the provision for the examination of the title, the completeness of the instrument that was executed, the taking possession of it by Lucy with no request or suggestion by either of the defendants that he give it back, are facts which furnish persuasive evidence that the execution of the contract was a serious business transaction rather than a casual, jesting matter as defendants now contend.
* * * *

In the field of contracts, as generally elsewhere, *we must look to the outward expression of a person as manifesting his intention rather than to his secret and unexpressed intention.* The law imputes to a person an intention corresponding to the reasonable meaning of his words and acts. [Emphasis added.]
* * * *

Whether the writing signed by the defendants and now sought to be enforced by the complainants was the result of a serious offer by Lucy and a serious acceptance by the defendants, or was a serious offer by Lucy and an acceptance in secret jest by the defendants, in either event it constituted a binding contract of sale between the parties.

Case 12.1 Continued

Decision and Remedy *The Supreme Court of Appeals of Virginia determined that the writing was an enforceable contract and reversed the ruling of the lower court. The Zehmers were required by court order to follow through with the sale of the Ferguson Farm to the Lucys.*

Impact of This Case on Today's Law *This is a classic case in contract law because it illustrates so clearly the objective theory of contracts with respect to determining whether a serious offer was intended. Today, the courts continue to apply the objective theory of contracts and routinely cite* Lucy v. Zehmer *as a significant precedent in this area.*

Critical Thinking

- **What If the Facts Were Different?** *Suppose that the day after Lucy signed the purchase agreement, he decided that he did not want the farm after all, and Zehmer sued Lucy to perform the contract. Would this change in the facts alter the court's decision that Lucy and Zehmer had created an enforceable contract? Why or why not?*

Situations in Which Intent May Be Lacking

The concept of intention can be further clarified by looking at statements that are *not* offers and situations in which the parties' intent to be bound might be questionable.

1. *Expressions of opinion.* An expression of opinion is not an offer. It does not indicate an intention to enter into a binding agreement.
2. *Statements of future intent.* A statement of an intention to do something in the future (such as "I plan to sell my Verizon stock") is not an offer.
3. *Preliminary negotiations.* A request or invitation to negotiate is not an offer. It only expresses a willingness to discuss the possibility of entering into a contract. Statements such as "Will you sell your farm?" or "I wouldn't sell my car for less than $8,000" are examples.
4. *Invitations to bid.* When a government entity or private firm needs to have construction work done, contractors are invited to submit bids. The invitation to submit bids is not an offer. The bids that contractors submit are offers, however, and the government entity or private firm can bind the contractor by accepting the bid.
5. *Advertisements and price lists.* In general, representations made in advertisements and price lists are treated not as offers to contract but as invitations to negotiate.[1]
6. *Live and online auctions.* In a live auction, a seller "offers" goods for sale through an auctioneer, but this is not an offer to form a contract. Rather, it is an invitation asking bidders to submit offers. In the context of an auction, a bidder is the offeror, and the auctioneer is the offeree. The offer is accepted when the auctioneer strikes the hammer.

The most familiar type of auction today takes place online through Web sites like eBay and eBid. "Offers" to sell an item on these sites generally are treated as invitations to negotiate. Unlike live auctions, online auctions are automated. Buyers can enter incremental bids on an item (without approving each price increase) up to a specified amount or without a limit.

Agreements to Agree. Traditionally, agreements to agree—that is, agreements to agree to the material terms of a contract at some future date—were not considered to be binding contracts. The modern view, however, is that agreements to agree may be enforceable agreements (contracts) if it is clear that the parties intended to be bound by the agreements. In other words, under the modern view the emphasis is on the parties' intent rather than on form.

■ **CASE IN POINT 12.2** After a person was injured and nearly drowned on a water ride at one of its amusement parks, Six Flags, Inc., filed a lawsuit against the manufacturer that had designed the ride. The defendant manufacturer claimed that the parties did not have a binding contract but had only engaged in preliminary negotiations that were never formalized in a construction contract.

The court, however, held that the evidence was sufficient to show an intent to be bound. The evidence included a faxed document specifying the details of the water ride, along with the parties' subsequent actions (having begun construction and written notes on the faxed document). The manufacturer was required to provide insurance for the water ride at Six Flags. In addition, its insurer was required to defend Six Flags in the personal-injury lawsuit that arose out of the incident.[2] ■

---

1. *Restatement (Second) of Contracts*, Section 26, Comment b.

2. *Six Flags, Inc. v. Steadfast Insurance Co.*, 474 F.Supp.2d 201 (D.Mass. 2007).

Preliminary Agreements. Increasingly, the courts are holding that a preliminary agreement constitutes a binding contract if the parties have agreed on all essential terms and no disputed issues remain to be resolved. In contrast, if the parties agree on certain major terms but leave other terms open for further negotiation, a preliminary agreement is not binding. The parties are bound only in the sense that they have committed themselves to negotiate the undecided terms in good faith in an effort to reach a final agreement.

In the following *Spotlight Case,* a dispute arose over an agreement to settle a case during the trial. One party claimed that the agreement, which was formed via e-mail, was binding. The other party claimed that the e-mail exchange was merely an agreement to work out the terms of a settlement in the future. Can an exchange of e-mails create a complete and unambiguous agreement?

Spotlight on Amazon.com

Case 12.2 Basis Technology Corp. v. Amazon.com, Inc.

Appeals Court of Massachusetts, 71 Mass.App.Ct. 29, 878 N.E.2d 952 (2008).

Background and Facts Basis Technology Corporation created software and provided technical services for a Japanese-language Web site belonging to Amazon.com, Inc. The agreement between the two companies allowed for separately negotiated contracts for additional services that Basis might provide to Amazon. At the end of 1999, Basis and Amazon entered into stock-purchase agreements. Later, Basis sued Amazon for various claims involving these securities and for failure to pay for services performed by Basis that were not included in the original agreement. During the trial, the two parties appeared to reach an agreement to settle out of court via a series of e-mail exchanges outlining the settlement. When Amazon reneged, Basis served a motion to enforce the proposed settlement. The trial judge entered a judgment against Amazon, which appealed.

In the Language of the Court
SIKORA, J. [Judge]
* * * *

* * * On the evening of March 23, after the third day of evidence and after settlement discussions, Basis counsel sent an e-mail with the following text to Amazon counsel:

[Amazon counsel]—This e-mail confirms the essential business terms of the settlement between our respective clients * * *. Basis and Amazon agree that they promptly will take all reasonable steps to memorialize in a written agreement, to be signed by individuals authorized by each party, the terms set forth below, as well as such other terms that are reasonably necessary to make these terms effective.

* * * *

[Amazon counsel], please contact me first thing tomorrow morning if this e-mail does not accurately summarize the settlement terms reached earlier this evening.
See you tomorrow morning when we report this matter settled to the Court.

At 7:26 A.M. on March 24, Amazon counsel sent an e-mail with a one-word reply: "correct." Later in the morning, in open court and on the record, both counsel reported the result of a settlement without specification of the terms.

On March 25, Amazon's counsel sent a facsimile of the first draft of a settlement agreement to Basis's counsel. The draft comported with all the terms of the e-mail exchange, and added some implementing and boilerplate [standard contract provisions] terms.
* * * *

[Within a few days, though,] the parties were deadlocked. On April 21, Basis served its motion to enforce the settlement agreement. Amazon opposed. * * * The motion and opposition presented the issues whether the e-mail terms were sufficiently complete and definite to form an agreement and whether Amazon had intended to be bound by them.
* * * *

We examine the text of the terms for the incompleteness and indefiniteness charged by Amazon. *Provisions are not ambiguous simply because the parties have developed different interpretations of them.* [Emphasis added.]

* * * *

We must interpret the document as a whole. In the preface to the enumerated terms, Basis counsel stated that the "e-mail confirms the essential business terms of the settlement between our respective clients," and that the parties "agree that they promptly will take all reasonable steps to memorialize" those terms. Amazon counsel concisely responded, "correct." Thus the "essential business terms" were resolved. The parties were proceeding to "memorialize" or record the settlement terms, not to create them.

* * * *

To ascertain intent, a court considers the words used by the parties, the agreement taken as a whole, and surrounding facts and circumstances. The essential circumstance of this disputed agreement is that it concluded a trial.

* * * As the trial judge explained in her memorandum of decision, she "terminated" the trial; she did not suspend it for exploratory negotiations. She did so in reliance upon the parties' report of an accomplished agreement for the settlement of their dispute.

* * * *

In sum, the deliberateness and the gravity attributable to a report of a settlement, especially during the progress of a trial, weigh heavily as circumstantial evidence of the intention of a party such as Amazon to be bound by its communication to the opposing party and to the court.

Decision and Remedy *The Appeals Court of Massachusetts affirmed the trial court's finding that Amazon intended to be bound by the terms of the March 23 e-mail. That e-mail constituted a complete and unambiguous statement of the parties' desire to be bound by the settlement terms.*

Critical Thinking

- **What If the Facts Were Different?** *Assume that, instead of exchanging e-mails, the attorneys for both sides had agreed by telephone to all of the terms actually included in their e-mail exchanges. Would the court have ruled differently? Why or why not?*
- **Legal Environment** *What does the result in this case suggest that a businessperson should do before agreeing to a settlement of a legal dispute?*

Definiteness of Terms The second requirement for an effective offer involves the definiteness of its terms. An offer must have reasonably definite terms so that a court can determine if a breach has occurred and give an appropriate remedy.[3] The specific terms required depend, of course, on the type of contract. Generally, a contract must include the following terms, either expressed in the contract or capable of being reasonably inferred from it:

1. The identification of the parties.
2. The identification of the object or subject matter of the contract (also the quantity, when appropriate), including the work to be performed, with specific identification of such items as goods, services, and land.
3. The consideration to be paid.
4. The time of payment, delivery, or performance.

An offer may invite an acceptance to be worded in such specific terms that the contract is made definite. ■**EXAMPLE 12.3** Nintendo of America, Inc., contacts your Play 2

Win Games store and offers to sell "from one to twenty-five Nintendo 3DS.XL gaming systems for $75 each. State number desired in acceptance." You agree to buy twenty systems. Because the quantity is specified in the acceptance, the terms are definite, and the contract is enforceable. ■

When the parties have clearly manifested their intent to form a contract, courts sometimes are willing to supply a missing term in a contract, especially a sales contract.[4] But a court will not rewrite a contract if the parties' expression of intent is too vague or uncertain to be given any precise meaning.

Communication The third requirement for an effective offer is communication—the offer must be communicated to the offeree. Ordinarily, one cannot agree to a bargain without knowing that it exists. ■ **CASE IN POINT 12.4** Adwoa Gyabaah was hit by a bus owned by Rivlab Transportation Corporation. Gyabaah filed a suit in a New York state court against the bus company. Rivlab's

---

3. *Restatement (Second) of Contracts*, Section 33.

4. See UCC 2–204. Article 2 of the UCC modifies general contract law by requiring *less* specificity, or definiteness of terms, in sales and lease contracts.

insurer offered to tender the company's policy limit of $1 million in full settlement of Gyabaah's claims. On the advice of her attorney, Jeffrey Aronsky, Gyabaah signed a release (a contract forfeiting the right to pursue a legal claim) to obtain the settlement funds.

The release, however, was not sent to Rivlab or its insurer, National Casualty. Moreover, Gyabaah claimed that she had not decided whether to settle. Two months later, Gyabaah changed lawyers and changed her mind about signing the release. Her former attorney, Aronsky, filed a motion to enforce the release so that he could obtain his fees from the settlement funds. The court denied the motion, and Aronsky appealed. The reviewing court held that there was no binding settlement agreement. The release was never delivered to Rivlab or its insurer nor was acceptance of the settlement offer otherwise communicated to them.[5] ∎

12–1b Termination of the Offer

The communication of an effective offer to an offeree gives the offeree the power to transform the offer into a binding, legal obligation (a contract) by an acceptance. This power of acceptance does not continue forever, though. It can be terminated either by action of the parties or by operation of law.

Termination by Action of the Parties An offer can be terminated by action of the parties in any of three ways: by revocation, by rejection, or by counteroffer.

Revocation. The offeror's act of revoking, or withdrawing, an offer is known as **revocation.** Unless an offer is irrevocable, the offeror usually can revoke the offer, as long as the revocation is communicated to the offeree before the offeree accepts. Revocation may be accomplished by either of the following:

1. Express repudiation of the offer (such as "I withdraw my previous offer of October 17").
2. Performance of acts that are inconsistent with the existence of the offer and are made known to the offeree (for instance, selling the offered property to another person in the offeree's presence).

In most states, a revocation becomes effective when the offeree or the offeree's *agent* (a person acting on behalf of the offeree) actually receives it. Therefore, a revocation sent via FedEx on April 1 and delivered at the offeree's residence or place of business on April 3 becomes effective on April 3. An offer made to the general public can be revoked in the same manner in which it was originally communicated. For instance, an offer made on specific Web sites or in particular newspapers can be revoked on the same Web sites or in the same newspapers.

Irrevocable Offers. Although most offers are revocable, some can be made irrevocable—that is, they cannot be revoked. One form of irrevocable offer is an **option contract.** An option contract is created when an offeror promises to hold an offer open for a specified period of time in return for a payment (consideration) given by the offeree. An option contract takes away the offeror's power to revoke the offer for the period of time specified in the option.

Option contracts are frequently used in conjunction with the sale or lease of real estate. ∎ **EXAMPLE 12.5** Tyler agrees to lease a house from Jackson, the property owner. The lease contract includes a clause stating that Tyler is paying an additional $15,000 for an option to purchase the property within a specified period of time. If Tyler decides not to purchase the house after the specified period has lapsed, he loses the $15,000, and Jackson is free to sell the property to another buyer. ∎

Rejection. If the offeree rejects the offer—by words or by conduct—the offer is terminated. Any subsequent attempt by the offeree to accept will be construed as a new offer, giving the original offeror (now the offeree) the power of acceptance.

Like a revocation, a rejection of an offer is effective only when it is actually received by the offeror or the offeror's agent. ∎ **EXAMPLE 12.6** Goldfinch Farms offers to sell specialty Maitake mushrooms to a Japanese buyer, Kinoko Foods. If Kinoko rejects the offer by sending a letter via U.S. mail, the rejection will not be effective (and the offer will not be terminated) until Goldfinch receives the letter. ∎

Merely inquiring about the "firmness" of an offer does not constitute rejection. ∎ **EXAMPLE 12.7** Raymond offers to buy Francie's digital pen for $100. She responds, "Is that your best offer?" A reasonable person would conclude that Francie has not rejected the offer but has merely made an inquiry. Francie could still accept and bind Raymond to the $100 price. ∎

Counteroffer. A **counteroffer** is a rejection of the original offer and the simultaneous making of a new offer. ∎ **EXAMPLE 12.8** Burke offers to sell his home to Lang for $270,000. Lang responds, "Your price is too high. I'll offer to purchase your house for $250,000." Lang's response is a counteroffer because it rejects Burke's offer to sell at $270,000 and creates a new offer by Lang to purchase the home for $250,000. ∎

At common law, the **mirror image rule** requires the offeree's acceptance to match the offeror's offer exactly—to

---

5. *Gyabaah v. Rivlab Transportation Corp.*, 102 A.D.3d 451, 958 N.Y.S.2d 109 (N.Y.A.D. 2013).

mirror the offer. Any change in, or addition to, the terms of the original offer automatically terminates that offer and substitutes the counteroffer. The counteroffer, of course, need not be accepted, but if the original offeror does accept the terms of the counteroffer, a valid contract is created.[6]

Termination by Operation of Law The power of the offeree to transform the offer into a binding, legal obligation can be terminated by operation of law through the occurrence of any of the following events:

1. Lapse of time.
2. Destruction of the specific subject matter of the offer.
3. Death or incompetence of the offeror or the offeree.
4. Supervening illegality of the proposed contract. (A statute or court decision that makes an offer illegal automatically terminates the offer.)

Lapse of Time. An offer terminates automatically by law when the period of time *specified in the offer* has passed. If the offer states that it will be left open until a particular date, then the offer will terminate at midnight on that day. If the offer states that it will be open for a number of days, this time period normally begins to run when the offeree *receives* the offer (not when it is formed or sent).

If the offer does not specify a time for acceptance, the offer terminates at the end of a *reasonable* period of time. What constitutes a reasonable period of time depends on the subject matter of the contract, business and market conditions, and other relevant circumstances. An offer to sell farm produce, for instance, will terminate sooner than

an offer to sell farm equipment. Farm produce is perishable and is also subject to greater fluctuations in market value.

Destruction, Death, or Incompetence. An offer is automatically terminated if the specific subject matter of the offer (such as a smartphone or a house) is destroyed before the offer is accepted.[7] Notice of the destruction is not required for the offer to terminate.

An offeree's power of acceptance is also terminated when the offeror or offeree dies or is legally incapacitated—*unless the offer is irrevocable.* ■ **EXAMPLE 12.9** Sybil Maven offers to sell commercial property to Westside Investment for $2 million. In June, Westside pays Maven $5,000 in exchange for her agreement to hold the offer open for ten months (forming an option contract). If Maven dies in July, her offer is not terminated, because it is irrevocable. Westside can purchase the property from Maven's estate at any time within the ten-month period. ■

In contrast, a revocable offer is personal to both parties and cannot pass to the heirs, guardian, or the estate of either party. This rule applies whether or not the other party had notice of the death or incompetence.

Supervening Illegality. A statute or court decision that makes an offer illegal automatically terminates the offer.[8] ■ **EXAMPLE 12.10** Lee offers to lend Kim $10,000 at an annual interest rate of 15 percent. Before Kim can accept the offer, a law is enacted that prohibits interest rates higher than 8 percent. Lee's offer is automatically terminated. (If the statute is enacted after Kim accepts the offer, a valid contract is formed, but the contract may still be unenforceable.) ■

Concept Summary 12.1 reviews the ways in which an offer can be terminated.

---

6. The mirror image rule has been greatly modified in regard to sales contracts. Section 2–207 of the UCC provides that a contract is formed if the offeree makes a definite expression of acceptance (such as signing a form in the appropriate location), even though the terms of the acceptance modify or add to the terms of the original offer.

7. *Restatement (Second) of Contracts*, Section 36.
8. *Restatement (Second) of Contracts*, Section 36.

Concept Summary 12.1

Methods by Which an Offer Can Be Terminated

By Action of the Parties	
	• Revocation
	• Rejection
	• Counteroffer

By Operation of Law	
	• Lapse of time
	• Destruction of the subject matter
	• Death or incompetence of the offeror or offeree
	• Supervening illegality

12–1c Acceptance

Acceptance is a voluntary act by the offeree that shows assent (agreement) to the terms of an offer. The offeree's act may consist of words or conduct. The acceptance must be unequivocal and must be communicated to the offeror.

Generally, only the person to whom the offer is made or that person's agent can accept the offer and create a binding contract. (See this chapter's *Digital Update* feature for a discussion of how parties can sometimes inadvertently accept a contract via e-mail or instant messages.)

DIGITAL UPDATE — Can Your E-Mails or Instant Messages Create a Valid Contract?

Instant messaging and e-mailing are among the most common forms of informal communication. Not surprisingly, parties considering an agreement often exchange offers and counteroffers via e-mail (and, to a lesser extent, instant messaging). The parties may believe that these informal electronic exchanges are for negotiation purposes only. But such communications can lead to the formation of valid contracts.

E-Mails and Settlements

After automobile accidents, the parties' attorneys sometimes exchange e-mails as part of the negotiation process. For instance, John Forcelli, who was injured in an automobile accident, sued the owner of the vehicle, Gelco Corporation. While the suit was pending, Gelco's insurance company's representative orally offered Forcelli a $230,000 settlement, which Forcelli accepted. The representative then sent an e-mail confirming the terms of the settlement, and Forcelli signed a notarized release.

A few days later, however, a New York trial court (unaware of the settlement) granted Gelco's motion for summary judgment and dismissed Forcelli's claims. Gelco then tried to rescind the settlement, claiming that the e-mail did not constitute a binding written settlement agreement. The trial court ruled against Gelco, and an appeal followed. The reviewing court affirmed. The e-mail contained all the necessary elements of contract.[a]

"Accidental" Contracts via E-Mails

When a series of e-mails signal intent to be bound, a contract may be formed, even though some language in the e-mails may be careless or accidental. What matters is whether a court determines that it is reasonable for the receiving party to believe that there is an agreement.

Indeed, e-mail contracting has become so common that only unusually strange circumstances will cause a court to reject such contracts.[b] Furthermore, under the Uniform Electronic Transactions Act (UETA), a contract "may not be denied legal effect solely because an electronic record was used in its formation." Most states have adopted this act, at least in part. (The UETA is discussed later in this chapter.)

Instant Messaging Can Create Valid Contract Modifications

Like e-mail exchanges, instant messaging conversations between individuals in the process of negotiations can result in the formation (or modification) of a contract. One case involved an online marketing service, CX Digital Media, Inc., which provides clients with advertising referrals from its network of affiliates.

CX Digital charges a fee for its services based on the number of referrals. One of its clients was Smoking Everywhere, Inc., a seller of electronic cigarettes. While the two companies were negotiating a change in contract terms via instant messaging, the issue of the maximum number of referrals per day came up. A CX Digital employee sent an instant message to a Smoking Everywhere executive asking about the maximum number. The executive responded, "NO LIMIT," and CX Digital's employee replied, "Awesome!"

After that, CX Digital referred a higher volume of sales leads than it had previously. Smoking Everywhere refused to pay for these additional referrals, claiming that the instant messaging chat did not constitute an enforceable modification of the initial contract. At trial, CX Digital prevailed. Smoking Everywhere had to pay more than $1 million for the additional sales leads.[c]

Critical Thinking *How can a company structure e-mail negotiations to avoid "accidentally" forming a contract?*

a. *Forcelli v. Gelco Corporation*, 109 A.D.3d 244, 972 N.Y.S.2d 570 (2013).
b. See, for example, *Beastie Boys v. Monster Energy Co.*, 983 F.Supp.2d 338 (S.D.N.Y. 2013).
c. *CX Digital Media, Inc. v. Smoking Everywhere, Inc.*, 2011 WL 1102782 (S.D.Fla. 2011).

Unequivocal Acceptance To exercise the power of acceptance effectively, the offeree must accept unequivocally. This is the *mirror image rule* previously discussed. An acceptance may be unequivocal even though the offeree expresses dissatisfaction with the contract. For instance, "I accept the offer, but can you give me a better price?" or "I accept, but please send a written contract" is an effective acceptance. (Notice how important each word is!)

An acceptance cannot impose new conditions or change the terms of the original offer. If it does, the acceptance may be considered a counteroffer, which is a rejection of the original offer. For instance, the statement "I accept the offer but only if I can pay on ninety days' credit" is a counteroffer and not an unequivocal acceptance.

Note that even when the additional terms are construed as a counteroffer, the other party can accept the terms by words or by conduct. ■ **CASE IN POINT 12.11** Lagrange Development is a nonprofit corporation in Ohio that acquires and rehabilitates real property. Sonja Brown presented Lagrange with a written offer to buy a particular house for $79,900. Lagrange's executive director, Terry Glazer, penciled in modifications to the offer—an increased purchase price of $84,200 and a later date for acceptance. Glazer initialed the changes and signed the document.

Brown initialed the date change but not the price increase, and did not sign the revised document. Nevertheless, Brown went through with the sale and received ownership of the property. When a dispute later arose as to the purchase price, a court found that Glazer's modification of the terms had constituted a counteroffer, which Brown had accepted by performance. Therefore, the contract was enforceable for the modified price of $84,200.[9] ■

Silence as Acceptance Ordinarily, silence cannot constitute acceptance, even if the offeror states, "By your silence and inaction, you will be deemed to have accepted this offer." An offeree should not be obligated to act affirmatively to reject an offer when no consideration (nothing of value) has passed to the offeree to impose such a duty.

In some instances, however, the offeree does have a duty to speak, and her or his silence or inaction will operate as an acceptance. Silence can constitute an acceptance when the offeree has had prior dealings with the offeror. ■ **EXAMPLE 12.12** Marabel's restaurant routinely receives shipments of produce from a certain supplier. That supplier notifies Marabel's that it is raising its prices because its crops were damaged by a late freeze. If the restaurant does not respond in any way, the silence may operate as an acceptance, and the supplier will be justified in continuing regular shipments. ■

Communication of Acceptance Whether the offeror must be notified of the acceptance depends on the nature of the contract. In a unilateral contract, the full performance of some act is called for. Acceptance is usually evident, and notification is therefore unnecessary (unless the law requires it or the offeror asks for it). In a bilateral contract, in contrast, communication of acceptance is necessary, because acceptance is in the form of a promise. The bilateral contract is formed when the promise is made rather than when the act is performed.

■ **CASE IN POINT 12.13** Powerhouse Custom Homes, Inc., owed $95,260.42 to 84 Lumber Company under a credit agreement. When Powerhouse failed to pay, 84 Lumber filed a suit to collect. During mediation, the parties agreed to a deadline for objections to whatever agreement they might reach. If there were no objections, the agreement would be binding.

Powerhouse then offered to pay less than the amount owed, but 84 Lumber did not respond. Powerhouse later argued that 84 Lumber had accepted the offer by not objecting to it within the deadline. The court ruled in 84 Lumber's favor for the entire amount of the debt. To form a contract, an offer must be accepted unequivocally. Powerhouse made an offer, but 84 Lumber did not communicate acceptance. Therefore, the parties did not reach an agreement on settlement.[10] ■

At issue in the following case was the validity and enforceability of a waiver of liability on the back page of a gym's membership agreement. In this case, the court had to determine whether the circumstances indicated that the offeree's acceptance of the agreement was unequivocal and clearly communicated.

---

9. *Brown v. Lagrange Development Corp.*, 2015 WL 223877 (Ohio App. 2015).

10. *Powerhouse Custom Homes, Inc. v. 84 Lumber Co.*, 307 Ga.App. 605, 705 S.E.2d 704 (2011).

Hinkal v. Pardoe

Superior Court of Pennsylvania, 2016 PA Super 11, 133 A.3d 738 (2016).

In the Language of the Court

Opinion by STABILE, J. [Judge]

* * * *

[Melinda Hinkal filed a suit in a Pennsylvania state court against personal trainer Gavin Pardoe and Gold's Gym, Inc., alleging that] she sustained a serious neck injury while using a piece of exercise equipment under * * * Pardoe's direction [at Gold's Gym. Hinkal] alleges that she suffered a rupture of the C5 disc in her neck requiring two separate surgeries. [Gold's and Pardoe] filed a Motion for Summary Judgment [asserting] that as a member of Gold's Gym [Hinkal] signed * * * a Membership Agreement [that] contains legally valid "waiver of liability" provisions, which in turn, bar [her] claims.

The trial court concluded that the waiver language set forth in Gold's Membership Agreement was valid and enforceable.

[Hinkal] filed a timely appeal to this [state intermediate appellate] Court.

* * * *

* * * Appellant [Hinkal] questions whether the waiver on the back page of her membership agreement is valid and enforceable. The language on the back page of the agreement reads in pertinent part as follows:

WAIVER OF LIABILITY; ASSUMP-TION OF RISK: Member acknowl-edges that the use of Gold's Gym's facilities, equipment, services and pro-grams involves an inherent risk of per-sonal injury to Member. * * * Member voluntarily agrees to assume all risks of personal injury to Member * * * and waives any and all claims or actions that Member may have against Gold's Gym * * * and any * * * employees * * * for * * * injuries arising from

use of any exercise equipment * * * in supervised or unsupervised activities.

The Gold's Gym Membership Agreement signed by Appellant further instructs:

Do not sign this Agreement until you have read both sides. The terms on each side of this form are a part of this Agreement. * * * By signing this Agreement, Member acknowledges that This Agreement is a contract that will become legally binding upon its acceptance.

The signature line follows immedi-ately and the words "Notice: See other side for important information" appear in bold typeface below the signature line.

* * * *

* * * Appellant * * * asserts that her claim is not barred by the "exclusion clause" on the back of the membership agreement. * * * Appellant contends the waiver is invalid because the waiver language appeared on the back of the agreement, she never read or was told to read the back of the agreement, and the clause was not "brought home" to her in a way that could suggest she was aware of the clause and its contents. However, * * * Appellant admitted she did not read the agreement prior to signing it. * * * Her failure to read her agreement does not render it either invalid or unenforceable. *The law of Pennsylvania is clear. One who is about to sign a contract has a duty to read that contract first.* * * * It is well established that, in the absence of fraud, the failure to read a contract before signing it is an unavailing excuse or defense and cannot justify an avoidance, modification or nulli-fication of the contract. [Emphasis added.]

[To support her claim, Appellant cites *Beck-Hummel v. Ski Shawnee, Inc.,*

a previous case before this court, but] the signed Gold's Gym membership agreement cannot be compared in any way to the unread and unsigned disclaimer on a ski facility ticket in [*Beck-Hummel.*]

* * * *

* * * In [*Beck-Hummel,*] the release provision was contained on the face of an entry ticket purchased for use of a ski facility. The ticket did not require a signature or an express acknowledgment that its terms were read and accepted before using the facility. Nothing about the ticket ensured that a purchaser would be aware of its release provision. The purchasers were mere recipients of the document. In short, there was not sufficient evidence to find conclusively that there was a meeting of the minds that part of the consideration for use of the facility was acceptance of a release provision. In stark contrast, here there is a written, signed and acknowledged agreement between the parties.

* * * *

Here, without reading it, Appel-lant signed the membership agreement, which included an unambiguous direc-tive not to sign before reading both sides, a clear pronouncement that the terms on both sides of the form are part of the agreement, and a straightforward statement that the agreement constitutes the entire agreement between the parties. * * * We find no genuine issue as to any material fact or any error in the lower court's determination that the waiver was valid and enforceable. Appellant is not entitled to relief based on [this] issue.

* * * *

Order affirmed.

Legal Reasoning Questions

1. What indicated that the terms in the agreement at issue in this case were accepted?

2. What were the appellant's arguments in support of her claim? Which of those contentions did the court imply was irrelevant? Why?

3. How did the court distinguish its conclusion in this case from its decision in *Beck-Hummel?*

Mode and Timeliness of Acceptance In bilateral contracts, acceptance must be timely. The general rule is that acceptance in a bilateral contract is timely if it is made before the offer is terminated. Problems may arise, though, when the parties involved are not dealing face to face. In such situations, the offeree should use an authorized mode of communication.

The Mailbox Rule. Acceptance takes effect, thus completing formation of the contract, at the time the offeree sends or delivers the communication via the mode expressly or impliedly authorized by the offeror. This is the so-called **mailbox rule,** also called the *deposited acceptance rule,* which the majority of courts follow. Under this rule, if the authorized mode of communication is the mail, then an acceptance becomes valid when it is dispatched (placed in the control of the U.S. Postal Service)—*not* when it is received by the offeror. (Note, however, that if the offer stipulates when acceptance will be effective, then the offer will not be effective until the time specified.)

The mailbox rule does not apply to instantaneous forms of communication, such as when the parties are dealing face to face, by telephone, by fax, and (usually) by e-mail. Under the Uniform Electronic Transactions Act, e-mail is considered sent when it either leaves the control of the sender or is received by the recipient. This rule takes the place of the mailbox rule when the parties have agreed to conduct transactions electronically and allows an e-mail acceptance to become effective when sent.

Authorized Means of Acceptance. A means of communicating acceptance can be expressly authorized by the offeror or impliedly authorized by the facts and circumstances of the situation.[11] An acceptance sent by means not expressly or impliedly authorized normally is not effective until it is received by the offeror.

When an offeror specifies how acceptance should be made (for instance, by overnight delivery), *express authorization* is said to exist. The contract is not formed unless the offeree uses that specified mode of acceptance. Moreover, both offeror and offeree are bound in contract the moment this means of acceptance is employed. ■ **EXAMPLE 12.14** Motorola Mobility, Inc., offers to sell 144 Atrix 4G smartphones and 72 Lapdocks to Call Me Plus phone stores. The offer states that Call Me Plus must accept the offer via FedEx overnight delivery. The acceptance is effective (and a binding contract is formed) the moment that Call Me Plus gives the overnight envelope containing the acceptance to the FedEx driver. ■

If the offeror does not expressly authorize a certain mode of acceptance, then acceptance can be made by *any reasonable means.*[12] Courts look at the prevailing business usages and the surrounding circumstances to determine whether the mode of acceptance used was reasonable.

Usually, the offeror's choice of a particular means in making the offer implies that the offeree can use the *same or a faster means* for acceptance. Thus, if the offer is made via Priority U.S. mail, it would be reasonable to accept the offer via Priority mail or by a faster method, such as overnight delivery.

Substitute Method of Acceptance. Sometimes, the offeror authorizes a particular method of acceptance, but the offeree accepts by a different means. In that situation, the acceptance may still be effective if the substituted method serves the same purpose as the authorized means.

Acceptance by a substitute method is not effective on dispatch, however. No contract will be formed until the acceptance is received by the offeror. ■ **EXAMPLE 12.15** Bennion's offer specifies acceptance via FedEx overnight delivery, but the offeree accepts instead by overnight delivery from UPS. The substitute method of acceptance will still be effective, but not until the offeror (Bennion) receives it from UPS. ■

12–2 Agreement in E-Contracts

Numerous contracts are formed online. Electronic contracts, or **e-contracts,** must meet the same basic requirements (agreement, consideration, contractual capacity, and legality) as paper contracts. Disputes concerning e-contracts, however, tend to center on contract terms and whether the parties voluntarily agreed to those terms.

Online contracts may be formed not only for the sale of goods and services but also for *licensing.* The "sale" of software generally involves a license, or a right to use the software, rather than the passage of title (ownership rights) from the seller to the buyer. ■ **EXAMPLE 12.16** Lauren wants to obtain software that will allow her to work on spreadsheets on her smartphone. She goes online and purchases GridMagic. During the transaction, she clicks on several on-screen "I agree" boxes to indicate her understanding that she is purchasing only the right to use the software, not ownership rights. After she agrees to these terms (the licensing agreement), she can download the software. ■

As you read through the following subsections, you will see that we typically refer to the offeror and the

---

11. *Restatement (Second) of Contracts,* Section 30, provides that an offer invites acceptance "by any medium reasonable in the circumstances," unless the offer specifies the means of acceptance.

12. *Restatement (Second) of Contracts,* Section 30. This is also the rule under UCC 2–206(1)(a).

offeree as a *seller* and a *buyer.* Keep in mind, though, that in many online transactions these parties would be more accurately described as a *licensor* and a *licensee.*

12–2a Online Offers

Sellers doing business via the Internet can protect themselves against contract disputes and legal liability by creating offers that clearly spell out the terms that will govern their transactions if the offers are accepted. All important terms should be conspicuous and easy to view.

Displaying the Offer The seller's Web site should include a hypertext link to a page containing the full contract so that potential buyers are made aware of the terms to which they are assenting. The contract generally must be displayed online in a readable format, such as a twelve-point typeface. All provisions should be reasonably clear.

Provisions to Include An important point to keep in mind is that the offeror (the seller) controls the offer and thus the resulting contract. The seller should therefore anticipate the terms he or she wants to include in a contract and provide for them in the offer. In some instances, a standardized contract form may suffice.

At a minimum, an online offer should include the following provisions:

1. *Acceptance of terms.* A clause that clearly indicates what constitutes the buyer's agreement to the terms of the offer, such as a box containing the words "I accept" that the buyer can click.
2. *Payment.* A provision specifying how payment for the goods (including any applicable taxes) must be made.
3. *Return policy.* A statement of the seller's refund and return policies.
4. *Disclaimer.* Disclaimers of liability for certain uses of the goods. For instance, an online seller of business forms may add a disclaimer that the seller does not accept responsibility for the buyer's reliance on the forms rather than on an attorney's advice.
5. *Limitation on remedies.* A provision specifying the remedies available to the buyer if the goods are found to be defective or if the contract is otherwise breached. Any limitation of remedies should be clearly spelled out.
6. *Privacy policy.* A statement indicating how the seller will use the information gathered about the buyer.
7. *Dispute resolution.* Provisions relating to dispute settlement, which we examine more closely in the following section.

Dispute-Settlement Provisions Online offers frequently include provisions relating to dispute settlement. For instance, an offer might include an arbitration clause specifying that any dispute arising under the contract will be arbitrated in a designated forum. The parties might also select the forum and the law that will govern any disputes.

Forum-Selection Clause. Many online contracts contain a **forum-selection clause** indicating the forum, or location (such as a court or jurisdiction), in which contract disputes will be resolved. Significant jurisdictional issues may arise when parties are at a great distance, as they often are when they form contracts via the Internet. A forum-selection clause will help to avert future jurisdictional problems and also help to ensure that the seller will not be required to appear in court in a distant state.

■ **CASE IN POINT 12.17** Scott Rosendahl enrolled in an online college, Ashford University. He claimed that the school's adviser had told him that Ashford offered one of the cheapest undergraduate degree programs in the country. In fact, it did not. Rosendahl later sued the school, claiming that it had violated unfair competition laws and false advertising laws and had engaged in fraud and negligent misrepresentation.

The university argued that its enrollment agreement clearly contained a requirement that all disputes be arbitrated. Rosendahl, like other students, had electronically assented to this agreement when he enrolled. Ashford presented the online application forms to the court, and the court dismissed Rosendahl's lawsuit. Rosendahl had agreed to arbitrate any disputes he had with Ashford.[13] ■

Choice-of-Law Clause. Some online contracts may also include a *choice-of-law clause,* specifying that any contract dispute will be settled according to the law of a particular jurisdiction, such as a state or country. Choice-of-law clauses are particularly common in international contracts, but they may also appear in e-contracts to specify which state's laws will govern in the United States.

12–2b Online Acceptances

The *Restatement (Second) of Contracts,* which is a compilation of common law contract principles, states that parties may agree to a contract "by written or spoken words or by other action or by failure to act."[14] The Uniform Commercial Code (UCC), which governs sales contracts, has a similar provision. Section 2–204 of the UCC states

---

13. *Rosendahl v. Bridgepoint Education, Inc.,* 2012 WL 667049 (S.D.Cal. 2012).
14. *Restatement (Second) of Contracts,* Section 19.

that any contract for the sale of goods "may be made in any manner sufficient to show agreement, including conduct by both parties which recognizes the existence of such a contract." The courts have used these provisions in determining what constitutes an online acceptance.

Click-On Agreements The courts have concluded that the act of clicking on a box labeled "I accept" or "I agree" can indicate acceptance of an online offer. The agreement resulting from such an acceptance is often called a **click-on agreement** (sometimes referred to as a *click-on license* or *click-wrap agreement*). Exhibit 12–1 shows a portion of a typical click-on agreement that accompanies a software package.

Generally, the law does not require that the parties have read all of the terms in a contract for it to be effective. Therefore, clicking on a box that states "I agree" to certain terms can be enough. The terms may be contained on a Web site through which the buyer is obtaining goods or services. They may also appear on a screen when software is downloaded from the Internet.

■ **CASE IN POINT 12.18** The "Terms of Use" that govern Facebook users' accounts include a forum-selection clause that provides for the resolution of all disputes in a court in Santa Clara County, California. To sign up for a Facebook account, a person must click on a box indicating that he or she has agreed to this term.

Mustafa Fteja was an active user of facebook.com when his account was disabled. He sued Facebook in a federal court in New York, claiming that it had disabled his Facebook page without justification and for discriminatory reasons. Facebook filed a motion to transfer the case to California under the forum-selection clause. The court found that the clause in Facebook's online contract was binding and transferred the case. When Fteja clicked on the button to accept the contract terms, he agreed to resolve all disputes with Facebook in Santa Clara County, California.[15] ■

Shrink-Wrap Agreements With a **shrink-wrap agreement** (or *shrink-wrap license*), the terms are expressed inside the box in which the goods are packaged. (The term *shrink-wrap* refers to the plastic that covers the box.) Usually, the party who opens the box is told that she or he agrees to the terms by keeping whatever is in the box. Similarly, when a purchaser opens a software package, he or she agrees to abide by the terms of the limited license agreement.

■ **EXAMPLE 12.19** Ava orders a new iMac from Big Ed's Electronics, which ships it to her. Along with the iMac, the box contains an agreement setting forth the terms of the sale, including what remedies are available.

---

15. *Fteja v. Facebook, Inc.*, 841 F.Supp.2d 829 (S.D.N.Y. 2012).

EXHIBIT 12–1 A Click-On Agreement Sample
This exhibit illustrates an online offer to form a contract. To accept the offer, the user simply scrolls down the page and clicks on the "Accept and Install" button.

The document also states that Ava's retention of the iMac for longer than thirty days will be construed as an acceptance of the terms. ∎

In most instances, a shrink-wrap agreement is not between a retailer and a buyer, but is between the manufacturer of the hardware or software and the ultimate buyer-user of the product. The terms generally concern warranties, remedies, and other issues associated with the use of the product.

Shrink-Wrap Agreements and Enforceable Contract Terms. In some cases, the courts have enforced the terms of shrink-wrap agreements in the same way as the terms of other contracts. These courts have reasoned that by including the terms with the product, the seller proposed a contract. The buyer could accept this contract by using the product after having an opportunity to read the terms. Thus, a buyer's failure to object to terms contained within a shrink-wrapped software package may constitute an acceptance of the terms by conduct.

Shrink-Wrap Terms That May Not Be Enforced. Sometimes, however, the courts have refused to enforce certain terms included in shrink-wrap agreements because the buyer did not expressly consent to them. An important factor is when the parties formed their contract.

If a buyer orders a product over the telephone, for instance, and is not informed of an arbitration clause or a forum-selection clause at that time, the buyer clearly has not expressly agreed to these terms. If the buyer discovers the clauses *after* the parties have entered into a contract, a court may conclude that those terms were proposals for additional terms and were not part of the contract.

Browse-Wrap Terms Like the terms of click-on agreements, **browse-wrap terms** can occur in transactions conducted over the Internet. Unlike click-on agreements, however, browse-wrap terms do not require Internet users to assent to the terms before downloading or using certain software. In other words, a person can install the software without clicking "I agree" to the terms of a license. Browse-wrap terms are often unenforceable because they do not satisfy the agreement requirement of contract formation.[16]

∎ **EXAMPLE 12.20** BrowseNet Corporation provides free downloadable "QuickLoad" software on its Web site. The site refers to a license agreement but the user does not have to view it or agree to its terms before downloading the software. One of the license terms requires all disputes to be submitted to arbitration in California. If a user sues BrowseNet in Washington State, the arbitration clause might not be enforceable, because users were not required to indicate their assent to the agreement. ∎

12–2c Federal Law on E-Signatures and E-Documents

An **e-signature** has been defined as "an electronic sound, symbol, or process attached to or logically associated with a record and executed or adopted by a person with the intent to sign the record."[17] In 2000, Congress enacted the Electronic Signatures in Global and National Commerce Act (E-SIGN Act).[18]

The E-SIGN Act provides that no contract, record, or signature may be "denied legal effect" solely because it is in electronic form. In other words, under this law, an electronic signature is as valid as a signature on paper, and an e-document can be as enforceable as a paper one. For an e-signature to be enforceable, however, the contracting parties must have agreed to use electronic signatures. For an electronic document to be valid, it must be in a form that can be retained and accurately reproduced.

E-Signature Technologies Electronic documents can be signed in a number of ways. E-signature technologies include encrypted digital signatures, names intended as signatures at the end of e-mail messages, and clicks on a Web page if the clicks include some means of identification.

Note that although courts do not question that documents can be signed electronically under the E-SIGN Act, some courts will question the validity of the signatures themselves. For instance, a court might find that a typed name at the bottom of e-mail is not admissible as the person's signature. For this reason, many businesses use special software, such as DocuSign or EchoSign, that is designed to create an e-signature that looks similar to a person's handwritten signature.

Exclusions The E-SIGN Act does not apply to all types of documents. Documents that are exempt include court papers, divorce decrees, evictions, foreclosures, health-insurance terminations, prenuptial agreements, and wills. Also, the only agreements governed by the UCC that fall under this law are those covered by Articles 2 and 2A (sales and lease contracts) and UCC 1–107 and 1–206.

---

16. See, for example, *Waldman v. New Chapter, Inc.*, 714 F.Supp.2d 398 (2010).

17. This definition is from the Uniform Electronic Transactions Act, discussed later in this chapter.
18. 15 U.S.C. Sections 7001 *et seq.*

Despite these limitations, the E-SIGN Act has significantly expanded online contracting.

12–2d Partnering Agreements

One way that online sellers and buyers can prevent disputes over signatures in their e-contracts, as well as disputes over the terms and conditions of those contracts, is to form partnering agreements. In a **partnering agreement,** a seller and a buyer who frequently do business with each other agree in advance on the terms and conditions that will apply to all transactions subsequently conducted electronically. The partnering agreement can also establish special access and identification codes to be used by the parties when transacting business electronically.

A partnering agreement reduces the likelihood that contract disputes will arise because the parties have agreed in advance to the terms and conditions that will accompany each sale. Furthermore, if a dispute does arise, a court or arbitration forum will be able to refer to the partnering agreement when determining the parties' intent.

12–3 The Uniform Electronic Transactions Act

The National Conference of Commissioners on Uniform State Laws and the American Law Institute promulgated the Uniform Electronic Transactions Act (UETA) in 1999. The UETA has been adopted, at least in part, by forty-eight states, resulting in more uniformity among state laws governing electronic transactions. Among other things, the UETA declares that a signature may not be denied legal effect or enforceability solely because it is in electronic form.

The primary purpose of the UETA is to remove barriers to e-commerce by giving the same legal effect to electronic records and signatures as is given to paper documents and signatures. As mentioned, the UETA broadly defines an *e-signature* as "an electronic sound, symbol, or process attached to or logically associated with a record and executed or adopted by a person with the intent to sign the record."[19] A **record** is "information that is inscribed on a tangible medium or that is stored in an electronic or other medium and is retrievable in perceivable [visual] form."[20]

12–3a The Scope and Applicability of the UETA

The UETA does not create new rules for electronic contracts. Rather, it establishes that records, signatures, and contracts may not be denied enforceability solely due to their electronic form.

The UETA does not apply to all writings and signatures. It covers only electronic records and electronic signatures *relating to a transaction.* A *transaction* is defined as an interaction between two or more people relating to business, commercial, or governmental activities.[21] The act specifically does not apply to wills or testamentary trusts or to transactions governed by the UCC (other than those covered by Articles 2 and 2A).[22] In addition, the provisions of the UETA allow the states to exclude its application to other areas of law.

12–3b The Federal E-SIGN Act and the UETA

Earlier, we discussed the provisions of the federal E-SIGN Act. Congress passed the E-SIGN Act in 2000, a year after the UETA was presented to the states for adoption. Thus, a significant issue was to what extent the federal E-SIGN Act preempted the UETA as adopted by the states.

The E-SIGN Act[23] explicitly provides that if a state has enacted the uniform version of the UETA, that law is not preempted by the E-SIGN Act. In other words, if the state has enacted the UETA without modification, state law will govern. The problem is that many states have enacted nonuniform (modified) versions of the UETA, usually to exclude other areas of state law from the UETA's terms. The E-SIGN Act specifies that those exclusions will be preempted to the extent that they are inconsistent with the E-SIGN Act's provisions.

The E-SIGN Act explicitly allows the states to enact alternative requirements for the use of electronic records or electronic signatures. Generally, however, the requirements must be consistent with the provisions of the E-SIGN Act, and the state must not give greater legal status or effect to one specific type of technology. Additionally, state laws that include alternative requirements, if enacted after the adoption of the E-SIGN Act, must specifically refer to the E-SIGN Act. The relationship between the UETA and the E-SIGN Act is illustrated in Exhibit 12–2.

---

19. UETA 102(8).
20. UETA 102(15).

21. UETA 2(12) and 3.
22. UETA 3(b).
23. 15 U.S.C. Section 7002(2)(A)(i).

EXHIBIT 12–2 The E-SIGN Act and the UETA

```
                    THE UNIFORM ELECTRONIC
                    TRANSACTIONS ACT (UETA)
                    ┌─────────┴─────────┐
                    ▼                   ▼
        The UETA is enacted     The UETA is enacted
        WITHOUT MODIFICATIONS   WITH MODIFICATIONS
                │                  ┌───┴────┐
                ▼                  ▼        ▼
        State law governs
```

State law governs

State law governs if:
- The state's procedures or requirements are consistent with the E-SIGN Act.
- The state does not give priority to one type of technology.
- The state law was enacted after the E-SIGN Act and refers to it.

The E-SIGN Act governs if:
- The modifications are inconsistent with the E-SIGN Act.

12–3c Highlights of the UETA

The UETA does not apply to a transaction unless each of the parties has previously agreed to conduct transactions by electronic means. The agreement may be explicit, or it may be implied by the conduct of the parties and the surrounding circumstances.[24] It may sometimes be reasonable to infer that a person who gives out a business card with an e-mail address on it has consented to transact business electronically, for instance. Agreement may also be inferred from an e-mail or even a verbal communication between the parties.

A person who has agreed to an electronic transaction can withdraw his or her consent and refuse to conduct further business electronically. In addition, the parties can agree to opt out of all or some of the terms of the UETA. If they do not do so, then the UETA terms will govern their electronic transactions.

Attribution of Signatures Under the UETA, if an electronic record or signature is the act of a particular person, the record or signature may be attributed to that person. If a person types her or his name at the bottom of an e-mail purchase order, for instance, that name qualifies as

a "signature." The signature is therefore attributed to the person whose name appears on the purchase order.

The UETA does not contain any express provisions about what constitutes fraud or whether an agent is authorized to enter into a contract. Under the UETA, other state laws control if any issues relating to agency, authority, forgery, or contract formation arise. If existing state law requires a document to be notarized, the UETA provides that this requirement is satisfied by the electronic signature of a notary public or other person authorized to verify signatures.

The Effect of Errors The UETA encourages, but does not require, the use of security procedures (such as encryption) to verify changes to electronic documents and to correct errors.

The parties themselves may agree to use a security procedure. If they do, and if one party does not follow the procedure and thus fails to detect an error, the party that followed procedure can legally avoid the effect of the error. When the parties have not agreed to use a security procedure, then other state laws (including contract law governing mistakes) will determine the effect of the error.

To avoid the effect of errors, a party must promptly notify the other party of the error and of her or his intent

---

24. UETA 5(b), and Comment 4B.

not to be bound by the error. In addition, the party must take reasonable steps to return any benefit received. Parties cannot avoid a transaction if they have benefited.

Timing An electronic record is considered *sent* when it is properly directed to the intended recipient in a form readable by the recipient's computer system. Once the electronic record leaves the control of the sender or comes under the control of the recipient, the UETA deems it to have been sent. An electronic record is considered *received* when it enters the recipient's processing system in a readable form—*even if no individual is aware of its receipt.*

12–4 International Treaties Affecting E-Contracts

Much of the e-commerce conducted on a worldwide basis involves buyers and sellers from the United States.

The preeminence of U.S. law in this area is likely to be challenged in the future, however, as Internet use continues to expand worldwide. Already, several international organizations have created their own regulations for global Internet transactions.

The United Nations Convention on the Use of Electronic Communications in International Contracts improves commercial certainty by determining an Internet user's location for legal purposes. The convention also establishes standards for creating functional equivalence between electronic communications and paper documents. In addition, it provides that e-signatures will be treated as the equivalent of signatures on paper documents.

Another treaty relevant to e-contracts is the Hague Convention on the Choice of Court Agreements. Although it does not specifically mention e-commerce, this convention provides more certainty regarding jurisdiction and recognition of judgments by other nations' courts, thereby facilitating both offline and online transactions.

Reviewing: Agreement in Traditional and E-Contracts

Shane Durbin wanted to have a recording studio custom-built in his home. He sent invitations to a number of local contractors to submit bids on the project. Rory Amstel submitted the lowest bid, which was $20,000 less than any of the other bids Durbin received. Durbin called Amstel to ascertain the type and quality of the materials that were included in the bid and to find out if he could substitute a superior brand of acoustic tiles for the same bid price. Amstel said he would have to check into the price difference. The parties also discussed a possible start date for construction.

Two weeks later, Durbin changed his mind and decided not to go forward with his plan to build a recording studio. Amstel filed a suit against Durbin for breach of contract. Using the information presented in the chapter, answer the following questions.

1. Did Amstel's bid meet the requirements of an offer? Explain.
2. Was there an acceptance of the offer? Why or why not?
3. Suppose that the court determines that the parties did not reach an agreement. Further suppose that Amstel, in anticipation of building Durbin's studio, had purchased materials and refused other jobs so that he would have time in his schedule for Durbin's project. Under what theory discussed in the chapter might Amstel attempt to recover these costs?
4. How is an offer terminated? Assuming that Durbin did not inform Amstel that he was rejecting the offer, was the offer terminated at any time described here? Explain.

Debate This . . . *The terms and conditions in click-on agreements are so long and detailed that no one ever reads the agreements. Therefore, the act of clicking on "I agree" is not really an acceptance.*

Terms and Concepts

acceptance 238	browse-wrap terms 244	counteroffer 236
agreement 231	click-on agreement 243	e-contract 241

Issue Spotters

1. Fidelity Corporation offers to hire Ron to replace Monica, who has given Fidelity a month's notice of intent to quit. Fidelity gives Ron a week to decide whether to accept. Two days later, Monica decides not to quit and signs an employment contract with Fidelity for another year. The next day, Monica tells Ron of the new contract. Ron immediately faxes a formal letter of acceptance to Fidelity. Do Fidelity and Ron have a contract? Why or why not? (See *Agreement.*)

2. Applied Products, Inc., does business with Beltway Distributors, Inc., online. Under the Uniform Electronic Transactions Act, what determines the effect of the electronic documents evidencing the parties' deal? Is a party's "signature" necessary? Explain. (See *The Uniform Electronic Transactions Act.*)

• **Check your answers to the Issue Spotters against the answers provided in Appendix D at the end of this text.**

Business Scenarios

12–1. Agreement. Ball e-mails Sullivan and inquires how much Sullivan is asking for a specific forty-acre tract of land Sullivan owns. Sullivan responds, "I will not take less than $60,000 for the forty-acre tract as specified." Ball immediately sends Sullivan a fax stating, "I accept your offer for $60,000 for the forty-acre tract as specified." Discuss whether Ball can hold Sullivan to a contract for the sale of the land. (See *Agreement.*)

12–2. Offer and Acceptance. Schmidt, the owner of a small business, has a large piece of used farm equipment for sale. He offers to sell the equipment to Barry for $10,000. Discuss the legal effects of the following events on the offer: (See *Agreement.*)

(a) Schmidt dies prior to Barry's acceptance, and at the time he accepts, Barry is unaware of Schmidt's death.

(b) The night before Barry accepts, fire destroys the equipment.

(c) Barry pays $100 for a thirty-day option to purchase the equipment. During this period, Schmidt dies, and later Barry accepts the offer, knowing of Schmidt's death.

(d) Barry pays $100 for a thirty-day option to purchase the equipment. During this period, Barry dies, and Barry's estate accepts Schmidt's offer within the stipulated time period.

Business Case Problems

12–3. Spotlight on Crime Stoppers—Communication.

 The Baton Rouge Crime Stoppers (BCS) offered a reward for information about the "South Louisiana Serial Killer." The information was to be provided via a hot line. Dianne Alexander had survived an attack by a person suspected of being the killer. She identified a suspect in a police photo lineup and later sought to collect the reward. BCS refused to pay because she had not provided information to them via the hot line. Had Alexander complied with the terms of the offer? Explain. [*Alexander v. Lafayette Crime Stoppers, Inc.,* 38 So.3d 282 (La. App. 3 Dist. 2010) (See *Agreement.*)

12–4. Business Case Problem with Sample Answer— Online Acceptances. Heather Reasonover opted to try

 Internet service from Clearwire Corp. Clearwire sent her a confirmation e-mail and a modem. When Reasonover plugged in the modem, an "I accept terms" box appeared. Without clicking on the box, Reasonover quit the page. She had not seen Clearwire's "Terms of Service," accessible only through its Web

site. Although the e-mail she received and the printed materials included with the model included URLs to the company's Web site, neither URL gave direct access to the "Terms of Service." A clause in the "Terms of Service" required subscribers to submit any dispute to arbitration. Is Reasonover bound to this clause? Why or why not? [*Kwan v. Clearwire Corp.,* 2012 WL 32380 (W.D.Wash. 2012)] (See *Agreement in E-Contracts.*)

• **For a sample answer to Problem 12–4, go to Appendix E at the end of this text.**

12–5. Acceptance. Judy Olsen, Kristy Johnston, and their mother, Joyce Johnston, owned seventy-eight acres of real property on Eagle Creek in Meagher County, Montana. When Joyce died, she left her interest in the property to Kristy. Kristy wrote to Judy, offering to buy Judy's interest or to sell her own interest to Judy. The letter said to "please respond to Bruce Townsend." In a letter to Kristy—not to Bruce—Judy accepted Kristy's offer to sell her interest. By that time, however, Kristy had made the same offer to sell her interest to their brother, Dave, and he had accepted. Did Judy and Kristy have an enforceable, binding contract? Or did Kristy's offer specifying one exclusive mode of acceptance mean that Judy's reply was not effective? Discuss. [*Olsen v. Johnston*, 368 Mont. 347, 301 P.3d 791 (2013)] (See *Agreement*.)

12–6. Agreement. Amy Kemper was seriously injured when her motorcycle was struck by a vehicle driven by Christopher Brown. Kemper's attorney wrote to Statewide Claims Services, the administrator for Brown's insurer, asking for "all the insurance money that Mr. Brown had under his insurance policy." In exchange, the letter indicated that Kemper would sign a "limited release" on Brown's liability, provided that it did not include any language requiring her to reimburse Brown or his insurance company for any of their incurred costs. Statewide then sent a check and release form to Kemper, but the release demanded that Kemper "place money in an escrow account in regards to any and all liens pending." Kemper refused the demand, claiming that Statewide's response was a counteroffer rather than an unequivocal acceptance of the settlement offer. Did Statewide and Kemper have an enforceable agreement? Discuss. [*Kemper v. Brown*, 325 Ga.App. 806, 754 S.E.2d 141 (2014)] (See *Agreement*.)

12–7. Requirements of the Offer. Technical Consumer Products, Inc. (TCP), makes and distributes energy-efficient lighting products. Emily Bahr was TCP's district sales manager in Minnesota, North Dakota, and South Dakota when the company announced the details of a bonus plan. A district sales manager who achieved 100 percent year-over-year sales growth and a 42 percent gross margin would earn 200 percent of his or her base salary as a bonus. TCP retained absolute discretion to modify the plan. Bahr's base salary was $42,500. Her final sales results for the year showed 113 percent year-over-year sales growth and a 42 percent gross margin. She anticipated a bonus of $85,945, but TCP could not afford to pay the bonuses as planned, and Bahr received only $34,229. In response to Bahr's claim for breach of contract, TCP argued that the bonus plan was too indefinite to be an offer. Is TCP correct? Explain. [*Bahr v. Technical Consumer Products, Inc.*, 601 Fed.Appx. 359 (6th Cir. 2015)] (See *Agreement*.)

12–8. Acceptance. Altisource Portfolio Solutions, Inc., is a global corporation that provides real property owners with a variety of services, including property preservation—repairs, debris removal, and so on. Lucas Contracting, Inc., is a small trade contractor in Carrollton, Ohio. On behalf of Altisource, Berghorst Enterprises, LLC, hired Lucas to perform preservation work on certain foreclosed properties in eastern Ohio.

When Berghorst did not pay for the work, Lucas filed a suit in an Ohio state court against Altisource. Before the trial, Lucas e-mailed the terms of a settlement. The same day, Altisource e-mailed a response that did not challenge or contradict Lucas's proposal and indicated agreement to it. Two days later, however, Altisource forwarded a settlement document that contained additional terms. Which proposal most likely satisfies the element of agreement to establish a contract? Explain. [*Lucas Contracting, Inc. v. Altisource Portfolio Solutions, Inc.*, __ Ohio App.3d __, 2016-Ohio-474, __ N.E.2d __ (2016)] (See *Agreement*.)

12–9. A Question of Ethics—E-Contract Disputes. Dewayne Hubbert, Elden Craft, Chris Grout, and Rhonda Byington bought computers from Dell Corp. through its Web site. Before buying, Hubbert and the others configured their own computers. To make a purchase, each buyer completed forms on five Web pages. On each page, Dell's "Terms and Conditions of Sale" were accessible by clicking on a blue hyperlink. A statement on three of the pages read, "All sales are subject to Dell's Term[s] and Conditions of Sale," but a buyer was not required to click an assent to the terms to complete a purchase. The terms were also printed on the backs of the invoices and on separate documents contained in the shipping boxes with the computers. Among those terms was a "Binding Arbitration" clause.

The computers contained Pentium 4 microprocessors, which Dell advertised as the fastest, most powerful Intel Pentium processors then available. In 2002, Hubbert and the others filed a suit in an Illinois state court against Dell, alleging that this marketing was false, misleading, and deceptive. The plaintiffs claimed that the Pentium 4 microprocessor was slower and less powerful, and provided poorer performance, than either a Pentium III or an AMD Athlon, and at a greater cost. Dell asked the court to compel arbitration. [Hubbert v. Dell Corp., 359 Ill.App.3d 976, 835 N.E.2d 113, 296 Ill.Dec. 258 (5 Dist. 2005)] (See *Agreement in E-Contracts*.)

(a) Should the court enforce the arbitration clause in this case? If you were the judge, how would you rule on this issue?

(b) Do you think shrink-wrap, click-on, and browse-wrap terms impose too great a burden on purchasers? Why or why not?

(c) An ongoing complaint about shrink-wrap, click-on, and browse-wrap terms is that sellers (often large corporations) draft them and buyers (typically individual consumers) do not read them. Should purchasers be bound in contract by terms that they have not even read? Why or why not?

Legal Reasoning Group Activity

12–10. E-Contracts. To download a specific application (app) to your smartphone or tablet device, usually you have to check a box indicating that you agree to the company's terms and conditions. Most individuals do so without ever reading those terms and conditions. Print out a specific set of terms and conditions from a downloaded app to use in this assignment. (See *Agreement in E-Contracts*.)

(a) One group will determine which of these terms and conditions are favorable to the company.

(b) Another group will determine which of these terms and conditions conceivably will be favorable to the individual.

(c) A third group will determine which terms and conditions, on net, favor the company too much.

Answers to the *Issue Spotters*

1. ***Do Fidelity and Ron have a contract? Why or why not?***
No. Revocation of an offer may be implied by conduct inconsistent with the offer. When the corporation hired someone else, and the offeree learned of the hiring, the offer was revoked. The acceptance was too late.

2. ***Under the Uniform Electronic Transactions Act, what determines the effect of the electronic documents evidencing the parties' deal? Is a party's "signature" necessary? Explain.***
First, it might be noted that the UETA does not apply unless the parties to a contract agree to use e-commerce in their transaction. In this deal, of course, the parties used e-commerce. The UETA removes barriers to e-commerce by giving the same legal effect to e-records and e-signatures as to paper documents and signatures. The UETA does not include rules for those transactions, however.

Sample Answers for *Business Case Problems with Sample Answer*

Problem 12–4. ***Online Acceptances.*** No. A shrink-wrap agreement is an agreement whose terms are expressed inside the box in which the goods are packaged. The party who opens the box may be informed that he or she agrees to the terms by keeping whatever is in the box. In many cases, the courts have enforced the terms of shrink-wrap agreements just as they enforce the terms of other contracts. But not all of the terms presented in shrink-wrap agreements have been enforced by the courts. One important consideration is whether the buyer had adequate notice of the terms.

A click-on agreement is formed when a buyer, completing a transaction on a computer, is required to indicate his or her assent to be bound by the terms of an offer by clicking on a button that says, for example, "I agree." In Reasonover's situation, no such agreement was formed with respect to Clearwire's "Terms of Service" (TOS). The e-mail did not give adequate notice of the TOS. It did not contain a direct link to the terms—accessing them required clicks on further links through the firm's homepage. The written, shrink-wrap materials accompanying the modem did not provide adequate notice of the TOS. There was only a reference to Clearwire's Web site in small print at the bottom of one page. Similarly, Reasonover's access to an "I accept terms" box did not establish notice of the terms. She did not click on the box but quit the page. Even if any of these references was sufficient notice, Reasonover kept the modem only because Clearwire told her that she could not return it.

In the actual case on which this problem is based, the court refused to compel arbitration on the basis of the clause in Clearwire's TOS.

CHAPTER

Consideration

The fact that a promise has been made does not mean the promise can or will be enforced. Under Roman law, a promise was not enforceable without a *causa*—that is, a reason for making the promise that was also deemed to be a sufficient reason for enforcing it.

Under the common law, a primary basis for the enforcement of promises is consideration. **Consideration** usually is defined as the value given in return for a promise (in a bilateral contract) or in return for a performance (in a unilateral contract). It is the inducement, price, or motive that causes a party to enter into an agreement.

As long as consideration is present, the courts generally do not interfere with contracts based on the amount of consideration paid. It is up to the contracting parties to determine how much their bargain is worth.

13–1 Elements of Consideration

Often, consideration is broken down into two parts: (1) something of *legally sufficient value* must be given in exchange for the promise, and (2) there must be a *bargained-for* exchange.

13–1a Legally Sufficient Value

To be legally sufficient, consideration must be something of value in the eyes of the law. The "something of legally sufficient value" may consist of the following:

1. A promise to do something that one has no prior legal duty to do.
2. The performance of an action that one is otherwise not obligated to undertake.
3. The refraining from an action that one has a legal right to undertake (called a **forbearance**).

Consideration in bilateral contracts normally consists of a promise in return for a promise. In a contract for the sale of goods, for instance, the seller promises to ship specific goods to the buyer, and the buyer promises to pay for those goods. Each of these promises constitutes consideration for the contract.

In contrast, unilateral contracts involve a promise in return for a performance (an action). ■ **EXAMPLE 13.1** Anita says to her neighbor, "When you finish painting the garage, I will pay you $800." Anita's neighbor paints the garage. The act of painting the garage is the consideration that creates Anita's contractual obligation to pay her neighbor $800. ■ Exhibit 13–1 illustrates how consideration differs by types of contracts.

What if, in return for a promise to pay, a person refrains from pursuing harmful habits (a forbearance), such as the use of tobacco and alcohol? Does such forbearance constitute legally sufficient consideration? This was the issue before the court in the following classic case concerning consideration.

Hamer v. Sidway

Court of Appeals of New York, Second Division, 124 N.Y. 538, 27 N.E. 256 (1891).

Background and Facts William E. Story, Sr., was the uncle of William E. Story II. In the presence of family members and others, the uncle promised to pay his nephew $5,000 ($76,000 in today's dollars) if he would refrain from drinking, using tobacco, swearing, and playing cards or billiards for

Case 13.1 Continued money until he reached the age of twenty-one. (Note that in 1869, when this contract was formed, it was legal in New York to drink and play cards for money before the age of twenty-one.)

The nephew agreed and fully performed his part of the bargain. When he reached the age of twenty-one, he wrote and told his uncle that he had kept his part of the agreement and was therefore entitled to $5,000. The uncle wrote a letter back indicating that he was pleased with his nephew's performance and saying "you shall have five thousand dollars, as I promised you." The uncle also said that the $5,000 was in the bank and that the nephew could "consider this money on interest." The nephew left the $5,000 in the care of his uncle, where it would earn interest under the terms and conditions of the letter.

The uncle died about twelve years later without having paid his nephew any part of the $5,000 and interest. The executor of the uncle's estate (Sidway, the defendant in this action) claimed that there had been no valid consideration for the promise. Sidway refused to pay the $5,000 (plus interest) to Hamer, a third party to whom the nephew had transferred his rights in the note. The court reviewed the case to determine whether the nephew had given valid consideration under the law.

In the Language of the Court

PARKER, J. [Justice]

* * * *

* * * Courts will not ask whether the thing which forms the consideration does in fact benefit the promisee or a third party, or is of any substantial value to any one. It is enough that something is promised, done, forborne, or suffered by the party to whom the promise is made as consideration for the promise made to him. *In general a waiver of any legal right at the request of another party is a sufficient consideration for a promise.* Any damage, or suspension, or forbearance of a right will be sufficient to sustain a promise. * * * Now, applying this rule to the facts before us, the promisee used tobacco, occasionally drank liquor, and he had a legal right to do so. That right he abandoned for a period of years upon the strength of the promise of the testator [his uncle] that for such forbearance he would give him $5,000. We need not speculate on the effort which may have been required to give up the use of those stimulants. It is sufficient that he restricted his lawful freedom of action within certain prescribed limits upon the faith of his uncle's agreement * * *. [Emphasis added.]

Decision and Remedy *The court ruled that the nephew had provided legally sufficient consideration by giving up smoking, drinking, swearing, and playing cards or billiards for money until he reached the age of twenty-one. Therefore, he was entitled to the funds.*

Impact of This Case on Today's Law *Although this case was decided more than a century ago, the principles enunciated by the court remain applicable to contracts formed today, including online contracts. For a contract to be valid and binding, consideration must be given, and that consideration must be something of legally sufficient value.*

Critical Thinking
- **What If the Facts Were Different?** *If the nephew had not had a legal right to engage in the behavior that he agreed to forgo, would the result in this case have been different? Explain.*

13–1b Bargained-for Exchange

The second element of consideration is that it must provide the basis for the bargain struck between the contracting parties. That is, the item of value must be given or promised by the promisor (offeror) in return for the promisee's promise, performance, or promise of performance.

This element of bargained-for exchange distinguishes contracts from gifts. ■ **EXAMPLE 13.2** Sheng-Li says to his son, "In consideration of the fact that you are not as wealthy as your brothers, I will pay you $5,000." The fact that the word *consideration* is used does not, by itself, mean that consideration has been given. Indeed, Sheng-Li's promise is not enforceable, because the son does not have to do anything in order to receive the $5,000 promised. Because the son does not need to give Sheng-Li something of legal value in return for his promise, there is no bargained-for exchange. Rather, Sheng-Li has simply stated his motive for giving his son a gift. ■

EXHIBIT 13–1 Consideration in Bilateral and Unilateral Contracts

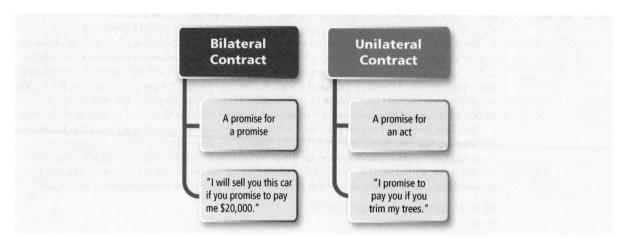

Sometimes, employers offer to cover the costs of employment-related education for their employees. The employees may then be required to repay their employers for all or a portion of the costs. At the center of the dispute in the following case was an agreement signed by an employee to reimburse his employer for educational costs. The question was whether the agreement met the requirement of a bargained-for exchange.

Case Analysis 13.2

USS–POSCO Industries v. Case

California Court of Appeal, First District, Division 1, 244 Cal.App.4th 197, 197 Cal.Rptr.3d 791 (2016).

In the Language of the Court

BANKE, J. [Judge]

* * * *

[USS–POSCO Industries (UPI) in Pittsburg, California,] hired [Floyd] Case in 2007. He initially worked as an entry-level Laborer and Side Trim Operator. As a condition of employment, Case joined Local 1440 of the United Steelworkers of America.

UPI faced a shortage of skilled Maintenance Technical Electrical (MTE) workers. To address this, UPI, after consultation with Local 1440, decided to implement a Learner Program. Thus, in June 2008, the company and Local 1440 entered into a Memorandum of Understanding (MOU) stating UPI would train up to 10 current employees, while continuing to pay their wages and benefits, in an effort to qualify them as MTEs. UPI and the union recognized "that, due to the strong demand

for Maintenance Technician Electrical [workers] the Company needs to retain successful candidates as employees for a reasonable period of time in order to recoup its substantial $46,000 investment in their training." UPI and the union therefore agreed UPI "may require candidates in the Learner Program to sign [a] Reimbursement Agreement that would require reimbursement for a portion of the training should a candidate voluntarily terminate employment within 30 months of completion of the Learner Program."

The Learner Program required 135 weeks of instruction, 90 weeks of on the job training and 45 weeks of classroom work (partially courses at a local community college, partially other courses). The goal was to complete training within 162 weeks, or just over three years. If a participant successfully completed the program and then passed UPI's MTE test,

he or she would be assigned to an MTE vacancy.

The MTE position and Learner Program aligned with Case's desire to work as an engineer. Case understood joining the Learner Program was voluntary. He also understood he did not need to go through the Learner Program or a similar formal educational program to obtain an MTE position. * * * A prospect could simply take and pass UPI's MTE test. However, Case did not attempt the test prior to participating in the Learner Program because he did not think he had the knowledge to pass. He was also unsure if he would pass if he undertook a self-study program. In any case, the Learner Program allowed him to get trained during the workday instead of after hours, and it would lead to higher pay. Accordingly, he applied for the program and was one of [the] selected participants.

Case 13.2 Continued

Case was informed of the reimbursement obligation during a training session for prospective participants. A presentation slide entitled "Repayment Agreement" told prospects they would "sign an agreement to reimburse a portion of their training cost should they voluntarily terminate employment within 30 months of program completion." The slide, consistent with the MOU, indicated the obligation would be "$46,000 prorated over 30 months."

Case was subsequently presented with a written reimbursement agreement and signed it without objection. Under that one-page agreement, Case acknowledged UPI would pay his "wages, benefits and training expenses" while he was in the Learner Program, but there would be no guarantee participation in the program would insure promotion, transfer, or continued employment with UPI. He further agreed that if he was fired for cause or voluntarily left UPI within 30 months after completing the program, he would, absent a compelling hardship such as a serious injury or family death, refund $30,000 of the expense of his training, less $1,000 per month of subsequent service at UPI.

Two months after completing the Learner Program and obtaining an MTE position, Case left UPI for Lawrence Livermore National Laboratory to work as a high voltage electrician.

* * * *

When Case refused to reimburse UPI, the company filed the instant lawsuit [in a California state court] alleging breach of contract * * * . UPI sought damages of $28,000—that is, $1,000 per month that remained in Case's 30-month earn-back period.

Case, in turn, filed a cross-complaint. [He] alleged the [reimbursement] agreement was unlawful because * * * it lacked consideration.

UPI subsequently moved for summary judgment on its complaint and Case's cross-complaint, asserting the reimbursement agreement was valid.

The trial court granted UPI's motion, and the parties thereafter stipulated to a judgment in favor of UPI in the amount of $28,000 plus prejudgment interest and costs. [The court also awarded UPI attorneys' fees of $80,000.]

[Case appealed the judgment to a state intermediate appellate court.]

Case maintains the reimbursement agreement * * * lacked consideration because UPI had no obligation to keep Case employed and, thus, no obligation to provide education, which Case views as "the only possible consideration listed in the Reimbursement Agreement."

Case's view of the bargained-for exchange is too constrained.

On entering the program, Case held a new position of Learner, which meant he would remain on UPI's payroll while *additionally* getting classroom and on-the-job training, the costs of which UPI would front. While Case was not guaranteed a promotion, transfer, or continued employment, exactly the same had been true with respect to his previous position. The exchange, frankly, is obvious: Case got continued wages and fronted education costs, and UPI got Case's agreement to repay those costs if he both completed the training and left the company before it could benefit from the investment. *That either Case or UPI could have terminated the agreement by ending the employment relationship at some point during the educational program does not render illusory the parties' bargained-for exchange*—or require us to ignore the substantial benefits Case obtained every day he spent on the payroll receiving advanced training with no upfront cost and potentially no cost at all to him. [Emphasis added.]

* * * *

The summary judgment in favor of UPI is affirmed.

Legal Reasoning Questions

1. What did Case view as "the only possible consideration" for his agreement to reimburse UPI for some of the cost of his employment-related education?

2. How did the court interpret Case's view of "the only possible consideration"? Why?

3. If UPI had simply offered to pay its employees' wages and training expenses during their participation in a program of instruction "subject entirely and exclusively to UPI's approval," would the element of bargained-for exchange have been met? Explain.

13–1c Adequacy of Consideration

Adequacy of consideration involves how much consideration is given. Essentially, adequacy of consideration concerns the fairness of the bargain.

The General Rule On the surface, when the items exchanged are of unequal value, fairness would appear to be an issue. Normally, however, a court will not question the adequacy of consideration based solely on the comparative value of the things exchanged.

In other words, the determination of whether consideration exists does not depend on a comparison of the values of the things exchanged. Something need not be of direct economic or financial value to be considered legally sufficient consideration. In many situations, the exchange of promises and potential benefits is deemed to be sufficient consideration.

Under the doctrine of freedom of contract, courts leave it up to the parties to decide what something is worth, and parties are usually free to bargain as they wish. If people could sue merely because they had entered into an unwise contract, the courts would be overloaded with frivolous suits.

When Voluntary Consent May Be Lacking

When there is a large disparity in the amount or value of the consideration exchanged, it may raise a red flag for a court to look more closely at the bargain. Shockingly inadequate consideration can indicate that fraud, duress, or undue influence was involved. ■ **EXAMPLE 13.3** Spencer pays $500 for an iPhone 7 that he later discovers is a fake (counterfeit). Because the device is not authentic, he could claim that there was no valid contract because of inadequate consideration and fraud. ■

Disparity in the consideration exchanged may also cause a judge to question whether the contract is so one sided that it is *unconscionable*.[1] For instance, an experienced appliance dealer induces a consumer to sign a contract written in complicated legal language. If the contract requires the consumer to pay twice the market value of the appliance, the disparity in value may indicate that the sale involved undue influence or fraud. A judge would thus want to make sure that the person voluntarily entered into this agreement.[2]

Concept Summary 13.1 provides a review of the main aspects of consideration.

---

1. Pronounced un-*kon*-shun-uh-bul.
2. For an example of an unconscionable home loan contract, see *Orcilla v. Big Sur, Inc.*, 244 Cal.App.4th 982, 198 Cal.Rptr.3d 715 (2016).

13–2 Agreements That Lack Consideration

Sometimes, one of the parties (or both parties) to an agreement may think that consideration has been exchanged when in fact it has not. Here, we look at some situations in which the parties' promises or actions do not qualify as contractual consideration.

13–2a Preexisting Duty

Under most circumstances, a promise to do what one already has a legal duty to do does not constitute legally sufficient consideration. The preexisting legal duty may be imposed by law or may arise out of a previous contract. A sheriff, for instance, has a duty to investigate crime and to arrest criminals. Hence, a sheriff cannot collect a reward for providing information leading to the capture of a criminal.

Likewise, if a party is already bound by contract to perform a certain duty, that duty cannot serve as consideration for a second contract. ■ **EXAMPLE 13.4** Ajax Contractors begins construction on a seven-story office building and after three months demands an extra $75,000 on its contract. If the extra $75,000 is not paid, the contractor will stop working. The owner of the land, finding no one else to complete the construction, agrees to pay the extra $75,000. The agreement is unenforceable because it is not supported by legally sufficient consideration. Ajax Contractors had a preexisting contractual duty to complete the building. ■

Concept Summary 13.1

Consideration

Elements of Consideration	Consideration is the value given in exchange for a promise that is necessary to form a contract. Consideration is often broken down into two elements: • *Legal value*—Something of legally sufficient value must be given in exchange for a promise. This may consist of a promise, a performance, or a forbearance. • *Bargained-for exchange*—There must be a bargained-for exchange.
Adequacy of Consideration	• Adequacy of consideration relates to how much consideration is given and whether a fair bargain was reached. • Courts will inquire into the adequacy of consideration (if the consideration is legally sufficient) only when fraud, undue influence, duress, or the lack of a bargained-for exchange may be involved.

Unforeseen Difficulties The rule regarding preexisting duty is meant to prevent extortion and the so-called holdup game. Nonetheless, if, during performance of a contract, extraordinary difficulties arise that were totally unforeseen at the time the contract was formed, a court may allow an exception to the rule. The key is whether the court finds that the modification is fair and equitable in view of circumstances not anticipated by the parties when the contract was made.[3]

Suppose that in *Example 13.4*, Ajax Contractors had asked for the extra $75,000 because it encountered a rock formation that no one knew existed. If the landowner agrees to pay the extra $75,000 to excavate the rock and the court finds that it is fair to do so, Ajax Contractors can enforce the agreement. If rock formations are common in the area, however, the court may determine that the contractor should have known of the risk. In that situation, the court may choose to apply the preexisting duty rule and prevent Ajax Contractors from obtaining the extra $75,000.

Rescission and New Contract The law recognizes that two parties can mutually agree to rescind, or cancel, their contract, at least to the extent that it is *executory* (still to be carried out). **Rescission**[4] is the unmaking of a contract so as to return the parties to the positions they occupied before the contract was made.

Sometimes, parties rescind a contract and make a new contract at the same time. When this occurs, it is often difficult to determine whether there was consideration for the new contract, or whether the parties had a preexisting duty under the previous contract. If a court finds there was a preexisting duty, then the new contract will be invalid because there was no consideration.

13–2b Past Consideration

Promises made in return for actions or events that have already taken place are unenforceable. These promises lack consideration in that the element of bargained-for exchange is missing. In short, you can bargain for something to take place now or in the future but not for something that has already taken place. Therefore, **past consideration** is no consideration.

■ **CASE IN POINT 13.5** Jamil Blackmon became friends with Allen Iverson when Iverson was a high school student who showed tremendous promise as an athlete. One evening, Blackmon suggested that Iverson use "The Answer" as a nickname in the summer league basketball tournaments. Blackmon said that Iverson would be "The Answer" to all of the National Basketball Association's woes. Later that night, Iverson said that he would give Blackmon 25 percent of any proceeds from the merchandising of products that used "The Answer" as a logo or a slogan. Because Iverson's promise was made in return for past consideration, it was unenforceable. In effect, Iverson stated his intention to give Blackmon a gift.[5] ■

In a variety of situations, an employer will often ask an employee to sign a *noncompete agreement,* also called a *covenant not to compete.* Under such an agreement, the employee agrees not to compete with the employer for a certain period of time after the employment relationship ends. When a current employee is required to sign a noncompete agreement, his or her employment is not sufficient consideration for the agreement, because the individual is already employed. To be valid, the agreement requires new consideration.

13–2c Illusory Promises

If the terms of the contract express such uncertainty of performance that the promisor has not definitely promised to do anything, the promise is said to be *illusory*—without consideration and unenforceable. A promise is illusory when it fails to bind the promisor.

■ **EXAMPLE 13.6** The president of Tuscan Corporation says to her employees, "If profits continue to be high, everyone will get a 10 percent bonus at the end of the year—if management agrees." This is an *illusory promise,* or no promise at all, because performance depends solely on the discretion of management. There is no bargained-for consideration. The statement indicates only that management may or may not do something in the future. Therefore, even though the employees work hard and profits remain high, the company is not obligated to pay the bonus now or later. ■

Option-to-Cancel Clauses Sometimes, option-to-cancel clauses in contracts present problems in regard to consideration. When the promisor has the option to cancel the contract before performance has begun, the promise is illusory.

■ **EXAMPLE 13.7** Abe contracts to hire Chris for one year at $5,000 per month, reserving the right to cancel the contract at any time. On close examination of these words, you can see that Abe has not actually agreed to hire Chris, as Abe could cancel without liability before Chris started performance. This contract is therefore illusory. ■

---

3. *Restatement (Second) of Contracts*, Section 73.
4. Pronounced reh-*sih*-zhen.

5. *Blackmon v. Iverson*, 324 F.Supp.2d 602 (E.D.Pa. 2003).

But if Abe instead reserves the right to cancel the contract at any time *after* Chris has begun performance by giving Chris *thirty days' notice,* the promise is not illusory. Abe, by saying that he will give Chris thirty days' notice, is relinquishing the opportunity (legal right) to hire someone else instead of Chris for a thirty-day period. If Chris works for one month and Abe then gives him thirty days' notice, Chris has an enforceable claim for two months' salary ($10,000). ■

Exhibit 13–2 illustrates some common situations in which promises or actions do not constitute contractual consideration.

Requirements and Output Contracts Problems with consideration may also arise in other types of contracts because of uncertainty of performance. Uncertain performance is characteristic of requirements and output contracts, for instance. In a *requirements contract,* a buyer and a seller agree that the buyer will purchase from the seller all of the goods of a designated type that the buyer needs, or requires. In an *output contract,* the buyer and seller agree that the buyer will purchase from the seller all of what the seller produces, or the seller's output. These types of contracts will be discussed further in a later chapter.

13–3 Settlement of Claims

Businesspersons and others often enter into contracts to settle legal claims. It is important to understand the nature of consideration given in these kinds of settlement agreements, or contracts. A claim may be settled through an *accord and satisfaction,* a *release,* or a *covenant not to sue.*

13–3a Accord and Satisfaction

In an **accord and satisfaction,** a debtor offers to pay, and a creditor accepts, a lesser amount than the creditor originally claimed was owed. The *accord* is the agreement. In the accord, one party undertakes to give or perform, and the other to accept, in satisfaction of a claim, something other than that on which the parties originally agreed. *Satisfaction* is the performance (usually payment) that takes place after the accord is executed.

A basic rule is that there can be no satisfaction unless there is first an accord. In addition, for accord and satisfaction to occur, the amount of the debt *must be in dispute.*

Liquidated Debts If a debt is *liquidated,* accord and satisfaction cannot take place. A **liquidated debt** is one whose amount has been ascertained, fixed, agreed on, settled, or exactly determined.

■ **EXAMPLE 13.8** Barbara Kwan signs an installment loan contract with her bank. In the contract, Kwan agrees to pay a set rate of interest on a specified amount of borrowed funds at monthly intervals for two years. Because both parties know the precise amount of the total obligation, it is a liquidated debt. ■

In the majority of states, a creditor's acceptance of a lesser sum than the entire amount of a liquidated debt is *not* satisfaction, and the balance of the debt is still legally owed. The reason for this rule is that the debtor has given no consideration to satisfy the obligation of paying the balance to the creditor. The debtor had a preexisting legal

EXHIBIT 13–2 Examples of Agreements That Lack Consideration

PREEXISTING DUTY	PAST CONSIDERATION	ILLUSORY PROMISES
When a person already has a legal duty to perform an action, there is no legally sufficient consideration.	When a person makes a promise in return for actions or events that have already taken place, there is no consideration.	When a person expresses contract terms with such uncertainty that the terms are not definite, the promise is illusory.
Example: A firefighter cannot receive a cash reward from a business owner for putting out a fire in a downtown commercial district. As a city employee, the firefighter had a duty to extinguish the fire.	*Example:* A real estate agent sold a friend's house without charging a commission, and in return, the friend promises to give the agent $1,000. The friend's promise is simply an intention to give a gift.	*Example:* A storeowner promises a $500 bonus to each employee who works Christmas Day, as long as the owner feels that they did their jobs well. The owner's promise is just a statement of something she may or may not do in the future.

obligation to pay the entire debt. (Of course, even with liquidated debts, creditors often do negotiate debt settlement agreements with debtors for a lesser amount than was originally owed. Creditors sometimes even forgive, or write off, a liquidated debt as uncollectable.)

Unliquidated Debts An **unliquidated debt** is the opposite of a liquidated debt. The amount of the debt is *not* settled, fixed, agreed on, ascertained, or determined, and reasonable persons may differ over the amount owed. In these circumstances, acceptance of a lesser sum operates as satisfaction, or discharge, of the debt because there is valid consideration. The parties give up a legal right to contest the amount in dispute.

13–3b Release

A **release** is a contract in which one party forfeits the right to pursue a legal claim against the other party. It bars any further recovery beyond the terms stated in the release.

A release will generally be binding if it meets the following requirements:

1. The agreement is made in good faith (honestly).
2. The release contract is in a signed writing (required in many states).
3. The contract is accompanied by consideration.[6]

---

6. Under the Uniform Commercial Code (UCC), a written, signed waiver or renunciation by an aggrieved party discharges any further liability for a breach, even without consideration.

Clearly, an individual is better off knowing the extent of his or her injuries or damages before signing a release. ■ **EXAMPLE 13.9** Lupe's car is damaged in an automobile accident caused by Dexter's negligence. Dexter offers to give her $3,000 if she will release him from further liability resulting from the accident. Lupe agrees and signs the release.

If Lupe later discovers that it will cost $4,200 to repair her car, she normally cannot recover the additional amount from Dexter. Lupe is limited to the $3,000 specified in the release. Lupe and Dexter voluntarily agreed to the terms in the release, which was in a signed writing, and sufficient consideration was present. The consideration was the legal right Lupe forfeited to sue to recover damages, should they be more than $3,000, in exchange for Dexter's promise to give her $3,000. ■

13–3c Covenant Not to Sue

Unlike a release, a **covenant not to sue** does not always bar further recovery. The parties simply substitute a contractual obligation for some other type of legal action based on a valid claim. Suppose that, in *Example 13.9*, Lupe agrees with Dexter not to sue for damages in a tort action if he will pay for the damage to her car. If Dexter fails to pay for the repairs, Lupe can bring an action against him for breach of contract.

As the following case illustrates, a covenant not to sue can form the basis for a dismissal of the claims of either party to the covenant.

Spotlight on Nike

Case 13.3 Already, LLC v. Nike, Inc.
Supreme Court of the United States, __ U.S. __, 133 S.Ct. 721, 184 L.Ed.2d 553 (2013).

Background and Facts Nike, Inc., designs, makes, and sells athletic footwear, including a line of shoes known as "Air Force 1." Already, LLC, also designs and markets athletic footwear, including the "Sugar" and "Soulja Boy" lines. Nike filed a suit in a federal district court against Already, alleging that Soulja Boys and Sugars infringed the Air Force 1 trademark. Already filed a counterclaim, contending that the Air Force 1 trademark was invalid. While the suit was pending, Nike issued a covenant not to sue. Nike promised not to raise any trademark claims against Already or any affiliated entity based on Already's existing footwear designs or any future Already designs that constituted a "colorable imitation" of Already's current products. Nike then filed a motion to dismiss its own claims and to dismiss Already's counterclaim. Already opposed the dismissal of its counterclaim, but the court granted Nike's motion. The U.S. Court of Appeals for the Second Circuit affirmed. Already appealed to the United States Supreme Court.

In the Language of the Court
Chief Justice *ROBERTS* delivered the opinion of the Court.
* * * *

Case 13.3 Continues

Case 13.3 Continued

* * * A defendant cannot automatically moot a case simply by ending its unlawful conduct once sued. [A matter is *moot* if it involves no actual controversy for the court to decide, and federal courts will dismiss moot cases.] Otherwise, a defendant could engage in unlawful conduct, stop when sued to have the case declared moot, then pick up where he left off, repeating this cycle until he achieves all his unlawful ends. Given this concern, * * * *a defendant claiming that its voluntary compliance moots a case bears the formidable burden of showing that it is absolutely clear the allegedly wrongful behavior could not reasonably be expected to recur.* [This is the voluntary cessation test. Emphasis added.]

* * * *

We begin our analysis with the terms of the covenant:

[Nike] unconditionally and irrevocably covenants to refrain from making *any* claim(s) or demand(s) * * * against Already or *any* of its * * * related business entities * * * [including] distributors * * * and employees of such entities and *all* customers * * * on account of any *possible* cause of action based on or involving trademark infringement * * * relating to the NIKE Mark based on the appearance of *any* of Already's current and/or previous footwear product designs, and *any* colorable imitations thereof, regardless of whether that footwear is produced * * * or otherwise used in commerce.

The breadth of this covenant suffices to meet the burden imposed by the voluntary cessation test.

In addition, Nike originally argued that the Sugars and Soulja Boys infringed its trademark; in other words, Nike believed those shoes were "colorable imitations" of the Air Force 1s. Nike's covenant now allows Already to produce all of its existing footwear designs—including the Sugar and Soulja Boy—and any "colorable imitation" of those designs. * * * It is hard to imagine a scenario that would potentially infringe Nike's trademark and yet not fall under the covenant. Nike, having taken the position in court that there is no prospect of such a shoe, would be hard pressed to assert the contrary down the road. If such a shoe exists, the parties have not pointed to it, there is no evidence that Already has dreamt of it, and we cannot conceive of it. It sits, as far as we can tell, on a shelf between Dorothy's ruby slippers and Perseus's winged sandals.

* * * *

* * * Given the covenant's broad language, and given that Already has asserted no concrete plans to engage in conduct not covered by the covenant, we can conclude the case is moot because the challenged conduct cannot reasonably be expected to recur.

Decision and Remedy *The United States Supreme Court affirmed the judgment of the lower court. Under the covenant not to sue, Nike could not file a claim for trademark infringement against Already, and Already could not assert that Nike's trademark was invalid.*

Critical Thinking
- **Economic** *Why would any party agree to a covenant not to sue?*
- **Legal Environment** *Which types of contracts are similar to covenants not to sue? Explain.*

See Concept Summary 13.2 to review the methods of settling claims.

13–4 Exceptions to the Consideration Requirement

There are some exceptions to the rule that only promises supported by consideration are enforceable. The following types of promises may be enforced despite the lack of consideration:

1. Promises that induce detrimental reliance, under the doctrine of *promissory estoppel*.
2. Promises to pay debts that are barred by a statute of limitations.
3. Promises to make charitable contributions.

13–4a Promissory Estoppel

Sometimes, individuals rely on promises to their detriment, and their reliance may form a basis for a court to infer contract rights and duties. Under the doctrine of **promissory estoppel** (also called *detrimental reliance*), a person who

Concept Summary 13.2

Settlement of Claims

Accord and Satisfaction	An *accord* is an agreement in which a debtor offers to pay a lesser amount than the creditor claims is owed. *Satisfaction* takes place when the accord is executed.
Release	An agreement in which, for consideration, a party forfeits the right to seek further recovery beyond the terms specified in the release.
Covenant Not to Sue	An agreement not to sue on a present, valid claim.

has reasonably and substantially relied on the promise of another may be able to obtain some measure of recovery.

Promissory estoppel is applied in a wide variety of contexts in which a promise is otherwise unenforceable, such as when a promise is made *without consideration*. Under this doctrine, a court may enforce an otherwise unenforceable promise to avoid the injustice that would otherwise result.

Requirements to Establish Promissory Estoppel For the promissory estoppel doctrine to be applied, the following elements are required:

1. There must be a clear and definite promise.
2. The promisor should have expected that the promisee would rely on the promise.
3. The promisee reasonably relied on the promise by acting or refraining from some act.
4. The promisee's reliance was definite and resulted in substantial detriment.
5. Enforcement of the promise is necessary to avoid injustice.

If these requirements are met, a promise may be enforced even though it is not supported by consideration.[7] In essence, the promisor will be **estopped** (prevented) from asserting the lack of consideration as a defense.

Promissory estoppel is similar in some ways to the doctrine of quasi contract. In both situations, a court, acting in the interests of equity, imposes contract obligations on the parties to prevent unfairness even though no actual contract exists. The difference is that with

quasi contract, no promise was made at all. In contrast, with promissory estoppel, an unenforceable promise was made and relied on but not performed.

Application of the Doctrine Promissory estoppel was originally applied to situations involving promises of gifts and of donations to charities. Later, courts began to apply the doctrine to avoid inequity or hardship in other situations, including business transactions, some employment relationships, and even disputes among family members.

■ **CASE IN POINT 13.10** Jeffrey and Kathryn Dow owned 125 acres of land in Corinth, Maine. The Dows regarded the land as their children's heritage, and the subject of the children's living on the land was often discussed within the family. With the Dows' permission, their daughter Teresa installed a mobile home and built a garage on the land. After Teresa married Jarrod Harvey, the Dows agreed to finance the construction of a house on the land for the couple. When Jarrod died in a motorcycle accident, however, Teresa financed the house with his life insurance proceeds. The construction cost about $200,000. Her father, Jeffrey, performed a substantial amount of carpentry and other work on the house.

Teresa then asked her parents for a deed to the property so that she could obtain a mortgage. They refused. Teresa sued her parents for promissory estoppel. Maine's highest court ruled in favor of Teresa's promissory estoppel claim. The court reasoned that the Dows' support and encouragement of their daughter's construction of a house on the land "conclusively demonstrated" their intent to transfer. For years, they had made general promises to convey the land to their children, including Teresa.

---

7. *Restatement (Second) of Contracts*, Section 90.

Teresa had reasonably relied on their promise in financing construction of a house to her detriment ($200,000). The court concluded that enforcing the promise was the only way to avoid injustice in this situation.[8] ■

13–4b Promises to Pay Debts Barred by a Statute of Limitations

Statutes of limitations in all states require a creditor to sue within a specified period to recover a debt. If the creditor fails to sue in time, recovery of the debt is barred by the statute of limitations.

A debtor who promises to pay a previous debt even though recovery is barred by the statute of limitations makes an enforceable promise. *The promise needs no consideration.* (Some states, however, require that it be in writing.) In effect, the promise extends the limitations period, and the creditor can sue to recover the entire debt or at least the amount promised. The promise can be implied if the debtor acknowledges the barred debt by making a partial payment.

---

8. *Harvey v. Dow*, 2011 ME 4, 11 A.3d 303 (2011).

13–4c Charitable Subscriptions

A charitable subscription is a promise to make a donation to a religious, educational, or charitable institution. Traditionally, such promises were unenforceable because they are not supported by legally sufficient consideration. A gift, after all, is the opposite of bargained-for consideration. The modern view, however, is to make exceptions to the general rule by applying the doctrine of promissory estoppel.

■ **EXAMPLE 13.11** A church solicits and receives pledges (commitments to contribute funds) from church members to erect a new church building. On the basis of these pledges, the church purchases land, hires architects, and makes other contracts that change its position. Because of the church's detrimental reliance, a court may enforce the pledges under the theory of promissory estoppel. Alternatively, a court may find consideration in the fact that each promise was made in reliance on the other promises of support or that the church trustees, by accepting the subscriptions, impliedly promised to complete the proposed undertaking. ■

Reviewing: Consideration

John operates a motorcycle repair shop from his home but finds that his business is limited by the small size of his garage. Driving by a neighbor's property, he notices a for-sale sign on a large, metal-sided garage. John contacts the neighbor and offers to buy the building, hoping that it can be dismantled and moved to his own property.

The neighbor accepts John's payment and makes a generous offer in return. If John will help him dismantle the garage, which will take a substantial amount of time, he will help John reassemble it after it has been transported to John's property. They agree to have the entire job completed within two weeks.

John spends every day for a week working with his neighbor to disassemble the building. In his rush to acquire a larger workspace, he turns down several lucrative repair jobs. Once the disassembled building has been moved to John's property, however, the neighbor refuses to help John reassemble it as he originally promised. Using the information presented in the chapter, answer the following questions.

1. Are the basic elements of consideration present in the neighbor's promise to help John reassemble the garage? Why or why not?
2. Suppose that the neighbor starts to help John but then realizes that putting the building back together will take much more work than dismantling it. Under which principle discussed in the chapter might the neighbor be allowed to ask for additional compensation?
3. What if John's neighbor made his promise to help reassemble the garage at the time he and John were moving it? Suppose he said, "Since you helped me take it down, I will help you put it back up." Would John be able to enforce this promise? Why or why not?
4. Under what doctrine discussed in the chapter might John seek to recover the profits he lost when he turned down repair jobs for one week?

Debate This . . . *Courts should not be able to rule on the adequacy of consideration. A deal is a deal.*

Terms and Concepts

accord and satisfaction 256	forbearance 250	release 257
consideration 250	liquidated debt 256	rescission 255
covenant not to sue 257	past consideration 255	unliquidated debt 257
estopped 259	promissory estoppel 258	

Issue Spotters

1. In September, Sharyn agrees to work for Totem Productions, Inc., at $500 a week for a year beginning January 1. In October, Sharyn is offered the same work at $600 a week by Umber Shows, Ltd. When Sharyn tells Totem about the other offer, a Totem representative tears up their contract and agrees that Sharyn will be paid $575. Is the new contract binding? Explain. (See *Agreements That Lack Consideration*.)

2. Before Maria starts her first year of college, Fred promises to give her $5,000 when she graduates. She goes to college, borrowing and spending far more than $5,000. At the beginning of the spring semester of her senior year, she reminds Fred of the promise. Fred sends her a note that says, "I revoke the promise." Is Fred's promise binding? Explain. (See *Exceptions to the Consideration Requirement*.)

• **Check your answers to the Issue Spotters against the answers provided in Appendix D at the end of this text.**

Business Scenarios

13–1. Preexisting Duty. Tabor is a buyer of file cabinets manufactured by Martin. Martin's contract with Tabor calls for delivery of fifty file cabinets at $40 per cabinet in five equal installments. After delivery of two installments (twenty cabinets), Martin informs Tabor that because of inflation, Martin is losing money. Martin will promise to deliver the remaining thirty cabinets only if Tabor will pay $50 per cabinet. Tabor agrees in writing to do so. Discuss whether Martin can legally collect the additional $100 on delivery to Tabor of the next installment of ten cabinets. (See *Agreements That Lack Consideration*.)

13–2. Consideration. Daniel, a recent college graduate, is on his way home for the Christmas holidays from his new job. He is caught in a snowstorm and is taken in by an elderly couple, who provide him with food and shelter. After the snowplows have cleared the road, Daniel proceeds home. Daniel's father, Fred, is most appreciative of the elderly couple's action and promises to pay them $500. The elderly couple, in need of funds, accept Fred's offer. Then, because of a dispute between Daniel and Fred, Fred refuses to pay the elderly couple the $500. Discuss whether the couple can hold Fred liable in contract for the services rendered to Daniel. (See *Agreements That Lack Consideration*.)

13–3. Accord and Satisfaction. Merrick grows and sells blueberries. Maine Wild Blueberry Co. agreed to buy all of Merrick's crop under a contract that left the price unliquidated. Merrick delivered the berries, but a dispute arose over the price. Maine Wild sent Merrick a check with a letter stating that the check was the "final settlement." Merrick cashed the check but filed a suit for breach of contract, claiming that he was owed more. What will the court likely decide in this case? Why? (See *Settlement of Claims*.)

Business Case Problems

13–4. Rescission. Farrokh and Scheherezade Sharabianlou signed a purchase agreement to buy a building owned by Berenstein Associates for $2 million. They deposited $115,000 toward the purchase. Before the deal closed, an environmental assessment of the property indicated the presence of chemicals used in dry cleaning. This substantially reduced the property's value. Do the Sharabianlous have a good argument for the return of their deposit and rescission of the contract Explain your answer. [*Sharabianlou v. Karp*, 181 Cal.App.4th 1133, 105 Cal.Rptr.3d 300 (1st Dist. 2010)] (See *Agreements That Lack Consideration*.)

13–5. Statute of Limitations. Leonard Kranzler loaned Lewis Saltzman $100,000. Saltzman made fifteen payments on the loan, but this did not repay the entire amount. More than ten years after the date of the loan, but less than two years after the date of the last payment, Kranzler filed a suit against Saltzman to recover the outstanding balance. Saltzman claimed that the suit was barred by a ten-year statute of limitations. Does Kranzler need to prove a new promise with new consideration to collect the unpaid debt? Explain. [*Kranzler v. Saltzman*, 407 Ill.App.3d 24, 942 N.E.2d 722, 347 Ill.Dec. 519 (1 Dist. 2011)] (See *Exceptions to the Consideration Requirement*.)

13–6. Spotlight on Kansas City Chiefs—Consideration. On Brenda Sniezek's first day of work for the Kansas

City Chiefs Football Club, she signed a document that purported to compel arbitration of any disputes that she might have with the Chiefs. In the document, Sniezek agreed to comply at all times with and be bound by the constitution and bylaws of the National Football League (NFL). She agreed to refer all disputes to the NFL Commissioner for a binding decision. On the Commissioner's decision, she agreed to release the Chiefs and others from any related claims. Nowhere in the document did the Chiefs agree to do anything. Was there consideration for the arbitration provision? Explain. [*Sniezek v. Kansas City Chiefs Football Club,* 402 S.W.3d 580 (Mo.App. W.D. 2013)] (See *Elements of Consideration.*)

13–7. Business Case Problem with Sample Answer—Consideration. Citynet, LLC, established an employee

incentive plan "to enable the Company to attract and retain experienced individuals." The plan provided that a participant who left Citynet's employment was entitled to "cash out" his or her entire vested balance. (When an employee's rights to a particular benefit become *vested,* they belong to that employee and cannot be taken away. The vested balance refers to the part of an account that goes with the employee if he or she leaves the company.) When Citynet employee Ray Toney terminated his employment, he asked to redeem his vested balance, which amounted to $87,000.48. Citynet refused, citing a provision of the plan that limited redemptions to no more than 20 percent annually. Toney filed a suit in a West Virginia state court against Citynet, alleging breach of contract. Citynet argued that the plan was not a contract but a discretionary bonus over which Citynet had sole discretion. Was the plan a contract? If so, what was the consideration? [*Citynet, LLC v. Toney,* 235 W.Va. 79, 772 S.E.2d 36 (2015)] (See *Elements of Consideration.*)

- For a sample answer to Problem 13–7, go to Appendix E at the end of this text.

13–8. Agreements That Lack Consideration. Arkansas-Missouri Forest Products, LLC (Ark-Mo), sells supplies to make wood pallets. Blue Chip Manufacturing (BCM) makes pallets. Mark Garnett, an owner of Ark-Mo, and Stuart Lerner, an owner of BCM, went into business together. Garnett and Lerner agreed that Ark-Mo would have a 30-percent ownership interest in their future projects. When Lerner formed Blue Chip Recycling, LLC (BCR), to manage a pallet repair facility in California, however, he allocated only a 5-percent interest to Ark-Mo. Garnett objected. In a "Telephone Deal," Lerner then promised Garnett that Ark-Mo would receive a 30-percent interest in their future projects in the Midwest, and Garnett agreed to forgo an ownership interest in BCR. But when Blue Chip III, LLC (BC III), was formed to operate a repair facility in the Midwest, Lerner told Garnett that he "was not getting anything." Ark-Mo filed a suit in a Missouri state court against Lerner, alleging breach of contract. Was there consideration to support the Telephone Deal? Explain. [*Arkansas-Missouri Forest Products, LLC v. Lerner,* ___ S.W.3d ___, 2016 WL 234889 (Mo.App. E.D. 2016)] (See *Agreements That Lack Consideration.*)

13–9. A Question of Ethics—Promissory Estoppel.

Claudia Aceves borrowed from U.S. Bank to buy a home. Two years later, she could no longer afford the monthly payments. The bank notified her that it planned to foreclose on her home. (Foreclosure is a process that allows a lender to repossess and sell the property that secures a loan.) *Aceves filed for bankruptcy. The bank offered to modify Aceves's mortgage if she would forgo bankruptcy. She agreed. Once she withdrew the filing, however, the bank foreclosed.* [Aceves v. U.S. Bank, N.A., *192 Cal.App.4th 218, 120 Cal.Rptr.3d 507 (2 Dist. 2011)]* (See *Exceptions to the Consideration Requirement.*)

(a) Could Aceves succeed on a claim of promissory estoppel? Why or why not?

(b) Did Aceves or U.S. Bank behave unethically? Discuss.

Legal Reasoning Group Activity

13–10. Preexisting Duty. Melissa Faraj owns a lot and wants to build a house according to a particular set of plans and specifications. She solicits bids from building contractors and receives three bids: one from Carlton for $160,000, one from Feldberg for $158,000, and one from Siegel for $153,000. She accepts Siegel's bid. One month after beginning construction of the house, Siegel contacts Faraj and tells her that because of inflation and a recent price hike for materials, his costs have gone up. He says he will not finish the house unless Faraj agrees to pay an extra $13,000. Faraj reluctantly agrees to pay the additional sum. (See *Agreements That Lack Consideration.*)

(a) One group will discuss whether a contractor can ever raise the price of completing construction because of inflation and the rising cost of materials.

(b) A second group will assume that after the house is finished, Faraj refuses to pay the extra $13,000. The group will decide whether Faraj is legally required to pay this additional amount.

(c) A third group will discuss the types of extraordinary difficulties that could arise during construction that would justify a contractor's charging more than the original bid.

Answers to the *Issue Spotters*

1. *Is the new contract binding? Explain.* Yes. The original contract was executory. The parties rescinded it and agreed to a new contract. If Sharyn had broken the contract to accept a contract with another employer, she might have been held liable for damages for the breach.

2. *Is Fred's promise binding? Explain.* Yes. Under the doctrine of detrimental reliance, or promissory estoppel, the promisee is entitled to payment of $5,000 from the promisor on graduation. There was a promise, on which the promisee relied, the reliance was substantial and definite (the promisee went to college for the full term, incurring considerable expenses, and will likely graduate), and it would only be fair to enforce the promise.

Sample Answers for *Business Case Problems with Sample Answer*

Problem 13–7. *Consideration.* Citynet's employee incentive plan was an offer for a unilateral contract. A Citynet employee who stayed on the job when he or she was under no obligation to do so could be considered to have accepted Citynet's offer and to have provided sufficient consideration to make the offer a binding and enforceable promise. Consideration has two elements—it must consist of something of legal value and must provide the basis for the bargain between the parties. A unilateral contract involves a promise in return for performance. The promisor becomes bound to the contract when the promisee performs—or, in many cases, begins to perform—the act. Both the promise and the performance have legal value.

Here, Citynet set up an employee incentive plan "to attract and retain experienced individuals." The plan provided that a participant who left Citynet's employ could "cash out" his or her entire vested balance. When Ray Toney terminated his employment and asked to redeem his vested balance, however, Citynet refused. But Toney had long stayed on the job when he did not have to. This was sufficient consideration to make Citynet's offer under the incentive plan a binding and enforceable contract with Toney.

In the actual case on which this problem is based, a West Virginia state court issued a judgment in Toney's favor. The West Virginia Supreme Court of Appeals affirmed, on the reasoning and principles stated above.

CHAPTER

Capacity and Legality

The first two requirements for a valid contract are agreement and consideration. This chapter examines the third and fourth requirements—*contractual capacity* and *legality*. The parties to the contract must have **contractual capacity**—the legal ability to enter into a contractual relationship. Courts generally presume the existence of contractual capacity, but in some situations, as when a person is very young or mentally incompetent, capacity may be lacking or questionable. Similarly, contracts calling for the performance of an illegal act are illegal and thus void—they are not contracts at all.

14–1 Contractual Capacity

Historically, the law has given special protection to those who bargain with the inexperience of youth and those who lack the degree of mental competence required by law. A person who has been determined by a court to be mentally incompetent, for instance, cannot form a legally binding contract with another party. In other situations, a party may have the capacity to enter into a valid contract but also have the right to avoid liability under it. Minors—or *infants,* as they are commonly referred to in legal terminology—usually are not legally bound by contracts. In this section, we look at the effect of youth, intoxication, and mental incompetence on contractual capacity.

14–1a Minors

Today, in almost all states, the **age of majority** (when a person is no longer a minor) for contractual purposes is eighteen years.[1] In addition, some states provide for the termination of minority on marriage.

Minority status may also be terminated by a minor's **emancipation,** which occurs when a child's parent or legal guardian relinquishes the legal right to exercise control over the child. Normally, minors who leave home to support themselves are considered emancipated. Several jurisdictions permit minors themselves to petition a court for emancipation. For business purposes, a minor may petition a court to be treated as an adult.

The general rule is that a minor can enter into any contract that an adult can, except contracts prohibited by law for minors (such as contracts to purchase tobacco or alcoholic beverages). A contract entered into by a minor, however, is voidable at the option of that minor, subject to certain exceptions. To exercise the option to avoid a contract, a minor need only manifest (clearly show) an intention not to be bound by it. The minor "avoids" the contract by disaffirming it.

Disaffirmance The legal avoidance, or setting aside, of a contractual obligation is referred to as **disaffirmance.** To disaffirm, a minor must express his or her intent, through words or conduct, not to be bound to the contract. The minor must disaffirm the entire contract, not merely a portion of it. For instance, the minor cannot decide to keep part of the goods purchased under a contract and return the remaining goods.

■ **CASE IN POINT 14.1** Fifteen-year-old Morgan Kelly was a cadet in her high school's Navy Junior Reserve Officer Training Corps. As part of the program, she visited a U.S. Marine Corps training facility. To enter the camp, she was required to sign a waiver that exempted the Marines from all liability for any injuries arising from her visit.

While participating in activities on the camp's confidence-building course, Kelly fell from the "Slide for Life" and suffered serious injuries. She filed a suit to recover her medical costs. The Marines asserted that she had signed their waiver of liability. Kelly claimed that she had disaffirmed the waiver when she filed suit. The court ruled in Kelly's favor. Liability waivers are generally

---

1. The age of majority may still be twenty-one for other purposes, such as the purchase and consumption of alcohol.

enforceable contracts, but a minor can avoid a contract by disaffirming it.[2] ∎

Note that an adult who enters into a contract with a minor cannot avoid his or her contractual duties on the ground that the minor can do so. Unless the minor exercises the option to disaffirm the contract, the adult party normally is bound by it. On disaffirming a contract, a minor normally can recover any property that he or she transferred to the adult as consideration, even if the property is in the possession of a third party.[3]

The question in the following case was whether a minor had effectively disaffirmed an agreement to arbitrate with her employer.

---

2. *Kelly v. United States*, 809 F.Supp.2d 429 (E.D.N.C. 2011).

---

3. Section 2–403(1) of the Uniform Commercial Code (UCC) allows an exception if the third party is a "good faith purchaser for value."

Case 14.1

PAK Foods Houston, LLC v. Garcia

Court of Appeals of Texas, Houston (14th District), 433 S.W.3d 171 (2014).

Background and Facts S.L., a female sixteen-year-old minor, worked at a KFC Restaurant operated by PAK Foods Houston, LLC. PAK Foods' policy was to resolve any dispute with an employee through arbitration. At the employer's request, S.L. signed an acknowledgment of this policy. S.L. was injured on the job and subsequently terminated her employment. S.L.'s mother, Marissa Garcia, filed a suit on S.L.'s behalf in a Texas state court against PAK Foods to recover the medical expenses for the injury. PAK Foods filed a motion to compel arbitration. The court denied the motion. "To the extent any agreement to arbitrate existed between S.L. and PAK Foods Houston, LLC, S.L. voided such agreement by filing this suit." PAK Foods appealed.

In the Language of the Court
Martha Hill *JAMISON,* Justice.
* * * *

* * * It is undisputed S.L. was a 16-year-old minor when the arbitration agreement was executed and she remained a minor during her employment by PAK Foods, including at the time of her injury. In Texas, the age of majority is 18 years.

*It has long been the law in Texas that a contract executed by a minor is not void, but it is voidable by the minor. * * * [A minor's contracts] may be either disaffirmed by the minor or ratified after the minor reaches majority. This means that the minor may set aside the entire contract at her option.* [Emphasis added.]

Appellees assert that S.L. elected to void any agreement to arbitrate by filing the underlying suit.
* * * *

PAK Foods argues that * * * S.L. was an at-will employee and did not execute an employment contract. PAK Foods also notes that S.L. did not notify PAK Foods prior to filing suit that she was voiding the arbitration agreement. These distinctions do not alter the settled law that a minor may void a contract at her election. The arbitration agreement is a contract with a minor, S.L., who had the option to disaffirm the contract.

While appellees assert that S.L. voided the agreement by filing suit, the mere filing of suit may not necessarily disaffirm an arbitration agreement. A party may file suit but later determine arbitration is appropriate. Here, appellees' original petition does not expressly disaffirm an agreement to arbitrate; the petition is silent about arbitration. However, appellees' response filed in opposition to the motion to compel arbitration is a definitive disaffirmance of any agreement to arbitrate. The response states in relevant part:

> S.L. was a minor at the time of her employment. * * * Contracts such as this Arbitration Agreement are voidable at her instance, and may be disaffirmed or repudiated by her or her guardian, * * * . Thus as S.L.'s disaffirmance of the Arbitration agreement has manifestly occurred with her termination of employment and election to file suit, she cannot be bound by the terms of the Arbitration Agreement.

S.L. was still a minor when she objected to arbitration and elected to void the contract. The record contains sufficient evidence of her election to support the trial court's fact finding. The trial court also did not abuse its discretion in concluding as a matter of law that S.L.'s action voided the contract.

Case 14.1 Continued **Decision and Remedy** *A state intermediate appellate court affirmed the decision of the lower court. A minor may disaffirm a contract at his or her option. S.L. opted to disaffirm the agreement to arbitrate by terminating her employment and filing the lawsuit.*

Critical Thinking
- **Legal Environment** *Could PAK Foods successfully contend that S.L.'s minority does not bar enforcement of the arbitration agreement because medical expenses are necessaries[a]? Discuss.*
- **Ethical** *Is it fair that a minor can work for an employer yet not be bound by a contract with the employer? Why or why not?*

a. *Necessaries* are basic needs, such as food, clothing, shelter, and medical services. As you will read shortly, minors can disaffirm contracts for necessaries but remain liable for the value of goods or services.

Disaffirmance within a Reasonable Time. A contract can ordinarily be disaffirmed at any time during minority or for a reasonable period after the minor reaches the age of majority.[4] What constitutes a "reasonable" time may vary, depending on the jurisdiction and to what extent the contract has been performed.

Minors' Obligations on Disaffirmance. Although all states' laws permit minors to disaffirm contracts, states differ on the extent of a minor's obligations on disaffirmance. Courts in most states hold that the minor need only return the goods (or other consideration) subject to the contract, provided the goods are in the minor's possession or control. Even if the minor returns damaged goods, the minor often is entitled to disaffirm the contract and obtain a full refund of the purchase price.

A growing number of states place an additional duty of restitution on the minor to restore the adult party to the position she or he held before the contract was made. These courts may hold a minor responsible for damage, ordinary wear and tear, and depreciation of goods that the minor used prior to disaffirmance.

■ **EXAMPLE 14.2** Sixteen-year-old Paul Dodson buys a pickup truck from a used-car dealer. The truck develops mechanical problems nine months later, but Dodson continues to drive it until it stops running. Then Dodson disaffirms the contract and attempts to return the truck to the dealer for a full refund. Dodson lives in a state that imposes a duty of restitution on minors. Therefore, he can disaffirm the contract but will not be entitled to a full refund of the purchase price. Dodson can only recover the fair market value of the truck in its current condition. ■

4. In some states, a minor who enters into a contract for the sale of land cannot disaffirm the contract until she or he reaches the age of majority.

Exceptions to a Minor's Right to Disaffirm State courts and legislatures have carved out several exceptions to the minor's right to disaffirm. For public-policy reasons, some contracts, such as marriage contracts and contracts to enlist in the armed services, cannot be avoided.

In addition, although ordinarily minors can disaffirm contracts even when they have misrepresented their age, a growing number of states have enacted laws to prohibit disaffirmance in such situations. Other states prohibit disaffirmance by minors who misrepresented their age while engaged in business as an adult.

Finally, a minor who enters into a contract for necessaries may disaffirm the contract but remains liable for the reasonable value of the goods. **Necessaries** are basic needs, such as food, clothing, shelter, and medical services. What is a necessary for one minor, however, may be a luxury for another, depending on the minors' customary living standard. Contracts for necessaries are enforceable only to the level of value needed to maintain the minor's standard of living.

Ratification In contract law, **ratification** is the act of accepting and giving legal force to an obligation that previously was not enforceable. A minor who has reached the age of majority can ratify a contract expressly or impliedly.

Express ratification takes place when the individual, on reaching the age of majority, states orally or in writing that he or she intends to be bound by the contract. *Implied* ratification takes place when the minor, on reaching the age of majority, indicates an intent to abide by the contract.

■ **EXAMPLE 14.3** Lin enters into a contract to sell her laptop to Andrew, a minor. If, on reaching the age of majority, Andrew e-mails Lin stating that he still agrees to buy the laptop, he has *expressly* ratified the contract. If, instead, Andrew takes possession of the laptop as a minor and continues to use it well after reaching the age of majority, he has *impliedly* ratified the contract. ∎

If a minor fails to disaffirm a contract within a reasonable time after reaching the age of majority, then the court must determine whether the conduct constitutes ratification or disaffirmance. Typically, courts presume that executed contracts (fully performed contracts) are ratified and that executory contracts (contracts not yet fully performed by both parties) are disaffirmed.

Parents' Liability As a general rule, parents are not liable for contracts made by minor children acting on their own, except contracts for necessaries, which parents are legally required to provide. As a consequence, businesses ordinarily require parents to cosign any contract made with a minor. The parents then become personally obligated under the contract to perform the conditions of the contract, even if their child avoids liability.

Concept Summary 14.1 reviews the rules relating to contracts by minors.

14–1b Intoxication

Intoxication is a condition in which a person's normal capacity to act or think is inhibited by alcohol or some other drug. A contract entered into by an intoxicated person can be either voidable or valid (and thus enforceable).

If the person was sufficiently intoxicated to lack mental capacity, then the agreement may be voidable even if the intoxication was purely voluntary. If, despite intoxication, the person understood the legal consequences of the agreement, the contract will be enforceable.

Courts look at objective indications of the intoxicated person's condition to determine if he or she possessed or lacked the required capacity. It is difficult to prove that a person's judgment was so severely impaired that he or she could not comprehend the legal consequences of entering into a contract. Therefore, courts rarely permit contracts to be avoided due to intoxication.

Disaffirmance If a contract is voidable because one party was intoxicated, that person has the option of disaffirming it while intoxicated and for a reasonable time after becoming sober. The person claiming intoxication typically must be able to return all consideration received unless the contract involved necessaries. Contracts for necessaries are voidable, but the intoxicated person is liable in quasi contract for the reasonable value of the consideration received.

Ratification An intoxicated person, after becoming sober, may ratify a contract expressly or impliedly, just as a minor may do on reaching majority. Implied ratification occurs when a person enters into a contract while intoxicated and fails to disaffirm the contract within a *reasonable*

Concept Summary 14.1

Contracts by Minors

The General Rule	• Contracts entered into by minors are *voidable* at the option of the minor.
Rules of Disaffirmance	• A minor may disaffirm the contract at any time while still a minor and within a reasonable time after reaching the age of majority. • Most states do not require restitution.
Exceptions to Basic Rules of Disaffirmance	• *Misrepresentation of age (or fraud)*—In many jurisdictions, misrepresentation of age prohibits the right of disaffirmance. • *Necessaries*—Minors remain liable for the reasonable value of necessaries (goods and services). • *Ratification*—After reaching the age of majority, a person can ratify a contract that he or she formed as a minor, thereby becoming fully liable for it.

Concept Summary 14.2

Contracts by Intoxicated Persons

The General Rules	• If a person was sufficiently intoxicated to lack the mental capacity to comprehend the legal consequences of entering into the contract, the contract may be *voidable* at the option of the intoxicated person. • If, despite intoxication, the person understood these legal consequences, the contract will be enforceable.
Rules of Disaffirmance	• An intoxicated person may disaffirm the contract at any time while intoxicated and for a reasonable time after becoming sober but must make full restitution. • Contracts for necessaries are voidable, but the intoxicated person is liable for the reasonable value of the goods or services.
Ratification	• After becoming sober, a person can ratify a contract that she or he formed while intoxicated, thereby becoming fully liable for it.

time after becoming sober. Acts or conduct inconsistent with an intent to disaffirm—such as the continued use of property purchased under a voidable contract—will also ratify the contract.

See Concept Summary 14.2 for a review of the rules relating to contracts by intoxicated persons.

14–1c Mental Incompetence

Contracts made by mentally incompetent persons can be void, voidable, or valid. We look here at the circumstances that determine when each of these classifications applies.

When the Contract Will Be Void If a court has previously determined that a person is mentally incompetent, any contract made by that person is void—no contract exists. On determining that someone is mentally incompetent, the court appoints a guardian to represent the individual. Only the guardian can enter into binding legal obligations on behalf of the mentally incompetent person.

When the Contract Will Be Voidable If a court has not previously judged a person to be mentally incompetent but the person was incompetent at the time the contract was formed, the contract may be voidable. The

contract is voidable if the person did not know he or she was entering into the contract or lacked the mental capacity to comprehend its nature, purpose, and consequences. In such situations, the contract is voidable (or can be ratified) at the option of the mentally incompetent person but not at the option of the other party.

■ **EXAMPLE 14.4** Larry agrees to sell his stock in Google, Inc., to Sergey for substantially less than its market value. At the time of the deal, Larry is confused about the purpose and details of the transaction, but he has not been declared incompetent. Nonetheless, if a court finds that Larry did not understand the nature and consequences of the contract due to a lack of mental capacity, he can avoid the sale. ■

When the Contract Will Be Valid A contract entered into by a mentally ill person (not previously declared incompetent) may be valid if the person had capacity *at the time the contract was formed*. Some people who are incompetent due to age or illness have *lucid intervals*—periods during which their intelligence, judgment, and will are temporarily restored. During such intervals, they will be considered to have legal capacity to enter into contracts.

See Concept Summary 14.3 for a review of the rules relating to contracts entered into by mentally incompetent persons.

Concept Summary 14.3

Contracts by Mentally Incompetent Persons

When the Contract Will Be Void	If a court has declared a person to be mentally incompetent and has appointed a legal guardian, any contract made by that person is void from the outset.
When the Contract Will Be Voidable	If a court has *not* declared a person mentally incompetent, but that person lacked the capacity to comprehend the subject matter, nature, and consequences of the agreement, then the contract is voidable at that person's option.
When the Contract Will Be Valid	If a court has *not* declared a person mentally incompetent and that person was able to understand the nature and effect of the contract at the time it was formed, then the contract is valid and enforceable.

14–2 Legality

For a contract to be valid and enforceable, it must be formed for a legal purpose. A contract to do something that is prohibited by federal or state statutory law is illegal and, as such, void from the outset and thus unenforceable. Additionally, a contract to commit a tortious act (such as an agreement to engage in defamation or fraud) is contrary to public policy and therefore illegal and unenforceable.

14–2a Contracts Contrary to Statute

Statutes often set forth rules specifying what may be included in contracts and what is prohibited. We now examine several ways in which contracts may be contrary to statute and thus illegal.

Contracts to Commit a Crime Any contract to commit a crime is in violation of a statute. Thus, a contract to sell illegal drugs in violation of criminal laws is unenforceable, as is a contract to hide a corporation's violation of securities laws or environmental regulations.

Sometimes, the object or performance of a contract is rendered illegal by a statute *after* the parties entered into the contract. In that situation, the contract is considered to be discharged (terminated) by law.

Usury Almost every state has a statute that sets the maximum rate of interest that can be charged for different types of transactions, including ordinary loans. A lender who makes a loan at an interest rate above the lawful maximum commits **usury.**

Although usurious contracts are illegal, most states simply limit the interest that the lender may collect on the contract to the lawful maximum interest rate in that state. In a few states, the lender can recover the principal amount of the loan but no interest. In addition, states can make exceptions to facilitate business transactions. For instance, many states exempt corporate loans from the usury laws, and nearly all states allow higher-interest-rate loans for borrowers who could not otherwise obtain loans.

Gambling Gambling is the creation of risk for the purpose of assuming it. Any scheme that involves the distribution of property by chance among persons who have paid valuable consideration for the opportunity (chance) to receive the property is gambling.

Traditionally, the states deemed gambling contracts illegal and thus void. Today, many states allow (and regulate) certain forms of gambling, such as horse racing, video poker machines, and charity-sponsored bingo. In addition, nearly all states allow state-operated lotteries and gambling on Native American reservations. Even in states that permit certain types of gambling, though, courts often find that gambling contracts are illegal.

■ **CASE IN POINT 14.5** Video poker machines are legal in Louisiana, but their use requires the approval of the state video gaming commission. Gaming Venture, Inc., did not obtain this approval before agreeing with

Tastee Restaurant Corporation to install poker machines in some of its restaurants. For this reason, when Tastee allegedly reneged on the deal by refusing to install the machines, a state court held that their agreement was an illegal gambling contract and therefore void.[5] ■

Licensing Statutes All states require members of certain professions—including physicians, lawyers, real estate brokers, accountants, architects, electricians, and stockbrokers—to have licenses. Some licenses are obtained only after extensive schooling and examinations, which indicate to the public that a special skill has been acquired. Others require only that the applicant be of good moral character and pay a fee.

Whether a contract with an unlicensed person is legal and enforceable depends on the purpose of the licensing statute. If the statute's purpose is to protect the public from unauthorized practitioners (such as unlicensed attorneys and electricians), then a contract involving an unlicensed practitioner is generally illegal and unenforceable. If the statute's purpose is merely to raise government revenues, however, a court may enforce the contract and fine the unlicensed person.

---

5. *Gaming Venture, Inc. v. Tastee Restaurant Corp.*, 996 So.2d 515 (La.App. 5 Cir. 2008).

■ **CASE IN POINT 14.6** The United Arab Emirates (UAE) held a competition for the design of a new embassy in Washington, D.C. Elena Sturdza—an architect licensed in Maryland but not in the District of Columbia—won. Sturdza and the UAE exchanged proposals, but the UAE stopped communicating with her before the parties had signed a contract. Later, Sturdza learned that the UAE had contracted with a District of Columbia architect to use another design. She filed a suit against the UAE for breach of contract.

Sturdza argued that the licensing statute should not apply to architects who submit plans in international architectural design competitions. The court held, however, that licensing requirements are necessary to ensure the safety of those who work in and visit buildings in the District of Columbia, as well as the safety of neighboring buildings. Because Sturdza was not a licensed architect in the District of Columbia, she could not recover on a contract to perform architectural services there.[6] ■

The following case involved a contract for the construction of an assisted living facility to be sanctioned by the state of Tennessee. On the project's completion, the facility was constructively delivered and accepted. At no time, however, was the party acting as the contractor licensed by the state to perform that function.

---

6. *Sturdza v. United Arab Emirates*, 11 A.3d 251 (D.C.App. 2011).

Case 14.2

McNatt v. Vestal

Court of Appeals of Tennessee, __ S.W.3d __, 2016 WL 659847 (2016).

Background and Facts Cecil McNatt contracted with Jane Vestal to build Henderson Villa, an assisted living facility, in Henderson, Tennessee, for $1.4 million. Three days later, McNatt formed a joint venture with M. S. Burton Construction Company to build two assisted living facilities, including Henderson Villa. Burton was licensed under the state's Contractors Licensing Act. McNatt was not. During the construction of Henderson Villa, McNatt remained onsite, selecting, supervising, and paying the subcontractors.

Following completion of the project, Vestal refused to pay the balance owed on the contract. McNatt filed a suit in a Tennessee state court against Vestal to collect. She filed a counterclaim, alleging breach of contract for his lack of a contractor's license. The court dismissed her claim and awarded him $96,280.11 in damages. Vestal appealed.

In the Language of the Court

Kenny *ARMSTRONG*, J. [Judge]

* * * *

Under Tennessee Code Annotated Section 62–6–103(a), it is "unlawful for any person, firm or corporation to engage in, or offer to engage in, contracting * * * unless the person, firm or corporation has been duly licensed under this part." "Contracting" is defined as when "any person or entity * * * offers to construct * * * or in any manner assume charge of the construction * * * for any building * * * for

Case 14.2 Continues

Case 14.2 Continued

which the total cost is twenty-five thousand dollars ($25,000) or more." "Any contractor * * * who is in violation of this part * * * shall not be permitted to recover any damages in any court other than actual documented expenses that can be shown by clear and convincing proof."

* * * *

The contract between McNatt and Vestal required payment in excess of $25,000. * * * *Merely offering to construct the assisted living facility constitutes contracting work, and the duties that McNatt performed under the contract fall within the definition of contracting work as well. Here, McNatt was not licensed at the time he made his offer to Vestal or at any time during the construction project.* [Emphasis added.]

* * * Tennessee Code Annotated Section 62–6–115 allows that entities engaged in a partnership may perform contracting work as long as one of the partners holds a contracting license.

* * * It is undisputed that McNatt and Burton Construction executed their agreement after McNatt executed his agreement with Vestal. * * * Because McNatt began performing contracting services before associating with Burton Construction, the subsequent association with Burton Construction does not cure his unlicensed contracting activity. We, therefore, conclude that the trial court erred in finding that McNatt did not violate the Contractors Licensing Act.

* * * *

At trial, [McNatt] presented an itemized list of costs [that] included architect fees, appraisal fees, interest paid on construction loans, application fees for licensure, charter fees, attorney's fees, insurance costs, payments to engineers, the costs of blueprints, gasoline, and an administrative fee. Upon review of the record, we conclude that the majority of these costs are supported by clear and convincing evidence. However, we conclude that the awards for [the] administrative duties and the costs of gas are not supported by clear and convincing evidence.

* * * *

* * * In subtracting these costs from the total costs presented at trial, we conclude that there is clear and convincing evidence to support an award of only $72,952.03.

Decision and Remedy *A state intermediate appellate court reversed the lower court's finding that McNatt had not violated the state Contractors Licensing Act and reduced the amount of his award. The appellate court affirmed the judgment as modified and remanded the case for further proceedings.*

Critical Thinking
- **Legal Environment** *In Tennessee, at common law, unlicensed contractors had no right to recover anything on their contracts. The Contractors Licensing Act changed this rule to permit unlicensed contractors to recover documented expenses proved by clear and convincing evidence. Why?*
- **What If the Facts Were Different?** *Suppose that McNatt had held a valid contractor's license when he entered into the contract with Vestal but that the license had expired while he was overseeing the construction of Henderson Villa. Would the result in that case have been different? Explain.*

14–2b Contracts Contrary to Public Policy

Although contracts involve private parties, some are not enforceable because of the negative impact they would have on society. These contracts are said to be *contrary to public policy.* Examples include a contract to commit an immoral act, such as selling a child, and a contract that prohibits marriage. Business contracts that may be against public policy include contracts in restraint of trade and unconscionable contracts or clauses.

Contracts in Restraint of Trade The United States has a strong public policy favoring competition in the economy. Thus, contracts in restraint of trade (anticompetitive agreements) generally are unenforceable because they are contrary to public policy. Typically, such contracts also violate one or more federal or state antitrust statutes.[7]

An exception is recognized when the restraint is reasonable and is contained in an ancillary (secondary or subordinate) clause in a contract. Such restraints often are included in contracts for the sale of an ongoing business and for employment contracts.

---

7. Federal statutes include the Sherman Antitrust Act, the Clayton Act, and the Federal Trade Commission Act.

Covenants Not to Compete and the Sale of an Ongoing Business. Many contracts involve a type of restraint called a **covenant not to compete,** or a restrictive covenant (promise). A covenant not to compete may be created when a merchant who sells a store agrees not to open a new store in a certain geographic area surrounding the old business. Such an agreement enables the seller to sell, and the purchaser to buy, the goodwill and reputation of an ongoing business without having to worry that the seller will open a competing business a block away. Provided the restrictive covenant is reasonable and is an ancillary part of the sale of an ongoing business, it is enforceable.

Covenants Not to Compete in Employment Contracts. Sometimes, agreements not to compete (also referred to as *noncompete agreements*) are included in employment contracts. People in middle- or upper-level management positions commonly agree not to work for competitors or not to start competing businesses for a specified period of time after termination of employment.

Noncompete agreements are legal in most states so long as the specified period of time (of restraint) is not excessive in duration and the geographic restriction is reasonable. What constitutes a reasonable time period may be shorter in the online environment than in conventional employment contracts. Because the geographical restrictions apply worldwide, the time restrictions may be shorter.

A restraint that is found to be overly broad will not be enforced. ■ **CASE IN POINT 14.7** An insurance firm in New York City, Brown & Brown, Inc., hired Theresa Johnson to perform actuarial analysis. On her first day of work, Johnson was asked to sign a nonsolicitation covenant. The covenant prohibited her from soliciting or servicing any of Brown's clients for two years after the termination of her employment.

Less than five years later, when Johnson's employment with Brown was terminated, she went to work for Lawley Benefits Group, LLC. Brown sued to enforce the covenant. A state appellate court ruled that the covenant was overly broad and unenforceable. It attempted to restrict Johnson from working for any of Brown's clients, without regard to whether she had had a relationship with those clients.[8] ■

Enforcement Issues. The laws governing the enforceability of covenants not to compete vary significantly from state to state. California prohibits the enforcement of covenants not to compete altogether. In some states, including Texas, such a covenant will not be enforced unless the

employee has received some benefit in return for signing the noncompete agreement. This is true even if the covenant is reasonable as to time and area. If the employee receives no benefit, the covenant will be deemed void.

Occasionally, depending on the jurisdiction, courts will *reform* covenants not to compete. If a covenant is found to be unreasonable in time or geographic area, the court may convert the terms into reasonable ones and then enforce the reformed covenant. Such court actions present a problem, though, in that the judge implicitly becomes a party to the contract. Consequently, courts usually resort to contract **reformation** only when necessary to prevent undue burdens or hardships.

Unconscionable Contracts or Clauses A court ordinarily does not look at the fairness or equity of a contract (or inquire into the adequacy of consideration). Persons are assumed to be reasonably intelligent, and the courts will not come to their aid just because they have made unwise or foolish bargains.

In certain circumstances, however, bargains are so oppressive that the courts relieve innocent parties of part or all of their duties. Such bargains are deemed **unconscionable**[9] because they are so unscrupulous or grossly unfair as to be "void of conscience." A contract can be unconscionable on either procedural or substantive grounds, as illustrated in Exhibit 14–1. The Uniform Commercial Code (UCC) incorporates the concept of unconscionability in its provisions regarding the sale and lease of goods.[10]

Procedural Unconscionability. *Procedural* unconscionability often involves inconspicuous print, unintelligible language ("legalese"), or the lack of an opportunity to read the contract or ask questions about its meaning. This type of unconscionability typically arises when a party's lack of knowledge or understanding of the contract terms deprived him or her of any meaningful choice.

Procedural unconscionability can also occur when there is such disparity in bargaining power between the two parties that the weaker party's consent is not voluntary. This type of situation often involves an *adhesion* contract, which is a contract written exclusively by one party and presented to the other on a take-it-or-leave-it basis.[11] In other words, the party to whom the contract is presented (usually a buyer or borrower) has no opportunity to negotiate its terms.

8. *Brown & Brown, Inc. v. Johnson,* 115 A.D.3d 52, 980 N.Y.S.2d 631 (2014).

9. Pronounced un-*kon*-shun-uh-bul.
10. See UCC 2–302 and 2A–719.
11. For a classic case involving an adhesion contract, see *Henningsen v. Bloomfield Motors, Inc.,* 32 N.J. 358, 161 A.2d 69 (1960).

EXHIBIT 14–1 Unconscionability

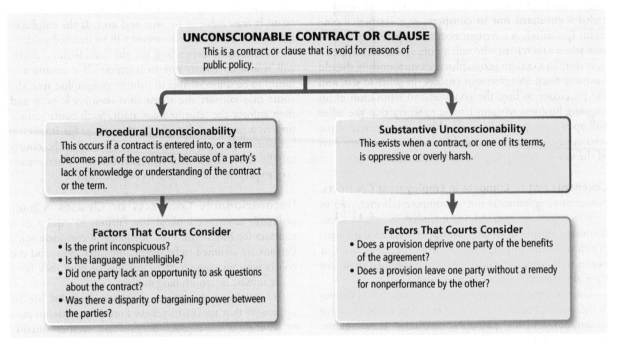

Not all adhesion contracts are unconscionable, only those that unreasonably favor the drafter. ■ **CASE IN POINT 14.8** Tiffany Brinkley committed to take six real estate investment training sessions at a cost of $4,195. She paid $850 and signed a retail installment contract promising to pay monthly payments on the balance to Monterey Financial Services. The contract contained an arbitration agreement. When a dispute arose, Brinkley stopped making payments and filed a lawsuit against Monterey in a California state court.

Monterey filed a motion to arbitrate, which the trial court granted. Brinkley appealed. She argued that the arbitration clause was procedurally unconscionable because it was part of an adhesion contract. The court, though, found that the arbitration clause was enforceable and dismissed the lawsuit. The court held that the "purported lack of meaningful choice did not render the arbitration provision in retail installment contract procedurally unconscionable."[12] ■

Substantive Unconscionability. *Substantive* unconscionability occurs when contracts, or portions of contracts, are oppressive or overly harsh. Courts generally focus on

provisions that deprive one party of the benefits of the agreement or leave that party without a remedy for nonperformance by the other.

Substantive unconscionability can arise in a wide variety of business contexts. For instance, a contract clause that gives the business entity unconstrained access to the courts but requires the other party to arbitrate any dispute with the firm may be unconscionable.

Exculpatory Clauses Often closely related to the concept of unconscionability are **exculpatory clauses,** which release a party from liability in the event of monetary or physical injury *no matter who is at fault.* Indeed, courts sometimes refuse to enforce such clauses on the ground that they are unconscionable.

Often Violate Public Policy. Most courts view exculpatory clauses with disfavor. Exculpatory clauses found in rental agreements for commercial property are frequently held to be contrary to public policy, and such clauses are almost always unenforceable in residential property leases. Courts also usually hold that exculpatory clauses are against public policy in the employment context. Thus, employers frequently cannot enforce exculpatory clauses in contracts with employees or independent contractors to avoid liability for work-related injuries.

---

12. *Brinkley v. Monterey Financial Services, Inc.*, 242 Cal.App.4th 314, 196 Cal.Rptr.3d 1 (2015). See also *Louisiana Extended Care Centers, LLC v. Bindon*, 180 So.3d 791 (2015).

■ **CASE IN POINT 14.9** Crum Motor Sales entered into an agreement with Martin County Coal Corporation to service Martin Coal's pickup trucks and light-duty vehicles. The parties agreed that when vehicles needed service, Crum Motor would pick up the vehicles from Martin Coal's mining site, repair them, and then bring them back. Martin Coal required Crum Motor to sign an indemnification agreement (exculpatory clause) for all injuries sustained on the mining site and to have insurance coverage.

A few years later, Philip Crum (an employee of Crum Motor) was driving on a road on the mining site when a falling boulder crushed the cab of his pickup. He was seriously injured and spent the rest of the year in a hospital and rehabilitation facility. Philip Crum and Crum Motor sued Martin Coal for negligence in maintaining the road and the site. Martin Coal counterclaimed, arguing that it was not liable under the indemnification agreement.

Crum Motor's insurance provider (Universal Underwriters) declined to represent the company in the lawsuit. Eventually, Martin Coal settled with Philip Crum and Crum Motor for $3.65 million and filed a suit against Universal Underwriters for that same amount. The court held that the indemnification agreement between Crum Motor and Martin Coal was against public policy and void. Therefore, Martin Coal was responsible for paying the settlement, not Crum Motor's insurance provider.[13] ■

When Courts Will Enforce Exculpatory Clauses. Courts do enforce exculpatory clauses if they are reasonable, do not violate public policy, and do not protect parties from liability for intentional misconduct. The language used must not be ambiguous, and the parties must have been in relatively equal bargaining positions.

Businesses such as health clubs, racetracks, amusement parks, skiing facilities, horse-rental operations, golf-cart concessions, and skydiving organizations frequently use exculpatory clauses to limit their liability for patrons' injuries. Because these services are not essential, the companies offering them have no relative advantage in bargaining strength, and anyone contracting for their services does so voluntarily. Courts also may enforce reasonable exculpatory clauses in loan documents, real estate contracts, and trust agreements. See this chapter's *Managerial Strategy* feature for more about exculpatory clauses that will not be considered unconscionable.

In the following case, the court considered whether an exculpatory clause that released "any Event sponsors and their agents and employees" from liability for future negligence was ambiguous.

---

13. *Martin County Coal Corp. v. Universal Underwriters Ins. Co.*, 727 F.3d 589 (6th Cir. 2013).

Holmes v. Multimedia KSDK, Inc.

Missouri Court of Appeals, Eastern District, Division Two, 395 S.W.3d 557 (2013).

In the Language of the Court

Kathianne *KNAUP CRANE,* Presiding Judge.

* * * *

* * * On or about May 12, 2009, plaintiff Colleen M. Holmes signed and dated an Entry Form for the 2009 Susan G. Komen Race for the Cure (the Event) to be held on Saturday, June 13, 2009 [in St. Louis, Missouri]. The one-page entry form contained a section titled, "RACE WAIVER AND RELEASE." This section contained the following language:

* * * I understand that my consent to these provisions is given in consideration for being permitted to participate in this Event. I further understand that I may be removed from this competition if I do not follow all the rules of this Event. I am a voluntary participant in this Event, and in good physical condition. I know that this Event is a potentially hazardous activity and I hereby voluntarily assume full and complete responsibility for, and the risk of, any injury or accident that may occur during my participation in this Event or while on the premises of this Event. I * * * hereby release and hold harmless and covenant not to file suit against The Susan G. Komen Breast Cancer Foundation, Inc., * * * D/B/A Susan G. Komen for the Cure, The St. Louis Affiliate of The Susan G. Komen Breast Cancer Foundation * * *, their Affiliates and any affiliated Individuals, any Event sponsors and their agents and employees, and all other persons or entities associated with this Event (collectively, the "Releasees") for any injury or damages I might suffer in connection with my participation in this Event or while on the premises of this Event. This release applies to any and all loss, liability, or claims I may have arising out of my participation in this Event, including but not limited to, personal injury or damage suffered by me or others, whether such losses, liabilities, or claims are caused by falls, contact with and/or the actions of other participants, contact with fixed or non-fixed

Case 14.3 Continues

Case 14.3 Continued

objects, contact with animals, conditions of the premises of the Event, negligence of the Releasees, risks not known to me or not reasonably foreseeable at this time, or otherwise.

On June 1, 2009, defendant Multimedia KSDK, Inc. (KSDK) executed a Race Sponsorship Agreement with the St. Louis Affiliate of the Event. This agreement governed the terms of KSDK's sponsorship of the Event in 2009. KSDK, as an Event sponsor, agreed to, and did, broadcast the Event. Defendants Lynn Beall and Michael Shipley, KSDK employees, were involved in arranging the live coverage.

On February 23, 2011, Mrs. Holmes and her husband, Rick W. Holmes (collectively, plaintiffs) filed a lawsuit in the Circuit Court of the City of St. Louis. Plaintiffs alleged that while Mrs. Holmes was a participant in the Event, she was caused to trip and fall over an audio-visual box, and she sustained injuries. Plaintiffs alleged that the audio-visual box was owned and operated by KSDK and was placed on the ground without barricades or warnings in a high pedestrian traffic area.

The circuit court entered summary judgment in defendants' favor on the grounds that plaintiffs' claims were barred by the language of the release, the release was not ambiguous, and the release applied to defendants. Plaintiffs appeal.

* * * *

[The plaintiffs] on appeal claim the release is ambiguous. Whether a release is ambiguous is a question of law. Interpretation of a release or settlement agreement is governed by the same principles as any other contract. * * * *Contract terms are ambiguous only if the language may be given more than one reasonable interpretation. Simply because parties disagree over the meaning of a contract does not mean that it is ambiguous.* [Emphasis added.]

* * * *

* * * Plaintiffs assert that the trial court erred in entering summary judgment because the release was ambiguous in that it did not clearly and explicitly set forth the individuals and entities it purported to release from liability. We disagree.

The release described the individuals and entities to be released in the following language:

> The St. Louis Affiliate of Susan G. Komen for the Cure, their affiliates, and any affiliated individuals, any Event sponsors and their agents and employees, and all other persons or entities associated with this Event.

Plaintiffs argue that the * * * language is ambiguous because it does not specifically name the individuals and entities being released. They contend that such specificity is required in a prospective release.

We have routinely held that the word "any" when used with a class in a release is all-inclusive, it excludes nothing, and it is not ambiguous. * * * *A release that releases claims against "any and all persons" is unambiguous and enforceable to bar claims against third parties who were not parties to the release, and it is not necessary that the release identify those persons by name or otherwise.* Thus, * * * the release of "any Event sponsors" unambiguously releases all Event sponsors without exclusion, and it is not necessary that each sponsor be named. [Emphasis added.]

However, plaintiffs argue that this reasoning does not apply to the use of "any" with classes of persons in a prospective release for future acts of negligence because courts require more specificity in a prospective release. We disagree.

Public policy disfavors but *does not* prohibit releases of future negligence. * * * To be enforceable in Missouri, exculpatory clauses must contain clear, unambiguous, unmistakable, and conspicuous language in order to release a party from his or her own future negligence. The exculpatory language must effectively notify a party that he or she is releasing the other party from claims arising from the other party's own negligence. * * * The words "negligence" or "fault" or their equivalents must be used conspicuously so that a clear and unmistakable waiver and shifting of risk occurs. There must be no doubt that a reasonable person agreeing to an exculpatory clause actually understands what future claims he or she is waiving.

* * * *

* * * [It is] not required that for a release of liability for future negligence to be effective, it must identify every individual sought to be released by name.

The release of "any Event sponsors and their agents and employees" from liability for future negligence clearly releases all Event sponsors and their agents and employees without exclusion. It is not ambiguous because it does not name each individual Event sponsor it purported to release from liability.

* * * *

The judgment of the trial court is affirmed.

Legal Reasoning Questions

1. When do courts enforce exculpatory clauses?

2. What are the specific requirements for an exculpatory clause to be enforceable in Missouri?

3. Was the exculpatory clause at issue in this case enforceable? Why or why not?

Creating Liability Waivers That Are Not Unconscionable

Blanket liability waivers that absolve a business from virtually every event, even those caused by the business's own negligence, are usually unenforceable because they are unconscionable. Exculpatory waivers are common, nonetheless. We observe such waivers in gym memberships, on ski lift tickets, on admissions tickets to sporting events, and in simple contracts for the use of campgrounds.

Typically, courts view liability waivers as voluntarily bargained for whether or not they have been read. Thus, a waiver included in the fine print on the back of an admission ticket or on an entry sign to a stadium may be upheld. In general, if such waivers are unambiguous and conspicuous, the assumption is that patrons have had a chance to read them and have accepted their terms.

Activities with Inherent Risks

Cases challenging liability waivers have been brought against skydiving operations, skiing operations, bobsledding operations, white-water rafting companies, and health clubs. For example, in *Bergin v. Wild Mountain, Inc.,*[a] an appellate court in Minnesota upheld a ski resort's liability waiver.

In that case, the plaintiff hit a snowmaking mound, which was "an inherent risk of skiing." Before the accident, the plaintiff had stated that he knew "that an inherent risk of serious injury in downhill skiing was hitting snowmaking mounds." Furthermore, he had not rejected the season pass that contained the

resort's exculpatory clause. Thus, the ski resort prevailed.

Overly Broad Waivers

While most liability waivers have survived legal challenges, some have not. In *Bagley v. Mt. Bachelor, Inc.,*[b] the Supreme Court of Oregon ruled against a ski resort's "very broad" liability waiver. The case involved an eighteen-year-old, Myles Bagley, who was paralyzed from the waist down after a snowboarding accident at Mt. Bachelor ski resort. The season pass that Bagley signed included a liability waiver. The waiver stated that the signer agreed not to sue the resort for injury even if "caused by negligence."

Bagley argued that the resort had created a dangerous condition because of the way it had set up a particular ski jump. He sued for $21.5 million and eventually won the right to go forward with his lawsuit. The Oregon Supreme Court found that, for various reasons, enforcement of the release would have been unconscionable. "Because the release is unenforceable, genuine issues of fact exist that preclude summary judgment in defendant's favor."

Business Questions

1. *If you are running a business, why would you opt to include overly broad waivers in your contracts with customers?*

2. *Under what circumstances would you, as a business owner, choose to aggressively defend your business against a customer's liability lawsuit?*

a. 2014 WL 996788 (Minn.App. 2014).

b. 356 Or. 543, 340 P.3d 27 (2014).

Discriminatory Contracts Contracts in which a party promises to discriminate on the basis of race, color, national origin, religion, gender, age, or disability are contrary to both statute and public policy. They are also unenforceable.[14] For instance, if a property owner promises in a contract not to sell the property to a member of a particular race, the contract is unenforceable. The public policy underlying these prohibitions is very strong, and the courts are quick to invalidate discriminatory contracts.

Exhibit 14–2 illustrates the types of contracts that may be illegal because they are contrary to statute or public policy.

14–2c Effect of Illegality

In general, an illegal contract is void—that is, the contract is deemed never to have existed, and the courts will not aid either party. In most illegal contracts, both parties are considered to be equally at fault—*in pari delicto.*[15] If the contract is executory (not yet fulfilled), neither party can enforce it. If it has been executed, neither party can recover damages.

Usually, the courts are not concerned if one wrongdoer in an illegal contract is unjustly enriched at the expense of the other. The main reason for this hands-off attitude is the belief that a plaintiff who has broken the law by entering into an illegal bargain should not be allowed to obtain help from the courts. Another justification is the

---

14. The major federal statute prohibiting discrimination is the Civil Rights Act of 1964, 42 U.S.C. Sections 2000e–2000e-17.

15. Pronounced in-*pah*-ree deh-*lick*-tow.

EXHIBIT 14–2 Contract Legality

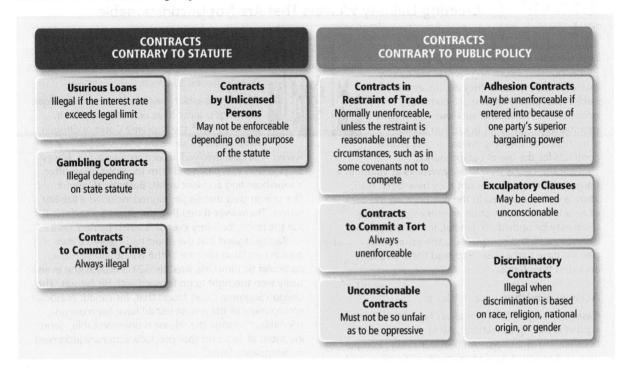

hoped-for deterrent effect. A plaintiff who suffers a loss because of an illegal bargain will presumably be deterred from entering into similar illegal bargains in the future.

There are, however, exceptions to the general rule that neither party to an illegal bargain can sue for breach and neither party can recover for performance rendered. We look at these exceptions next.

Justifiable Ignorance of the Facts Sometimes, one of the parties to a contract has no reason to know that the contract is illegal and thus is relatively innocent. That party can often recover any benefits conferred in a partially executed contract. In this situation, the courts will not enforce the contract but will allow the parties to return to their original positions.

Sometimes, a court may permit an innocent party who has fully performed under the contract to enforce the contract against the guilty party. ■ **EXAMPLE 14.10** A trucking company contracts with Gillespie to carry crates filled with goods to a specific destination for the normal fee of $5,000. The trucker delivers the crates and later finds out that they contained illegal goods. Although the law specifies that the shipment, use, and sale of the goods were illegal, the trucker, being an innocent party, can still legally collect the $5,000 from Gillespie. ■

Members of Protected Classes When a statute is clearly designed to protect a certain class of people, a member of that class can enforce a contract in violation of the statute even though the other party cannot. ■ **EXAMPLE 14.11** Statutes prohibit certain employees (such as flight attendants and pilots) from working more than a certain number of hours per month. An employee who is required to work more than the maximum can recover for those extra hours of service. ■

Other examples of statutes designed to protect a particular class of people are state statutes that regulate the sale of insurance. If an insurance company violates a statute when selling insurance, the purchaser can still enforce the policy and recover from the insurer.

Withdrawal from an Illegal Agreement If the illegal part of a bargain has not yet been performed, the party rendering performance can withdraw from the contract and recover the performance or its value. ■ **EXAMPLE 14.12** Sam and Jim decide to wager (illegally) on the outcome of a boxing match. Each deposits cash with a stakeholder, who agrees to pay the winner of the bet. At this point, each party has performed part of the agreement. Before payment occurs, either party is entitled to withdraw from the bargain by giving notice of repudiation to the stakeholder. ■

Contract Illegal through Fraud, Duress, or Undue Influence Often, one party to an illegal contract is more at fault than the other. When one party uses fraud, duress, or undue influence to induce another party to enter into an illegal bargain, the second party will be allowed to recover for the performance or its value.

Severable, or Divisible, Contracts A contract that is *severable*, or divisible, consists of distinct parts that can be performed separately, with separate consideration provided for each part. With an *indivisible* contract, in contrast, complete performance by each party is essential, even if the contract contains a number of seemingly separate provisions.

If a contract is divisible into legal and illegal portions, a court may enforce the legal portion but not the illegal one, so long as the illegal portion does not affect the essence of the bargain. This approach is consistent with the courts' basic policy of enforcing the legal intentions of the contracting parties whenever possible.

■ **EXAMPLE 14.13** Cole signs an employment contract that includes an overly broad and thus illegal covenant not to compete. In that situation, a court might allow the employment contract to be enforceable but reform the unreasonably broad covenant by converting its terms into reasonable ones. Alternatively, the court could declare the covenant illegal (and thus void) and enforce the remaining employment terms. ■

A contract clause stating that the parties intend the contract terms to be enforced to "the fullest extent possible" indicates that the parties regard their contract as divisible. In the event of a dispute, the parties intend that the court will strike out the illegal terms and enforce the rest.

Reviewing: Capacity and Legality

Renee Beaver started racing go-karts competitively in 2016, when she was fourteen. Many of the races required her to sign an exculpatory clause to participate, which she or her parents regularly signed. In 2018, right before her sixteenth birthday, Renee participated in the annual Elkhart Grand Prix, a series of races in Elkhart, Indiana. During the event in which she drove, a piece of foam padding used as a course barrier was torn from its base and ended up on the track. A portion of the padding struck Beaver in the head, and another portion was thrown into oncoming traffic, causing a multikart collision during which she sustained severe injuries. Beaver filed an action against the race organizers for negligence. The race organizers could not locate the exculpatory clause that Beaver had supposedly signed. The organizers argued that she must have signed one to enter the race, but even if she had not signed one, her actions showed her intent to be bound by its terms. Using the information presented in the chapter, answer the following questions.

1. Did Beaver have the contractual capacity to enter a contract with an exculpatory clause? Why or why not?
2. Assuming that Beaver did, in fact, sign the exculpatory clause, did she later disaffirm or ratify the contract? Explain.
3. Now assume that Beaver stated that she was eighteen years old at the time she signed the exculpatory clause. How might this affect her ability to disaffirm or ratify the contract?
4. If Beaver did not actually sign the exculpatory clause, could a court conclude that she impliedly accepted its terms by participating in the race? Why or why not?

Debate This . . . *After agreeing to an exculpatory clause or purchasing some item, minors often seek to avoid the contracts. Today's minors are far from naïve and should not be allowed to avoid their contractual obligations.*

Terms and Concepts

age of majority 263	emancipation 263	reformation 271
contractual capacity 263	exculpatory clause 272	unconscionable 271
covenant not to compete 271	necessaries 265	usury 268
disaffirmance 263	ratification 265	

Issue Spotters

1. Joan, who is sixteen years old, moves out of her parents' home and signs a one-year lease for an apartment at Kenwood Apartments. Joan's parents tell her that she can return to live with them at any time. Unable to pay the rent, Joan moves back to her parents' home two months later. Can Kenwood enforce the lease against Joan? Why or why not? (See *Contractual Capacity*.)

2. Sun Airlines, Inc., prints on its tickets that it is not liable for any injury to a passenger caused by the airline's negligence. If the cause of an accident is found to be the airline's negligence, can it use the clause as a defense to liability? Why or why not? (See *Legality*.)

• **Check your answers to the Issue Spotters against the answers provided in Appendix D at the end of this text.**

Business Scenarios

14–1. Covenants Not to Compete. A famous New York City hotel, Hotel Lux, is noted for its food as well as its luxury accommodations. Hotel Lux contracts with a famous chef, Chef Perlee, to become its head chef at $30,000 per month. The contract states that should Perlee leave the employment of Hotel Lux for any reason, he will not work as a chef for any hotel or restaurant in New York, New Jersey, or Pennsylvania for a period of one year. During the first six months of the contract, Hotel Lux heavily advertises Perlee as its head chef, and business at the hotel is excellent. Then a dispute arises between the hotel's management and Perlee, and Perlee terminates his employment. One month later, he is hired by a famous New Jersey restaurant just across the New York state line. Hotel Lux learns of Perlee's employment through a large advertisement in a New York City newspaper. It seeks to enjoin (prevent) Perlee from working in that restaurant as a chef for one year. Discuss how successful Hotel Lux will be in its action. (See *Legality*.)

14–2. Capacity. Joanne is a seventy-five-year-old widow who survives on her husband's small pension. Joanne has become increasingly forgetful, and her family worries that she may have Alzheimer's disease (a brain disorder that seriously affects a person's ability to carry out daily activities). No physician has diagnosed her, however, and no court has ruled on her legal competence. One day while she is out shopping, Joanne stops by a store that is having a sale on pianos and enters into a fifteen-year installment contract to buy a grand piano. When the piano arrives the next day, Joanne seems confused and repeatedly asks the delivery person why a piano is being delivered. Joanne claims that she does not recall buying a piano. Explain whether this contract is void, voidable, or valid. Can Joanne avoid her contractual obligation to buy the piano? If so, how? (See *Contractual Capacity*.)

Business Case Problems

14–3. Business Case Problem with Sample Answer— Unconscionable Contracts or Clauses. Geographic

 Expeditions, Inc. (GeoEx), which guided climbs up Mount Kilimanjaro, required climbers to sign a release to participate in an expedition. The form mandated the arbitration of any dispute in San Francisco and limited damages to the cost of the trip. GeoEx told climbers that the terms were nonnegotiable and were the same as terms imposed by other travel firms. Jason Lhotka died on a GeoEx climb. His mother filed a suit against GeoEx. GeoEx sought arbitration. Was the arbitration clause unconscionable? Why or why not? [*Lhotka v. Geographic Expeditions, Inc.,* 181 Cal.App.4th 816, 104 Cal.Rptr.3d 844 (1 Dist. 2010)] (See *Legality*.)

• **For a sample answer to Problem 14–3, go to Appendix E at the end of this text.**

14–4. Mental Incompetence. Dorothy Drury suffered from dementia and chronic confusion. When she became unable to manage her own affairs, including decisions about medical and financial matters, her son Eddie arranged for her

move to an assisted living facility. During admission, she signed a residency agreement, which included an arbitration clause. After she sustained injuries in a fall at the facility, a suit was filed to recover damages. The facility asked the court to compel arbitration. Was Dorothy bound to the residency agreement? Discuss. [*Drury v. Assisted Living Concepts, Inc.,* 245 Or.App. 217, 262 P.3d 1162 (2011)] (See *Contractual Capacity*.)

14–5. Licensing Statutes. PEMS Co. International, Inc., agreed to find a buyer for Rupp Industries, Inc., for a commission of 2 percent of the purchase price, which was to be paid by the buyer. Using PEMS's services, an investment group bought Rupp for $20 million and changed its name to Temp-Air, Inc. PEMS asked Temp-Air to pay a commission on the sale. Temp-Air refused, arguing that PEMS had acted as a broker in the deal without a license. The applicable statute defines a broker as any person who deals with the sale of a business. If this statute was intended to protect the public, can PEMS collect its commission? Explain. [*PEMS Co. International, Inc. v. Temp-Air, Inc.,* 2011 WL 69098 (Minn.App. 2011)] (See *Legality*.)

14–6. Minors. D.V.G. (a minor) was injured in a one-car auto accident in Hoover, Alabama. The vehicle was covered by an insurance policy issued by Nationwide Mutual Insurance Co. Stan Brobston, D.V.G.'s attorney, accepted Nationwide's offer of $50,000 on D.V.G.'s behalf. Before the settlement could be submitted to an Alabama state court for approval, D.V.G. died from injuries received in a second, unrelated auto accident. Nationwide argued that it was not bound to the settlement, because a minor lacks the capacity to contract and so cannot enter into a binding settlement without court approval. Should Nationwide be bound to the settlement? Why or why not? [*Nationwide Mutual Insurance Co. v. Wood,* 121 So.3d 982 (Ala. 2013)] (See *Contractual Capacity.*)

14–7. Adhesion Contracts. David Desgro hired Paul Pack to inspect a house that Desgro wanted to buy. Pack had Desgro sign a standard-form contract that included a twelve-month limit for claims based on the agreement. Pack reported that the house had no major problems, but after Desgro bought it, he discovered issues with the plumbing, insulation, heat pump, and floor support. Thirteen months after the inspection, Desgro filed a suit in a Tennessee state court against Pack. Was Desgro's complaint filed too late, or was the contract's twelve-month limit unenforceable? Discuss. [*Desgro v. Pack,* 2013 WL 84899 (Tenn.App. 2013)] (See *Legality.*)

14–8. Legality. Sue Ann Apolinar hired a guide through Arkansas Valley Adventures, LLC, for a rafting excursion on the Arkansas River. At the outfitter's office, Apolinar signed a release that detailed potential hazards and risks, including "overturning," "unpredictable currents," "obstacles" in the water, and "drowning." The release clearly stated that her signature discharged Arkansas Valley from liability for all claims arising in connection with the trip. On the river, while attempting to maneuver around a rapid, the raft capsized. The current swept Apolinar into a logjam where, despite efforts to save her, she drowned. Her son, Jesus Espinoza, Jr., filed a suit in a federal district court against the rafting company, alleging negligence. What are the arguments for and against enforcing the release that Apolinar signed? Discuss. [*Espinoza v. Arkansas Valley Adventures, LLC,* 809 F.3d 1150 (10th Cir. 2016)] (See *Legality.*)

14–9. A Question of Ethics—Covenants Not to Compete. *Brendan Coleman created and marketed Clinex, a software billing program. Later, Retina Consultants, P.C., a medical practice, hired Coleman as a software engineer. Together, they modified the Clinex program to create Clinex-RE. Coleman signed an agreement to the effect that he owned Clinex, Retina owned Clinex-RE, and he would not market Clinex in competition with Clinex-RE. After Coleman quit Retina, he withdrew funds from a Retina bank account and marketed both forms of the software to other medical practices. At trial, the court entered a judgment enjoining (preventing) Coleman from marketing the software that was in competition with the software he had developed for Retina Consultants. The court also obligated Coleman to return the funds taken from the company's bank account. Coleman appealed. [Coleman v. Retina Consultants, P.C., 286 Ga. 317, 687 S.E.2d 457 (2009)] (See Legality.)*

(a) Should the court uphold the noncompete clause? If so, why? If not, why not?

(b) Should the court require Coleman to return the funds he withdrew from the company's accounts? Discuss fully.

(c) Did Coleman's behavior after he left the company influence the court's decision? Explain your answer.

Legal Reasoning Group Activity

14–10. Covenants Not to Compete. Assume that you are part of a group of executives at a large software corporation. The company is considering whether to incorporate covenants not to compete into its employment contracts. You know that there are some issues with the enforceability of these covenants, and you want to make an informed decision. (See *Legality.*)

(a) One group should make a list of what interests are served by enforcing covenants not to compete.

(b) A second group should create a list of what interests are served by refusing to enforce covenants not to compete.

(c) A third group is to consider whether a court should reform (and then enforce) a covenant not to compete that it determines is illegal. The group should create an argument for and an argument against reformation.

Answers to the *Issue Spotters*

1. *Can Kenwood enforce the lease against Joan? Why or why not?* No. Joan is a minor and may disaffirm this contract. Because the apartment was a necessary, however, she remains liable for the reasonable value of her occupancy of the apartment.

2. *If the cause of an accident is found to be the airline's negligence, can it use the clause as a defense to liability? Why or why not?* No. Generally, an exculpatory clause (a clause attempting to absolve parties of negligence or other wrongs) is not enforced if the party seeking its enforcement is involved in a business that is important to the public as a matter of practical necessity, such as an airline. Because of the essential nature of such services, this party has an advantage in bargaining strength and could insist that anyone contracting for its services agree not to hold it liable.

Sample Answers for *Business Case Problems with Sample Answer*

Problem 14–3. *Unconscionable Contracts or Clauses.* In this case, the agreement that restricted the buyer's options for resolution of a dispute to arbitration and limited the amount of damages was both procedurally and substantively unconscionable. Procedural unconscionability concerns the manner in which the parties enter into a contract. Substantive unconscionability can occur when a contract leaves one party to the agreement without a remedy for the nonperformance of the other.

Here, GeoEx told customers that the arbitration terms in its release form were nonnegotiable and that climbers would encounter the same requirements with any other travel company. This amounted to procedural unconscionability, underscoring the customers' lack of bargaining power. The imbalance resulted in oppressive terms, with no real negotiation and an absence of meaningful choice. Furthermore, the restriction on forum (San Francisco) and the limitation on damages (the cost of the trip)—with no limitation on GeoEx's damages—amounted to substantive unconscionability. In the actual case on which this problem is based, the court ruled that the agreement was unconscionable.

CHAPTER

Mistakes, Fraud, and Voluntary Consent

An otherwise valid contract may still be unenforceable if the parties have not genuinely agreed to its terms. A lack of *voluntary consent* (assent) can be used as a defense to the contract's enforceability.

Voluntary consent may be lacking because of a mistake, misrepresentation, undue influence, or duress—in other words, because there is no true "meeting of the minds." Generally, a party who demonstrates that he or she did not truly agree to the terms of a contract has a choice. That party can choose either to carry out the contract or to rescind (cancel) it and thus avoid the entire transaction. In this chapter, we examine the kinds of factors that may indicate a lack of voluntary consent.

15–1 Mistakes

We all make mistakes, so it is not surprising that mistakes are made when contracts are formed. In certain circumstances, contract law allows a contract to be avoided on the basis of mistake.

It is important to distinguish between *mistakes of fact* and *mistakes of value or quality*. Only a mistake of fact makes a contract voidable. Also, the mistake must involve some *material fact*—a fact that a reasonable person would consider important when determining his or her course of action.

Mistakes of fact occur in two forms—*bilateral* and *unilateral*. A unilateral mistake is made by only *one* of the parties. A bilateral, or mutual, mistake is made by *both* of the contracting parties. We look next at these two types of mistakes and illustrate them graphically in Exhibit 15–1.

15–1a Unilateral Mistakes of Fact

A **unilateral mistake** is made by only one of the parties. In general, a unilateral mistake does not give the mistaken party any right to relief from the contract. Normally, the contract is enforceable.

■ **EXAMPLE 15.1** Elena intends to sell her jet ski for $2,500. When she learns that Chin is interested in buying a used jet ski, she sends him an e-mail offering to sell the jet ski to him. When typing the e-mail, however, she mistakenly keys in the price of $1,500. Chin immediately sends Elena an e-mail reply accepting her offer. Even though Elena intended to sell her personal jet ski for $2,500, she has made a unilateral mistake and is bound by the contract to sell it to Chin for $1,500. ■

This general rule has at least two exceptions.[1] The contract may not be enforceable if:

1. The *other* party to the contract knows or should have known that a mistake of fact was made.
2. The error was due to a *substantial* mathematical mistake in addition, subtraction, division, or multiplication and was made inadvertently and without gross (extreme) negligence. If, for instance, a contractor's bid was significantly low because he or she made a mistake in addition when totaling the estimated costs, any contract resulting from the bid normally may be rescinded.

Of course, in both situations, the mistake must still involve some material fact.

15–1b Bilateral (Mutual) Mistakes of Fact

A **bilateral mistake** is a "mutual misunderstanding concerning a basic assumption on which the contract was made."[2] Note that, as with unilateral mistakes, the mistake must be about a material fact.

---

1. The *Restatement (Second) of Contracts*, Section 153, liberalizes the general rule to take into account the modern trend of allowing avoidance even though only one party has been mistaken.
2. *Restatement (Second) of Contracts*, Section 152.

EXHIBIT 15–1 Mistakes of Fact

Either Party Can Rescind the Contract When both parties are mistaken about the same material fact, the contract can be rescinded by either party. ■ **CASE IN POINT 15.2** Coleman Holdings LP bought a parcel of real estate subject to setback restrictions imposed in a document entitled "Partial Release of Restrictions" that effectively precluded building a structure on the property. Lance and Joanne Eklund offered to buy the parcel from Coleman, intending to combine it with an adjacent parcel and build a home. Coleman gave the Eklunds a title report that referred to the "Partial Release of Restrictions," but they were not given a copy of the release.

Mistakenly believing that the document released restrictions on the property, the Eklunds did not investigate further. Meanwhile, Coleman also mistakenly believed that the setback restrictions had been removed. After buying the property and discovering the restrictions, the Eklunds filed a suit in a Nevada state court against Coleman, seeking rescission of the sale. The court ordered the deal rescinded. The Nevada Supreme Court affirmed the order. "The parties made a mutual mistake in their mutual belief that the parcel had no setback restrictions."[3] ■

When the Parties Reasonably Interpret a Term Differently A word or term in a contract may be subject to more than one reasonable interpretation. If the parties to the contract attach materially different meanings to the term, a court may allow the contract to be rescinded because there has been no true "meeting of the minds." ■ **CASE IN POINT 15.3** L&H Construction Company contracted with Circle Redmont, Inc., to make a cast-iron staircase and a glass flooring system. Redmont's original proposal was to "engineer, fabricate, and

install" the staircase and flooring system, but installation was later dropped from the deal as a cost-cutting measure. The final contract stated that payment was due on "Supervision of Installation," although "install" appeared elsewhere in the contract. L&H insisted that installation was included and sued Redmont. The court found that the word *install* in the phrase "engineer, fabricate, and install" was the result of a mutual mistake. Both parties understood that Redmont would only supervise the installation, not perform it. Therefore, Redmont was not required to install the staircase and flooring.[4] ■

15–1c Mistakes of Value

If a mistake concerns the future market value or quality of the object of the contract, the mistake is one of *value,* and the contract normally is enforceable. ■ **EXAMPLE 15.4** Sung buys a violin from Bev for $250. Although the violin is very old, neither party believes that it is valuable. Later, however, an antiques dealer informs the parties that the violin is rare and worth thousands of dollars. Here, both parties were mistaken, but the mistake is a mistake of *value* rather than a mistake of *fact.* Because mistakes of value do not warrant contract rescission, Bev cannot rescind the contract. ■

The reason that mistakes of value do not affect the enforceability of contracts is that value is variable. Depending on the time, place, and other circumstances, the same item may be worth considerably different amounts. When parties form a contract, their agreement establishes the value of the object of their transaction— for the moment. Each party is considered to have assumed the risk that the value will change in the future or prove

---

3. *Coleman Holdings Limited Partnership v. Eklund,* 2015 WL 428567 (Nev. Sup.Ct. 2015).

4. *L&H Construction Co. v. Circle Redmont, Inc.,* 55 So.3d 630 (Fla.App. 2011).

to be different from what he or she thought. Without this rule, almost any party who did not receive what she or he considered a fair bargain could argue mistake.

15–2 Fraudulent Misrepresentation

Although fraud is a tort, the presence of fraud also affects the authenticity of the innocent party's consent to the contract. When an innocent party is fraudulently induced to enter into a contract, the contract usually can be avoided, because that party has not *voluntarily* consented to its terms.[5] The innocent party can either rescind the contract and be restored to her or his original position or enforce the contract and seek damages for any harms resulting from the fraud.

Generally, fraudulent misrepresentation refers only to misrepresentation that is consciously false and is intended to mislead another. The person making the fraudulent

misrepresentation knows or believes that the assertion is false or knows that she or he does not have a basis (stated or implied) for the assertion.[6] Typically, fraudulent misrepresentation consists of the following elements:

1. A misrepresentation of a material fact must occur.
2. There must be an intent to deceive.
3. The innocent party must justifiably rely on the misrepresentation.
4. To collect damages, a party must have been harmed as a result of the misrepresentation.

Like other actions based in the common law, a cause of action based on fraud can be subject to a statute of limitations. Of course, a cause based on a statute can also be subject to a statute of limitations. The limitations periods governing these actions may be different. In the following case, the issue was which limit to apply to a specific fraud claim—the three-year limit that applied to certain statute-based actions or the six-year limit that applied to common law actions.

---

5. *Restatement (Second) of Contracts*, Sections 163 and 164.

6. *Restatement (Second) of Contracts*, Section 162.

Case 15.1

Schneiderman v. Trump Entrepreneur Initiative, LLC

New York Supreme Court, Appellate Division, First Department, 137 A.D.3d 409, 26 N.Y.S.3d 66 (2016).

Background and Facts Donald Trump and Michael Sexton formed Trump University, LLC—later known as Trump Entrepreneur Initiative, LLC (TEI)—to sell courses in real estate investing. To attract students, Trump made a promotional video. In it, he said, "We're going to have professors that are absolutely terrific—terrific people, terrific brains, successful, the best. . . . All people that are hand-picked by me."

New York Attorney General Eric Schneiderman brought a proceeding in a New York state court against TEI, Trump, and Sexton, alleging that they had operated an illegal educational institution between 2005 and 2011. The attorney general sought an injunction, damages, penalties, and restitution under a state statute that provided for these remedies in cases of "persistent fraud." TEI was charged with intentionally misleading more than 5,000 students, including over 600 New York residents, into paying as much as $35,000 each to participate in its programs. Among other things, according to the attorney general, Trump did not handpick the instructors as he claimed.

The court dismissed the claim on the ground that it exceeded a three-year limit imposed on all statutory causes of action. The court also held that the specific statute did not provide the state with an independent cause of action for fraud. The attorney general appealed.

In the Language of the Court
MAZZARELLI, J.P. [Justice Presiding], RENWICK, SAXE, MOSKOWITZ, J.J. [Justices]
* * * *

* * * [New York] Executive Law Section 63(12) states, in relevant part:

Whenever any person shall engage in repeated fraudulent or illegal acts or otherwise demonstrate persistent fraud or illegality in the carrying on, conducting or transaction of business, the attorney general may apply * * * to the supreme court of the state of New York * * * for an order enjoining the continuance of such business activity or of any fraudulent or illegal acts and directing restitution and damages * * * and the court may award [such] relief * * * as it may deem proper.

Case 15.1 Continued * * * *

[In its ruling, the lower court cited *People v. Charles Schwab & Co., Inc.,* 109 A.D.3d 445, 971 N.Y.S.2d 267 (1 Dept. 2013).] In *Charles Schwab,* the Attorney General had brought an enforcement action asserting claims under Section 63(12) * * * . The court dismissed the Section 63(12) claim.

On appeal to this Court, * * * we found that the court had properly dismissed that claim, stating that the section does not create independent claims, but merely authorizes the Attorney General to seek injunctive and other relief * * * in cases involving persistent fraud.

Although the holding of *Charles Schwab* purported to be based on the [New York] Court of Appeals' ruling in *State v. Cortelle Corp.,* 38 N.Y.2d 83, 378 N.Y.S.2d 654, 341 N.E.2d 223 (1975), *Cortelle* does not, in fact, hold that the Attorney General cannot bring a standalone cause of action for fraud under Executive Law Section 63(12).

* * * *

In *Cortelle,* the Court of Appeals [found] that * * * causes of action [under Section 63(12)] addressing * * * allegedly fraudulent practices did not rely on liabilities, penalties, or forfeitures created or imposed by statute. *Specifically, Section 63(12) did not make unlawful the alleged fraudulent practices, but only provided standing in the Attorney General to seek redress and additional remedies for recognized wrongs which pre-existed the statute.* [Emphasis added.]

* * * *

* * * Other New York courts addressing that issue * * * have generally allowed for independent causes of action for fraud under Section 63(12).

* * * *

Thus, *Charles Schwab* does not comport with prevailing authority.

* * * Hence, we hold that the Attorney General is, in fact, authorized to bring a cause of action for fraud under Section 63(12).

Decision and Remedy *A state intermediate appellate court reversed the lower court's dismissal of the fraud claim, holding that the three-year limit on statutory causes of action did not apply. Because material issues of fact still existed as to that claim, however, the court remanded the case for further proceedings.*

Critical Thinking

- **Legal Environment** *The statute at the center of this case provides for remedies that may not be available at common law. Why would those additional remedies be sought, and when would they most likely be awarded?*
- **What If the Facts Were Different?** *Suppose that Trump University, or Trump Entrepreneur Initiative, had offered courses in real estate investing only online. Would the result in this case have been different? Explain.*

15–2a Misrepresentation Has Occurred

The first element of proving fraud is to show that misrepresentation of a material fact has occurred. This misrepresentation can occur by words or actions. For instance, the statement "This sculpture was created by Michelangelo" is a misrepresentation of fact if another artist sculpted the statue. Similarly, if a customer asks to see only paintings by Jasper Johns and the gallery owner immediately leads the customer to paintings that were not done by Johns, the owner's actions can be a misrepresentation.

Misrepresentation by Conduct Misrepresentation also occurs when a party takes specific action to conceal a fact that is material to the contract.[7] Therefore, if a seller, by her or his actions, prevents a buyer from learning of some fact that is material to the contract, such behavior constitutes misrepresentation by conduct.

■ **CASE IN POINT 15.5** Actor Tom Selleck contracted to purchase a horse named Zorro for his daughter from Dolores Cuenca. Cuenca acted as though Zorro were fit to ride in competitions, when in reality the horse was unfit for this use because of a medical condition. Selleck filed a lawsuit against Cuenca for wrongfully concealing the horse's condition and won. A jury awarded Selleck more than $187,000 for Cuenca's misrepresentation by conduct.[8] ■

Statements of Opinion Statements of opinion and representations of future facts (predictions) generally are

---

7. *Restatement (Second) of Contracts,* Section 160.

8. *Selleck v. Cuenca,* Case No. GIN056909, North County of San Diego, California, decided September 9, 2009.

not subject to claims of fraud. Statements such as "This land will be worth twice as much next year" and "This car will last for years and years" are statements of opinion, not fact. A fact is objective and verifiable, whereas an opinion is usually subject to debate. Contracting parties should know the difference and should not rely on statements of opinion.

Here, as in other areas of contract law, every person is expected to exercise care and judgment when entering into contracts. The law will not come to the aid of one who simply makes an unwise bargain. Nevertheless, in certain situations, such as when a naïve purchaser relies on an opinion from an expert, the innocent party may be entitled to rescission or reformation. (*Reformation* occurs when a court alters the terms of a contract to prevent undue hardships or burdens.)

■ **CASE IN POINT 15.6** In a classic case, an instructor at an Arthur Murray dance school told Audrey Vokes, a widow without family, that she had the potential to become an accomplished dancer. The instructor sold her 2,302 hours of dancing lessons for a total amount of $31,090.45 (equivalent to $146,000 in 2018). When it became clear to Vokes that she did not, in fact, have the potential to be an excellent dancer, she sued the school for fraudulent misrepresentation. The court held that because the dance school had superior knowledge about dance potential, the instructor's statements could be considered statements of fact rather than opinion.[9] ■

Misrepresentation of Law Misrepresentation of law *ordinarily* does not entitle a party to relief from a contract. ■ **EXAMPLE 15.7** Camara has a parcel of property that she is trying to sell to Pike. Camara knows that a local ordinance prohibits the construction of anything higher than three stories on the property. Nonetheless, she tells Pike, "You can build a condominium a hundred stories high on this land if you want to." Pike buys the land and later discovers that Camara's statement was false. Normally, Pike cannot avoid the contract, because people are assumed to know local zoning laws. ■

Exceptions to this rule occur when the misrepresenting party is in a profession that is known to require greater knowledge of the law than the average citizen possesses. For instance, if Camara, in *Example 15.7*, had been a lawyer or a real estate broker, her willful misrepresentation of the area's zoning laws probably would have constituted fraud.

Misrepresentation by Silence Ordinarily, neither party to a contract has a duty to come forward and disclose facts. Therefore, courts typically do not set aside contracts because a party did not volunteer pertinent information. ■ **EXAMPLE 15.8** Jim is selling a car that has been in an accident and has been repaired. He does not need to volunteer this information to a potential buyer. If, however, the purchaser asks Jim if the car has had extensive bodywork and he lies, he has committed a fraudulent misrepresentation. ■

In general, if a seller knows of a serious potential problem that the buyer cannot reasonably be expected to discover, the seller may have a duty to speak. Usually, the seller must disclose only **latent defects**—that is, defects that could not readily be ascertained. Because a buyer of a house could easily discover the presence of termites through an inspection, for instance, termites may not qualify as a latent defect. Also, when the parties are in a *fiduciary relationship*—one of trust, such as partners, physician and patient, or attorney and client—they have a duty to disclose material facts. Failure to do so may constitute fraud.

15–2b Intent to Deceive

The second element of fraud is knowledge on the part of the misrepresenting party that facts have been falsely represented. This element, normally called *scienter*,[10] or "guilty knowledge," signifies that there was an *intent to deceive*.

Scienter clearly exists if a party knows that a fact is not as stated. ■ **EXAMPLE 15.9** Richard Wright applies for a position as a business law professor two weeks after his release from prison. On his résumé, he lies and says that he was a corporate president for fourteen years and taught business law at another college. After he is hired, his probation officer alerts the school to Wright's criminal history. The school immediately fires him. If Wright sues the school for breach of his employment contract, he is unlikely to succeed. Because Wright clearly exhibited an intent to deceive the college by not disclosing his history, the school can rescind his employment contract without incurring liability. ■

Scienter also exists if a party makes a statement that he or she believes is not true or makes a statement recklessly, without regard to whether it is true or false. Finally, this element is met if a party says or implies that a statement is made on some basis, such as personal knowledge or personal investigation, when it is not.

Innocent Misrepresentation What if a person makes a statement that she or he believes to be true but that actually misrepresents material facts? In this situation, the person is guilty only of an **innocent misrepresentation,** not of fraud. When an innocent misrepresentation occurs, the aggrieved party can rescind the contract but usually cannot seek damages.

---

9. *Vokes v. Arthur Murray, Inc.*, 212 So.2d 906 (Fla.App. 1968).

10. Pronounced sy-en-ter.

EXAMPLE 15.10 Parris tells Roberta that a tract of land contains 250 acres. Parris is mistaken—the tract contains only 215 acres—but Parris had no knowledge of the mistake. Roberta relies on the statement and contracts to buy the land. Even though the misrepresentation is innocent, Roberta can avoid the contract if the misrepresentation is material. ■

Negligent Misrepresentation Sometimes, a party makes a misrepresentation through carelessness, believing the statement is true, which can constitute **negligent misrepresentation.** Negligent misrepresentation occurs if the party does not exercise reasonable care in uncovering or disclosing facts, or use the skill and competence required by his or her business or profession.

EXAMPLE 15.11 Kirk, an operator of a weight scale, certifies the weight of Sneed's commodity. If Kirk knows that the scale's accuracy has not been checked for more than three years, his action may constitute negligent misrepresentation. ■

In almost all states, such negligent misrepresentation is equal to *scienter,* or knowingly making a misrepresentation. In effect, negligent misrepresentation is treated as fraudulent misrepresentation, even though the misrepresentation was not purposeful. In negligent misrepresentation, culpable ignorance of the truth supplies the intention to mislead, even if the defendant can claim, "I didn't know."

15–2c Justifiable Reliance on the Misrepresentation

The third element of fraud is reasonably *justifiable reliance* on the misrepresentation of fact. The deceived party must have a justifiable reason for relying on the misrepresentation. Also, the misrepresentation must be an important factor (but not necessarily the sole factor) in inducing the deceived party to enter into the contract. Reliance is not justified if the innocent party knows the true facts or relies on obviously extravagant statements (such as, "this pickup truck will get fifty miles to the gallon").

EXAMPLE 15.12 Meese, a securities broker, offers to sell BIM stock to Packer. Meese assures Packer that BIM shares are blue chip securities—that is, they are stable, have limited risk, and yield a good return on investment over time. In reality, Meese knows nothing about the quality of BIM stock and does not believe the truth of what he is saying. Thus, Meese's statement is an intentional misrepresentation of a material fact. If Packer is induced by Meese's statement to enter into a contract to buy the stock, he probably can avoid the contract. Packer justifiably relied on his broker's misrepresentation of material fact. ■

The same rule applies to defects in property sold. If the defects would be obvious on inspection, the buyer cannot justifiably rely on the seller's representations. If the defects are hidden or latent, as previously discussed, the buyer is justified in relying on the seller's statements.

In the following case, the receiver for a car wash assured the buyer that the property would be "appropriately winterized," but it was not. Was the buyer justified in relying on the seller's representations? (A *receiver,* also called a *trustee,* is an independent, impartial party appointed by a bankruptcy court to manage property in bankruptcy and dispose of it in an orderly manner for the benefit of the creditors.)

Case Analysis 15.2

Cronkelton v. Guaranteed Construction Services, LLC

Court of Appeals of Ohio, Third District, 988 N.E.2d 656, 2013-Ohio-328 (2013).

In the Language of the Court
PRESTON, P.J. [Presiding Judge]
* * * *

The case before this Court stems from a real estate transaction for a foreclosed car wash in Bellefontaine, Ohio. [A court had appointed Patrick Shivley to be a receiver for the protection of the property, which was offered for sale by Huntington Bank. Clifford] Cronkelton filed a complaint against appellants [Guaranteed Construction Services, LLC, and Shivley] in the Logan County

Court of Common Pleas following his purchase of the car wash. Cronkelton asserted * * * fraud.
* * * *

* * * The trial court held a jury trial on the fraud claim. The jury returned a verdict for Cronkelton.

* * * The trial court filed its judgment entry recording the jury's verdict for Cronkelton and awarding Cronkelton $43,671 in compensatory damages, $66,000 in punitive damages, and $30,000 for attorney fees. [Guaranteed Construction

Services and Shivley filed an appeal.]
* * * *

* * * [At the trial] Cronkelton testified that he first inspected the foreclosed car wash at the end of November 2009. At that time, Cronkelton tested the equipment and knew that some of the pieces of equipment were fully functioning and some were not. * * * Shortly thereafter, Cronkelton called Shivley to discuss the winterization of the property. Cronkelton testified:

Case 15.2 Continues

So I called him, said, hey, it's going to freeze here this week. * * * It's supposed to get down to like ten degrees, have you got it winterized, you know. If it's not winterized, I'm not interested in the property. If it freezes, I'm not interested in the property at all. And he guaranteed me. He said, no, it will be taken care of. We don't have a problem. That's my job as receiver. I'll take care of it.

After the phone call, Shivley sent Cronkelton an e-mail dated December 7, 2009 that stated:

As per our phone conversation Guaranteed [Construction Services] will winterize the Car Wash with the anticipation of reopening the wash in the near future. Within this Winterization we will put antifreeze and secure floor heating as well as blow water out of all lines in self serve bays as well as empty tanks, etc. We will leave the heat on at a minimal level in the pump room. * * * We will complete all of this on Wednesday, December 9, 2009.

[Guaranteed Construction Services hired Strayer Company to winterize the property. But on December 10, Strayer's owner sent a memo to Guaranteed Construction Services and Shivley stating that the building was not designed to be winterized and that the only way to avoid problems was to leave the heat on. Shivley knew Huntington Bank had shut off the heat because the property was not generating income. In March 2010, Shivley informed Huntington of damage to the property as a result of freezing. Shivley did not share any of this information with Cronkelton.]

Cronkelton testified that they closed on the property in June and he received the keys at that time. Cronkelton testified that he immediately went to the property:

I opened the door, and the huge canisters that I was telling you about were all busted. The tops had been exploded off the top of them. * * * You could see pipes that were busted * * *. So it was clear at that time that this whole thing had froze up, and the extent of the damage could not even be, you know, detailed at that point.

* * * *

* * * Appellants argue Cronkelton unjustifiably relied on Shivley's statements about the car wash's condition because Cronkelton had the opportunity to inspect the property prior to closing.

* * * *

* * * Whether or not reliance on a material misrepresentation was justified under the facts of a case is a question for the trier of fact. Consequently, we must determine whether the jury's decision is supported by competent, credible evidence.

In the present case, it is undisputed that the damage caused by freezing was open and obvious upon inspection, that Cronkelton did inspect the property in November 2009, and that he could have inspected the property again before signing the purchase agreement. Cronkelton

testified regarding why he did not inspect the property after November 2009:

* * * [Shivley] wrote me this e-mail, guaranteed me it was taken care of in detail what he was going to do, so I had no reason. And because * * * he was appointed by the Court, I don't know how much more I could have done to know that I could trust him.

* * * The jury found that Cronkelton had reasonably relied on Shivley's representations.

The jury's finding was supported by competent, credible evidence. * * * *When determining whether reliance is justifiable, courts consider the various circumstances involved, such as the nature of the transaction, the form and materiality of the transaction, the form and materiality of the representation, the relationship of the parties, the respective intelligence, experience, age, and mental and physical condition of the parties, and their respective knowledge and means of knowledge.* [Emphasis added.]

Cronkelton relied on representations made by Shivley * * *. As a receiver, Shivley had a fiduciary duty to the assets under his control. Under the circumstances of this case, Cronkelton had a reasonable basis to believe that Shivley, who was acting as an arm of the court, would take the promised steps to winterize the property.

* * * *

* * * We affirm the judgment of the trial court.

Legal Reasoning Questions

1. In evaluating a claim of fraud, what factors does a court consider in determining whether reliance was justifiable?

2. In this case, what did the jury find with respect to the plaintiff's claim of reliance? What was the appellate court's opinion of this finding?

3. Did Shivley's misrepresentations rise to the level of fraud? Explain.

15–2d Injury to the Innocent Party

Most courts do not require a showing of injury when the action is to rescind the contract. These courts hold that because rescission returns the parties to the positions they held before the contract was made, a showing of injury to the innocent party is unnecessary.

In contrast, to recover damages caused by fraud, proof of harm is universally required. The measure of damages is ordinarily equal to the property's value had it been delivered as represented, less the actual price paid for the property. (Additionally, because fraud actions necessarily involve wrongful conduct, courts may also sometimes award punitive damages, which are not ordinarily available in contract actions.)

In the following case, a real estate investor claimed that a seller's failure to disclose material facts about the property affected its value. The court had to determine not only if the seller's conduct constituted fraud, but also whether the fraud had caused harm to the property value.

Case 15.3

Fazio v. Cypress/GR Houston I, LP

Court of Appeals of Texas, First District, 403 S.W.3d 390 (2013).

Background and Facts Peter Fazio began talks with Cypress/GR Houston I, LP, to buy retail property whose main tenant was a Garden Ridge store. In performing a background investigation, Fazio and his agents became concerned about Garden Ridge's financial health. Nevertheless, after being assured that Garden Ridge had a positive financial outlook, Fazio sent Cypress a letter of intent to buy the property for $7.67 million "[b]ased on the currently reported absolute net income of $805,040.00." Cypress then agreed to provide all information in its possession, but it failed to disclose the following:

1. A consultant for Garden Ridge had recently requested a $240,000 reduction in the annual rent as part of a restructuring of the company's real estate leases.
2. Cypress's bank was so concerned about Garden Ridge's financial health that it had required a personal guaranty of the property's loan.

The parties entered into a purchase agreement, but Garden Ridge went into bankruptcy shortly after the deal closed. Fazio, along with other members of his family, sued Cypress for fraud after he was forced to sell the property three years later for only $3.75 million. A jury found in Fazio's favor. Although the jury agreed that Cypress had failed to disclose a material fact, however, it determined that Fazio was not entitled to any damages. The jury concluded that the fraud had not negatively affected the value of the property at the time it was sold to Fazio. Thus, no damages had been proximately caused by the fraud. The trial court entered a judgment notwithstanding the verdict in favor of Cypress, and Fazio appealed.

In the Language of the Court

Jane BLAND, Justice.

In this suit arising from the sale of land, we examine the appropriate measure of damages for a sale obtained through fraudulent inducement. A jury concluded that the seller of the land had failed to disclose material information to the buyer about the financial state of a commercial tenant who leased the land. But the jury further concluded that the buyers suffered nothing in damages proximately caused by the fraud, measured at the time of the sale, and it awarded no damages * * * . The trial court entered a take-nothing judgment [a judgment in which the plaintiff will receive no damages or other relief] in favor of the seller.
* * * *

The Fazios appeal the trial court's judgment against them on their claim for fraudulent inducement, contending that the trial court erred in disregarding the jury's * * * findings in their favor.
* * * *

There are two measures of direct damages in a fraud case: out-of-pocket and benefit-of-the-bargain. Out-of-pocket damages measure the difference between the amount the buyer paid and the value of the property the buyer received. Benefit-of-the-bargain damages measure the difference between the value of the property as represented and the actual value of the property. Both measures are determined at the time of the sale induced by the fraud. [Emphasis added.]

Losses that arise after the time of sale may be recoverable as consequential damages in appropriate cases. Consequential damages must be foreseeable and directly traceable to the misrepresentation and result from it. * * * Consequential damages must be explicitly premised on findings that the losses were foreseeable and directly traceable to the misrepresentation.

Case 15.3 Continues

Case 15.3 Continued

* * * *

* * * [The jury was] instructed * * * to determine the difference between the fraud-induced price that the Fazios paid for the property and the actual value of the property they received when they purchased it. * * * The question correctly focused the jury on the time of the sale, *because direct damages for fraud, including out-of-pocket damages, are properly measured at the time of the sale induced by the fraud—in this case, when the purchase agreement was executed—and not at some future time.* The jury responded that such damages were $0. It found other sorts of incidental and consequential damage to be $0 as well. [Emphasis added.]

* * * *

* * * The trial court properly * * * accorded judgment based on the jury's zero damages finding.

Decision and Remedy *A state intermediate appellate court affirmed the trial court's judgment based on the jury's finding. Fazio was not entitled to damages, because the misrepresentation (fraud) had not negatively affected the property's value at the time Fazio purchased the property.*

Critical Thinking
- **Ethical** *Was Cypress's conduct unethical? Why or why not?*
- **Social** *What does the decision in this case suggest to sellers of commercial real estate and others who engage in business negotiations?*

15–3 Undue Influence

Undue influence arises from relationships in which one party can greatly influence another party, thus overcoming that party's free will. A contract entered into under excessive or undue influence lacks voluntary consent and is therefore voidable.[11]

15–3a One Party Dominates the Other

In various types of relationships, one party may have the opportunity to dominate and unfairly influence another party. Minors and elderly people, for instance, are often under the influence of guardians (persons who are legally responsible for them). If a guardian induces a young or elderly ward (a person whom the guardian looks after) to enter into a contract that benefits the guardian, the guardian may have exerted undue influence. Undue influence can arise from a number of fiduciary relationships, such as physician-patient, parent-child, husband-wife, or guardian-ward situations.

The essential feature of undue influence is that the party being taken advantage of does not, in reality, exercise free will in entering into a contract. It is not enough that a person is elderly or suffers from some physical or mental impairment. There must be clear and convincing evidence that the person did not act out of her or his free

will.[12] Similarly, the existence of a fiduciary relationship alone is insufficient to prove undue influence.[13]

15–3b Presumption of Undue Influence in Certain Situations

When the dominant party in a fiduciary relationship benefits from that relationship, a presumption of undue influence arises. The dominant party must exercise the utmost good faith in dealing with the other party. When a contract enriches the dominant party, the court will often *presume* that the contract was made under undue influence.

■ **EXAMPLE 15.13** Erik is the guardian for Kinsley, his ward. Erik is the dominant party in this relationship. On Kinsley's behalf, he enters into a contract from which he benefits financially. If Kinsley challenges the contract, the court will likely presume that the guardian has taken advantage of his ward. To rebut (refute) this presumption, Erik has to show that he made full disclosure to Kinsley and that consideration was present. He must also show that Kinsley received, if available, independent and competent advice before completing the transaction. Unless the presumption can be rebutted, the contract will be rescinded. ■

---

11. *Restatement (Second) of Contracts*, Section 177.

12. See, for example, *Ayers v. Shaffer*, 286 Va. 212, 748 S.E.2d 83 (2013).
13. See, for example, *Sleepy Hollow Ranch LLC v. Robinson*, 373 S.W.3d 485 (Mo.App. 2012).

15–4 Duress

Agreement to the terms of a contract is not voluntary if one of the parties is *forced* into the agreement. The use of threats to force a party to enter into a contract constitutes **duress.** Similarly, the use of blackmail or extortion to induce consent to a contract is duress. Duress is both a defense to the enforcement of a contract and a ground for the rescission of a contract.

15–4a The Threatened Act Must Be Wrongful or Illegal

To establish duress, there must be proof of a threat to do something that the threatening party has no right to do. Generally, for duress to occur, the threatened act must be wrongful or illegal. It also must render the person who is threatened incapable of exercising free will. A threat to exercise a legal right, such as the right to sue someone, ordinarily does not constitute duress.

■ **EXAMPLE 15.14** Joan accidentally drives into Olin's car at a stoplight. Joan has no automobile insurance, but she has substantial assets. At the scene, Olin claims to have suffered whiplash and tells Joan that he will agree not to file a lawsuit against her if she pays him $5,000. Joan initially refuses, but Olin says, "If you don't pay me $5,000 right now, I'm going to sue you for $25,000." Joan then gives Olin a check for $5,000 to avoid the lawsuit. The next day, Joan stops payment on the check. When Olin later sues to enforce their oral settlement agreement for $5,000, Joan claims duress as a defense to its enforcement. In this situation, because Olin had a right to sue Joan, his threat to sue her does not constitute duress. A court normally would not consider the threat of a civil suit to be duress. ■

15–4b Economic Duress

Economic need generally is not sufficient to constitute duress, even when one party exacts a very high price for an item that the other party needs. If the party exacting the price also creates the need, however, *economic duress* may be found.[14]

■ **EXAMPLE 15.15** The Internal Revenue Service (IRS) assesses a large tax and penalty against Weller. Weller retains Eyman, the accountant who prepared the

tax returns on which the assessment was based, to challenge the assessment. Two days before the deadline for filing a reply with the IRS, Eyman declines to represent Weller unless he signs a very expensive contingency-fee agreement for the services.

In this situation, a court might find that the agreement is unenforceable because of economic duress. Eyman threatened only to withdraw his services, something that he was legally entitled to do. However, he delayed the withdrawal until two days before the IRS deadline. It would have been impossible at that late date to obtain adequate representation elsewhere. Therefore, Weller can argue that he was forced either to sign the contract or to lose his right to challenge the IRS assessment. ■

15–5 Adhesion Contracts and Unconscionability

Sometimes, the terms of a contract are dictated by a party with overwhelming bargaining power. The signer must agree to those terms or go without the commodity or service in question. In these situations, questions concerning voluntary consent may arise. (Many such contracts include arbitration provisions, as discussed in this chapter's *Ethics Today* feature.)

Adhesion contracts are written *exclusively* by one party and presented to the other party on a take-it-or-leave-it basis. These contracts often use standard forms, which give the adhering party no opportunity to negotiate the contract terms.

15–5a Standard-Form Contracts

Standard-form contracts often contain fine-print provisions that shift a risk ordinarily borne by one party to the other. A variety of businesses use such contracts. Life insurance policies, residential leases, loan agreements, and employment agency contracts are often standard-form contracts. To avoid enforcement of the contract or of a particular clause, the plaintiff normally must show that the contract or particular term is *unconscionable.*

■ **CASE IN POINT 15.16** Gregory and Stephanie Smith bought a house in Summerville, South Carolina, that was built by D. R. Horton, Inc. The standard purchase agreement they signed included a "Warranties and Dispute Resolution Section" that contained an arbitration clause and limited Horton's liability. After the Smiths moved in, they found extensive defects in the home. The Smiths

---

14. For a decision discussing the requirements for establishing economic duress, see *Cate Street Capital, Inc. v. DG Whitefield, LLC,* 2014 WL 8382756 (N.H.Super. 2014).

filed a lawsuit against Horton and numerous subcontractors for negligence, breach of contract, breach of warranties, and unfair trade practices.

Horton moved to compel arbitration, but the trial court denied the motion, holding that the arbitration clause was unconscionable. Horton appealed. The reviewing court affirmed the lower court's decision. The standard-form contract's "Warranties and Dispute Resolution Section" required binding arbitration of certain disputes and included "an entire host of attempted waivers of important legal remedies." Therefore, the court found that it was oppressive, unconscionable, and unenforceable. The Smiths could sue Horton and its subcontractors for the alleged defects.[15] ∎

15. *Smith v. D.R. Horton, Inc.,* 403 S.C. 10, 742 S.E.2d 37 (2013).

15–5b Unconscionability and the Courts

Technically, unconscionability under Section 2–302 of the Uniform Commercial Code (UCC) applies only to contracts for the sale of goods. Many courts, however, have broadened the concept and applied it in other situations.

It is important to note here that the UCC gives courts a great degree of discretion to invalidate or strike down a contract or clause as being unconscionable. As a result, some states have *not* adopted Section 2–302 of the UCC. In those states, the legislature and the courts prefer to rely on traditional notions of fraud, undue influence, and duress.

See Concept Summary 15.1 for a review of the factors that may indicate a lack of voluntary consent.

Concept Summary 15.1

Factors That May Indicate a Lack of Voluntary Consent

Mistakes	• *Bilateral (mutual) mistake*—If both parties are mistaken about a material fact, either party can avoid the contract. If the mistake relates to the value or quality of the subject matter, either party can enforce the contract. • *Unilateral mistake*—Generally, the mistaken party is bound by the contract, unless the other party knows or should have known of the mistake, or the mistake is an inadvertent mathematical error that is committed without gross negligence.
Fraudulent Misrepresentation	• A misrepresentation of a material fact has occurred. • There has been an intent to deceive. • The innocent party has justifiably relied on the misrepresentation. • To collect damages, a party must have been harmed as a result of the misrepresentation.
Undue Influence and Duress	• *Undue influence*—Arises from special relationships, in which one party's free will has been overcome by the undue influence of another. Usually, the contract is voidable. • *Duress*—Defined as the use of threats to force a party to enter into a contract out of fear; for example, the threat of violence or economic pressure. The party forced to enter into the contract can rescind the contract.
Adhesion Contracts and Unconscionability	• Concerns one-sided bargains in which one party has substantially superior bargaining power and can dictate the terms of a contract. • Unconscionability can occur in standard-form contracts and take-it-or-leave-it (adhesion) contracts.

ETHICS TODAY

Forced Arbitration: Right or Wrong?

Knowingly or not, many consumers sign contracts that include arbitration clauses. Such clauses require that dissatisfied consumers submit to arbitration, rather than pursue litigation through the court system. Not surprisingly, there is a growing movement in protest of arbitration clauses of this kind, which some believe are unfair to consumers.

Governing Arbitration Law

For the most part, federal law encourages arbitration through the Federal Arbitration Act (FAA).[a] Generally, federal courts have ruled in favor of contracts with arbitration clauses if those clauses provide a meaningful way for consumers to seek redress for alleged harms.

Over the past few years, the United States Supreme Court has held that the FAA preempts state courts' interpretations of arbitration clauses. For instance, in *AT&T Mobility, LLC v. Concepcion,*[b] the Court ruled that federal law preempts state laws that bar enforcement of arbitration clauses prohibiting class-action suits. Later, in *DIRECTV, Inc. v. Imburgia,*[c] the Court again upheld an arbitration clause, citing the *Concepcion* case. The Court stated that the FAA "is the law of the United States, and [the] *Concepcion* [case] is an authoritative interpretation of the act." The Court stated that "the judges of every State must follow it" because of the supremacy clause of the U.S. Constitution.

Federal Attempts to Circumvent the Supreme Court's Decisions

Even within the federal government, certain entities wish to reduce the use of arbitration clauses in consumer contracts. In the fall of 2015, the Consumer Financial Protection Bureau announced that it would seek to implement new rules barring contracts from substituting private arbitration for class-action litigation. Such rules would apply to checking accounts, credit cards, and other financial products. If that federal agency is successful, it will undoubtedly face litigation that will go to the Supreme Court.

Why Arbitration Is So Prevalent

Many corporations favor arbitration clauses in consumer contracts because arbitration is less expensive than litigation. Arbitration is certainly the preferred remedy for disputes involving relatively small sums—disputes over cell phone contracts, for instance. While individuals may feel that they are at a disadvantage if they are forced to go to arbitration, for the economy as a whole, there are benefits. In particular, according to some estimates, the rate of growth in liability costs has fallen relative to the growth in the economy since 2003. Ultimately, consumers on average pay lower costs for products and services when corporations spend less on litigation.

Critical Thinking *What might happen if arbitration clauses were prohibited in all consumer contracts?*

---

a. 9 U.S.C. Sections 1 *et seq.*
b. 563 U.S. 333, 131 S.Ct. 1740, 179 L.Ed.2d 742 (2011). See also *American Express Co. v. Italian Colors Restaurant,* ___ U.S. ___, 133 S.Ct. 2304, 186 L.Ed.2d 417 (2013).
c. ___ U.S. ___, 135 S.Ct. 1547, 191 L.Ed.2d 636 (2015).

Reviewing: Mistakes, Fraud, and Voluntary Consent

Chelene had been a caregiver for Marta's eighty-year-old mother, Janis, for nine years. Shortly before Janis passed away, Chelene convinced her to buy Chelene's house for Marta. The elderly woman died before the papers were signed, however. Four months later, Marta used her inheritance to buy Chelene's house without having it inspected. The house was built in the 1950s, and Chelene said it was in "perfect condition." Nevertheless, one year after the purchase, the basement started leaking. Marta had the paneling removed from the basement walls and discovered that the walls were bowed inward and cracked. Marta then had a civil engineer inspect the basement walls, and he found that the cracks had been caulked and painted over before the paneling was installed. He concluded that the "wall failure" had existed "for at least thirty years" and that the basement walls were "structurally unsound." Using the information presented in the chapter, answer the following questions.

Continues

1. Can Marta avoid the contract on the ground that both parties made a mistake about the condition of the house? Explain.
2. Can Marta sue Chelene for fraudulent misrepresentation? Why or why not? What element or elements might be lacking?
3. Now assume that Chelene knew that the basement walls were cracked and bowed and that she had hired someone to install paneling before she offered to sell the house. Did she have a duty to disclose this defect to Marta? Could a court find that Chelene's silence in this situation constituted misrepresentation? Explain.
4. Can Marta obtain rescission of the contract based on undue influence? If the sale to Janis had been completed before her death, could Janis have obtained rescission based on undue influence? Explain.

Debate This . . . *The concept of* caveat emptor *("let the buyer beware") should be applied to all sales, including those of real property.*

Terms and Concepts

adhesion contract 289
bilateral mistake 280
duress 289
innocent misrepresentation 284

latent defect 284
negligent misrepresentation 285
scienter 284
undue influence 288

unilateral mistake 280
voluntary consent 280

Issue Spotters

1. In selling a house, Matt tells Ann that the wiring, fixtures, and appliances are of a certain quality. Matt knows nothing about the quality, but it is not as specified. Ann buys the house. On learning the true quality, Ann confronts Matt. He says he wasn't trying to fool her, he was only trying to make a sale. Can she rescind the deal? Why or why not? (See *Fraudulent Misrepresentation*.)

2. Elle, an accountant, certifies several audit reports for Flite Corporation, her client, knowing that Flite intends to use the reports to obtain loans from Good Credit Company (GCC). Elle believes that the reports are true and does not intend to deceive GCC, but she does not check the reports before certifying them. Can Elle be held liable to GCC? Why or why not? (See *Fraudulent Misrepresentation*.)

- **Check your answers to the Issue Spotters against the answers provided in Appendix D at the end of this text.**

Business Scenarios

15–1. Undue Influence. Juan is an elderly man who lives with his nephew, Samuel. Juan is totally dependent on Samuel's support. Samuel tells Juan that unless he transfers a tract of land he owns to Samuel for a price 35 percent below its market value, Samuel will no longer support and take care of him. Juan enters into the contract. Discuss fully whether Juan can set aside this contract. (See *Undue Influence*.)

15–2. Fraudulent Misrepresentation. Grano owns a forty-room motel on Highway 100. Tanner is interested in purchasing the motel. During the course of negotiations, Grano tells Tanner that the motel netted $30,000 during the previous year and that it will net at least $45,000 the next year. The motel books, which Grano turns over to Tanner before the purchase, clearly show that Grano's motel netted only $15,000 the previous year. Also, Grano fails to tell Tanner that a bypass to Highway 100 is being planned that will redirect most traffic away from the front of the motel. Tanner purchases the motel. During the first year under Tanner's operation, the motel nets only $18,000. At this time, Tanner learns of the motel's previous low profits and the planned bypass. Tanner wants Grano to return the purchase price. Discuss fully Tanner's probable success in getting his funds back. (See *Fraudulent Misrepresentation*.)

15–3. Voluntary Consent. Discuss whether either of the following contracts will be unenforceable on the ground that voluntary consent is lacking:

(a) Simmons finds a stone in his pasture that he believes to be quartz. Jenson, who also believes that the stone is quartz, contracts to purchase it for $10. Just before delivery, the stone is discovered to be a diamond worth $1,000. (See *Mistakes.*)

(b) Jacoby's barn is burned to the ground. He accuses Goldman's son of arson and threatens to have the prosecutor bring a criminal action unless Goldman agrees to pay him $5,000. Goldman agrees to pay. (See *Duress.*)

Business Case Problems

15–4. Fraudulent Misrepresentation. Ricky and Sherry Wilcox hired Esprit Log and Timber Frame Homes to build a log house, which the Wilcoxes intended to sell. They paid Esprit $125,260 for materials and services. They eventually sold the home for $1,620,000 but sued Esprit due to construction delays. The logs were supposed to arrive at the construction site precut and predrilled, but that did not happen. It took five extra months to build the house while the logs were cut and drilled one by one. The Wilcoxes claimed that the interest they paid on a loan for the extra construction time cost them about $200,000. The jury agreed and awarded them that much in damages, plus $250,000 in punitive damages and $20,000 in attorneys' fees. Esprit appealed, claiming that the evidence did not support the verdict because the Wilcoxes had sold the house for a good price. Is Esprit's argument credible? Why or why not? How should the court rule? [*Esprit Log and Timber Frame Homes, Inc. v. Wilcox,* 302 Ga.App. 550, 691 S.E.2d 344 (2010)] (See *Fraudulent Misrepresentation.*)

15–5. Fraudulent Misrepresentation. Charter One Bank owned a fifteen-story commercial building. A fire inspector told Charter that the building's drinking-water and fire-suppression systems were linked, which violated building codes. Without disclosing this information, Charter sold the building to Northpoint Properties, Inc. Northpoint spent $280,000 to repair the water and fire-suppression systems and filed a suit against Charter One. Is the seller liable for not disclosing the building's defects? Discuss. [*Northpoint Properties, Inc. v. Charter One Bank,* 2011-Ohio-2512 (Ohio App. 8 Dist. 2011)] (See *Fraudulent Misrepresentation.*)

15–6. Standard-Form Contracts. David Desgro hired Paul Pack to inspect a house that Desgro wanted to buy. Pack had Desgro sign a standard-form contract that included a twelve-month limit for claims based on the agreement. Pack reported that the house had no major problems, but after Desgro bought it, he discovered issues with the plumbing, insulation, heat pump, and floor support. Thirteen months after the inspection, Desgro filed a suit in a Tennessee state court against Pack. Was Desgro's complaint filed too late, or was the contract's twelve-month limit unenforceable? Discuss. [*Desgro v. Pack,* 2013 WL 84899 (Tenn.App. 2013)] (See *Adhesion Contracts and Unconscionability.*)

15–7. Business Case Problem with Sample Answer— Fraudulent Misrepresentation. Joy Pervis and Brenda Pauley worked together as talent agents in Georgia. When Pervis "discovered" actress Dakota Fanning, Pervis sent Fanning's audition tape to Cindy Osbrink, a talent agent in California. Osbrink agreed to represent Fanning in California and to pay 3 percent of Osbrink's commissions to Pervis and Pauley, who agreed to split the payments equally. Six years later, Pervis told Pauley that their agreement with Osbrink had expired and there would be no more payments. Nevertheless, Pervis continued to receive payments from Osbrink. Each time Pauley asked about commissions, however, Pervis replied that she was not receiving any. Do these facts evidence fraud? Explain. [*In re Pervis,* 512 Bankr. 348 (N.D.Ga. 2014)] (See *Fraudulent Misrepresentation.*)

- **For a sample answer to Problem 15–7, go to Appendix E at the end of this text.**

15–8. Fraudulent Misrepresentation. Vianna Stibal owns and operates the ThetaHealing Institute of Knowledge (THInK) in Idaho Falls, Idaho. ThetaHealing is Stibal's "self-discovered" healing method. In her book *Go Up and Seek God,* Stibal stated that she had been diagnosed with cancer and had cured herself using ThetaHealing. But Stibal's representation that she cured herself of cancer was false, and she knew it—her medical records did not confirm a cancer diagnosis. Believing Stibal's claim, Kara Alexander traveled from New York to Idaho to pay for, and attend, classes in ThetaHealing from Stibal. Later, Alexander began to question the validity of her THInK degree. What are the elements of a cause of action for fraudulent misrepresentation? Do the facts in this situation meet these requirements? Discuss. [*Alexander v. Stibal,* 160 Idaho 10, 368 P.3d 630 (2016)] (See *Fraudulent Misrepresentation.*)

15–9. A Question of Ethics—Mistake. On behalf of BRJM, LLC, Nicolas Kepple offered Howard Engelsen $210,000 for a parcel of land known as lot five on the north side of Barnes Road in Stonington, Connecticut. Engelsen's company, Output Systems, Inc., owned the land. Engelsen had the lot surveyed and obtained an appraisal. The appraiser determined that the property was 3.0 acres in size. It thus could not be subdivided because it did not *meet the town's minimum legal requirement of 3.7 acres for subdivision. The appraiser then valued the property at $277,000. Engelsen responded to Kepple's offer of $210,000 with a counteroffer of $230,000, which Kepple accepted. On May 3, 2002, the parties signed a contract. When Engelsen refused to go through with the deal, BRJM filed a suit in a Connecticut state court against Output, seeking specific performance and other relief. The defendant asserted the defense of mutual mistake on at least two grounds. [BRJM, LLC v. Output Systems, Inc., 100 Conn. App. 153, 917 A.2d 605 (2007)]* (See *Mistakes.*)

(a) In the counteroffer, Engelsen asked Kepple to remove from their contract a clause requiring written confirmation of the availability of a "free split," which meant that the property could be subdivided without the town's prior approval. Kepple agreed. After signing the contract, Kepple learned that the property was *not* entitled to a free split. Would this circumstance qualify as a mistake on which the defendant could avoid the contract? Discuss.

(b) After signing the contract, Engelsen obtained a second appraisal that established the size of lot five as 3.71 acres, which meant that it could be subdivided, and valued the property at $490,000. Can the defendant avoid the contract on the basis of a mistake in the first appraisal? Explain.

Legal Reasoning Group Activity

15–10. Fraudulent Misrepresentation. Radiah Givens was involved romantically with Joseph Rosenzweig. She moved into an apartment on which he made the down payment. She signed the mortgage, but he made the payments and paid household expenses. They later married. She had their marriage annulled, however, when she learned that he was married to someone else. Rosenzweig then filed a suit against her to collect on the mortgage. (See *Fraudulent Misrepresentation.*)

(a) The first group should decide whether Rosenzweig committed fraud.

(b) The second group should evaluate whether Rosenzweig's conduct was deceitful, and if so, whether his deceitfulness should affect the decision in this case.

(c) The third group should consider how fraud is related to ethics. Can a contracting party act ethically and still commit fraud? How?

Answers to the *Issue Spotters*

1. *Can she rescind the deal? Why or why not?* Yes. Rescission may be granted on the basis of fraudulent misrepresentation. The elements of fraudulent misrepresentation include intent to deceive, or *scienter*. *Scienter* exists if a party makes a statement recklessly, without regard to whether it is true or false, or if a party says or implies that a statement is made on some basis such as personal knowledge or personal investigation when it is not.

2. *Can Elle be held liable to GCC? Why or why not?* Yes. The accountant may be liable on the ground of negligent misrepresentation. A misrepresentation is negligent if a person fails to exercise reasonable care in disclosing material facts or does not use the skill and competence required by his or her business or profession.

Sample Answers for *Business Case Problems with Sample Answer*

Problem 15–7. *Fraudulent Misrepresentation.* Yes, the facts in this problem evidence fraud. There are three elements to fraud: (1) the misrepresentation of a material fact, (2) an intent to deceive, and (3) an innocent party's justifiable reliance on the misrepresentation. To collect damages, the innocent party must suffer an injury.

Here, Pervis represented to Pauley that no further commission would be paid by Osbrink. This representation was false—despite Pervis's statement to the contrary, Osbrink continued to send payments to Pervis. Pervis knew the representation was false, as shown by the fact that she made it more than once during the time that she was continuing to receive payments from Osbrink. Each time Pauley asked about commissions, Pervis replied that she was not receiving any. Pauley's reliance on her business associate's statements was justified and reasonable. And for the purpose of recovering damages, Pauley suffered an injury in the amount of her share of the commissions that Pervis received as a result of the fraud.

In the actual case on which this problem is based, Pauley filed a suit in a Georgia state court against Pervis, who filed for bankruptcy in a federal bankruptcy court to stay the state action. The federal court held Pervis liable on the ground of fraud for the amount of the commissions that were not paid to Pauley and denied Pervis a discharge of the debt.

CHAPTER

The Writing Requirement in Our Digital World

A contract that is otherwise valid may still be unenforceable if it is not in the proper form. Certain types of contracts are required to be in writing or evidenced by a memorandum or an electronic record. An agreement subject to the writing requirement does not necessarily have to be written on paper. An exchange of e-mails that evidences the parties' contract can be sufficient, provided that they are "signed," or agreed to, by the party against whom enforcement is sought.

In this chapter, we examine the kinds of contracts that require a writing and some exceptions to the writing requirement. We also discuss the *parol evidence rule,* which courts follow when determining whether evidence that is extraneous, or external, to written contracts may be admissible at trial.

16–1 The Statute of Frauds

Every state has a statute that stipulates what types of contracts must be in writing. We refer to such a statute as the **Statute of Frauds.** The origins of these statutes can be traced to early English law.

16–1a Origins of the Statute

At early common law, parties to a contract were not allowed to testify if a dispute arose. This led to the practice of hiring third party witnesses. As early as the seventeenth century, the English recognized that this practice created many problems and enacted a statute to help deal with them.

The statute, passed by the English Parliament in 1677, was known as "An Act for the Prevention of Frauds and Perjuries." The act established that certain types of contracts, to be enforceable, had to be evidenced by a writing and signed by the party against whom enforcement was sought. The primary purpose of the statute was to ensure that, for certain types of contracts, there was reliable evidence of the contracts and their terms.

16–1b State Legislation

Today, although each state has a statute modeled after the English act, the statutes vary slightly from state to state. All states require certain types of contracts to be in writing or evidenced by a written memorandum or an electronic record. In addition, the party or parties against whom enforcement is sought must have signed the contract, unless certain exceptions apply (as discussed later in this chapter). Recall that in the context of electronic communications, a party's name typed at the bottom of an e-mail can qualify as a signature.

The actual name of the Statute of Frauds is misleading because the statute does not apply to fraud. Rather, it denies enforceability to certain contracts that do not comply with its writing requirements. The primary purpose of the statute is to prevent harm to innocent parties by requiring written evidence of agreements concerning important transactions. A contract that is oral when it is required to be in writing is normally voidable by a party who later does not wish to follow through with the agreement.

16–2 Contracts That Require a Writing

The following types of contracts are generally required to be in writing or evidenced by a written memorandum or electronic record:

1. Contracts involving interests in land.
2. Contracts that cannot *by their terms* be performed within one year from the day after the date of formation.

3. Collateral, or secondary, contracts, such as promises to answer for the debt or duty of another and promises by the administrator or executor of an estate to pay a debt of the estate personally—that is, out of her or his own pocket.

4. Promises made in consideration of marriage.

5. Under the Uniform Commercial Code (UCC), contracts for the sale of goods priced at $500 or more.

16–2a Contracts Involving Interests in Land

A contract calling for the sale of land is not enforceable unless it is in writing or evidenced by a written memorandum. Land is *real property* and includes all physical objects that are permanently attached to the soil, such as buildings, fences, trees, and the soil itself.

The Statute of Frauds operates as a *defense* to the enforcement of an oral contract for the sale of land. ■ **EXAMPLE 16.1** Skylar contracts orally to sell his property in Fair Oaks to Beth. If he later decides not to sell, under most circumstances, Beth cannot enforce the contract. ■

The Statute of Frauds also requires written evidence of contracts for the transfer of other interests in land, such as mortgage agreements and leases. Similarly, an agreement that includes an option to purchase real property must be in writing for the option to be enforced.

Generally, for a land sale contract to be enforceable under the Statute of Frauds, the contract must describe the property being transferred with sufficient certainty for it to be identified. ■ **CASE IN POINT 16.2** Talat Solaiman and Sabina Chowdhury agreed to buy a convenience store and gas station owned by Mohammad Salim for $975,000 and gave Salim a $25,000 security deposit. They signed a handwritten contract, which was later typed up, but the contract described the property only by its street address (199 Upper Riverdale Road, Jonesboro, GA 30236).

When Solaiman and Chowdhury decided not to go through with the deal, Salim kept their deposit and filed a breach of contract lawsuit. The court held that the parties' purchase agreement was unenforceable because it did not sufficiently describe the real property to be purchased. To comply with the Statute of Frauds, "a contract must describe the property . . . with the same degree of certainty as that required in a deed conveying realty." Therefore, the contract was void, and Salim had to return the buyers' security deposit.[1] ■

The issue in the following case was whether a contract for a sale of land sufficiently identified the property and the sellers.

---

1. *Salim v. Solaiman*, 302 Ga.App. 607, 691 S.E.2d 389 (2010).

Case Analysis 16.1

Sloop v. Kiker
Court of Appeals of Arkansas, Division III, 2016 Ark. App. 125 (2016).

In the Language of the Court
Cliff HOOFMAN, Judge
* * * *

[Russell and Sally] Kiker * * * own a house on 134.5 acres in Newton County [Arkansas]. On January 26, 2012, [Mona] Sloop contracted to purchase the house and the land for $850,000. The contract contained the following down-payment provision:

The *nonrefundable down payment shall be $350,000,* due upon execution of this contract by both parties * * *. Time is of the essence in satisfying the terms of this contract. In the event closing does not occur on or before August 31, 2013, this contract shall be null and void, the down payment

shall be retained by Seller. Buyer, if then occupying the property shall vacate the property * * *.

Sloop made the $350,000 down payment on January 26, 2012. That same day, the parties executed two additional documents: a warranty deed and a lease/caretaker agreement. The deed recited that the Kikers * * * conveyed the property to Sloop * * *. It further contained a full metes-and-bounds description of the property, which the contract had described only by street address. The lease/caretaker agreement essentially allowed Sloop to live on the property as a tenant until the $500,000 balance due was paid, subject to an August 31, 2013 deadline. Sloop assumed occupancy of

the property in the summer of 2012.

* * * As the August 31, 2013 deadline approached, [Sloop] informed the Kikers that she would * * * not be able to pay the balance by that date.

* * * On or about September 6, 2013, the Kikers served Sloop with a notice to vacate the premises. The notice stated that the lease/caretaker agreement had expired and that Sloop had missed the August 31, 2013 deadline to pay the balance due on the property, requiring her to forfeit her $350,000 nonrefundable down payment.

Sloop refused to vacate the property, and the Kikers filed suit against her in

Case 16.1 Continued

Newton County Circuit Court. Their complaint sought an order removing Sloop from the property and a declaration that they were entitled to retain the $350,000 down payment. Sloop voluntarily abandoned the property a month after the complaint was filed, but she filed a counterclaim asking that the Kikers return her $350,000 down payment.

The Kikers moved for summary judgment, arguing that the real-estate contract unambiguously provided that the $350,000 down payment was nonrefundable, given that Sloop had failed to pay the balance due by August 31, 2013. Sloop responded that * * * the parties' contract violated the Statute of Frauds because it lacked a sufficient property description and failed to identify the sellers.

After a hearing, the circuit court entered an order granting the Kikers' motion for summary judgment * * *

on the ground that any uncertainties in the real-estate contract were cured by the warranty deed—a clear reference to Sloop's Statute-of-Frauds argument. Sloop now appeals from the summary-judgment order.

* * * *

* * * Sloop argues that the circuit court erred in determining that the parties' real-estate contract satisfied the Statute of Frauds. We see no error on this point.

The Statute of Frauds provides that a contract for the sale of land must be in writing to be enforceable. Additionally, the contract must contain certain essential information, such as the terms and conditions of the sale, the price to be paid, the time for payment, and a description of the property. [Emphasis added.]

Sloop contends that the contract in this case was deficient because it did not name the Kikers * * * as sellers of the

property and did not contain a sufficient description of the property. However, as noted by the circuit court, the warranty deed that the parties executed on the same day as the real-estate contract named the Kikers * * * as grantors and provided a formal, legal description of the property. Generally, instruments executed at the same time by the same parties, for the same purpose, and in the course of the same transaction, are, in the eyes of the law, one instrument and will be read and construed together. Moreover, if a contract furnishes a means by which realty can be identified—a key to the property's location—the Statute of Frauds is satisfied. Here, the contract's designation of the premises by street address met this requirement.

* * * *

Affirmed.

Legal Reasoning Questions

1. Why does the Statute of Frauds require that a contract for a sale of land contain a sufficient description of the property?
2. How did the court construe the deed and the contract in this case—as one instrument or as separate documents? Why?
3. What effect did the court's construction of the deed and the contract have on the outcome in this case? Explain.

16–2b The One-Year Rule

A contract that cannot, *by its own terms,* be performed within one year *from the day after* the contract is formed must be in writing to be enforceable.[2] The reason for this rule is that the parties' memory of their contract's terms is not likely to be reliable for longer than a year. Disputes are unlikely to occur until some time after the contracts are made, and if the terms have not been put into writing, resolving such disputes is difficult.

Time Period Starts the Day after the Contract Is Formed The one-year period begins to run *the day after the contract is made.* ■ **EXAMPLE 16.3** Superior University forms a contract with Kimi San stating that San will teach three courses in history during the coming academic year (September 15 through June 15). If the contract is formed in March, it must be in writing to be

enforceable—because it cannot be performed within one year. If the contract is not formed until July, however, it does not have to be in writing to be enforceable—because it can be performed within one year. ■

Must Be Objectively Impossible to Perform within One Year The test for determining whether an oral contract is enforceable under the one-year rule is whether performance is *possible* within one year. It does not matter whether the agreement is *likely* to be performed during that period.

When performance of a contract is objectively impossible during the one-year period, the contract must be in writing (or a record) to be enforceable. ■ **EXAMPLE 16.4** A contract to provide five crops of tomatoes to be grown on a specific farm in Illinois would be objectively impossible to perform within one year. No farmer in Illinois can grow five crops of tomatoes in a single year. ■

If performance is possible within one year under the contract's terms, the contract does not fall under the

---

2. *Restatement (Second) of Contracts,* Section 130.

Statute of Frauds and need not be in writing. ■ **EXAMPLE 16.5** Janine enters into a contract to create a carving of President Barack Obama's face on a mountainside, similar to the carvings of other presidents' faces on Mount Rushmore. It is technically possible—although not very likely—that the contract could be performed within one year. (Mount Rushmore took over fourteen years to complete.) Therefore, Janine's contract need not be in writing to be enforceable. ■

Exhibit 16–1 graphically illustrates the one-year rule.

16–2c Collateral Promises

A **collateral promise,** or secondary promise, is one that is ancillary (subsidiary) to a principal transaction or primary contractual relationship. In other words, a collateral promise is one made by a third party to assume the debts or obligations of a primary party to a contract if that party does not perform. Any collateral promise of this nature falls under the Statute of Frauds and therefore must be in writing to be enforceable.

Primary versus Secondary Obligations To understand this concept, it is important to distinguish between primary and secondary promises and obligations. A promise to pay another person's debt (or other obligation) that is *not conditioned on the person's failure to pay (or perform)* is a primary obligation. A promise to pay another's debt *only if that party fails to pay* is a secondary obligation. A contract in which a party assumes a primary obligation normally does not need to be in writing to

be enforceable, whereas a contract assuming a secondary obligation does.

■ **EXAMPLE 16.6** Connor tells Leanne Lu, an orthodontist, that he will pay for the services provided for Connor's niece, Allison. Because Connor has assumed direct financial responsibility for his niece's debt, this is a primary obligation and need not be in writing to be enforceable. In contrast, if Connor commits to paying Allison's orthodontist bill only if her mother does not, it is a secondary obligation. In that situation, Lu must have a signed writing or record proving that Connor assumed this secondary obligation for it to be enforced. ■

Exhibit 16–2 illustrates the concept of a collateral promise.

An Exception—The "Main Purpose" Rule An oral promise to answer for the debt of another is covered by the Statute of Frauds *unless* the guarantor's main purpose in incurring a secondary obligation is to secure a personal benefit. This type of contract need not be in writing.[3] The assumption is that a court can infer from the circumstances of a particular case whether the "leading objective" of the guarantor was to secure a personal benefit. In this situation, the guarantor is, in effect, answering for (guaranteeing) her or his own debt.

■ **EXAMPLE 16.7** Carlie Braswell contracts with Winsom Manufacturing Company to have some machines custom-made for her factory. She promises Newform Supply, Winsom's supplier, that if Newform continues to

---

3. *Restatement (Second) of Contracts,* Section 116.

EXHIBIT 16–1 The One-Year Rule

Under the Statute of Frauds, contracts that by their terms are impossible to perform within one year from the day after the date of contract formation must be in writing to be enforceable. Put another way, if it is at all possible to perform an oral contract within one year from the day after the contract is made, the contract will fall outside the Statute of Frauds and be enforceable.

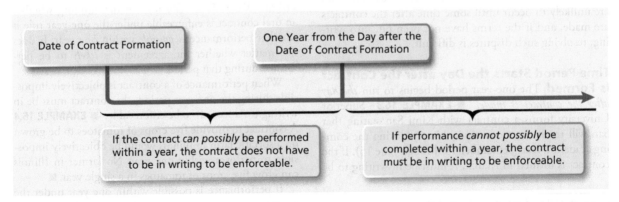

EXHIBIT 16–2 Collateral Promises

A collateral (secondary) promise is one made by a third party (C, in this exhibit) to a creditor (B, in this exhibit) to pay the debt of another (A, in this exhibit), who is primarily obligated to pay the debt. Under the Statute of Frauds, collateral promises must be in writing to be enforceable.

deliver the materials to Winsom for the production of the custom-made machines, she will guarantee payment. This promise need not be in writing, even though the effect may be to pay the debt of another. This is because Braswell's main purpose in forming the contract is to secure a benefit for herself. ■

Another typical application of the main purpose rule occurs when one creditor guarantees a debtor's debt to another creditor to forestall litigation. A creditor might do this to allow the debtor to remain in business long enough to generate profits sufficient to pay *both* creditors. In this situation, the guaranty does not need to be in writing to be enforceable.

16–2d Promises Made in Consideration of Marriage

A unilateral promise to make a monetary payment or to give property in consideration of a promise to marry must be in writing. In other words, if a mother promises to pay a man $20,000 if he marries her daughter, that promise must be in writing to be enforceable. ■ **EXAMPLE 16.8** Evan promises to buy Celeste a condo in Maui if she marries him. Celeste would need written evidence of Evan's promise to enforce it. ■

The same rule applies to **prenuptial agreements**—agreements made before marriage that define each partner's ownership rights in the other partner's property. Prenuptial agreements must be in writing to be enforceable. ■ **EXAMPLE 16.9** Before marrying country singer Keith Urban, actress Nicole Kidman entered into a prenuptial agreement with him. Kidman agreed that if the couple divorced, she would pay Urban $640,000 for every year they had been married, unless Urban had started to use drugs again. In that event, he would receive nothing. ■

16–2e Contracts for the Sale of Goods

The Uniform Commercial Code (UCC) includes Statute of Frauds provisions that require written evidence or an electronic record of a contract for the sale of goods priced at $500 or more. (This low threshold amount may be increased in the future.)

A writing that will satisfy the UCC requirement need only state the quantity term (6,000 boxes of cotton gauze, for instance). The contract will not be enforceable for any quantity greater than that set forth in the writing.

Other agreed-on terms can be omitted or stated imprecisely in the writing, as long as they adequately reflect both parties' intentions. A written memorandum or series of communications evidencing a contract will suffice, provided that the writing is signed by the party against whom enforcement is sought. The writing normally need not designate the buyer or the seller, the terms of payment, or the price.

16–3 Exceptions to the Writing Requirement

Exceptions to the writing requirement are made in certain circumstances. We describe those situations here.

16–3a Partial Performance

When a contract has been partially performed and the parties cannot be returned to their positions prior to the contract's formation, a court may grant *specific performance.* Specific performance is an equitable remedy that requires performance of the contract according to its precise terms. Courts may sometimes grant specific performance of an oral contract. The parties must prove that an oral contract existed, of course.

In cases involving oral contracts for the transfer of interests in land, courts usually look at whether justice is better served by enforcing the oral contract when partial performance has taken place. For instance, if the purchaser has paid part of the price, taken possession, and made valuable improvements to the property, a court may grant specific performance.

In some states, mere reliance on certain types of oral contracts is enough to remove them from the Statute of Frauds.[4] Under the UCC, an oral contract for the sale of goods is enforceable to the extent that a seller accepts payment or a buyer accepts delivery of the goods.[5] ■ **EXAMPLE 16.10** Cooper orders twenty chairs from an online seller. After ten chairs have been delivered and accepted, Cooper repudiates (denies the existence of) the contract. In that situation, the seller can enforce the contract (and obtain payment) to the extent of the ten chairs already accepted by Cooper. ■

Partial performance is an unmistakable indication that one party believes there is a contract. In the following case, the court considered whether, by accepting partial performance, the other party indicated that it also understood that a contract was in effect.

---

4. *Restatement (Second) of Contracts*, Section 129.
5. UCC 2–201(3)(c).

Case 16.2

NYKCool A.B.ᵃ v. Pacific Fruit, Inc.

United States Court of Appeals, Second Circuit, 507 Fed.Appx. 83 (2013).

Company Profile *NYKCool A.B., based in Stockholm, Sweden, provides maritime transportation for hire. It is a subsidiary of NYKReefers Limited, which operates as a subsidiary of Nippon Yusen Kabushiki Kaisha, one of the world's largest shipping companies. NYKCool has a fleet of more than fifty ships and has offices in Argentina, Brazil, Chile, Ecuador, Japan, New Zealand, South Africa, the United Kingdom, and the United States. NYKCool focuses on transporting perishables, especially fruit. To reduce the number of empty containers, the firm disperses its large fleet around the globe in cost-efficient patterns and carries other cargoes on its vessels' return trips.*

Background and Facts Pacific Fruit, Inc., exports cargo from Ecuador. NYKCool and Pacific entered into a written contract with a two-year duration, under which NYKCool agreed to transport weekly shipments of bananas from Ecuador to California and Japan. At the end of the period, the parties agreed to extend the deal. Due to a disagreement over one of the terms, a new contract was never signed, but the parties' trade continued.

After nearly four more years of performance between 2005 and 2008, a dispute arose over unused cargo capacity and unpaid freight charges. An arbitration panel of the Society of Maritime Arbitrators found that Pacific Fruit was liable to NYKCool for $8,787,157 for breach of contract. NYKCool filed a petition in a federal district court to confirm the award. Pacific Fruit appealed the judgment in NYKCool's favor, contending that the arbitration panel "manifestly disregarded" the law when it concluded that the parties had an enforceable contract.

In the Language of the Court
Robert A. *KATZMANN,* Barrington D. *PARKER* and Richard C. *WESLEY,* Circuit Judges.
* * * *

On appeal, Pacific Fruit first contends that the arbitration panel manifestly disregarded the New York contract law by concluding that Pacific Fruit * * * entered into an oral contract with NYKCool, under which NYKCool agreed to transport weekly shipments of [Pacific Fruit's] bananas from Ecuador

---

a. The initials *A.B.* stand for *Aktiebolag,* which is the Swedish term for "limited company."

Case 16.2 Continued

to California and Japan for the period between 2005 and 2008. In order to vacate an arbitration award for manifest disregard of the law, a court must conclude that the arbitrator knew of the relevant legal principle, appreciated that this principle controlled the outcome of the disputed issue, and nonetheless willfully flouted the governing law by refusing to apply it. This rigorous standard ensures that awards are vacated on grounds of manifest disregard only in those exceedingly rare instances where some egregious [shocking] impropriety on the part of the arbitrator is apparent. As such, the standard essentially bars review of whether an arbitrator misconstrued a contract.

Here, we detect no manifest disregard of the law in the arbitration panel's conclusion that the parties had entered into a binding oral contract for the period between 2005 and 2008. In particular, we agree with the panel's conclusion that *the parties' substantial partial performance on the contract weighs strongly in favor of contract formation.* It is undisputed that in 2005 and 2006 NYKCool transported 30 million boxes of cargo for [Pacific Fruit] on over 100 voyages, for which it received $70 million dollars in payments even though there was no written contract in place. Moreover, *the parties' behavior during 2005 and 2006 strongly suggests that they believed themselves subject to a binding agreement.* Notably, the parties engaged in extensive renegotiation of the terms of the contract when [Pacific Fruit] began facing difficulties meeting its cargo commitments. In these circumstances, the panel cannot be said to have engaged in egregious impropriety in concluding that the parties intended to enter a binding oral agreement. [Emphasis added.]

* * * *

For the foregoing reasons, the Order of the district court confirming the arbitration award is hereby AFFIRMED.

Decision and Remedy *The U.S. Court of Appeals for the Second Circuit affirmed the judgment of the lower court. The appellate court reasoned that "the parties' substantial partial performance on the contract weighs strongly in favor of contract formation."*

Critical Thinking

- **Legal Environment** *What circumstance in this case demonstrates most strongly that Pacific did not truly believe that it did not have a contract with NYKCool? Explain.*
- **Economic** *How can a carrier avoid losses under a contract that obligates it only to transport cargo one way and not on the return voyage?*

16–3b Admissions

If a party against whom enforcement of an oral contract is sought "admits" under oath that a contract for sale was made, the contract will be enforceable.[6] The party's admission can occur at any stage of the court proceedings, such as during a deposition or other discovery, pleadings, or testimony.

If a party admits a contract subject to the UCC, the contract is enforceable, but only to the extent of the quantity admitted.[7] ■ **EXAMPLE 16.11** Rachel, the president of Bistro Corporation, admits under oath that an oral agreement was made with Commercial Kitchens, Inc., to buy certain equipment for $10,000. A court will enforce the agreement only to the extent admitted ($10,000), even if Commercial Kitchens claims that the agreement involved $20,000 worth of equipment. ■

16–3c Promissory Estoppel

An oral contract that would otherwise be unenforceable under the Statute of Frauds may be enforced in some states under the doctrine of promissory estoppel. Recall that if a person justifiably relies on another's promise to his or her detriment, a court may *estop* (prevent) the promisor from denying that a contract exists. Section 139 of the *Restatement (Second) of Contracts* provides that in these circumstances, an oral promise can be enforceable notwithstanding the Statute of Frauds.

For the promise to be enforceable, the promisee must have justifiably relied on it to her or his detriment, and the reliance must have been foreseeable to the person making the promise. In addition, there must be no way

---

6. *Restatement (Second) of Contracts*, Section 133.
7. UCC 2–201(3)(b).

to avoid injustice except to enforce the promise. (Note the similarities between promissory estoppel and the doctrine of partial performance discussed previously. Both require reasonable reliance and operate to estop a party from claiming that no contract exists.)

16-3d Special Exceptions under the UCC

Special exceptions to the writing requirement apply to sales contracts. Oral contracts for customized goods may be enforced in certain circumstances. Another exception has to do with oral contracts *between merchants* that have been confirmed in a written memorandum. We will examine these exceptions in more detail when we discuss the UCC's Statute of Frauds provisions in a later chapter.

Exhibit 16–3 graphically summarizes the types of contracts that fall under the Statute of Frauds and the various exceptions that apply.

16-4 Sufficiency of the Writing

A written contract will satisfy the writing requirement, as will a written memorandum or an electronic record that evidences the agreement and is signed by the party against whom enforcement is sought. The signature need not be placed at the end of the document but can be anywhere in the writing. A signature can consist of a typed name or even just initials.

16-4a What Constitutes a Writing?

A writing can consist of any order confirmation, invoice, sales slip, check, fax, or e-mail—or such items in combination. The written contract need not consist of a single document in order to constitute an enforceable contract. One document may incorporate another document by expressly referring to it. Several documents may form a single contract if they are physically attached, such as by staple, paper clip, or glue. Several documents may form a single contract even if they are only placed in the same envelope.

■ **EXAMPLE 16.12** Simpson orally agrees to sell some land next to a shopping mall to Terro Properties. Simpson gives Terro an unsigned memo that contains a legal description of the property, and Terro gives Simpson an unsigned first draft of their real estate contract. Simpson sends Terro a signed letter that refers to the memo and to the first and final drafts of the contract. Terro sends Simpson an unsigned copy of the final draft of the contract with a signed check stapled to it. Together, the documents can constitute a writing sufficient to satisfy the writing requirement and bind both parties to the terms of the contract. ■

EXHIBIT 16–3 Business Contracts and the Writing Requirement

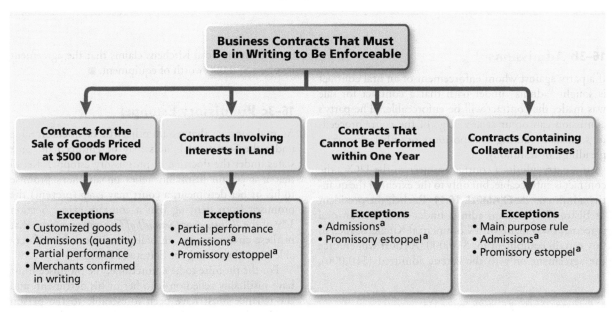

Business Contracts That Must Be in Writing to Be Enforceable

Contracts for the Sale of Goods Priced at $500 or More	Contracts Involving Interests in Land	Contracts That Cannot Be Performed within One Year	Contracts Containing Collateral Promises
Exceptions • Customized goods • Admissions (quantity) • Partial performance • Merchants confirmed in writing	**Exceptions** • Partial performance • Admissions[a] • Promissory estoppel[a]	**Exceptions** • Admissions[a] • Promissory estoppel[a]	**Exceptions** • Main purpose rule • Admissions[a] • Promissory estoppel[a]

a. Some states follow Section 133 (on admissions) and Section 139 (on promissory estoppel) of the *Restatement (Second) of Contracts.*

16–4b What Must Be Contained in the Writing?

A memorandum or note evidencing an oral contract need only contain the essential terms of the contract, not every term. There must, of course, also be some indication that the parties voluntarily agreed to the terms. As mentioned, under the UCC, a writing evidencing a contract for the sale of goods need only state the quantity and be signed by the party against whom enforcement is sought.

Under most state laws, the writing must also name the parties and identify the subject matter, the consideration, and the essential terms with reasonable certainty. In addition, contracts for the sale of land often are required to state the price and describe the property with sufficient clarity to allow them to be determined without reference to outside sources.

Note that because only the party against whom enforcement is sought must have signed the writing, a contract may be enforceable by one of its parties but not by the other. For instance, if a person borrows funds to purchase a home but does not sign a loan contract, the lender cannot enforce the contract but the borrower probably can.[8]

16–5 The Parol Evidence Rule

Sometimes, a written contract does not include—or contradicts—an oral understanding reached by the parties before or at the time of contracting. For instance, a landlord might tell a person who agrees to rent an apartment that cats are allowed, whereas the lease contract clearly states that no pets are permitted. In deciding such disputes, the courts look to a common law rule called the *parol evidence rule*.

Under the **parol evidence rule,** if a court finds that a written contract represents the complete and final statement of the parties' agreement, it will not allow either party to present parol evidence. *Parol evidence* is testimony or other evidence of communications between the parties that is not contained in the contract itself. A party normally *cannot* present any evidence of the following if that evidence contradicts or varies the terms of the written contract:

1. Negotiations prior to contract formation.
2. Agreements prior to contract formation.

3. Oral agreements contemporaneous with (at the same time as) contract formation.[9]

16–5a Exceptions to the Parol Evidence Rule

Because of the rigidity of the parol evidence rule, the courts have created the following exceptions:

1. *Contracts subsequently modified.* Evidence of any subsequent modification (oral or written) of a written contract can be introduced in court. Oral modifications may not be enforceable under the Statute of Frauds, however (for instance, a modification that increases the price of the goods being sold to more than $500). Also, oral modifications will not be enforceable if the original contract provides that any modification must be in writing.[10]

2. *Voidable or void contracts.* Oral evidence can be introduced in all cases to show that the contract was voidable or void (for example, induced by mistake, fraud, or misrepresentation). The reason is simple: if deception led one of the parties to agree to the terms of a written contract, oral evidence attesting to the fraud should not be excluded. Courts frown on bad faith and are quick to allow such evidence when it establishes fraud.

3. *Contracts containing ambiguous terms.* When the terms of a written contract are ambiguous and require interpretation, evidence is admissible to show the meaning of the terms. ■ **CASE IN POINT 16.13** Pamela Watkins bought a home from Sandra Schexnider. Their agreement stated that Watkins would make payments on the mortgage until the note was paid in full, when "the house" would become hers. The agreement also stipulated that she would pay for insurance on "the property." The home was destroyed in a hurricane, and the insurance proceeds paid off the mortgage. Watkins claimed that she owned the land, but Schexnider argued that she had sold only the house. The court found that because "the house" term in the contract was ambiguous, parol evidence was admissible. The court also concluded that the parties had intended to transfer ownership of both the house and the land, and ordered that title to the property be transferred to Watkins.[11] ■

4. *Incomplete contracts.* When the written contract is incomplete in that it lacks one or more of the essential terms, the courts allow additional evidence to "fill in the gaps."

---

8. See, for example, *Beneficial Homeowner Service Corp. v. Steele,* 30 Misc.3d 1208(A), 958 N.Y.S.2d 644 (2011).

9. *Restatement (Second) of Contracts,* Section 213.
10. UCC 2–209(2), (3).
11. *Watkins v. Schexnider,* 31 So.3d 609 (La.App. 3 Cir. 2010).

5. *Prior dealing, course of performance, or usage of trade.* Under the UCC, evidence can be introduced to explain or supplement a written contract by showing a prior dealing, course of performance, or usage of trade.[12] This is because when buyers and sellers deal with each other over extended periods of time, certain customary practices develop. These practices are often overlooked in writing the contract, so courts allow the introduction of evidence to show how the parties have acted in the past. Usage of trade—practices and customs generally followed in a particular industry—can also shed light on the meaning of certain contract provisions. Thus, evidence of trade usage may be admissible. We will discuss these terms in further detail later in the context of sales contracts.

6. *Contracts subject to an orally agreed-on condition precedent.* Sometimes the parties agree that a condition must be fulfilled before a party is required to perform the contract. This is called a *condition precedent.* If the parties have orally agreed on a condition precedent that

does not conflict with the terms of their written agreement, a court may allow parol evidence to prove the oral condition. The parol evidence rule does not apply here because the existence of the entire written contract is subject to an orally agreed-on condition. Proof of the condition does not alter or modify the written terms but affects the *enforceability* of the written contract.

7. *Contracts with an obvious or gross clerical (or typographic) error that clearly would not represent the agreement of the parties.* Parol evidence is admissible to correct an obvious typographic error. ■ **EXAMPLE 16.14** Davis agrees to lease office space from Stone Enterprises for $3,000 per month. The signed written lease provides for a monthly payment of $300 rather than the $3,000 agreed to by the parties. Because the error is obvious, Stone Enterprises will be allowed to admit parol evidence to correct the mistake. ■

In the following case, an appellate court considered whether the trial court should have admitted parol evidence regarding the terms of an apartment lease.

12. UCC 1–205, 2–202.

Case 16.3

Frewil, LLC v. Price

Court of Appeals of South Carolina, 411 S.C. 525, 769 S.E.2d 250 (2015).

Background and Facts Madison Price and Carter Smith were planning to attend the College of Charleston in South Carolina. They contacted Frewil, LLC, about renting an apartment at the beginning of the fall semester. They asked if the apartment had a washer/dryer and dishwasher, and were told yes. The lease did not expressly state that the unit contained those appliances, but it provided that any overflow from a washing machine or dishwasher was the responsibility of the tenant and that the dishwasher had to be clean for a refund of the security deposit.

When Price and Smith arrived to move in, the apartment had no washer/dryer or dishwasher and no connections for them. The students found housing elsewhere. Frewil filed a suit in a South Carolina state court against Price and Smith, claiming breach of contract. The defendants sought to introduce parol evidence to challenge Frewil's claim. The court denied the request and issued a judgment in Frewil's favor. Price and Smith appealed.

In the Language of the Court
KONDUROS, J. [Judge]
* * * *

* * * If a writing, on its face, appears to express the whole agreement between the parties, parol evidence cannot be admitted to add another term thereto. However, *where a contract is silent as to a particular matter, and ambiguity thereby arises, parol evidence may be admitted to supply the deficiency and establish the true intent. For, generally, parol evidence is admissible to show the true meaning of an ambiguous written contract.* Such a contract is one capable of being understood in more ways than just one, or an agreement unclear in meaning because it expresses its purpose in an indefinite manner. When an agreement is ambiguous, the court may consider the circumstances surrounding its execution in determining the intent. Where the contract is susceptible of more than one interpretation, the ambiguity will be resolved against the party who prepared the contract. It would be virtually impossible for a contract to encompass all of the many possibilities which may be encountered by the parties. Indeed, neither law, nor equity,

Case 16.3 Continued

requires every term or condition to be set forth in a contract. If a situation is unaddressed in a contract, the court may look to the circumstances surrounding the bargain as an aid in determining the parties' intent. [Emphasis added.]

In this case, the [lower] court relied upon * * * the lease itself to conclude the girls had breached the lease as a matter of law. However, if a contract is subject to more than one interpretation, it is ambiguous and parol evidence is admissible. Frewil contends, and the [lower] court found, the lease unambiguously states the unit does not contain a washer/dryer or dishwasher. However, the lease states any overflow from washing machines or dishwashers is the responsibility of the tenant. Additionally, the Security Deposit Agreement * * * indicates the dishwasher must be clean in order for the tenant to receive a return of the security deposit. The lease does not explicitly indicate what appliances are or are not in the unit. Because the lease is ambiguous on this point, parol evidence was admissible. As these appliances are mentioned and Price and Smith allege they were told the washer/dryer and dishwasher were included, the [lower] court erred in concluding the lease * * * precluded any challenge to Frewil's breach of contract claim as a matter of law.

Decision and Remedy *A state intermediate appellate court reversed the judgment of the lower court. The court noted that, "the lease was ambiguous thereby permitting the introduction of parol evidence."*

Critical Thinking
- **Economic** *How does the parol evidence rule save time and money for the parties to a dispute and the court that hears it? Discuss.*

16–5b Integrated Contracts

In determining whether to allow parol evidence, courts consider whether the written contract is intended to be the complete and final statement of the terms of the agreement. If it is, the contract is referred to as an **integrated contract,** and extraneous evidence (evidence from outside the contract) is excluded.

■ **EXAMPLE 16.15** TKTS, Inc., offers to sell Gwen season tickets to the Dallas Cowboys football games in Cowboys Stadium. Prices and seat locations are indicated in diagrams in a brochure that accompanies the offer. Gwen responds, listing her seat preference. TKTS sends her the tickets, along with a different diagram showing seat locations. Also enclosed is a document that reads, "This is the entire agreement of the parties," which Gwen signs and returns. When Gwen goes to the first game, she discovers that her seat is not where she expected, based on the brochure. Under the parol evidence rule, however, the brochure is not part of the parties' agreement. The document that Gwen signed was identified as the parties' entire contract. Therefore, she cannot introduce in court any evidence of prior negotiations or agreements that contradict or vary the contract's terms. ■

A contract can be either completely or partially integrated. If it contains all of the terms of the parties' agreement, it is completely integrated. If it contains only some of the terms that the parties agreed on and not others, it is partially integrated. If the contract is only partially integrated, evidence of consistent additional terms is admissible to supplement the written agreement.[13] Note that for both completely and partially integrated contracts, courts exclude any evidence that *contradicts* the writing. Parol evidence is allowed only to add to the terms of a partially integrated contract. Exhibit 16–4 illustrates the relationship between integrated contracts and the parol evidence rule.

16–6 The Statute of Frauds in the International Context

The Convention on Contracts for the International Sale of Goods (CISG) governs international sales contracts between citizens of countries that have ratified the convention (agreement). Article 11 of the CISG does not incorporate any Statute of Frauds provisions. Rather, it states that a "contract for sale need not be concluded in or evidenced by writing and is not subject to any other requirements as to form."

Article 11 accords with the legal customs of most nations, which no longer require contracts to meet certain

---

13. *Restatement (Second) of Contracts,* Section 216; and UCC 2–202.

EXHIBIT 16–4 The Parol Evidence Rule

formal or writing requirements to be enforceable. Even England, the nation that created the original Statute of Frauds in 1677, has repealed all of it except the provisions relating to collateral promises and to transfers of interests in land. Many other countries that once had such statutes have also repealed all or parts of them. Some civil law countries, such as France, have never required certain types of contracts to be in writing.

Reviewing: The Writing Requirement in Our Digital World

Evelyn Vollmer orally agreed to loan Danny Lang $150,000 to make an investment in a local nightclub. The loan was to be repaid from the profits received from the investment. Their agreement was never memorialized in writing, however. Eighteen months later, Lang had paid only $15,000 on the loan from the profits from the business. Vollmer filed a lawsuit alleging breach of contract. Using the information presented in the chapter, answer the following questions.

1. Lang claimed that repayment of the loan would "almost certainly" take over a year and that his agreement with Vollmer was therefore unenforceable because it was not in writing. Is he correct? Explain.
2. Suppose that a week after Vollmer gave Lang the funds, she sent him an e-mail containing the terms of their loan agreement with her named typed at the bottom. Lang did not respond to the e-mail. Is this sufficient as a writing under the Statute of Frauds?
3. Assume that at trial the court finds that the contract falls within the Statute of Frauds. Further assume that the state in which the court sits recognizes every exception to the Statute of Frauds discussed in the chapter. What exception provides Vollmer with the best chance of enforcing the oral contract in this situation?
4. Suppose that at trial, Lang never raises the argument that the parties' agreement violates the Statute of Frauds, and the court rules in favor of Vollmer. Then Lang appeals and raises the Statute of Frauds for the first time. What exception can Vollmer now argue?

Debate This . . . *Many countries have eliminated the Statute of Frauds except for sales of real estate. The United States should do the same.*

Terms and Concepts

collateral promise 298
integrated contract 305

parol evidence rule 303
prenuptial agreement 299

Statute of Frauds 295

Issue Spotters

1. GamesCo orders $800 worth of game pieces from Midstate Plastic, Inc. Midstate delivers, and GamesCo pays for $450 worth. GamesCo then says it wants no more pieces from Midstate. GamesCo and Midstate have never dealt with each other before and have nothing in writing. Can Midstate enforce a deal for the full $800? Explain your answer. (See *Contracts That Require a Writing.*)

2. Paula orally agrees to work with Next Corporation in New York City for two years. Paula moves her family and begins work. Three months later, Paula is fired for no stated cause. She sues for reinstatement and back pay. Next Corporation argues that there is no written contract between them. What will the court say? (See *Exceptions to the Writing Requirement.*)

• **Check your answers to the Issue Spotters against the answers provided in Appendix D at the end of this text.**

Business Scenarios

16–1. The One-Year Rule. On May 1, by telephone, Yu offers to hire Benson to perform personal services. On May 5, Benson returns Yu's call and accepts the offer. Discuss fully whether this contract falls under the Statute of Frauds in the following circumstances: (See *Contracts That Require a Writing.*)

(a) The contract calls for Benson to be employed for one year, with the right to begin performance immediately.

(b) The contract calls for Benson to be employed for nine months, with performance of services to begin on September 1.

(c) The contract calls for Benson to submit a written research report, with a deadline of two years for submission.

16–2. Collateral Promises. Mallory promises a local hardware store that she will pay for a lawn mower that her brother is purchasing on credit if the brother fails to pay the debt. Must this promise be in writing to be enforceable? Why or why not? (See *Contracts That Require a Writing.*)

Business Case Problems

16–3. The Parol Evidence Rule. Evangel Temple Assembly of God leased a facility from Wood Care Centers, Inc., to house evacuees who had lost their homes in Hurricane Katrina. One clause in the lease contract said that Evangel could terminate the lease at any time by giving Wood Care notice and paying 10 percent of the balance remaining on the lease. Another clause stated that if the facility was not given a property tax exemption (as a church), Evangel had the option to terminate the lease without making the 10 percent payment. Nine months later, the last of the evacuees left the facility, and Evangel notified Wood Care that it would end the lease. Wood Care demanded the 10 percent payment. Is parol evidence admissible to interpret this lease? Why or why not? [*Wood Care Centers, Inc. v. Evangel Temple Assembly of God of Wichita Falls*, 307 S.W.3d 816 (Tex.App.—Fort Worth 2010)] (See *The Parol Evidence Rule.*)

16–4. Sufficiency of the Writing. Newmark & Co. Real Estate, Inc., contacted 2615 East 17 Street Realty, LLC, to lease certain real property on behalf of a client. Newmark e-mailed the landlord a separate agreement for the payment of Newmark's commission. The landlord e-mailed it back with a separate demand to pay the commission in installments. Newmark revised the agreement and e-mailed a final copy to the landlord. Does the agreement qualify as a writing under the Statute of Frauds? Explain. [*Newmark & Co. Real Estate, Inc. v. 2615 East 17 Street Realty, LLC*, 80 A.D.3d 476, 914 N.Y.S.2d 162 (1 Dept. 2011)] (See *Sufficiency of the Writing.*)

16–5. Business Case Problem with Sample Answer— The Parol Evidence Rule. Rimma Vaks and her husband, Steven Mangano, executed a written contract with Denise Ryan and Ryan Auction Co. to auction their furnishings. The six-page contract provided a detailed summary of the parties' agreement. It addressed the items to be auctioned, how reserve prices would be determined, and the amount of Ryan's commission. When a dispute arose between the parties, Vaks and Mangano sued Ryan for breach of contract. Vaks and Mangano asserted that, before they executed the contract, Ryan made various oral representations that were inconsistent with the terms of their written agreement. Assuming that their written contract was valid, can Vaks and Mangano recover for breach of an oral contract? Why or why not? [*Vaks v. Ryan*, 2012 WL 194398 (Mass.App. 2012)] (See *The Parol Evidence Rule*.)

- **For a sample answer to Problem 16–5, see Appendix E at the end of this text.**

16–6. Promises Made in Consideration of Marriage.

After twenty-nine years of marriage, Robert and Mary Lou Tuttle were divorced. They admitted in court that before they were married, they had signed a prenuptial agreement. They agreed that the agreement had stated that each would keep his or her own property and anything derived from that property. Robert came into the marriage owning farmland, while Mary Lou owned no real estate. During the marriage, ten different parcels of land, totaling about six hundred acres, were acquired, and two corporations, Tuttle Grain, Inc., and Tuttle Farms, Inc., were formed. A copy of the prenuptial agreement could not be found. Can the court enforce the agreement without a writing? Why or why not? [*In re Marriage of Tuttle*, 2013 WL 164035 (Ill.App. 5 Dist. 2013)] (See *Contracts That Require a Writing*.)

16–7. Promises Made in Consideration of Marriage.

Before their marriage, Linda and Gerald Heiden executed a prenuptial agreement. The agreement provided that "no spouse shall have any right in the property of the other spouse, even in the event of the death of either party." The description of Gerald's separate property included a settlement from a personal injury suit. Twenty-four years later, Linda filed for divorce. The court ruled that the prenuptial agreement applied only in the event of death, not divorce, and entered a judgment that included a property division and spousal

support award. The ruling disparately favored Linda, whose monthly income with spousal support would be $4,467, leaving Gerald with only $1,116. Did the court interpret the Heidens' prenuptial agreement correctly? Discuss. [*Heiden v. Heiden*, 2015 WL 849006 (Mich.App. 2015)] (See *Contracts That Require a Writing*.)

16–8. A Question of Ethics—Exceptions to the Writing Requirement.

 Madeline Castellotti was the sole shareholder of Whole Pies, Inc., which owns John's Pizzeria in New York City. Her other assets included a 51 percent interest in a real estate partnership, a residence on Staten Island, and various bank accounts. When Madeline's son, Peter Castellotti, was going through a divorce, Madeline wanted to prevent Peter's then-wife Rea from benefiting from any of Madeline's assets. With this purpose in mind, she removed Peter from her will, leaving her daughter Lisa Free as the sole beneficiary. Lisa orally agreed to provide Peter with half of the income generated by the assets after their mother's death if his divorce was still pending and to transfer half of the assets after the divorce was final. In reliance on those promises, Peter agreed to pay the property taxes for the estate. Madeline died and Peter paid the taxes, but Lisa reneged on the deal. Peter filed a suit in a New York state court against his sister to recover. [Castellotti v. Free, 138 A.D.3d 198, 27 N.Y.S.3d 507 (1 Dept. 2016)] (See *Exceptions to the Writing Requirement*.)

(a) Should the court enforce the promise? On what legal theory?

(b) If the court enforces the promise, should Rea get a share of what Peter and his mother and sister were "hiding"? Discuss.

Legal Reasoning Group Activity

16–9. The Writing Requirement.

Jason Novell, doing business as Novell Associates, hired Barbara Meade to work for him. The parties orally agreed on the terms of employment, including payment of a share of the company's income to Meade, but they did not put anything in writing. Two years later, Meade quit. Novell then told Meade that she was entitled to $9,602—25 percent of the difference between the accounts receivable and the accounts payable as of Meade's last day of work. Meade disagreed and demanded more than $63,500—25 percent of the revenue from all invoices, less the cost of materials and outside processing, for each of the years that she had worked for Novell. Meade filed a lawsuit against Novell for breach of contract. (See *The Statute of Frauds*.)

(a) The first group should decide whether the parties had an enforceable contract.

(b) The second group should decide whether the parties' oral agreement falls within any exception to the Statute of Frauds.

(c) The third group should discuss how the lawsuit would be affected if Novell admitted that the parties had an oral contract under which Meade was entitled to 25 percent of the difference between accounts receivable and accounts payable as of the day Meade quit.

Answers to the *Issue Spotters*

1. *Can Midstate enforce a deal for the full $800? Explain your answer.* No. Under the UCC, a contract for a sale of goods priced at $500 or more must be in writing to be enforceable. In this case, the contract is not enforceable beyond the quantity already delivered and paid for.

2. *Next Corporation argues that there is no written contract between them. What will the court say?* The court might conclude that under the doctrine of promissory estoppel, the employer is estopped from claiming the lack of a written con-

tract as a defense. The oral contract may be enforced because the employer made a promise on which the employee justifiably relied in moving to New York, the reliance was foreseeable, and injustice can be avoided only by enforcing the promise. If the court strictly enforces the Statute of Frauds, however, the employee may be without a remedy.

Sample Answers for *Business Case Problems with Sample Answer*

Problem 16–5. *The Parol Evidence Rule.* Vaks and Mangano may not recover for breach of an oral contract. Under the parol evidence rule, if there is a written contract representing the complete and final statement of the parties' agreement, a party may not introduce any evidence of past agreements. Here, the writ-

ten agreement was an integrated contract because the parties intended it to be a complete and final statement of the terms of their agreement. Vaks and Mangano therefore may not introduce evidence of any inconsistent oral representations made before the contract was executed.

CHAPTER

Third Party Rights

Once it has been determined that a valid and legally enforceable contract exists, attention can turn to the rights and duties of the parties to the contract. A contract is a private agreement between the parties who have entered into it, and traditionally these parties alone have rights and liabilities under the contract. This principle is referred to as **privity of contract.** A *third party*—one who is not a direct party to a particular contract—normally does not have rights under that contract.

There are exceptions to the rule of privity of contract. For instance, privity of contract is not required to recover damages under product liability laws. Hence, a person injured by a defective product can still recover damages even though she or he was not the buyer of the product. In this chapter, we look at two other exceptions. One exception allows a party to a contract to transfer the rights or duties arising from the contract to another person through an *assignment* (of rights) or a *delegation* (of duties). The other exception involves a *third party beneficiary contract*—a contract in which the parties to the contract intend that the contract benefit a third party.

17–1 Assignments and Delegations

In a bilateral contract, the two parties have corresponding rights and duties. One party has a *right* to require the other to perform some task, and the other has a *duty* to perform it. The transfer of contractual *rights* to a third party is known as an **assignment.** The transfer of contractual *duties* to a third party is known as a **delegation.** An assignment or a delegation occurs *after* the original contract was made.

17–1a Assignments

Assignments are important because they are used in many types of business financing. Lending institutions, such as banks, frequently assign their rights to receive payments under their loan contracts to other firms, which pay for those rights. ■ **EXAMPLE 17.1** Tia obtains a loan from a bank to finance an online business venture. She may later receive a notice from the bank stating that it has transferred (assigned) its rights to receive payments on the loan to another firm. When it is time to repay the loan, Tia must make the payments to that other firm. ■

Financial institutions that make *mortgage* loans (loans to enable prospective home buyers to purchase land or a home) often assign their rights to collect the mortgage payments to a third party, such as PNC Mortgage.

Following the assignment, the home buyers are notified that they must make future payments not to the bank that loaned them the funds but to the third party.

Billions of dollars change hands daily in the business world in the form of assignments of rights in contracts. If it were not possible to transfer contractual rights, many businesses could not continue to operate.

The Effect of an Assignment In an assignment, the party assigning the rights to a third party is known as the **assignor,**[1] and the party receiving the rights is the **assignee.**[2] Other traditional terms used to describe the parties in assignment relationships are **obligee** (the person to whom a duty, or obligation, is owed) and **obligor** (the person who is obligated to perform the duty).

Extinguishes the Rights of the Assignor. When rights under a contract are assigned unconditionally, the rights of the assignor are extinguished.[3] The third party (the assignee) has a right to demand performance from the other original party to the contract. The assignee takes only those rights that the assignor originally had, however.

■ **EXAMPLE 17.2** Brower is obligated by contract to pay Horton $1,000. Brower is the obligor because she

---

1. Pronounced uh-*sye*-nore.
2. Pronounced uh-*sye*-nee.
3. *Restatement (Second) of Contracts,* Section 317.

EXHIBIT 17-1 Assignment Relationships

In the assignment relationship illustrated here, Horton assigns his *rights* under a contract that he made with Brower to a third party, Kuhn. Horton thus becomes the *assignor* and Kuhn the *assignee* of the contractual rights. Brower, the *obligor*, now owes performance to Kuhn instead of Horton. Horton's original contractual rights are extinguished after assignment.

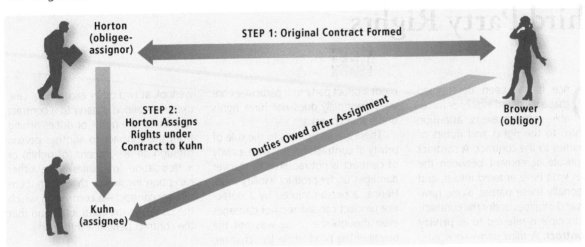

owes an obligation, or duty, to Horton. Horton is the obligee, the one to whom the obligation is owed. If Horton then assigns his right to receive the $1,000 to Kuhn, Horton is the assignor and Kuhn is the assignee. Kuhn now becomes the obligee because Brower owes Kuhn the $1,000. Here, a valid assignment of a debt exists. Kuhn (the assignee-obligee) is entitled to enforce payment in court if Brower (the obligor) does not pay him the $1,000. (Horton is no longer entitled to enforce payment because the assignment extinguished his original contract rights.) ∎ These concepts are illustrated in Exhibit 17–1.

In the following case, a lender assigned its rights to loan payments from a borrower. The court had to decide whether the borrower owed the payments to the assignee.

Case 17.1

Hosch v. Colonial Pacific Leasing Corp.

Court of Appeals of Georgia, 313 Ga.App. 873, 722 S.E.2d 778 (2012).

Background and Facts Edward Hosch entered into four loan agreements with Citicapital Commercial Corporation to finance the purchase of heavy construction equipment. A few months later, Citicapital merged into Citicorp Leasing, Inc., which was then renamed GE Capital Commercial, Inc. One year later, GE Capital assigned the loans to Colonial Pacific Leasing Corporation. When Hosch defaulted on the loans, Colonial provided a notice of default and demanded payment. Hosch failed to repay the loans, so Colonial sued to collect the amount due. The trial court granted summary judgment to Colonial and entered final judgment against Hosch. On appeal, Hosch argued that there was insufficient evidence that the loans had been assigned to Colonial.

In the Language of the Court

McFADDEN, Judge.

* * * *

Hosch contends that the trial court erred in granting Colonial's motion for summary judgment because there is no evidence that the contracts were assigned to Colonial. However, the contention is refuted by the record, which includes affidavits of a GE litigation specialist, a written assignment and other documents establishing that Hosch's four loans were assigned to Colonial. Hosch has presented no contradictory evidence showing that the loans were not assigned to Colonial, and instead submitted his own affidavit stating that he had not been notified of any such assignment. However, the loan

Case 17.1 Continued agreements expressly provide that the lender may transfer or assign any or all of its rights under the agreements without notice to or the consent of Hosch.

"A party may assign to another a contractual right to collect payment, including the right to sue to enforce the right. But an assignment must be in writing in order for the contractual right to be enforceable by the assignee." Because the record, as noted above, contains a written assignment of the loans to Colonial, as well as other evidence of the assignment, the trial court did not err in granting summary judgment to Colonial. [Emphasis added.]

Decision and Remedy *The Georgia appellate court found sufficient evidence that GE Capital had assigned the loans to Colonial. It therefore affirmed the trial court's judgment for Colonial.*

Critical Thinking

- **Legal Environment** *Do borrowers benefit from the fact that lenders may freely assign their rights under loan agreements? If so, how?*
- **What If the Facts Were Different?** *Suppose that Hosch had sold the equipment financed by the loans from Citicapital to a third party. Would Hosch still have been liable to Colonial Pacific? Why or why not?*

Assignee's Rights Are Subject to the Same Defenses. The assignee's rights are subject to the defenses that the obligor has against the assignor. In other words, the assignee obtains only those rights that the assignor originally had.

■ **EXAMPLE 17.3** Returning to *Example 17.2,* suppose Brower owes Horton the $1,000 under a contract in which Brower agreed to buy Horton's Surface Pro 4. When Brower decided to purchase the tablet, she relied on Horton's fraudulent misrepresentation that it had an Intel Core i7 processor. When Brower discovers that its processor is an Intel i3, she tells Horton that she is going to return the device to him and cancel the contract. Even though Horton has assigned his "right" to receive the $1,000 to Kuhn, Brower need not pay Kuhn the $1,000. Brower can raise the defense of Horton's fraudulent misrepresentation to avoid payment. ■

Form of the Assignment. In general, an assignment can take any form, oral or written. Naturally, it is more difficult to prove that an oral assignment occurred, so it is advisable to put all assignments in writing. Of course, assignments covered by the Statute of Frauds—such as an assignment of an interest in land—must be in writing to be enforceable. In addition, most states require contracts for the assignment of wages to be in writing.[4] There are other assignments that must be in writing as well.

Rights That Cannot Be Assigned As a general rule, all rights can be assigned. Exceptions are made, however, under certain circumstances. Some of these exceptions are listed here and described in more detail in the following subsections:

1. The assignment is prohibited by statute.
2. The contract is personal.
3. The assignment significantly changes the risk or duties of the obligor.
4. The contract prohibits assignment.

When a Statute Prohibits Assignment. When a statute expressly prohibits assignment of a particular right, that right cannot be assigned. ■ **EXAMPLE 17.4** Quincy is an employee of Specialty Travel, Inc. Specialty is an employer bound by workers' compensation statutes in its state, and thus Quincy is a covered employee. Quincy is injured on the job and begins to collect monthly workers' compensation checks. In need of a loan, Quincy borrows from Draper, assigning to Draper all of her future workers' compensation benefits. A state statute prohibits the assignment of *future* workers' compensation benefits, and thus such rights cannot be assigned. ■

When a Contract Is Personal in Nature. If a contract is for personal services, the rights under the contract normally cannot be assigned unless all that remains is a monetary payment.[5] ■ **EXAMPLE 17.5** Anton signs a contract to be a tutor for Marisa's children. Marisa then attempts to assign to Roberto (who also has children) her right to Anton's services. Roberto cannot enforce the contract against Anton. Roberto's children may be more difficult to tutor than Marisa's. Thus, if Marisa could assign her rights to Anton's services to Roberto, it would change the nature of Anton's obligation. Because personal services are unique to the person rendering them, rights to receive personal services are likewise unique and cannot be assigned. ■

---

4. See, for example, California Labor Code Section 300.

5. *Restatement (Second) of Contracts*, Sections 317 and 318.

Note that when legal actions involve personal rights, they are considered personal in nature and cannot be assigned. For instance, personal-injury tort claims generally are nonassignable as a matter of public policy. Thus, if Elizabeth is injured by Randy's defamation, she cannot assign to someone else her right to sue Randy for damages.

When an Assignment Will Significantly Change the Risk or Duties of the Obligor. A right cannot be assigned if the assignment will significantly increase or alter the risks to or the duties of the obligor.[6] ■ **EXAMPLE 17.6** Larson owns a hotel. To insure it, he takes out a policy with Southeast Insurance. The policy insures against fire, theft, floods, and vandalism. Larson attempts to assign the insurance policy to Hewitt, who also owns a hotel.

The assignment is ineffective because it substantially alters Southeast Insurance's *duty of performance.* An insurance company evaluates the particular risk of a certain party and tailors its policy to fit that risk. If the policy is assigned to a third party, the insurance risk is materially altered because the insurance company may have no information on the third party. Therefore, the assignment will not operate to give Hewitt any rights against Southeast Insurance. ■

When the Contract Prohibits Assignment. When a contract specifically stipulates that a right cannot be assigned, then *ordinarily* it cannot be assigned. Note that restraints on the power to assign operate only against the parties themselves. They do not prohibit an assignment by operation of law, such as an assignment pursuant to bankruptcy or death.

6. Section 2–210(2) of the Uniform Commercial Code (UCC).

Whether such an *antiassignment clause* is effective depends, in part, on how it is phrased. A contract that states that *any* assignment is void effectively prohibits any assignment. ■ **EXAMPLE 17.7** Ramirez agrees to build a house for Carmen. Their contract states "This contract cannot be assigned by Carmen without Ramirez's consent. Any assignment without such consent renders the contract void." This antiassignment clause is effective, and Carmen cannot assign her rights without obtaining Ramirez's consent. ■

The general rule that a contract can prohibit assignment has several exceptions:

1. A contract cannot prevent an assignment of the right to receive funds. This exception exists to encourage the free flow of funds and credit in modern business settings.
2. The assignment of rights in real estate often cannot be prohibited because such a prohibition is contrary to public policy in most states. Prohibitions of this kind are called restraints against **alienation** (transfer of land ownership).
3. The assignment of *negotiable instruments* (such as checks and promissory notes) cannot be prohibited.
4. In a contract for the sale of goods, the right to receive damages for breach of contract or payment of an account owed may be assigned even though the sales contract prohibits such an assignment.[7]

The lease and purchase agreement in the following case contained an antiassignment clause. The court had to decide whether the clause was enforceable.

7. UCC 2–210(2).

Case 17.2

Bass-Fineberg Leasing, Inc. v. Modern Auto Sales, Inc.

Court of Appeals of Ohio, Ninth District, Medina County, __ N.E.3d __, 2015-Ohio-46 (2015).

Background and Facts Bass-Fineberg Leasing, Inc., leased a tour bus to Modern Auto Sales, Inc., and Michael Cipriani. The lease included an option to buy the bus. The lease prohibited Modern Auto and Cipriani from assigning their rights without Bass-Fineberg's written consent. Later, Cipriani left the bus with Anthony Allie at BVIP Limo Services, Ltd., for repairs. Modern Auto and Cipriani did not pay for the repairs. At the same time, they defaulted on the lease payments to Bass-Fineberg.

While BVIP retained possession of the bus, Allie signed an agreement with Cipriani to buy it and to make an initial $5,000 payment to Bass-Fineberg. Bass-Fineberg filed an action in an Ohio state court against Modern Auto, Cipriani, BVIP, and Allie to regain possession of the bus. The court ordered the bus returned to Bass-Fineberg and the $5,000 payment refunded to Allie. All of the parties appealed.

In the Language of the Court
WHITMORE, Judge.
* * * *

* * * Bass-Fineberg argues that the purported contract between Cipriani and Allie was void because Cipriani could not assign his rights or obligations under the lease without the written consent of

Case 17.2 Continued

Bass-Fineberg. * * * BVIP responds that if the contract was void, then the parties should be returned to their pre-contract status, including refunding its $5,000 payment. We agree with Bass-Fineberg that there was not a valid contract between Allie and Cipriani, but we agree with BVIP as to the effect of that invalidity, namely that it was entitled to have its $5,000 returned.

Ohio enforces anti-assignment clauses where there is clear contractual language prohibiting an assignment. Violations of a non-assignment provision in a contract render the resulting agreement null and void. [Emphasis added.]

* * * *

The lease between Bass-Fineberg and Modern Auto and Cipriani contained the following provision:

MODERN AUTO AND CIPRIANI ACKNOWLEDGE THAT MODERN AUTO AND CIPRIANI MAY NOT ASSIGN OR IN ANY WAY TRANSFER OR DISPOSE OF ALL OR ANY PART OF MODERN AUTO AND CIPRIANI'S RIGHTS OR OBLIGATIONS UNDER THIS LEASE * * * WITHOUT BASS-FINEBERG'S PRIOR WRITTEN CONSENT.

This clear contractual language prohibited Modern Auto and Cipriani from transferring their rights or obligations under the lease agreement unless Bass-Fineberg consented in writing.

The purported agreement between Cipriani and Allie attempted to transfer Cipriani's right to purchase the bus to Allie and some of Cipriani's payment obligations to Allie. [David] Libman, Bass-Fineberg's lease sales manager, did not sign the agreement between Allie and Cipriani. Nor did the parties introduce evidence of anyone else from Bass-Fineberg providing written consent to the attempted assignment.

As the lease agreement prohibited an assignment without Bass-Fineberg's consent, the agreement between Cipriani and Allie was void. If a contract is void, then an obligation under it never existed. In such circumstances, the one who made a payment is entitled to a refund.

Decision and Remedy *A state intermediate appellate court affirmed the lower court's order. The contract between Cipriani and Allie was void because Cipriani could not assign his rights under the lease without Bass-Fineberg's written consent. Because the contract was void, the parties were to be returned to their pre-contract status, which included a refund of the $5,000 payment.*

Critical Thinking

• **Economic** *The repairs to the bus cost $1,341.50. Who should pay this amount? Why?*

Notice of Assignment Once a valid assignment of rights has been made, the assignee should notify the obligor of the assignment. For instance, in *Example 17.2*, when Horton assigns to Kuhn his right to receive the $1,000 from Brower, Kuhn (the assignee) should notify Brower (the obligor) of the assignment.

Giving notice is not legally necessary to establish the validity of the assignment: an assignment is effective immediately, whether or not notice is given. Two major problems arise, however, when notice of the assignment is not given to the obligor.

Priority Issues. If the assignor assigns the same right to two different persons, the question arises as to which one has priority—that is, which one has the right to the performance by the obligor. The rule most often observed in the United States is that the first assignment in time is the first in right. Nevertheless, some states follow the English rule, which basically gives priority to the first assignee who gives notice.

■ **EXAMPLE 17.8** Jason owes Alexis $5,000 under a contract. Alexis first assigns the claim to Carmen, who does not give notice to Jason. Alexis then assigns it to Dorman, who notifies Jason. In most states, Carmen would have priority because the assignment to her was first in time. In some states, however, Dorman would have priority because he gave first notice. ■

Potential for Discharge by Performance to the Wrong Party. Until the obligor has notice of an assignment, the obligor can discharge his or her obligation by performance to the assignor (the obligee). Performance by the obligor to the assignor constitutes a discharge to the assignee. Once the obligor receives proper notice, however, only performance to the assignee can discharge the obligor's obligations.

■ **EXAMPLE 17.9** Recall that Alexis, the obligee in *Example 17.8*, assigned to Carmen her right to collect $5,000 from Jason, and Carmen did not give notice to Jason. Jason subsequently pays Alexis the $5,000.

Although the assignment was valid, Jason's payment to Alexis is a discharge of the debt. Carmen's failure to notify Jason of the assignment causes her to lose the right to collect the $5,000 from Jason. (Note that Carmen still has a claim against Alexis for the $5,000.) If Carmen had given Jason notice of the assignment, Jason's payment to Alexis would not have discharged the debt. ■

17–1b Delegations

Just as a party can transfer rights through an assignment, a party can also transfer duties. Duties are not assigned, however, they are *delegated*. The party delegating the duties is the **delegator,** and the party to whom the duties are delegated is the **delegatee.** Normally, a delegation of duties does not relieve the delegator of the obligation to perform in the event that the delegatee fails to do so.

No special form is required to create a valid delegation of duties. As long as the delegator expresses an intention to make the delegation, it is effective. The delegator need not even use the word *delegate*. Exhibit 17–2 illustrates delegation relationships.

Duties That Cannot Be Delegated As a general rule, any duty can be delegated. There are, however, some exceptions to this rule. Delegation is prohibited in the following circumstances:

1. When special trust has been placed in the obligor or when performance depends on the personal skill or talents of the obligor.
2. When performance by a third party will vary materially from that expected by the obligee.
3. When the contract expressly prohibits delegation.

When the Duties Are Personal in Nature. When special trust has been placed in the obligor or when performance depends on the personal skill or talents of the obligor, contractual duties cannot be delegated. ■ **EXAMPLE 17.10** O'Brien, who is impressed with Brodie's ability to perform veterinary surgery, contracts with Brodie to have her perform surgery on O'Brien's prize-winning stallion in July. Brodie later decides that she would rather spend the summer at the beach, so she delegates her duties under the contract to Lopez, who is also a competent veterinary surgeon. The delegation is not effective without O'Brien's consent, no matter how competent Lopez is, because the contract is for *personal* performance. ■

In contrast, nonpersonal duties may be delegated. Assume that in *Example 17.10,* Brodie has contracted with O'Brien to pick up and deliver a large horse trailer to O'Brien's property. Brodie delegates this duty to Lopez, who owns a towing business. This delegation is effective because the performance required is of a *routine* and *nonpersonal* nature.

EXHIBIT 17–2 Delegation Relationships

In the delegation relationship illustrated here, Brower delegates her *duties* under a contract that she made with Horton to a third party, Kuhn. Brower thus becomes the *delegator* and Kuhn the *delegatee* of the contractual duties. Kuhn now owes performance of the contractual duties to Horton. Note that a delegation of duties normally does not relieve the delegator (Brower) of liability if the delegatee (Kuhn) fails to perform the contractual duties.

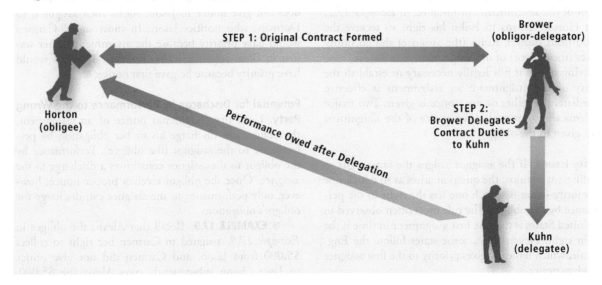

STEP 1: Original Contract Formed

Brower
(obligor-delegator)

Horton
(obligee)

Performance Owed after Delegation

STEP 2:
Brower Delegates
Contract Duties
to Kuhn

Kuhn
(delegatee)

When Performance by a Third Party Will Vary Materially from That Expected by the Obligee. When performance by a third party will vary materially from that expected by the obligee under the contract, contractual duties cannot be delegated. ■ **EXAMPLE 17.11** Jared, a wealthy investor, established the company Heaven Sent to provide grants of capital to struggling but potentially successful businesses. Jared contracted with Merilyn, whose judgment Jared trusted, to select the recipients of the grants. Later, Merilyn delegated this duty to Donald. Jared did not trust Donald's ability to select worthy recipients. This delegation is not effective because it materially alters Jared's expectations under the contract with Merilyn. ■

When the Contract Prohibits Delegation. When the contract expressly prohibits delegation by including an antidelegation clause, the duties cannot be delegated. ■ **EXAMPLE 17.12** Stark, Ltd., contracts with Belisario, a certified public accountant, to perform its annual audits for five years. The contract prohibits delegation. Belisario cannot delegate the duty to perform the audit to another accountant—not even an accountant at the same firm. ■

Effect of a Delegation If a delegation of duties is enforceable, the obligee must accept performance from the delegatee. The obligee can legally refuse performance from the delegatee only if the duty is one that cannot be delegated. ■ **EXAMPLE 17.13** Bryan has a duty to pick up and deliver metal fabrication equipment to Alicia's property. Bryan delegates his duty to Liam. Alicia (the obligee) must accept performance from Liam (the delegatee). ■

A valid delegation of duties does not relieve the delegator of obligations under the contract. Although there are exceptions, generally the obligee can sue both the delegatee and the delegator for nonperformance. Therefore, in *Example 17.13*, if Liam (the delegatee) fails to perform, Bryan (the delegator) is still liable to Alicia, and Alicia normally can sue Bryan, Liam, or both.

Concept Summary 17.1 outlines the basic principles of the laws governing assignments and delegations.

Concept Summary 17.1

Assignment and Delegations

Which Rights Can Be Assigned, and Which Duties Can Be Delegated?	All rights can be assigned *unless:* • A statute expressly prohibits assignment. • The contract is for personal services. • The assignment will materially alter the obligor's risk or duties. • The contract prohibits assignment. All duties can be delegated *unless:* • Performance depends on the obligor's personal skills or talents or special trust has been placed in the obligor. • Performance by a third party will materially vary from that expected by the obligee. • The contract prohibits delegation.
What If the Contract Prohibits Assignment or Delegation?	No rights can be assigned *except:* • Rights to receive funds. • Ownership rights in real estate. • Rights to negotiable instruments. • Rights to damages for breach of a sales contract or payments under a sales contract. No duties can be delegated.
What Is the Effect on the Original Party's Rights?	• On a valid assignment, effective immediately, the original party (assignor) no longer has any rights under the contract. • On a valid delegation, if the delegatee fails to perform, the original party (delegator) is liable to the obligee (who may also hold the delegatee liable).

17–1c Assignment of "All Rights"

When a contract provides for an "assignment of all rights," this wording may create both an assignment of rights and a delegation of duties.[8] Typically, this occurs when general words are used, such as "I assign the contract" or "I assign all my rights under the contract." A court normally will construe such words as implying both an assignment of rights and a delegation of any duties of performance. Thus, the assignor remains liable if the assignee fails to perform the contractual obligations.

17–2 Third Party Beneficiaries

Another exception to the doctrine of privity of contract arises when the contract is intended to benefit a third party. The original parties to a contract can agree that the contract performance should be rendered to or directly benefit a third person. When this happens, the third person becomes an *intended* **third party beneficiary** of the contract. As the **intended beneficiary** of the contract, the third party has legal rights and can sue the promisor directly for breach of the contract.

17–2a Who Is the Promisor?

Who, though, is the promisor? In a bilateral contract, both parties to the contract make promises that can be

enforced, so the court has to determine which party made the promise that benefits the third party. That person is the promisor. In effect, allowing a third party to sue the promisor directly circumvents the "middle person" (the promisee) and thus reduces the burden on the courts. Otherwise, the third party would sue the promisee, who would then sue the promisor.

■ **CASE IN POINT 17.14** The classic case that gave third party beneficiaries the right to bring a suit directly against a promisor was decided in 1859. The case involved three parties—Holly, Lawrence, and Fox. Holly had borrowed $300 from Lawrence. Shortly thereafter, Holly loaned $300 to Fox, who in return promised Holly that he would pay Holly's debt to Lawrence on the following day. When Lawrence failed to obtain the $300 from Fox, he sued Fox to recover the funds. The court had to decide whether Lawrence could sue Fox directly (rather than suing Holly). The court held that when "a promise [is] made for the benefit of another, he for whose benefit it is made may bring an action for its breach."[9] ■

In the following case, the third party beneficiary was a former front woman for a band. The promisor was the band's recording company and distributor. The promisee was a corporation formed by the band members to receive the band's royalties. The contract involved the payment of those royalties. The question before the court was whether the third party could sue for breach of contract when the promisee lacked the capacity to bring the suit.

---

8. *Restatement (Second) of Contracts*, Section 328; UCC 2–210(3), (4).

9. *Lawrence v. Fox*, 20 N.Y. 268 (1859).

Case Analysis 17.3

Bozzio v. EMI Group, Ltd.
United States Court of Appeals, Ninth Circuit, 811 F.3d 1144 (2016).

In the Language of the Court
CHRISTEN, Circuit Judge:
    * * * *

In 1980, Dale Bozzio * * * , Terry Bozzio, and Warren Cuccurullo founded the band Missing Persons. * * * As the band's front woman, [Dale] Bozzio personified the sound and the look of the new wave scene in 1980s Los Angeles.

Capitol Records signed the band and * * * the individual artists in 1982. Their agreement provided that the artists comprising Missing Persons would create master recordings that Capitol would sell and license. In return, Capitol promised to "pay royalties at rates ranging from 20% to 24% for sales in the United States and Canada,

and from 7% to 8% for sales in the rest of the world." The agreement also provided that the artists would receive 50% of Capitol's net royalties from licensing.

In 1983, Bozzio and the other band members formed Missing Persons, Inc., a California corporation, to serve as a loan-out company through which they would provide services to Capitol. A loan-out corporation is a legal fiction employed for the financial benefit of successful artists and entertainers. It is a duly organized corporation, typically wholly owned by an artist, the sole function of which is to "loan out" the services of the artist-owner to producers and other potential employers.

Capitol subsequently entered into a new contract, called the Loan-Out Agreement, with Missing Persons, Inc. The Loan-Out Agreement substituted Missing Persons, Inc. in place of the individual band members in the original * * * Agreement and required Capitol to pay all artist royalties to Missing Persons, Inc., not to the artists. It also stated that Missing Persons, Inc. was to receive all contractual benefits, and that it, not Capitol, was to pay the individual artists all required royalties and advances. As part of the Loan-Out Agreement, each band member executed an Artist Declaration * * * . Bozzio's

Case 17.3 Continued

declaration states that she "agrees to look solely to Missing Persons, Inc. for the payment of her fees and/or royalties * * *, and will not assert any claims in this regard against Capitol."

The music group disbanded in 1986, and, as of July 1, 1988, Missing Persons, Inc. was suspended under California Revenue and Taxation Code Section 23301 due to failure to pay [its] taxes. The parties do not dispute that Missing Persons, Inc. remains a suspended corporation.
* * * *

In 2012, Bozzio filed a * * * suit in [a federal district court in] the Northern District of California. The * * * complaint alleges breach of contract and other claims against EMI Group, Ltd., Capitol Records, LLC, [and others] (collectively, "Capitol"). Specifically, the complaint alleges that Capitol failed to "properly account for and pay its recording artists and music producers for income it has received, and continues to receive, from the licenses of its recorded music catalog for the sale of digital downloads, ringtones (or mastertones), and streaming music." It requests declaratory judgment, injunctive relief, restitution, and attorneys' fees.

Capitol moved to dismiss Bozzio's complaint * * *. Capitol primarily argued that Bozzio could not file suit because she expressly agreed in the Artist Declaration to "look solely to" the loan-out corporation for royalty payments and promised to "not assert any claim in this regard against Capitol." Bozzio countered that she was an intended third-party beneficiary of the Loan-Out Agreement with an individual right to sue that is separate from the corporation's. According to Bozzio, the Artist Declarations "only prohibit an artist from asserting a claim against EMI when there is a dispute among individual band members over the internal allocation and

distribution of royalties that have already been properly accounted for and paid by the record label."

* * * The district court granted Capitol's motion to dismiss. * * * The court * * * concluded that allowing Bozzio to sue as a third-party beneficiary of the recording contract would permit her to "use the corporate entity to contract, and gain the benefits of the corporate form, yet allow her to retain the right to sue as an individual, third party beneficiary even when the corporation could not, on account of its failure to comply with its corporate obligations * * *." Bozzio timely appealed [to the U.S. Court of Appeals for the Ninth Circuit].
* * * *

* * * On appeal, Bozzio argues that the suspended status of the contracting corporate party is irrelevant when the party bringing the action is a third-party beneficiary of the contract, and the district court's dismissal of the * * * complaint on that basis constitutes reversible error. We agree with Bozzio that the district court erred in holding that, even if Bozzio is a third-party beneficiary, she cannot bring an action while Missing Persons, Inc. is suspended.
* * * *

The parties have not cited, and we have not found, any California case holding that a third-party beneficiary cannot sue the promisor for breach of contract when the promisee is a suspended corporation.
* * * *

* * * *California courts do not consider the incapacity of the promisee to a contract to be an absolute bar to a lawsuit by a third-party beneficiary.* [Emphasis added.]
* * * *

When sitting in diversity jurisdiction, this court will follow a state supreme court's interpretation * * *. Where the

state's highest court has not decided an issue, this court looks for guidance to decisions by intermediate appellate courts of the state * * *. Here, the California Supreme Court has not decided whether a promisee corporation's suspended status precludes suit by a third-party beneficiary of the contract, but * * * the California Court of Appeal [has] suggested that a third-party beneficiary suit may go forward notwithstanding the promisee's incapacity to sue. Therefore, the district court erred in its determination that a third-party beneficiary cannot state a claim if the promisee is a suspended corporation.
* * * *

In light of the above, it was an error to grant the motion to dismiss on the ground that Missing Persons, Inc. was a suspended corporation.
* * * *

Capitol strenuously argues that by agreeing "not to assert any claims * * * against Capitol," Bozzio waived her right to sue as a third-party beneficiary. Bozzio counters that this "look solely to" clause was intended to prohibit an artist from asserting a claim against Capitol only "when there is a dispute among individual band members over the internal allocation and distribution of royalties that have already been properly accounted for and paid by the record label to the artists' musical group or loan-out corporation." Nothing in the record forecloses Bozzio's reading of this contract language.

We agree with Bozzio that whether she forfeited the ability to sue as a third-party beneficiary is a fact-bound inquiry ill-suited to resolution at the motion to dismiss stage. On remand, a record can be developed that will allow consideration of Bozzio's claim that she was an intended third-party beneficiary of the Agreement.
* * * *

REVERSED AND REMANDED.

Legal Reasoning Questions

1. What did the lower court rule with respect to the plaintiff's complaint in this case? Why?

2. Did the appellate court agree or disagree with the lower court's ruling? Why?

3. Which issues remain to be determined in this case? Which court will make those determinations initially? Why?

17–2b Types of Intended Beneficiaries

The law traditionally recognized two types of intended third party beneficiaries: creditor beneficiaries and donee beneficiaries.

Creditor Beneficiary One type of intended beneficiary is a *creditor beneficiary*. Like the plaintiff in *Case in Point 17.14*, a creditor beneficiary benefits from a contract in which one party (the promisor) promises another party (the promisee) to pay a debt that the promisee owes to a third party (the creditor beneficiary).

■ **CASE IN POINT 17.15** Autumn Allan owned a condominium unit in a Texas complex located directly beneath a condo unit owned by Aslan Koraev. Over the course of two years, Allan's unit suffered eight incidents of water and sewage incursion as a result of plumbing problems and misuse of appliances in Koraev's unit. Allan sued Koraev for breach of contract and won.

Koraev appealed, arguing that he had no contractual duty to Allan. The court found that Allan was an intended third party beneficiary of the contract between Koraev and the condominium owners' association. Because the governing documents stated that each owner had to comply strictly with their provisions, failure to comply created grounds for an action by the condominium association or by an aggrieved (wronged) owner. Here, Allan was clearly an aggrieved owner and could sue Koraev directly for his failure to perform his contract duties to the condominium association.[10] ■

Donee Beneficiary Another type of intended beneficiary is a *donee beneficiary*. When a contract is made for the express purpose of giving a *gift* to a third party, the third party (the donee beneficiary) can sue the promisor directly to enforce the promise.[11]

The most common donee beneficiary contract is a life insurance contract. ■ **EXAMPLE 17.16** Ang (the promisee) pays premiums to Standard Life, a life insurance company. Standard Life (the promisor) promises to pay a certain amount upon Ang's death to anyone Ang designates as a beneficiary. The designated beneficiary is a donee beneficiary under the life insurance policy and can enforce the promise made by the insurance company to pay her or him on Ang's death. ■

The Modern View Most third party beneficiaries do not fit neatly into either the creditor beneficiary or the donee beneficiary category. Thus, the modern view adopted by the *Restatement (Second) of Contracts* does not draw clear lines between the types of intended beneficiaries. Today, courts frequently distinguish only between *intended beneficiaries* (who can sue to enforce contracts made for their benefit) and *incidental beneficiaries* (who cannot sue, as will be discussed shortly).

17–2c When the Rights of an Intended Beneficiary Vest

An intended third party beneficiary cannot enforce a contract against the original parties until the rights of the third party have *vested*, which means the rights have taken effect and cannot be taken away. Until these rights have vested, the original parties to the contract—the promisor and the promisee—can modify or rescind the contract without the consent of the third party.

When do the rights of third parties vest? The majority of courts hold that the rights vest when any of the following occurs:

1. When the third party demonstrates express consent to the agreement, such as by sending a letter, a note, or an e-mail acknowledging awareness of, and consent to, a contract formed for her or his benefit.
2. When the third party materially alters his or her position in detrimental reliance on the contract. For instance, a person contracts to have a home built in reliance on the receipt of funds promised to him or her in a donee beneficiary contract.
3. When the conditions for vesting are satisfied. For instance, the rights of a beneficiary under a life insurance policy vest when the insured person dies.[12]

If the contract expressly reserves to the contracting parties the right to cancel, rescind, or modify the contract, the rights of the third party beneficiary are subject to any changes that result. If the original contract reserves the right to revoke the promise or change the beneficiary, the vesting of the third party's rights does not terminate that power.[13] In most life insurance contracts, for instance, the policyholder reserves the right to change the designated beneficiary.

17–2d Incidental Beneficiaries

Sometimes, a third person receives a benefit from a contract even though that person's benefit is not the reason the contract was made. Such a person is known as an **incidental beneficiary**. Because the benefit is *unintentional*,

---

10. *Allan v. Nersesova*, 307 S.W.3d 564 (Tx.App.—Dallas 2010).
11. This principle was first enunciated in *Seaver v. Ransom*, 224 N.Y. 233, 120 N.E. 639 (1918).
12. *Restatement (Second) of Contracts*, Section 311.
13. Defenses against third party beneficiaries are given in the *Restatement (Second) of Contracts*, Section 309.

an incidental beneficiary cannot sue to enforce the contract.

■ **CASE IN POINT 17.17** Spectators at the infamous boxing match in which Mike Tyson was disqualified for biting his opponent's ear sued Tyson and the fight's promoters for a refund on the basis of breach of contract. The spectators claimed that they were third party beneficiaries of the contract between Tyson and the fight's promoters. The court, however, held that the spectators could not sue because they were not in contractual privity with the defendants. Any benefits they received from the contract were incidental to the contract. According to the court, the spectators got what they paid for: "the right to view whatever event transpired."[14] ■

17–2e Intended versus Incidental Beneficiaries

In determining whether a third party beneficiary is an intended or an incidental beneficiary, the courts focus on intent, as expressed in the contract language and implied by the surrounding circumstances. Any beneficiary who is not deemed an intended beneficiary is considered incidental. Exhibit 17–3 illustrates the distinction between intended beneficiaries and incidental beneficiaries.

---

14. *Castillo v. Tyson*, 268 A.D.2d 336, 701 N.Y.S.2d 423 (Sup.Ct.App.Div. 2000).

Although no single test can embrace all possible situations, courts often apply the *reasonable person* test: Would a reasonable person in the position of the beneficiary believe that the promisee intended to confer on the beneficiary the right to enforce the contract? In addition, the presence of one or more of the following factors strongly indicates that the third party is an intended beneficiary to the contract:

1. Performance is rendered directly to the third party.
2. The third party has the right to control the details of performance.
3. The third party is expressly designated as a beneficiary in the contract.

■ **CASE IN POINT 17.18** New York City decided to build a state-of-the-art forensic biology (DNA testing) laboratory next to Bellevue Hospital in Manhattan. The project was designed to be a fifteen-story structure with a two-level basement. The city turned the project over to the Dormitory Authority of the State of New York (DASNY), which oversees public projects. DASNY contracted with Perkins Eastman Architects, P.C., to provide architectural services for the project. Perkins hired Samson Construction Company to excavate the site and lay the foundation. Unfortunately, Samson's excavation of the site caused adjacent structures, including a building, sidewalks, roadbeds, sewers, and water systems, to "settle," sustaining about $37 million in damage.

EXHIBIT 17–3 Third Party Beneficiaries

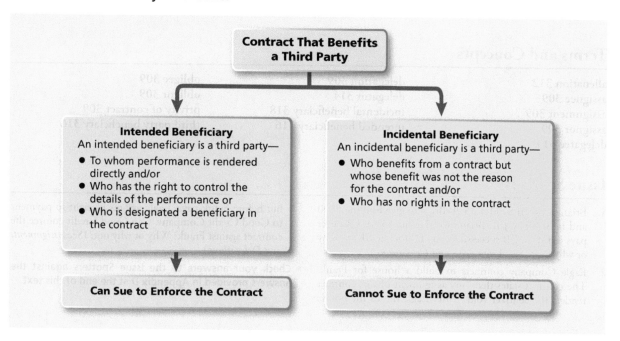

Contract That Benefits a Third Party

Intended Beneficiary
An intended beneficiary is a third party—
- To whom performance is rendered directly and/or
- Who has the right to control the details of the performance or
- Who is designated a beneficiary in the contract

Can Sue to Enforce the Contract

Incidental Beneficiary
An incidental beneficiary is a third party—
- Who benefits from a contract but whose benefit was not the reason for the contract and/or
- Who has no rights in the contract

Cannot Sue to Enforce the Contract

DASNY and the city filed a suit in a New York state court against Samson and Perkins, alleging breach of contract. The lower court dismissed the claim, finding that because the city was not named in the contract between Samson and Perkins, it was not a third party beneficiary. A state intermediate appellate court reversed. "The City raised an issue of fact whether it is an intended third party beneficiary of the contract. The contract expressly states that a City agency will operate the DNA laboratory, and the City retained control over various aspects of the project."[15] ■

---

15. *Dormitory Authority of the State of New York v. Samson Construction Co.,* 137 A.D.3d 433, 27 N.Y.S.3d 114 (1 Dept. 2016).

Reviewing: Third Party Rights

Myrtle Jackson owns several commercial buildings that she leases to businesses, one of which is a restaurant. The lease states that tenants are responsible for securing all necessary insurance policies but the landlord is obligated to keep the buildings in good repair. The owner of the restaurant, Joe McCall, tells his restaurant manager to purchase insurance, but the manager never does so. Jackson tells her son-in-law, Rob Dunn, to perform any necessary maintenance for the buildings. Dunn knows that the ceiling in the restaurant needs repair but fails to do anything about it.

One day a customer, Ian Faught, is dining in the restaurant when a chunk of the ceiling falls on his head and fractures his skull. Faught files suit against the restaurant and discovers that there is no insurance policy in effect. Faught then files a suit against Jackson. He argues that he is an intended third party beneficiary of the lease provision requiring the restaurant to carry insurance and thus can sue Jackson for failing to enforce that provision. Using the information presented in the chapter, answer the following questions.

1. Can Jackson delegate her duty to maintain the buildings to Dunn? Why or why not?
2. Who can be held liable for Dunn's failure to fix the ceiling, Jackson or Dunn? Why?
3. Was Faught an intended third party beneficiary of the lease between Jackson and McCall? Why or why not?
4. Suppose that Jackson tells Dan Stryker, a local builder to whom she owes $50,000, that he can collect the rents from the buildings' tenants until the debt is satisfied. Is this a valid assignment? Why or why not?

Debate This . . . *As a matter of public policy, personal-injury tort claims cannot be assigned. This public policy is wrong and should be changed.*

Terms and Concepts

alienation 312	delegation 309	obligee 309
assignee 309	delegator 314	obligor 309
assignment 309	incidental beneficiary 318	privity of contract 309
assignor 309	intended beneficiary 316	third party beneficiary 316
delegatee 314		

Issue Spotters

1. Brian owes Jeff $100. Ed tells Brian to give him the $100 and he will pay Jeff. Brian gives Ed the $100. Ed never pays Jeff. Can Jeff successfully sue Ed for the $100? Why or why not? (See *Assignments and Delegations.*)

2. Eagle Company contracts to build a house for Frank. The contract states that "any assignment of this contract renders the contract void." After Eagle builds the house, but before Frank pays, Eagle assigns its right to payment to Good Credit Company. Can Good Credit enforce the contract against Frank? Why or why not? (See *Assignments and Delegations.*)

• Check your answers to the Issue Spotters against the answers provided in Appendix D at the end of this text.

Business Scenarios

17–1. Assignment. Five years ago, Hensley purchased a house. At that time, being unable to pay the full purchase price, she borrowed funds from Thrift Savings and Loan, which in turn took a mortgage at 6.5 percent interest on the house. The mortgage contract did not prohibit the assignment of the mortgage. Then Hensley secured a new job in another city and sold the house to Sylvia. The purchase price included payment to Hensley of the value of her equity and the assumption of the mortgage debt still owed to Thrift. At the time the contract between Hensley and Sylvia was made, Thrift did not know about or consent to the sale. On the basis of these facts, if Sylvia defaults in making the mortgage payments to Thrift, what are Thrift's rights? Discuss. (See *Assignments and Delegations.*)

17–2. Assignment. Marsala, a college student, signs a one-year lease agreement that runs from September 1 to August 31. The lease agreement specifies that the lease cannot be assigned without the landlord's consent. In late May, Marsala decides not to go to summer school and assigns the balance of the lease (three months) to a close friend, Fred. The landlord objects to the assignment and denies Fred access to the apartment. Marsala claims that Fred is financially sound and should be allowed the full rights and privileges of an assignee.

Discuss fully who is correct, the landlord or Marsala. (See *Assignments and Delegations.*)

17–3. Third Party Beneficiaries. Wilken owes Rivera $2,000. Howie promises Wilken that he will pay Rivera the $2,000 in return for Wilken's promise to give Howie's children guitar lessons. Is Rivera an intended beneficiary of the Howie-Wilken contract? Explain. (See *Third Party Beneficiaries.*)

17–4. Delegation. Inez has a specific set of plans to build a sailboat. The plans are detailed, and any boatbuilder can construct the boat. Inez secures bids, and the low bid is made by the Whale of a Boat Corp. Inez contracts with Whale to build the boat for $4,000. Whale then receives unexpected business from elsewhere. To meet the delivery date in the contract with Inez, Whale delegates its obligation to build the boat, without Inez's consent, to Quick Brothers, a reputable boatbuilder. When the boat is ready for delivery, Inez learns of the delegation and refuses to accept delivery, even though the boat is built to her specifications. Discuss fully whether Inez is obligated to accept and pay for the boat. Would your answer be any different if Inez had not had a specific set of plans but had instead contracted with Whale to design and build a sailboat for $4,000? Explain. (See *Assignments and Delegations.*)

Business Case Problems

17–5. Duties That Cannot Be Delegated. Bruce Albea Contracting, Inc., was the general contractor on a state highway project. Albea subcontracted the asphalt work to APAC-Southeast, Inc. Their contract prohibited any delegation without Albea's consent. In midproject, APAC delegated its duties to Matthews Contracting Co. Although Albea allowed Matthews to finish the work, Albea did not pay APAC for its work on the project. Albea argued that APAC had violated the antidelegation clause, rendering their contract void. Is Albea correct? Explain. [*Western Surety Co. v. APAC-Southeast, Inc.,* 302 Ga.App. 654, 691 S.E.2d 234 (2010)] (See *Assignments and Delegations.*)

17–6. Notice of Assignment. Arnold Kazery was the owner of a hotel leased to George Wilkinson. The lease included renewal options of ten years each. When Arnold transferred his interest in the property to his son, Sam, no one notified Wilkinson. For the next twenty years, Wilkinson paid the rent to Arnold and renewed the lease by notice to Arnold. When Wilkinson wrote to Arnold that he was exercising another option to renew, Sam filed a suit against him, claiming that the lease was void. Did Wilkinson give proper notice to renew? Discuss. [*Kazery v. Wilkinson,* 52 So.3d 1270 (Miss.App. 2011)] (See *Assignments and Delegations.*)

17–7. Business Case Problem with Sample Answer—Third Party Beneficiary. David and Sandra Dess con-tracted with Sirva Relocation, LLC, to assist in selling their home. In their contract, the Desses agreed to disclose all information about the property on which Sirva "and other prospective buyers may rely in deciding whether and on what terms to purchase the Property." The Kincaids contracted with Sirva to buy the house. After the closing, they discovered dampness in the walls, defective and rotten windows, mold, and other undisclosed problems. Can the Kincaids bring an action against the Desses for breach of their contract with Sirva? Why or why not? [*Kincaid v. Dess,* 298 P.3d 358 (2013)] (See *Third Party Beneficiaries.*)

- **For a sample answer to Problem 17–7, go to Appendix E at the end of this text.**

17–8. Third Party Beneficiaries. Randy Jones is an agent for Farmers Insurance Co. of Arizona. Through Jones, Robert and Marcia Murray obtained auto insurance with Farmers. On Jones's advice, the Murrays increased the policy's limits over the minimums required by the state of Arizona, except for uninsured/underinsured motorist coverage, for which Jones made no recommendation. Later, the Murrays' seventeen-year-old daughter, Jessyka, was in an accident that involved both an uninsured motorist and an underinsured motorist. She sustained a traumatic brain injury that permanently incapacitated her. Does Jessyka have standing to bring a claim against Jones and Farmers as a third party to her parents' contract for auto insurance? Explain. [*Lucas Contracting, Inc. v. Altisource Portfolio Solutions, Inc.*, __ N.E.2d __, 2016-Ohio-474 (Ohio App. 2016)] (See *Third Party Beneficiaries*.)

17–9. A Question of Ethics—Assignment and Delegation. *Premier Building & Development, Inc., entered into a list-* 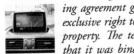 *ing agreement giving Sunset Gold Realty, LLC, the exclusive right to find a tenant for some commercial property. The terms of the listing agreement stated that it was binding on both parties and "their . . . assigns." Premier Building did not own the property at the time but had the option to purchase it. To secure financing for the*

project, Premier Building established a new company called Cobblestone Associates. Premier Building then bought the property and conveyed it to Cobblestone the same day. Meanwhile, Sunset Gold found a tenant for the property, and Cobblestone became the landlord. Cobblestone acknowledged its obligation to pay Sunset Gold for finding a tenant, but it later refused to pay Sunset Gold's commission. Sunset Gold then sued Premier Building and Cobblestone for breach of the listing agreement. [Sunset Gold Realty, LLC v. Premier Building & Development, Inc., 133 Conn.App. 445, 36 A.3d 243 (2012)] (See *Assignments and Delegations*.)

(a) Is Premier Building relieved of its contractual duties if it assigned the contract to Cobblestone? Why or why not?

(b) Given that Sunset Gold performed its obligations under the listing agreement, did Cobblestone behave unethically in refusing to pay Sunset Gold's commission? Why or why not?

Legal Reasoning Group Activity

17–10. Assignment. The Smiths buy a house. They borrow 80 percent of the purchase price from the local ABC Savings and Loan. Before they make their first payment, ABC transfers the right to receive mortgage payments to Citibank. (See *Assignments and Delegations*.)

(a) The first group will outline what would happen if the Smiths continued to make all their payments to ABC Savings and Loan because ABC never notified them of the assignment.

(b) The second group will describe what would happen if the Smiths were notified by ABC of the assignment, but continued to make payments to ABC.

(c) A third group will determine what would happen if the Smiths failed to make any payments on the loan. Which financial institution would have the right to repossess their house?

Answers to the *Issue Spotters*

1. *Can Jeff successfully sue Ed for the $100? Why or why not?* Yes. When one person makes a promise with the intention of benefiting a third person, the third person can sue to enforce it. This is a third party beneficiary contract. The third party in this problem is an intended beneficiary.

2. *Can Good Credit enforce the contract against Frank? Why or why not?* Yes. Generally, if a contract clearly states that a right is not assignable, no assignment will be effective, but there are exceptions. Assignment of the right to receive monetary payment cannot be prohibited.

Sample Answers for *Business Case Problems with Sample Answer*

Problem 17–7. *Third Party Beneficiary.* Yes, the Kincaids can bring an action against the Desses for breach of their contract with Sirva. A third person becomes an intended third party beneficiary of a contract when the original parties to the contract expressly agree that the performance should be rendered to or directly benefit a third person. As the intended beneficiary of a contract, a third party has legal rights and can sue the promisor directly for breach of the contract.

Here, the Desses agreed in their contract with Sirva to disclose all information about their property. They further agreed that Sirva and "other prospective buyers" could rely on the Desses' disclosure in deciding "whether and on what terms to purchase the Property." The Kincaids were not direct parties to the contract between Sirva and the Desses, but the Kincaids were "other prospective buyers." Thus, the language of the contract indicated that the Kincaids were intended by Sirva and the Desses to be third party beneficiaries of it. As intended beneficiaries of the contract, the Kincaids could sue the Desses directly for its breach.

In the actual case on which this problem is based, the Kincaids filed a suit in a Kansas state court against the Desses. From a judgment in the Desses' favor (for lack of privity), the Kincaids appealed. A state intermediate appellate court reversed on the basis of the reasoning stated above and remanded the case for trial.

CHAPTER

Performance and Discharge

The most common way to **discharge,** or terminate, contractual duties is by the **performance** of those duties. For instance, a buyer and seller enter into an agreement via e-mail for the sale of a 2018 Lexus RX for $44,000. This contract will be discharged by performance when the buyer pays $44,000 to the seller and the seller transfers possession of the Lexus to the buyer.

In a perfect world, every party who signed a contract would perform his or her duties completely and in a timely fashion, thereby discharging the contract. The real world is more complicated. Events often occur that affect our performance or our ability to perform contractual duties. In addition, the duty to perform under a contract is not always *absolute*. It may instead be *conditioned* on the occurrence or nonoccurrence of a certain event. The legal environment of business requires the identification of some point at which the parties can reasonably know that their duties have ended.

18–1 Conditions

In most contracts, promises of performance are not expressly conditioned or qualified. Instead, they are *absolute promises.* They must be performed, or the parties promising the acts will be in breach of contract.
■ **EXAMPLE 18.1** Paloma Enterprises contracts to sell a truckload of organic produce to Tran for $10,000. The parties' promises are unconditional: Paloma will deliver the produce to Tran, and Tran will pay $10,000 to Paloma. The payment does not have to be made if the produce is not delivered. ■

In some situations, however, performance is *conditioned*. A **condition** is a qualification in a contract based on a possible future event. The occurrence or nonoccurrence of the event will trigger the performance of a legal obligation or terminate an existing obligation under a contract.[1] If the condition is not satisfied, the obligations of the parties are discharged.

Three types of conditions can be present in contracts: conditions *precedent,* conditions *subsequent,* and *concurrent* conditions. Conditions can also be classified as *express* or *implied.*

18–1a Conditions Precedent

A condition that must be fulfilled before a party's performance can be required is called a **condition precedent.** The condition precedes the absolute duty to perform.

A contract to lease university housing, for instance, may be conditioned on the person's being a student at the university. ■ **CASE IN POINT 18.2** James Maciel leased an apartment in a university-owned housing facility for Regent University (RU) students in Virginia. The lease ran until the end of the fall semester. Maciel had an option to renew the lease semester by semester as long as he maintained his status as an RU student.

When Maciel told RU that he intended to withdraw, the university told him that he had to move out of the apartment by May 31, the final day of the semester. Maciel asked for two additional weeks, but the university denied the request. On June 1, RU changed the locks on the apartment. Maciel entered through a window and e-mailed the university that he planned to stay "for another one or two weeks." He was convicted of trespassing. He appealed, arguing that he had "legal authority" to occupy the apartment. The reviewing court affirmed his conviction. "Regent's deadline was consistent with the lease agreement, and Maciel's eligibility to reside in student housing was *conditioned* upon his status as a Regent student." In other words, being enrolled as a student in RU was a condition precedent to living in its student housing.[2] ■

---

1. The *Restatement (Second) of Contracts*, Section 224, defines a condition as "an event, not certain to occur, which must occur, unless its nonoccurrence is excused, before performance under a contract becomes due."

2. *Maciel v. Commonwealth*, 2011 WL 65942 (Va.App. 2011).

Life insurance contracts frequently specify that certain conditions, such as passing a physical examination, must be met before the insurance company will be obligated to perform under the contract. In addition, many contracts are conditioned on an independent appraisal of value. ■ **EXAMPLE 18.3** iMotors offers to buy Gabe's 1959 Thunderbird only if an appraiser estimates that it can be restored for less than a certain price. Therefore, the parties' obligations are conditional. If the condition is not satisfied—that is, if the appraiser deems the cost to be above that price—their obligations are discharged. ■

18–1b Conditions Subsequent

When a condition operates to terminate a party's absolute promise to perform, it is called a **condition subsequent.** The condition follows, or is subsequent to, the time at which the absolute duty to perform arose. If the condition occurs, the party's duty to perform is discharged. ■ **EXAMPLE 18.4** A law firm hires Julie Mendez, a recent law school graduate. Their contract provides that the firm's obligation to continue employing Mendez is discharged if Mendez fails to pass the bar exam by her second attempt. This is a condition subsequent because a failure to pass the exam—and thus to obtain a license to practice law—would discharge a duty (employment) that has already arisen. ■

Generally, conditions precedent are common, and conditions subsequent are rare. Indeed, the *Restatement (Second) of Contracts* does not use the terms *condition subsequent* and *condition precedent* but refers to both simply as conditions.[3]

18–1c Concurrent Conditions

When each party's performance is conditioned on the other party's performance or tender of performance (offer to perform), **concurrent conditions** are present. These conditions exist only when the contract expressly or impliedly calls for the parties to perform their respective duties *simultaneously.*

■ **EXAMPLE 18.5** If Janet Feibush promises to pay for goods when Hewlett-Packard delivers them, the parties' promises to perform are mutually dependent. Feibush's duty to pay for the goods does not become absolute until Hewlett-Packard either delivers or tenders the goods. Likewise, Hewlett-Packard's duty to deliver the goods does not become absolute until Feibush tenders or actually makes payment. Therefore, neither can recover from the other for breach without first tendering performance. ■

Exhibit 18–1 reviews the types of conditions.

3. *Restatement (Second) of Contracts,* Section 224.

EXHIBIT 18–1 Conditions of Performance

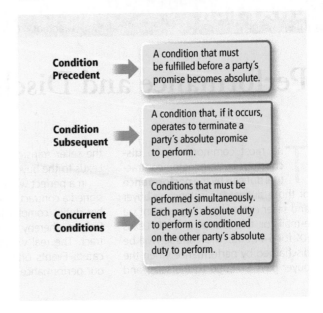

18–1d Express and Implied Conditions

Conditions can also be classified as express or implied in fact. *Express conditions* are provided for by the parties' agreement. Although no particular words are necessary, express conditions are normally prefaced by the words *if, provided, after,* or *when.* For instance, most automobile insurance policies include what is known as a cooperation clause. This clause states that if the insured person is involved in an accident, he or she must cooperate with the insurance company in the defense of any claim or lawsuit.

Implied conditions are understood to be part of the agreement, but they are not found in the express language of the agreement. Courts may imply conditions from the purpose of the contract or from the intent of the parties. Conditions are often implied when they are inherent in the actual performance of the contract.

18–2 Discharge by Performance

The great majority of contracts, as noted earlier, are discharged by performance. The contract comes to an end when both parties fulfill their respective duties by performing the acts they have promised.

Performance can also be accomplished by *tender.* **Tender** is an unconditional offer to perform by a person who is ready, willing, and able to do so. Therefore, a seller who places goods at the disposal of a buyer has tendered delivery and can demand payment. A buyer who offers to pay for goods has tendered payment and can demand delivery of the goods.

Once performance has been tendered, the party making the tender has done everything possible to carry out the terms of the contract. If the other party then refuses to perform, the party making the tender can sue for breach of contract. There are two basic types of performance—*complete performance* and *substantial performance*.

18–2a Complete Performance

When a party performs exactly as agreed, there is no question as to whether the contract has been performed. When a party's performance is perfect, it is said to be complete. Normally, conditions expressly stated in a contract must fully occur in all respects for complete performance (strict performance) of the contract to take place. Any deviation breaches the contract and discharges the other party's obligation to perform.

Most construction contracts, for instance, require the builder to meet certain specifications. If the specifications are conditions, complete performance is required to avoid material breach (*material breach* will be discussed shortly). If the conditions are met, the other party to the contract must then fulfill her or his obligation to pay the builder.

If the parties to the contract did not expressly make the specifications a condition, however, and the builder fails to meet the specifications, performance is not complete. What effect does such a failure have on the other party's obligation to pay? The answer is part of the doctrine of *substantial performance*.

18–2b Substantial Performance

A party who in good faith performs substantially all of the terms of a contract can enforce the contract against the other party under the doctrine of substantial performance. The basic requirements for performance to qualify as substantial performance are as follows:

1. The party must have performed in good faith. Intentional failure to comply with the contract terms is a breach of the contract.
2. The performance must not vary greatly from the performance promised in the contract. An omission, variance, or defect in performance is considered minor if it can easily be remedied by compensation (monetary damages).
3. The performance must create substantially the same benefits as those promised in the contract.

Courts Must Decide Courts decide whether the performance was substantial on a case-by-case basis, examining all of the facts of the particular situation. ■ **CASE IN POINT 18.6** Eugene Pegg had been an electrician in North Dakota for thirty years and had brought a large customer, Sungold, with him through several employers. When an acquaintance, Kelly Kohn, started Kohn Electric, LLC, Pegg approached him to become partners.

Kohn and Pegg orally agreed that Pegg could become a partner in Kohn Electric if he contributed $10,000 in capital and the Sungold account. In return, Pegg was to receive 10 percent of the gross revenue generated by the Sungold account, among other things. Pegg paid $9,152.49 for a pickup truck titled in Kohn Electric's name and paid for tools and equipment for the business. Later, the relationship soured, and Pegg quit. Pegg sued in a state court to recover the proceeds due under the agreement. Kohn denied that they were partners, but he paid Pegg $9,152.49 for the truck.

The state court found that there was an oral partnership agreement and that Pegg had substantially performed by contributing the pickup and bringing in the Sungold account. Therefore, he was entitled to damages in an amount equal to 10 percent of the gross revenue generated from the Sungold account. The court's decision was affirmed on appeal.[4] ■

Effect on Duty to Perform If one party's performance is substantial, the other party's duty to perform remains absolute. In other words, the parties must continue performing under the contract. For instance, the party who substantially performed is entitled to payment. If performance is not substantial, there is a material breach (to be discussed shortly), and the nonbreaching party is excused from further performance.

Measure of Damages Because substantial performance is not perfect, the other party is entitled to damages to compensate for the failure to comply with the contract. The measure of the damages is the cost to bring the object of the contract into compliance with its terms, if that cost is reasonable under the circumstances.

What if the cost is unreasonable? Then the measure of damages is the difference in value between the performance rendered and the performance that would have been rendered if the contract had been performed completely.

The following case is a classic illustration that there is no exact formula for deciding when a contract has been substantially performed.

---

4. *Pegg v. Kohn*, 861 N.W.2d 764, 2015 ND 79 (2015).

Jacob & Youngs v. Kent

Court of Appeals of New York, 230 N.Y. 239, 129 N.E. 889 (1921).

Background and Facts The plaintiff, Jacob & Youngs, Inc., was a builder that had contracted with George Kent to construct a country residence for him. A specification in the building contract required that "all wrought-iron pipe must be well galvanized, lap welded pipe of the grade known as 'standard pipe' of Reading manufacture." Jacob & Youngs installed substantially similar pipe that was not of Reading manufacture. When Kent became aware of the difference, he ordered the builder to remove all of the plumbing and replace it with the Reading type. To do so would have required removing finished walls that encased the plumbing—an expensive and difficult task. The builder explained that the plumbing was of the same quality, appearance, value, and cost as Reading pipe. When Kent nevertheless refused to pay the $3,483.46 still owed for the work, Jacob & Youngs sued to compel payment. The trial court ruled in favor of Kent. The plaintiff appealed, and the appellate court reversed the trial court's decision. Kent then appealed to the Court of Appeals of New York, the state's highest court.

In the Language of the Court

CARDOZO, Justice.

* * * *

* * * The courts never say that one who makes a contract fills the measure of his duty by less than full performance. They do say, however, that *an omission, both trivial and innocent, will sometimes be atoned [compensated] for by allowance of the resulting damage, and will not always be the breach of a condition[.]* [Emphasis added.]

* * * Where the line is to be drawn between the important and the trivial cannot be settled by a formula. * * * *We must weigh the purpose to be served, the desire to be gratified, the excuse for deviation from the letter, [and] the cruelty of enforced adherence. Then only can we tell whether literal fulfillment is to be implied by law as a condition.* [Emphasis added.]

* * * We think the measure of the allowance is not the cost of replacement, which would be great, but the difference in value, which would be either nominal or nothing. * * * The owner is entitled to the money which will permit him to complete, unless the cost of completion is grossly and unfairly out of proportion to the good to be attained.

Decision and Remedy New York's highest court affirmed the appellate court's decision, holding that Jacob & Youngs had substantially performed the contract.

Impact of This Case on Today's Law At the time of the Jacob & Youngs case, some courts did not apply the doctrine of substantial performance to disputes involving breaches of contract. This landmark decision contributed to a developing trend toward equity and fairness in those circumstances. Today, an unintentional and trivial deviation from the terms of a contract will not prevent its enforcement but will permit an adjustment in the value of its performance.

Critical Thinking

- **Legal Environment** *The New York Court of Appeals found that Jacob & Youngs had substantially performed the contract. To what, if any, remedy was Kent entitled?*

18–2c Performance to the Satisfaction of Another

Contracts often state that completed work must personally satisfy one of the parties or a third person. The question then is whether this satisfaction becomes a condition precedent, requiring actual personal satisfaction or approval for discharge, or whether the performance need only satisfy a *reasonable person.*

When the Contract Is Personal When the subject matter of the contract is *personal*, the obligation is conditional, and performance must actually satisfy the party specified in the contract. For instance, contracts for portraits, works of art, and tailoring are considered personal because they involve matters of personal taste. Therefore, only the personal satisfaction of the party fulfills the condition. (An exception exists, of course, if a court finds that the party is expressing dissatisfaction simply to avoid payment or otherwise is not acting in good faith.)

Reasonable Person Standard Most other contracts need to be performed only to the satisfaction of a reasonable person unless they *expressly state otherwise*. When the subject matter of the contract is mechanical, courts are more likely to find that the performing party has performed satisfactorily if a reasonable person would be satisfied with what was done. ■ **EXAMPLE 18.7** Mason signs a contract with Jen to mount a new heat pump on a concrete platform to her satisfaction. Such a contract normally need only be performed to the satisfaction of a reasonable person. ■

When contracts require performance to the satisfaction of a third party with superior knowledge or training in the subject matter—such as a supervising engineer—the courts are divided. A majority of courts require the work to be satisfactory to a reasonable person, but some courts require the personal satisfaction of the third party designated in the contract. (Again, the personal judgment must be made honestly, or the condition will be excused.)

18–2d Material Breach of Contract

A **breach of contract** is the nonperformance of a contractual duty. The breach is *material* when performance is

not at least substantial.[5] As mentioned earlier, when there is a material breach, the nonbreaching party is excused from the performance of contractual duties. That party can also sue the breaching party for damages resulting from the breach.

■ **EXAMPLE 18.8** When country singer Garth Brooks's mother died, he donated $500,000 to a hospital in his hometown in Oklahoma to build a new women's health center named after his mother. After several years passed and the health center was not built, Brooks demanded a refund. The hospital refused, claiming that while it had promised to honor his mother in some way, it had not promised to build a women's health center. Brooks sued for breach of contract. A jury determined that the hospital's failure to build a women's health center and name it after Brooks's mother was a material breach of the contract. The jury awarded Brooks $1 million in damages. ■

Material versus Minor Breach If the breach is *minor* (not material), the nonbreaching party's duty to perform is not entirely excused, but it can sometimes be suspended until the breach has been remedied. Once the minor breach has been cured, the nonbreaching party must resume performance of the contractual obligations.

Both parties in the following case were arguably in breach of their contract. Which party's breach was material?

---

5. *Restatement (Second) of Contracts*, Section 241.

Case Analysis 18.2

Kohel v. Bergen Auto Enterprises, L.L.C.

Superior Court of New Jersey, Appellate Division, 2013 WL 439970 (2013).

In the Language of the Court
PER CURIAM. [By the Whole Court]
* * * *

On May 24, 2010, plaintiffs Marc and Bree Kohel entered into a sales contract with defendant Bergen Auto Enterprises, L.L.C. d/b/a Wayne Mazda Inc. (Wayne Mazda), for the purchase of a used 2009 Mazda. Plaintiffs agreed to pay $26,430.22 for the Mazda and were credited $7,000 as a trade-in, for their 2005 Nissan Altima. As plaintiffs still owed $8,118.28 on the Nissan, Wayne Mazda assessed plaintiffs a net pay-off of

this amount and agreed to remit the balance due to satisfy the outstanding lien.

Plaintiffs took possession of the Mazda with temporary plates and left the Nissan with defendant. A few days later, a representative of defendant advised plaintiffs that the Nissan's vehicle identification tag (VIN tag) was missing. The representative claimed it was unable to sell the car and offered to rescind the transaction. Plaintiffs refused.

When the temporary plates on the Mazda expired on June 24, 2010, defendant refused to provide plaintiffs with

the permanent plates they had paid for. In addition, defendant refused to pay off plaintiffs' outstanding loan on the Nissan, as they had agreed. As a result, plaintiffs were required to continue to make monthly payments on both the Nissan and the Mazda.

On July 28, 2010, plaintiffs filed a complaint in [a New Jersey state court] against Wayne Mazda * * * . Plaintiffs alleged breach of contract.
* * * *

Case 18.2 Continues

Case 18.2 Continued

On February 2, 2012, the court rendered an oral decision finding that there was a breach of contract by Wayne Mazda * * * . On February 17, 2012, the court entered judgment in the amount of $5,405.17 in favor of plaintiffs against Wayne Mazda. [The defendant appealed to a state intermediate appellate court.]

* * * *

Defendant argues that plaintiffs' delivery of the Nissan without a VIN tag was, itself, a breach of the contract of sale and precludes a finding that defendant breached the contract. However, the trial court found that plaintiffs were not aware that the Nissan lacked a VIN tag when they offered it in trade. Moreover, defendant's representatives examined the car twice before accepting it in trade and did not notice the missing VIN until they took the car to an auction where they tried to sell it.

There is a material distinction in plaintiffs' conduct, which the court found unintentional, and defendant's refusal to release the permanent plates for which the plaintiffs had paid, an action the court concluded was done to maintain "leverage." [Emphasis added.]

* * * The evidence * * * indicated that * * * the problem with the missing VIN tag could be rectified. Marc Kohel applied and paid for a replacement VIN tag at Meadowlands [Nissan for $35.31]. While he initially made some calls to Meadowlands, he did not follow up in obtaining the VIN tag after the personnel at Wayne Mazda began refusing to take his calls.

* * * The court concluded that "Wayne Mazda didn't handle this as— as adroitly [skillfully] as they could * * * ." Kevin DiPiano, identified in the complaint as the owner and/or CEO of Wayne Mazda, would not even take [the plaintiffs'] calls to discuss this matter. The court found:

> Mr. DiPiano could have been a better businessman, could have been a little bit more compassionate or at least responsive, you know? He was not. He acted like he didn't care. That obviously went a long way to infuriate the plaintiffs. I don't blame them for being infuriated.

* * * *

* * * Here, plaintiffs attempted to remedy the VIN tag issue but this resolution was frustrated by defendant's unreasonable conduct. We thus reject defendant's argument that plaintiffs' failure to obtain the replacement VIN tag amounted to a repudiation of the contract.

* * * *

Affirmed.

Legal Reasoning Questions

1. What is a material breach of contract? When a material breach occurs, what are the nonbreaching party's options?
2. What is a minor breach of contract? When a minor breach occurs, is the nonbreaching party excused from performance? Explain.
3. In this case, the defendant—Wayne Mazda—argued that the plaintiffs should not be granted relief for the defendant's breach. What were the defendant's main arguments in support of this position?

Underlying Policy Note that any breach entitles the nonbreaching party to sue for damages, but only a material breach discharges the nonbreaching party from the contract. The policy underlying these rules allows a contract to go forward when only minor problems occur but allows it to be terminated if major difficulties arise. Exhibit 18–2 reviews how performance can discharge a contract.

18–2e Anticipatory Repudiation

Before either party to a contract has a duty to perform, one of the parties may refuse to carry out his or her contractual obligations. This is called **anticipatory repudiation**[6] of the contract.

Repudiation Is a Material Breach When an anticipatory repudiation occurs, it is treated as a material breach of the contract, and the nonbreaching party is permitted to bring an action for damages immediately. The nonbreaching party can file suit even though the scheduled time for performance under the contract may still be in the future. Until the nonbreaching party treats an early repudiation as a breach, however, the repudiating party can retract the anticipatory repudiation by proper notice and restore the parties to their original obligations.[7]

An anticipatory repudiation is treated as a present, material breach for two reasons. First, the nonbreaching party should not be required to remain ready and willing to perform when the other party has already repudiated the contract. Second, the nonbreaching party should have the opportunity to seek a similar contract elsewhere and may have a duty to do so to minimize his or her loss.[8]

---

6. *Restatement (Second) of Contracts*, Section 253; Section 2–610 of the Uniform Commercial Code (UCC).

7. See UCC 2–611.

8. The doctrine of anticipatory repudiation first arose in the landmark case of *Hochster v. De La Tour*, 2 Ellis and Blackburn Reports 678 (1853). An English court recognized the delay and expense inherent in a rule requiring a nonbreaching party to wait until the time of performance before suing on an anticipatory repudiation.

EXHIBIT 18–2 Discharge by Performance

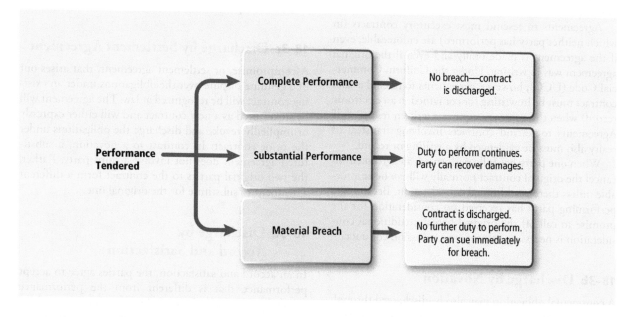

Anticipatory Repudiation and Market Prices

Quite often, anticipatory repudiation occurs when performance of the contract would be extremely unfavorable to one of the parties because of a sharp fluctuation in market prices.

■ **EXAMPLE 18.9** Mobile X enters into an e-contract to manufacture and sell 100,000 smartphones to Best Com, a global telecommunications company. Delivery is to be made two months from the date of the contract. One month later, three inventory suppliers raise their prices to Mobile X. Because of these higher prices, Mobile X stands to lose $500,000 if it sells the smartphones to Best Com at the contract price.

Mobile X immediately sends an e-mail to Best Com, stating that it cannot deliver the 100,000 smartphones at the contract price. Even though you may sympathize with Mobile X, its e-mail is an anticipatory repudiation of the contract. Best Com can treat the repudiation as a material breach and immediately pursue remedies, even though the contract delivery date is still a month away. ■

18–2f Time for Performance

If no time for performance is stated in a contract, a *reasonable time* is implied.[9] If a specific time is stated, the parties must usually perform by that time. Unless time is expressly stated to be vital, though, a delay in

performance will not destroy the performing party's right to payment.

When time is expressly stated to be "of the essence" or vital, the parties normally must perform within the stated time period because the time element becomes a condition. Even when the contract states that time is of the essence, however, a court may find that a party who fails to complain about the other party's delay has waived the breach of the time provision.

18–3 Discharge by Agreement

Any contract can be discharged by agreement of the parties. The agreement can be contained in the original contract, or the parties can form a new contract for the express purpose of discharging the original contract.

18–3a Discharge by Mutual Rescission

As mentioned in previous chapters, *rescission* is the process by which a contract is canceled or terminated and the parties are returned to the positions they occupied prior to forming it. For **mutual rescission** to take place, the parties must make another agreement that also satisfies the legal requirements for a contract. There must be an *offer,* an *acceptance,* and *consideration.* Ordinarily, if the parties agree to rescind the original contract, their promises not to perform the acts stipulated in the

9. See UCC 2–204.

original contract will be legal consideration for the second contract (the rescission).

Agreements to rescind most executory contracts (in which neither party has performed) are enforceable, even if the agreement is made orally and even if the original agreement was in writing. Under the Uniform Commercial Code (UCC), however, agreements to rescind a sales contract must be in writing (or contained in an electronic record) when the contract requires a written rescission.[10] Agreements to rescind contracts involving transfers of realty also must be evidenced by a writing or record.

When one party has fully performed, an agreement to cancel the original contract normally will *not* be enforceable unless there is additional consideration. Because the performing party has received no consideration for the promise to call off the original bargain, additional consideration is necessary to support a rescission contract.

18–3b Discharge by Novation

A contractual obligation may also be discharged through novation. A **novation** occurs when both of the parties to a contract agree to substitute a third party for one of the original parties. The requirements of a novation are as follows:

1. A previous valid obligation.
2. An agreement by all parties to a new contract.
3. The extinguishing of the old obligation (discharge of the prior party).
4. A new contract that is valid.

■ **EXAMPLE 18.10** Union Corporation contracts to sell its pharmaceutical division to British Pharmaceuticals, Ltd. Before the transfer is completed, Union, British Pharmaceuticals, and a third company, Otis Chemicals, execute a new agreement to transfer all of British Pharmaceuticals' rights and duties in the transaction to Otis Chemicals. As long as the new contract is supported by consideration, the novation will discharge the original contract (between Union and British Pharmaceuticals) and replace it with the new contract (between Union and Otis Chemicals). ■

A novation expressly or impliedly revokes and discharges a prior contract. The parties involved may expressly state in the new contract that the old contract is now discharged. If the parties do not expressly discharge the old contract, it will be impliedly discharged if the new contract's terms are inconsistent with the old contract's terms. It is this immediate discharge of the prior contract that distinguishes a novation from both an accord and satisfaction, discussed shortly, and an assignment of all rights.

18–3c Discharge by Settlement Agreement

A compromise, or settlement agreement, that arises out of a genuine dispute over the obligations under an existing contract will be recognized at law. The agreement will be substituted as a new contract and will either expressly or impliedly revoke and discharge the obligations under the prior contract. In contrast to a novation, a substituted agreement does not involve a third party. Rather, the two original parties to the contract form a different agreement to substitute for the original one.

18–3d Discharge by Accord and Satisfaction

In an accord and satisfaction, the parties agree to accept performance that is different from the performance originally promised. An *accord* is a contract to perform some act to satisfy an existing contractual duty that is not yet discharged.[11] A *satisfaction* is the performance of the accord agreement. An accord and its satisfaction discharge the original contractual obligation.

Once the accord has been made, the original obligation is merely suspended until the accord agreement is fully performed. If it is not performed, the obligee (the one to whom performance is owed) can file a lawsuit based on either the original obligation or the accord. ■ **EXAMPLE 18.11** Fahreed has a judgment against Ling for $8,000. Later, both parties agree that the judgment can be satisfied by Ling's transfer of his automobile to Fahreed. This agreement to accept the auto in lieu of $8,000 in cash is the accord. If Ling transfers the car to Fahreed, the accord is fully performed, and the debt is discharged. If Ling refuses to transfer the car, the accord is breached. Because the original obligation was merely suspended, Fahreed can sue Ling to enforce the original judgment for $8,000 in cash or bring an action for breach of the accord. ■

18–4 Discharge by Operation of Law

Under specified circumstances, contractual duties may be discharged by operation of law. These circumstances include material alteration of the contract, the running

---

10. UCC 2–209(2), (4).

11. *Restatement (Second) of Contracts*, Section 281.

of the statute of limitations, bankruptcy, and the impossibility or impracticability of performance.

18–4a Material Alteration of the Contract

To discourage parties from altering written contracts, the law allows an innocent party to be discharged when the other party has materially altered a written contract without consent. For instance, suppose that a party alters a material term of a contract, such as the stated quantity or price, without the knowledge or consent of the other party. In this situation, the party who was unaware of the alteration can treat the contract as discharged.

18–4b Statutes of Limitations

As mentioned earlier in this text, statutes of limitations restrict the period during which a party can sue on a particular cause of action. After the applicable limitations period has passed, a suit can no longer be brought. The limitations period for bringing suits for breach of oral contracts usually is two to three years, and for written contracts, four to five years. Parties generally have ten to twenty years to file for recovery of amounts awarded in judgments, depending on state law.

Lawsuits for breach of a contract for the sale of goods usually must be brought within four years after the cause of action has accrued.[12] A cause of action for a sales contract generally accrues when the breach occurs, even if the aggrieved party is not aware of the breach. A breach of warranty normally occurs when the seller delivers the goods to the buyer. By their original agreement, the parties can reduce this four-year period to not less than one year, but they cannot agree to extend it.

18–4c Bankruptcy

A proceeding in bankruptcy attempts to allocate the debtor's assets to the creditors in a fair and equitable fashion. Once the assets have been allocated, the debtor receives a **discharge in bankruptcy.** A discharge in bankruptcy ordinarily prevents the creditors from enforcing most of the debtor's contracts. Partial payment of a debt *after* discharge in bankruptcy will not revive the debt.

18–4d Impossibility of Performance

After a contract has been made, supervening events (such as a fire) may make performance impossible in an objective sense. This is known as **impossibility of performance** and can discharge a contract.[13] The doctrine of impossibility of performance applies only when the parties could not have reasonably foreseen, at the time the contract was formed, the event that rendered performance impossible. Performance may also become so difficult or costly due to some unforeseen event that a court will consider it commercially unfeasible, or impracticable, as will be discussed later in the chapter.

Objective impossibility ("It can't be done") must be distinguished from *subjective impossibility* ("I'm sorry, I simply can't do it"). An example of subjective impossibility occurs when a party cannot deliver goods on time because of freight car shortages or cannot make payment on time because the bank is closed. In effect, in each of these situations the party is saying, "It is impossible for *me* to perform," not "It is impossible for *anyone* to perform." Accordingly, such excuses do not discharge a contract, and the nonperforming party is normally held in breach of contract.

When Performance Is Impossible Three basic types of situations may qualify as grounds for the discharge of contractual obligations based on impossibility of performance:[14]

1. *When one of the parties to a personal contract dies or becomes incapacitated prior to performance.* ■ **EXAMPLE 18.12** Frederic, a famous dancer, contracts with Ethereal Dancing Guild to play a leading role in its new ballet. Before the ballet can be performed, Frederic becomes ill and dies. His personal performance was essential to the completion of the contract. Thus, his death discharges the contract and his estate's liability for his nonperformance. ■

2. *When the specific subject matter of the contract is destroyed.* ■ **EXAMPLE 18.13** A-1 Farm Equipment agrees to sell Gunther the green tractor on its lot and promises to have the tractor ready for Gunther to pick up on Saturday. On Friday night, however, a truck veers off the nearby highway and smashes into the tractor, destroying it beyond repair. Because the contract was for this specific tractor, A-1's performance is rendered impossible owing to the accident. ■

3. *When a change in law renders performance illegal.* ■ **EXAMPLE 18.14** Hopper contracts with Playlist, Inc., to create a Web site through which users can post and share movies, music, and other forms of digital entertainment. Hopper goes to work. Before the site is operational, however, Congress passes the No Online Piracy in Entertainment (NOPE) Act.

---

12. Section 2–725 of the UCC contains this four-year limitation period.

13. *Restatement (Second) of Contracts*, Section 261.
14. *Restatement (Second) of Contracts*, Sections 262–266; UCC 2–615.

The NOPE Act makes it illegal to operate a Web site on which copyrighted works are posted without the copyright owners' consent. In this situation, the contract is discharged by operation of law. The purpose of the contract has been rendered illegal, and contract performance is objectively impossible. ■

The following case involved a financial institution participating in the federal Troubled Asset Relief Program (TARP). Could the institution assert TARP's prohibition on "golden parachute" payments as a defense to a breach of contract action brought by one of its former senior executive officers?

Case 18.3

Hampton Roads Bankshares, Inc. v. Harvard

Virginia Supreme Court, 291 Va. 42, 781 S.E.2d 172 (2016).

Background and Facts Scott Harvard was a senior executive officer of Hampton Roads Bankshares, Inc. (HRB), headquartered in Virginia Beach, Virginia. Harvard's employment contract included a "golden parachute"—a payment of approximately three times his average annual compensation if he quit.

In 2008, during the Great Recession, Congress enacted the Emergency Economic Stabilization Act (EESA) "to restore liquidity and stability to the financial system."[a] EESA included the Troubled Asset Relief Program (TARP), which allowed the government to buy "troubled assets" from financial institutions to promote market stability. TARP barred participating institutions from making golden parachute payments, defined as "any payment to a senior executive officer for departure from a company for any reason."

HRB participated in TARP. Later, Harvard quit the firm and filed a suit in a Virginia state court against HRB to obtain his golden parachute payment. The court ordered HRB to make the payment. HRB appealed to the Virginia Supreme Court.

In the Language of the Court

Opinion by Justice William C. MIMS.

* * * *

The defense of impossibility of performance is an established principle of contract law. In Virginia, *it is well settled that where impossibility is due to domestic law, to the death or illness of one who by the terms of the contract was to do an act requiring his personal performance, or to the fortuitous destruction or change in the character of something to which the contract related, or which by the terms of the contract was made a necessary means of performance, the promisor will be excused, unless he either expressly agreed in the contract to assume the risk of performance, whether possible or not, or the impossibility was due to his fault.* [Emphasis added.]

Harvard does not dispute that EESA directly bars HRB from making the severance payment to Harvard upon the termination of his employment, because the payment falls within the definition of a prohibited "golden parachute payment." Moreover, Harvard does not suggest that HRB expressly agreed in the contract to assume the risk of performance, whether possible or not. Nor could he; the * * * Employment Agreement clearly places the risk of * * * the law regulating golden parachute payments on Harvard.

On December 31, 2008, Harvard agreed [with HRB to amend] the Employment Agreement [to provide that it] "will be interpreted, administered and construed to, comply with EESA."

By its plain language, the amended Employment Agreement must be read to comply with EESA. Nothing therein exempts the agreement from * * * EESA * * * or places the risk of performance * * * on HRB.

* * * *

There is nothing in the record that would suggest HRB refused to make the golden parachute payment in bad faith. After Harvard terminated his employment, HRB sought guidance from [the U.S. Department of the] Treasury regarding its contractual obligation to make the disputed golden parachute payment, and whether it could perform that obligation in light of EESA. In response, Treasury provided informal guidance indicating that HRB could not make the payment and comply with EESA. Where, as here, the government has clearly expressed its intent to enforce the law, and the promisor cannot in

---

a. 12 U.S.C. Section 5201.

Case 18.3 Continued good faith perform its contractual obligation without violating the law, the promisor is discharged from its obligation.

Decision and Remedy *The Virginia Supreme Court reversed the order of the lower court, which "erred when it ordered HRB to make the golden parachute payment despite the federal prohibition on such payments found in EESA." Under EESA, payment of the golden parachute would violate the law.*

Critical Thinking

- **Legal Environment** *What advantage does the discharge of a contractual obligation under the rule applied in this case offer to the contract's parties? Discuss.*
- **Ethical** *Did HRB violate any ethical duty by refusing to make Harvard's golden parachute payment? Explain.*

Temporary Impossibility An occurrence or event that makes performance temporarily impossible operates to suspend performance until the impossibility ceases.

Performance Normally Is Only Delayed. Once the temporary event ends, the parties ordinarily must perform the contract as originally planned. ■ **CASE IN POINT 18.15** Keefe Hurwitz contracted to sell his home in Louisiana to Wesley and Gwendolyn Payne for $241,500. Four days later, Hurricane Katrina made landfall and caused extensive damage to the house. The cost of repairs was estimated at $60,000. Hurwitz refused to pay for the repairs only to sell the property to the Paynes for the previously agreed-on price. The Paynes filed a lawsuit to enforce the contract. Hurwitz argued that Hurricane Katrina had made it impossible for him to perform and had discharged his duties under the contract. The court, however, ruled that Hurricane Katrina had caused only a temporary impossibility. Hurwitz was required to pay for the necessary repairs and to perform the contract as written. He could not obtain a higher purchase price to offset the cost of the repairs.[15] ■

Performance Can Be Discharged. Sometimes, the lapse of time and the change in circumstances surrounding the contract make it substantially more burdensome for the parties to perform the promised acts. In that situation, the contract is discharged. ■ **CASE IN POINT 18.16** In 1942, actor Gene Autry was drafted into the U.S. Army. Being drafted rendered his contract with a Hollywood movie company temporarily impossible to perform, and it was suspended until the end of World War II in 1945. When Autry got out of the army, the purchasing power of the dollar had declined so much that performance of the contract would have been substantially burdensome to him. Therefore, the contract was discharged.[16] ■

It can be difficult to predict how a court will—or should—rule on whether performance is impossible in a particular situation, as discussed in this chapter's *Ethics Today* feature.

18–4e Commercial Impracticability

Courts may also excuse parties from their performance when it becomes much more difficult or expensive than the parties originally contemplated at the time the contract was formed. In one classic case, for example, a court held that a contract could be discharged because a party would otherwise have had to pay ten times more than the original estimate to excavate a certain amount of gravel.[17]

For someone to invoke the doctrine of **commercial impracticability** successfully, however, the anticipated performance must become *significantly* more difficult or costly.[18] In addition, the added burden of performing *must not have been foreseeable by the parties when the contract was made.*

18–4f Frustration of Purpose

Closely allied with the doctrine of commercial impracticability is the doctrine of **frustration of purpose.** In principle, a contract will be discharged if supervening

---

15. *Payne v. Hurwitz*, 978 So.2d 1000 (La.App. 1st Cir. 2008).

16. *Autry v. Republic Productions*, 30 Cal.2d 144, 180 P.2d 888 (1947).
17. *Mineral Park Land Co. v. Howard*, 172 Cal. 289, 156 P. 458 (1916).
18. *Restatement (Second) of Contracts*, Section 264.

ETHICS TODAY

When Is Impossibility of Performance a Valid Defense?

The doctrine of impossibility of performance is applied only when the parties could not have reasonably foreseen, at the time the contract was formed, the event or events that rendered performance impossible. In some cases, the courts may seem to go too far in holding that the parties should have foreseen certain events or conditions. Such a holding means that the parties cannot avoid their contractual obligations under the doctrine of impossibility of performance.

Actually, courts today are more likely to allow parties to raise this defense than courts in the past, which rarely excused parties from performance under the impossibility doctrine. Indeed, until the latter part of the nineteenth century, courts were reluctant to discharge a contract even when performance appeared to be impossible.

Generally, the courts must balance the freedom of parties to contract (and thereby assume the risks involved) against the injustice that may result when certain contractual obligations are enforced. If the courts allowed parties to raise impossibility of performance as a defense to contractual obligations more often, freedom of contract would suffer.

Critical Thinking *Why might those entering into contracts be worse off in the long run if the courts increasingly accepted impossibility of performance as a defense?*

---

circumstances make it impossible to attain the purpose both parties had in mind when they made the contract. As with commercial impracticability and impossibility, the supervening event must not have been reasonably foreseeable at the time the contract was formed.

There are some differences between these doctrines, however. Commercial impracticability usually involves an event that increases the cost or difficulty of performance. In contrast, frustration of purpose typically involves an event that decreases the value of what a party receives under the contract.[19]

See Exhibit 18–3 for a summary of the ways in which a contract can be discharged.

---

19. See, for instance, *Direct Supply, Inc. v. Specialty Hospitals of America, LLC,* 935 F.Supp.2d 137 (D.C.Cir. 2013).

EXHIBIT 18–3 Contract Discharge

BY OPERATION OF LAW	BY PERFORMANCE	BY AGREEMENT
• Material alteration • Statutes of limitations • Bankruptcy • Impossibility or impracticability of performance • Frustration of purpose	• Complete • Substantial	• Mutual rescission • Novation • Settlement agreement • Accord and satisfaction

BY FAILURE OF A CONDITION	BY BREACH
If performance is conditional, duty to perform does not become absolute until that condition occurs.	• Material breach • Anticipatory repudiation

Reviewing: Performance and Discharge

Val's Foods signs a contract to buy 1,500 pounds of basil from Sun Farms, a small organic herb grower, as long as an independent organization inspects the crop and certifies that it contains no pesticide or herbicide residue. Val's has a contract with several restaurant chains to supply pesto and intends to use Sun Farms' basil in the pesto to fulfill these contracts. While Sun Farms is preparing to harvest the basil, an unexpected hailstorm destroys half the crop. Sun Farms attempts to purchase additional basil from other farms, but it is late in the season, and the price is twice the normal market price. Sun Farms is too small to absorb this cost and immediately notifies Val's that it will not fulfill the contract. Using the information presented in the chapter, answer the following questions.

1. Suppose that the basil does not pass the chemical-residue inspection. Which concept discussed in the chapter might allow Val's to refuse to perform the contract in this situation?
2. Under which legal theory or theories might Sun Farms claim that its obligation under the contract has been discharged by operation of law? Discuss fully.
3. Suppose that Sun Farms contacts every basil grower in the country and buys the last remaining chemical-free basil anywhere. Nevertheless, Sun Farms is able to ship only 1,475 pounds to Val's. Would this fulfill Sun Farms' obligations to Val's? Why or why not?
4. Now suppose that Sun Farms sells its operations to Happy Valley Farms. As a part of the sale, all three parties agree that Happy Valley will provide the basil as stated under the original contract. What is this type of agreement called?

Debate This . . . *The doctrine of commercial impracticability should be abolished.*

Terms and Concepts

anticipatory repudiation 328
breach of contract 327
commercial impracticability 333
concurrent conditions 324
condition 323

condition precedent 323
condition subsequent 324
discharge 323
discharge in bankruptcy 331
frustration of purpose 333

impossibility of performance 331
mutual rescission 329
novation 330
performance 323
tender 324

Issue Spotters

1. Ready Foods contracts to buy two hundred carloads of frozen pizzas from Stealth Distributors. Before Ready or Stealth starts performing, can the parties call off the deal? What if Stealth has already shipped the pizzas? Explain your answers. (See *Discharge by Performance.*)
2. C&D Services contracts with Ace Concessions, Inc., to service Ace's vending machines. Later, C&D wants Dean Vending Services to assume the duties under a new contract. Ace consents. What type of agreement is this? Are Ace's obligations discharged? Why or why not? (See *Discharge by Agreement.*)

- **Check your answers to the Issue Spotters against the answers provided in Appendix D at the end of this text.**

Business Scenarios

18–1. Conditions of Performance. The Caplans contract with Faithful Construction, Inc., to build a house for them for $360,000. The specifications state "all plumbing bowls and fixtures . . . to be Crane brand." The Caplans leave on vacation, and during their absence, Faithful is unable to buy and install Crane plumbing fixtures. Instead, Faithful installs Kohler brand fixtures, an equivalent in the industry. On completion of the building contract, the Caplans inspect the work, discover the substitution, and refuse to accept the house, claiming Faithful has breached the conditions set forth in the specifications. Discuss fully the Caplans' claim. (See *Conditions.*)

18–2. Discharge by Agreement. Junior owes creditor Iba $1,000, which is due and payable on June 1. Junior has been in a car accident, has missed a great deal of work, and consequently will not have the funds on June 1. Junior's father, Fred, offers to pay Iba $1,100 in four equal installments if Iba will discharge Junior from any further liability on the debt. Iba accepts. Is this transaction a novation or an accord and satisfaction? Explain. (See *Discharge by Agreement.*)

18–3. Impossibility of Performance. In the following situations, certain events take place after the contracts are formed. Discuss which of these contracts are discharged because the events render the contracts impossible to perform. (See *Discharge by Operation of Law.*)

(a) Jimenez, a famous singer, contracts to perform in your nightclub. He dies prior to performance.

(b) Raglione contracts to sell you her land. Just before title is to be transferred, she dies.

(c) Oppenheim contracts to sell you one thousand bushels of apples from her orchard in the state of Washington. Because of a severe frost, she is unable to deliver the apples.

(d) Maxwell contracts to lease a service station for ten years. His principal income is from the sale of gasoline. Because of an oil embargo by foreign oil-producing nations, gasoline is rationed, cutting sharply into Maxwell's gasoline sales. He cannot make his lease payments.

Business Case Problems

18–4. Business Case Problem with Sample Answer—Material Breach. The Northeast Independent School District in Bexar County, Texas, hired STR Constructors, Ltd., to renovate a middle school. STR subcontracted the tile work in the school's kitchen to Newman Tile, Inc. (NTI). The project had already fallen behind schedule. As a result, STR allowed other workers to walk over and damage the newly installed tile before it had cured, forcing NTI to constantly redo its work. Despite NTI's requests for payment, STR remitted only half the amount due under their contract. When the school district refused to accept the kitchen, including the tile work, STR told NTI to quickly make repairs. A week later, STR terminated their contract. Did STR breach the contract with NTI? Explain. [*STR Constructors, Ltd. v. Newman Tile, Inc.*, 395 S.W.3d 383 (Tex.App.—El Paso 2013)] (See *Discharge by Performance.*)

- For a sample answer to Problem 18–4, go to Appendix E at the end of this text.

18–5. Conditions of Performance. Russ Wyant owned Humble Ranch in Perkins County, South Dakota. Edward Humble, whose parents had previously owned the ranch, was Wyant's uncle. Humble held a two-year option to buy the ranch. The option included specific conditions. Once it was exercised, the parties had thirty days to enter into a purchase agreement, and the seller could become the buyer's lender by matching the terms of the proposed financing. After the option was exercised, the parties engaged in lengthy negotiations. Humble did not respond to Wyant's proposed purchase agreement nor advise him of available financing terms before the option expired, however. Six months later, Humble filed a suit against Wyant to enforce the option. Is Humble entitled to specific performance? Explain. [*Humble v. Wyant*, 843 N.W.2d 334 (S.Dak. 2014)] (See *Conditions.*)

18–6. Discharge by Operation of Law. Dr. Jake Lambert signed an employment agreement with Baptist Health Services, Inc., to provide cardiothoracic surgery services to Baptist Memorial Hospital–North Mississippi, Inc., in Oxford, Mississippi. Complaints about Lambert's behavior arose almost immediately. He was evaluated by a team of doctors and psychologists, who diagnosed him as suffering from obsessive-compulsive personality disorder and concluded that he was unfit to practice medicine. Based on this conclusion, the hospital suspended his staff privileges. Citing the suspension, Baptist Health Services claimed that Lambert had breached his employment contract. What is Lambert's best defense to this claim? Explain. [*Baptist Memorial Hospital–North Mississippi, Inc. v. Lambert*, 157 So.3d 109 (Miss.App. 2015)] (See *Discharge by Operation of Law.*)

18–7. Conditions. H&J Ditching & Excavating, Inc., was hired by JRSF, LLC, to perform excavating and grading work on Terra Firma, a residential construction project in West Knox County, Tennessee. Cornerstone Community Bank financed the project with a loan to JRSF. As the work progressed, H&J received payments totaling 90 percent of the price on its contract. JRSF then defaulted on the loan from Cornerstone, and Cornerstone foreclosed and took possession of the property. H&J filed a suit in a Tennessee state court against the bank to recover the final payment on its contract. The bank responded that H&J had not received its payment because it had failed to obtain an engineer's certificate of final completion, a condition under its contract with JRSF. H&J responded that it had completed all the work it had contracted to do. What type of contract condition does obtaining the engineer's certificate represent? Is H&J entitled to the final payment? Discuss. [*H&J Ditching & Excavating, Inc. v. Cornerstone Community Bank*, __ S.W.3d __, 2016 WL 675554 (Tenn.App. 2016)] (See *Conditions.*)

18–8. A Question of Ethics—Conditions. *King County,* *Washington, hired Frank Coluccio Construction Co. (FCCC) to act as general contractor for a public works project involving the construction of a small utility tunnel under the Duwamish Waterway. FCCC hired Donald B. Murphy Contractors, Inc. (DBM), as a subcontractor. DBM was responsible for constructing an access shaft at the eastern end of the tunnel. Problems arose during construction, including a "blow-in" of the access shaft that caused it to fill with water, soil, and debris. FCCC and DBM incurred substantial expenses from the repairs and delays. Under the project contract, King County was supposed to buy an insurance policy to "insure against physical loss or damage by perils included under an 'All-Risk' Builder's Risk policy." Any claim under this policy was to be filed through the insured. King County, which had general property damage insurance, did not obtain an all-risk builder's risk policy. For the losses attributable to the blow-in, FCCC and DBM submitted builder's risk claims, which the county denied. FCCC filed a suit in a Washington state court against King County, alleging, among other claims, breach of contract. [Frank Coluccio Construction Co. v. King County, 136 Wash.App. 751, 150 P.3d 1147 (Div. 1 2007)]* (See *Conditions.*)

(a) King County's property damage policy specifically excluded, at the county's request, coverage of tunnels. The county drafted its contract with FCCC to require the all-risk builder's risk policy and authorize itself to "sponsor" claims. When FCCC and DBM filed their claims, the county secretly colluded with its property damage insurer to deny payment. What do these facts indicate about the county's ethics and legal liability in this situation?

(b) Could DBM, as a third party to the contract between King County and FCCC, maintain an action on the contract against King County? Discuss.

(c) All-risk insurance is a promise to pay on the "fortuitous" (accidental) happening of a loss or damage from any cause except those that are specifically excluded. Payment usually is not made on a loss that, at the time the insurance was obtained, the claimant subjectively knew would occur. If a loss results from faulty workmanship on the part of a contractor, should the obligation to pay under an all-risk policy be discharged? Explain.

18–9. Special Case Analysis—Material Breach. Go to Case Analysis 18.2, *Kohel v. Bergen Auto Enterprises, L.L.C.* Read the excerpt, and answer the following questions.

(a) Issue: This case involved allegations of breach of contract involving which parties and for what actions?

(b) Rule of Law: What is the difference between a *material* breach and a *minor* breach of contract?

(c) Applying the Rule of Law: How did the court determine which party was in material breach of the contract in this case?

(d) Conclusion: Was the defendant liable for breach? Why or why not?

Legal Reasoning Group Activity

18–10. Anticipatory Repudiation. ABC Clothiers, Inc., has a contract with Taylor & Sons, a retailer, to deliver one thousand summer suits to Taylor's place of business on or before May 1. On April 1, Taylor receives a letter from ABC informing him that ABC will not be able to make the delivery as scheduled. Taylor is very upset, as he had planned a big ad campaign. (See *Discharge by Performance.*)

(a) The first group will discuss whether Taylor can immediately sue ABC for breach of contract (on April 2).

(b) Now suppose that Taylor's son, Tom, tells his father that they cannot file a lawsuit until ABC actually fails to deliver the suits on May 1. The second group will decide who is correct, Taylor senior or Tom.

(c) Assume that Taylor & Sons can either file immediately or wait until ABC fails to deliver the goods. The third group will evaluate which course of action is better, given the circumstances.

Answers to the *Issue Spotters*

1. *Before Ready or Stealth starts performing, can the parties call off the deal? What if Stealth has already shipped the pizzas? Explain your answers.* Contracts that are executory on both sides—contracts on which neither party has performed—can be rescinded solely by agreement. Contracts that are executed on one side—contracts on which one party has performed—can be rescinded only if the party who has performed receives consideration for the promise to call off the deal.

2. *What type of agreement is this? Are Ace's obligations discharged? Why or why not?* This is a novation because it substitutes a new party for an original party, by agreement of all the parties. The requirements are a previous valid obligation, an agreement of all the parties to a new contract, extinguishment of the old obligation, and a new, valid contract. Ace's obligations are discharged.

Sample Answers for *Business Case Problems with Sample Answer*

Problem 18–4. *Material Breach.* Yes, STR breached the contract with NTI. A breach of contract is the nonperformance of a contractual duty. A breach is *material* when performance is not at least substantial. On a material breach, the nonbreaching party is excused from performance. If a breach is *minor*, the nonbreaching party's duty to perform can sometimes be suspended until the breach has been remedied, but the duty to perform is not entirely excused. Once a minor breach has been cured, the nonbreaching party must resume performance. Any breach—material or minor—entitles the nonbreaching party to sue for damages.

In this problem, NTI had to redo its work constantly because STR permitted its employees and the employees of other subcontractors to walk over and damage the newly installed tile.

Furthermore, despite NTI's requests for payment, STR remitted only half the amount due under their contract. Thus, NTI was deprived of at least half of the money it was owed under the contract. And STR terminated the contract, apparently wrongfully and without cause—the tile work would have been completed satisfactorily if STR had not allowed other workers to trample on the newly installed tile before it had cured.

In the actual case on which this problem is based, when STR refused to pay NTI and then terminated their contract, the subcontractor filed a suit in a Texas state court to recover. From a jury verdict in NTI's favor, STR appealed. A state intermediate appellate court affirmed. "The evidence presented was legally sufficient for the jury to conclude that STR materially breached the contract."

CHAPTER

Breach of Contract and Remedies

When one party breaches a contract, the other party—the nonbreaching party—can choose one or more of several remedies. (Does changing terms of service on a social networking site constitute a breach of contract? See this chapter's *Digital Update* feature for a look at this issue.) A *remedy* is the relief provided for an innocent party when the other party has breached the contract. It is the means employed to enforce a right or to redress an injury.

The most common remedies available to a nonbreaching party include *damages, rescission* and *restitution, specific performance,* and *reformation.* Courts distinguish between *remedies at law* and *remedies in equity.* The remedy at law normally is monetary damages. Usually, a court will not award equitable remedies—such as rescission and restitution, specific performance, and reformation—unless the remedy at law is inadequate.

19–1 Damages

A breach of contract entitles the nonbreaching party to sue for monetary damages. In contract law, damages compensate the nonbreaching party for the loss of the bargain (whereas tort law damages compensate for harm suffered as a result of another's wrongful act). Often, courts say that innocent parties are to be placed in the position they would have occupied had the contract been fully performed.[1]

Realize at the outset, though, that collecting damages through a court judgment requires litigation, which can be expensive and time consuming. Also keep in mind that court judgments are often difficult to enforce, particularly if the breaching party does not have sufficient assets to pay the damages awarded. For these reasons, most parties settle their lawsuits for damages (or other remedies) prior to trial.

19–1a Types of Damages

There are four broad categories of damages:

1. Compensatory (to cover direct losses and costs).
2. Consequential (to cover indirect and foreseeable losses).
3. Punitive (to punish and deter wrongdoing).
4. Nominal (to recognize wrongdoing when no monetary loss is shown).

Compensatory and punitive damages were discussed in the context of tort law. Here, we look at these types of damages, as well as consequential and nominal damages, in the context of contract law.

Compensatory Damages Damages that compensate the nonbreaching party for the *loss of the bargain* are known as *compensatory damages.* These damages compensate the injured party only for damages actually sustained and proved to have arisen directly from the loss of the bargain caused by the breach of contract. They simply replace what was lost because of the wrong or damage and, for this reason, are often said to "make the person whole."

■ **CASE IN POINT 19.1** Janet Murley was the vice president of marketing at Hallmark Cards, Inc., until Hallmark eliminated her position as part of a corporate restructuring. Murley and Hallmark entered into a separation agreement under which she agreed not to work in the greeting card industry for eighteen months and not to disclose or use any of Hallmark's confidential information. In exchange, Hallmark gave Murley a $735,000 severance payment.

---

1. *Restatement (Second) of Contracts,* Section 347.

DIGITAL UPDATE

When Do Changes in Social Media Terms of Service Constitute a Breach of Contract?

Hundreds of millions of individuals use some form of social media. To do so, they must agree to certain terms of service.

The Terms of Service Are a Contract

When you use social media or other services on the Internet or download an app for a mobile device, you normally have to indicate that you accept the terms of service associated with that service or app. Of course, users rarely, if ever, actually read those terms. They simply click on "accept" and start using the service. By clicking on "accept," however, those users are entering into a contract.

Instagram Changes Its Terms of Service

A few years ago, Instagram changed its terms of service to give it the right to transfer and otherwise use content placed on the site by users. The new terms appeared to allow Instagram to do this without compensating users. The terms also limited users' ability to bring class-action lawsuits against Instagram, limited the damages they could recover to $100, and required arbitration of any disputes.

Lucy Funes, an Instagram user in California, filed a class-action lawsuit against Instagram on behalf of herself and other users.[a] The suit claimed breach of contract and breach of the covenant of good faith and fair dealing that a contract implies. Instagram subsequently modified the language that appeared to give it the right to use photos without compensation. It retained other controversial terms, however, including the mandatory arbitration clause and a provision allowing it to place ads in conjunction with user content.

Instagram Seeks Dismissal of the Lawsuit

Funes contended that Instagram had breached their contract by changing its terms of service. Instagram argued that Funes could not claim breach of contract. The reason was that she—and other users—had been given thirty days' notice before the new terms of service took effect. Because Funes continued to use her account after that thirty-day period, Instagram maintained, in effect, she agreed to the new terms.

Instagram Changes Its Policies

Instagram continues to use its revised terms of service agreement. As mentioned, it abandoned some of its previous changes and denied any intention to sell user content. In the terms of service, Instagram states that it does "not claim ownership of any content user's post on or through the service."

Nonetheless, the terms state clearly that each user "hereby grants to Instagram a non-exclusive, fully paid and royalty-free, transferable, sublicensable, worldwide license to use content that the user posts." That means that Instagram can reassign the rights or relicense the work to any other party for free or for a fee. The user—anyone who posts on Instagram—need not be compensated or even given notice.

Critical Thinking *Within Instagram's current terms of service is the following statement: "we may not always identify paid services, sponsored content, or commercial communications as such." Is it ethical for Instagram to post advertisements without identifying them as advertisements? Discuss.*

a. *Funes v. Instagram, Inc.,* 3:12-CV06482-WHA (N.D.Cal. 2012). See also *Rodriguez v. Instagram, LLC,* 2013 WL 3732883 (N.D.Cal. 2013).

After eighteen months, Murley took a job with Recycled Paper Greetings (RPG) for $125,000 and disclosed confidential Hallmark information to RPG. Hallmark sued for breach of contract and won. The jury awarded $860,000 in damages (the $735,000 severance payment and $125,000 that Murley received from RPG). Murley appealed. The appellate court held that Hallmark was entitled only to the return of the $735,000 severance payment. Hallmark was not entitled to the other $125,000 because that additional award would have left Hallmark better off than if Murley had not breached the contract.[2] ■

There is a two-step process to determine whether a breach of contract has resulted in compensable damages. First, it must be established that there was a contract between the parties and a breach of that contract. Next, it must be proved that the breach caused damages. The following case concerned the second step of this process.

2. *Hallmark Cards, Inc. v. Murley,* 703 F.3d 456 (8th Cir. 2013).

Baird v. Owens Community College

Court of Appeals of Ohio, Tenth District, Franklin County, __ N.E.2d __, 2016-Ohio-537 (2016).

In the Language of the Court

BRUNNER, J. [Judge]

* * * *

[Carrianne Baird and the other sixty-one] plaintiffs-appellants * * * are former students in the registered nursing program of defendant-appellee, Owens Community College. The college lost its accreditation from the National League for Nursing Accreditation Commission ("NLNAC") in 2009.[a] The program remains approved by the Ohio Board of Nursing, which permits successful graduates to take the National Council Licensure Examination ("NCLEX") for their nursing license. Although the college received notice via a letter dated July 27, 2009 that the accreditation had been denied, it did not formally notify its students until it issued a letter on September 26, 2009, after classes for the fall semester already had begun. The appellants sued [in an Ohio state court] for breach of contract.

* * * The court [did not determine whether there was a contract between the college and the students or whether such a contract was breached by the loss of accreditation, but only] concluded that the loss of accreditation did not affect the students' ability to take the state licensing examination, and therefore that appellants suffered no actual damages from the alleged breach of contract. [The court issued a summary judgment in favor of the college.]

* * * *

On appeal from the summary judgment against them, appellants [contend that] the trial court erred when it granted the Motion for Summary Judgment of the Defendant-Appellee because the evidence creates a genuine issue of material fact as to whether Appellee's breach of the contract caused damages.

* * * *

a. In 2013, the NLNAC changed its name and is now known as the Accreditation Commission for Education in Nursing.

After the appellee lost its NLNAC accreditation graduates feared that they would face barriers to licensing, employment or further education in their field. Some programs, including The Ohio State University RN [registered nursing] to BSN [bachelor of science in nursing] option, would accept only nurses who received an associate's degree or diploma in nursing from an institution with NLNAC accreditation. In support of their allegations of damages, appellants submitted the * * * testimony of various "sample plaintiffs." * * * Carianne Baird stated that she could not attend the University of Toledo's RN to MSN [master of science in nursing] program without submitting a "portfolio" that would not have been required if appellee had maintained its accreditation. Other institutions would not accept her for continuing nursing education because her associate's degree is not from an NLNAC accredited institution.

Kelsey Darbyshire testified * * * that Lima Memorial Hospital required applicants to have graduated from an accredited nursing school. She indicated on her application that she did not graduate from an accredited program, and had no response. Miracle Huffman * * * applied to the U.S. Department of Veterans Affairs for psychiatric nurse practitioner positions and has received no response. She testified that the Veterans Affairs requires an NLNAC accredited degree, and she does not have it.

* * * *

* * * None of the appellants submitted sufficient evidence of economic damages based on their rejection from specific employment or a higher degree program. *However, a claimant's inability to demonstrate a specific denial of employment due to the program's loss of accreditation does not defeat damages on account of lost earning capacity * * *. The measure of damages for impairment of earning capacity is the difference between the amount*

which the plaintiff was capable of earning before his injury and that which he is capable of earning thereafter. The claimant must offer sufficient proof of any future impairment and also sufficient evidence of the extent of prospective damages flowing from the impairment. In order to recover for impaired earning capacity, the plaintiff must prove by sufficient evidence that he is reasonably certain to incur such damages in the future. * * * The [lower] court * * * should have considered whether each of the appellants suffered impaired earning capacity or other compensable damages and what those damages would be to place them in the same position that they would have enjoyed if appellee had performed its contract. [Emphasis added.]

Since there exists a genuine issue of material fact concerning damages, the [lower] court * * * must also determine, in addition to whether any appellant can prove diminished earning capacity, whether any appellant produced sufficient evidence that appellee breached its contract with her or him.

When a student enrolls in a college or university, pays his or her tuition and fees, and attends such school, the resulting relationship may reasonably be construed as being contractual in nature. The terms of such a contract may be found in the college or university catalog, handbook, and/or other guidelines supplied to the students.

On the first page of the registered nursing section of the course book appellee provided to students, appellee listed its NLNAC accreditation foremost, and according to appellants, providing an NLNAC accredited education was part and parcel of appellee's "deal" with each of them. By contrast, appellee urges that a text box in another part of the course book contains a disclaimer for changes in circumstance, stating that it "reserves the

Case 19.1 Continued

right to modify rules, policies, fees, program requirements, course scheduling and courses offered during any specific semester, and any other matter, without notice."

Appellee submits that summary judgment should be affirmed on the * * * basis that this language effectively excludes the loss of NLNAC accreditation from the contractual relationship

between it and its students. Without more evidence, or a more explicit disclaimer, we find that genuine issues remain to preclude summary judgment.

* * * *

* * * We remand this matter to the [lower] court * * * to ascertain as to each of the appellants whether the appellant has offered sufficient evidence to avoid

summary judgment on whether appellee has breached its contract to her or him in losing its NLNAC accreditation, and if such a breach is determined from the evidence, whether she or he has set forth sufficient evidence to create a material issue of fact in support of a claim for diminished earning capacity.

Legal Reasoning Questions

1. In this case, what was the basis for the students' suit?

2. What was the college's argument against the students' allegations?

3. In whose favor did the court rule? Why? What remains to be determined?

Standard Measure. The standard measure of compensatory damages is the difference between the value of the breaching party's promised performance under the contract and the value of her or his actual performance. This amount is reduced by any loss that the injured party has avoided.

■ **EXAMPLE 19.2** Randall contracts to perform certain services exclusively for Hernandez during the month of March for $4,000. Hernandez cancels the contract and is in breach. Randall is able to find another job during March but can earn only $3,000. He can sue Hernandez for breach and recover $1,000 as compensatory damages. Randall can also recover from Hernandez the amount that he spent to find the other job. ■ Expenses that are caused directly by a breach of contract—such as those incurred to obtain performance from another source—are known as **incidental damages.**

Note that the measure of compensatory damages often varies by type of contract. Certain types of contracts deserve special mention.

Sale of Goods. In a contract for the sale of goods, the usual measure of compensatory damages is an amount equal to the difference between the contract price and the market price.[3] ■ **EXAMPLE 19.3** Medik Laboratories contracts to buy ten model UTS network servers from Cal Industries for $4,000 each. Cal Industries, however, fails to deliver the ten servers to Medik. The market price of the servers at the time Medik learns of the breach is

$4,500. Therefore, Medik's measure of damages is $5,000 (10 × $500), plus any incidental damages (expenses) caused by the breach. ■

Sometimes, the buyer breaches when the seller has not yet produced the goods. In that situation, compensatory damages normally equal lost profits on the sale, not the difference between the contract price and the market price.

Sale of Land. Ordinarily, because each parcel of land is unique, the remedy for a seller's breach of a contract for a sale of real estate is specific performance. That is, the buyer is awarded the parcel of property for which she or he bargained. (*Specific performance* will be discussed more fully later in this chapter.) The majority of states follow this rule.

When the *buyer* is the party in breach, the measure of damages is typically the difference between the contract price and the market price of the land. The same measure is used when specific performance is not available (because the seller has sold the property to someone else, for example).

A minority of states apply a different rule when the seller breaches the contract and the breach is not deliberate (intentional).[4] These states limit the prospective buyer's damages to a refund of any down payment made plus any expenses incurred (such as fees for title searches, attorneys, and escrows). Thus, the minority rule

---

3. More specifically, the amount is the difference between the contract price and the market price at the time and place at which the goods were to be delivered or tendered. See Sections 2–708 and 2–713 of the Uniform Commercial Code (UCC).

4. "Deliberate" breaches include the seller's failure to convey (transfer title to) the land because the market price has gone up. "Nondeliberate" breaches include the seller's failure to convey the land because of a problem with the title. For instance, the discovery of an unknown easement that gives another party a right of use over the property would be a problem with the title.

effectively returns purchasers to the positions they occupied prior to the sale, rather than giving them the benefit of the bargain.

Construction Contracts. The measure of damages in a building or construction contract varies depending on which party breaches and when the breach occurs.

1. *Breach by owner.* The owner may breach at three different stages—before, during, or after performance. If the owner breaches *before performance has begun,* the contractor can recover only the profits that would have been made on the contract. (Profits equal the total contract price less the cost of materials and labor.) If the owner breaches *during performance,* the contractor can recover the profits plus the costs incurred in partially constructing the building. If the owner breaches *after the construction has been completed,* the contractor can recover the entire contract price, plus interest.

2. *Breach by contractor.* When the construction contractor breaches the contract—either by failing to begin construction or by stopping work partway through the project—the measure of damages is the cost of completion. The cost of completion includes reasonable compensation for any delay in performance. If the contractor finishes late, the measure of damages is the loss of use.

3. *Breach by both owner and contractor.* When the performance of both parties—the construction contractor and the owner—falls short of what their contract required, the courts attempt to strike a fair balance in awarding damages.

■ **CASE IN POINT 19.4** Jamison Well Drilling, Inc., contracted to drill a well for Ed Pfeifer for $4,130. Jamison drilled the well and installed a storage tank. The well did not comply with state health department requirements, however, and failed repeated tests for bacteria. The health department ordered the well to be abandoned and sealed. Pfeifer used the storage tank but paid Jamison nothing. Jamison filed a suit to recover. The court held that Jamison was entitled to $970 for the storage tank but was not entitled to the full contract price because the well was not usable.[5] ■

The rules concerning the measurement of damages in breached construction contracts are summarized in Exhibit 19–1.

Consequential Damages Foreseeable damages that result from a party's breach of contract are called **consequential damages,** or *special damages.* They differ from compensatory damages in that they are caused by special circumstances beyond the contract itself. They flow from

---

5. *Jamison Well Drilling, Inc. v. Pfeifer,* 2011 Ohio 521 (2011).

EXHIBIT 19–1 Measurement of Damages—Breach of Construction Contracts

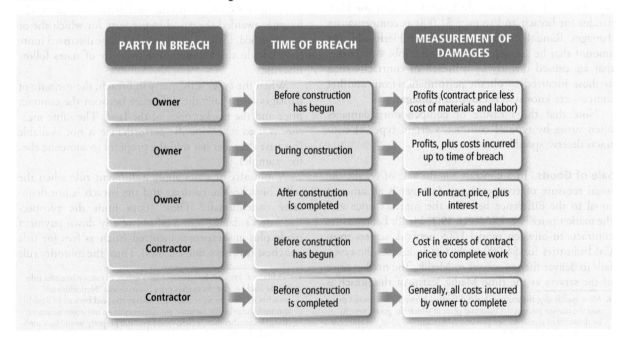

PARTY IN BREACH	TIME OF BREACH	MEASUREMENT OF DAMAGES
Owner	Before construction has begun	Profits (contract price less cost of materials and labor)
Owner	During construction	Profits, plus costs incurred up to time of breach
Owner	After construction is completed	Full contract price, plus interest
Contractor	Before construction has begun	Cost in excess of contract price to complete work
Contractor	Before construction is completed	Generally, all costs incurred by owner to complete

the consequences, or results, of a breach. When a seller fails to deliver goods, knowing that the buyer is planning to use or resell those goods immediately, a court may award consequential damages for the loss of profits from the planned resale.

■ **EXAMPLE 19.5** Marty contracts to buy a certain quantity of Quench, a specialty sports drink, from Nathan. Nathan knows that Marty has contracted with Ruthie to resell and ship the Quench within hours of its receipt. The beverage will then be sold to fans attending the Super Bowl. Nathan fails to deliver the Quench on time. Marty can recover the consequential damages—the loss of profits from the planned resale to Ruthie—caused by the nondelivery. (If Marty purchases Quench from another vender, he can also recover compensatory damages for any difference between the contract price and the market price.) ■

For the nonbreaching party to recover consequential damages, the breaching party must have known (or had reason to know) that special circumstances would cause the nonbreaching party to suffer an additional loss.[6]

Punitive Damages Punitive damages are very seldom awarded in lawsuits for breach of contract. Because punitive damages are designed to punish a wrongdoer and set an example to deter similar conduct in the future, they have no legitimate place in contract law. A contract is simply a civil relationship between the parties. The law may compensate one party for the loss of the bargain—no more and no less. When a person's actions cause both a breach of contract and a tort (such as fraud), however, punitive damages may be available.

Nominal Damages When no actual damage or financial loss results from a breach of contract and only a technical injury is involved, the court may award **nominal damages** to the innocent party. Awards of nominal damages are often small, such as one dollar, but they do establish that the defendant acted wrongfully. Most lawsuits for nominal damages are brought as a matter of principle under the theory that a breach has occurred and some damages must be imposed regardless of actual loss.

■ **EXAMPLE 19.6** Jackson contracts to buy potatoes from Stanley at fifty cents a pound. Stanley breaches the contract and does not deliver the potatoes. In the meantime, the price of potatoes has fallen. Jackson is able to buy them in the open market at half the price he contracted for with Stanley. He is clearly better off because of Stanley's breach. Thus, because Jackson sustained only a technical injury and suffered no monetary loss, he is likely to be awarded only nominal damages if he brings a suit for breach of contract. ■

19–1b Mitigation of Damages

In most situations, when a breach of contract occurs, the innocent injured party is held to a duty to mitigate, or reduce, the damages that he or she suffers. Under this doctrine of **mitigation of damages,** the duty owed depends on the nature of the contract.

Rental Agreements Some states require a landlord to use reasonable means to find a new tenant if a tenant abandons the premises and fails to pay rent. If an acceptable tenant is found, the landlord is required to lease the premises to this tenant to mitigate the damages recoverable from the former tenant.

The former tenant is still liable for the difference between the amount of the rent under the original lease and the rent received from the new tenant. If the landlord has not taken reasonable steps to find a new tenant, a court will likely reduce any award made by the amount of rent the landlord could have received had he or she done so.

Employment Contracts In the majority of states, a person whose employment has been wrongfully terminated owes a duty to mitigate the damages that he or she suffered. In other words, a wrongfully terminated employee has a duty to take a similar job if one is available.

If the employee fails to mitigate, the damages awarded will be equivalent to the person's former salary less the income he or she would have received in a similar job obtained by reasonable means. The employer has the burden of proving that such a job existed and that the employee could have been hired. Normally, the employee is under no duty to take a job of a different type and rank.

19–1c Liquidated Damages versus Penalties

A **liquidated damages** provision in a contract specifies that a certain dollar amount is to be paid in the event of a *future* default or breach of contract. (*Liquidated* means determined, settled, or fixed.)

Liquidated damages differ from penalties. Like liquidated damages, a **penalty** specifies a certain amount

---

6. This rule was first enunciated in *Hadley v. Baxendale,* 156 Eng.Rep. 145 (1854).

to be paid in the event of a default or breach of contract. Unlike liquidated damages, it is designed to penalize the breaching party, not to make the innocent party whole.

Liquidated damages provisions usually are enforceable. In contrast, if a court finds that a provision calls for a penalty, the agreement as to the amount will not be enforced. Recovery will be limited to actual damages.

Enforceability To determine if a particular provision is for liquidated damages or for a penalty, a court must answer two questions:

1. When the contract was entered into, was it apparent that damages would be difficult to estimate in the event of a breach?
2. Was the amount set as damages a reasonable estimate and not excessive?[7]

If the answers to both questions are yes, the provision normally will be enforced. If either answer is no, the provision usually will not be enforced.

In the following *Spotlight Case,* the court had to decide whether a clause in a contract was an enforceable liquidated damages provision or an unenforceable penalty.

7. *Restatement (Second) of Contracts,* Section 356(1).

Spotlight on Liquidated Damages

Case 19.2 Kent State University v. Ford

Court of Appeals of Ohio, Eleventh District, Portage County, 26 N.E.3d 868, 2015-Ohio-41 (2015).

Background and Facts Gene Ford signed a five-year contract with Kent State University in Ohio to work as the head coach for the men's basketball team. The contract provided that if Ford quit before the end of the term, he would pay liquidated damages to the school. The amount was to equal his salary ($300,000) multiplied by the number of years remaining on the contract. Laing Kennedy, Kent State's athletic director, told Ford that the contract would be renegotiated within a few years. Four years before the contract expired, however, Ford left Kent State and began to coach for Bradley University at an annual salary of $700,000. Kent State filed a suit in an Ohio state court against Ford, alleging breach of contract. The court enforced the liquidated damages clause and awarded the university $1.2 million. Ford appealed, arguing that the liquidated damages clause in his employment contract was an unenforceable penalty.

In the Language of the Court
Diane V. GRENDELL, J. [Judge]
* * * *

* * * The parties agreed on an amount of damages, stated in clear terms in Ford's * * * employment contract. * * * *It is apparent that such damages were difficult, if not impossible, to determine.* * * * The departure of a university's head basketball coach may result in a decrease in ticket sales, impact the ability to successfully recruit players and community support for the team, and require a search for both a new coach and additional coaching staff. Many of these damages cannot be easily measured or proven. This is especially true given the nature of how such factors may change over the course of different coaches' tenures with a sports program or team. [Emphasis added.]
* * * *

* * * Kennedy's statements to Ford that the contract would be renegotiated within a few years made it clear that Kent State desired Ford to have long-term employment, which was necessary to establish the stability in the program that would benefit recruitment, retention of assistant coaching staff, and community participation and involvement. The breach of the contract impacted all of these areas.
* * * *

Regarding the alleged unreasonableness of the damages, * * * based on the record, we find that the damages were reasonable. * * * Finding a coach of a similar skill and experience level as Ford, which was gained based partially on the investment of Kent State in his development, would have an increased cost. This is evident from the fact that Ford was able to more than double his yearly salary when hired

Case 19.2 Continued

by Bradley University. The salary Ford earned at Bradley shows the loss of market value in coaching experienced by Kent State, $400,000 per year, for four years. Although this may not have been known at the time the contract was executed, it could have been anticipated, and was presumably why Kent State wanted to renegotiate the contract * * * . There was also an asserted decrease in ticket sales, costs associated with the trips for the coaching search, and additional potential sums that may be expended.

* * * *

As discussed extensively above, there was justification for seeking liquidated damages to compensate for Kent State's losses, and, thus, there was a valid compensatory purpose for including the clause. * * * Given all of the circumstances and facts in this case, and the consideration of the factors above, we cannot find that the liquidated damages clause was a penalty. [Emphasis added.]

Decision and Remedy *A state intermediate appellate court affirmed the lower court's award. At the time Ford's contract was entered into, ascertaining the damages resulting from a breach was "difficult, if not impossible." The court found, "based on the record, . . . that the damages were reasonable." Thus, the clause was not a penalty—it had "a valid compensatory purpose."*

Critical Thinking

- **Cultural** *How does a college basketball team's record of wins and losses, and its ranking in its conference, support the court's decision in this case?*

Liquidated Damages Common in Certain Contracts Liquidated damages provisions are frequently used in construction contracts. For instance, a provision requiring a construction contractor to pay $300 for every day he or she is late in completing the project is a liquidated damages provision. Such provisions are also common in contracts for the sale of goods.[8] In addition, contracts with entertainers and professional athletes often include liquidated damages provisions.

■ **EXAMPLE 19.7** Johnny Chavis, formerly the defensive coordinator for the Louisiana State University (LSU) football team, had a liquidated damages provision in his employment contract with LSU. The clause stated that if he quit with less than eleven months remaining on his contract term, he would owe no damages. If he left with more than eleven months remaining, he would owe LSU $400,000 in liquidated damages. When Chavis and LSU could not agree on terms to renew their contract, which was set to expire at the end of 2015, Chavis gave his thirty-day notice. He then took a position at Texas A&M. Chavis gave notice on January 5, 2015, which meant his employment would officially end on February 4, with less than eleven months left on his contract term. LSU demanded that he pay the $400,000 damages, however, because he had allegedly started recruiting for Texas A&M before February 1. Chavis claimed that he owed LSU nothing, but the dispute has not yet been resolved. ■

---

8. Section 2–718(1) of the UCC specifically authorizes the use of liquidated damages provisions.

19–2 Equitable Remedies

Sometimes, damages are an inadequate remedy for a breach of contract. In these situations, the nonbreaching party may ask the court for an equitable remedy. Equitable remedies include rescission and restitution, specific performance, and reformation.

19–2a Rescission and Restitution

Rescission is essentially an action to undo, or terminate, a contract—to return the contracting parties to the positions they occupied prior to the transaction.[9] When fraud, a mistake, duress, undue influence, misrepresentation, or lack of capacity to contract is present, unilateral rescission is available. Rescission may also be available by statute.[10] The failure of one party to perform entitles the other party to rescind the contract. The rescinding party must give prompt notice to the breaching party.

Restitution Generally, to rescind a contract, both parties must make **restitution** to each other by returning

---

9. The rescission discussed here is unilateral rescission, in which only one party wants to undo the contract. In mutual rescission, both parties agree to undo the contract. Mutual rescission discharges the contract. Unilateral rescission generally is available as a remedy for breach of contract.

10. Many states have statutes allowing individuals who enter "home solicitation contracts" to rescind those contracts within three business days for any reason. See, for example, California Civil Code Section 1689.5.

goods, property, or funds previously conveyed.[11] If the property or goods can be returned, they must be. If the goods or property have been consumed, restitution must be made in an equivalent dollar amount.

Essentially, restitution involves the plaintiff's recapture of a benefit conferred on the defendant that has unjustly enriched her or him. ■ **EXAMPLE 19.8** Katie contracts with Mikhail to design a house for her. Katie pays Mikhail $9,000 and agrees to make two more payments of $9,000 (for a total of $27,000) as the design progresses. The next day, Mikhail calls Katie and tells her that he has taken a position with a large architectural firm in another state and cannot design the house. Katie decides to hire another architect that afternoon. Katie can obtain restitution of the $9,000. ■

---

11. *Restatement (Second) of Contracts*, Section 370.

Restitution Is Not Limited to Rescission Cases

Restitution may be appropriate when a contract is rescinded, but the right to restitution is not limited to rescission cases. Because an award of restitution basically returns something to its rightful owner, a party can seek restitution in actions for breach of contract, tort actions, and other types of actions.

Restitution can be obtained, for instance, when funds or property have been transferred by mistake or because of fraud or incapacity. Similarly, restitution may be available when there has been misconduct by a party in a confidential or other special relationship. Even in criminal cases, a court can order restitution of funds or property obtained through embezzlement, conversion, theft, or copyright infringement.

As mentioned, one of the bases that a court may use to order the rescission of a contract is fraud. That was the ground for the order of rescission in the following case.

Case 19.3

Clara Wonjung Lee, DDS, Ltd. v. Robles

Appellate Court of Illinois, First District, 2014 WL 976776 (2014).

Background and Facts Clara Lee agreed to buy Rosalina Robles's dental practice and to lease her dental offices in Chicago, Illinois. The price was $267,000, with $133,500 allocated to goodwill—that is, the market value of the business's good reputation. After Lee took over the practice, *Chicago Magazine* and other local media revealed that Gary Kimmel, one of Robles's dentists, had illegally treated underage prostitutes in the practice's offices after hours. The media reported that Kimmel was under investigation by federal officials for this and other activities.

Lee filed a suit in an Illinois state court against Robles, seeking to rescind the contract. Lee alleged that Robles had deliberately withheld the information about Kimmel and that this information "adversely impacted the desirability and economic value of the practice." The court ruled in Lee's favor and awarded rescission and damages, which included the purchase price less Lee's unpaid rent and a portion of her income during her ownership of the practice. Robles appealed.

In the Language of the Court

Justice *LIU* delivered the judgment of the court:

* * * *

Section 6 of the Purchase Agreement required that Dr. Robles, as "seller, shall disclose to Dr. Lee, any material or significant information and/or charges that have occurred in the practice, (including but not limited to any pending litigation, actions, threatened actions by the Illinois State Board of Dental Examiners, or from any other governmental agency that materially alter the desirability or economic potential of the assets) up to the time of the date of transfer." *The question then was whether Dr. Robles had a duty to disclose the information she had about Dr. Kimmel's activities and the federal investigation to Dr. Lee.* Defendants offered no evidence to rebut the testimony of both Dr. Lee and [Bruce Lowery, a business appraiser], who indicated that such information would have been material to a reasonable dentist's decision to purchase the practice. Based on such evidence, we agree with the trial court's holding that information about Dr. Kimmel's activities and his association with the practice was material to Dr. Lee's decision to acquire the practice and to enter into the loan, and that Dr. Robles had a duty to disclose it to Dr. Lee under section 6 of the Purchase Agreement. [Emphasis added.]

Case 19.3 Continued

* * * Defendants' actions were purposeful and not the result of any mistake or accident. Dr. Robles' nondisclosure was designed to prevent plaintiffs from gaining relevant information that may have caused them to not proceed with the sale transaction.

* * * Here, the trial judge had the opportunity to assess the credibility of the witnesses and to weigh the evidence presented at trial. In doing so, he concluded that Dr. Robles had knowledge of the investigations involving Dr. Kimmel's illicit use of the dental practice and that she deliberately withheld the information from Dr. Lee. Despite evidence that she had been interviewed by the FBI and by *Chicago Magazine* about Dr. Kimmel's activities, Dr. Robles testified that she was unaware of the nature of such activities. The * * * court characterized Dr. Robles' testimony as "incredible." We hold that no opposite conclusion is clearly evident from the record.

Accordingly, we find that the * * * court's judgment was consistent with the manifest weight of the evidence presented at trial.

Decision and Remedy *A state intermediate court affirmed the lower court's award of rescission and damages. Robles's nondisclosure was "designed to prevent Lee from gaining relevant information" that "would have been material to a reasonable dentist's decision to purchase the practice."*

Critical Thinking

- **Legal Environment** *When rescission is awarded, what is the measure of recovery? What did the recovery include in this case?*

19–2b Specific Performance

The equitable remedy of **specific performance** calls for the performance of the act promised in the contract. This remedy is attractive to a nonbreaching party because it provides the exact bargain promised in the contract. It also avoids some of the problems inherent in a suit for damages, such as collecting a judgment and arranging another contract. In addition, the actual performance may be more valuable than the monetary damages.

Normally, however, specific performance will not be granted unless the party's legal remedy (monetary damages) is inadequate.[12] For this reason, contracts for the sale of goods rarely qualify for specific performance. The legal remedy—monetary damages—is ordinarily adequate in such situations because substantially identical goods can be bought or sold in the market. Only if the goods are unique will a court grant specific performance. For instance, paintings, sculptures, or rare books or coins are so unique that monetary damages will not enable a buyer to obtain substantially identical substitutes in the market.

Sale of Land A court may grant specific performance to a buyer in an action for a breach of contract involving the sale of land. In this situation, the legal remedy of monetary damages may not compensate the buyer adequately. After all, every parcel of land is unique: the same land in the same location obviously cannot be obtained elsewhere. Only when specific performance is unavailable (such as when the seller has sold the property to someone else) will monetary damages be awarded instead.

A seller of land can also seek specific performance of the contract. ■ **CASE IN POINT 19.9** Developer Charles Ghidorzi formed Crabtree Ridge, LLC, for the sole purpose of purchasing twenty-three acres of vacant land from Cohan Lipp, LLC. Crabtree signed a contract agreeing to pay $3.1 million for the land, which would be developed and paid for in three phases. When an environmental survey showed that the land might contain some wetlands that could not be developed, Crabtree backed out of the deal. Lipp sued Crabtree for breach of contract, seeking specific performance. The court held that Lipp was entitled to specific performance of the land-sale contract.[13] ■

Contracts for Personal Services Contracts for personal services require one party to work personally for another party. Courts generally refuse to grant specific performance of personal-service contracts. One reason is that to order a party to perform personal services against his or her will amounts to a type of involuntary servitude.[14]

---

12. *Restatement (Second) of Contracts*, Section 359.

13. *Cohan Lipp, LLC v. Crabtree Ridge, LLC*, 358 Wis.2d 711, 856 N.W.2d 346 (2014).

14. Involuntary servitude, or slavery, is contrary to the public policy expressed in the Thirteenth Amendment to the U.S. Constitution. A court can, however, enter an order (injunction) prohibiting a person who breached a personal-service contract from engaging in similar contracts for a period of time in the future.

Moreover, the courts do not want to monitor contracts for personal services, which usually require the exercise of personal judgment or talent. ■ **EXAMPLE 19.10** Nicole contracts with a surgeon to perform surgery to remove a tumor on her brain. If he refuses, the court would not compel (nor would Nicole want) the surgeon to perform under those circumstances. A court cannot ensure meaningful performance in such a situation.[15] ■

19–2c Reformation

Reformation is an equitable remedy used when the parties have *imperfectly* expressed their agreement in writing. Reformation allows a court to rewrite the contract to reflect the parties' true intentions.

Exhibit 19–2 graphically summarizes the remedies, including reformation, that are available to the nonbreaching party.

Fraud or Mutual Mistake Is Present Courts order reformation most often when fraud or mutual mistake (for example, a clerical error) is present. Typically, a party seeks reformation so that some other remedy may then be pursued.

■ **EXAMPLE 19.11** If Carson contracts to buy a forklift from Yoshie but their contract mistakenly refers to a crane, a mutual mistake has occurred. Accordingly, a court can reform the contract so that it conforms to the parties' intentions and accurately refers to the forklift being sold. ■

---

15. Similarly, courts often refuse to order specific performance of construction contracts because courts are not set up to operate as construction supervisors or engineers.

Written Contract Incorrectly States the Parties' Oral Agreement A court will also reform a contract when two parties enter into a binding oral contract but later make an error when they attempt to put the terms into writing. Normally, a court will allow into evidence the correct terms of the oral contract, thereby reforming the written contract.

Covenants Not to Compete Courts also may reform contracts that contain a written covenant not to compete. Such covenants are often included in contracts for the sale of ongoing businesses and in employment contracts. The agreements restrict the area and time in which one party can directly compete with the other party.

A covenant not to compete may be for a valid and legitimate purpose, but may impose unreasonable area or time restraints. In such instances, some courts will reform the restraints by making them reasonable and will then enforce the entire contract as reformed. Other courts will throw out the entire restrictive covenant as illegal. Thus, when businesspersons create restrictive covenants, they must make sure that the restrictions imposed are reasonable.

■ **CASE IN POINT 19.12** Cardiac Study Center, Inc., a medical practice group, hired Dr. Robert Emerick. Later, Emerick became a shareholder of Cardiac and signed an agreement that included a covenant not to compete. The covenant stated that a physician who left the group promised not to practice competitively in the surrounding area for a period of five years.

After Cardiac began receiving complaints from patients and other physicians about Emerick, it terminated his employment. Emerick sued Cardiac, claiming

EXHIBIT 19–2 Remedies for Breach of Contract

that the covenant not to compete that he had signed was unreasonable and should be declared illegal. Ultimately, a state appellate court held that the covenant was both reasonable and enforceable. Cardiac had a legitimate interest in protecting its existing client base and prohibiting Emerick from taking its clients.[16] ■

19-3 Recovery Based on Quasi Contract

In some situations, when no actual contract exists, a court may step in to prevent one party from being unjustly enriched at the expense of another party. Quasi contract is a legal theory under which an obligation is imposed in the absence of an agreement.

The legal obligation arises because the law considers that the party accepting the benefits has made an implied promise to pay for them. Generally, when one party has conferred a benefit on another party, justice requires that the party receiving the benefit pay the reasonable value for it. The party conferring the benefit can recover in *quantum meruit*,[17] which means "as much as he or she deserves."

19-3a When Quasi Contract Is Used

Quasi contract allows a court to act as if a contract exists when there is no actual contract or agreement between the parties. Therefore, if the parties have entered into a contract concerning the matter in controversy, a court normally will not impose a quasi contract. A court can also use this theory when the parties entered into a contract, but it is unenforceable for some reason.

Quasi-contractual recovery is often granted when one party has partially performed under a contract that is unenforceable. It provides an alternative to suing for damages and allows the party to recover the reasonable value of the partial performance. Depending on the case, the amount of the recovery may be measured either by the benefit received or by the detriment suffered.

■ **EXAMPLE 19.13** Ericson contracts to build two oil derricks for Petro Industries. The derricks are to be built over a period of three years, but the parties do not make a written contract. Thus, the writing requirement will bar enforcement of the contract.[18] After Ericson completes one derrick, Petro Industries informs him that it will not pay for the derrick. Ericson can sue Petro Industries under the theory of quasi contract. ■

19-3b The Requirements of Quasi Contract

To recover under the theory of quasi contract, the party seeking recovery must show the following:

1. The party has conferred a benefit on the other party.
2. The party conferred the benefit with the reasonable expectation of being paid.
3. The party did not act as a volunteer in conferring the benefit.
4. The party receiving the benefit would be unjustly enriched if allowed to retain the benefit without paying for it.

Applying these requirements to *Example 19.13*, Ericson can sue in quasi contract because all of the conditions for quasi-contractual recovery have been fulfilled. Ericson conferred a benefit on Petro Industries by building the oil derrick. Ericson built the derrick with the reasonable expectation of being paid. He was not intending to act as a volunteer. The derrick conferred an obvious benefit on Petro Industries. Petro Industries would be unjustly enriched if it was allowed to keep the derrick without paying Ericson for the work. Therefore, Ericson should be able to recover in *quantum meruit* the reasonable value of the oil derrick that was built, which is ordinarily equal to its fair market value.

Concept Summary 19.1 reviews all of the equitable remedies, including quasi contract, that may be available in the event that a contract is breached.

19-4 Waiver of Breach

Under certain circumstances, a nonbreaching party may be willing to accept a defective performance of the contract. This knowing relinquishment of a legal right (that is, the right to require satisfactory and full performance) is called a **waiver**.

19-4a Consequences of a Waiver of Breach

When a waiver of a breach of contract occurs, the party waiving the breach cannot take any later action on it. In effect, the waiver erases the past breach, and the contract continues as if the breach had never occurred. Of course, the waiver of breach of contract extends only to the matter waived and not to the whole contract.

---

16. *Emerick v. Cardiac Study Center, Inc.,* 166 Wash.App. 1039 (2012).
17. Pronounced *kwahn*-tuhm *mehr*-oo-wit.
18. Contracts that by their terms cannot be performed within one year must be in writing to be enforceable.

Concept Summary 19.1

Equitable Remedies

Rescission and Restitution	• *Rescission*—A remedy whereby a contract is canceled and the parties are restored to the original positions that they occupied prior to the transaction. • *Restitution*—When a contract is rescinded, both parties must make restitution to each other by returning the goods, property, or funds previously conveyed.
Specific Performance	• An equitable remedy calling for the performance of the act promised in the contract. • Only available when monetary damages would be inadequate and never available in personal-service contracts.
Reformation	• An equitable remedy allowing a contract to be reformed, or rewritten, to reflect the parties' true intentions. • Available when an agreement is imperfectly expressed in writing, such as when a mutual mistake has occurred.
Recovery Based on Quasi Contract	• An equitable theory under which a party who confers a benefit on another—with the reasonable expectation of being paid—can seek a court order for the fair market value of the benefit conferred.

19–4b Reasons for Waiving a Breach

Businesspersons often waive breaches of contract to obtain whatever benefit is still possible out of the contract. ■ **EXAMPLE 19.14** A seller, Purdue Resources, contracts with a buyer, Bladco Enterprises, to deliver ten thousand tons of coal on or before November 1. The contract calls for Bladco to pay by November 10 for coal delivered. Because of a coal miners' strike, coal is hard to find. Purdue breaches the contract by not tendering delivery until November 5. Bladco will likely choose to waive the seller's breach, accept delivery of the coal, and pay as contracted. ■

19–4c Waiver of Breach and Subsequent Breaches

Ordinarily, a waiver by a contracting party will not operate to waive subsequent, additional, or future breaches of contract. This is always true when the subsequent breaches are unrelated to the first breach. ■ **EXAMPLE 19.15** Ashton owns a multimillion-dollar apartment complex that is under construction. Ashton allows the contractor to complete a stage of construction late. By doing so, Ashton waives his right to sue for the delay. Ashton does not, however, waive the right to sue for failure to comply with engineering specifications on the same job. ■

Pattern-of-Conduct Exception A waiver can extend to subsequent defective performance if a reasonable person would conclude that similar defective performance in the future will be acceptable. Therefore, a *pattern of conduct* that waives a number of successive breaches will operate as a continued waiver. To change this result, the nonbreaching party should give notice to the breaching party that full performance will be required in the future.

Effect on the Contract The party who has rendered defective or less-than-full performance remains liable for the damages caused by the breach of contract. In effect, the waiver operates to keep the contract going. The waiver prevents the nonbreaching party from declaring the contract at an end or rescinding the contract. The contract continues, but the nonbreaching party can recover damages caused by the defective or less-than-full performance.

19–5 Contract Provisions Limiting Remedies

A contract may include provisions stating that no damages can be recovered for certain types of breaches or that damages will be limited to a maximum amount. A contract may also provide that the only remedy for breach is replacement, repair, or refund of the purchase price. Finally, a contract may provide that one party can seek injunctive relief if the other party breaches the contract. Provisions stating that no damages can be recovered are called *exculpatory clauses*. Provisions that affect the availability of certain remedies are called *limitation-of-liability clauses*.

19–5a The UCC Allows Sales Contracts to Limit Remedies

The Uniform Commercial Code (UCC) provides that in a contract for the sale of goods, remedies can be limited. We will examine the UCC provisions on limited remedies in a later chapter in the context of contracts for the sale or lease of goods.[19]

---

19. See UCC 2–719(1).

19–5b Enforceability of Limitation-of-Liability Clauses

Whether a limitation-of-liability clause in a contract will be enforced depends on the type of breach that is excused by the provision. Normally, a provision excluding liability for fraudulent or intentional injury will not be enforced. Likewise, a clause excluding liability for illegal acts, acts that are contrary to public policy, or violations of law will not be enforced. A clause that excludes liability for negligence may be enforced in some situations when the parties have roughly equal bargaining positions.

■ **CASE IN POINT 19.16** Engineering Consulting Services, Ltd. (ECS), contracted with RSN Properties, Inc., a real estate developer. ECS was to perform soil studies for $2,200 and render an opinion on the use of septic systems in a particular subdivision being developed. A clause in the contract limited ECS's liability to RSN to the value of the engineering services or the sum of $50,000, whichever was greater.

ECS concluded that most of the lots were suitable for septic systems, so RSN proceeded with the development. RSN constructed the roads and water lines to the subdivision in reliance on ECS's conclusions, which turned out to be incorrect. RSN sued ECS for breach of contract and argued that the limitation of liability was against public policy and unenforceable. The court, however, enforced the limitation-of-liability clause as "a reasonable allocation of risks in an arm's-length business transaction."[20] ■

---

20. *RSN Properties, Inc. v. Engineering Consulting Services, Ltd.*, 301 Ga.App. 52, 686 S.E.2d 853 (2009).

Reviewing: Breach of Contract and Remedies

Kyle Bruno enters a contract with X Entertainment to be a stuntman in a movie. Bruno is widely known as the best motorcycle stuntman in the business, and the movie to be produced, *Xtreme Riders,* has numerous scenes involving high-speed freestyle street-bike stunts. Filming is set to begin August 1 and end by December 1 so that the film can be released the following summer. Both parties to the contract have stipulated that the filming must end on time to capture the profits from the summer movie market. The contract states that Bruno will be paid 10 percent of the net proceeds from the movie for his stunts.

The contract also includes a liquidated damages provision, which specifies that if Bruno breaches the contract, he will owe X Entertainment $1 million. In addition, the contract includes a limitation-of-liability clause stating that if Bruno is injured during filming, X Entertainment's liability is limited to nominal damages. Using the information presented in the chapter, answer the following questions.

1. One day, while Bruno is preparing for a difficult stunt, he gets into an argument with the director and refuses to perform any stunts at all. Can X Entertainment seek specific performance of the contract? Why or why not?
2. Suppose that while performing a high-speed wheelie on a motorcycle, Bruno is injured by the intentionally reckless act of an X Entertainment employee. Will a court be likely to enforce the limitation-of-liability clause? Why or why not?

Continues

3. What factors would a court consider to determine whether the $1 million liquidated damages provision constitutes valid damages or is a penalty?

4. Suppose that there was no liquidated damages provision (or the court refused to enforce it) and X Entertainment breached the contract. The breach caused the release of the film to be delayed until after summer. Could Bruno seek consequential (special) damages for lost profits from the summer movie market in that situation? Explain.

Debate This . . . *Courts should always uphold limitation-of-liability clauses, whether or not the two parties to the contract had equal bargaining power.*

Terms and Concepts

consequential damages 342
incidental damages 341
liquidated damages 343
mitigation of damages 343

nominal damages 343
penalty 343
quantum meruit 349
reformation 348

restitution 345
specific performance 347
waiver 349

Issue Spotters

1. Greg contracts to build a storage shed for Haney, who pays Greg in advance, but Greg completes only half the work. Haney pays Ipswich $500 to finish the shed. If Haney sues Greg, what will be the measure of recovery? (See *Damages*.)

2. Lyle contracts to sell his ranch to Marley, who is to take possession on June 1. Lyle delays the transfer until August 1. Marley incurs expenses in providing for cattle that he bought for the ranch. When they made the contract, Lyle had no reason to know of the cattle. Is Lyle liable for Marley's expenses in providing for the cattle? Why or why not? (See *Damages*.)

• **Check your answers to the Issue Spotters against the answers provided in Appendix D at the end of this text.**

Business Scenarios

19–1. Liquidated Damages. Cohen contracts to sell his house and lot to Windsor for $100,000. The terms of the contract call for Windsor to pay 10 percent of the purchase price as a down payment. The terms further stipulate that if the buyer breaches the contract, Cohen will retain the deposit as liquidated damages. Windsor pays the deposit, but because her expected financing of the $90,000 balance falls through, she breaches the contract. Two weeks later, Cohen sells the house and lot to Ballard for $105,000. Windsor demands her $10,000 back, but Cohen refuses, claiming that Windsor's breach and the contract terms entitle him to keep the deposit. Discuss who is correct. (See *Damages*.)

19–2. Specific Performance. In which of the following situations would specific performance be an appropriate remedy? Discuss fully. (See *Equitable Remedies*.)

(a) Thompson contracts to sell her house and lot to Cousteau. Then, on finding another buyer willing to pay a higher purchase price, she refuses to deed the property to Cousteau.

(b) Amy contracts to sing and dance in Fred's nightclub for one month, beginning May 1. She then refuses to perform.

(c) Hoffman contracts to purchase a rare coin owned by Erikson, who is breaking up his coin collection. At the last minute, Erikson decides to keep his coin collection intact and refuses to deliver the coin to Hoffman.

(d) ABC Corp. has three shareholders: Panozzo, who owns 48 percent of the stock; Chang, who owns another 48 percent; and Ryan, who owns 4 percent. Ryan contracts to sell her 4 percent to Chang. Later, Ryan refuses to transfer the shares to Chang.

Business Case Problems

19–3. Liquidated Damages and Penalties. Planned Pethood Plus, Inc., is a veterinarian-owned clinic. It borrowed $389,000 from KeyBank at an interest rate of 9.3 percent per year for ten years. The loan had a "prepayment penalty" clause that clearly stated that if the loan was repaid early, a specific formula would be used to assess a lump-sum payment to extinguish the obligation. The sooner the loan was paid off, the higher the prepayment penalty. After a year, the veterinarians decided to pay off the loan. KeyBank invoked a prepayment penalty of $40,525.92, which was equal to 10.7 percent of the balance due. The veterinarians sued, contending that the prepayment requirement was unenforceable because it was a penalty. The bank countered that the amount was not a penalty but liquidated damages and that the sum was reasonable. The trial court agreed with the bank, and the veterinarians appealed. Was the loan's prepayment charge reasonable, and should it have been enforced? Why or why not? [*Planned Pethood Plus, Inc. v. KeyCorp, Inc.,* 228 P.3d 262 (Colo.App. 2010)] (See *Damages.*)

19–4. Measure of Damages. Before buying a house, Dean and Donna Testa hired Ground Systems, Inc. (GSI), to inspect the sewage and water disposal system. GSI reported a split system with a watertight septic tank, a wastewater tank, a distribution box, and a leach field. The Testas bought the house. Later, Dean saw that the system was not as GSI described—there was no distribution box or leach field, and there was only one tank, which was not watertight. The Testas arranged for the installation of a new system and sold the house. Assuming that GSI is liable for breach of contract, what is the measure of damages? [*Testa v. Ground Systems, Inc.,* 206 N.J. 330, 20 A.3d 435 (App.Div. 2011)] (See *Damages.*)

19–5. Business Case Problem with Sample Answer—Consequential Damages. After submitting the high bid at a foreclosure sale, David Simard entered into a contract to purchase real property in Maryland for $192,000. Simard defaulted (failed to pay) on the contract. A state court ordered the property to be resold at Simard's expense, as required by state law. The property was then resold for $163,000, but the second purchaser also defaulted. The court then ordered a second resale, resulting in a final price of $130,000. Assuming that Simard is liable for consequential damages, what is the extent of his liability? Is he liable for losses and expenses related to the first resale? If so, is he also liable for losses and expenses related to the second resale? Why or why not? [*Burson v. Simard,* 35 A.3d 1154 (Md. 2012)] (See *Damages.*)

- For a sample answer to Problem 19–5, go to Appendix E at the end of this text.

19–6. Liquidated Damages. Cuesport Properties, LLC, sold a condominium in Anne Arundel County, Maryland, to Critical Developments, LLC. As part of the sale, Cuesport agreed to build a wall between Critical Developments' unit and an adjacent unit within thirty days of closing. If Cuesport failed to do so, it was to pay $126 per day until completion. This was an estimate of the amount of rent that Critical Developments would lose until the wall was finished and the unit could be rented. Actual damages were otherwise difficult to estimate at the time of the contract. The wall was built on time, but without a county permit, and it did not comply with the county building code. Critical Developments did

not modify the wall to comply with the code until 260 days after the date of the contract deadline for completion of the wall. Does Cuesport have to pay Critical Developments $126 for each of the 260 days? Explain. [*Cuesport Properties, LLC v. Critical Developments, LLC,* 209 Md.App. 607, 61 A.3d 91 (2013)] (See *Damages.*)

19–7. Limitation-of-Liability Clauses. Mia Eriksson was a seventeen-year-old competitor in horseback-riding events. Her riding coach was Kristi Nunnink. Eriksson signed an agreement that released Nunnink from all liability except for damages caused by Nunnink's "direct, willful and wanton negligence." During an event at Galway Downs in Temecula, California, Eriksson's horse struck a hurdle. She fell from the horse and the horse fell on her, causing her death. Her parents, Karan and Stan Eriksson, filed a suit in a California state court against Nunnink for wrongful death. Is the limitation-of-liability agreement that Eriksson signed likely to be enforced in her parents' case? If so, how will it affect their claim? Explain. [*Eriksson v. Nunnink,* 233 Cal.App.4th 708, 183 Cal.Rptr.3d 234 (4 Dist. 2015)] (See *Contract Provisions Limiting Remedies.*)

19–8. Damages. Robert Morris was a licensed insurance agent working for his father's independent insurance agency when he contacted Farmers Insurance Exchange in Alabama about becoming a Farmers agent. According to Farmers' company policy, Morris was an unsuitable candidate due to his relationship with his father's agency. But no Farmers representative told Morris of this policy, and none of the documents that he signed expressed it. Farmers trained Morris and appointed him its agent. About three years later, however, Farmers terminated the appointment for "a conflict of interest because his father was in the insurance business." Morris filed a suit in an Alabama state court against Farmers, claiming that he had been fraudulently induced to leave his father's agency to work for Farmers. If Morris was successful, what type of damages was he most likely awarded? What was the measure of damages? Discuss. [*Farmers Insurance Exchange v. Morris,* __ So.3d __, 2016 WL 661671 (Ala. 2016)] (See *Damages.*)

19–9. A Question of Ethics—Remedies. *On a weekday, Tamara Cohen, a real estate broker, showed a townhouse owned by Ray and Harriet Mayer to Jessica Seinfeld, the wife of comedian Jerry Seinfeld. On the weekend, when Cohen was unavailable because her religious beliefs prevented her from working, the Seinfelds revisited the townhouse on their own and agreed to buy it. The contract stated that the "buyers will pay buyer's real estate broker's fees." [Cohen v. Seinfeld, 15 Misc.3d 1118(A), 839 N.Y.S.2d 432 (Sup. 2007)] (See Equitable Remedies.)*

(a) Is Cohen entitled to payment even though she was not available to show the townhouse to the Seinfelds on the weekend? Explain.

(b) What obligation do parties involved in business deals owe to each other with respect to their religious beliefs? How might the situation in this case have been avoided?

Legal Reasoning Group Activity

19–10. Breach and Remedies. Frances Morelli agreed to sell Judith Bucklin a house in Rhode Island for $177,000. The sale was supposed to be closed by September 1. The contract included a provision that "if Seller is unable to convey good, clear, insurable, and marketable title, Buyer shall have the option to: (a) accept such title as Seller is able to convey without reduction of the Purchase Price, or (b) cancel this Agreement and receive a return of all Deposits."

An examination of the public records revealed that the house did not have marketable title. Bucklin offered Morelli additional time to resolve the problem, and the closing did not occur as scheduled. Morelli decided that "the deal was over" and offered to return the deposit. Bucklin refused and, in mid-October, decided to exercise her option to accept the house without marketable title. She notified Morelli, who did not respond. She then filed a lawsuit against Morelli in a state court. (See *Damages.*)

(a) One group will discuss whether Morelli breached the contract and will decide in whose favor the court should rule.

(b) A second group will assume that Morelli did breach the contract and will determine what the appropriate remedy is in this situation.

UNIT

Application and Ethics

Fantasy Sports—Legal Gambling?

A *fantasy sport* involves games in which the participants compile imaginary teams made up of real players in a professional sport. As in real sports, fantasy sports team owners draft, trade, and drop players. The teams are grouped into leagues and compete based on the statistical performance of the players in actual games.

Fantasy sports is a multibillion-dollar industry that includes more than three hundred companies, ranging from small start-ups to large corporations. For example, CBSSports.com, which offers fantasy sports games on its Web site, is a brand operated by CBS Interactive, a division of CBS Corporation. More than 50 million U.S. adults play fantasy sports.

One of the most important issues confronting the industry is whether participation in fantasy sports constitutes illegal gambling.

Do Fantasy Sports Constitute Gambling under State Law?

To *gamble* is to play a game of chance or bet on the outcome of an uncertain event in the hope of winning. State laws concerning the legality of gambling vary. Even in states where most forms of gambling are illegal, however, some activities that would otherwise fall within the definition of gambling are allowed.

Consideration, Reward, and Chance In most states, an activity constitutes gambling if it involves consideration, reward, and chance. Most courts construe *consideration* narrowly in this context, limiting it to money or valuable property exchanged for a chance to win a prize. Some courts apply the term more broadly to any form of legal detriment exchanged for a chance to win.

A *reward* is the prize for winning. Courts generally hold that the reward, or prize, must be something tangible, regardless of its value.[1]

Chance requires that an activity's outcome be determined unpredictably by factors outside a participant's control, not by judgment, practice, or skill. Most states deem an activity to involve chance if greater than 50 percent of the outcome is determined by outside factors.

Entry Fees, Prizes, and Skill In states that apply these three elements to determine whether an activity constitutes gambling, the lack of any one of them argues in favor of an activity's lawfulness. For example, fantasy sports leagues that offer free entry for participants lack the element of consideration. Games that do not include prizes lack the element of reward.

Other fantasy sports games are not so clearly legal. For example, a game that extends for less than a full professional sports season involves a greater degree of chance and is thus less likely to qualify as legal.[2] The shorter the time, the less opportunity a participant's skill has to offset such factors as a player's health, the decisions of a team manager or coach, and weather. There is also less time for participants to negotiate trades and manage their fantasy teams.

Continues

---

1. See, for example, *State of Arkansas v. 26 Gaming Machines*, 356 Ark. 47, 145 S.W.3d 368 (2004).
2. See *Three Kings Holdings, L.L.C. v. Six*, 45 Kan.App.2d 1043, 255 P.3d 1218 (2011).

Application and Ethics

Stricter Standards The standards are stricter in some states. For example, states that apply the contract definition of *consideration*—something of legally sufficient value—to fantasy sports games will not exempt a game simply because there is no entry fee.

Some states interpret the element of chance to involve *any* chance. In those states, all fantasy sports games violate gambling laws. Other states have indicated or expressly stated that the games are illegal.[3]

Does Federal Law Define Fantasy Sports as Gambling?

Most federal laws related to gambling were enacted to help states enforce their gambling laws. There are, however, at least two federal acts that may apply to fantasy sports.

"Wagering Schemes" The professional sports industry lobbied Congress to enact the Professional and Amateur Sports Protection Act (PAPSA)[4] in 1992. This act prohibits, with certain exceptions, the operation of a "wagering scheme" based on a game in which "professional or amateur athletes participate."

It is not likely that PAPSA would apply to fantasy sports generally—most professional sports leagues operate their own fantasy sports Web sites and endorse seasonal play. But the act could apply to *daily* fantasy sports games—games played over a brief period, such as a week or a single day, rather than an entire sports season. Their sponsors emphasize payouts and prizes, giving daily games the appearance of "wagering schemes."

Skill of the Participants The Unlawful Internet Gambling Enforcement Act (UIGEA) of 2006[5] prohibits persons "engaged in the business of betting" to "knowingly accept" funds "in connection with the participation of another person in unlawful Internet gambling." Under the act, "unlawful Internet gambling" is knowingly transmitting a bet, via the Internet, if the bet is otherwise illegal where it is "initiated, received, or . . . made." In other words, if a person places a bet in a state in which gambling is illegal, a business that accepts the bet violates the UIGEA, regardless of the business's location.[6]

The UIGEA exempts fantasy sports games in which, among other requirements, the "outcomes reflect the relative knowledge and skill of the participants and are determined predominantly by the performance of individuals . . . in multiple real-world sporting events." It is likely that *daily* fantasy sports games do not meet this requirement. Their short duration decreases the effect of a participant's skill and increases the effect of luck on the result.

Daily Fantasy Sports—Skill or Gamble?

DraftKings and FanDuel operate daily fantasy sports (DFS) Web sites. In the fall of 2015, the two companies saturated the media with advertising, emphasizing million-dollar payouts. Then, in early October, DraftKings employee Brian Haskell allegedly used inside information to beat more than 200,000 other participants and win $350,000 in a game on FanDuel's site. DraftKings denied the allegation. Both companies announced, "Nothing is more important . . . than the integrity of the games we offer to our customers."

---

3. These states include Arizona, Iowa, Louisiana, Montana, and Washington.
4. 28 U.S.C. Sections 3701–3704.
5. 31 U.S.C. Sections 5361–5367.
6. See *Interactive Media Entertainment and Gaming Association Inc. v. Attorney General of United States*, 580 F.3d 113 (3d Cir. 2009).

Application and Ethics

Before the end of the month, the Federal Bureau of Investigation and U.S. Department of Justice opened an investigation. ESPN announced that it would stop running segments sponsored by DraftKings. The National Collegiate Athletic Association (NCAA) barred DraftKings and FanDuel from advertising at NCAA championship events and prohibited student athletes from participating in DFS. The National Football League limited the amount of money its players could win from DFS.

Meanwhile, a dozen states began considering new fantasy sports legislation. The Nevada Gaming Control Board ruled that DFS should be considered gambling and banned DFS sites from operating in the state. New York Attorney General Eric Schneiderman, characterizing DFS as games of chance rather than skill, ordered DraftKings and FanDuel to stop accepting "wagers" from New York residents.

> Daily fantasy sports companies are engaged in illegal gambling . . . , causing the same kinds of social and economic harms as other forms of illegal gambling. . . . Daily fantasy sports is neither victimless nor harmless, and it is clear that DraftKings and FanDuel are the leaders of a massive, multi-billion-dollar scheme intended to evade the law and fleece sports fans across the country.[7]

Ethical Connection

DraftKings and FanDuel contend that they are not taking bets—that the games on their sites involve more skill than luck. They have a legal right to argue this point in a New York state court on a challenge to the order of the state's attorney general. And, in the best interest of their owners and customers, they may have an ethical duty to challenge the order.

In the meantime, do the two sites have an ethical duty to *comply* with the order? Or do they have an ethical obligation to *defy* the order to play to completion the games that New York residents started? The sites might thereby gain additional support for their argument to challenge the attorney general. Or their open defiance might undercut any sympathy a court might have for their situation. It is a judgment call—an ethical gamble—and the question for the sites might be, "Do you feel lucky?"

Ethics Question *Is gambling less ethical than trading in securities or funding a start-up? Why?*

Critical Thinking *What is the most significant factor in determining whether fantasy sports games constitute gambling? Explain.*

---

7. Press Release, New York State Office of the Attorney General, *A.G. Schneiderman Issues Cease-and-Desist Letters to FanDuel and DraftKings, Demanding That Companies Stop Accepting Illegal Wagers in New York State* (Nov. 11, 2015) (http://www .ag.ny.gov/press-release/ag-schneiderman-issues-cease-and-desist-letters-fanduel-and-draftkings-demanding).

Answers to the *Issue Spotters*

1. *If Haney sues Greg, what will be the measure of recovery?* A nonbreaching party is entitled to his or her benefit of the bargain under the contract. Here, the innocent party is entitled to be put in the position she would have been in if the contract had been fully performed. The measure of the benefit is the cost to complete the work ($500). These are compensatory damages.

2. *Is Lyle liable for Marley's expenses in providing for the cattle? Why or why not?* No. To recover damages that flow from the consequences of a breach but that are caused by circumstances beyond the contract (consequential damages), the breaching party must know, or have reason to know, that special circumstances will cause the nonbreaching party to suffer the additional loss. That was not the circumstance in this problem.

Sample Answers for *Business Case Problems with Sample Answer*

Problem 19–5. *Consequential Damages.* Simard is liable only for the losses and expenses related to the first resale. Simard could reasonably have anticipated that his breach would require another sale and that the sales price might be less than what he had agreed to pay. Therefore, he should be liable for the difference between his sales price and the first resale price ($29,000), plus any expenses arising from the first resale. Simard is not liable, however, for any expenses and losses related to the second resale. After all, Simard did not cause the second purchaser's default, and he could not reasonably have foreseen that default as a probable result of his breach.

Domestic and International Sales and Lease Contracts

CHAPTER

Warranties

Most goods are covered by some type of warranty designed to protect buyers. In sales and lease law, a warranty is an assurance or guarantee by the seller or lessor about the quality and features of the goods being sold or leased.

The Uniform Commercial Code (UCC) has numerous rules governing product warranties as they occur in sales and lease contracts. Articles 2 (on sales) and 2A (on leases) designate several types of warranties that can arise in a sales or lease contract, including warranties of title, express warranties, and implied warranties. In addition, federal law imposes certain requirements on warranties.

Because a warranty imposes a duty on the seller or lessor, a breach of warranty is a breach of the seller's or lessor's promise. Assuming that the parties have not agreed to limit or modify the remedies available, if the seller or lessor breaches a warranty, the buyer or lessee can sue to recover damages. Under some circumstances, a breach of warranty can allow the buyer or lessee to rescind (cancel) the agreement.

23–1 Warranties of Title

Under the UCC, three types of title warranties—*good title, no liens,* and *no infringements*—can automatically arise in sales and lease contracts [UCC 2–312, 2A–211]. Normally, a seller or lessor can disclaim or modify these title warranties only by including *specific language* in the contract. For instance, sellers may assert that they are transferring only such rights, title, and interest as they have in the goods.

23–1a Good Title

In most sales, sellers warrant that they have good and valid title to the goods sold and that the transfer of the title is rightful [UCC 2–312(1)(a)]. If the buyer subsequently learns that the seller did not have valid title to the goods that were purchased, the buyer can sue the seller for breach of this warranty.

■ **EXAMPLE 23.1** Alexis steals two iPads from Camden and sells them to Emma, who does not know that they are stolen. If Camden discovers that Emma has the iPads, then he has the right to reclaim them from her. When Alexis sold Emma the iPads, Alexis *automatically* warranted to Emma that the title conveyed was valid and that its transfer was rightful. Because a thief has no title to stolen goods, Alexis breached the warranty of

title imposed by UCC 2–312(1)(a) and became liable to Emma for appropriate damages. ■

23–1b No Liens

A second warranty of title protects buyers and lessees who are *unaware* of any encumbrances against goods at the time the contract is made [UCC 2–312(1)(b), 2A–211(1)]. (Such encumbrances—that is, claims, charges, or liabilities—are usually called *liens.*[1]) This warranty protects buyers who, for instance, unknowingly purchase goods that are subject to a creditor's security interest. (A *security interest* in this context is an interest in the goods that secures payment or performance of an obligation.) If a creditor legally repossesses the goods from a buyer *who had no actual knowledge of the security interest,* the buyer can recover from the seller for breach of warranty. (In contrast, a buyer who has *actual knowledge of a security interest* has no recourse against a seller.)

■ **EXAMPLE 23.2** Henderson buys a used boat from Loring for cash. A month later, Barish proves that she has a valid security interest in the boat and that Loring, who has missed five payments, is in default. Barish then repossesses the boat from Henderson. Henderson demands his cash back from Loring. Under Section 2–312(1)(b),

---

1. Pronounced *leens.*

Henderson has legal grounds to recover from Loring. As a seller of goods, Loring warrants that the goods are delivered free from any security interest or other lien of which the buyer has no knowledge. ∎

Article 2A affords similar protection for lessees. Section 2A–211(1) provides that during the term of the lease, no claim of any third party will interfere with the lessee's enjoyment of the leasehold interest.

23–1c No Infringements

A third type of warranty of title arises automatically when the seller or lessor is a merchant. A merchant-seller or lessor warrants that the buyer or lessee takes the goods *free of infringements* from any copyright, trademark, or patent claims of a third person[2] [UCC 2–312(3), 2A–211(2)].

Notice in Sales Contracts If the buyer is subsequently sued by a third party holding copyright, trademark, or patent rights in the goods, then this warranty is breached. The buyer *must notify the seller* of the litigation within a reasonable time to enable the seller to decide whether to defend the lawsuit. The seller then decides whether to defend the buyer and bear all expenses in the action.

If the seller agrees in a writing to defend and to pay the expenses, then the buyer must turn over control of the litigation to the seller. Otherwise, the buyer is barred from any remedy against the seller for liability established by the litigation [UCC 2–607(3)(b), 2–607(5)(b)]. Thus, if a buyer wins at trial but did not notify the seller of the litigation, the buyer cannot sue the seller to recover the expenses of the lawsuit.

Notice in Lease Contracts In situations that involve leases rather than sales, Article 2A provides for the same notice of infringement litigation [UCC 2A–516(3)(b), 2A–516(4)(b)]. After being notified of the lawsuit, the lessor (or supplier, in a finance lease) who agrees to pay all expenses can demand that the lessee turn over the control of the litigation. Failure to provide notice normally bars any subsequent remedy against the lessor for liability established by the litigation.

There is an exception for leases to individual consumers for personal, family, or household purposes. A consumer who fails to notify the lessor within a reasonable time does not lose his or her remedy against the lessor for whatever liability is established in the litigation [UCC 2A–516(3)(b)].

---

2. Recall that *merchant* is defined in UCC 2–104(1) as a person who deals in goods of the kind involved in the sales contract or who, by occupation, presents himself or herself as having knowledge or skill peculiar to the goods involved in the transaction.

23–2 Express Warranties

A seller or lessor can create an **express warranty** by making representations concerning the quality, condition, description, or performance potential of the goods.

23–2a Statements That Create Express Warranties

Under UCC 2–313 and 2A–210, express warranties arise when a seller or lessor indicates any of the following:

1. That the goods conform to any *affirmation* (declaration that something is true) *of fact or promise* that the seller or lessor makes to the buyer or lessee about the goods. Such affirmations or promises are usually made during the bargaining process. ∎ **EXAMPLE 23.3** D. J. Vladick, a salesperson at Home Depot, tells a customer, "These drill bits will easily penetrate stainless steel—and without dulling." Vladick's statement is an express warranty. ∎

2. That the goods conform to any *description* of them. ∎ **EXAMPLE 23.4** A label reads "Crate contains one Kawasaki Brute Force 750 4X4i EPS ATV," and a contract calls for the delivery of a "wool coat." Both statements create express warranties that the goods sold conform to the descriptions. ∎

3. That the goods conform to any *sample or model* of the goods shown to the buyer or lessee. ∎ **EXAMPLE 23.5** Melissa Faught orders a stainless steel 5500 Super Angel juicer for $1,100 after seeing a dealer demonstrate its use at a health fair. The Super Angel is shipped to her. When the juicer arrives, it is an older model, not the 5500 model. This is a breach of an express warranty because the dealer warranted that the juicer would be the same model used in the demonstration. ∎

Express warranties can be found in a seller's or lessor's advertisement, brochure, or promotional materials, in addition to being made orally or in an express warranty provision in a sales or lease contract.

See Concept Summary 23.1 for a review of warranties of title and express warranties.

23–2b Basis of the Bargain

To create an express warranty, a seller or lessor does not have to use formal words, such as *warrant* or *guarantee*. It is only necessary that a reasonable buyer or lessee would regard the representation as being part of the basis of the bargain [UCC 2–313(2), 2A–210(2)].

The UCC does not explicitly define the phrase "basis of the bargain." Generally, it means that the buyer or

Concept Summary 23.1

Warranties of Title and Express Warranties

Warranties of Title	• *Good title*—A seller warrants that he or she has the right to pass good and rightful title to the goods [UCC 2–312(1)(a)]. • *No liens*—A seller warrants that the goods sold are free of any encumbrances, such as claims, charges, or liabilities (usually called *liens*). A lessor warrants that the lessee will not be disturbed in her or his possession of the goods by the claims of a third party [UCC 2–312(1)(b), 2A–211(1)]. • *No infringements*—A merchant-seller warrants that the goods are free of infringement claims (claims that a patent, trademark, or copyright has been infringed) by third parties. Lessors make similar warranties [UCC 2–312(3), 2A–211(2)].
Express Warranties	• Under UCC 2–313 and 2A–210, an express warranty arises when a seller or lessor indicates any of the following as part of the sale or bargain: • An affirmation of fact or promise. • A description of the goods. • A sample or model shown as conforming to the contract goods. • Under the Magnuson-Moss Warranty Act, an express written warranty covering consumer goods priced at more than $25, *if made*, must be labeled as either a full warranty or a limited warranty.

lessee must have relied on the representation at the time of entering into the agreement. Therefore, a court must determine in each case whether a representation was made at such a time and in such a way that it induced the buyer or lessee to enter into the contract.

23–2c Statements of Opinion and Value

Only statements of fact create express warranties. A seller or lessor who states an opinion about or recommends the goods thus does not create an express warranty [UCC 2–313(2), 2A–210(2)].

■ **CASE IN POINT 23.6** Kathleen Arthur underwent a surgical procedure for neck pain. Her surgeon implanted an Infuse Bone Graft device made by Medtronic, Inc. Although the device was not approved for this use, a sales representative for Medtronic allegedly had told the surgeon that the Infuse device could be appropriate for this surgery. The surgery did not resolve Arthur's neck pain, and she developed numbness in her arm and fingers. She filed a breach of warranty claim against Medtronic, alleging that the salesperson's statements created an express warranty. The court dismissed Arthur's case, however. The alleged statements of a sales representative on whether it was "appropriate" to use the Infuse device

in such a procedure were opinion and did not create an express warranty.[3] ■

Similarly, a seller or lessor who makes a statement about the value or worth of the goods does not create an express warranty. Thus, a statement such as "this is worth a fortune" or "anywhere else you'd pay $10,000 for it" usually does not create a warranty.

Opinions by Experts Ordinarily, statements of opinion do not create warranties. If the seller or lessor is an expert, however, and gives an opinion as an expert to a layperson, then a warranty may be created. ■ **EXAMPLE 23.7** Stephen is an art dealer and an expert in seventeenth-century paintings. If Stephen tells Lauren, a purchaser, that in his opinion a particular painting is by Rembrandt, Stephen has warranted the accuracy of his opinion. ■

Reasonable Reliance It is not always easy to determine whether a statement constitutes an express warranty or puffery ("seller's talk"). The reasonableness of the buyer's or lessee's reliance appears to be the controlling criterion in many cases. ■ **EXAMPLE 23.8** A salesperson's statements that a ladder will "never break" and will "last

---

3. *Arthur v. Medtronic, Inc.,* 123 F.Supp.3d 1145 (E.D.Mo. 2015).

a lifetime" are so clearly improbable that they do not create a warranty. No reasonable buyer would rely on such statements. ■

Additionally, the context in which a statement is made may be relevant in determining the reasonableness of a buyer's or lessee's reliance. For instance, a reasonable person is more likely to rely on a written statement made in an advertisement than on a statement made orally by a salesperson. ■ **CASE IN POINT 23.9** Lennox International, Inc., makes heating, ventilating, and air conditioning (HVAC) systems. T & M Solar and Air Conditioning, Inc., is a California corporation that contracts to install HVAC systems. T & M became interested in Lennox solar panel systems. Lennox advertised that the systems could run through the existing HVAC system, rather than through an electrical panel. This meant that the systems, unlike traditional solar panel systems, could be installed without modifying the electrical panels in a residence.

Lennox representatives repeatedly assured T & M that their systems would operate as advertised and would pass National Electric Code requirements. Lennox sent representatives to California to advertise the systems to potential clients of T & M. T & M ordered and paid for six Lennox systems for customers. The systems that Lennox supplied could not be operated or installed as promised, however, and T & M ultimately had to remove them from customers' homes at its own expense. T & M filed suit, alleging breach of an express warranty. The court found that T & M had ordered the Lennox systems precisely because they could operate through the HVAC system without modification of existing electrical panels. That was sufficient evidence of reasonable reliance to justify a trial.[4] ■

In the following case, the plaintiffs relied on the word *premium* and similar general terms in automobile advertisements as the basis for a claim against the automobile's manufacturer.

---

4. *T & M Solar and Air Conditioning, Inc. v. Lennox International, Inc.*, 83 F.Supp.3d 855 (N.D.Cal. 2015).

Spotlight on Nissan

Case 23.1 Hurst v. Nissan North America Inc.

Missouri Court of Appeals, Western District, __ S.W.3d __, 2016 WL 1128297 (2016).

Background and Facts Nissan North America, Inc., makes and sells Infiniti autos, including a sport utility vehicle called the FX. According to Nissan, its marketing brochures for the FX contain many statements that are meant to convey "an overall image of a very refined vehicle" and a promise of "premium automotive machinery."

Robert Hurst bought an Infiniti FX that, with other models made at the same time, developed dashboard bubbling. Hurst and other FX owners with bubbling dashboards filed a suit in a Missouri state court against the automaker under the Missouri Merchandising Practices Act (MMPA). The plaintiffs alleged that Nissan violated the MMPA by making representations in its brochures that were not in accord with the facts regarding the quality of the FX.

A jury issued a verdict in the plaintiffs' favor and awarded damages. Nissan filed a motion for a judgment notwithstanding the verdict, which the court denied. Nissan appealed, arguing that the alleged misrepresentations were not actionable statements of fact but puffery.

In the Language of the Court
JAMES EDWARD WELSH, Judge
* * * *

* * * The MMPA bars an "assertion that is not in accord with the facts," and deceptions in advertising that have a tendency "to create a false impression."

Many statements made in advertising, however, are not actionable statements of fact but are merely the puffing of wares, sales propaganda, or other expression of opinion. *A seller may puff his wares or express his opinion about the quality and value of his goods even to the point of exaggeration without incurring liability. Indeed, puffing of wares, sales propaganda, and other expressions of opinion are common, are permitted, and should be expected.* [Emphasis added.]

Puffing of wares and expressions of opinion are mutually exclusive from statements of fact. *A factual claim is a statement that (1) admits of being adjudged true or false in a way that (2) admits of empirical*

Case 23.1 Continued

verification. To be actionable, the statement must be a specific and measurable claim, capable of being proved false or of being reasonably interpreted as a statement of objective fact. Generally, opinions are not actionable. * * * If a statement is a specific, measurable claim or can be reasonably interpreted as being a factual claim, *i.e.,* one capable of verification, the statement is one of fact. Conversely, if the statement is not specific and measurable, and cannot be reasonably interpreted as providing a benchmark by which the veracity of the statement can be ascertained, the statement constitutes puffery. [Emphasis added.]

Thus, a pasta maker may declare that it is "America's Favorite Pasta" and Papa John's may proclaim "Better Ingredients. Better Pizza" without incurring liability. * * * Such statements are unquantifiable, not susceptible of exact knowledge, and are not capable of being proved false or of being reasonably interpreted as a statement of objective fact.

None of the statements that Hurst complains about are capable of being proved false or capable of being reasonably interpreted as a statement of objective fact. Statements that the FX was a "premium" vehicle with a "premium automotive experience," a "leader in style," a "luxury" car, a "superior product representing excellent value," and a vehicle of "uncompromising style and luxury" are classic examples of statements not susceptible of exact knowledge. They are very general statements and are not capable of being proved false or of being reasonably interpreted as a statement of objective fact. The advertising employed by Nissan was merely dealer's talk, trade talk, puffing of manufacturer's wares, and sales propaganda, and the statements used in the advertising were mere statements of opinion, promises, expectations, and estimates, which are not actionable.

Decision and Remedy *A state intermediate appellate court reversed the judgment of the lower court and remanded the case for the entry of a judgment in favor of Nissan. Hurst had not shown that Nissan made an actionable misrepresentation in its advertising for the FX. The statements Hurst relied on were not statements of fact but statements of opinion.*

Critical Thinking

- **Legal Environment** *The court in the* Nissan *case indicated that the word* premium *may be considered puffing when viewed in isolation. Is the term also puffing when considered in a broader context? Explain.*
- **What If the Facts Were Different?** *Suppose that the court in the* Nissan *case had held the defendant liable based on the statements in its marketing brochures. What impact would this holding likely have on the results in future cases? Discuss.*

23-3 Implied Warranties

An **implied warranty** is one that *the law derives* by inference from the nature of the transaction or the relative situations or circumstances of the parties. Under the UCC, merchants impliedly warrant that the goods they sell or lease are merchantable and, in certain circumstances, fit for a particular purpose. In addition, an implied warranty may arise from a course of dealing or usage of trade. These three types of implied warranties are illustrated in Exhibit 23–1 and examined in the following subsections.

23-3a Implied Warranty of Merchantability

Every sale or lease of goods made by a merchant who deals in goods of the kind sold or leased automatically gives rise to an **implied warranty of merchantability** [UCC 2–314, 2A–212]. Thus, a merchant who is in the business of selling ski equipment makes an implied warranty of merchantability every time he sells a pair of skis. A neighbor selling her skis at a garage sale does not (because she is not in the business of selling goods of this type).

Merchantable Goods To be *merchantable,* goods must be "reasonably fit for the ordinary purposes for which such goods are used." They must be of at least average, fair, or medium-grade quality. The quality must be comparable to quality that will pass without objection in the trade or market for goods of the same description. The warranty of merchantability may be breached even though the merchant did not know or could not have discovered that a product was defective (not merchantable).

To be merchantable, the goods must also be adequately packaged and labeled. In addition, they must

EXHIBIT 23–1 Types of Implied Warranties

conform to the promises or affirmations of fact made on the container or label, if any. Of course, merchants are not absolute insurers against *all* accidents arising in connection with the goods. A bar of soap is not unmerchantable merely because a user could slip and fall by stepping on it.

The implied warranty of merchantability may be breached when the warrantor has unsuccessfully attempted to repair or replace defective parts. ■ **CASE IN POINT 23.10** Ilan Brand leased a new Hyundai Genesis from Allen Hyundai. The next day, when he was driving on an interstate highway, the sunroof began opening and closing, although Brand was not pushing the sunroof buttons. He immediately returned the vehicle to the Hyundai dealer. He was told it had a defective sunroof switch, which would be repaired within 24 hours. In spite of the dealer's assurances, however, the problem was not repaired. Ten days later, Brand—who still had not been able to pick up the vehicle—attempted to rescind the lease. Hyundai would not allow him to do so.

Brand then filed an action for breach of the implied warranty of merchantability in state court. The trial court dismissed the case, but the appellate court reversed. The reviewing court held that a reasonable jury could conclude that the opening and closing of the sunroof constituted

a safety hazard and therefore breached the implied warranty of merchantability. The court remanded the case for a jury trial.[5] ■

Merchantable Food The serving of food or drink to be consumed on or off the premises is also treated as a sale of goods and subject to the implied warranty of merchantability [UCC 2–314(1)]. "Merchantable" food is food that is fit to eat.

Courts generally determine whether food is fit to eat on the basis of consumer expectations. Consumers should reasonably expect to find on occasion bones in fish fillets, cherry pits in cherry pie, a nutshell in a package of shelled nuts, and the like. Such substances are, after all, natural to the ingredients or the finished food product. In contrast, consumers would not reasonably expect to find an inchworm in a can of peas or a piece of glass in a soft drink.

In the following classic case, the court had to determine whether one should reasonably expect to find a fish bone in fish chowder.

---

5. *Brand v. Hyundai Motor America*, 226 Cal.App.4th 1538, 173 Cal.Rptr.3d 454 (4th Dist. 2014).

Webster v. Blue Ship Tea Room, Inc.

Supreme Judicial Court of Massachusetts, 347 Mass. 421 198 N.E.2d 309 (1964).

Background and Facts Blue Ship Tea Room, Inc., was located in Boston in an old building overlooking the ocean. Priscilla Webster, who had been born and raised in New England, went to the restaurant and ordered fish chowder. The chowder was milky in color. After three or four spoonfuls, she felt something lodged in her throat. As a result, she underwent two esophagoscopies (procedures in which an instrument is used to look into the throat). In the second esophagoscopy, a fish bone was found and removed. Webster filed a suit against the restaurant in a Massachusetts state court for breach of the implied warranty of merchantability. The jury rendered a verdict for Webster, and the restaurant appealed to the state's highest court.

In the Language of the Court

REARDON, Justice.

[The plaintiff] ordered a cup of fish chowder. Presently, there was set before her "a small bowl of fish chowder." * * * After 3 or 4 [spoonfuls] she was aware that something had lodged in her throat because she "couldn't swallow and couldn't clear her throat by gulping and she could feel it." This misadventure led to two esophagoscopies at the Massachusetts General Hospital, in the second of which, on April 27, 1959, a fish bone was found and removed. The sequence of events produced injury to the plaintiff which was not insubstantial.

We must decide whether a fish bone lurking in a fish chowder, about the ingredients of which there is no other complaint, constitutes a breach of implied warranty under applicable provisions of the Uniform Commercial Code * * * . As the judge put it in his charge [jury instruction], "Was the fish chowder fit to be eaten and wholesome? * * * Nobody is claiming that the fish itself wasn't wholesome. * * * But the bone of contention here—I don't mean that for a pun—but was this fish bone a foreign substance that made the fish chowder unwholesome or not fit to be eaten?"

* * * *

[We think that it] is not too much to say that a person sitting down in New England to consume a good New England fish chowder embarks on a gustatory [taste-related] adventure which may entail the removal of some fish bones from his bowl as he proceeds. We are not inclined to tamper with age-old recipes by any amendment reflecting the plaintiff's view of the effect of the Uniform Commercial Code upon them. We are aware of the heavy body of case law involving foreign substances in food, but we sense a strong distinction between them and those relative to unwholesomeness of the food itself, [for example,] tainted mackerel, and a fish bone in a fish chowder. * * * We consider that the joys of life in New England include the ready availability of fresh fish chowder. *We should be prepared to cope with the hazards of fish bones, the occasional presence of which in chowders is, it seems to us, to be anticipated, and which, in the light of a hallowed tradition, do not impair their fitness or merchantability.* [Emphasis added.]

Decision and Remedy *The Supreme Judicial Court of Massachusetts "sympathized with a plaintiff who has suffered a peculiarly New England injury" but entered a judgment for the defendant, Blue Ship Tea Room. A fish bone in fish chowder is not a breach of the implied warranty of merchantability.*

Impact of This Case on Today's Law *This classic case, phrased in memorable language, was an early application of the UCC's implied warranty of merchantability to food products. The case established the rule that consumers should expect to find, on occasion, elements of food products that are natural to the product (such as fish bones in fish chowder). Courts today still apply this rule.*

Critical Thinking

- **E-Commerce** *If Webster had made the chowder herself from a recipe that she had found on the Internet, could she have successfully brought an action against its author for a breach of the implied warranty of merchantability? Explain.*

23–3b Implied Warranty of Fitness for a Particular Purpose

The **implied warranty of fitness for a particular purpose** arises in the sale or lease of goods when a seller or lessor (merchant or nonmerchant) knows *both* of the following:

1. The particular purpose for which a buyer or lessee will use the goods.
2. That the buyer or lessee is relying on the skill and judgment of the seller or lessor to select suitable goods [UCC 2–315, 2A–213].

Particular versus Ordinary Purpose A "particular purpose" of the buyer or lessee differs from the "ordinary purpose for which goods are used" (merchantability). Goods can be merchantable but unfit for a particular purpose.

■ **EXAMPLE 23.11** Sheryl needs a gallon of paint to match the color of her living room walls—a light shade somewhere between coral and peach. She takes a sample to Sherwin-Williams and requests a gallon of paint of that color. Instead, the salesperson gives her a gallon of bright blue paint. Here, the salesperson has not breached any warranty of implied merchantability—the bright blue paint is of high quality and suitable for interior walls. The salesperson has breached an implied warranty of fitness for a particular purpose, though, because the paint is not the right color for Sheryl's purpose (to match her living room walls). ■

Knowledge and Reliance Requirements A seller or lessor need not have actual knowledge of the buyer's or lessee's particular purpose. It is sufficient if a seller or lessor "has reason to know" the purpose. For an implied warranty to be created, however, the buyer or lessee must have *relied* on the skill or judgment of the seller or lessor in selecting or furnishing suitable goods. Moreover, the seller or lessor must have reason to know that the buyer or lessee is relying on her or his judgment or skill.

■ **EXAMPLE 23.12** Carlos Fuentes tells Tyrone, a salesperson at GamerPC, that he is looking for a new PC, such as the Cyberpower Black Pearl or Velocity Raptor Signature Edition, to use for gaming. Fuentes's statement implies that he needs a PC with a video card that is capable of running fast-paced video games with detailed graphics. Tyrone recommends and sells to Carlos a computer that does not have a video card and is too slow to run such video games. By doing so, Tyrone has breached the implied warranty of fitness for a particular purpose. ■

23–3c Warranties Implied from Prior Dealings or Trade Custom

Implied warranties can also arise (or be excluded or modified) as a result of course of dealing or usage of trade [UCC 2–314(3), 2A–212(3)]. Without evidence to the contrary, when both parties to a sales or lease contract have knowledge of a well-recognized trade custom, the courts will infer that both parties intended for that custom to apply to their contract.

■ **EXAMPLE 23.13** Industry-wide custom is to lubricate a new car before it is delivered. If a dealer fails to lubricate a car, the dealer can be held liable to a buyer for damages resulting from the breach of an implied warranty. (This would also be negligence on the part of the dealer.) ■

23–3d Lemon Laws

Purchasers of defective automobiles—called "lemons"—may have remedies in addition to those offered by the UCC. All of the states and the District of Columbia have enacted *lemon laws*. Basically, state lemon laws provide remedies to consumers who buy automobiles that repeatedly fail to meet standards of quality and performance.

Although lemon laws vary by state, typically they apply to automobiles under warranty that are defective in a way that significantly affects the vehicle's value or use. Lemon laws do not necessarily cover used-car purchases (unless the car is covered by a manufacturer's extended warranty) or vehicles that are leased.[6]

Seller Has Had the Opportunity to Remedy Defect Generally, the car's owner must notify the dealer or manufacturer of the defect and give the dealer or manufacturer a number of opportunities to remedy it (usually four). If the seller fails to cure the problem despite a reasonable number of attempts (as specified by state law), the buyer may be entitled to a new car, replacement of defective parts, or return of all consideration paid. Buyers who prevail in a lemon-law dispute may also be entitled to reimbursement of their attorneys' fees.

Arbitration Often Required In many states, even after the dealer or manufacturer has failed to cure the defect, the owner cannot take the case directly to court.

---

6. Note that in some states, such as California, these laws may extend beyond automobile purchases and apply to other consumer goods.

Instead, the owner must submit the complaint to the arbitration program specified in the manufacturer's warranty.

Decisions by arbitration panels are binding on the manufacturer—that is, cannot be appealed by the manufacturer to the courts—but usually are not binding on the purchaser. Most major automobile companies operate their own arbitration panels. All arbitration boards must meet state and/or federal standards of impartiality, and some states have established mandatory government-sponsored arbitration programs for lemon-law disputes.

23–3e Magnuson-Moss Warranty Act

The Magnuson-Moss Warranty Act of 1975[7] was designed to prevent deception in warranties by making them easier to understand.

Applies Only to Consumer Transactions The Magnuson-Moss Warranty Act modifies UCC warranty rules to some extent when *consumer* transactions are involved. The UCC, however, remains the primary codification of warranty rules for commercial transactions.

Under the Magnuson-Moss Act, no seller is *required* to give a written warranty for consumer goods sold. If a seller chooses to make an express written warranty, however, and the cost of the consumer goods is more than $25, the warranty must be labeled as either "full" or "limited."

A *full warranty* requires free repair or replacement of any defective part. If the product cannot be repaired within a reasonable time, the consumer has the choice of a refund or a replacement without charge. A full warranty can be for an unlimited or a limited time period, such as a "full twelve-month warranty."

A *limited warranty* is one in which the buyer's recourse is limited in some fashion, such as to replacement of an item. The fact that only a limited warranty is being given must be conspicuously stated.

Requires Certain Disclosures The Magnuson-Moss Act further requires the warrantor to make certain disclosures fully and conspicuously in a single document in "readily understood language." The seller must disclose the name and address of the warrantor, specifically what is warranted, and the procedures for enforcing the warranty. The seller must also clarify that the buyer has legal rights and explain limitations on warranty relief.

---

7. 15 U.S.C. Sections 2301–2312.

23–4 Overlapping Warranties

Sometimes, two or more warranties are made in a single transaction. An implied warranty of merchantability, an implied warranty of fitness for a particular purpose, or both can exist in addition to an express warranty. ■ **EXAMPLE 23.14** A sales contract for a new car states that "this car engine is warranted to be free from defects for 36,000 miles or thirty-six months, whichever occurs first." This statement creates an express warranty against all defects, as well as an implied warranty that the car will be fit for normal use. ■

23–4a When the Warranties Are Consistent

The rule under the UCC is that express and implied warranties are construed as *cumulative* if they are consistent with one another [UCC 2–317, 2A–215]. In other words, courts interpret two or more warranties as being in agreement with each other unless this construction is unreasonable. If it is unreasonable for the two warranties to be consistent, then the court looks at the intention of the parties to determine which warranty is dominant.

23–4b Conflicting Warranties

If the warranties are *inconsistent,* the courts usually apply the following rules to interpret which warranty is most important:

1. *Express* warranties displace inconsistent *implied* warranties, except implied warranties of fitness for a particular purpose.
2. Samples take precedence over inconsistent general descriptions.
3. Exact or technical specifications displace inconsistent samples or general descriptions.

■ **EXAMPLE 23.15** Innova, Ltd., leases a high-speed server from Vernon Sources. The contract contains an express warranty concerning the speed of the CPU and the application programs that the server is capable of running. Innova does not realize that the speed expressly warranted in the contract is insufficient for its needs until it tries to run the software and the server slows to a crawl.

Because Innova made it clear that it was leasing the server to perform certain tasks, Innova files an action against Vernon for breach of the implied warranty of fitness for a particular purpose. In this situation, Innova normally will prevail. Although the express warranty on CPU speed takes precedence over the implied warranty of merchantability, it normally does not take precedence over an implied warranty of fitness for a particular purpose. ■

23-5 Warranty Disclaimers and Limitations on Liability

The UCC generally permits warranties to be disclaimed or limited by specific and unambiguous language, provided that this is done in a manner that protects the buyer or lessee from surprise. Because each type of warranty is created in a different way, the manner in which a seller or lessor can disclaim warranties varies with the type of warranty.

23-5a Express Warranties

A seller or lessor can disclaim all oral express warranties by including in the contract a written disclaimer. The disclaimer must be in language that is clear and conspicuous and must be called to a buyer's or lessee's attention [UCC 2–316(1), 2A–214(1)]. This allows the seller or lessor to avoid false allegations that oral warranties were made. It also ensures that only representations made by properly authorized individuals are included in the bargain.

Note that a buyer or lessee must be made aware of any warranty disclaimers or modifications *at the time the contract is formed.* In other words, the seller or lessor cannot modify any warranties or disclaimers made during the bargaining process without the consent of the buyer or lessee.

23-5b Implied Warranties

Normally, unless circumstances indicate otherwise, the implied warranties of merchantability and fitness are disclaimed by an expression such as "as is" or "with all faults." Both parties must be able to clearly understand from the language used that there are no implied warranties [UCC 2–316(3)(a), 2A–214(3)(a)]. (Note, however, that some states have passed consumer protection statutes that forbid "as is" sales or make it illegal to disclaim warranties of merchantability on consumer goods.)

■ **CASE IN POINT 23.16** Mandy Morningstar advertised a "lovely, eleven-year-old mare" with extensive jumping ability for sale. After examining the horse twice, Sue Hallett contracted to buy the horse. She signed a contract that described the horse as an eleven-year-old mare being sold "as is." Shortly after the purchase, a veterinarian determined that the horse was actually sixteen years old and in no condition for jumping. Hallett stopped payment, and Morningstar filed a lawsuit for breach of contract.

The court held that the statement in the contract describing the horse as eleven years old constituted an express warranty, which Morningstar had breached. The "as is" clause effectively disclaimed any implied warranties (of merchantability and fitness for a particular purpose, such as jumping). It did not, however, disclaim the express warranty concerning the horse's age.[8] ■

In the following case, the court explained the rationale behind the effect of an "as is" clause.

---

8. *Morningstar v. Hallett*, 858 A.2d 125 (Pa.Super.Ct. 2004).

Case Analysis 23.3

Roberts v. Lanigan Auto Sales

Court of Appeals of Kentucky, 406 S.W.3d 882 (2013).

In the Language of the Court

VANMETER, Judge:

* * * *

* * * [Evan] Roberts purchased a used vehicle from Lanigan [Auto Sales] in September 2009. Roberts and Lanigan executed a purchase contract, which contained a clause stating the vehicle is "sold as is * * * without any guarantee express or implied." Following the purchase, Roberts independently obtained a report which indicated that the vehicle had previously been involved in an accident and

suffered damage to the undercarriage of the vehicle.

Roberts filed the underlying action [in a Kentucky state court] alleging that Lanigan * * * committed fraud by omitting, suppressing, and concealing the vehicle's prior damage and accident history in order to induce Roberts into purchasing the vehicle. Lanigan maintained it never represented that the vehicle had not been damaged or involved in a wreck and filed a * * * motion to dismiss the action for failure to state a claim upon

which relief can be granted. * * * The trial court * * * dismissed Roberts' action on the basis that the purchase contract, which contained the express term "sold as is," barred his action for fraud. This appeal followed.

On appeal, Roberts argues the trial court erred by dismissing his action because the "sold as is" clause in the purchase contract did not bar his action for fraud. We disagree.

* * * *

Case 23.3 Continued

[Kentucky Revised Statute] 355.2–316 [Kentucky's version of UCC 2–316] seeks to provide a structure for construing both oral representations and written disclaimers within an agreement for the sale of goods. To carry out that purpose, the statute provides that, "unless the circumstances indicate otherwise, all implied warranties are excluded by expressions like 'as is,' 'with all faults' or other language which in common understanding calls the buyer's attention to the exclusion of warranties."

* * * *An "as is" clause in a sales contract is understood to mean that the buyer takes the entire risk as to the quality of the goods involved. * * * A valid "as is" agreement prevents a buyer from holding a seller liable if the thing sold turns out to be worth less than the price paid, because it is impossible for the buyer's injury on account of this disparity to have been caused by the seller and the sole cause of the buyer's injury is the buyer himself or herself.* Thus, by agreeing to purchase something "as is," a buyer agrees to make his or her own appraisal of the bargain and to accept the risk that he or she may

be wrong, and the seller gives no assurances, express or implied, concerning the value or condition of the thing sold. [Emphasis added.]

In an action for fraud, a party must prove by clear and convincing evidence that (1) the seller made a material misrepresentation to the buyer, (2) which was false, (3) known by the seller to be false, (4) made with the intent to be relied upon, (5) was reasonably relied upon and (6) caused injury. Here, Roberts executed a written sales contract which stated the car was "sold as is" and acknowledging, "I hereby make this purchase knowingly without any guarantee expressed or implied by this dealer or his agent." * * * The effect of the "sold as is" clause is to shift the assumption of risk regarding the value or condition of the vehicle to Roberts despite any express or implied warranties that were made by Lanigan. Since the only claimed injury concerns the value or condition of the car sold, and because the sole cause of such an injury is the buyer himself, Roberts is unable to prove that the seller's representation caused the injury.

Furthermore, by agreeing to buy the vehicle "as is," Roberts agreed to make his own assessment of the condition of the vehicle in spite of Lanigan's representations. Thus, he cannot later claim that he reasonably relied on those representations when agreeing to purchase the vehicle.

This is not to say that an "as is" clause bars any claim of fraud; when circumstances indicate otherwise, express or implied warranties may not be disclaimed by a written contract. Different circumstances could support an action for fraud despite an "as is" clause when the injury results in consequential damages, [that is,] injury to a person or property as a result of a breach of warranty, rather than an injury as a result of decreased value of the goods. Our holding here merely follows the rationale that an "as is" clause transfers the risk to the buyer that the condition or value of the goods is not what the seller represents. In accordance with that rationale, the trial court did not err by dismissing Roberts' action.

The order of the [trial court] is affirmed.

Legal Reasoning Questions

1. What language in a sales contract excludes all implied warranties?

2. How does an "as is" clause in a sales contract affect the bargain between the buyer and the seller?

3. In this case, what did the court rule on the effect of the "as is" clause? Why?

Disclaimer of the Implied Warranty of Merchantability To specifically disclaim an implied warranty of merchantability, a seller or lessor must mention the word *merchantability*. The disclaimer need not be written, but if it is, the writing must be conspicuous [UCC 2–316(2), 2A–214(4)].

Under the UCC, a term or clause is conspicuous when it is written or displayed in such a way that a reasonable person would notice it. Conspicuous terms include words set in capital letters, in a larger font size, or in a different color so as to be set off from the surrounding text.

Disclaimer of the Implied Warranty of Fitness
To disclaim an implied warranty of fitness for a particular

purpose, the disclaimer must be in a writing and must be conspicuous. The writing does not have to mention the word *fitness*. It is sufficient if, for instance, the disclaimer states, "There are no warranties that extend beyond the description on the face hereof."

23–5c Buyer's or Lessee's Examination or Refusal to Inspect

If a buyer or lessee examines the goods (or a sample or model) as fully as desired, there is no implied warranty with respect to defects that are found or that could be found on a reasonable examination [UCC 2–316(3)(b), 2A–214(2)(b)]. Also, if a buyer or lessee refuses to examine the goods on the seller's or lessor's request that he or she do so, there is no implied warranty with respect to reasonably evident defects.

■ **EXAMPLE 23.17** Janna buys a table at Gershwin's Home Store. No express warranties are made. Gershwin asks Janna to inspect the table before buying it, but she refuses. Had Janna inspected the table, she would have noticed that one of its legs was obviously cracked, which made it unstable. Janna takes the table home and sets a lamp on it. The table later collapses, and the lamp starts a fire that causes significant damage. Janna normally will not be able to hold Gershwin's liable for breach of the warranty of merchantability, because she refused to examine the table as Gershwin requested. Janna therefore assumed the risk that the table was defective. ■

23-5d Warranty Disclaimers and Unconscionability

The UCC sections dealing with warranty disclaimers do not refer specifically to unconscionability as a factor.

Ultimately, however, the courts will test warranty disclaimers with reference to the UCC's unconscionability standards [UCC 2–302, 2A–108]. Factors such as lack of bargaining position, "take-it-or-leave-it" choices, and a buyer's or lessee's failure to understand or know of a warranty disclaimer will be relevant to the issue of unconscionability.

23-5e Statutes of Limitations

A cause of action for breach of contract under the UCC must be commenced within four years after the breach occurs (unless the parties agree to a shorter period). An action for breach of warranty accrues when the seller or lessor *tenders* delivery, even if the buyer or lessee is unaware of the breach at that time [UCC 2–725(2), 2A–506(2)]. In addition, the nonbreaching party usually must notify the breaching party within a reasonable time after discovering the breach or be barred from pursuing any remedy [UCC 2–607(3)(a), 2A–516(3)].

Reviewing: Warranties

Shalene Kolchek bought a Great Lakes spa from Val Porter, a dealer who was selling spas at the state fair. Porter told Kolchek that Great Lakes spas were "top of the line" and "the Cadillac of spas." He also indicated that the spa she was buying was "fully warranted for three years." Kolchek signed an installment contract. Then, Porter handed her the manufacturer's paperwork and arranged for the spa to be delivered and installed for her. Three months later, Kolchek noticed that one corner of the spa was leaking onto her new deck and causing damage. She complained to Porter, but he did nothing about the problem. Kolchek's family continued to use the spa. Using the information presented in the chapter, answer the following questions.

1. Did Porter's statement that the spa was "top of the line" and "the Cadillac of spas" create any type of warranty? Why or why not?
2. If the paperwork provided to Kolchek after her purchase indicated that the spa had no warranty, would this be an effective disclaimer under the Uniform Commercial Code? Explain.
3. Can Kolchek sue Porter for breach of the implied warranty of merchantability because the spa leaked? Explain.
4. Suppose that one year later, Pacific Credit Union contacted Kolchek and claimed that it had a security interest in the spa. Would this be a breach of any of the title warranties discussed in the chapter? Explain.

Debate This . . . *No express warranties should be created by the oral statements made by salespersons about a product.*

Terms and Concepts

express warranty 426	implied warranty of fitness for a	implied warranty of
implied warranty 429	particular purpose 432	merchantability 429

Issue Spotters

1. General Construction Company (GCC) tells Industrial Supplies, Inc., that it needs an adhesive to do a particular job. Industrial provides a five-gallon bucket of a certain brand. When it does not perform to GCC's specifications, GCC sues Industrial, which claims, "We didn't expressly promise anything." What should GCC argue? (See *Implied Warranties.*)

2. Stella bought a cup of coffee at the Roasted Bean Drive-Thru. The coffee had been heated to 190 degrees and consequently had dissolved the inside of the cup. When Stella lifted the lid, the cup collapsed, spilling the contents on her lap. To recover for third-degree burns on her thighs, Stella filed a suit against the Roasted Bean. Can Stella recover for breach of the implied warranty of merchantability? Why or why not? (See *Implied Warranties.*)

- **Check your answers to the Issue Spotters against the answers provided in Appendix D at the end of this text.**

Business Scenarios

23–1. Implied Warranties. Moon, a farmer, needs to install a two-thousand-pound piece of equipment in his barn. This will require lifting the equipment thirty feet up into a hayloft. Moon goes to Davidson Hardware and tells Davidson that he needs some heavy-duty rope to be used on his farm. Davidson recommends a one-inch-thick nylon rope, and Moon purchases two hundred feet of it. Moon ties the rope around the piece of equipment; puts the rope through a pulley; and, with a tractor, lifts the equipment off the ground. Suddenly, the rope breaks. The equipment crashes to the ground and is severely damaged. Moon files a suit against Davidson for breach of the implied warranty of fitness for a particular purpose. Discuss how successful Moon will be in his suit. (See *Implied Warranties.*)

23–2. Warranty Disclaimers. Tandy purchased a washing machine from Marshall Appliances. The sales contract included a provision explicitly disclaiming all express or implied warranties, including the implied warranty of merchantability. The disclaimer was printed in the same size and color as the rest of the contract. The machine never functioned properly. Tandy sought a refund of the purchase price, claiming that Marshall had breached the implied warranty of merchantability. Can Tandy recover the purchase price, notwithstanding the warranty disclaimer in the contract? Explain. (See *Warranty Disclaimers and Limitations on Liability.*)

Business Case Problems

23–3. Express Warranties. Videotape is recorded magnetically. The magnetic particles that constitute the recorded image are bound to the tape's polyester base. The binder that holds the particles to the base breaks down over time. This breakdown, which is called *sticky shed syndrome,* causes the image to deteriorate. The Walt Disney Co. made many of its movies available on tape. Buena Vista Home Entertainment, Inc., sold the tapes, which it described as part of a "Gold Collection" or "Masterpiece Collection." The advertising included such statements as "Give Your Children the memories of a lifetime—Collect Each Timeless Masterpiece!" and "Available for a Limited Time Only!"

Charmaine Schreib and others who bought the tapes filed a suit in an Illinois state court against Disney and Buena Vista, alleging, among other things, breach of warranty. The plaintiffs claimed that the defendants' marketing promised the tapes would last for generations. In reality, the tapes were as subject to sticky shed syndrome as other tapes. Did the ads create an express warranty? In whose favor should the court rule on this issue? Explain. [*Schreib v. Walt Disney Co.,* 2006 WL 573008 (Ill.App. 1 Dist. 2006)] (See *Express Warranties.*)

23–4. Implied Warranties. Peter and Tanya Rothing operated Diamond R Stables near Belgrade, Montana, where they bred, trained, and sold horses. Arnold Kallestad owned a ranch in Gallatin County, Montana, where he grew hay and grain, and raised Red Angus cattle. For more than twenty years, Kallestad had sold between three hundred and one thousand tons of hay annually, sometimes advertising it for sale in the *Bozeman Daily Chronicle.* In 2001, the Rothings bought hay from Kallestad for $90 a ton. They received delivery on April 23. In less than two weeks, at least nine of the Rothings' horses exhibited symptoms of poisoning that was diagnosed as botulism. Before the outbreak was over, nineteen animals had died. Robert Whitlock, associate professor of medicine and the director of the Botulism Laboratory at the University of Pennsylvania, concluded that Kallestad's hay was the source. The Rothings filed a suit in a Montana state court against Kallestad, claiming, in part, breach of the implied warranty of merchantability. Kallestad asked the court to dismiss this claim on the ground that, if botulism had been present, it had been in no way foreseeable. Should the court grant this request? Why or why not? [*Rothing v.*

Kallestad, 337 Mont. 193, 159 P.3d 222 (2007)] (See *Implied Warranties.*)

23–5. Spotlight on Apple—Implied Warranties.

Alan Vitt purchased an iBook G4 laptop computer from Apple, Inc. Shortly after the one-year warranty expired, the laptop failed to work due to a weakness in the product manufacture. Vitt sued Apple, arguing that the laptop should have lasted "at least a couple of years," which Vitt believed was a reasonable consumer expectation for a laptop. Vitt claimed that Apple's descriptions of the laptop as "durable," "rugged," "reliable," and "high performance" were affirmative statements concerning the quality and performance of the laptop, which Apple did not meet. How should the court rule? Why? [*Vitt v. Apple Computer, Inc.,* 469 Fed.Appx. 605 (9th Cir. 2011)] (See *Implied Warranties.*)

23–6. Business Case Problem with Sample Answer—Implied Warranties.

Bariven, S.A., agreed to buy 26,000 metric tons of powdered milk for $123.5 million from Absolute Trading Corp. to be delivered in shipments from China to Venezuela. After the first three shipments, China halted dairy exports due to the presence of melamine in some products. Absolute assured Bariven that its milk was safe, and when China resumed dairy exports, Absolute delivered sixteen more shipments. Tests of samples of the milk revealed that it contained dangerous levels of melamine. Did Absolute breach any implied warranties? Discuss. [*Absolute Trading Corp. v. Bariven S.A.,* 503 Fed.Appx. 694 (11th Cir. 2013)] (See *Implied Warranties.*)

- **For a sample answer to Problem 23–6, go to Appendix E at the end of this text.**

23–7. Express Warranties.
Charity Bell bought a used Toyota Avalon from Awny Gobran of Gobran Auto Sales, Inc. The odometer showed that the car had been driven 147,000 miles. Bell asked whether it had been in any accidents. Gobran replied that it was in good condition. The parties signed a warranty disclaimer that the vehicle was sold "as is." Problems with the car arose the same day as the purchase. Gobran made a few ineffectual attempts to repair it before refusing to do more. Meanwhile, Bell obtained a vehicle history report from Carfax, which showed that the Avalon had been damaged in an accident and that its last reported odometer reading was 237,271. Was the "as is" disclaimer sufficient to put Bell on notice that the odometer reading could be false and that the car might have been in an accident? Can Gobran avoid any liability that might otherwise be imposed because Bell did not obtain the Carfax report until *after* she bought the car? Discuss. [*Gobran Auto Sales Inc. v. Bell,* 335 Ga.App. 873, 783 S.E.2d 389 (2016)] (See *Warranty Disclaimers and Limitations on Liability.*)

23–8. A Question of Ethics—Lemon Laws.

Randal Schweiger bought a 2008 Kia Spectra EX from Kia Motors America, Inc., for his stepdaughter, April Kirichkow. The cost was $17,231, plus sales tax, fees, and other items. April had trouble starting the car. The Kia dealership replaced various parts of the motor several times but was unable to fix the problem. Schweiger sought a refund under the state's lemon law. When they could not agree on the amount, Schweiger filed a suit in a Wisconsin state court against Kia. From a judgment in Schweiger's favor, Kia appealed. [Schweiger v. Kia Motors America, Inc., *347 Wis.2d 550, 830 N.W.2d 723 (2013)]* (See *Implied Warranties.*)

(a) Kia offered a refund of $3,306.24. Should this offer bar Schweiger's claim for a refund? Why or why not?

(b) Schweiger claimed that Kia's offer did not include the $1,301 cost of a service contract. Kia argued that the "payoff to the lender" of $13,060.16, which Schweiger agreed was the correct amount, "would by definition refund the cost of the service contract." The court found "no logical basis" for this argument. Is it ethical for a party to argue a position for which there is no logical basis? Discuss.

Legal Reasoning Group Activity

23–9. Warranties.
Milan purchased saffron extract, marketed as "America's Hottest New Way to a Flat Belly," online from Dr. Chen. The Web site stated that recently published studies showed a significant weight loss (more than 25 percent) for people who used pure saffron extract as a supplement *without diet and exercise.* Dr. Chen said that the saffron suppresses appetite by increasing levels of serotonin, which reduces emotional eating. Milan took the extract as directed without any resulting weight loss. (See *Express Warranties.*)

(a) The first group will determine whether Dr. Chen's Web site made any express warranty on the saffron extract or its effectiveness in causing weight loss.

(b) The second group will discuss whether the implied warranty of merchantability applies to the purchase of weight-loss supplements.

(c) The third group will decide if Dr. Chen's sale of saffron extract breached the implied warranty of fitness for a particular purpose.

Answers to the *Issue Spotters*

1. **When it does not perform to GCC's specifications, GCC sues Industrial, which claims, "We didn't expressly promise anything." What should GCC argue?** The buyer should argue that the seller breached an implied warranty of fitness for a particular purpose. An implied warranty of fitness for a particular purpose arises when a seller knows a particular purpose for which a buyer will use goods and that the buyer is relying on the seller's skill and judgment to select suitable goods.

2. **Can Stella recover for breach of the implied warranty of merchantability? Why or why not?** Yes, Stella can recover from Roasted Bean for breach of the implied warranty of merchant-ability. An implied warranty of merchantability arises in every sale of goods sold by a merchant who deals in goods of the kind. Goods that are merchantable are fit for the ordinary purposes for which such goods are used. A sale of food or drink is a sale of goods. Merchantable food is food that is fit to eat or drink on the basis of consumer expectations. A consumer should reasonably expect hot coffee to be hot, but not to be so scalding that it causes third-degree burns.

Sample Answers for *Business Case Problems with Sample Answer*

Problem 23–6. *Implied Warranties.* Yes, Absolute breached the implied warranties of merchantability and fitness for a particular purpose. Under the UCC, merchants impliedly warrant that the goods they sell or lease are merchantable and, in certain circumstances, fit for a particular purpose. To be merchant-able, goods must be "reasonably fit for the ordinary purposes for which such goods are used." They must be at least average, fair, or medium-grade quality—quality that will pass without objection in the trade or market for the goods. For example, merchantable food is food that is fit to eat. To be fit for a particular purpose, the seller must know (or have reason to know) the purpose for which the buyer will use the goods and that the buyer is relying on the judgment of the seller to select suitable goods.

In this problem, Bariven agreed to buy 26,000 metric tons of powdered milk for $123.5 million from Absolute Trading Corp. to be delivered in shipments from China to Venezuela. Absolute assured Bariven that its milk was safe, but tests of samples of the milk revealed that it contained dangerous levels of melamine. This is not quality that will pass without objection in the market for the goods. Nor is milk contaminated with melamine "reasonably fit for the ordinary purposes for which such goods are used." The value of the milk as food was impaired because it was potentially lethal and thus not fit to be consumed. Absolute had reason to know the purpose for which Bariven bought the milk and that the buyer was relying on Absolute to select safe milk. In view of the potential hazards and liabilities of the contaminated milk, Absolute was in breach of the implied warranties of merchantability and fitness for a particular purpose.

In the actual case on which this problem is based, Bariven revoked its acceptance of the first nineteen shipments of the milk and canceled the twentieth. From a decision against Absolute in its suit against Bariven, the seller appealed. The U.S. Court of Appeals for the Eleventh Circuit affirmed. Bariven's revocation was not invalid because "the value of the milk was impaired."

Agency and Employment

BUSINESS LAW

CLARKSON · MILLER · CROSS

CHAPTER

Agency Formation and Duties

One of the most common, important, and pervasive legal relationships is that of **agency.** In an agency relationship involving two parties, one of the parties, called the *agent,* agrees to represent or act for the other, called the *principal.* The principal has the right to control the agent's conduct in matters entrusted to the agent.

Agency relationships are crucial in the business world. By using agents, a principal can conduct multiple business operations at the same time in different locations. Indeed, the only way that certain business entities can function is through their agents. For instance, a corporate officer is an agent who serves in a representative capacity for the corporation. The officer has the authority to bind the corporation to a contract. Only through its officers can corporations enter into contracts.

Most employees are also considered to be agents of their employers.

Today, however, the United States is experiencing a trend toward a so-called *gig economy,* which centers on short-term, independent workers who are not employees. Companies like Uber and Lyft (discussed in this chapter's feature) provide evidence of this trend. This type of on-demand employment raises questions related to agency, making agency an increasingly important topic for students of business law and the legal environment to understand.

32–1 Agency Relationships

Section 1(1) of the *Restatement (Third) of Agency*[1] defines *agency* as "the fiduciary relation [that] results from the manifestation of consent by one person to another that the other shall act in his [or her] behalf and subject to his [or her] control, and consent by the other so to act." In other words, in a principal-agent relationship, the parties have agreed that the agent will act *on behalf and instead of* the principal in negotiating and transacting business with third parties.

The term **fiduciary** is at the heart of agency law. This term can be used both as a noun and as an adjective. When used as a noun, it refers to a person having a duty created by his or her undertaking to act primarily for another's benefit in matters connected with the undertaking. When used as an adjective, as in the phrase *fiduciary relationship,* it means that the relationship involves trust and confidence.

Agency relationships commonly exist between employers and employees. Agency relationships may sometimes also exist between employers and independent contractors who are hired to perform special tasks or services.

32–1a Employer-Employee Relationships

Normally, all employees who deal with third parties are deemed to be agents. A salesperson in a department store, for instance, is an agent of the store's owner (the principal) and acts on the owner's behalf. Any sale of goods made by the salesperson to a customer is binding on the principal. Similarly, most representations of fact made by the salesperson with respect to the goods sold are binding on the principal.

Because employees who deal with third parties generally are deemed to be agents of their employers, agency law and employment law overlap considerably. Agency relationships, however, can exist outside

---

1. The *Restatement (Third) of Agency* is an authoritative summary of the law of agency and is often referred to by judges in their decisions and opinions.

an employer-employee relationship, so agency law has a broader reach than employment law. Additionally, agency law is based on the common law, whereas much employment law is statutory law.

Employment laws (state and federal) apply only to the employer-employee relationship. Statutes governing Social Security, withholding taxes, workers' compensation, unemployment compensation, workplace safety, and employment discrimination apply only if an employer-employee relationship exists. *These laws do not apply to independent contractors.*

32–1b Employer–Independent Contractor Relationships

Independent contractors are not employees because, by definition, those who hire them have no control over the details of their work performance. Section 2 of the *Restatement (Third) of Agency* defines an **independent contractor** as follows:

> [An independent contractor is] a person who contracts with another to do something for him [or her] but who is not controlled by the other nor subject to the other's right to control with respect to his [or her] physical conduct in the performance of the undertaking. He [or she] may or may not be an agent.

Building contractors and subcontractors are independent contractors. A property owner who hires a contractor and subcontractors to complete a project does not control the details of the way they perform their work. Truck drivers who own their vehicles and hire out on a per-job basis are independent contractors, but truck drivers who drive company trucks on a regular basis usually are employees. See this chapter's *Ethics Today* feature for a discussion of disputes involving the classification of drivers working for Uber and Lyft.

The relationship between a principal and an independent contractor may or may not involve an agency relationship. To illustrate: A homeowner who hires a real estate broker to sell her house has contracted with an independent contractor (the broker). The homeowner has also established an agency relationship with the broker for the specific purpose of selling the property. Another example is an insurance agent, who is both an independent contractor and an agent of the insurance company for which he sells policies. (Note that an insurance *broker*, in contrast, normally is an agent of the person obtaining insurance and not of the insurance company.)

32–1c Determination of Employee Status

The courts are frequently asked to determine whether a particular worker is an employee or an independent contractor. How a court decides this issue can have a significant effect on the rights and liabilities of the parties. Employers are required to pay certain taxes, such as Social Security and unemployment taxes, for employees but not for independent contractors. Therefore, workers may benefit from obtaining employee status in some situations.

Criteria Used by the Courts In deciding whether a worker is categorized as an employee or an independent contractor, courts often consider the following questions:

1. *How much control does the employer exercise over the details of the work?* If the employer exercises considerable control over the details of the work and the day-to-day activities of the worker, this indicates employee status. This is perhaps the most important factor weighed by the courts in determining employee status.
2. *Is the worker engaged in an occupation or business distinct from that of the employer?* If so, this points to independent-contractor, not employee, status.
3. *Is the work usually done under the employer's direction or by a specialist without supervision?* If the work is usually done under the employer's direction, this indicates employee status.
4. *Does the employer supply the tools at the place of work?* If so, this indicates employee status.
5. *For how long is the person employed?* If the person is employed for a long period of time, this indicates employee status.
6. *What is the method of payment—by time period or at the completion of the job?* Payment by time period, such as once every two weeks or once a month, indicates employee status.
7. *What degree of skill is required of the worker?* If a great degree of skill is required, this may indicate that the person is an independent contractor hired for a specialized job and not an employee.

Whether a worker is an employee or an independent contractor can affect the employer's liability for the worker's actions. An employer normally is not responsible for the actions of an independent contractor. In the following case, the court had to determine the status of an auto service company and its tow truck driver who assaulted the passenger of a vehicle the company had been hired to tow.

Coker v. Pershad

Superior Court of New Jersey, Appellate Division, 2013 WL 1296271 (2013).

Background and Facts AAA North Jersey, Inc., contracted with Five Star Auto Service to perform towing and auto repair services for AAA. Terence Pershad, the driver of a tow truck for Five Star, responded to a call to AAA for assistance by the driver of a car involved in an accident in Hoboken, New Jersey. Pershad got into a fight with Nicholas Coker, a passenger in the car, and assaulted Coker with a knife.

Coker filed a suit in a New Jersey state court against Pershad, Five Star, and AAA. The court determined that Pershad was Five Star's employee and that Five Star was an independent contractor, not AAA's employee. Thus, AAA was "not responsible for the alleged negligence of its independent contractor, defendant Five Star, in hiring Mr. Pershad." Five Star entered into a settlement with Coker. Coker appealed the ruling in AAA's favor.

In the Language of the Court

PER CURIAM.

* * * *

The important difference between an employee and an independent contractor is that one who hires an independent contractor has no right of control over the manner in which the work is to be done. [Emphasis added.]

* * * *

* * * Plaintiff [Coker] argues AAA controlled the means and method of the work performed by Five Star. * * * Factors * * * [that] determine whether a principal maintains the right of control over an individual or a corporation claimed to be an independent contractor [include]:

   (a) the extent of control which, by the agreement, the master may exercise over the details of the work;

   (b) whether or not the one employed is engaged in a distinct occupation or business;

   (c) the kind of occupation, with reference to whether, in the locality, the work is usually done under the direction of the employer or by a specialist without supervision;

   (d) the skill required in the particular occupation;

   (e) whether the employer or the workman supplies the * * * tools * * * ;

   (f) the length of time for which the person is employed * * * .

Applying these factors to the facts of this case, it is clear AAA did not control the manner and means of Five Star's work. The Agreement specifically stated Five Star was an independent contractor. Five Star purchased its own trucks and any other necessary equipment. AAA assigned jobs to Five Star and Five Star completed the work without any further supervision by AAA. Five Star chose the employees to send on towing calls and the trucks and equipment the employees would use.

Five Star was also in business for itself and performed auto repair services for principals and customers other than AAA. Five Star hired and fired its own employees * * * .

* * * *

Plaintiff also argues Five Star should be considered to be controlled by AAA because "providing towing and other roadside assistance is arguably the focus of the regular business of AAA." * * * [But] AAA is an automobile club that provides a wide variety of services to its members. It contracts with numerous service providers, such as gas stations, motels and other businesses, to provide these services. Thus, AAA is not solely in the towing business.

* * * AAA had used Five Star to provide towing services for approximately eight years and there is nothing in the record to demonstrate it lacked the skill needed to provide these services.

Decision and Remedy *A state intermediate appellate court affirmed the lower court's ruling. AAA could not be held liable for the actions of Five Star, its independent contractor, because "AAA did not control the manner and means of Five Star's work."*

Critical Thinking

- **Legal** *Five Star's contract with AAA required Five Star to be available to provide service for AAA members. Does this support Coker's argument that Five Star was AAA's employee? Why or why not?*

ETHICS TODAY

Is It Fair to Classify Uber and Lyft Drivers as Independent Contractors?

The transportation-for-hire world has changed dramatically since Uber, Lyft, and other transportation-sharing companies came onto the scene. Uber started in San Francisco in 2009. Today, its services are available in one form or another in about 60 countries and more than 300 cities worldwide. Its main competitor, Lyft, was launched in 2012 and operates in more than 200 U.S. cities. The growth in transportation sharing has not been without its set-backs, though. Most of them involve laws that have prohibited Uber and Lyft from operating in certain cities, as well as lawsuits by drivers claiming that they were misclassified.

Classification of Workers

Workers in the United States generally fall into two categories: employees and independent contractors. Employment laws, including minimum wage and anti-discrimination statutes, cover employees. Such laws do not cover most independent contractors. Enter the digital age of on-demand workers who obtain job assignments via apps.

Workers for Lyft, Uber, and similar companies choose when and where they will perform their duties. They do not choose how much they will be paid, however. For them, employment is a take-it-or-leave-it proposition. They electronically accept the platform terms of the apps, or they obtain no work assignments.

Some critics of this contractual system argue that there should be a new category of workers with "dependent-contractor" status who receive some of the protections traditionally given only to employees. Certain aspects of current labor law would be attached to the relationships between dependent contractors and their employers.

Worker Misclassification Lawsuits

A number of former or current Uber and Lyft drivers have pursued legal remedies to change their job classification and to obtain better benefits. In California, for instance, two federal court judges allowed separate lawsuits to go before juries on the question of whether on-demand drivers should be considered employees rather than independent contractors.[a]

In a similar case, rather than go to court, Lyft settled a worker misclassification lawsuit for $12.25 million. The suit, which was settled in 2016, had been brought in 2013. The settlement did not achieve a reclassification of Lyft drivers as employees. Basically, Lyft agreed to change its terms of service to conform to California's independent contractor status regulations. For instance, the company can no longer deactivate drivers' accounts without reason and without warning the drivers. Drivers have to be given a fair hearing first. Even though the lawsuit and the agreement were California based, the new terms of service will apply to all Lyft's drivers nationwide.

Competitors Sue Uber

In many cities, competitors, especially taxi drivers, have sued Uber. These lawsuits have involved claims of unfair competition, lack of minimum wages, and unsafe vehicles. A taxi driver sued Uber in northern California, for instance, but a federal district court ruled in favor of Uber's request for summary judgment.[b]

Another suit was brought in Pennsylvania. In this one, Checker Cab of Philadelphia claimed that Uber was violating Pennsylvania's unfair competition law. Checker Cab sought a preliminary injunction to prevent Uber from taking away its customers. The federal district court refused to grant an injunction, however, because Checker Cab failed to show irreparable harm. That decision was upheld on appeal.[c]

Critical Thinking *What choices do disgruntled Uber and Lyft drivers have?*

a. *Cotter v. Lyft, Inc.,* 60 F.Supp.3d 1067 (N.D.Cal. 2015); *O'Connor v. Uber Technologies, Inc., et al.,* Case No. C-13-3826 EMC (N.D.Cal. 2015).
b. *Rosen v. Uber Technologies, Inc.,* __ F.Supp.3d __, 2016 WL 704078 (N.D.Cal. 2016).
c. *Checker Cab of Philadelphia v. Uber Technologies, Inc.,* __ Fed.Appx. __, 2016 WL 929310 (3d Cir. 2016).

Criteria Used by the IRS The Internal Revenue Service (IRS) has established its own criteria for determining whether a worker is an independent contractor or an employee. The most important factor is the degree of control the business exercises over the worker.

The IRS tends to closely scrutinize a firm's classification of its workers because, as mentioned, employers can avoid certain tax liabilities by hiring independent contractors instead of employees. Even when a firm has classified a worker as an independent contractor, the IRS may decide that the worker is actually an employee. If the IRS decides that an employee is misclassified, the employer will be responsible for paying any applicable Social Security, withholding, and unemployment taxes due for that employee.

Employee Status and "Works for Hire" Ordinarily, a person who creates a copyrighted work is the owner of it—unless it is a "work for hire." Under the Copyright Act, any copyrighted work created by an employee within the scope of her or his employment at the request of the employer is a "work for hire." The employer owns the copyright to the work.

In contrast, when an employer hires an independent contractor—such as a freelance artist, writer, or computer programmer—the independent contractor normally owns the copyright. An exception is made if the parties agree in writing that the work is a "work for hire" and the work falls into one of nine specific categories. The nine categories include audiovisual works, collective works (such as magazines), motion pictures, textbooks, tests, and translations.

■ **CASE IN POINT 32.1** As a freelance contractor, Brian Cooley created two sculptures of dinosaur eggs for the National Geographic Society for use in connection with an article in its magazine, *National Geographic*. Cooley spent hundreds of hours researching, designing, and constructing the sculptures. National Geographic hired Louis Psihoyos to photograph Cooley's sculptures for the article. Cooley and Psihoyos had separate contracts with National Geographic in which each transferred the copyrights in their works to National Geographic for a limited time.

The rights to the works were returned to the artists at different times after publication. Psihoyos then began licensing his photographs of Cooley's sculptures to third parties in return for royalties. He digitized the photographs and licensed them to various online stock photography companies, and they appeared in several books published by Penguin Group. Cooley sued Psihoyos for copyright infringement.

Psihoyos argued that he owned the photos and could license them however he saw fit, but a federal district court disagreed. The court found that Psihoyos did not have an unrestricted right to use and license the photos. When Psihoyos reproduced an image of a Cooley sculpture, he reproduced the sculpture, which infringed on Cooley's copyright. Therefore, the court granted a summary judgment to Cooley.[2] ■

---

2. *Cooley v. Penguin Group (USA), Inc.*, 31 F.Supp.3d 599 (S.D.N.Y. 2014).

32–2 Formation of the Agency Relationship

Agency relationships normally are consensual. They come about by voluntary consent and agreement between the parties. Normally, the agreement need not be in writing, and consideration is not required.

A person must have contractual capacity to be a principal.[3] The idea is that those who cannot legally enter into contracts directly should not be allowed to do so indirectly through an agent. Any person can be an agent, however, regardless of whether he or she has the capacity to contract (including minors).

An agency relationship can be created for any legal purpose. An agency relationship created for a purpose that is illegal or contrary to public policy is unenforceable. ■ **EXAMPLE 32.2** Archer (as principal) contracts with Burke (as agent) to sell illegal narcotics. The agency relationship is unenforceable because selling illegal narcotics is a felony and is contrary to public policy. If Burke sells the narcotics and keeps the profits, Archer cannot sue to enforce the agency agreement. ■

An agency relationship can arise in four ways: by agreement of the parties, by ratification, by estoppel, and by operation of law.

32–2a Agency by Agreement

Most agency relationships are based on an express or implied agreement that the agent will act for the principal and that the principal agrees to have the agent so act. An agency agreement can take the form of an express written contract or be created by an oral agreement. ■ **EXAMPLE 32.3** Reese asks Grace, a gardener, to contract with others for the care of his lawn on a regular basis. If Grace agrees, an agency relationship exists between Reese and Grace for the lawn care. ■

An agency agreement can also be implied by conduct. ■ **CASE IN POINT 32.4** Gilbert Bishop was admitted to a nursing home, Laurel Creek Health Care Center, suffering from various physical ailments. He was not able to use his hands well enough to write but was otherwise mentally competent. Bishop's sister offered to sign the admission papers for him, but it was Laurel Creek's

---

3. Note that some states allow a minor to be a principal. When a minor is permitted to be a principal, any resulting contracts will be voidable by the minor principal but *not* by the adult third party.

policy to have the patient's spouse sign the forms if the patient could not.

Bishop's sister then brought his wife, Anna, to the hospital to sign the paperwork, which included a mandatory arbitration clause. Later, when the family filed a lawsuit against Laurel Creek, the nursing home sought to enforce the arbitration clause. Ultimately, a Kentucky appellate court held that Bishop was bound by the contract and the arbitration clause his wife had signed. Bishop's conduct had indicated that he was giving his wife authority to act as his agent in signing the admission papers.[4] ■

32–2b Agency by Ratification

On occasion, a person who is in fact not an agent (or who is an agent acting outside the scope of her or his authority) makes a contract on behalf of another (a principal). If the principal approves or affirms that contract by word or by action, an agency relationship is created by *ratification*. Ratification involves a question of intent, and intent can be expressed by either words or conduct.

32–2c Agency by Estoppel

Sometimes, a principal causes a third person to believe that another person is the principal's agent, and the third person acts to his or her detriment in reasonable reliance on that belief. When this occurs, the principal is "estopped to deny" (prevented from denying) the agency relationship. The principal's actions have created the *appearance* of an agency that does not in fact exist, creating an agency by estoppel.

The Third Party's Reliance Must Be Reasonable
The third person must prove that he or she *reasonably* believed that an agency relationship existed.[5] Facts and circumstances must show that an ordinary, prudent person familiar with business practice and custom would have been justified in concluding that the agent had authority.

Created by the Principal's Conduct
Note that the acts or declarations of a purported *agent* in and of themselves do not create an agency by estoppel. Rather, it is the deeds or statements of the *principal* that create an agency by estoppel. ■ **CASE IN POINT 32.5** Francis Azur

was president and chief executive officer of ATM Corporation of America. Michelle Vanek was Azur's personal assistant. Among other duties, she reviewed his credit-card statements. For seven years, Vanek took unauthorized cash advances from Azur's credit-card account with Chase Bank. The charges appeared on at least sixty-five monthly statements.

When Azur discovered Vanek's fraud, he fired her and closed the account. He filed a suit against Chase, arguing that the bank should not have allowed Vanek to take cash advances. The court concluded that Azur (the principal) had given the bank reason to believe that Vanek (the agent) had authority. Therefore, Azur was estopped (prevented) from denying Vanek's authority.[6] ■

32–2d Agency by Operation of Law

The courts may find an agency relationship in the absence of a formal agreement in other situations as well. This may occur in family relationships, such as when one spouse purchases certain basic necessaries and charges them to the other spouse's account. The courts often rule that a spouse is liable for payment for the necessaries because of either a social policy or a legal duty to supply necessaries to family members.

Agency by operation of law may also occur in emergency situations. If an agent cannot contact the principal and failure to act would cause the principal substantial loss, the agent may take steps beyond the scope of her or his authority. For instance, a railroad engineer may contract on behalf of his or her employer for medical care for an injured motorist hit by the train.

Concept Summary 32.1 reviews the various ways in which agency relationships are formed.

32–3 Duties of Agents and Principals

Once the principal-agent relationship has been created, both parties have duties that govern their conduct. As discussed previously, the principal-agent relationship is *fiduciary*—based on trust. In a fiduciary relationship, each party owes the other the duty to act with the utmost good faith. In this section, we examine the various duties of agents and principals.

---

4. *Laurel Creek Health Care Center v. Bishop*, 2010 WL 985299 (Ky.App. 2010).
5. These concepts also apply when a person who is, in fact, an agent undertakes an action that is beyond the scope of her or his authority.

6. *Azur v. Chase Bank, USA, N.A.*, 601 F.3d 212 (3d Cir. 2010).

Concept Summary 32.1

Formation of the Agency Relationship

By Agreement
- The agency relationship is formed through express consent (oral or written) or implied by conduct.

By Ratification
- The principal either by act or by agreement ratifies the conduct of a person who is not, in fact, an agent.

By Estoppel
- The principal causes a third person to believe that another person is the principal's agent, and the third person acts to his or her detriment in reasonable reliance on that belief.

By Operation of Law
- The agency relationship is based on a social or legal duty—such as the need to support family members. Or, it is formed in emergency situations when the agent is unable to contact the principal and failure to act outside the scope of the agent's authority would cause the principal substantial loss.

32–3a Agent's Duties to the Principal

Generally, the agent owes the principal five duties—performance, notification, loyalty, obedience, and accounting (see Exhibit 32–1).

Performance An implied condition in every agency contract is the agent's agreement to use reasonable diligence and skill in performing the work. When an agent fails to perform his or her duties, liability for breach of contract may result.

Standard of Care. The degree of skill or care required of an agent is usually that expected of a reasonable person under similar circumstances. Generally, this is interpreted to mean ordinary care. If an agent has represented herself or himself as possessing special skills, however, the agent is expected to exercise the degree of skill claimed. Failure to do so constitutes a breach of the agent's duty.

Gratuitous Agents. Not all agency relationships are based on contract. In some situations, an agent acts gratuitously—that is, without payment. A gratuitous agent cannot be liable for breach of contract because there is no contract. He or she is subject only to tort liability. Once a gratuitous agent has begun to act in an agency capacity, he or she has the duty to continue to perform in that capacity. A gratuitous agent must perform in an acceptable manner and is subject to the same standards of care and duty to perform as other agents.

■ **EXAMPLE 32.6** Bower's friend Alcott is a real estate broker. Alcott offers to sell Bower's vacation home at no charge. If Alcott never attempts to sell the home, Bower has no legal cause of action to force her to do so. If Alcott does attempt to sell the home to Friedman, but then performs so negligently that the sale falls through, Bower can sue Alcott for negligence. ■

Notification An agent is required to notify the principal of all matters that come to her or his attention concerning the subject matter of the agency. This is the *duty of notification,* or the duty to inform.

■ **EXAMPLE 32.7** Perez, an artist, is about to negotiate a contract to sell a series of paintings to Barber's Art Gallery for $25,000. Perez's agent learns that Barber is insolvent and will be unable to pay for the paintings. The agent has a duty to inform Perez of Barber's insolvency because it is relevant to the subject matter of the agency, which is the sale of Perez's paintings. ■

Generally, the law assumes that the principal is aware of any information acquired by the agent that is relevant to the agency—regardless of whether the agent actually passes on this information to the principal. It is a basic tenet of agency law that notice to the agent is notice to the principal.

EXHIBIT 32–1 Duties of the Agent

Loyalty Loyalty is one of the most fundamental duties in a fiduciary relationship. Basically, the agent has the duty to act *solely for the benefit of his or her principal* and not in the interest of the agent or a third party. For instance, an agent cannot represent two principals in the same transaction unless both know of the dual capacity and consent to it.

Maintain Confidentiality. The duty of loyalty also means that any information or knowledge acquired through the agency relationship is confidential. It is a breach of loyalty to disclose such information either during the agency relationship or after its termination. Typical examples of confidential information are trade secrets and customer lists compiled by the principal.

Actions Must Benefit the Principal. The agent's loyalty must be undivided. The agent's actions must be strictly for the benefit of the principal and must not result in any secret profit for the agent.

■ **EXAMPLE 32.8** Don contracts with Leo, a real estate agent, to negotiate the purchase of an office building. Leo discovers that the property owner will sell the building only as a package deal with another parcel. So Leo buys the two properties, intending to resell the building to Don. Leo has breached his fiduciary duty. As a real estate agent, Leo has a duty to communicate all offers to Don, his principal, and not to purchase the property secretly and then resell it to Don. Leo is required to act in Don's best interests and can become the purchaser in this situation only with Don's knowledge and approval. ■

In the following case, an employer alleged that a former employee had breached his duty of loyalty by planning a competing business while still working for the employer.

Spotlight on Taser International

Case 32.2 Taser International, Inc. v. Ward
Court of Appeals of Arizona, Division 1, 224 Ariz. 389, 231 P.3d 921 (2010).

Background and Facts Taser International, Inc., develops and makes electronic control devices, commonly called stun guns, as well as accessories for electronic control devices, including a personal video and audio recording device called the TASER CAM.

Steve Ward was Taser's vice president of marketing when he began to explore the possibility of developing and marketing devices of his own design, including a clip-on camera. Ward talked to

Case 32.2 Continues

Case 32.2 Continued

patent attorneys and a product development company and completed most of a business plan. After he resigned from Taser, he formed Vievu, LLC, to market his clip-on camera.

Ten months after Ward resigned, Taser announced the AXON, a product that provides an audio-video record of an incident from the visual perspective of the person involved. Taser then filed a suit in an Arizona state court against Ward, alleging that he had breached his duty of loyalty to Taser. The court granted Taser's motion for a summary judgment in the employer's favor. Ward appealed.

In the Language of the Court
PORTLEY, Judge.

* * * *

* * * An agent is under the duty to act with entire good faith and loyalty for the furtherance of the interests of his principal in all matters concerning or affecting the subject of his agency.

One aspect of this broad principle is that an employee is precluded from actively competing with his or her employer during the period of employment.

Although an employee may not compete prior to termination, the employee may take action during employment, not otherwise wrongful, to prepare for competition following termination of the agency relationship. Preparation cannot take the form of acts in direct competition with the employer's business. [Emphasis added.]

* * * *

It is undisputed that, prior to his resignation, Ward did not solicit or recruit any Taser employees, distributors, customers, or vendors; he did not buy, sell, or incorporate any business; he did not acquire office space or other general business services; he did not contact or enter into any agreements with suppliers or manufacturers for his proposed clip-on camera; and he did not sell any products. However, Ward did begin developing a business plan, counseled with several attorneys, explored and abandoned the concept of an eyeglass-mounted camera device, and engaged, to some extent, in the exploration and development of a clip-on camera device.

Ward argues that his pre-termination activities did not constitute active competition but were merely lawful preparation for a future business venture. Taser contends, however, that "this case is * * * about developing a rival design during employment, knowing full well TASER has sold such a device and continues to develop a second-generation product."

* * * *

* * * Assuming Taser was engaged in the research and development of a recording device during Ward's employment, assuming Ward knew or should have known of those efforts, and assuming Taser's device would compete with Ward's concept, substantial design and development efforts by Ward during his employment would constitute direct competition with the business activities of Taser and would violate his duty of loyalty. In the context of a business which engages in research, design, development, manufacture, and marketing of products, we cannot limit "competition" to just actual sales of competing products.

Decision and Remedy *A state intermediate appellate court agreed with Taser that an employee may not actively compete with his employer before his employment is terminated. But the parties disputed the extent of Ward's pre-termination efforts, creating a genuine issue of material fact that could not be resolved on a motion for summary judgment. The appellate court thus reversed the lower court's decision in Taser's favor and remanded the case for further proceedings.*

Critical Thinking
- **Legal Environment** *Did Ward breach any duties owed to his employer in addition to his alleged breach of the duty of loyalty? Discuss.*
- **What If the Facts Were Different?** *Suppose that Ward's pre-termination activities focused on a product that was not designed to compete with Taser's products. Would these efforts have breached the duty of loyalty? Why or why not?*

Obedience When acting on behalf of the principal, an agent has a duty to follow all lawful and clearly stated instructions of the principal. Any deviation from such instructions is a violation of this duty.

During emergency situations, however, when the principal cannot be consulted, the agent may deviate from the instructions without violating this duty. Whenever instructions are not clearly stated, the agent can fulfill the duty of obedience by acting in good faith and in a manner reasonable under the circumstances.

Accounting Unless the agent and principal agree otherwise, the agent must keep and make available to the principal an account of all property and funds received and paid out on the principal's behalf. This includes gifts from third parties in connection with the agency. ■ **EXAMPLE 32.9** Marla is a salesperson for Roadway Supplies. Knife River Construction gives Marla a new tablet as a gift for prompt deliveries of Roadway's paving materials. The tablet belongs to Roadway. ■

The agent has a duty to maintain a separate account for the principal's funds and must not intermingle these funds with the agent's personal funds. If a licensed professional (such as an attorney) violates this duty, he or she may be subject to disciplinary action by the licensing authority (such as the state bar association). Of course, the professional will also be liable to his or her client (the principal) for failure to account.

32–3b Principal's Duties to the Agent

The principal also has certain duties to the agent (as shown in Exhibit 32–2). These duties relate to compensation, reimbursement and indemnification, cooperation, and safe working conditions.

Compensation In general, when a principal requests certain services from an agent, the agent reasonably expects payment. For instance, when an accountant or an attorney is asked to act as an agent, an agreement to compensate the

agent for this service is implied. The principal therefore has a duty to pay the agent for services rendered.

Unless the agency relationship is gratuitous and the agent does not act in exchange for payment, the principal must pay the agreed-on value for the agent's services. If no amount has been expressly agreed on, then the principal owes the agent the customary compensation for such services. The principal also has a duty to pay that compensation in a timely manner.

■ **CASE IN POINT 32.10** Keith Miller worked as a sales representative for Paul M. Wolff Company, a subcontractor specializing in concrete-finishing services. Sales representatives at Wolff are paid a 15 percent commission on projects that meet a 35 percent gross profit threshold. The commission is paid after the projects are completed. When Miller resigned, he asked for commissions on fourteen projects for which he had secured contracts but which had not yet been completed. Wolff refused, so Miller sued.

The court found that "an agent is entitled to receive commissions on sales that result from the agent's efforts," even after the employment or agency relationship ends. Miller had met the gross profit threshold on ten of the unfinished projects, and therefore, he was entitled to more than $21,000 in commissions.[7] ■

Reimbursement and Indemnification Whenever an agent disburses funds at the request of the principal, the principal has a duty to reimburse the agent. The principal must also reimburse the agent (even a gratuitous

---

7. *Miller v. Paul M. Wolff Co.*, 178 Wash.App. 957, 316 P.3d 1113 (2014).

EXHIBIT 32–2 Duties of the Principal

DUTIES OF THE PRINCIPAL			
Compensation	**Reimbursement and Indemnification**	**Cooperation**	**Safe Working Conditions**
Principal must pay the agreed-on (or reasonable) value for the agent's services.	Principal must reimburse the agent for any funds paid out at the principal's request, as well as for necessary expenses.	Principal must cooperate with and assist an agent in performing his or her duties.	Principal must provide a safe working environment for agents and employees.

agent) for any necessary expenses incurred in the course of the reasonable performance of her or his agency duties. Agents cannot recover for expenses incurred as a result of their own misconduct or negligence, though.

Subject to the terms of the agency agreement, the principal has the duty to *indemnify* (compensate) an agent for liabilities incurred because of authorized and lawful acts and transactions. For instance, if the agent, on the principal's behalf, forms a contract with a third party, and the principal fails to perform the contract, the third party may sue the agent for damages. In this situation, the principal is obligated to compensate the agent for any costs incurred by the agent as a result of the principal's failure to perform the contract.

Additionally, the principal must indemnify the agent for the value of benefits that the agent confers on the principal. The amount of indemnification usually is specified in the agency contract. If it is not, the courts will look to the nature of the business and the type of loss to determine the amount. Note that this rule applies to acts by gratuitous agents as well.

Cooperation A principal has a duty to cooperate with the agent and to assist the agent in performing his or her duties. The principal must do nothing to prevent that performance.

For instance, when a principal grants an agent an exclusive territory, the principal creates an **exclusive agency,** in which the principal cannot compete with the agent or appoint or allow another agent to compete. If the principal does so, he or she violates the exclusive agency and is exposed to liability for the agent's lost profits.

■ **EXAMPLE 32.11** Penny (the principal) creates an exclusive agency by granting Andrew (the agent) a territory within which only Andrew may sell Penny's organic skin care products. If Penny starts to sell the products herself within Andrew's territory—or permits another agent to do so—Penny has failed to cooperate with the agent. Because she has violated the exclusive agency, Penny can be held liable for Andrew's lost sales or profits. ■

In the following case, a pair of potential homebuyers entered into an agreement with a realtor to act as the buyers' exclusive agent in locating and purchasing property. Later, the buyers executed an exclusive agency agreement with a different realtor. Neither agent knew about the other until the buyers found a home that they liked and bought it.

Case Analysis 32.3

NRT New England, LLC v. Jones
Appellate Court of Connecticut, 162 Conn.App. 840, 134 A.3d 632 (2016).

In the Language of the Court
HARPER, J. [Judge]
    * * * *

The defendant [Christopher Jones] met Andrea Woolston, a licensed realtor working as an independent contractor [for NRT New England, LLC, doing business as Coldwell Banker Residential Brokerage], in October 2010. The defendant expressed to Woolston a desire to purchase a home for himself and his then fiancée, Katherine Wiltshire. One of the first things Woolston asked the defendant was whether he was represented by another agent. The defendant responded that he was not. After a number of conversations about the defendant's needs and wishes, the parties executed an exclusive right to represent buyer agreement (agreement), which established, among other things, that Woolston was the defendant's

exclusive agent for finding, negotiating, and purchasing property. Over the next several months, Woolston devoted a substantial amount of time searching for properties for the defendant to purchase. Specifically, Woolston researched available properties at six town halls in the communities in which the defendant was interested. She showcased a number of properties personally to the defendant and Wiltshire and introduced many more to them through e-mail. Woolston and the defendant had at least twenty appointments where they viewed multiple properties. Additionally, Woolston visited many properties alone to determine if they were suitable for the defendant. Altogether, Woolston spent hundreds of hours seeking a suitable home for the defendant.

The agreement was in effect from January 11, 2011 until July 11, 2011,

and set forth the geographical area that the defendant was interested in and the rate of compensation for the plaintiff's services. With respect to geographical area, the parties agreed that Woolston would seek properties in Killingworth, Guilford, Essex, Old Saybrook, Deep River, Lyme, and Old Lyme [Connecticut]. With respect to compensation, the defendant agreed to pay the plaintiff a commission equal to 2.5 percent of the purchase price of the property "if the [buyer] or any person or entity acting on the [buyer's] behalf purchases, options, exchanges, leases or trades any property, through the efforts of anyone, including the [buyer]." The agreement imposed the following duties on the defendant: "The [buyer] will not deal directly with any other broker, agent or licensee during the term of this agreement. The [buyer] will notify other brokers, agents or licensees at first contact that the [buyer] is being exclusively represented by [NRT]. The [buyer] will disclose to [NRT] any past and/or current contacts for any real property or with any other real estate broker or agent."

On May 10, 2011, the defendant informed Woolston via e-mail that he and Wiltshire purchased property at 300 Vineyard Point Road in Guilford for $1,375,000. The defendant learned of this property on May 4, 2011, from Mary Jane Burt, a realtor with H. Pearce Real Estate (H. Pearce), who previously had represented Wiltshire with the sale of her house in Hamden [Connecticut]. Woolston subsequently confronted the defendant and eventually learned that he and Wiltshire previously had executed an exclusive right to represent buyer agreement with Burt and H. Pearce. This agreement was in effect from August 1, 2010, until August 1, 2011, and contained a provision designating Burt as the exclusive agent for the defendant and Wiltshire. Thus, at the time the defendant purchased the property in Guilford, he was under contract for exclusive agency with both Woolston and Burt. The defendant never told Woolston or Burt that he had two agreements in effect at the same time. Woolston notified her superiors of what had transpired.

* * * [NRT] filed a * * * complaint [in a Connecticut state court] against the defendant [for] breach of contract * * *. After a trial * * *, the court * * * found that the plaintiff had proven * * * breach of contract * * * and damages. * * * The court awarded the plaintiff $34,375 in damages [which represented 2.5 percent of the purchase price for the Vineyard Point property] plus attorney's fees and costs. This appeal followed.

* * * *

The defendant * * * claims that the agreement was unenforceable. Specifically, he argues that the court improperly * * * found that it was inequitable to deny the plaintiff recovery.

* * * *

There is ample evidence in the record to support the court's conclusion that denying the plaintiff relief would be inequitable. Woolston testified, and the defendant himself conceded, that she rendered a significant amount of services to the defendant over several months. Specifically, Woolston researched properties at town halls for availability and encumbrances, contacted property owners, arranged personal visits, prepared and presented literature to the defendant on available properties, and attended appointments with the defendant and Wiltshire. Woolston spent hundreds of hours working for the defendant in total.

The defendant, on the other hand, accepted Woolston's services while under contract with another agent in violation of the agreement. Indeed, the defendant acknowledged that he was untruthful with Woolston at the beginning of their relationship when he told her that he was not represented by another agent. In fact, he was scheduling appointments and viewing properties with both Woolston and Burt at approximately the same time in May 2011. For example, the defendant e-mailed Woolston on May 2, 2011, thanking her for showing him a property. Approximately one week later, the defendant e-mailed Woolston to inform her that he viewed 300 Vineyard Point Road with Burt and had "put in an all cash bid that has been accepted."

The defendant nevertheless argues that it would not be inequitable to deny recovery to the plaintiff because Woolston performed no services in connection with his purchase of 300 Vineyard Point Road. We are not persuaded. *The defendant agreed to pay a commission "equal to 2.5% of the purchase price if the [buyer] or any person or entity acting on the [buyer's] behalf purchases * * * any property, through the efforts of anyone, including the [buyer], where an agreement to purchase the property was entered into during the term of this agreement."* However unjust this result may seem to the defendant in hindsight, we cannot say it is inequitable because it is precisely what he agreed to. [Emphasis added.]

* * * *

The judgment is affirmed.

Legal Reasoning Questions

1. What is the advantage to a principal of an exclusive agency agreement? What was the advantage to Jones of his agreement with Woolston? Discuss.

2. Why, in addition to damages, was the plaintiff awarded attorneys' fees and costs?

3. Jones's agreement with Woolston provided that on the purchase of the property, NRT "will, whenever feasible, seek compensation from the seller or the seller's agent." The court determined that it was not feasible. Why would it not be reasonable in this situation to ask the seller of the property to pay part of Woolston's commission?

Safe Working Conditions The common law requires the principal to provide safe working premises, equipment, and conditions for all agents and employees. The principal has a duty to inspect working areas and to warn agents and employees about any unsafe situations. When the agent is an employee, the employer's liability is frequently covered by state workers' compensation insurance. In addition, federal and state statutes often require the employer to meet certain safety standards.

32–4 Rights and Remedies of Agents and Principals

In general, for every duty of the principal, the agent has a corresponding right, and vice versa. When one party to the agency relationship violates his or her duty to the other party, the nonbreaching party is entitled to a remedy. The remedies available arise out of contract and tort law. These remedies include monetary damages, termination of the agency relationship, an injunction, and required accountings.

32–4a Agent's Rights and Remedies against the Principal

The agent has the right to be compensated, to be reimbursed and indemnified, and to have a safe working environment. An agent also has the right to perform agency duties without interference by the principal.

Tort and Contract Remedies Remedies of the agent for breach of duty by the principal follow normal contract and tort remedies. ■ **EXAMPLE 32.12** Aaron Hart, a builder who has just constructed a new house, contracts with a real estate agent, Fran Boller, to sell the house. The contract calls for the agent to have an exclusive ninety-day listing and to receive 6 percent of the selling price when the home is sold. Boller holds several open houses and shows the home to a number of potential buyers.

One month before the ninety-day listing terminates, Hart agrees to sell the house to another buyer—not one to whom Boller has shown the house—after the ninety-day listing expires. Hart and the buyer agree that Hart will reduce the price of the house by 3 percent because he will sell it directly and thus will not have to pay Boller's commission. If Boller learns of Hart's actions, she can terminate the agency relationship and sue Hart for the 6 percent commission she should have earned on the sale of the house. ■

Demand for an Accounting An agent can also withhold further performance and demand that the principal give an accounting. For instance, a sales agent may demand an accounting if the agent and principal disagree on the amount of commissions the agent should have received for sales made during a specific period.

No Right to Specific Performance When the principal-agent relationship is not contractual, the agent has no right to specific performance. An agent can recover for past services and future damages but cannot force the principal to allow him or her to continue acting as an agent.

32–4b Principal's Rights and Remedies against the Agent

In general, a principal has contract remedies for an agent's breach of fiduciary duties. The principal also has tort remedies if the agent engages in misrepresentation, negligence, deceit, libel, slander, or trespass. In addition, any breach of a fiduciary duty by an agent may justify the principal's termination of the agency. The main actions available to the principal are constructive trust, avoidance, and indemnification.

Constructive Trust Anything that an agent obtains by virtue of the employment or agency relationship belongs to the principal. An agent commits a breach of fiduciary duty if he or she secretly retains benefits or profits that, by right, belong to the principal. Therefore, the agent holds such property in a *constructive trust* (an equitable trust imposed for reasons of fairness) for the principal. ■ **EXAMPLE 32.13** Lee, a purchasing agent for Metcalf, receives cash rebates from a customer. If Lee keeps the rebates for himself, he violates his fiduciary duty to his principal, Metcalf. On finding out about the cash rebates, Metcalf can sue Lee and recover them. ■

Avoidance When an agent breaches the agency agreement or agency duties under a contract, the principal has a right to avoid any contract entered into with the agent. This right of avoidance is at the election of the principal.

Indemnification In certain situations, when a principal is sued by a third party for an agent's negligent conduct, the principal can sue the agent for indemnification—that is, for an equal amount of damages. The same holds true if the agent violates the principal's instructions.
■ **EXAMPLE 32.14** Parker (the principal) owns a used-car lot where Moore (the agent) works as a salesperson. Parker tells Moore to make no warranties for the used cars. Moore is eager to make a sale to Walters, a customer, and adds a 50,000-mile warranty for the car's engine. Parker may be liable to Walters for engine failure, but if Walters sues Parker, Parker normally can then sue Moore for indemnification for violating his instructions. ■

Sometimes, though, it is difficult to distinguish between instructions of the principal that limit an agent's authority and those that are merely advice. ■ **EXAMPLE 32.15** Gutierrez (the principal) owns an office supply company, and Logan (the agent) is the manager. Gutierrez tells Logan, "Don't purchase any more inventory this month." Gutierrez goes on vacation. A large order comes in from a local business, and the inventory on hand is insufficient to meet it. What is Logan to do? In this situation, Logan probably has the inherent authority to purchase more inventory despite Gutierrez's command. It is unlikely that Logan would be required to indemnify Gutierrez in the event that the local business subsequently canceled the order. ■

Reviewing: Agency Formation and Duties

James Blatt hired Marilyn Scott to sell insurance for the Massachusetts Mutual Life Insurance Company. Their contract stated, "Nothing in this contract shall be construed as creating the relationship of employer and employee." The contract was terminable at will by either party. Scott financed her own office and staff, was paid according to performance, had no taxes withheld from her checks, and could legally sell products of Massachusetts Mutual's competitors. Blatt learned that Scott was simultaneously selling insurance for Perpetual Life Insurance Corporation, one of Massachusetts Mutual's fiercest competitors. Blatt therefore withheld client contact information from Scott. Scott complained to Blatt that he was inhibiting her ability to sell insurance for Massachusetts Mutual. Blatt subsequently terminated their contract. Scott filed a suit in a New York state court against Blatt and Massachusetts Mutual. Scott claimed that she had lost sales for Massachusetts Mutual—and commissions—as a result of Blatt's withholding contact information from her. Using the information presented in the chapter, answer the following questions.

1. Who is the principal and who is the agent in this scenario? By which method was an agency relationship formed between Scott and Blatt?
2. What facts would the court consider most important in determining whether Scott was an employee or an independent contractor?
3. How would the court most likely rule on Scott's employee status? Why?
4. Which of the four duties that Blatt owed Scott in their agency relationship has probably been breached?

Debate This . . . *All works created by independent contractors should be considered works for hire under copyright law.*

Terms and Concepts

agency 606
exclusive agency 616

fiduciary 606

independent contractor 607

Issue Spotters

1. Winona contracted with XtremeCast, a broadcast media firm, to cohost an Internet-streaming sports program. Winona and XtremeCast signed a new contract for each episode. In each contract, Winona agreed to work a certain number of days for a certain salary. During each broadcast, Winona was free to improvise her performance. She had no other obligation to work for Xtreme-Cast. Was Winona an independent contractor? (See *Agency Relationships*.)

2. Dimka Corporation wants to build a new mall on a specific tract of land. Dimka contracts with Nadine to buy the property. There is a substantial difference between the price that Dimka is willing to pay and the price at which the owner is willing to sell. When Nadine learns of this, she wants to buy the land and sell it to Dimka herself. Can she do this? Discuss. (See *Duties of Agents and Principals*.)

• **Check your answers to the Issue Spotters against the answers provided in Appendix D at the end of this text.**

Business Scenarios

32–1. Agency Formation. Paul Gett is a well-known, wealthy financial expert living in the city of Torris. Adam Wade, Gett's friend, tells Timothy Brown that he is Gett's agent for the purchase of rare coins. Wade even shows Brown a local newspaper clipping mentioning Gett's interest in coin collecting. Brown, knowing of Wade's friendship with Gett, contracts with Wade to sell a rare coin valued at $25,000 to Gett. Wade takes the coin and disappears with it. On the payment due date, Brown seeks to collect from Gett, claiming that Wade's agency made Gett liable. Gett does not deny that Wade was a friend, but he claims that Wade was never his agent. Discuss fully whether an agency was in existence at the time the contract for the rare coin was made. (See *Formation of the Agency Relationship*.)

32–2. Duty of Loyalty. Peter hires Alice as an agent to sell a piece of property he owns. The price is to be at least $30,000. Alice discovers that the fair market value of Peter's property is actually at least $45,000 and could be higher because a shopping mall is going to be built nearby. Alice forms a real estate partnership with her cousin Carl. Then she prepares for Peter's signature a contract for the sale of the property to Carl for $32,000. Peter signs the contract. Just before closing and passage of title, Peter learns about the shopping mall and the increased fair market value of his property. Peter refuses to deed the property to Carl. Carl claims that Alice, as Peter's agent, solicited a price above that agreed on when the agency was created and that the contract is therefore binding and enforceable. Discuss fully whether Peter is bound to this contract. (See *Duties of Agents and Principals*.)

32–3. Employee versus Independent Contractor. Stephen Hemmerling was a driver for the Happy Cab Co. Hemmerling paid certain fixed expenses and followed various rules relating to the use of the cab, the hours that could be worked, and the solicitation of fares, among other things. Rates were set by the state. Happy Cab did not withhold taxes from Hemmerling's pay. While driving the cab, Hemmerling was injured in an accident and filed a claim for workers' compensation benefits in a state court. Such benefits are not available to independent contractors. On what basis might the court hold that Hemmerling was an employee? Explain. (See *Agency Relationships*.)

Business Case Problems

32–4. Agency by Ratification. Wesley Hall, an independent contractor managing property for Acree Investments, Ltd., lost control of a fire he had set to clear ten acres of Acree land. The runaway fire burned seventy-eight acres of Earl Barrs's property. Russell Acree, one of the owners of Acree Investments, had previously owned the ten acres, but he had put it into the company and was no longer the principal owner. Hall had worked for Russell Acree in the past and had told the state forestry department that he was burning the land for Acree. Barrs sued Russell Acree for the acts of his agent, Hall. In his suit, Barrs noted that Hall had been an employee of Russell Acree, Hall had talked about burning the land "for Acree," and Russell Acree had apologized to Barrs for the fire. Barrs also pointed out that Acree Investments had not been identified as the principal property owner until Barrs filed his lawsuit. Barrs argued that those facts were sufficient to create an agency by ratification to impose liability on Russell Acree. Was Barrs's agency by ratification claim valid? Why or why not? [*Barrs v. Acree*, 691 S.E.2d 575 (Ga.App. 2010)] (See *Formation of the Agency Relationship*.)

32–5. Employment Relationships. William Moore owned Moore Enterprises, a wholesale tire business. William's son, Jonathan, worked as a Moore Enterprises employee while he was in high school. Later, Jonathan started his own business, called Morecedes Tire. Morecedes regrooved tires and sold them to businesses, including Moore Enterprises. A decade after Jonathan started Morecedes, William offered him work with Moore Enterprises. On the first day, William told Jonathan to load certain tires on a trailer but did not tell him how to do it. Was Jonathan an independent contractor? Discuss. [*Moore v. Moore*, 152 Idaho 245, 269 P.3d 802 (2011)] (See *Agency Relationships*.)

32–6. Agent's Duties to Principal. William and Maxine Miller were shareholders of Claimsco International, Inc. They filed a suit against the other shareholders, Michael Harris and Kenneth Hoxie, and the accountant who worked for all of them—John Verchota. Among other things, the Millers alleged that Verchota had breached a duty that he owed them. They claimed that at Harris's instruction, Verchota had taken various actions that placed them at a disadvantage to the other shareholders. Verchota had allegedly adjusted Claimsco's books to maximize the Millers' financial liabilities, for instance, and had falsely reported distributions of income to them without actually transferring that income. Which duty are the Millers referring to? If the allegations can be proved, did Verchota breach this duty? Explain. [*Miller v. Harris*, 2013 IL App (2d) 120512, 985 N.E.2d 671 (2 Dist. 2013)] (See *Duties of Agents and Principals*.)

32–7. Business Case Problem with Sample Answer— Determining Employee Status. Nelson Ovalles worked as a cable installer for Cox Rhode Island Telecom, LLC, under an agreement with a third party, M&M Communications, Inc. The agreement stated that no employer-employee relationship existed between Cox and M&M's technicians, including Ovalles. Ovalles was required to designate his affiliation with Cox on his work van, clothing, and identification badge. Cox had minimal contact with him, however, and had limited power to control how he performed his duties. Cox supplied cable wire and similar items, but the equipment was delivered to M&M, not to Ovalles. On a workday, while Ovalles was fulfilling a work order, his van rear-ended a car driven by Barbara Cayer. Is Cox liable to Cayer? Explain. [*Cayer v. Cox*

Rhode Island Telecom, LLC, 85 A.3d 1140 (R.I. 2014)] (See *Agency Relationships*.)

- **For a sample answer to Problem 32–7, go to Appendix E at the end of this text.**

32–8. Agency Relationships. Standard Oil of Connecticut, Inc., sells home heating, cooling, and security systems. Standard schedules installation and service appointments with its customers and then contracts with installers and technicians to do the work. The company requires an installer or technician to complete a project by a certain time but to otherwise "exercise independent judgment and control in the execution of any work." The installers and technicians are licensed and certified by the state. Standard does not train them, provide instruction manuals, supervise them at customers' homes, or inspect their work. The installers and technicians use their own equipment and tools, and they can choose which days they work. Standard pays a set rate per project. According to criteria used by the courts, are these installers and technicians independent contractors or employees? Why? [*Standard Oil of Connecticut, Inc. v. Administrator, Unemployment Compensation Act*, 320 Conn. 611, __ A.3d __ (2016)] (See *Agency Relationships*.)

32–9. A Question of Ethics—Agency Formation and Duties. *Western Fire Truck, Inc., contracted with Emergency* *One, Inc. (EO), to be its exclusive dealer in Colorado and Wyoming through December 2003. James Costello, a Western salesperson, was authorized to order EO vehicles for his customers. Without informing Western, Costello e-mailed EO about Western's difficulties in obtaining cash to fund its operations. He asked about the viability of Western's contract and his possible employment with EO. On EO's request, and in disregard of Western's instructions, Costello sent some payments for EO vehicles directly to EO. In addition, Costello, with EO's help, sent a competing bid to a potential Western customer. EO's representative e-mailed Costello, "You have my permission to kick [Western's] ass." In April 2002, EO terminated its contract with Western. At about the same time, a Western manager discovered Costello's e-mails saying that he was dissatisfied with the company and fired Costello. Western filed a suit in a Colorado state court, alleging that Costello had breached his duty as an agent and that EO had aided and abetted the breach. [*Western Fire Truck, Inc. v. Emergency One, Inc., 134 P.3d 570 (Colo.App. 2006)]* (See *Formation of the Agency Relationship*.)*

(a) Was there an agency relationship between Western and Costello? Western required monthly reports from its sales staff, but Costello did not report regularly. Does this indicate that Costello was not Western's agent? In determining whether an agency relationship exists, is the right to control or the fact of control more important? Explain.

(b) Did Costello owe Western a duty? If so, what was the duty? Did Costello breach it? If so, how?

(c) A Colorado state statute allows a court to award punitive damages in "circumstances of fraud, malice, or willful and wanton conduct." Did any of these circumstances exist in this case? Should punitive damages be assessed against either defendant? Why or why not?

Legal Reasoning Group Activity

32–10. Agent's Duties to Principal. John Warren wanted to buy a condominium in California. Hildegard Merrill was the agent for the seller. Because Warren's credit rating was poor, Merrill told him he needed a co-borrower to obtain a mortgage at a reasonable rate. Merrill said that her daughter Charmaine would "go on title" until the loan and sale were complete if Warren would pay her $10,000. Merrill also offered to defer her commission on the sale as a loan to Warren so that he could make a 20 percent down payment on the property. He agreed to both plans.

Merrill secured the mortgage in Charmaine's name alone by misrepresenting her daughter's address, business, and income. To close the sale, Merrill had Warren remove his name from the title to the property. In October, Warren moved into the condominium, repaid Merrill the amount of her deferred commission, and began paying the mortgage. Within a few months, Merrill had Warren evicted. Warren subsequently filed a suit against Merrill and Charmaine. (See *Duties of Agents and Principals*.)

(a) The first group will determine who among these parties was in an agency relationship.

(b) The second group will discuss the basic duty that an agent owes a principal and decide whether that duty was breached here.

Answers to the *Issue Spotters*

1. ***Was Winona an independent contractor?*** Yes. An independent contractor is a person who contracts with another—the principal—to do something but who is neither controlled by the other nor subject to the other's right to control with respect to the performance. Independent contractors are not employees, because those who hire them have no control over the details of their performance.

2. ***When Nadine learns of this, she wants to buy the land and sell it to Dimka herself. Can she do this? Discuss.*** No. Nadine, as an agent, is prohibited from taking advantage of the agency relationship to obtain property that the principal (Dimka Corporation) wants to purchase. This is the duty of loyalty that arises with every agency relationship.

Sample Answers for *Business Case Problems with Sample Answer*

Problem 32–7. ***Determining Employee Status.*** No, Cox is not liable to Cayer for any injuries or damage that she sustained in the accident with Ovalles. Generally, an employer is not liable for physical harm caused to a third person by the negligent act of an independent contractor in the performance of a contract. This is be cause the employer does not have the right to control the details of the performance. In determining whether a worker has the status of an independent contractor, how much control the employer can exercise over the details of the work is the most important factor weighed by the courts.

In this problem, Ovalles worked as a cable installer for Cox under an agreement with M&M. The agreement disavowed any employer-employee relationship between Cox and M&M's installers. Ovalles was required to designate his affiliation with Cox on his van, clothing, and an ID badge. But Cox had minimal contact with Ovalles and limited power to control the manner in which he performed his work. Cox supplied cable wire and other equipment, but these items were delivered to M&M, not Ovalles. These facts indicate that Ovalles was an independent contractor, not an employee. Thus, Cox was not liable to Cayer for the harm caused to her by Ovalles when his van rear-ended Cayer's car.

In the actual case on which this problem is based, the court issued a judgment in Cox's favor. The Rhode Island Supreme Court affirmed, applying the principles stated above to arrive at the same conclusion.

CHAPTER

Agency Liability and Termination

We have already discussed how agency relationships are formed and the duties of the principal and agent in that relationship. This chapter deals with another important aspect of agency law—the liability of principals and agents to third parties.

We look first at the liability of principals for contracts formed by agents with third parties. Generally, the liability of the principal will depend on whether the agent was authorized to form the contract. The second part of the chapter deals with an agent's liability to third parties in contract and tort. It also discusses the principal's liability to third parties because of an agent's torts. The chapter concludes with a discussion of how agency relationships are terminated.

33–1 Scope of Agent's Authority

The liability of a principal to third parties with whom an agent contracts depends on whether the agent had the authority to enter into legally binding contracts on the principal's behalf. An agent's authority can be either *actual* (express or implied) or *apparent*. If an agent contracts outside the scope of his or her authority, the principal may still become liable by ratifying the contract.

33–1a Express Authority

Express authority is authority declared in clear, direct, and definite terms. Express authority can be given orally or in writing.

The Equal Dignity Rule In most states, the **equal dignity rule** requires that if the contract being executed is or must be in writing, then the agent's authority must also be in writing. (Recall that a writing includes an electronic record.) Failure to comply with the equal dignity rule can make a contract voidable *at the option of the principal.* The law regards the contract at that point as a mere offer. If the principal decides to accept the offer, the acceptance must be ratified, or affirmed, in writing.

■ **EXAMPLE 33.1** Paloma (the principal) orally asks Austin (the agent) to sell a ranch that Paloma owns. Austin finds a buyer and signs a sales contract on behalf of Paloma to sell the ranch. Because a contract for an interest in realty must be in writing, the equal dignity rule applies. The buyer cannot enforce the contract unless Paloma subsequently ratifies Austin's agency status *in a writing.* Once the sales contract is ratified, either party can enforce rights under the contract. ■

Modern business practice allows several exceptions to the equal dignity rule:

1. An executive officer of a corporation normally can conduct *ordinary* business transactions without obtaining written authority from the corporation.
2. When the agent acts in the presence of the principal, the rule does not apply.
3. When the agent's act of signing is merely a formality, then the agent does not need written authority to sign. ■ **EXAMPLE 33.2** Sandra Healy (the principal) negotiates a contract but is called out of town the day it is to be signed. If Healy orally authorizes Derek Santini to sign, the oral authorization is sufficient. ■

Power of Attorney Giving an agent a **power of attorney** confers express authority.[1] The power of attorney is a written document and is usually notarized. (A document is notarized when a **notary public**—a person authorized to attest to the authenticity of signatures—signs, dates, and imprints the document with her or his seal of authority.) Most states have statutory provisions for creating a power of attorney.

---

1. An agent who holds a power of attorney is called an *attorney-in-fact* for the principal. The holder does not have to be an attorney-at-law (and often is not).

A power of attorney can be *special* (permitting the agent to perform specified acts only), or it can be *general* (permitting the agent to transact all business for the principal). Because a general power of attorney (see Exhibit 33–1) grants extensive authority to the agent, it should be used with great caution and usually only in exceptional circumstances. Ordinarily, a power of attorney terminates on the incapacity or death of the person giving the power.[2]

---

2. A *durable* power of attorney, however, continues to be effective despite the principal's incapacity or death. An elderly person, for instance, might grant a durable power of attorney to provide for the handling of property and investments or specific health-care needs should he or she become incompetent.

EXHIBIT 33–1 A Sample General Power of Attorney

GENERAL POWER OF ATTORNEY

Know All Men by These Presents:

That I, _____ , hereinafter referred to as PRINCIPAL, in the County of _____
State of _____ , do(es) appoint _____ as my true and lawful attorney.

In principal's name, and for principal's use and benefit, said attorney is authorized hereby;

(1) To demand, sue for, collect, and receive all money, debts, accounts, legacies, bequests, interest, dividends, annuities, and demands as are now or shall hereafter become due, payable, or belonging to principal, and take all lawful means, for the recovery thereof and to compromise the same and give discharges for the same;

(2) To buy and sell land, make contracts of every kind relative to land, any interest therein or the possession thereof, and to take possession and exercise control over the use thereof;

(3) To buy, sell, mortgage, hypothecate, assign, transfer, and in any manner deal with goods, wares and merchandise, choses in action, certificates or shares of capital stock, and other property in possession or in action, and to make, do, and transact all and every kind of business of whatever nature;

(4) To execute, acknowledge, and deliver contracts of sale, escrow instructions, deeds, leases including leases for minerals and hydrocarbon substances and assignments of leases, covenants, agreements and assignments of agreements, mortgages and assignments of mortgages, conveyances in trust, to secure indebtedness or other obligations, and assign the beneficial interest thereunder, subordinations of liens or encumbrances, bills of lading, receipts, evidences of debt, releases, bonds, notes, bills, requests to reconvey deeds of trust, partial or full judgments, satisfactions of mortgages, and other debts, and other written instruments of whatever kind and nature, all upon such terms and conditions as said attorney shall approve.

GIVING AND GRANTING to said attorney full power and authority to do all and every act and thing whatsoever requisite and necessary to be done relative to any of the foregoing as fully to all intents and purposes as principal might or could do if personally present.

All that said attorney shall lawfully do or cause to be done under the authority of this power of attorney is expressly approved.

Dated: _____   /s/ _____

State of _____
County of _____   } SS.
On _____ , before me, the undersigned, a Notary Public in and for said
State, personally appeared _____

_____

known to me to be the person _____ whose name _____ subscribed
to the within instrument and acknowledged that _____ executed the same.

Witness my hand and official seal.   (Seal) _____
                                                    Notary Public in and for said State.

33–1b Implied Authority

An agent has the **implied authority** to do what is reasonably necessary to carry out express authority and accomplish the objectives of the agency. Authority can also be implied by custom or inferred from the position the agent occupies.

■ **EXAMPLE 33.3** Archer is employed by Packard Grocery to manage one of its stores. Packard has not expressly stated that Archer has authority to contract with third persons. Nevertheless, authority to manage a business implies authority to do what is reasonably required (as is customary or can be inferred from a manager's position) to operate the business. This includes forming contracts to hire employees, buying merchandise and equipment, and advertising the products sold in the store. ■

Note, however, that an agent's implied authority cannot contradict his or her express authority. Thus, if a principal has limited an agent's express authority, then the fact that the agent customarily would have such authority is irrelevant. ■ **EXAMPLE 33.4** Juanita Alvarez is the owner of six Baja Tacos restaurants. Alvarez (the principal) strictly forbids the managers (agents) of her taco shops from entering into contracts to hire additional workers. Therefore, the fact that managers customarily would have authority to hire employees is immaterial. ■

33–1c Apparent Authority

Actual authority (express or implied) arises from what the principal makes clear *to the agent*. Apparent authority, in contrast, arises from what the principal causes a third party to believe. An agent has **apparent authority** when the principal, by either word or action, causes a *third party* reasonably to believe that the agent has authority to act, even though the agent has no express or implied authority.

A Pattern of Conduct Apparent authority usually comes into existence through a principal's pattern of conduct over time. ■ **EXAMPLE 33.5** Bailey is a traveling salesperson. She solicits orders for goods but does not carry them with her. She normally would not have the implied authority to collect payments from customers on behalf of the principal. Suppose that she does accept payments from Corgley Enterprises, however, and submits them to the principal's accounting department for processing. If the principal does nothing to stop Bailey from continuing this practice, a pattern develops over time, and the principal confers apparent authority on Bailey to accept payments from Corgley. ■

At issue in the following *Spotlight Case* was whether the manager of a horse breeding operation had the authority to bind the farm's owner in a contract guaranteeing breeding rights.

Spotlight on Apparent Authority of Managers

Case 33.1 Lundberg v. Church Farm, Inc.

Court of Appeals of Illinois, 502 N.E.2d 806, 151 Ill.App.3d (1986).

Background and Facts Gilbert Church owned a horse breeding farm managed by Herb Bagley. Advertisements for the breeding rights to one of Church Farm's stallions, Imperial Guard, directed all inquiries to "Herb Bagley, Manager." Vern and Gail Lundberg bred Thoroughbred horses. The Lundbergs contacted Bagley and executed a preprinted contract giving them breeding rights to Imperial Guard "at Imperial Guard's location," subject to approval of the mares by Church. Bagley handwrote a statement on the contract that guaranteed the Lundbergs "six live foals in the first two years." He then signed it "Gilbert G. Church by H. Bagley."

The Lundbergs bred four mares, which resulted in one live foal. Church then moved Imperial Guard from Illinois to Oklahoma. The Lundbergs sued Church for breaching the contract by moving the horse. Church claimed that Bagley was not authorized to sign contracts for Church or to change or add terms, but only to present preprinted contracts to potential buyers. Church testified that although Bagley was his farm manager and the contact person for breeding rights, Bagley had never before modified the preprinted forms or signed Church's name on them. The jury found in favor of the Lundbergs and awarded $147,000 in damages. Church appealed.

In the Language of the Court

Justice UNVERZAGT delivered the opinion of the court.

* * * *

* * * *Defendant contends that plaintiffs have failed to establish that Bagley had apparent authority to negotiate and sign the Lundberg contract for Church Farm * * *.*

Case 33.1 Continued

*The party asserting an agency has the burden of proving its existence * * * but may do so by inference and circumstantial evidence. * * * Additionally, an agent may bind his principal by acts which the principal has not given him actual authority to perform, but which he appears authorized to perform. * * * An agent's apparent authority is that authority which "the principal knowingly permits the agent to assume or which he holds his agent out as possessing. It is the authority that a reasonably prudent man, exercising diligence and discretion, in view of the principal's conduct, would naturally suppose the agent to possess." [Emphasis added.]*

Plaintiffs produced evidence at trial that Gil Church approved the Imperial Guard advertisement listing Herb Bagley as Church Farm's manager, and directing all inquiries to him. Church also permitted Bagley to live on the farm and to handle its daily operations. Bagley was the only person available to visitors to the farm. Bagley answered Church Farm's phone calls, and there was a preprinted signature line for him on the breeding rights package.

The conclusion is inescapable that Gil Church affirmatively placed Bagley in a managerial position giving him complete control of Church Farm and its dealings with the public. We believe that this is just the sort of "holding out" of an agent by a principal that justifies a third person's reliance on the agent's authority.

We cannot accept defendant's contention that the Lundbergs were affirmatively obligated to seek out Church to ascertain the actual extent of Bagley's authority. Where an agent has apparent authority to act, the principal will be liable in spite of any undisclosed limitations the principal has placed on that authority.

Decision and Remedy *The state appellate court affirmed the lower court's judgment in favor of the Lundbergs for $147,000. Because Church allowed circumstances to lead the Lundbergs to believe Bagley had the authority to negotiate and sign the contract, Church was bound by Bagley's actions.*

Critical Thinking

- **Legal Environment** *The court held that Church had allowed the Lundbergs to believe that Bagley was his agent. What steps could Church have taken to protect himself against a finding of apparent authority?*
- **Ethical** *Does a principal have an ethical responsibility to inform an unaware third party that an apparent agent does not in fact have the authority to act on the principal's behalf? Explain.*

Apparent Authority and Estoppel A court can apply the doctrine of agency by estoppel when a principal has given a third party reason to believe that an agent has authority to act. If the third party honestly relies on the principal's representations to his or her detriment, the principal may be *estopped* (prevented) from denying that the agent had authority.

33–1d Emergency Powers

When an unforeseen emergency demands action by the agent to protect or preserve the property and rights of the principal, but the agent is unable to communicate with the principal, the agent has emergency power. ■ **EXAMPLE 33.6** Rob Fulsom is an engineer for Pacific Drilling Company. While Fulsom is acting within the scope of his employment, he is severely injured in an accident on an oil rig many miles from home. Acosta, the rig supervisor, directs Thompson, a physician, to give medical aid to Fulsom and to charge Pacific for the medical services.

Acosta, an agent, has no express or implied authority to bind the principal, Pacific Drilling, for Thompson's medical services. Because of the emergency situation, however, the law recognizes Acosta as having authority to act appropriately under the circumstances. ■

33–1e Ratification

Ratification occurs when the principal affirms, or accepts responsibility for, an agent's *unauthorized* act. When ratification occurs, the principal is bound to the agent's act, and the act is treated as if it had been authorized by the principal *from the outset*. Ratification can be either express or implied.

If the principal does not ratify the contract, the principal is not bound, and the third party's agreement with the agent is viewed as merely an unaccepted offer. Because the third party's agreement is an unaccepted offer, the third party can revoke it at any time, without liability, before the principal ratifies the contract. The agent, however, may be liable to the third party for misrepresenting her or his authority.

The requirements for ratification can be summarized as follows:

1. The agent must have acted on behalf of an identified principal who subsequently ratifies the action.
2. The principal must know all of the material facts involved in the transaction. If a principal ratifies a contract without knowing all of the facts, the principal can rescind (cancel) the contract.[3]
3. The principal must affirm the agent's act in its entirety.
4. The principal must have the legal capacity to authorize the transaction at the time the agent engages in the act and at the time the principal ratifies. The third party must also have the legal capacity to engage in the transaction.
5. The principal's affirmation (ratification) must occur before the third party withdraws from the transaction.

6. The principal must observe the same formalities when ratifying the act as would have been required to authorize it initially.

Concept Summary 33.1 summarizes the rules concerning an agent's authority to bind the principal and a third party.

33–2 Liability for Contracts

Liability for contracts formed by an agent depends on how the principal is classified and on whether the actions of the agent were authorized or unauthorized. Principals are classified as disclosed, partially disclosed, or undisclosed.[4]

1. A **disclosed principal** is a principal whose identity is known by the third party at the time the contract is made by the agent.

---

3. Note that if the third party has changed position in reliance on the apparent contract, the principal can still rescind the contract but must reimburse the third party for any costs.

4. *Restatement (Third) of Agency*, Section 1.04(2).

Concept Summary 33.1

Authority of an Agent to Bind the Principal and a Third Party

Express Authority	**Definition:** Authority expressly given by the principal to the agent.	**Effect:** Principal and third party are bound in contract.
Implied Authority	**Definition:** Authority implied (1) by custom, (2) from the position in which the principal has placed the agent, or (3) because such authority is necessary if the agent is to carry out expressly authorized duties and responsibilities.	**Effect:** Principal and third party are bound in contract.
Apparent Authority	**Definition:** Authority created when the conduct of the principal leads a third party to believe that the principal's agent has authority.	**Effect:** Principal and third party are bound in contract.
Unauthorized Acts	**Definition:** Acts committed by an agent that are outside the scope of his or her express, implied, or apparent authority.	**Effect:** Principal and third party are not bound in contract—*unless* the principal ratifies prior to the third party's withdrawal.

2. A **partially disclosed principal** is a principal whose identity is not known by the third party. Nevertheless, the third party knows that the agent is or *may* be acting for a principal at the time the contract is made. ■ **EXAMPLE 33.7** Eileen has contracted with a real estate agent to sell certain property. She wishes to keep her identity a secret, but the agent makes it clear to potential buyers of the property that he is acting in an agency capacity. In this situation, Eileen is a partially disclosed principal. ■

3. An **undisclosed principal** is a principal whose identity is totally unknown by the third party. In addition, the third party has no knowledge that the agent is acting in an agency capacity at the time the contract is made.

33–2a Authorized Acts

If an agent acts within the scope of her or his authority, normally the principal is obligated to perform the contract regardless of whether the principal was disclosed, partially disclosed, or undisclosed. Whether the *agent may also be held liable* under the contract, however, depends on the disclosed, partially disclosed, or undisclosed status of the principal.

Disclosed or Partially Disclosed Principal A disclosed or partially disclosed principal is liable to a third party for a contract made by the agent. If the principal is disclosed, the agent has no contractual liability for the nonperformance of the principal or the third party. If the principal is partially disclosed, in most states the agent is also treated as a party to the contract. Thus, the third party can hold the agent liable for contractual nonperformance.[5]

■ **CASE IN POINT 33.8** Stonhard, Inc., makes epoxy and urethane flooring and installs it in industrial and commercial buildings. Marvin Sussman contracted with Stonhard to install flooring at a Blue Ridge Farms food-manufacturing facility in Brooklyn, New York. Sussman did not disclose that he was acting as an agent for the facility's owner, Blue Ridge Foods, LLC, at the time of the contract.

When Stonhard was not paid for the flooring it installed, it filed a suit against the facility, its owner, and Sussman to recover damages for breach of contract. The lower court dismissed the complaint against Sussman personally, but on appeal a reviewing court reversed that decision. The contract had been signed by Sussman "of Blue Ridge Farms." That evidence indicated that

Sussman was acting as an agent for a partially disclosed principal, in that the agency relationship was known, but not the principal's identity. "As an agent for an undisclosed [or partially disclosed] principal, Sussman became personally liable under the contract."[6] ■

Undisclosed Principal When neither the fact of an agency relationship nor the identity of the principal is disclosed, the undisclosed principal is bound to perform just as if the principal had been fully disclosed at the time the contract was made.

■ **CASE IN POINT 33.9** Bobby Williams bought a car at Sherman Henderson's auto repair business in Louisiana for $3,000. Henderson (the agent) negotiated and made the sale for the car's owner, Joe Pike (the principal), whose name was not disclosed. Williams drove the car to Memphis, Tennessee, where his daughter was a student. Three days after the sale, the car's engine caught fire. Williams extinguished the blaze and contacted Henderson. The next day, the vehicle was stolen from a parking lot outside Williams's daughter's apartment.

Williams filed a suit in a Louisiana state court against Pike (the principal) and Henderson (the agent). The court awarded Williams $2,000, plus the costs of the suit, adding that if Williams had returned the car, it would have awarded him the entire price. A state appellate court affirmed. Both Pike and Henderson—the undisclosed principal and his agent—were liable to Williams.[7] ■

Indemnification. When a principal's identity is undisclosed and the agent is forced to pay the third party, the agent is entitled to be *indemnified* (compensated) by the principal. The principal had a duty to perform, even though his or her identity was undisclosed,[8] and failure to do so will make the principal ultimately liable.

Performance. Once the undisclosed principal's identity is revealed, the third party generally can elect to hold either the principal or the agent liable on the contract. Conversely, the undisclosed principal can require the third party to fulfill the contract, *unless* one of the following is true:

1. The undisclosed principal was expressly excluded as a party in the written contract.

---

5. *Restatement (Third) of Agency,* Section 6.02.

6. *Stonhard, Inc. v. Blue Ridge Farms, LLC,* 114 A.D.3d 757, 980 N.Y.S.2d 507 (2 Dept. 2014).
7. *Williams v. Pike,* 58 So.3d 525 (La.App. 2 Cir. 2011).
8. If the agent is a gratuitous agent, and the principal accepts the benefits of the agent's contract with a third party, then the principal will be liable to the agent on the theory of quasi contract.

2. The contract is a negotiable instrument signed by the agent with no indication of signing in a representative capacity.[9]
3. The performance of the agent is personal to the contract, thus allowing the third party to refuse the principal's performance.

33–2b Unauthorized Acts

If an agent has no authority but nevertheless contracts with a third party, the *principal* cannot be held liable on the contract. It does not matter whether the principal was disclosed, partially disclosed, or undisclosed. The *agent* is liable.

■ **EXAMPLE 33.10** Chu signs a contract for the purchase of a truck, purportedly acting as an agent under authority granted by Navarro. In fact, Navarro has not given Chu any such authority. Navarro refuses to pay for the truck, claiming that Chu had no authority to purchase it. The seller of the truck is entitled to hold Chu liable for payment. ■

Implied Warranty If the principal is disclosed or partially disclosed, and the agent contracts with a third party without authorization, the agent is liable to the third party. The agent's liability here is based on his or her breach of the *implied warranty of authority*, not on the breach of the contract itself.[10] An agent impliedly warrants that he or she has the authority to enter a contract on behalf of the principal.

■ **EXAMPLE 33.11** Pinnell, a reclusive artist, hires Auber to solicit offers for particular paintings from various galleries, but does not authorize her to enter into sales agreements. Olaf, a gallery owner, offers to buy two of Pinnell's paintings for an upcoming show. If Auber draws up a sales contract with Olaf, she impliedly warrants that she has the authority to enter into sales contracts on behalf of Pinnell. If Pinnell does not agree to ratify Auber's sales contract, Olaf cannot hold Pinnell liable, but he can hold Auber liable for breaching the implied warranty of authority. ■

Third Party's Knowledge Note that if the third party knows at the time the contract is made that the agent does not have authority, then the agent is not liable. Similarly, if the agent expresses to the third party *uncertainty* as to

the extent of her or his authority, the agent is not personally liable.

33–2c Actions by E-Agents

Although in the past standard agency principles applied only to *human* agents, today these same agency principles also apply to e-agents. An electronic agent, or **e-agent,** is a semiautonomous software program that is capable of executing specific tasks, such as searching through many databases and retrieving relevant information for the user.

The Uniform Electronic Transactions Act (UETA), which was discussed previously, sets forth provisions relating to the principal's liability for the actions of e-agents. According to Section 15 of the UETA, e-agents can enter into binding agreements on behalf of their principals—at least, in those states that have adopted the act. Thus, if consumers place an order over the Internet, and the company (principal) takes the order via an e-agent, the company cannot later claim that it did not receive the order.

The UETA also stipulates that if an e-agent does not provide an opportunity to prevent errors at the time of the transaction, the other party to the transaction can avoid the transaction. Therefore, if an e-agent fails to provide an on-screen confirmation of a purchase or sale, the other party can avoid the effect of any errors. ■ **EXAMPLE 33.12** Bigelow wants to purchase three copies of three different books (a total of nine items). The e-agent mistakenly records an order for thirty-three of a single book and does not provide an on-screen verification of the order. If thirty-three books are then sent to Bigelow, he can avoid the contract to purchase them. ■

33–3 Liability for Torts and Crimes

Obviously, any person, including an agent, is liable for his or her own torts and crimes. Whether a principal can also be held liable for an agent's torts and crimes depends on several factors, which we examine here. In some situations, a principal may be held liable not only for the torts of an agent but also for torts committed by an independent contractor.

33–3a Principal's Tortious Conduct

A principal who acts through an agent may be liable for harm resulting from the principal's own negligence or recklessness. Thus, a principal may be liable if he or she gives improper instructions, authorizes the use of improper materials or tools, or establishes improper rules that result in the agent's committing a tort.

---

9. Under the Uniform Commercial Code (UCC), only the agent is liable if the instrument neither names the principal nor shows that the agent signed in a representative capacity [UCC 3–402(b)(2)].
10. The agent is not liable on the contract because the agent was never intended personally to be a party to the contract.

■ **EXAMPLE 33.13** Parker knows that Audrey's driver's license has been suspended but nevertheless tells her to use the company truck to deliver some equipment to a customer. If someone is injured as a result, Parker will be liable for his own negligence in instructing Audrey to drive without a valid license. ■

33–3b Principal's Authorization of Agent's Tortious Conduct

Similarly, a principal who authorizes an agent to commit a tort may be liable to persons or property injured thereby, because the act is considered to be the principal's. ■ **EXAMPLE 33.14** Pedro directs his agent, Andy, to cut the corn on specific acreage, which neither of them has the right to do. The harvest is therefore a trespass (a tort), and Pedro is liable to the owner of the corn. ■

Note that an agent acting at the principal's direction can be liable, along with the principal, for committing the tortious act even if the agent was unaware that the act was wrong. Assume in *Example 33.14* that Andy, the agent, did not know that Pedro lacked the right to harvest the corn. Andy can nonetheless be held liable to the owner of the field for damages, along with Pedro, the principal.

33–3c Liability for Agent's Misrepresentation

A principal is exposed to tort liability whenever a third person sustains a loss due to the agent's misrepresentation. The principal's liability depends on whether the agent was actually or apparently authorized to make representations and whether the representations were made within the scope of the agency. The principal is always directly responsible for an agent's misrepresentation made within the scope of the agent's authority.

■ **EXAMPLE 33.15** Ainsley is a demonstrator for Pavlovich's products. Pavlovich sends Ainsley to a home show to demonstrate the products and to answer questions from consumers. Pavlovich has given Ainsley authority to make statements about the products. If Ainsley makes only true representations, all is fine. But if he makes false claims, Pavlovich will be liable for any injuries or damages sustained by third parties in reliance on Ainsley's false representations. ■

Apparent Implied Authority When a principal has placed an agent in a position of apparent authority—making it possible for the agent to defraud a third party—the principal may also be liable for the agent's fraudulent acts. For instance, partners in a partnership generally have the apparent implied authority to act as agents of the firm. Thus, if one of the partners commits a tort or a crime, the partnership itself—and often the other partners personally—can be held liable for the loss.

■ **EXAMPLE 33.16** Saulheim & Company is a securities brokerage firm that operates as a partnership and provides various financial services. The firm's managing partner, Dan Saulheim, is caught embezzling funds that clients have turned over to the firm for investment. After he is convicted, other partners in the firm claim that they are not liable for losses resulting from his illegal activities. In this situation, other partners may be liable if a court finds that Saulheim had apparent implied authority to act in the ordinary course of the partnership's business. Thus, the firm, as principal, is liable, and the personal assets of the individual partners, as agents, can be used to pay the firm's liability. ■

Innocent Misrepresentation Tort liability based on fraud requires proof that a material misstatement was made knowingly and with the intent to deceive. An agent's *innocent* misstatements in a contract or warranty transaction can also provide grounds for the third party's rescission of the contract and the award of damages. Justice dictates that when a principal knows that an agent is not accurately advised of facts but does not correct either the agent's or the third party's impressions, the principal is responsible. The point is that the principal is always directly responsible for an agent's misrepresentation made within the scope of authority.

33–3d Liability for Agent's Negligence

An agent is liable for his or her own torts. A principal may also be liable for harm an agent causes to a third party under the doctrine of ***respondeat superior,***[11] a Latin term meaning "let the master respond." Under the doctrine of *respondeat superior*, the principal-employer is liable for any harm caused to a third party by an agent-employee in the course or scope of employment. The doctrine imposes **vicarious liability,** or indirect liability, because the principal-employer is being held liable for torts committed by an agent-employee.

When an agent commits a negligent act in such a situation, *both* the agent and the principal are liable. ■ **EXAMPLE 33.17** Aegis hires SDI to provide landscaping services for its property. An herbicide sprayed by

---

11. Pronounced ree-*spahn*-dee-uht soo-*peer*-ee-your. The doctrine of *respondeat superior* applies not only to employer-employee relationships but also to other principal-agent relationships in which the principal has the right of control over the agent.

SDI employee David Hoggatt enters the Aegis building through the air-conditioning system and caused Catherine Warner, an Aegis employee, to suffer a heart attack. If Warner sues, both SDI (principal) and Hoggatt (agent) can be held liable for negligence. ∎

The Doctrine of *Respondeat Superior*

The doctrine of *respondeat superior* is similar to the theory of strict liability in that liability is imposed regardless of fault. At early common law, a servant (employee) was viewed as the master's (employer's) property. The master was deemed to have absolute control over the servant's acts and was held strictly liable for them, no matter how carefully the master supervised the servant. Although employers today are not masters of their employees, control is still a central concept to liability. This chapter's *Global Insight* feature discusses whether nations that follow Islamic law recognize the doctrine of *respondeat superior.*

Underlying Rationale. The rationale for the doctrine of *respondeat superior* is based on the social duty that requires every person to manage his or her affairs so as not to injure another. This duty applies even when a person acts through an agent (controls the conduct of another).

Public Policy. Generally, public policy requires that an injured person be afforded effective relief, and a business enterprise is usually better able to provide that relief than is an individual employee. Employers normally carry liability insurance to cover any damages awarded as a result of such lawsuits. They are also able to spread the cost of risk over the entire business enterprise.

Application Today. The courts have applied the doctrine of *respondeat superior* for nearly two centuries. It continues to have practical implications in all situations involving principal-agent (employer-employee) relationships. Today, the small-town store with one clerk and the multinational corporation with thousands of employees are equally subject to the doctrine.

Determining the Scope of Employment

The key to determining whether a principal may be liable for the torts of an agent under the doctrine of *respondeat superior* is whether the torts are committed within the scope of the agency. Courts may consider the following factors in determining whether a particular act occurred within the course and scope of employment:

1. Whether the employee's act was authorized by the employer.
2. The time, place, and purpose of the act.
3. Whether the act was one commonly performed by employees on behalf of their employers.
4. The extent to which the employer's interest was advanced by the act.
5. The extent to which the private interests of the employee were involved.

GLOBAL INSIGHT — Islamic Law and *Respondeat Superior*

The doctrine of *respondeat superior* is well established in the legal systems of the United States and most Western countries. As you have already read, under this doctrine, employers can be held liable for the acts of their employees. The doctrine of *respondeat superior* is not universal, however. Most Middle Eastern countries, for example, do not follow this doctrine.

Codification of Islamic Law

Islamic law, as codified in the *sharia*, holds to a strict belief that responsibility for human actions lies with the individual and cannot be vicariously (indirectly) extended to others. This belief and other concepts of Islamic law are based on the writings of Muhammad, the seventh-century prophet whose revelations form the basis of the Islamic religion and, by extension, the

sharia. Muhammad's prophecies are documented in the Koran (Qur'an), which is the principal source of the *sharia.*

An Exception

Islamic law does allow for an employer to be responsible for an employee's actions when the actions result from a direct order given by the employer to the employee. This principle also applies to contractual obligations. Note that the master is responsible *only* if direct orders were given. Otherwise stated, unless an employee is obeying a direct order of the employer, liability for the employee's actions does not extend to the employer.

Critical Thinking *How would U.S. society be affected if employers could not be held vicariously liable for their employees' torts?*

6. Whether the employer furnished the means or instrumentality (such as a truck or a machine) by which an injury was inflicted.

7. Whether the employer had reason to know that the employee would perform the act in question and whether the employee had done it before.

8. Whether the act involved the commission of a serious crime.

In the following case, the court had to determine whether or not a dump truck operator was the employee of a concrete services contractor.

Case 33.2

Asphalt & Concrete Services, Inc. v. Perry

Court of Special Appeals of Maryland, 221 Md.App. 235, 108 A.3d 558 (2015).

Background and Facts Asphalt & Concrete Services, Inc. (ACS), was working on a play pad at St. John Regional Catholic School in Frederick, Maryland. ACS project manager Blake Wood contacted William Johnson at Higher Power Trucking, LLC, to arrange for a dump truck to haul material from a quarry to the job site. One day, while Johnson was driving the dump truck between the job site and the quarry, the truck struck and injured Moran Perry, who was crossing an intersection.

To recover for his injuries, Perry filed a lawsuit in a Maryland state court against ACS. Perry alleged that Johnson's negligence in operating the dump truck was the proximate cause of his injuries and that Johnson was ACS's employee. ACS, however, claimed that Johnson was an independent contractor. A jury agreed with Perry and awarded him $529,500 in damages. The court issued a judgment in Perry's favor, and ACS appealed.

In the Language of the Court

GRAEFF, J. [Judge]

* * * *

* * * Pursuant to the doctrine of *respondeat superior*, an employer may be found liable for torts committed by its employee while acting in the scope of employment. ACS does not dispute this well-established rule, but it argues that the evidence showed that Mr. Johnson was not its employee.

* * * Maryland courts have traditionally considered five criteria in determining whether or not an employer/employee relationship exists between two parties. *These criteria, developed from the common law standard for determining the master/servant relationship, include (1) the power to select and hire the employee, (2) the payment of wages, (3) the power to discharge, (4) the power to control the employee's conduct, and (5) whether the work is part of the regular business of the employer.* [Emphasis added.]

Of the five factors, the factor of control stands out as the most important. * * * Whether the employer has the right to control and direct the employee in the performance of the work and in the manner in which the work is to be done is the decisive, or controlling, test.

* * * *

Here, * * * the evidence indicated as follows: (1) ACS called Mr. Johnson directly to reserve his trucking services; (2) Mr. Wood spoke only to Mr. Johnson when calling Higher Power; (3) ACS directed Mr. Johnson to go to the * * * quarry to pick up materials for the play pad project and gave him the time to be there for the pick-up; (4) Mr. Johnson was required to bring the materials directly to the job site after his truck was loaded, and if Mr. Johnson did not deliver the materials promptly, ACS had the right to dock his pay or to no longer employ him; (5) ACS paid Mr. Johnson on an hourly basis from the time he picked up his first load until ACS dismissed him from the job site; (6) after Mr. Johnson delivered his first load of materials, ACS directed him to return to the quarry to pick up and bring back additional materials; and (7) at the job site, Mr. Johnson was obligated to follow ACS's directions in terms of where to drop the materials, how much material to drop, and how many times he would need to return to the quarry. Based on that evidence, a jury could find that Mr. Johnson was subject to ACS's control, and ACS was liable for Mr. Johnson's negligence pursuant to the doctrine of *respondeat superior*.

Case 33.2 Continues

Case 33.2 Continued

Decision and Remedy *The state intermediate appellate court affirmed the jury's finding with respect to Johnson's status as ACS's employee. The court disagreed, however, with the lower court's admission of certain evidence that may have influenced the jury's finding of proximate cause for Perry's injuries. As a result, the court reversed the judgment on this ground and remanded the case for a new trial.*

Critical Thinking
- **Economic** *Why did ACS contend that Johnson was not its employee? Discuss.*

The Distinction between a "Detour" and a "Frolic" A useful insight into the concept of "scope of employment" can be gained from Judge Baron Parke's classic distinction between a "detour" and a "frolic" in the case of *Joel v. Morison* (1834).[12] In this case, the English court held that if a servant merely took a detour from his master's business, the master will be responsible. If, however, the servant was on a "frolic of his own" and not in any way "on his master's business," the master will not be liable.

■ **EXAMPLE 33.18** While driving his employer's vehicle to call on a customer, Mandel decides to stop at a store—which is three blocks off his route—to take care of a personal matter. As Mandel approaches the store, he negligently runs into a parked vehicle owned by Chan. In this situation, because Mandel's detour from the employer's business is not substantial, he is still acting within the scope of employment, and the employer is liable.

But suppose instead that Mandel decides to pick up a few friends in another city for cocktails and in the process negligently runs his vehicle into Chan's. In this situation, the departure from the employer's business is substantial—Mandel is on a "frolic" of his own. Thus, the employer normally will not be liable to Chan for damages. ■

Employee Travel Time An employee going to and from work or to and from meals usually is considered to be outside the scope of employment. If travel is part of a person's position, however, as it is for a traveling salesperson, then travel time is normally considered within the scope of employment. For such an employee, the entire business trip, including the return trip home, is within the scope of employment unless there is a significant departure from the employer's business.

Notice of Dangerous Conditions The employer is charged with knowledge of any dangerous conditions discovered by an employee and pertinent to the employment situation.

---
12. 6 Car. & P. 501, 172 Eng.Rep. 1338 (1834).

■ **EXAMPLE 33.19** Brad, a maintenance employee in Martin's apartment building, notices a lead pipe protruding from the ground in the building's courtyard. Brad neglects either to fix the pipe or to inform Martin of the danger. John trips on the pipe and is injured. Martin is charged with knowledge of the dangerous condition regardless of whether Brad actually informed him. That knowledge is imputed to the employer by virtue of the employment relationship. ■

33–3e Liability for Agent's Intentional Torts

Most intentional torts that individuals commit have no relation to their employment, and their employers will not be held liable. Nevertheless, under the doctrine of *respondeat superior*, the employer can be liable for intentional torts that an employee commits within the course and scope of employment. For instance, a department store owner is liable when a security guard who is a store employee commits the tort of false imprisonment while acting within the scope of employment. Similarly, a nightclub owner is liable when a "bouncer" commits the tort of assault and battery while on the job.

In addition, an employer who knows or should know that an employee has a propensity for committing tortious acts is liable for the employee's acts even if they would not ordinarily be considered within the scope of employment. ■ **EXAMPLE 33.20** Chaz, the owner of the Comedy Club, hires Alec as a bouncer for the club even though he knows that Alec has a history of arrests for criminal assault and battery. In this situation, Chaz may be liable if Alec viciously attacks a customer in the parking lot after hours. ■

An employer is also liable for permitting an employee to engage in reckless actions that can injure others. ■ **EXAMPLE 33.21** The owner of Bates Trucking observes an employee smoking while filling containerized trucks with highly flammable liquids. Failure to stop the employee will cause the employer to be liable for any injuries that result if a truck explodes. ∎ Needless to say, most employers purchase liability insurance to cover their potential liability for employee conduct in many situations.

Whether an agent's allegedly tortious conduct fell within the scope of the agent's employment, making the principal vicariously liable, was at the heart of the dispute in the following case.

M.J. v. Wisan

Utah Supreme Court, 2016 UT 13, __ P.3d __ (2016).

In the Language of the Court

Associate Chief Justice *LEE* * * * :

* * * *

[The United Effort Plan Trust ("UEP Trust" or the "Trust") was formed in Utah by members of the Fundamental-ist Church of Jesus Christ of Latter-Day Saints ("FLDS Church"). The Trust] members deeded their property to the UEP Trust to be managed by Church leaders. Church leaders, who were also trustees, then used this property to min-ister to the needs of the members.

* * * *

[At the time of the events leading up to this case,] the Trust was operated for the express purpose of furthering the doctrines of the FLDS Church, includ-ing the practice of * * * marriage involv-ing underage girls.

* * * *

[Later, as a result of unrelated litiga-tion, a state court reformed the Trust] by excising the purpose of advancing the religious doctrines and goals of the FLDS Church to the degree that any of these were illegal, including * * * sexual activity between adults and minors. [The court appointed Bruce Wisan to head the Trust.]

* * * *

[Later] M.J., a former member of the FLDS Church and beneficiary of the UEP Trust, [filed this suit in a Utah state court against Wisan, as head of the Trust, alleging that] when she was fourteen years old, she was forced to marry Allen Steed, her first cousin. The wedding was performed by Warren Jeffs, who at the time was acting president of both the FLDS Church and * * * the Trust. * * * M.J. claims that Steed repeat-edly sexually assaulted and raped her

* * * . She requested a divorce from Steed on multiple occasions, but Jeffs refused to allow it. He also refused to let M.J. live * * * separately from her husband.

* * * She seeks to hold * * * the Trust vicariously liable for intentional inflic-tion of emotional distress.

* * * M.J. * * * claims that Jeffs and other trustees were acting "in further-ance of the trust administration and within the scope of their authority," and thus contends that the Trust should be liable under the doctrine of *respondeat superior.*

* * * *

The Trust filed a series of motions for summary judgment. All of those motions were denied. The Trust then filed [this] petition for review.

* * * *

* * * Under [Utah Code Section 75–7–1010, Utah's version of Section 1010 of the Uniform Trust Code,] a trust is liable for the trustee's acts per-formed "in the course of administering the trust."

* * * The terms of the statute, in con-text, are quite clear. "In the course of" *is the traditional formulation of the standard for vicarious liability under the doctrine of* respondeat superior. *We accordingly inter-pret the Uniform Trust Act as incorporat-ing the established standard of* respondeat superior *liability.* Thus, under [Section 75–7–1010] a trust is liable for the acts of a trustee when the trustee was acting within the scope of his responsibility as a trustee. [Emphasis added.]

* * * *

The difficult question for the law in this field has been to define the line between a course of conduct sub-ject to the employer's control and an

independent course of conduct not con-nected to the prin-cipal. *An independent course of conduct is a matter so removed from the agent's duties that the law, in fairness, eliminates the principal's vicarious liability.* Such a course of conduct is one that represents a departure from, not an escalation of, conduct involved in performing assigned work or other conduct that an employer permits or controls. [Emphasis added.]

Our cases have identified three factors of relevance to this inquiry: (1) whether the agent's conduct is of the general kind the agent is employed to perform; (2) whether the agent is acting within the hours of the agent's work and the ordinary spatial boundaries of the employment; and (3) whether the agent's acts were motivated, at least in part, by the purpose of serving the principal's interest.

* * * In the case law of a number of states, spatial and time boundaries are no longer essential hallmarks of an agency relationship. Instead, the law now recognizes that agents may interact on an employer's behalf with third parties although the employee is neither situated on the employer's premises nor continu-ously or exclusively engaged in perform-ing assigned work.

A number of courts have also ques-tioned the viability of the requirement that an agent's acts be motivated in some part by an intention to serve the princi-pal's purposes.

* * * In [some] jurisdictions, * * * courts avoid the use of motive or inten-tion to determine whether an employee's tortious conduct falls within the scope of employment and adopt a different

Case 33.3 Continues

Case 33.3 Continued

standard for identifying the tie between the tortfeasor's employment and the tort. One such standard is whether the tort is a generally foreseeable consequence of the enterprise undertaken by the employer or is incident to it—in other words, whether the agent's conduct is not so unusual or startling that it seems unfair to include the loss resulting from it in the employer's business costs, or whether the tort was engendered by the employment or an outgrowth of it. Another considers whether the employment furnished the specific impetus for a tort or increased the general risk that the tort would occur. These tests leave to the finder of fact the challenge of determining whether a tortfeasor's employment did more than create a happenstance opportunity to commit the tort.

* * * To resolve this case we need not choose * * * between the purpose or motive test * * * and the alternative formulations * * * because we find that the Trust's attempts to defeat its liability on summary judgment fail under any of the * * * formulations.

We do openly endorse one particular aspect of * * * the doctrine of *respondeat superior*, however. Specifically * * * we hold that an agent need not be acting within the hours of the employee's work and the ordinary spatial boundaries of the employment in order to be acting within the course of his employment. * * * We acknowledge that in today's business world much work is performed for an employer away from a defined work space and outside of a limited work shift. And we accordingly reject the Trust's attempt to escape liability on the ground that Jeffs's acts as a trustee were not performed while he was on the Trust's clock or at a work space designated for his work for the Trust. Instead we hold that the key question is whether Jeffs was acting within the scope of employment when performing work assigned by the employer or engaging in a course of conduct subject to the employer's control.

[The Trust argues] that settled case-law establishes "as a matter of law that the sexual misconduct of an employee is outside the scope of employment." Granted, there are many cases that so conclude * * * and some of those cases * * * turn principally on the ground that * * * an agent who commits a sexual assault * * * cannot be viewed as advancing, even in part, the purposes of his principal. Yet some of the cases in this field (particularly more recent ones) * * * adopt * * * a standard that turns not on motive or purpose but on foreseeability, or on whether the employee's acts were engendered by or an outgrowth of the employment, or the employment furnished the impetus for the tort.

* * * *

And we conclude that this is one of those cases. Given Jeffs's unique role as leader of the FLDS Church, and in light of the unusual, troubling function of * * * marriage involving young brides in the FLDS culture, we hold that a reasonable factfinder could conclude that Jeffs was acting within the scope of his role as a trustee in directing Steed to engage in sexual activity with M.J.

* * * *

* * * We affirm the denial of the Trust's motions for summary judgment on that basis.

Legal Reasoning Questions

1. Why do some courts apply a standard for imposing vicarious liability that does not rely on motive or purpose to determine whether an agent's tortious conduct falls within the scope of employment?

2. Why, in some states, are the boundaries of work time and space no longer essential factors in determining the scope of employment in an agency relationship?

3. Who does the result in this case benefit? Why?

33–3f Liability for Independent Contractor's Torts

Generally, an employer is not liable for physical harm caused to a third person by the negligent act of an independent contractor in the performance of the contract. This is because the employer does not have *the right to control* the details of an independent contractor's performance.

Courts make an exception to this rule when the contract involves unusually hazardous activities, such as blasting operations, the transportation of highly volatile chemicals, or the use of poisonous gases. In these situations, strict liability is imposed, and an employer cannot be shielded from liability merely by using an independent contractor.

33–3g Liability for Agent's Crimes

An agent is liable for his or her own crimes. A principal or employer normally is *not* liable for an agent's crime even if the crime was committed within the scope of authority or employment. An exception to this rule is made when the principal or employer participated in the crime by conspiracy or other action.

In addition, in some jurisdictions, a principal may be liable under specific statutes if an agent, in the course and scope of employment, violates certain regulations. For instance, a principal might be liable for an agent's violation of sanitation rules or regulations governing prices, weights, or the sale of liquor.

33–4 Termination of an Agency

Agency law is similar to contract law in that both an agency and a contract may be terminated by an act of the parties or by operation of law. Once the relationship between the principal and the agent has ended, the agent no longer has the right (*actual* authority) to bind the principal. For an agent's *apparent* authority to be terminated, though, third persons may also need to be notified that the agency has been terminated.

33–4a Termination by Act of the Parties

An agency may be terminated by certain acts of the parties, which are listed and described in Exhibit 33–2. Bases for termination by act of the parties include lapse of time, achievement of purpose, occurrence of a specific event, mutual agreement, and at the option of one party.

When an agency agreement specifies the time period during which the agency relationship will exist, the agency ends when that time period expires. If no definite time is stated, then the agency continues for a reasonable time and can be terminated at will by either party. What constitutes a reasonable time depends on the circumstances and the nature of the agency relationship.

The parties can, of course, mutually agree to end their agency relationship. In addition, as a general rule, either party can terminate the agency relationship without the agreement of the other. The act of termination is called *revocation* if done by the principal and *renunciation* if done by the agent. Note, however, that the terminating party may face liability if the termination is wrongful.

EXHIBIT 33–2 Termination by Act of the Parties

METHOD	RULES	ILLUSTRATION
1. Lapse of Time.	Agency terminates automatically at the end of the stated time.	Page lists her property for sale with Alex, a real estate agent, for six months. The agency ends in six months.
2. Purpose Achieved.	Agency terminates automatically on the completion of the purpose for which it was formed.	Calvin, a cattle rancher, hires Abe as his agent in the purchase of fifty breeding stock. The agency ends when the cattle have been purchased.
3. Occurrence of a Specific Event.	Agency normally terminates automatically on the event's occurrence.	Meredith appoints Allen to handle her business affairs while she is away. The agency terminates when Meredith returns.
4. Mutual Agreement.	Agency terminates when both parties consent to end the agency relationship.	Linda and Greg agree that Greg will no longer be her agent in procuring business equipment.
5. At the Option of One Party (*revocation*, if by principal; *renunciation*, if by agent).	Either party normally has a right to terminate the agency relationship. Wrongful termination can lead to liability for breach of contract.	When Patrick becomes ill, he informs Alice that he is revoking her authority to be his agent.

Wrongful Termination Although both parties have the *power* to terminate the agency, they may not always possess the *right* to do so. Wrongful termination can subject the canceling party to a lawsuit for breach of contract. ■ **EXAMPLE 33.22** Rawlins has a one-year employment contract with Munro to act as agent in return for $65,000. Munro has the *power* to discharge Rawlins before the contract period expires. But if he does so, he can be sued for breaching the contract, because he had no *right* to terminate the agency. ■

Even in an agency at will—in which either party may terminate at any time—the principal who wishes to terminate must give the agent *reasonable* notice. The notice must be at least sufficient to allow the agent to recoup his or her expenses and, in some situations, to make a normal profit.

Agency Coupled with an Interest A special rule applies to an *agency coupled with an interest.* In an **agency coupled with an interest,** the agent has some legal right to (an interest in) the property that is the subject of the agency. This type of agency is not an agency in the usual sense because it is created for the agent's benefit instead of for the principal's benefit.

■ **EXAMPLE 33.23** Sylvia owns Harper Hills, a vacation home. She needs some cash right away, so she enters into an agreement with Rob under which Rob will lend her $10,000. In return, she will grant Rob a one-half interest in Harper Hills and "the exclusive right to sell" it. The loan is to be repaid out of the sale's proceeds. Rob is Sylvia's agent, and their relationship is an agency coupled with an interest. The agency was created when the loan agreement was made for the purpose of securing the loan. Therefore, Rob's agency power is irrevocable. ■

An agency coupled with an interest should not be confused with a situation in which the agent merely derives proceeds or profits from the sale of the subject matter. Many agents are paid a commission for their services, but the agency relationship involved does not constitute an agency coupled with an interest. For instance, a real estate agent who merely receives a commission from the sale of real property does not have a beneficial interest in the property itself.

Notice of Termination When the parties terminate an agency, it is the principal's duty to inform any third parties who know of the existence of the agency that it has been terminated. No particular form is required for notice of termination to be effective. The principal can personally notify the agent, or the agent can learn of the termination through some other means.

Although an agent's actual authority ends when the agency is terminated, an agent's *apparent authority* continues until the third party receives notice (from any source) that such authority has been terminated. ■ **EXAMPLE 33.24** Manning bids on a shipment of steel, and Stone is hired as an agent to arrange transportation for the shipment. When Stone learns that Manning has lost the bid, Stone's authority to make the transportation arrangement terminates. ■

If the principal knows that a third party has dealt with the agent, the principal is expected to notify that person *directly.* For third parties who have heard about the agency but have not yet dealt with the agent, *constructive notice* is sufficient.[13] If the agent's authority is written, however, normally it must be revoked in writing (unless the written document contains an expiration date).

33–4b Termination by Operation of Law

Certain events terminate agency authority automatically because their occurrence makes it impossible for the agent to perform or improbable that the principal would continue to want performance. We look at these events here. Note that when an agency terminates by operation of law, there is no duty to notify third persons—unless the agent's authority is coupled with an interest.

1. *Death or insanity.* The general rule is that the death or insanity of either the principal or the agent automatically and immediately terminates an ordinary agency relationship.[14] Knowledge of the death or insanity is not required. ■ **EXAMPLE 33.25** Grey sends Bosley to Japan to purchase a rare book. Before Bosley makes the purchase, Grey dies. Bosley's agent status is terminated at the moment of Grey's death, even though Bosley does not know that Grey has died. ■ (Some states, however, have enacted statutes that change the common law rule to require an agent's knowledge of the principal's death before termination.)

---

13. With *constructive notice* of a fact, knowledge of the fact is imputed by law to a person if he or she could have discovered the fact through proper diligence. Constructive notice is often accomplished by publication in a newspaper.

14. An exception to this rule exists in the bank-customer relationship. A bank, as agent, can continue to exercise specific types of authority after the customer's death or insanity and can continue to pay checks drawn by the customer for ten days after death.

2. *Impossibility.* When the specific subject matter of an agency is destroyed or lost, the agency terminates. ■ **EXAMPLE 33.26** Pedro employs Vasquez to sell Pedro's house. Prior to any sale, the house is destroyed by fire. Vasquez's agency and authority to sell the house terminate. ■ Similarly, when it is impossible for the agent to perform the agency lawfully because of a change in the law, the agency terminates.

3. *Changed circumstances.* Sometimes, an event occurs that has such an unusual effect on the subject matter of the agency that the agent can reasonably infer that the principal will not want the agency to continue. In such situations, the agency terminates. ■ **EXAMPLE 33.27** Baird hires Joslen to sell a tract of land for $40,000. Subsequently, Joslen learns that there is oil under the land and that the land is therefore worth $1 million. The agency and Joslen's authority to sell the land for $40,000 are terminated. ■

4. *Bankruptcy.* If either the principal or the agent petitions for bankruptcy, the agency is *usually* terminated. In certain circumstances, such as when the agent's financial status is irrelevant to the purpose of the agency, the agency relationship may continue. Insolvency, as distinct from bankruptcy, does not necessarily terminate the relationship. (An *insolvent* person is one who cannot pay debts as they come due or whose liabilities exceed his or her assets.)

5. *War.* When the principal's country and the agent's country are at war with each other, the agency is terminated. In this situation, the agency is automatically suspended or terminated because there is no way to enforce the legal rights and obligations of the parties.

See Concept Summary 33.2 for a synopsis of the rules governing the termination of an agency by operation of law.

Concept Summary 33.2

Agency Termination by Operation of Law

Death or Insanity	Termination of the agency is automatic on the death or insanity of either the principal or the agent—except when the agency is coupled with an interest.
Impossibility	Agency termination occurs any time the agency cannot be performed because of an event beyond the parties' control, such as the destruction of the specific subject matter.
Changed Circumstances	When events are so unusual that it would be inequitable to allow the agency to exist, the agency will terminate.
Bankruptcy	Bankruptcy petition—but not mere insolvency—usually terminates the agency.
War between Countries	War between the principal's country and the agent's country automatically suspends or terminates agency because there is no way to enforce legal rights.

Reviewing: Agency Liability and Termination

Lynne Meyer, on her way to a business meeting and in a hurry, stopped at a Buy-Mart store for a new car charger for her smartphone. There was a long line at one of the checkout counters, but a cashier, Valerie Watts, opened another counter and began loading the cash drawer. Meyer told Watts that she was in a hurry and asked Watts to work faster. Instead, Watts slowed her pace. At this point, Meyer hit Watts. It is not clear whether Meyer hit Watts intentionally or, in an attempt to retrieve the car charger, hit her inadvertently.

In response, Watts grabbed Meyer by the hair and hit her repeatedly in the back of the head, while Meyer screamed for help. Management personnel separated the two women and questioned them about the incident. Watts was immediately fired for violating the store's no-fighting policy. Meyer subsequently sued Buy-Mart, alleging that the store was liable for the tort (assault and battery) committed by its employee. Using the information presented in the chapter, answer the following questions.

1. Under what doctrine discussed in this chapter might Buy-Mart be held liable for the tort committed by Watts?
2. What is the key factor in determining whether Buy-Mart is liable under this doctrine?
3. How is Buy-Mart's potential liability affected by whether Watts's behavior constituted an intentional tort or a tort of negligence?
4. Suppose that when Watts applied for the job at Buy-Mart, she disclosed in her application that she had previously been convicted of felony assault and battery. Nevertheless, Buy-Mart hired Watts as a cashier. How might this fact affect Buy-Mart's liability for Watts's actions?

Debate This . . . *The doctrine of* respondeat superior *should be modified to make agents solely liable for their tortious (wrongful) acts committed within the scope of employment.*

Terms and Concepts

agency coupled with an interest 636	express authority 622	ratification 625
apparent authority 624	implied authority 624	*respondeat superior* 629
disclosed principal 626	notary public 622	undisclosed principal 627
e-agent 628	partially disclosed principal 627	vicarious liability 629
equal dignity rule 622	power of attorney 622	

Issue Spotters

1. Davis contracts with Estee to buy a certain horse on her behalf. Estee asks Davis not to reveal her identity. Davis makes a deal with Farmland Stables, the owner of the horse, and makes a down payment. Estee does not pay the rest of the price. Farmland Stables sues Davis for breach of contract. Can Davis hold Estee liable for whatever damages he has to pay? Why or why not? (See *Liability for Contracts*.)

2. Vivian, owner of Wonder Goods Company, employs Xena as an administrative assistant. In Vivian's absence, and without authority, Xena represents herself as Vivian and signs a promissory note in Vivian's name. In what circumstance is Vivian liable on the note? (See *Liability for Contracts*.)

• **Check your answers to the Issue Spotters against the answers provided in Appendix D at the end of this text.**

Business Scenarios

33–1. Unauthorized Acts. Janell Arden is a purchasing agent–employee for the A&B Coal Supply partnership. Arden has authority to purchase the coal needed by A&B to satisfy the needs of its customers. While Arden is leaving a coal mine from which she has just purchased a large quantity of coal, her car breaks down. She walks into a small roadside grocery store for help. While there, she encounters Will Wilson, who owns 360 acres back in the mountains with all mineral rights. Wilson, in need of cash, offers to sell Arden the property for $1,500 per acre.

On inspection of the property, Arden forms the opinion that the subsurface contains valuable coal deposits. Arden contracts to purchase the property for A&B Coal Supply, signing the contract "A&B Coal Supply, Janell Arden, agent." The closing date is August 1. Arden takes the contract to the partnership. The managing partner is furious, as A&B is not in the property business. Later, just before closing, both Wilson and the partnership learn that the value of the land is at least $15,000 per acre. Discuss the rights of A&B and Wilson concerning the land contract. (See *Liability for Contracts*.)

33–2. Respondeat Superior. ABC Tire Corp. hires Arnez as a traveling salesperson and assigns him a geographic area and time schedule in which to solicit orders and service customers. Arnez is given a company car to use in covering the territory. One day, Arnez decides to take his personal car to cover part of his territory. It is 11:00 A.M., and Arnez has just finished calling on all customers in the city of Tarrytown. His next appointment is at 2:00 P.M. in the city of Austex, twenty miles down the road. Arnez starts out for Austex, but halfway there he decides to visit a former college roommate who runs a farm ten miles off the main highway. Arnez is enjoying his visit with his former roommate when he realizes that it is 1:45 P.M. and that he will be late for the appointment in Austex. Driving at a high speed down the country road to reach the main highway, Arnez crashes his car into a tractor, severely injuring Thomas, the driver of the tractor. Thomas claims that he can hold ABC Tire Corp. liable for his injuries. Discuss fully ABC's liability in this situation. (See *Liability for Torts and Crimes*.)

Business Case Problems

33–3. Liability Based on Apparent Authority. Summerall Electric Co. and other subcontractors were hired by National Church Services, Inc. (NCS), which was the general contractor on a construction project for the Church of God at Southaven. As work progressed, payments from NCS to the subcontractors were late and eventually stopped altogether. The church had paid NCS in full for the entire project beforehand, but apparently NCS had mismanaged the project. When payments from NCS stopped, the subcontractors filed mechanic's liens for the value of the work they had performed but for which they had not been paid. The subcontractors sued the church, contending that it was liable for the payments because NCS was its agent on the basis of either actual or apparent authority. Was NCS an agent for the church, thereby making the church liable to the subcontractors? Explain your reasoning. [*Summerall Electric Co. v. Church of God at Southaven*, 25 So.3d 1090 (Miss.App. 2010)] (See *Scope of Agent's Authority*.)

33–4. Disclosed Principal. To display desserts in restaurants, Mario Sclafani ordered refrigeration units from Felix Storch, Inc. Felix faxed a credit application to Sclafani. The application was faxed back with a signature that appeared to be Sclafani's. Felix delivered the units. When they were not paid for, Felix filed a suit against Sclafani to collect. Sclafani denied that he had seen the application or signed it. He testified that he referred all credit questions to "the girl in the office." Who was the principal? Who was the agent? Who is liable on the contract? Explain. [*Felix Storch, Inc. v. Martinucci Desserts USA, Inc.*, 30 Misc.3d 1217, 924 N.Y.S.2d 308 (Suffolk Co. 2011)] (See *Liability for Contracts*.)

33–5. Liability for Contracts. Thomas Huskin and his wife entered into a contract to have their home remodeled by House Medic Handyman Service. Todd Hall signed the contract as an authorized representative of House Medic. It turned out that House Medic was a fictitious name for Hall Hauling, Ltd. The contract did not indicate this, however, and Hall did not inform the Huskins about Hall Hauling. When a contract dispute later arose, the Huskins sued Todd Hall personally for breach of contract. Can Hall be held personally liable? Why or why not? [*Huskin v. Hall*, 2012 WL 553136 (Ohio Ct.App. 2012)] (See *Liability for Contracts*.)

33–6. Business Case Problem with Sample Answer— Agent's Authority. Basic Research, L.L.C., advertised its products on television networks owned by Rainbow Media Holdings, Inc., through an ad agency, Icebox Advertising, Inc. As Basic's agent, Icebox had the express authority to buy ads from Rainbow on Basic's behalf, but the authority was limited to buying ads with cash in advance. Despite this limit, Rainbow sold ads to Basic through Icebox on credit. Basic paid Icebox for the ads, but Icebox did not pass all of the payments on to Rainbow. Icebox filed for bankruptcy. Can Rainbow recoup the unpaid amounts from Basic? Explain. [*American Movie Classics v. Rainbow Media Holdings*, 508 Fed.Appx. 826 (10th Cir. 2013)] (See *Scope of Agent's Authority*.)

- For a sample answer to Problem 33–6, go to Appendix E at the end of this text.

33–7. Agent's Authority. Terry Holden's stepmother, Rosie, was diagnosed with amyotrophic lateral sclerosis (ALS), and Terry's wife, Susan, became Rosie's primary caregiver. Rosie executed a durable power of attorney appointing Susan as her agent. Susan opened a joint bank account with Rosie at Bank of America, depositing $9,643.62 of Rosie's funds. Susan used some of the money to pay for "household expenses to keep us going while we were taking care of her." Rosie died three months later. Terry's father, Charles, as executor of Rosie's estate, filed a petition in a Texas state court against Susan for an accounting. What general duty did Susan owe Rosie as her agent? What does an agent's duty of accounting require? Did Susan breach either of these duties? Explain.

[*Holden v. Holden*, 456 S.W.3d 642 (Tex.App.—Tyler 2015)] (See *Scope of Agent's Authority*.)

33–8. Scope of Agent's Authority. Kindred Nursing Centers East, LLC, owns and operates Whitesburg Gardens, a long-term care and rehabilitation facility, in Huntsville, Alabama. Lorene Jones was admitted to the facility following knee-replacement surgery. Jones's daughter, Yvonne Barbour, signed the admission forms required by Whitesburg Gardens as her mother's representative in her presence. Jones did not object. The forms included an "Alternative Dispute Resolution Agreement," which provided for binding arbitration in the event of a dispute between "the Resident" (Jones) and "the Facility" (Whitesburg Gardens). Six days later, Jones was transferred to a different facility. After recovering from the surgery, she filed a suit in an Alabama state court against Kindred, alleging substandard care on a claim of negligence. Can Jones be compelled to submit her claim to arbitration? Explain. [*Kindred Nursing Centers East, LLC v. Jones*, __ So.3d __, 2016 WL 762450 (Ala. 2016)] (See *Scope of Agent's Authority*.)

33–9. A Question of Ethics—Vicarious Liability. *Jamie* *Paliath worked as a real estate agent for Home Town Realty of Vandalia, LLC (the principal, a real estate broker). Torri Auer, a California resident, relied on Paliath's advice and assistance to buy three rental properties in Ohio. Before the sales, Paliath had represented that each property was worth approximately twice as much as what Auer would pay and that there was a waiting list of prospective tenants. Paliath also stated that all of the property needed work* and agreed to do the work for a specified price. Nearly a year later, substantial work was still needed, and only a few of the units had been rented. Auer sued Paliath and Home Town Realty for fraudulent misrepresentation. [*Auer v. Paliath*, *140 Ohio St.3d 276, 17 N.E.3d 561, 2014-Ohio-3632 (2014)*] (See *Liability for Torts and Crimes*.)

(a) Were Paliath's representations to Auer within the scope of her employment? Explain. Will the court hold the principal (Home Town Realty) liable for the misrepresentations of the agent (Paliath)?

(b) What is the ethical basis for imposing vicarious liability on a principal for an agent's tort?

33–10. Special Case Analysis—Liability for Torts and Crimes. Go to Case Analysis 33.3, *M.J. v. Wisan.* Read the excerpt and answer the following questions.

(a) **Issue:** What conduct was at the center of the dispute in this case? Who did the plaintiff allege was liable for this conduct? Which of these parties was the principal, and which was the agent?

(b) **Rule of Law:** What rule applied to determine the liability of the parties for the conduct in dispute?

(c) **Applying the Rule of Law:** What factors did the court indicate could be considered in deciding whether to impose liability in this case?

(d) **Conclusion:** How did the court rule on the question of vicarious liability?

Legal Reasoning Group Activity

33–11. Liability for Independent Contractor's Torts. Dean Brothers Corp. owns and operates a steel drum manufacturing plant. Lowell Wyden, the plant superintendent, hired Best Security Patrol, Inc. (BSP), a security company, to guard Dean property and "deter thieves and vandals." Some BSP security guards, as Wyden knew, carried firearms. Pete Sidell, a BSP security guard, was not certified as an armed guard but nevertheless came to work with his gun (in a briefcase).

While working at the Dean plant on October 31, Sidell fired his gun at Tyrone Gaines, in the belief that Gaines was an intruder. The bullet struck and killed Gaines. Gaines's mother filed a lawsuit claiming that her son's death was the result of BSP's negligence, for which Dean was responsible. (See *Liability for Torts and Crimes*.)

(a) The first group will determine what the plaintiff's best argument is to establish that Dean is responsible for BSP's actions.

(b) The second group will discuss Dean's best defense and formulate arguments to support it.

Answers to the *Issue Spotters*

1. **Can Davis hold Estee liable for whatever damages he has to pay? Why or why not?** Yes. A principal has a duty to indemnify an agent for liabilities incurred because of authorized and lawful acts and transactions and for losses suffered because of the principal's failure to perform his or her duties.

2. **In what circumstance is Vivian liable on the note?** When a person enters into a contract on another's behalf without the authority to do so, the other may be liable on the contract if he or she approves or affirms that contract. In other words, the employer-principal would be liable for the note in this problem on ratifying it. Whether the employer-principal ratifies the note or not, the unauthorized agent is most likely also liable for it.

Sample Answers for *Business Case Problems with Sample Answer*

Problem 33–6. *Agent's Authority.* No, Rainbow cannot recoup the unpaid amounts from Basic. Express authority is authority declared in clear, direct, and definite terms. Express authority can be given orally or in writing. In most states, if the contract being executed is or must be in writing, then the agent's authority must also be in writing. Otherwise, the contract may be avoided (or ratified) by the principal. If it is ratified, the ratification must be in writing. An agent has the implied authority to do what is reasonably necessary to carry out express authority. For example, authority to manage a business implies authority to do what is reasonably required to operate the business. But an agent's implied authority cannot contradict his or her express authority. Thus, if a principal has limited an agent's express authority, then the fact that the agent customarily would have such authority is irrelevant.

In this problem, Basic Research advertised its products on television networks owned by Rainbow Media Holdings through an ad agency, Icebox Advertising. Basic paid Icebox for the ads, but Icebox did not make all of the payments to Rainbow. Icebox filed for bankruptcy. Rainbow cannot recover what it was owed from Basic. As Basic's agent, Icebox had the express authority to buy ads from Rainbow on Basic's behalf, but that authority was limited to purchasing ads with cash in advance. Thus, Icebox did not have the authority—express or implied—to buy ads on Basic's credit. And Basic did not ratify the contracts that represented purchases on credit.

In the actual case on which this problem is based, on Basic's appeal from a judgment in Rainbow's favor, the U.S. Court of Appeals for the Tenth Circuit reversed that judgment and ruled in Basic's favor.

APPENDIX
How to Brief Cases and Analyze Case Problems

How to Brief Cases

To fully understand the law with respect to business, you need to be able to read and understand court decisions. To make this task easier, you can use a method of case analysis that is called *briefing*. There is a fairly standard procedure that you can follow when you "brief" any court case. You must first read the case opinion carefully. When you feel you understand the case, you can prepare a brief of it.

Although the format of the brief may vary, typically it will present the essentials of the case under headings such as the following:

1. **Citation.** Give the full citation for the case, including the name of the case, the date it was decided, and the court that decided it.
2. **Facts.** Briefly indicate (a) the reasons for the lawsuit; (b) the identity and arguments of the plaintiff(s) and defendant(s), respectively; and (c) the lower court's decision—if appropriate.
3. **Issue.** Concisely phrase, in the form of a question, the essential issue before the court. (If more than one issue is involved, you may have two—or even more—questions here.)
4. **Decision.** Indicate here—with a "yes" or "no," if possible—the court's answer to the question (or questions) in the *Issue* section above.
5. **Reason.** Summarize as briefly as possible the reasons given by the court for its decision (or decisions) and the case or statutory law relied on by the court in arriving at its decision.

An Example of a Briefed Sample Court Case

As an example of the format used in briefing cases, we present here a briefed version of the sample court case that was presented in Chapter 1 in Exhibit 1–6.

ROSA AND RAYMOND PARKS INSTITUTE FOR SELF DEVELOPMENT v. TARGET CORPORATION
United States Court of Appeals, Eleventh Circuit, 812 F.3d 824 (2016).

FACTS In December 1955, on a bus in Montgomery, Alabama, Rosa Parks refused to give up her seat to a white man in violation of the city's segregation law. This "courageous act" sparked the modern civil rights movement. Parks's role in "the most significant social movement in the history of the United States" has been chronicled in books and movies, and featured on mementoes, some of which are offered for sale by Target Corp. The Rosa and Raymond Parks Institute for Self Development is a Michigan firm that owns Parks's name and likeness. The Institute filed a suit in a federal district court against Target, alleging misappropriation in violation of the Institute's right of publicity. The court dismissed the complaint. The Institute appealed to the U.S. Court of Appeals for the Eleventh Circuit.

ISSUE Are Target's sales of books, movies, and other items that depict or discuss Rosa Parks and the modern civil rights movement protected by Michigan's common-law qualified privilege?

DECISION Yes. The U.S. Court of Appeals for the Eleventh Circuit affirmed the lower court's decision to dismiss the Institute's complaint. The items offered for sale by Target that feature or discuss Rosa Parks and her role in history are protected by Michigan's qualified privilege protecting matters of public interest.

REASON Michigan's common-law right of publicity prohibits the commercial use of a person's name or likeness without his or her consent. But this privacy right has limits. It "must yield to the qualified privilege to communicate on matters of public interest." The court recognized that "Rosa Parks is a figure of great historical significance and the civil rights movement a matter of legitimate and important public interest." The items identified by the Institute and sold by Target are "*bona fide* works" discussing Parks and her role in the modern civil rights movement. The items "communicate information, express opinions, recite grievances, and protest claimed abuses on behalf of a movement whose existence and objectives continue to be of the highest public interest and concern." Therefore, they fall within Michigan's qualified privilege.

A Review of the Briefed Sample Court Case

Here, we provide a review of the briefed case to indicate the kind of information that is contained in each section.

CITATION The name of the case is *Rosa and Raymond Parks Institute for Self Development v. Target Corporation*. The Rosa and Raymond Parks Institute for Self Development is the plaintiff. Target is the defendant. The U.S. Court of Appeals for the Eleventh Circuit decided this case in 2016. The citation states that this case can be found in Volume 812 of the *Federal Reporter, Third Series,* on page 824.

FACTS The *Facts* section identifies the plaintiff and the defendant. It also describes the events leading up to this suit and the allegations made by the plaintiff in the suit. Because this case is a decision of one of the U.S. courts of appeals, the lower court's ruling, the party appealing, and sometimes the appellant's contention on appeal are included here.

ISSUE The *Issue* section presents the central issue (or issues) decided by the court. In this case, the court considers whether the sales of books and other items that depict or discuss Rosa Parks and the modern civil rights movement are protected by Michigan's common-law qualified privilege.

DECISION The *Decision* section includes the court's decision on the issues before it. The decision reflects the opinion of the judge or justice hearing the case. In this case, the court decided that the items offered for sale focusing on or featuring Rosa Parks and her role in history fall within Michigan's qualified privilege, which protects depictions and discussions of matters of public interest. Decisions by appellate courts are frequently phrased in reference to the lower court's decision. That is, the appellate court may "affirm" the lower court's ruling or "reverse" it. A case may also be remanded, or sent back to the lower court, for further proceedings.

REASON The *Reason* section includes references to the relevant laws and legal principles that the court applied in coming to the conclusion arrived at in the case. The relevant law here includes Michigan's common-law qualified privilege protecting the use of others' names and likenesses in depictions and discussions of matters in the pubic interest. This section also explains the court's application of the law to the facts in this case.

Analyzing Case Problems

In addition to learning how to brief cases, students also find it helpful to know how to analyze case problems. Part of the study of business law and the legal environment usually involves analyzing case problems, such as those included in this text at the end of each chapter.

For each case problem in this book, we provide the relevant background and facts of the lawsuit and the issue before the court. When you are assigned one of these problems, your job will be to determine how the court should decide the issue, and why. In other words, you will need to engage in legal analysis and reasoning. Here, we offer some suggestions on how to make this task less daunting. We begin by presenting a SAMPLE PROBLEM:

> While Janet Lawson, a famous pianist, was shopping in Quality Market, she slipped and fell on a wet floor in one of the aisles. The floor had recently been mopped by one of the store's employees, but there were no signs warning customers that the floor in that area was wet. As a result of the fall, Lawson injured her right arm and was unable to perform piano concerts for the next six months. Had she been able to perform the scheduled concerts, she would have earned approximately $60,000 over that period of time. Lawson sued Quality Market for this amount, plus another $10,000 in medical expenses. She claimed that the store's failure to warn customers of the wet floor constituted negligence and therefore the market was liable for her injuries. Will the court agree with Lawson? Discuss.

Understand the Facts

This may sound obvious, but before you can analyze or apply the relevant law to a specific set of facts, you must clearly understand those facts. In other words, you should read through the case problem carefully—more than once, if necessary—to make sure you understand the identity of the plaintiff(s) and defendant(s) in the case and the progression of events that led to the lawsuit.

In the sample case problem just given, the identity of the parties is fairly obvious. Janet Lawson is the one bringing the suit; therefore, she is the plaintiff. Quality Market, against whom she is bringing the suit, is the defendant. Some of the case problems you may work on have multiple plaintiffs or defendants. Often, it is helpful to use abbreviations for the parties. To indicate a reference to a plaintiff, for example, the *pi* symbol—π—is often used, and a defendant is denoted by a *delta*—Δ—a triangle.

The events leading to the lawsuit are also fairly straightforward. Lawson slipped and fell on a wet floor, and she contends that Quality Market should be liable for her injuries because it was negligent in not posting a sign warning customers of the wet floor.

When you are working on case problems, realize that the facts should be accepted as they are given. For example, in our sample problem, it should be accepted that the floor was wet and that there was no sign. In other words, avoid making conjectures, such as "Maybe the floor wasn't too wet," or "Maybe an employee was getting a sign to put up," or "Maybe someone stole the sign." Questioning the facts as they are presented only adds confusion to your analysis.

Legal Analysis and Reasoning

Once you understand the facts given in the case problem, you can begin to analyze the case. The IRAC method is a helpful tool to use in the legal analysis and reasoning process. IRAC is an acronym for Issue, Rule, Application, Conclusion. Applying this method to our sample problem would involve the following steps:

1. First, you need to decide what legal **issue** is involved in the case. In our sample case, the basic issue is whether Quality Market's

failure to warn customers of the wet floor constituted negligence. As discussed in the text, negligence is a *tort*—a civil wrong. In a tort lawsuit, the plaintiff seeks to be compensated for another's wrongful act. A defendant will be deemed negligent if he or she breached a duty of care owed to the plaintiff and the breach of that duty caused the plaintiff to suffer harm.

2. Once you have identified the issue, the next step is to determine what **rule of law** applies to the issue. To make this determination, you will want to review carefully the text of the chapter in which the relevant rule of law for the problem appears. Our sample case problem involves the tort of negligence. The applicable rule of law is the tort law principle that business owners owe a duty to exercise reasonable care to protect their customers ("business invitees"). Reasonable care, in this context, includes either removing—or warning customers of—*foreseeable* risks about which the owner *knew* or *should have known.* Business owners need not warn customers of "open and obvious" risks, however. If a business owner breaches this duty of care (fails to exercise the appropriate degree of care toward customers), and the breach of duty causes a customer to be injured, the business owner will be liable to the customer for the customer's injuries.

3. The next—and usually the most difficult—step in analyzing case problems is the **application** of the relevant rule of law to the specific facts of the case you are studying. In the sample problem, applying the tort law principle just discussed presents few difficulties. An employee of the store had mopped the floor in the aisle where Lawson slipped and fell, but no sign was present indicating that the floor was wet. That a customer might fall on a wet floor is clearly a foreseeable risk. Therefore, the failure to warn customers about the wet floor was a breach of the duty of care owed by the business owner to the store's customers.

4. Once you have completed Step 3 in the IRAC method, you should be ready to draw your **conclusion.** In our sample problem, Quality Market is liable to Lawson for her injuries, because the market's breach of its duty of care caused Lawson's injuries.

The fact patterns in the business scenarios and case problems presented in this text are not always as simple as those presented in our sample problem. Often, for example, a case has more than one plaintiff or defendant. A case may also involve more than one issue and have more than one applicable rule of law. Furthermore, in some case problems the facts may indicate that the general rule of law should not apply.

For example, suppose that a store employee advised Lawson not to walk on the floor in the aisle because it was wet, but Lawson decided to walk on it anyway. This fact could alter the outcome of the case because the store could then raise the defense of assumption of risk. Nonetheless, a careful review of the chapter text should always provide you with the knowledge you need to analyze the problem thoroughly and arrive at accurate conclusions.

The Constitution of the United States

Preamble

We the People of the United States, in Order to form a more perfect Union, establish Justice, insure domestic Tranquility, provide for the common defence, promote the general Welfare, and secure the Blessings of Liberty to ourselves and our Posterity, do ordain and establish this Constitution for the United States of America.

Article I

Section 1. All legislative Powers herein granted shall be vested in a Congress of the United States, which shall consist of a Senate and House of Representatives.

Section 2. The House of Representatives shall be composed of Members chosen every second Year by the People of the several States, and the Electors in each State shall have the Qualifications requisite for Electors of the most numerous Branch of the State Legislature.

No Person shall be a Representative who shall not have attained to the Age of twenty five Years, and been seven Years a Citizen of the United States, and who shall not, when elected, be an Inhabitant of that State in which he shall be chosen.

Representatives and direct Taxes shall be apportioned among the several States which may be included within this Union, according to their respective Numbers, which shall be determined by adding to the whole Number of free Persons, including those bound to Service for a Term of Years, and excluding Indians not taxed, three fifths of all other Persons. The actual Enumeration shall be made within three Years after the first Meeting of the Congress of the United States, and within every subsequent Term of ten Years, in such Manner as they shall by Law direct. The Number of Representatives shall not exceed one for every thirty Thousand, but each State shall have at Least one Representative; and until such enumeration shall be made, the State of New Hampshire shall be entitled to chuse three, Massachusetts eight, Rhode Island and Providence Plantations one, Connecticut five, New York six, New Jersey four, Pennsylvania eight, Delaware one, Maryland six, Virginia ten, North Carolina five, South Carolina five, and Georgia three.

When vacancies happen in the Representation from any State, the Executive Authority thereof shall issue Writs of Election to fill such Vacancies.

The House of Representatives shall chuse their Speaker and other Officers; and shall have the sole Power of Impeachment.

Section 3. The Senate of the United States shall be composed of two Senators from each State, chosen by the Legislature thereof, for six Years; and each Senator shall have one Vote.

Immediately after they shall be assembled in Consequence of the first Election, they shall be divided as equally as may be into three Classes. The Seats of the Senators of the first Class shall be vacated at the Expiration of the second Year, of the second Class at the Expiration of the fourth Year, and of the third Class at the Expiration of the sixth Year, so that one third may be chosen every second Year; and if Vacancies happen by Resignation, or otherwise, during the Recess of the Legislature of any State, the Executive thereof may make temporary Appointments until the next Meeting of the Legislature, which shall then fill such Vacancies.

No Person shall be a Senator who shall not have attained to the Age of thirty Years, and been nine Years a Citizen of the United States, and who shall not, when elected, be an Inhabitant of that State for which he shall be chosen.

The Vice President of the United States shall be President of the Senate, but shall have no Vote, unless they be equally divided.

The Senate shall chuse their other Officers, and also a President pro tempore, in the Absence of the Vice President, or when he shall exercise the Office of President of the United States.

The Senate shall have the sole Power to try all Impeachments. When sitting for that Purpose, they shall be on Oath or Affirmation. When the President of the United States is tried, the Chief Justice shall preside: And no Person shall be convicted without the Concurrence of two thirds of the Members present.

Judgment in Cases of Impeachment shall not extend further than to removal from Office, and disqualification to hold and enjoy any Office of honor, Trust, or Profit under the United States: but the Party convicted shall nevertheless be liable and subject to Indictment, Trial, Judgment, and Punishment, according to Law.

Section 4. The Times, Places and Manner of holding Elections for Senators and Representatives, shall be prescribed in each State by the Legislature thereof; but the Congress may at any time by Law make or alter such Regulations, except as to the Places of chusing Senators.

The Congress shall assemble at least once in every Year, and such Meeting shall be on the first Monday in December, unless they shall by Law appoint a different Day.

Section 5. Each House shall be the Judge of the Elections, Returns, and Qualifications of its own Members, and a Majority of each shall constitute a Quorum to do Business; but a smaller Number may adjourn from day to day, and may be authorized to compel the Attendance of absent Members, in such Manner, and under such Penalties as each House may provide.

Each House may determine the Rules of its Proceedings, punish its Members for disorderly Behavior, and, with the Concurrence of two thirds, expel a Member.

Each House shall keep a Journal of its Proceedings, and from time to time publish the same, excepting such Parts as may in their Judgment require Secrecy; and the Yeas and Nays of the

Members of either House on any question shall, at the Desire of one fifth of those Present, be entered on the Journal.

Neither House, during the Session of Congress, shall, without the Consent of the other, adjourn for more than three days, nor to any other Place than that in which the two Houses shall be sitting.

Section 6. The Senators and Representatives shall receive a Compensation for their Services, to be ascertained by Law, and paid out of the Treasury of the United States. They shall in all Cases, except Treason, Felony and Breach of the Peace, be privileged from Arrest during their Attendance at the Session of their respective Houses, and in going to and returning from the same; and for any Speech or Debate in either House, they shall not be questioned in any other Place.

No Senator or Representative shall, during the Time for which he was elected, be appointed to any civil Office under the Authority of the United States, which shall have been created, or the Emoluments whereof shall have been increased during such time; and no Person holding any Office under the United States, shall be a Member of either House during his Continuance in Office.

Section 7. All Bills for raising Revenue shall originate in the House of Representatives; but the Senate may propose or concur with Amendments as on other Bills.

Every Bill which shall have passed the House of Representatives and the Senate, shall, before it become a Law, be presented to the President of the United States; If he approve he shall sign it, but if not he shall return it, with his Objections to the House in which it shall have originated, who shall enter the Objections at large on their Journal, and proceed to reconsider it. If after such Reconsideration two thirds of that House shall agree to pass the Bill, it shall be sent together with the Objections, to the other House, by which it shall likewise be reconsidered, and if approved by two thirds of that House, it shall become a Law. But in all such Cases the Votes of both Houses shall be determined by Yeas and Nays, and the Names of the Persons voting for and against the Bill shall be entered on the Journal of each House respectively. If any Bill shall not be returned by the President within ten Days (Sundays excepted) after it shall have been presented to him, the Same shall be a Law, in like Manner as if he had signed it, unless the Congress by their Adjournment prevent its Return in which Case it shall not be a Law.

Every Order, Resolution, or Vote, to which the Concurrence of the Senate and House of Representatives may be necessary (except on a question of Adjournment) shall be presented to the President of the United States; and before the Same shall take Effect, shall be approved by him, or being disapproved by him, shall be repassed by two thirds of the Senate and House of Representatives, according to the Rules and Limitations prescribed in the Case of a Bill.

Section 8. The Congress shall have Power To lay and collect Taxes, Duties, Imposts and Excises, to pay the Debts and provide for the common Defence and general Welfare of the United States; but all Duties, Imposts and Excises shall be uniform throughout the United States;

To borrow Money on the credit of the United States;

To regulate Commerce with foreign Nations, and among the several States, and with the Indian Tribes;

To establish an uniform Rule of Naturalization, and uniform Laws on the subject of Bankruptcies throughout the United States;

To coin Money, regulate the Value thereof, and of foreign Coin, and fix the Standard of Weights and Measures;

To provide for the Punishment of counterfeiting the Securities and current Coin of the United States;

To establish Post Offices and post Roads;

To promote the Progress of Science and useful Arts, by securing for limited Times to Authors and Inventors the exclusive Right to their respective Writings and Discoveries;

To constitute Tribunals inferior to the supreme Court;

To define and punish Piracies and Felonies committed on the high Seas, and Offenses against the Law of Nations;

To declare War, grant Letters of Marque and Reprisal, and make Rules concerning Captures on Land and Water;

To raise and support Armies, but no Appropriation of Money to that Use shall be for a longer Term than two Years;

To provide and maintain a Navy;

To make Rules for the Government and Regulation of the land and naval Forces;

To provide for calling forth the Militia to execute the Laws of the Union, suppress Insurrections and repel Invasions;

To provide for organizing, arming, and disciplining, the Militia, and for governing such Part of them as may be employed in the Service of the United States, reserving to the States respectively, the Appointment of the Officers, and the Authority of training the Militia according to the discipline prescribed by Congress;

To exercise exclusive Legislation in all Cases whatsoever, over such District (not exceeding ten Miles square) as may, by Cession of particular States, and the Acceptance of Congress, become the Seat of the Government of the United States, and to exercise like Authority over all Places purchased by the Consent of the Legislature of the State in which the Same shall be, for the Erection of Forts, Magazines, Arsenals, dock-Yards, and other needful Buildings;—And

To make all Laws which shall be necessary and proper for carrying into Execution the foregoing Powers, and all other Powers vested by this Constitution in the Government of the United States, or in any Department or Officer thereof.

Section 9. The Migration or Importation of such Persons as any of the States now existing shall think proper to admit, shall not be prohibited by the Congress prior to the Year one thousand eight hundred and eight, but a Tax or duty may be imposed on such Importation, not exceeding ten dollars for each Person.

The privilege of the Writ of Habeas Corpus shall not be suspended, unless when in Cases of Rebellion or Invasion the public Safety may require it.

No Bill of Attainder or ex post facto Law shall be passed.

No Capitation, or other direct, Tax shall be laid, unless in Proportion to the Census or Enumeration herein before directed to be taken.

No Tax or Duty shall be laid on Articles exported from any State.

No Preference shall be given by any Regulation of Commerce or Revenue to the Ports of one State over those of another: nor shall Vessels bound to, or from, one State be obliged to enter, clear, or pay Duties in another.

No Money shall be drawn from the Treasury, but in Consequence of Appropriations made by Law; and a regular Statement and Account of the Receipts and Expenditures of all public Money shall be published from time to time.

No Title of Nobility shall be granted by the United States: And no Person holding any Office of Profit or Trust under them, shall, without the Consent of the Congress, accept of any present, Emolument, Office, or Title, of any kind whatever, from any King, Prince, or foreign State.

Section 10. No State shall enter into any Treaty, Alliance, or Confederation; grant Letters of Marque and Reprisal; coin Money; emit Bills of Credit; make any Thing but gold and silver Coin a Tender in Payment of Debts; pass any Bill of Attainder, ex post facto Law, or Law impairing the Obligation of Contracts, or grant any Title of Nobility.

No State shall, without the Consent of the Congress, lay any Imposts or Duties on Imports or Exports, except what may be absolutely necessary for executing its inspection Laws: and the net Produce of all Duties and Imposts, laid by any State on Imports or Exports, shall be for the Use of the Treasury of the United States; and all such Laws shall be subject to the Revision and Controul of the Congress.

No State shall, without the Consent of Congress, lay any Duty of Tonnage, keep Troops, or Ships of War in time of Peace, enter into any Agreement or Compact with another State, or with a foreign Power, or engage in War, unless actually invaded, or in such imminent Danger as will not admit of delay.

Article II

Section 1. The executive Power shall be vested in a President of the United States of America. He shall hold his Office during the Term of four Years, and, together with the Vice President, chosen for the same Term, be elected, as follows:

Each State shall appoint, in such Manner as the Legislature thereof may direct, a Number of Electors, equal to the whole Number of Senators and Representatives to which the State may be entitled in the Congress; but no Senator or Representative, or Person holding an Office of Trust or Profit under the United States, shall be appointed an Elector.

The Electors shall meet in their respective States, and vote by Ballot for two Persons, of whom one at least shall not be an Inhabitant of the same State with themselves. And they shall make a List of all the Persons voted for, and of the Number of Votes for each; which List they shall sign and certify, and transmit sealed to the Seat of the Government of the United States, directed to the President of the Senate. The President of the Senate shall, in the Presence of the Senate and House of Representatives, open all the Certificates, and the Votes shall then be counted. The Person having the greatest Number of Votes shall be the President, if such Number be a Majority of the whole Number of Electors appointed; and if there be more than one who have such Majority, and have an equal Number of Votes, then the House of Representatives shall immediately chuse by Ballot one of them for President; and if no Person have a Majority, then from the five highest on the List the said House shall in like Manner chuse the President. But in chusing the President, the Votes shall be taken by States, the Representation from each State having one Vote; A quorum for this Purpose shall consist of a Member or Members from two thirds of the States, and a Majority of all the States shall be necessary to a Choice. In every Case, after the Choice of the President, the Person having the greater Number of Votes of the Electors shall be the Vice President. But if there should remain two or more who have equal Votes, the Senate shall chuse from them by Ballot the Vice President.

The Congress may determine the Time of chusing the Electors, and the Day on which they shall give their Votes; which Day shall be the same throughout the United States.

No person except a natural born Citizen, or a Citizen of the United States, at the time of the Adoption of this Constitution, shall be eligible to the Office of President; neither shall any Person be eligible to that Office who shall not have attained to the Age of thirty five Years, and been fourteen Years a Resident within the United States.

In Case of the Removal of the President from Office, or of his Death, Resignation or Inability to discharge the Powers and Duties of the said Office, the same shall devolve on the Vice President, and the Congress may by Law provide for the Case of Removal, Death, Resignation or Inability, both of the President and Vice President, declaring what Officer shall then act as President, and such Officer shall act accordingly, until the Disability be removed, or a President shall be elected.

The President shall, at stated Times, receive for his Services, a Compensation, which shall neither be increased nor diminished during the Period for which he shall have been elected, and he shall not receive within that Period any other Emolument from the United States, or any of them.

Before he enter on the Execution of his Office, he shall take the following Oath or Affirmation: "I do solemnly swear (or affirm) that I will faithfully execute the Office of President of the United States, and will to the best of my Ability, preserve, protect and defend the Constitution of the United States."

Section 2. The President shall be Commander in Chief of the Army and Navy of the United States, and of the Militia of the several States, when called into the actual Service of the United States; he may require the Opinion, in writing, of the principal Officer in each of the executive Departments, upon any Subject relating to the Duties of their respective Offices, and he shall have Power to grant Reprieves and Pardons for Offenses against the United States, except in Cases of Impeachment.

He shall have Power, by and with the Advice and Consent of the Senate to make Treaties, provided two thirds of the Senators present concur; and he shall nominate, and by and with the Advice and Consent of the Senate, shall appoint Ambassadors, other public Ministers and Consuls, Judges of the supreme

Court, and all other Officers of the United States, whose Appointments are not herein otherwise provided for, and which shall be established by Law; but the Congress may by Law vest the Appointment of such inferior Officers, as they think proper, in the President alone, in the Courts of Law, or in the Heads of Departments.

The President shall have Power to fill up all Vacancies that may happen during the Recess of the Senate, by granting Commissions which shall expire at the End of their next Session.

Section 3. He shall from time to time give to the Congress Information of the State of the Union, and recommend to their Consideration such Measures as he shall judge necessary and expedient; he may, on extraordinary Occasions, convene both Houses, or either of them, and in Case of Disagreement between them, with Respect to the Time of Adjournment, he may adjourn them to such Time as he shall think proper; he shall receive Ambassadors and other public Ministers; he shall take Care that the Laws be faithfully executed, and shall Commission all the Officers of the United States.

Section 4. The President, Vice President and all civil Officers of the United States, shall be removed from Office on Impeachment for, and Conviction of, Treason, Bribery, or other high Crimes and Misdemeanors.

Article III

Section 1. The judicial Power of the United States, shall be vested in one supreme Court, and in such inferior Courts as the Congress may from time to time ordain and establish. The Judges, both of the supreme and inferior Courts, shall hold their Offices during good Behaviour, and shall, at stated Times, receive for their Services a Compensation, which shall not be diminished during their Continuance in Office.

Section 2. The judicial Power shall extend to all Cases, in Law and Equity, arising under this Constitution, the Laws of the United States, and Treaties made, or which shall be made, under their Authority;—to all Cases affecting Ambassadors, other public Ministers and Consuls;—to all Cases of admiralty and maritime Jurisdiction;—to Controversies to which the United States shall be a Party;—to Controversies between two or more States;—between a State and Citizens of another State;—between Citizens of different States;—between Citizens of the same State claiming Lands under Grants of different States, and between a State, or the Citizens thereof, and foreign States, Citizens or Subjects.

In all Cases affecting Ambassadors, other public Ministers and Consuls, and those in which a State shall be a Party, the supreme Court shall have original Jurisdiction. In all the other Cases before mentioned, the supreme Court shall have appellate Jurisdiction, both as to Law and Fact, with such Exceptions, and under such Regulations as the Congress shall make.

The Trial of all Crimes, except in Cases of Impeachment, shall be by Jury; and such Trial shall be held in the State where the said Crimes shall have been committed; but when not committed within any State, the Trial shall be at such Place or Places as the Congress may by Law have directed.

Section 3. Treason against the United States, shall consist only in levying War against them, or, in adhering to their Enemies, giving them Aid and Comfort. No Person shall be convicted of Treason unless on the Testimony of two Witnesses to the same overt Act, or on Confession in open Court.

The Congress shall have Power to declare the Punishment of Treason, but no Attainder of Treason shall work Corruption of Blood, or Forfeiture except during the Life of the Person attainted.

Article IV

Section 1. Full Faith and Credit shall be given in each State to the public Acts, Records, and judicial Proceedings of every other State. And the Congress may by general Laws prescribe the Manner in which such Acts, Records and Proceedings shall be proved, and the Effect thereof.

Section 2. The Citizens of each State shall be entitled to all Privileges and Immunities of Citizens in the several States.

A Person charged in any State with Treason, Felony, or other Crime, who shall flee from Justice, and be found in another State, shall on Demand of the executive Authority of the State from which he fled, be delivered up, to be removed to the State having Jurisdiction of the Crime.

No Person held to Service or Labour in one State, under the Laws thereof, escaping into another, shall, in Consequence of any Law or Regulation therein, be discharged from such Service or Labour, but shall be delivered up on Claim of the Party to whom such Service or Labour may be due.

Section 3. New States may be admitted by the Congress into this Union; but no new State shall be formed or erected within the Jurisdiction of any other State; nor any State be formed by the Junction of two or more States, or Parts of States, without the Consent of the Legislatures of the States concerned as well as of the Congress.

The Congress shall have Power to dispose of and make all needful Rules and Regulations respecting the Territory or other Property belonging to the United States; and nothing in this Constitution shall be so construed as to Prejudice any Claims of the United States, or of any particular State.

Section 4. The United States shall guarantee to every State in this Union a Republican Form of Government, and shall protect each of them against Invasion; and on Application of the Legislature, or of the Executive (when the Legislature cannot be convened) against domestic Violence.

Article V

The Congress, whenever two thirds of both Houses shall deem it necessary, shall propose Amendments to this Constitution, or, on the Application of the Legislatures of two thirds of the several States, shall call a Convention for proposing Amendments, which, in either Case, shall be valid to all Intents and Purposes, as part of this Constitution, when ratified by the Legislatures of three fourths of the several States, or by Conventions in three fourths thereof, as the one or the other Mode of Ratification may be proposed by the Congress; Provided that no

Amendment which may be made prior to the Year One thousand eight hundred and eight shall in any Manner affect the first and fourth Clauses in the Ninth Section of the first Article; and that no State, without its Consent, shall be deprived of its equal Suffrage in the Senate.

Article VI

All Debts contracted and Engagements entered into, before the Adoption of this Constitution shall be as valid against the United States under this Constitution, as under the Confederation.

This Constitution, and the Laws of the United States which shall be made in Pursuance thereof; and all Treaties made, or which shall be made, under the Authority of the United States, shall be the supreme Law of the Land; and the Judges in every State shall be bound thereby, any Thing in the Constitution or Laws of any State to the Contrary notwithstanding.

The Senators and Representatives before mentioned, and the Members of the several State Legislatures, and all executive and judicial Officers, both of the United States and of the several States, shall be bound by Oath or Affirmation, to support this Constitution; but no religious Test shall ever be required as a Qualification to any Office or public Trust under the United States.

Article VII

The Ratification of the Conventions of nine States shall be sufficient for the Establishment of this Constitution between the States so ratifying the Same.

Amendment I [1791]

Congress shall make no law respecting an establishment of religion, or prohibiting the free exercise thereof; or abridging the freedom of speech, or of the press; or the right of the people peaceably to assembly, and to petition the Government for a redress of grievances.

Amendment II [1791]

A well regulated Militia, being necessary to the security of a free State, the right of the people to keep and bear Arms, shall not be infringed.

Amendment III [1791]

No Soldier shall, in time of peace be quartered in any house, without the consent of the Owner, nor in time of war, but in a manner to be prescribed by law.

Amendment IV [1791]

The right of the people to be secure in their persons, houses, papers, and effects, against unreasonable searches and seizures, shall not be violated, and no Warrants shall issue, but upon probable cause, supported by Oath or affirmation, and particularly describing the place to be searched, and the persons or things to be seized.

Amendment V [1791]

No person shall be held to answer for a capital, or otherwise infamous crime, unless on a presentment or indictment of a Grand Jury, except in cases arising in the land or naval forces, or in the Militia, when in actual service in time of War or public danger; nor shall any person be subject for the same offence to be twice put in jeopardy of life or limb; nor shall be compelled in any criminal case to be a witness against himself, nor be deprived of life, liberty, or property, without due process of law; nor shall private property be taken for public use, without just compensation.

Amendment VI [1791]

In all criminal prosecutions, the accused shall enjoy the right to a speedy and public trial, by an impartial jury of the State and district wherein the crime shall have been committed, which district shall have been previously ascertained by law, and to be informed of the nature and cause of the accusation; to be confronted with the witnesses against him; to have compulsory process for obtaining witnesses in his favor, and to have the Assistance of Counsel for his defence.

Amendment VII [1791]

In Suits at common law, where the value in controversy shall exceed twenty dollars, the right of trial by jury shall be preserved, and no fact tried by jury, shall be otherwise re-examined in any Court of the United States, than according to the rules of the common law.

Amendment VIII [1791]

Excessive bail shall not be required, nor excessive fines imposed, nor cruel and unusual punishments inflicted.

Amendment IX [1791]

The enumeration in the Constitution, of certain rights, shall not be construed to deny or disparage others retained by the people.

Amendment X [1791]

The powers not delegated to the United States by the Constitution, nor prohibited by it to the States, are reserved to the States respectively, or to the people.

Amendment XI [1795]

The Judicial power of the United States shall not be construed to extend to any suit in law or equity, commenced or prosecuted against one of the United States by Citizens of another State, or by Citizens or Subjects of any Foreign State.

Amendment XII [1804]

The Electors shall meet in their respective states, and vote by ballot for President and Vice-President, one of whom, at least, shall not be an inhabitant of the same state with themselves; they shall name in their ballots the person voted for as

President, and in distinct ballots the person voted for as Vice-President, and they shall make distinct lists of all persons voted for as President, and of all persons voted for as Vice-President, and of the number of votes for each, which lists they shall sign and certify, and transmit sealed to the seat of the government of the United States, directed to the President of the Senate;—The President of the Senate shall, in the presence of the Senate and House of Representatives, open all the certificates and the votes shall then be counted;—The person having the greatest number of votes for President, shall be the President, if such number be a majority of the whole number of Electors appointed; and if no person have such majority, then from the persons having the highest numbers not exceeding three on the list of those voted for as President, the House of Representatives shall choose immediately, by ballot, the President. But in choosing the President, the votes shall be taken by states, the representation from each state having one vote; a quorum for this purpose shall consist of a member or members from two-thirds of the states, and a majority of all states shall be necessary to a choice. And if the House of Representatives shall not choose a President whenever the right of choice shall devolve upon them, before the fourth day of March next following, then the Vice-President shall act as President, as in the case of the death or other constitutional disability of the President.—The person having the greatest number of votes as Vice-President, shall be the Vice-President, if such number be a majority of the whole number of Electors appointed, and if no person have a majority, then from the two highest numbers on the list, the Senate shall choose the Vice-President; a quorum for the purpose shall consist of two-thirds of the whole number of Senators, and a majority of the whole number shall be necessary to a choice. But no person constitutionally ineligible to the office of President shall be eligible to that of Vice-President of the United States.

Amendment XIII [1865]

Section 1. Neither slavery nor involuntary servitude, except as a punishment for crime whereof the party shall have been duly convicted, shall exist within the United States, or any place subject to their jurisdiction.

Section 2. Congress shall have power to enforce this article by appropriate legislation.

Amendment XIV [1868]

Section 1. All persons born or naturalized in the United States, and subject to the jurisdiction thereof, are citizens of the United States and of the State wherein they reside. No State shall make or enforce any law which shall abridge the privileges or immunities of citizens of the United States; nor shall any State deprive any person of life, liberty, or property, without due process of law; nor deny to any person within its jurisdiction the equal protection of the laws.

Section 2. Representatives shall be apportioned among the several States according to their respective numbers, counting the whole number of persons in each State, excluding Indians not taxed. But when the right to vote at any election for the choice of electors for President and Vice President of the United States, Representatives in Congress, the Executive and Judicial officers of a State, or the members of the Legislature thereof, is denied to any of the male inhabitants of such State, being twenty-one years of age, and citizens of the United States, or in any way abridged, except for participation in rebellion, or other crime, the basis of representation therein shall be reduced in the proportion which the number of such male citizens shall bear to the whole number of male citizens twenty-one years of age in such State.

Section 3. No person shall be a Senator or Representative in Congress, or elector of President and Vice President, or hold any office, civil or military, under the United States, or under any State, who having previously taken an oath, as a member of Congress, or as an officer of the United States, or as a member of any State legislature, or as an executive or judicial officer of any State, to support the Constitution of the United States, shall have engaged in insurrection or rebellion against the same, or given aid or comfort to the enemies thereof. But Congress may by a vote of two-thirds of each House, remove such disability.

Section 4. The validity of the public debt of the United States, authorized by law, including debts incurred for payment of pensions and bounties for services in suppressing insurrection or rebellion, shall not be questioned. But neither the United States nor any State shall assume or pay any debt or obligation incurred in aid of insurrection or rebellion against the United States, or any claim for the loss or emancipation of any slave; but all such debts, obligations and claims shall be held illegal and void.

Section 5. The Congress shall have power to enforce, by appropriate legislation, the provisions of this article.

Amendment XV [1870]

Section 1. The right of citizens of the United States to vote shall not be denied or abridged by the United States or by any State on account of race, color, or previous condition of servitude.

Section 2. The Congress shall have power to enforce this article by appropriate legislation.

Amendment XVI [1913]

The Congress shall have power to lay and collect taxes on incomes, from whatever source derived, without apportionment among the several States, and without regard to any census or enumeration.

Amendment XVII [1913]

Section 1. The Senate of the United States shall be composed of two Senators from each State, elected by the people thereof, for six years; and each Senator shall have one vote. The electors in each State shall have the qualifications requisite for electors of the most numerous branch of the State legislatures.

Section 2. When vacancies happen in the representation of any State in the Senate, the executive authority of such State shall issue writs of election to fill such vacancies: *Provided,* That the legislature of any State may empower the executive thereof to make temporary appointments until the people fill the vacancies by election as the legislature may direct.

Section 3. This amendment shall not be so construed as to affect the election or term of any Senator chosen before it becomes valid as part of the Constitution.

Amendment XVIII [1919]

Section 1. After one year from the ratification of this article the manufacture, sale, or transportation of intoxicating liquors within, the importation thereof into, or the exportation thereof from the United States and all territory subject to the jurisdiction thereof for beverage purposes is hereby prohibited.

Section 2. The Congress and the several States shall have concurrent power to enforce this article by appropriate legislation.

Section 3. This article shall be inoperative unless it shall have been ratified as an amendment to the Constitution by the legislatures of the several States, as provided in the Constitution, within seven years from the date of the submission hereof to the States by the Congress.

Amendment XIX [1920]

Section 1. The right of citizens of the United States to vote shall not be denied or abridged by the United States or by any State on account of sex.

Section 2. Congress shall have power to enforce this article by appropriate legislation.

Amendment XX [1933]

Section 1. The terms of the President and Vice President shall end at noon on the 20th day of January, and the terms of Senators and Representatives at noon on the 3d day of January, of the years in which such terms would have ended if this article had not been ratified; and the terms of their successors shall then begin.

Section 2. The Congress shall assemble at least once in every year, and such meeting shall begin at noon on the 3d day of January, unless they shall by law appoint a different day.

Section 3. If, at the time fixed for the beginning of the term of the President, the President elect shall have died, the Vice President elect shall become President. If the President shall not have been chosen before the time fixed for the beginning of his term, or if the President elect shall have failed to qualify, then the Vice President elect shall act as President until a President shall have qualified; and the Congress may by law provide for the case wherein neither a President elect nor a Vice President elect shall have qualified, declaring who shall then act as President, or the manner in which one who is to act shall be selected, and such person shall act accordingly until a President or Vice President shall have qualified.

Section 4. The Congress may by law provide for the case of the death of any of the persons from whom the House of Representatives may choose a President whenever the right of choice shall have devolved upon them, and for the case of the death of any of the persons from whom the Senate may choose a Vice President whenever the right of choice shall have devolved upon them.

Section 5. Sections 1 and 2 shall take effect on the 15th day of October following the ratification of this article.

Section 6. This article shall be inoperative unless it shall have been ratified as an amendment to the Constitution by the legislatures of three-fourths of the several States within seven years from the date of its submission.

Amendment XXI [1933]

Section 1. The eighteenth article of amendment to the Constitution of the United States is hereby repealed.

Section 2. The transportation or importation into any State, Territory, or possession of the United States for delivery or use therein of intoxicating liquors, in violation of the laws thereof, is hereby prohibited.

Section 3. This article shall be inoperative unless it shall have been ratified as an amendment to the Constitution by conventions in the several States, as provided in the Constitution, within seven years from the date of the submission hereof to the States by the Congress.

Amendment XXII [1951]

Section 1. No person shall be elected to the office of the President more than twice, and no person who has held the office of President, or acted as President, for more than two years of a term to which some other person was elected President shall be elected to the office of President more than once. But this Article shall not apply to any person holding the office of President when this Article was proposed by the Congress, and shall not prevent any person who may be holding the office of President, or acting as President, during the term within which this Article becomes operative from holding the office of President or acting as President during the remainder of such term.

Section 2. This article shall be inoperative unless it shall have been ratified as an amendment to the Constitution by the legislatures of three-fourths of the several States within seven years from the date of its submission to the States by the Congress.

Amendment XXIII [1961]

Section 1. The District constituting the seat of Government of the United States shall appoint in such manner as the Congress may direct:

A number of electors of President and Vice President equal to the whole number of Senators and Representatives in Congress to which the District would be entitled if it were a State, but in no event more than the least populous state; they shall be in addition to those appointed by the states, but they shall be considered, for the purposes of the election of President and Vice President, to be electors appointed by a state; and they shall meet in the District and perform such duties as provided by the twelfth article of amendment.

Section 2. The Congress shall have power to enforce this article by appropriate legislation.

Amendment XXIV [1964]

Section 1. The right of citizens of the United States to vote in any primary or other election for President or Vice President, for electors for President or Vice President, or for Senator or Representative in Congress, shall not be denied or abridged by the United States, or any State by reason of failure to pay any poll tax or other tax.

Section 2. The Congress shall have power to enforce this article by appropriate legislation.

Amendment XXV [1967]

Section 1. In case of the removal of the President from office or of his death or resignation, the Vice President shall become President.

Section 2. Whenever there is a vacancy in the office of the Vice President, the President shall nominate a Vice President who shall take office upon confirmation by a majority vote of both Houses of Congress.

Section 3. Whenever the President transmits to the President pro tempore of the Senate and the Speaker of the House of Representatives his written declaration that he is unable to discharge the powers and duties of his office, and until he transmits to them a written declaration to the contrary, such powers and duties shall be discharged by the Vice President as Acting President.

Section 4. Whenever the Vice President and a majority of either the principal officers of the executive departments or of such other body as Congress may by law provide, transmit to the President pro tempore of the Senate and the Speaker of the House of Representatives their written declaration that the President is unable to discharge the powers and duties of his office, the Vice President shall immediately assume the powers and duties of the office as Acting President.

Thereafter, when the President transmits to the President pro tempore of the Senate and the Speaker of the House of Representatives his written declaration that no inability exists, he shall resume the powers and duties of his office unless the Vice President and a majority of either the principal officers of the executive department or of such other body as Congress may by law provide, transmit within four days to the President pro tempore of the Senate and the Speaker of the House of Representatives their written declaration that the President is unable to discharge the powers and duties of his office. Thereupon Congress shall decide the issue, assembling within forty-eight hours for that purpose if not in session. If the Congress, within twenty-one days after receipt of the latter written declaration, or, if Congress is not in session, within twenty-one days after Congress is required to assemble, determines by two-thirds vote of both Houses that the President is unable to discharge the powers and duties of his office, the Vice President shall continue to discharge the same as Acting President; otherwise, the President shall resume the powers and duties of his office.

Amendment XXVI [1971]

Section 1. The right of citizens of the United States, who are eighteen years of age or older, to vote shall not be denied or abridged by the United States or by any State on account of age.

Section 2. The Congress shall have power to enforce this article by appropriate legislation.

Amendment XXVII [1992]

No law, varying the compensation for the services of the Senators and Representatives, shall take effect, until an election of Representatives shall have intervened.

Index

Brazil, 300
breach, 3, 6, 24, 37, 44-45, 47, 49, 54-55,
68, 99, 113-114, 123, 126-127, 133-134,
164, 215, 217-218, 221-222, 225, 228, 235,
247, 249, 253, 257, 261-263, 269, 276, 284,
290, 296, 300, 304-309, 312, 315-323,
323-332, 334-338, 338-354, 358, 359,
425-428, 430-439, 612-614, 617-618,
620-621, 627-628, 635-636, 638-639
   anticipatory, 328-329, 334-335, 337
   buyer, 247, 249, 261, 284, 296, 300, 304,
          321, 323, 323-324, 331, 336,
          341, 343, 347, 350, 352-354,
          425-428, 430, 432-436, 439,
          617-618, 627
   defined, 3, 99, 113, 269, 290, 332, 426
   discharge by, 324, 329-330, 335-337
   good faith, 99, 217, 221-222, 257, 325,
          327, 339, 614
   in contract, 217, 312, 338, 341
   material, 68, 217, 247, 262, 284, 290,
          308, 325, 327-331, 334,
          336-338, 340-342, 346-347,
          426, 435, 614, 628
   seller, 6, 247, 249, 284, 296, 300, 304,
          323-324, 331, 336, 341, 343,
          346-347, 350, 354, 425-428,
          430, 432-436, 439, 617, 621,
          628
Bribery, 102-103
bribes, 103
brief, 10, 20, 50, 61, 65-67, 225, 356
Britain, 32
broadcasting, 77, 226
brokerage firms, 629
brokers, 269, 278, 284-285, 353, 607, 612,
616-617, 640
Brown v. Entertainment Merchants
Association, 143
Browse-wrap terms, 244, 247, 249
budget, 107
building, 4, 43, 70, 96, 101, 120, 124, 126,
150, 169, 221, 225, 247, 254, 260-262, 263,
269, 281, 286, 293, 296, 319-320, 322, 326,
335, 342, 349, 353, 431, 607, 613, 627, 630,
632
Building codes, 70, 293, 353
business, 1, 2-5, 7, 9-10, 12, 14, 19, 25-26,
26-34, 37-38, 41, 44, 46-48, 50, 55, 58-59,
68-70, 70-72, 74-75, 78, 80, 82-89, 89-98,
100-110, 112-116, 123-124, 127, 131-134,
134, 139, 142, 148-150, 150, 152, 156-157,
159, 163-165, 167-168, 170, 216, 221,
228-231, 232, 234-237, 241-242, 244-246,
248, 250, 256, 258-263, 263, 265-266, 268,
270-273, 275, 278, 280, 282, 284-285,
288-289, 292-293, 295, 299, 302, 306-309,
309, 312, 314-315, 320-321, 323, 323, 325,
335-338, 345-346, 348, 351-353, 356, 358,
429, 437-439, 606-609, 611, 613-614, 616,
619-622, 622-624, 627, 629-632, 634-635,
638-639, 641
   accountability, 85
   defined, 3, 14, 28, 72, 89, 113, 244-245,
          634
   expertise, 30, 127
   long-run profits, 90
   profitability, 110
   social responsibility, 96, 104-105
   unfairness, 259
   wrongful interference with, 123, 133
Business association, 98
Business contracts, 55, 102, 270, 302
Business decision making, 2-3, 94, 97
Business entities, 75, 83, 258, 272, 606

corporations, 75, 83, 606
partnerships, 83
Business ethics, 1, 89-90, 93, 102-106
   cases, 90, 93, 103, 105
   corporate social responsibility, 104-105
   defined, 89
   global, 90, 102, 105-106
   international business, 102
   making ethical, 104-105
   moral minimum, 104
   profit maximization, 89-90
   standards, 102, 106
   studying, 89
Business firms, 31, 78, 103, 112, 164
Business for profit, 133
Business invitee, 127, 131-132, 134
Business law, 2, 7, 10, 124, 127, 168, 284,
606
Business organization, 94
   corporations, 94
Business plan, 614
Business Process Pragmatism, 97, 101, 104
Business Process Pragmatism™, 97, 101,
104
Business Roundtable, 94
business service, 614
business torts, 123, 168
   intentional torts, 123
Businesspeople, 91, 97, 235
Buyer, 31, 120, 125, 137, 156, 168, 216,
233, 236, 241-245, 247, 249-250, 250, 256,
261, 271, 278, 280, 283-285, 287, 292, 296,
299-300, 304, 309, 321, 323-324, 323, 331,
336, 341, 343, 347, 350, 352-354, 425-428,
430, 432-436, 439, 616-618, 622, 624, 627
   acceptance by, 241
   default, 321, 343, 425
   overview, 216
   performance, 168, 236, 249, 250, 256,
          300, 304, 309, 323, 323-324,
          331, 336, 341, 347, 350, 352,
          425-426, 432, 616, 618, 627
   performance by, 256
   remedies for, 283, 618
   security interests, 425-426, 436
Bylaws, 262

C

California, 10, 14-18, 24-25, 32-33, 39, 46,
48, 74, 88, 96, 105, 108, 119, 125, 138, 143,
163, 169, 226, 228, 243-244, 252-253, 262,
271-272, 283, 293, 300-301, 311, 316-317,
339, 345, 353, 428, 432, 609, 621, 640
call, 42, 47, 62, 67, 70, 73, 83, 97-98, 105,
118, 151, 167, 220, 241, 261, 286, 307, 324,
328, 330, 335, 338, 344, 346-347, 350, 352,
357, 426, 435, 608, 618, 625, 632
Camera, 10, 60, 613-614
cams, 613
Canada, 150, 167, 316
canceled checks, 121
Cancellation, 6, 104
capacity, 30, 47, 83, 95-96, 103, 113, 139,
149, 215, 217, 222-224, 231, 241, 263,
266-268, 277-279, 300, 316, 340-341, 345,
606, 610, 612-613, 626-628
   contract, 30, 47, 103, 215, 217, 222-224,
          231, 241, 263, 266-268,
          277-279, 300, 316, 340-341,
          345, 606, 610, 612-613,
          626-628
   contractual, 217, 223-224, 231, 241, 263,
          277-279, 316, 340-341, 610,
          627

defined, 113, 223
capital, 5, 289, 310-311, 315, 325, 435, 623
Carbon dioxide, 24, 148
cards, 106, 108-109, 125, 230, 246,
250-251, 291, 338-339, 432, 611
   ATM, 611
   check, 106, 230
   credit, 106, 108-109, 125, 230, 291, 611
CARE, 7, 26, 29, 47, 51, 68-69, 70, 85, 114,
117, 122, 124-127, 130-131, 133-134,
134-135, 137-138, 140, 150, 154, 229, 251,
272, 284-286, 292, 295, 307, 328, 610-612,
616, 623, 632, 639-640
   due, 135, 137, 140, 150, 229, 610, 623
   ordinary, 135, 140, 611-612
   reasonable, 29, 51, 114, 124-127, 130,
          134-135, 134, 137, 140, 150,
          285-286, 295, 611-612, 616
   slight, 126
carrier, 301
Cars, 16, 31, 46, 48, 50-52, 59, 82-83, 89,
107, 124-125, 128-129, 133, 135, 148, 219,
224, 230, 231-233, 252, 257, 265, 279,
284-286, 289, 327-328, 330-331, 336, 429,
432-433, 435, 438, 608, 618, 620, 622, 627,
632, 638-639
case analysis, 19, 29, 54, 81, 88, 100, 115,
136, 161, 169, 218, 240, 252, 273, 285, 296,
316, 327, 337, 340, 434, 616, 633, 640
case law, 3, 5, 11, 15, 19, 24-26, 431, 633
   defined, 3
   finding, 15, 25-26
   old, 19, 431, 633
Case names, 17
case reporters, 7, 17
Cases
   briefing, 20
   sample, 15, 19-23, 25-26, 47-48, 69-70,
          87, 89, 105, 110, 133-134,
          149-150, 168-170, 229, 231,
          243, 248, 250, 262-263, 278,
          280, 293, 295, 307, 309, 321,
          323, 336, 338, 340, 353, 358,
          427, 432, 435, 438-439,
          620-622, 639, 641
Cash advances, 230, 611, 639, 641
Cash value, 220
Categorical imperative, 95, 104, 110
Caterpillar, 144
causation, 35, 126-128, 131, 136, 144
   foreseeability, 128, 136
   in fact, 35
   in product liability, 136
   legal cause, 128
   proximate, 128, 131, 136
   proximate cause, 128, 131, 136
Cause
   superseding, 129-130, 132
   superseding cause, 129-130, 132
caveat emptor, 292
CBS, 160, 355
CD, 105, 161-163
cell phones, 291
Cellphones, 57
Certificate
   stock, 623
Certification mark, 155, 167
certiorari, 40, 45
Chancellor, 6
Chancery courts, 6
Charitable subscriptions, 260
Charles Schwab, 283
charter, 270, 293
Chats, 238
Chattel, 124

I5